Implicit Motives

IMPLICIT MOTIVES

Edited by
Oliver C. Schultheiss
Friedrich-Alexander University

Joachim C. Brunstein
Justus-Liebig University

OXFORD
UNIVERSITY PRESS
2010

OXFORD
UNIVERSITY PRESS

Oxford University Press, Inc., publishes works that further Oxford University's
objective of excellence in research, scholarship, and education.

Oxford   New York
Auckland   Cape Town   Dar es Salaam   Hong Kong   Karachi
Kuala Lumpur   Madrid   Melbourne   Mexico City   Nairobi
New Delhi   Shanghai   Taipei   Toronto

With offices in
Argentina   Austria   Brazil   Chile   Czech Republic   France   Greece
Guatemala   Hungary   Italy   Japan   Poland   Portugal   Singapore
South Korea   Switzerland   Thailand   Turkey   Ukraine   Vietnam

Published by Oxford University Press, Inc.
198 Madison Avenue, New York, New York 10016

www.oup.com

Oxford is a registered trademark of Oxford University Press, Inc.

Library of Congress Cataloging-in-Publication Data

Implicit motives / edited by Oliver C. Schultheiss, Joachim C. Brunstein.
   p.   cm.
   ISBN 978-0-19-533515-6
   1. Motivation (Psychology)   I. Schultheiss, Oliver C., 1967–   II. Brunstein,
Joachim C.
   BF503.I47 2010
   153.8—dc22
                                                            2009021960

9 8 7 6 5 4 3 2 1

Printed in the United States of America on acid-free paper

Contents

Contributors

Nicola Baumann
University of Trier

Michael Bender
Tilburg University

Virginia Blankenship
Northern Arizona University

Richard E. Boyatzis
Case Western Reserve University

Joachim C. Brunstein
Justus-Liebig University

Scott E. Cassidy
College of William & Mary

Tanya Cotler
Adelphi University

Andrew J. Elliot
University of Rochester

Stefan Engeser
Technishe Univesität München

Daniel Fishman
Adelphi University

Eugene M. Fodor
Clarkson University

Julie L. Hall
University of Michigan

Jan Hofer
University of Osnabrück

Miguel Kazén
University of Osnabrück

Stephen P. Kelner, Jr.
Egon Zehnder International Inc.

Julius Kuhl
University of Osnabrück

Thomas A. Langens
University of Wuppertal

Laura A. Maruskin
College of William & Mary

Joyce S. Pang
Nanyang Technological
University

Falko Rheinberg
University of Potsdam

Clemens H. Schmitt
Justus-Liebig University

Oliver C. Schultheiss
Friedrich-Alexander University

Steven J. Stanton
Duke University

Todd M. Thrash
College of William & Mary

Joel Weinberger
Derner Institute, Adelphi University

David G. Winter
University of Michigan

Barbara A. Woike
Barnard College, Columbia University

Introduction

This volume continues a loose series of edited books (Atkinson, 1958; Smith, 1992) dedicated to the examination of human motivation and behavior through the lens of implicit motives, enduring non-conscious needs that drive humans' behavior toward the attainment of specific classes of incentives. In the following, we will sketch out a brief history of research on implicit motives, portray the basic principles guiding implicit motive research, and provide an overview of the chapters featured in this book.

The Excitement of the Early Years : 1948 to 1961

Research on implicit motives started when in the late 1940s David McClelland, who was then a new faculty member at Wesleyan University, teamed up with graduate student John Atkinson to measure motivational needs in humans. They decided to start with hunger motivation as a model need system but did not want to rely on people's introspective reports of hunger because they doubted the validity of such self-reports. McClelland (1984) later traced his doubts about self-report to his observations as a young man who noted the striking difference between the values people avowed to in church on Sundays and their actual behavior throughout the rest of the week. "I never put much faith in what people say their values are on questionnaires, because I don't believe that these statements bear very much relationship to what they in fact do or even to the values that *implicitly* guide their lives. This also gave me a strong belief in the reality of unconscious values or motives, which were obviously affecting what they did in ways that were quite unknown to themselves" (p. 4, italics in original).

McClelland and Atkinson were looking for a way to assess the need for food that bypassed research participants' introspective reports on how hungry they felt. According to Atkinson (in Winter, 1998), the decision to measure hunger motivation with a variant of the Thematic Apperception Test (TAT), Morgan & Murray's (1935) device to tap into unconscious needs, was due to a lucky coincidence: "We were talking about this first experiment in Dave's office. Bob Knapp walked from one side to the other and he said, 'Why don't you try the TAT?', and then walked out the door." (Winter, 1998, p.139)

The decision to use the TAT was due to serendipity; the rest is history. McClelland and Atkinson's original work on the effects of food deprivation on TAT story content was extremely promising (Atkinson & McClelland, 1948). Individuals who had fasted for 16 hours wrote stories about pictures suggestive of food that dealt with the procurement of food and with deprivation states; individuals who had just had breakfast did not imbue their stories with this kind of imagery. Thus, Atkinson and McClelland had used an experimental manipulation of a motivational need (food deprivation versus no deprivation) and studied its effect on the themes research participants wrote about in their stories. In later research, the themes identified in experimental motive arousal studies of this kind were codified and used to assess individual differences in motivational needs in individuals who had been tested under neutral conditions. This was based on the assumption that individuals who showed a lot of motive imagery in their stories in the absence of situational motive arousal must be chronically high in this motivational need whereas individuals with little motive imagery are not.

Despite the initial success with identifying imagery differences in stories written by hungry and full research participants, hunger as a motivational need was soon abandoned in favor of the need to achieve because it was felt that this need was more relevant for individuals' success in specific jobs and life in general. Within only a handful of years, McClelland, Atkinson, and their collaborators conducted ground-breaking research on the assessment of the need for achievement (or *n* Achievement, as it was named to adhere to Murray's, 1938, original terminology). The harvest of this research was published as *The Achievement Motive* (McClelland, Atkinson, Clark, & Lowell, 1953), a book that remains highly readable and thought-stimulating to this day and contains many ideas and findings whose implications still await thorough study.

The years after the publication of *The Achievement Motive* saw a rapid proliferation of the measurement approach to motivation introduced by McClelland and Atkinson. Enthusiasm for the new motivational concepts and measurement approach quickly spread beyond the confines of Harvard University, where David McClelland received an appointment in the early 1950s, and the University of Michigan, where John Atkinson continued his work after graduating from Wesleyan. In quick succession, TAT-based measures of other motivational needs were developed, such as the needs for power, affiliation, and sex, and validated in studies on task performance, perception, attitudes, developmental processes, and other validity criteria. Researchers also dedicated considerable effort to understanding the picture story coding methods used for the assessment of motives. Many of these studies were published or reprinted in the first edited volume dedicated solely to theory and research dealing with implicit motives, Atkinson's (1958) *Motives in Fantasy, Action, and Society*.

The early years also portended what would come to be a hallmark of implicit motive research, namely the application of motivational measures and concepts beyond the confines of psychological science. Soon after the initial work on the assessment and validation of the need for achievement was completed, McClelland started to explore the usefulness of this motive for the explanation of economic phenomena and their cultural precursors. These ideas were formulated for the first time in a contribution to the Nebraska Symposium on Motivation series (McClelland, 1955) and culminated in the publication of *The Achieving Society* (McClelland, 1961), an exciting intellectual tour-de-force through history, mythology, religion, sociology, and particularly economics. In the book, McClelland linked Protestant values to child-rearing practices that fostered high achievement motivation and, as a consequence, entrepreneurial activity. He also demonstrated for several different countries and historical eras that periods of increases in collective achievement motivation preceded periods of economic growth. *The Achieving Society* represents the crowning accomplishment of the field's early years, pushing the boundaries of what motivational science (and psychology more generally) can be applied to and account for, and showcasing the impressive validity and predictive power of content-coding methods for the assessment of motivational needs.

Consolidation, Confusion, and Conflict: 1961 to 1989

For roughly the next three decades, work on implicit motives branched out further, first continuing to gain interest among researchers, but then slipping into stagnation in the later years. The factors that contributed to its initially increasing popularity included Atkinson's development of a rigorous and highly influential theory of achievement motivation that was originally published in 1957 but had its main impact on psychology and other social sciences in the 1960s and 1970s. Atkinson later took theorizing a big step further by developing, with David Birch, the dynamics of action theory (Atkinson & Birch, 1970), a highly advanced and complex account of the laws governing the ebb and flow of motivation and the change from one activity to the next.

Meanwhile, McClelland and his associates intensified their efforts to apply motivational concepts to real-world phenomena in business settings and economic development. One such effort was the attempt to train small business owners in an entire Indian town to think and act like a person high in the need for achievement and thereby to improve the local economy (McClelland & Winter, 1969). Another success story of the second phase in the field's history was the emerging realization that implicit motives were associated with specific psychophysiological responses and health outcomes. Steele (1973), in his pioneering dissertation, was able to document a link between aroused power motivation and excretion of sympathetic catecholamines, as measured in urine levels. With a time lag of 10 years, this discovery led to an intensive and productive exploration of the role of implicit motives in health and disease and the physiological mechanisms involved in it (for a summary, see McClelland, 1989).

Despite these successes, the enthusiasm of the early years started to wear off, an effect that is, perhaps, inevitable in any line of research whose early promise of boundless validity and applicability finally has to give way to a realistic acknowledgment of the boundaries of its concepts and the limitations of its measures. But work on implicit motives also came under fire from critics (e.g., Entwisle, 1972; Fineman, 1977; Klinger, 1971), and the leading researchers of the field took an amazingly long time to muster convincing rebuttals to the inappropriate criticisms and to learn from the appropriate ones.

It is ironic and also tragic that the very principle on which implicit motive research is built—that people cannot validly report on their motivational needs, and, therefore, indirect assessment methods have to be employed—was ignored by many researchers at the fringes of the field, some of whom then complained that measures of implicit motives did not correlate with self-report measures and did not predict the same outcomes as these self-report measures (e.g., Entwisle, 1972; Fineman, 1977). Others simply developed self-report measures for the motivational needs studied by implicit motive researchers and declared these new assessment tools to be able to tap the same constructs as the more time-consuming picture story content-coding motive measures. As a consequence, scores of questionnaire measures of the "achievement motive" and other motivational needs have been developed and established under the same construct name as measures of implicit needs, and entire theories have been built on findings obtained with them, despite the fact that these questionnaire measures do not substantially correlate with implicit motive measures. A novice entering the field of human motivation today is faced with the daunting task of figuring out that self-report and indirect measures of presumably the same motive do not measure the same thing or predict the same kinds of outcomes, despite having the same construct name. McClelland, Koestner, and Weinberger (1989) later commented on this state of affairs: "Another way to react to this lack of correlation is to take it seriously, to insist that at a minimum, psychologists should not call by the same name two measures that do not correlate with one another [...]." (p. 691).

To some extent, however, this state of affairs was also a homemade problem, reflecting a lack of careful theorizing in the field of implicit motives itself, theorizing that was commensurate with basic assumptions and research findings. True, Atkinson (1957) had developed the influential risk-taking theory of achievement motivation. But in doing so, he abandoned a basic assumption of his earlier work—that motivational needs operate unconsciously—and integrated a self-report measure of fear of failure into his research and theorizing, thereby perhaps giving others the impression that questionnaires can be used, after all, to validly assess motivational needs. Atkinson's later work on the dynamics of action, although developed in part to account for the lacking internal consistency of implicit motive measures, ranged far beyond the domain of the empirical data—too far, perhaps, to provide a useful conceptual framework for predicting, testing, and interpreting effects of implicit motives empirically. McClelland, on the other hand, had witnessed the rise and fall of Clark Hull's general theory of behavior while he was a graduate student at Yale University and therefore was ambivalent about the usefulness of theories: "My *primary* loyalty is to the phenomenon, to the empirical fact—and if it messes up somebody's theory, so much the worse for the theory" (McClelland, 1984, p. 28, italics in original).

What was missing at the very core of implicit motive research was an explicit recognition that it is not sufficient to postulate that people have no insight into their motivational needs and then prove the point by showing that self-report measures of motivation do not correlate with implicit motive measures. That only leads to the question: If they are not correlated, which is better at predicting relevant criteria? The issue of statistical independence then becomes an issue of competing validity, and only one type of construct can win the race. What needs to be added to the independence of the predictors is, at a minimum, a conceptual and empirical specification of which kinds of outcomes are affected by each type of measure.

A study by deCharms, Morrison, Reitman, and McClelland (1955) provided the clues necessary to arrive at such a model. The researchers assessed participants' implicit achievement motive and also the value they explicitly placed on achievement. Then they had them work on a classic validity correlate of the implicit motive (an anagram task) and on a task that required them to ascribe achievement-related traits to a target person. The implicit achievement motive predicted performance on the anagram task, but not the traits participants ascribed to the target. In contrast, the degree to which participants rated achievement as something valuable predicted their trait ascriptions, but not their anagram task performance. What this study suggested, then, was that implicit motivational needs predict behavioral performance and that self-attributed motives predict verbal choices and attitudes.

Either this set of findings was so perfectly compatible with McClelland's and his colleagues' way of thinking about conscious and unconscious levels of motivation that they did not fully realize its significance for a person unfamiliar with their views on motivation (i.e., someone outside of the field of implicit motives), or they failed to grasp that they had just identified a rift between levels of behavior that was much more general and pervasive than the mere dissociation of the predictor measures of implicit and self-attributed motivation. Whatever the reason, McClelland and his associates never made much of these findings for the next 25 years.

But in light of waxing criticism of implicit motive measures and waning interest in implicit motive research, McClelland finally realized that something more was needed than an insistence on the validity of the implicit motive measure. After all, as long as implicit and self-attributed motives were in competition with each other and one was presented as a valid measure, where, exactly, did that leave the other?

McClelland (1980) provided the first grudging acknowledgement that self-reports of motivation might also have some validity, but in a different domain of behavior than implicit motives. Using data from studies on academic and life success, early socialization, and other validity correlates, he showed that implicit motives and self-attributed needs (which he termed "values") predicted different kinds of behavior: implicit motives, long-term behavioral trends in unstructured situations; and self-attributed motives, short-term behavior on questionnaires and in response to specific, clear-cut situational demands. At the same time, he questioned the evidence proponents of self-report measures of motivation cited for the reliability and validity of their constructs. In particular, he denied that self-report measures of motivation assessed anything motivational at all. Although many of his arguments against self-report measures of motivation were incisive and still deserve careful consideration and a principled response by anyone who considers using self-report measures of motivation, this half-hearted concession did not yet resolve the antagonism that the field of implicit motive research had developed with the rest of personality psychology, then a notoriously self-report-prone field of research.

Conceptual Refinement and Reinvigoration: 1989 until Now

During the 1980s, McClelland kept working on a way to integrate conscious and nonconscious forms of motivation into a coherent account of motivated behavior (McClelland, 1985, 1987). Meanwhile, the rest of psychology caught up with implicit motive research. Cognitive psychology, which for a long time had put its trust in common-coding models of information processing, started to realize that information that is processed consciously takes a different route and has different properties than information that is processed outside of consciousness (e.g., Squire, 1986). Concepts like implicit perception, implicit memory, and implicit learning started to become popular, and the paradigms to test and separate them from explicit forms of cognition were developed (Kihlstrom, 1990). Social psychologists began to realize that attitudes can be processed and represented implicitly, outside of conscious awareness, and can dissociate from explicit, conscious attitudes (e.g., Devine, 1989). Neuropsychologists had known at least since the 1950s that the brain has several dissociable systems for perceiving, processing, and storing information, only some of which are involved in conscious memory and control of behavior (e.g., Corkin, 1968). In short, psychology collectively realized that the human psyche operates on more than one level, and that this can be robustly demonstrated across many different mental functions (Kihlstrom, 1990).

So the time was ripe when in 1989, McClelland, Koestner, and Weinberger published a seminal paper, "How do self-attributed and implicit motives differ?," in *Psychological Review*. In this article, they proposed that implicit motives respond to task-intrinsic incentives and influence operant behaviors (i.e., behavior in unstructured situations), whereas self-attributed (or explicit) motives respond to social incentives and influence respondent behaviors (i.e., behaviors in response to a specific social demand or expectation). Besides formulating for the first time a comprehensive, conceptually symmetric model for conscious and nonconscious levels of motivational control over behavior, McClelland et al. also introduced new terms for existing measures and constructs that have been adopted by most researchers in this field since then. For one, they coined the term *implicit motive* in analogy to Schachter's (1987) implicit memory concept to denote nonconscious motivational needs assessed through indirect means and contrasted it with the term *explicit motive*, which denoted the motivational needs and strivings that people consciously ascribe to themselves. A second change in terminology was the switch from TAT to Picture Story Exercise (PSE) as the official name for the picture story methods commonly used to assess implicit motives. The change reflects the fact that motive researchers have rarely used Murray's (1943) original TAT stimuli or the administration procedures associated with it. Instead, they frequently used pictures coming from other sources, administered the test in group settings in which participants would write their stories under timed conditions instead of having them tell their stories to an interviewer, and they used empirically derived content-coding systems for scoring the stories instead of coding systems developed based on psychodynamic theories or clinicians' consensus (Winter, 1999).

A meta-analysis by Spangler (1992) soon corroborated the fundamental validity of McClelland et al.'s (1989) two-systems model. Spangler found that across hundreds of studies, the implicit achievement motive was indeed a powerful predictor of operant behaviors, particularly if suitable task incentives were present, but not of respondent behaviors, and that the reverse was true of the explicit achievement motive. These findings and McClelland et al.'s (1989) detailed model of motivation went a long way toward reconciling implicit motive research with the mainstream of personality psychology and convincing a new generation of researchers that the implicit motive construct was worth investigating.

This development was further facilitated by the publication of a second edited volume dedicated to the theory and assessment of implicit motives and related constructs, Smith's (1992) *Motivation And Personality: Handbook of Thematic Content Analysis*. The book featured, besides new and reprinted chapters on conceptual issues related to implicit motive measurement and validity, coding manuals for classic, revised, and new measures of implicit motives as well as cognitive styles that are expressed in people's storytelling. It also contains chapters summarizing the validation of each coding system and, in the appendix, training materials for the acquisition of coding skills in all of the featured systems. Together with Atkinson (1958), this book represents an authoritative and comprehensive source for the reader who is interested in learning how to code text for motivational imagery.

Perhaps a third, albeit less visible, promoter of the rejuvenated interest in implicit motives was the fact that since the 1970s, David Winter had developed an integrated coding system for the assessment of motivational imagery in political speeches and historical documents (Winter, 1991). This running text system allows researchers to code achievement, power, and affiliation imagery in one run, using simplified coding rules. Although developed for other purposes than for use with the PSE, many researchers have started using Winter's running text system for coding PSE stories due to its efficiency and comprehensiveness.

So after a time of stagnation, research on implicit motives was off to a fresh start, benefitting from the fact that the zeitgeist in academic psychology had finally caught up with its basic assumptions, from new and better models, and a greater and more refined choice of coding systems. A factor that has also started to play into the rapidly increasing sophistication of implicit motive research is the fact that cognitive psychology has developed models and instruments that now help motive researchers tease apart the domains and boundaries of influence of implicit and explicit motives on a variety of processes, such as attention, learning, and memory. And biopsychological approaches to motivation, with their conceptual rigor and precision, hold particular promise for understanding the neurobiological foundations of implicit motives and the behaviors affected by them (Berridge, 2004; LeDoux, 2002). So perhaps it is not too much to hope for if we predict that after decades of relative separation from the mainstream of psychological research, the implicit motive construct will become a useful ingredient of affective neuroscience approaches to explaining behavior, one of the most rapidly growing disciplines of psychology.

We will not go into much detail about the specific developments in motive research after 1989; these are described at length in the many excellent chapters contained in this book. Instead, as a measure of the resurgence of interest in implicit motive research, we would like to note that implicit motives are featured at length in several popular textbooks of personality psychology (Carver & Scheier, 2007; Larsen & Buss, 2008; McAdams, 2009; Winter, 1996), many of which are enjoying widespread use in undergraduate courses and are frequently updated in new editions. The *Handbook of Personality* (John, Robins, & Pervin, 2008), a defining resource for the field of personality psychology and the training of graduate students, now features in its third edition a chapter on implicit motives for the first time (Schultheiss, 2008). Its companion *Handbook of Research Methods in Personality Psychology* (Robins, Fraley, & Krueger, 2007) contains a chapter dedicated to implicit motive assessment (Schultheiss & Pang, 2007). Thus, the implicit motive construct enjoys continued as well as newfound popularity among personality psychologists and also in other disciplines, and we are confident that its impact will continue to increase as more researchers start using in their own work the conceptual and methodological tools developed by motive researchers. The purpose of this book is to document the more recent developments in implicit motive research and to be a resource for colleagues who would like to familiarize themselves with established and emergent theories and measurement approaches in the field.

Common Principles of Implicit Motive Research

Research in the field of implicit motives is defined by a set of common principles and assumptions about what implicit motives are, how they can be assessed, and how they operate. We have already mentioned some of them above; nevertheless, we think it is helpful to be absolutely clear about the assumptions guiding the study of implicit motives because they often are not made fully explicit in the work. Assumptions are fundamental, broad hypotheses underlying the actual, narrow hypotheses and the way they are tested. As such, they might be wrong (slightly or wholly) and not only for the sake of falsifiability, but also for rational and principled development of models and theories, they need to be spelled out. So here are, in brief, the common principles guiding most of the work presented by the contributors to this volume:

1. Implicit Motives Are Nonconscious and Cannot Be Measured Through Self-Report

As we have pointed out previously, this assumption has guided the field from the very beginning and has also been supported in numerous studies that have examined the correlation between the motivational needs that individuals attribute to themselves and PSE measures of the same motivational needs. Across studies and motive domains, the correlation is close to 0. This is even the case when the explicit measure is made as similar as possible to the implicit measure, as Schultheiss, Yankova, Dirlikov, and Schad (2009) have recently demonstrated.

2. Situational Arousal of a Motivational Need Is Associated with Characteristic Changes in Thought Content and Other Nondeclarative Markers of Motivation

This was Atkinson and McClelland's (1948) fundamental insight and idea: We may not know how a motive is manifested in behavior, but we can find a way to arouse it and then examine how thought content as manifested in picture stories changes as a function of the arousal. Virtually all motive measures were derived following this basic principle or at least validated through their convergence with measures developed in this way. There can be considerable variation in the type of situational arousal, ranging from food deprivation (Atkinson & McClelland, 1948) to subliminal tachistoscopic priming with brief sentences (Siegel & Weinberger, 1998). Although most studies so far have used changes in imaginative stories written after the situational arousal had taken place, and thought content may be a good place to start looking for arousal-induced changes, there is no a priori reason why this approach could not also be extended to other markers of aroused motivational states.

3. Motives Represent Capacities for Specific Affective Experiences; They Orient, Select, and Energize Behavior

Starting with McClelland et al.'s (1953) work, motive researchers have conceived of motives as dispositions to seek out certain incentives for the affective changes they elicit. Because a person with a strong motive is a person who has a strong affective response to an incentive, the person orients attention toward cues predicting the possibility of such an affective experience, selects through learning predictive cues and instrumental behaviors that will allow approach toward and attainment of the incentive, and executes such behaviors with increased vigor and energy. These properties represent the hallmarks of motivation in studies with animals and humans alike (Berridge, 2004; McClelland, 1987; Schultheiss, 2008).

4. Motives Interact with Situational Incentives to Shape Behavior

This interactional view of motivation is part and parcel of classic and modern theories of motivation (e.g., Lewin, 1935; Toates, 1986) and has been a fundamental assumption of implicit motive research from the very beginning. For example, in the domain of achievement motivation, one and the same situational incentive (e.g., a task of moderate difficulty) may elicit dramatically different responses (e.g., an increase or a decrease in effort expenditure) depending on the strength of an individual's implicit motive to achieve. Conversely, the behavioral effects of implicit motives can markedly differ when critical situational features are varied in laboratory settings or real-life situations. For instance, the implicit achievement motive predicts response latencies on a mental concentration task when participants receive feedback that their performance deteriorates but not when the feedback indicates that that they are doing well (Brunstein & Maier, 2005). Motive researchers generally adhere to Lewin's (1935) view that behavior might best be understood as the product of person and situation variables and thus seek to elucidate how implicit motives interact with environmental cues to generate meaningful patterns of behavior both within and across situations.

5. Motives Have Pervasive Effects Across Several Levels of Psychological Functioning

Because early researchers—McClelland in particular—kept pushing the envelope with regard to how far the influence of implicit motive reaches, we now know that motives can have detectable effects at many levels: in the biological basement of brain and body; at the first-floor level of individuals' cognitive, affective, and behavioral functioning; and all the way up to the attic of societal, historic, and economic phenomena—a pretty breathtaking span of validity for a construct! But perhaps this span is not surprising because motives can be viewed as individual manifestations and elaborations of fundamental systems that have guided the behavior of our species in phylogenetic timespans (including historic time) and in many different environments and situations. They are bound to have marked effects on behavior at all levels.

6. There Is a Limited Number of Implicit Motives

Power, affiliation, and achievement, the motives this volume focuses on, are not the only basic motivational needs, and others, such as hunger or sex, also deserve more attention in research. However, the list of potential motives is not endless and in all likelihood limited to the small number of phylogenetically evolved motivational systems biopsychologists have described in some detail now (see, for instance, Panksepp, 1998).

Overview of the Book

The book is divided into four parts. The first part, titled "Motive Systems," provides an overview of past and current research and theorizing on the "Big Three" of motivation research, the needs for power, achievement, and affiliation. In Chapter 1, Fodor portrays the power motive as an ambivalent force behind human behavior: sometimes beneficial, such as when power motivation fuels creativity; sometimes detrimental, such as when power-motivated individuals become stressed by dominance challenges or elicit ingratiating behavior in members of their work teams. Pang, in Chapter 2, chronicles the metamorphoses of the achievement motive, from its beginnings in *The Achievement Motive* (McClelland et al., 1953) and Atkinson's (1957) influential risk-taking theory, to the work of Heinz Heckhausen (1963) in Germany who dissected the motive into a hope of success and a fear of failure component, all the way to the latest rigorous research efforts to identify the correlates of achievement hope and fear in the thoughts and behaviors of research participants. Weinberger, Cotler, and Fishman chronicle and discuss the measurement and validity of the affiliation motive in Chapter 3. Like the achievement motive, the affiliation motive consists of hope and fear components with different validity correlates: a capacity for closeness and love, also called intimacy motivation, and a fear of rejection and loneliness, captured to a large extent in classical measures of affiliation motivation. As Weinberger, Cotler, and Fishman point out, this distinction deserves greater attention in future measurement and theorizing about the motivational need to affiliate. Langens's chapter on activity inhibition concludes the section on motive systems. Activity inhibition does not represent an implicit motive in its own right, but it has been identified as an important implicit measure of self-regulation that frequently influences the expression of motives in behavior. Because it was derived atheoretically, as a lucky finding in one of the first attempts to aid language analysis through the use of the computer in the 1960s, its impact on the behavioral expression of power and affiliation motivation was long regarded as a slight embarrassment by scholars in the field. The situation has rapidly changed in recent years, however, because researchers have started to study activity inhibition in its own right and have gained important insights into the properties and functions of this construct. The fascinating findings from this research, to which Langens has made key contributions, are summarized in Chapter 4.

The second section of this book is titled "Assessment of Implicit Motives," and the chapters in it deal with various overarching issues in motive assessment. In Chapter 5, Pang gives a state-of-the-art account of the craft of motive assessment based on content coding of picture stories. Her contribution provides excellent guidance for all the major decisions that have to be made and issues that need to be considered if a researcher wants to employ implicit motive measures: which and how many pictures to select, whether to pretest pictures, which coding systems to use, how to train coders, how to ensure high interrater reliability, and much more. Her chapter features descriptive information about the pull of a large array of frequently used pictures for the motivational needs for power, achievement, and affiliation—information that will help make the compilation of suitable picture sets for the assessment of a given motive or sets of motives less of an art and more of an exact science. Pang also sketches out her own work on a new coding system for *n* Achievement, which separates hope of success and fear of failure based on sophisticated motivational arousal experiments.

Brunstein and Schmitt (Chapter 6) present the exciting results of their efforts to develop and validate an alternative approach to motive assessment based on the Implicit Association Test (IAT; Greenwald, McGhee, & Schwartz, 1998), an approach that promises a highly overdue extension of the measurement basis of implicit motives. As they demonstrate in considerable detail, their IAT measure of *n* Achievement shows convergent validity with a classic PSE measure of *n* Achievement, predicts the same criterion (physiological indicators of effort investment of easy, medium, and difficult tasks), and fails to overlap with self-report measures of achievement motivation.

Finally, Blankenship discusses the use of the computer in motivational theory and assessment in Chapter 7. In the past, computers have been used for the development and validation of a sophisticated theory of motivational processes, Atkinson and Birch's (1970) dynamics of action theory, and Blankenship highlights the basic assumptions behind this theory and its application in computer simulations that illustrate how stable motives can give rise to variable behavior. She also discusses how the computer can be used in the assessment of motives and in the analysis of thematic content in the stories collected from research participants.

By being the longest of the book, the third section titled "Basic Concepts and Processes" reflects the fact that the field of implicit motive research has been reinvigorated in recent years by a broad and rigorous exploration of the conceptual foundations and implications of the implicit motive construct. In Chapter 8, Bender and Woike summarize others' and their own impressive work on the effects of implicit motives on memory processes. Motives enhance memory for events and episodes of daily life, particularly when these episodes are affectively charged. Integrating motivational and cognitive models of memory, Bender and Woike portray the effects of motives on each stage of information processing contributing to this robust and pervasive effect.

In Chapter 9, Stanton, Hall, and Schultheiss discuss the nature of motive-specific incentives, whose properties have not been identified and described satisfactorily for a long time. They suggest that implicit motives respond preferentially to nonverbal incentive stimuli and contrast this mode of functioning with explicit motives, which respond primarily to verbal incentives. They also present a more specific model derived from the nonverbal-processing hypothesis, motivational field theory, which holds that nonverbal emotional signals of a sender serve as motivational incentives for the perceiver, an effect that depends critically on the perceiver's implicit motives.

Hall, Stanton, and Schultheiss then descend into the biological basement of motives in Chapter 10. As these authors point out, evidence for a strong and specific biological basis for each of the major three implicit motives has been accumulating since the 1960s, and this evidence may be among the strongest for the validity of the implicit motive construct because it gets very close to the actual neurophysiological substrates of motivation. Hall, Stanton, and Schultheiss provide a review of the older literature on the biopsychology of motives and integrate it with more recent work on the behavioral endocrinology of the big three motives. They also report findings from recent brain imaging work on the role of the needs for power, affiliation, and achievement on brain activation responses to facial expressions of emotion.

The next two chapters of this section deal with a fundamental and pervasive finding in motive research and its implications: the statistical independence between implicit motives and the motivational needs and strivings people ascribe to themselves on questionnaires. Thrash, Cassidy, Maruskin, and Elliot (Chapter 11) provide a careful and thought-stimulating analysis of the methodological and conceptual reasons for the low overlap between implicit and explicit motives. They also discuss a variety of moderators that influence the degree to which people's implicit motives and self-attributed needs converge and that have emerged in research conducted over the past 10 years. In Chapter 12, Brunstein then discusses the consequences of the matches and mismatches between implicit motives and explicit goal strivings for emotional well-being. His review of the literature clearly shows that although implicit motives and explicit goals represent independently operating systems for the regulation of behavior, they interact in shaping feelings of elation and dejection that depend on the degree to which individuals succeed or fail at motive-congruent goals. In tandem, the chapters by Thrash et al. and Brunstein emphasize the validity of the basic assumption of implicit motive research—that people generally do not have introspective access to their motivational needs—and demonstrate how the concepts and methods developed by the field can be used for addressing one of the fundamental issues of psychology since Freud, the independence of and dynamic interactions between conscious and unconscious realms of the psychic apparatus.

Baumann, Kazén, and Kuhl (Chapter 13) present a principled conceptual account of implicit motives from the perspective of personality systems interaction (PSI) theory. PSI theory holds that affective and cognitive macrosystems interact in shaping people's volitional, motivational, and self-regulatory adjustment to situational demands and affordances. According to Baumann, Kazén, and Kuhl, implicit motives are rooted in one of the cognitive macrosystems, extension memory, and moderate the interactions between and typical config-urations of affective and cognitive systems. PSI theory also yields a new, more differentiated measurement approach for the assessment of each of the big three motives, the Operant Motive Test, whose measurement credentials the authors describe and discuss in this chapter.

The fourth and final section of the book deals with "Interdisciplinary and Applied Aspects" of implicit motives. Winter (Chapter 14) discusses the political and historical correlates of implicit motives and provides a breathtaking vista of the findings he and his collaborators have collected over the years. His research shows that the motivational needs of political leaders predict their behavior in office and that the secret to belligerent or peaceful resolutions of conflicts between countries is the degree to which the communication between the parties involved reflects power-related or affiliative themes. Here is hope that some fundamental laws driving the course of history can be identified and measured empirically and that this knowledge may one day be used to predict and prevent violent conflicts.

Since McClelland's (1961) seminal work on the cultural origins and corre-lates of the achievement motive, one of the strengths of research of implicit motives has been its focus on the cross-cultural commonalities of and differ-ences between the eliciting conditions and behavioral manifestations of moti-vational needs. Like few others in recent years, Hofer has pushed the limits on the effects of culture on motives with his rigorous and painstaking work on cultural influences on motives and their effects on well-being and behavior in Germany, Costa Rica, Zambia, and other countries. He provides an overview of the key findings resulting from this impressive research program and integrates them with earlier work in Chapter 15.

In contrast to the long tradition of cross-cultural work on motives, their role in clinically relevant syndromes and disorders has received scarce attention in research. This is particularly amazing in light of the fact that implicit motives play a critical role in people's emotional well-being (see Chapter 12), and it therefore appears likely that they also might influence the occurrence of mood disorders. Weinberger, Cotler, and Fishman (Chapter 16) are the first to explore the role of implicit motives as vulnerabilities for and protective factors against psychological problems. Their work on oneness motivation, a member of the family of affiliative needs, indicates that this disposition is associated with beneficial outcomes of psychotherapy and may promote mental health.

Boyatzis and Kelner, in Chapter 17, discuss the role of competencies, which are rooted in, and are measured through similar content-coding procedures as, implicit motives in business and management contexts. Competency assess-ment has been used successfully to identify individuals who will show superior performance in specific jobs. Boyatzis and Kelner provide an overview of the links between job competencies and other measures of managerial success and job-related emotional intelligence.

Last but not least, Rheinberg and Engeser summarize their work on motivational training of teachers, students, and their parents in Chapter 18. In groundbreaking studies conducted over the past 30 years, Rheinberg has shown that motivational training can help reduce fear of failure in the classroom and bolster hope of success through the setting of individual norms instead of social norms. Rheinberg and Engeser also discuss the issue of motivational competence, that is, individuals' ability to accurately perceive the strength of their implicit motives and to set their goals accordingly. Many of Rheinberg's findings are presented in English language here for the first time.

Science is a collaborative effort, and good scientific concepts need the nurture and care of many brilliant and creative minds. This is also true for research on implicit motives in general and the path that has led us to the conception and publication of this volume in particular. We thank our excellent, knowledgeable contributors for bearing with us through the various stages of this book. Without them and the work that they present here the field would be in a state of intellectual anemia; thanks to them, it is brimming with exciting new ideas, theories, and measures. Thanks to them, we have every reason to hope for future growth and groundbreaking new insights in the field of implicit motives!

We are grateful to our students who have, with their enthusiasm, curiosity, and sharp minds, pushed us to go where in many instances we would not have gone on our own, who have made the process of research and discovery exciting and addictive fun for us, and who have shared the road with us on the way toward a better understanding of motivational phenomena. At Friedrich-Alexander University (1989 until 2000), these were Ruth Grässmann, Sven Hoyer, Harry Jankowski, Melitta Kosmann, Matthias Mehl, Birgit Nawroth, Petra Rothe, and Udo Wolf (nee Lautenschlager). At the University of Potsdam: Katharina Thiele, Anja Dargel, Cornelia Glaser, Jens Gebauer, and Norman Geissler. At the University of Michigan, Ann Arbor: Albert Bertram, Alexstine Davis, Ben Dirlikov, Anja Fiedler, Jessica Hale, Julie Hall, Nicolette Jones, Casey Kley, Scott Liening, Jeffrey MacInnes, Elizabeth Meier, Tiffiany Murray, Joyce Pang, Kathrin Riebel, Ekjyot Saini, Daniel Schad, Steven Stanton, Cynthia Torges, Wendy Treynor, Mark Villacorta, Kathryn Welsh, Alexi Wisher, Michelle Wirth, and Diana Yankova. At the University of Giessen: Clemens Schmitt, Christian Schmirl, and Michael Förster. At Friedrich-Alexander University (since 2007): Bettina Glaiber, Miriam Frisch, Martin Köllner, Annette Kordik, Jennifer Kullmann, Alexandra Mader, Vilma Maksimovaite, Mariya Patalakh, Maika Rawolle, Ramona Roch, Andreas Rösch, Anja Schiepe, Anne Stab, and Stacie Stahnke.

We owe a particular debt to our mentors, colleagues, and collaborators, who generously shared their time, resources, insights, and skills with us and without whom we would not have prospered and grown as scientists in the way we did: Kent Berridge, Stephanie Brown, Kenneth Campbell, Andy Elliot, Phoebe

Ellsworth, Barb Fredrickson, Rich Gonzalez, Dave McClelland, Heinz Heckhausen, Richard Hackmann, Günter Maier, Erhard Olbrich, Patti Reuter-Lorenz, Wolfgang Rohde, Norbert Schwarz, Todd Thrash, Brenda Volling, Christian Waugh, David Winter, and Carolyn Yoon.

A very special thanks to Heidi Reichmann and Judith Fisher for helping us with finalizing the manuscript and getting it ready for submission, to Susannah Goss for her competent translation of Chapter 18, and to Lori Handelman and Aaron Van Dorn at Oxford University Press for their patient and professional handling of the production of this volume.

To our families, our partners, and our children: you have given us love and support throughout the entire duration of this book project, despite the fact that because of the book, we spent many evenings and weekends hunched over the computer instead of with you. Thank you for your patience and understanding and for helping us balance our lives when we lost sight of the fact that there is a world outside the word processor.

Erlangen and Giessen, April 2009
Oliver C. Schultheiss
Joachim C. Brunstein

References

Atkinson, J. W. (1957). Motivational determinants of risk-taking behavior. *Psychological Review, 64,* 359–372.

Atkinson, J. W. (1958). *Motives in fantasy, action, and society: A method of assessment and study.* Princeton, NJ: Van Nostrand.

Atkinson, J. W., & Birch, D. (1970). *The dynamics of action.* New York: Wiley.

Atkinson, J. W., & McClelland, D. C. (1948). The projective expression of needs. II. The effects of different intensities of the hunger drive on thematic apperception. *Journal of Experimental Psychology, 28,* 643–658.

Berridge, K. C. (2004). Motivation concepts in behavioral neuroscience. *Physiology and Behavior, 81*(2), 179–209.

Brunstein, J. C., & Maier, G. W. (2005). Implicit and self-attributed motives to achieve: Two separate but interacting needs. *Journal of Personality and Social Psychology, 89*(2), 205–222.

Carver, C. S., & Scheier, M. F. (2007). *Perspectives on personality* (6th ed.). Boston: Allyn and Bacon.

Corkin, S. (1968). Acquisition of motor skill after bilateral medial temporal-lobe excision. *Neuropsychologia, 6,* 225–264.

deCharms, R., Morrison, H. W., Reitman, W., & McClelland, D. C. (1955). Behavioral correlates of directly and indirectly measured achievement motivation. In D. C. McClelland (Ed.), *Studies in motivation* (pp. 414–423). New York: Appleton-Century-Crofts.

Devine, P. G. (1989). Stereotypes and prejudice: Their automatic and controlled components. *Journal of Personality and Social Psychology, 56*, 5–18.

Entwisle, D. R. (1972). To dispel fantasies about fantasy-based measures of achievement motivation. *Psychological Bulletin, 77*, 377–391.

Fineman, S. (1977). The achievement motive construct and its measurement: Where are we now? *British Journal of Psychology, 68*, 1–22.

Greenwald, A. G., McGhee, D. E., & Schwartz, J. L. K. (1998). Measuring individual differences in implicit cognition: The implicit association test. *Journal of Personality and Social Psychology, 74*, 1464–1480.

Heckhausen, H. (1963). *Hoffnung und Furcht in der Leistungsmotivation [Hope and fear components of achievement motivation].* Meisenheim am Glan, Germany: Anton Hain.

John, O. P., Robins, R. W., & Pervin, L. A. (Eds.). (2008). *Handbook of personality: Theory and research* (3rd ed.). New York: Guilford.

Kihlstrom, J. F. (1990). The psychological unconscious. In L. A. Pervin (Ed.), *Handbook of personality. Theory and research* (pp. 445–464). New York: Guilford.

Klinger, E. (1971). *Structure and functions of fantasy.* New York: Wiley & Sons.

Larsen, R. J., & Buss, D. M. (2008). *Personality psychology: Domains of knowledge about human nature* (3rd ed.). New York: McGraw Hill.

LeDoux, J. E. (2002). *The synaptic self.* New York: Viking.

Lewin, K. (1935). *A dynamic theory of personality. Selected papers.* New York: McGraw-Hill.

McAdams, D. P. (2009). *The person: An introdcution to the science of personality psychology* (5th ed.). Hoboken, NJ: Wiley.

McClelland, D. C. (1955). Some social consequences of achievement motivation. In M. R. Jones (Ed.), *Nebraska Symposium on Motivation* (Vol. III, pp. 41–65). Lincoln, NE: University of Nebraska Press.

McClelland, D. C. (1961). *The achieving society.* New York: Free Press.

McClelland, D. C. (1980). Motive dispositions. The merits of operant and respondent measures. In L. Wheeler (Ed.), *Review of personality and social psychology* (Vol. 1, pp. 10–41). Beverly Hills, CA: Sage.

McClelland, D. C. (1984). *Motives, personality, and society. Selected papers.* New York: Praeger.

McClelland, D. C. (1985). How motives, skills, and values determine what people do. *American Psychologist, 40*, 812–825.

McClelland, D. C. (1987). *Human motivation.* New York: Cambridge University Press.

McClelland, D. C. (1989). Motivational factors in health and disease. *American Psychologist, 44*, 675–683.

McClelland, D. C., Atkinson, J. W., Clark, R. A., & Lowell, E. L. (1953). *The achievement motive.* New York: Appleton-Century-Crofts.

McClelland, D. C., Koestner, R., & Weinberger, J. (1989). How do self-attributed and implicit motives differ? *Psychological Review, 96*, 690–702.

McClelland, D. C., & Winter, D. G. (1969). *Motivating economic achievement: Accelerating economic development through psychological training.* New York: Free Press.

Morgan, C., & Murray, H. A. (1935). A method for investigating fantasies: The Thematic Apperception Test. *Archives of Neurology and Psychiatry, 34*, 289–306.

Murray, H. A. (1938). *Explorations in personality.* New York: Oxford University Press.

Murray, H. A. (1943). *Thematic Apperception Test.* Cambridge, MA: Harvard University Press.

Panksepp, J. (1998). *Affective neuroscience: The foundations of human and animal emotions.* New York: Oxford University Press.

Robins, R. W., Fraley, R. C., & Krueger, R. F. (Eds.). (2007). *Handbook of research methods in personality psychology.* New York: Guilford.

Schacter, D. L. (1987). Implicit memory: History and current status. *Journal of Experimental Psychology Learning, Memory, and Cognition, 13*, 501–518.

Schultheiss, O. C. (2008). Implicit motives. In O. P. John, R. W. Robins, & L. A. Pervin (Eds.), *Handbook of personality: Theory and research* (3rd ed., pp. 603–633). New York: Guilford.

Schultheiss, O. C., & Pang, J. S. (2007). Measuring implicit motives. In R. W. Robins, R. C. Fraley, & R. Krueger (Eds.), *Handbook of research methods in personality psychology* (pp. 322–344). New York: Guilford.

Schultheiss, O. C., Yankova, D., Dirlikov, B., & Schad, D. J. (2009). Are implicit and explicit motive measures statistically independent? A fair and balanced test using the Picture Story Exercise and a cue- and response-matched questionnaire measure. *Journal of Personality Assessment, 91*, 72–81.

Siegel, P., & Weinberger, J. (1998). Capturing the "mommy and I are one" merger fantasy: The oneness motive. In R. F. Bornstein & J. M. Masling (Eds.), *Empirical perspectives on the psychoanalytic unconscious* (pp. 71–97). Washington, DC: American Psychological Association.

Smith, C. P. (Ed.). (1992). *Motivation and personality: Handbook of thematic content analysis.* New York: Cambridge University Press.

Spangler, W. D. (1992). Validity of questionnaire and TAT measures of need for achievement: Two meta-analyses. *Psychological Bulletin, 112*, 140–154.

Squire, L. R. (1986). Mechanisms of memory. *Science, 232*(4758), 1612–1619.

Steele, R. S. (1973). *The physiological concomitants of psychogenic motive arousal in college males.* Unpublished dissertation thesis, Harvard University, Boston, MA.

Toates, F. (1986). *Motivational systems.* Cambridge, UK: Cambridge University Press.

Winter, D. G. (1991). Measuring personality at a distance: Development of an integrated system for scoring motives in running text. In D. J. Ozer, J. M. Healy, & A. J. Stewart (Eds.), *Perspectives in personality* (Vol. 3, pp. 59–89). London: Jessica Kingsley.

Winter, D. G. (1996). *Personality: Analysis and interpretation of lives.* New York: McGraw-Hill.

Winter, D. G. (1998). The contributions of David McClelland to personality assessment. *Journal of Personality Assessment, 71*, 129–145.

Winter, D. G. (1999). Linking personality and "scientific" psychology: The development of empirically derived Thematic Apperception Test measures. In L. Gieser & M. I. Stein (Eds.), *Evocative images: The Thematic Apperception Test and the art of projection* (pp. 107–124). Washington, DC: American Psychological Association.

SECTION 1

Motive Systems

Chapter 1
Power Motivation

EUGENE M. FODOR
Clarkson University

Introduction

Need for power (*n* Power) is conceptualized as a desire to influence, control, or impress others and, as a corollary, to receive acclaim or at least recognition for these power-motivated behaviors. As a motive, it both energizes behavior and channels it toward objectives that fulfill the basic need (Carver & Scheier, 2008). The operational definition of *n* Power most in use arose with the coding system developed by David Winter (1973, 1992) in relation to what researchers now term the Picture Story Exercise (PSE; McClelland, Koestner, & Weinberger, 1989; Winter, 1999). McClelland et al. conceived the PSE as a measure of *implicit motives*—that is, motives not readily accessible to the conscious mind but nevertheless capable of shaping people's feelings and overt behavior in important ways. The term "implicit" seemed appropriate because evidence for the motive is inferred from what people write in response to picture cues. Unlike the self-report inventories that personality psychologists more commonly use, people are not *explicitly* describing themselves. The present chapter explores the *n* Power concept from its origins through the various research applications that it has spawned. Influenced in large degree by Robert MacCleod (1975), one of my professors in graduate school, I believe that we can best understand a psychological concept by tracing it back to its historical origins. For that reason, much of the chapter does exactly that and then shows how current research interests arise in logical fashion from those intellectual roots. Special attention centers on a few topics and issues that have most caught my attention over the years. These include concern about the reliability of the PSE, the important distinction between implicit and explicit motives, and the concept of power stress.

Measuring Power Motivation

For research-oriented psychologists, the essence of a theoretical concept is its operational definition. As already mentioned, the operational definition of the power motive is the PSE. Presented with individual pictures, the research participant taking the PSE writes 5-minute stories that essentially answer the following questions:

1. What is happening? Who are the people?
2. What has led up to this situation? That is, what has happened in the past?
3. What is being thought? What is wanted? By whom?
4. What will happen? What will be done?

Written instructions exhort participants to write *vivid, imaginative, dramatic* stories, the pictures serving only as a rough guide and not to be viewed as constraining.

An Illustrative Example

Here is a story that is high in power imagery, written by a student who obtained the highest overall *n* Power score in a recent study. The story illustrates some of the scoring categories (italicized phrases) in Winter's scoring system. The picture shows a man and a woman performing a trapeze act.

> The people are *Superwoman* and *her arch nemesis Rhinosorous (sic) Man*. She is finally going to catch him and rid the world of his evil ways. Up to this point, Rhino Man has been *terrorizing the world in his attempt to gain ultimate control. He wants to make every person his servant.* Superwoman *wants to rid the world of his evil ways. The only way she can do this is to knock him into the next galaxy. The people of the world will be forever grateful for her services. For her efforts she will be made Honorary Princess of the World.* She can travel anywhere and do anything she wants all over the world.

Each coding category evidenced in the story receives a score of 1 but does not receive an additional score if it recurs again throughout the story. The first two sentences establish the theme of the story as one of power imagery (coded as Pow Im) and signal that the coder proceed in search of additional categories. If no power imagery occurs, the story receives a score of 0. Power motivation involves concerns about status, either positive or negative, so the name designation *Superwoman* implies positive prestige of a key actor (Pa+) and the designation *Rhinosorous Man* later described as terrorizing the world suggests negative prestige of a key actor (Pa-). Reference to the recognition that comes with status constitutes power imagery, the reasoning goes, regardless of whether status is positive or negative. Terrorizing the world qualifies as instrumental activity oriented toward achieving the power goal (I). Wanting to make every person his servant expresses Rhinosorous Man's need to achieve control over others (N). Wanting to rid the world of Rhinosorous Man's evil ways again expresses a need for control (N), now for Superwoman, but does not receive an additional score. In contemplating how to achieve this goal, Superwoman is showing instrumental activity (I) insofar as she is planning a means to exert power, but because instrumental activity already occurs in the person of Rhinosorous Man, the student writing the story does not receive an additional +1 score. The statement of gratitude from the world at large signifies that Superwoman has produced a momentous and far-reaching effect (Eff) and, like Pa+ and Pa-, indicates thoughts of prestige and recognition. Becoming *Honorary Princess of the World* can be seen either as a further elaboration of Eff or as Pa+. There are additional scoring categories that do not occur in the foregoing story, but the ones mentioned give an idea of how the system works. Total score for this story tallies out at 6. Rarely does a single story command a score higher than 6, although a total score of 11 is theoretically possible.

The remaining five coding categories are as follows:

Ga+ (anticipation of success in pursuit of the power goal)
Ga- (anticipation of failure to attain the power goal)
G+ (positive affect associated with success at achieving the power goal)
G- (negative affect associated with failure to achieve the power goal)
Bw (a block in the external world outside the actor that represents an at least temporary barrier to power goal attainment).

The difference between the Ga's and the G's is that the former occur *prior to* culmination of the power-motivated act and the latter subsequent to its completion. Ga- and G-, although they signal anticipated or actual failure in the quest for power, nevertheless factor into the total score because they suggest that the individual is thinking about the exercise of power.

Winter (1973, p. 250) devised a schematic diagram (Fig. 1.1) to illustrate the behavioral sequence reflected in the *n* Power coding system. He conceptualizes the motivational process as consisting of four distinguishable parts: (1) wishes, anticipations, and affective states, along with status attributions (Pa+ and Pa-) likely to accompany these states of mind, (2) possible blockage to expression of the power need, (3) instrumental activity directed toward the goal of achieving

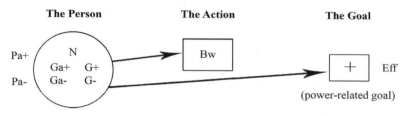

Figure 1.1 Schematic diagram of the *n* Power coding system.

impact, which on occasions may circumvent Bw, and (4) attainment of the power goal, perhaps resulting in the desired Eff.

The foregoing story combines both the beneficent and malevolent inclinations toward which the power motive may impel people. Reflecting on the question of whether power motivation is a good or bad influence on the human condition, Winter (1973) said it well:

> To me, power is like *fire*: it can do useful things; it can be fun to play with and to watch; but it must be constantly guarded and trimmed back, lest it burn and destroy. (p. xviii)

Genesis of the Winter Scoring System

Building upon Veroff (1957) and Ullman's (1972) insights on *n* Power and *n* Influence, respectively, and in an attempt to integrate these two formulations with the one he began in his doctoral dissertation (Winter, 1967), Winter (1973) proceeded to develop the scoring system that has guided most of the more recent research on power motivation. The procedure Winter chose was both conceptual and empirical. He showed a group of MBA students a film of the 1961 inauguration and speech of President John F. Kennedy. The film conceptually captured key elements of what we mean in common parlance by the term power, notably, the personal charisma of John Kennedy himself and the grandeur of the occasion (the transfer of elected executive power). A control group of MBA students observed a film in which a businessman discussed science demonstration equipment. Immediately after seeing the film, each group took a six-story version of the PSE. They also completed some questionnaires. The group who saw the Kennedy film endorsed such feelings as pride, leadership, identification with a cause, respect, and fascination. President Kennedy appeared to affect them as a heroic, powerful figure. The control group reported essentially neutral feelings without power connotations.

What Winter then did was empirically search for scoring categories that differentiated between stories written by those MBA students who saw the Kennedy film versus those who witnessed the demonstration of scientific equipment. A priori ideas of what was "power" guided his search in large part but were superseded by empirical evidence when that evidence showed disagreement with those preconceived expectations. As a final test of procedural adequacy, Winter applied the emerging scoring system to MBA students from the original sample whose protocols he had set aside and not scored and whose group membership (aroused versus neutral) he did not know (blind scoring). For example, the Eff category (registered impact felt by another) was prevalent among stories written by MBA students who observed the Kennedy video but rare among those exposed to the equipment demonstration. Some research participants who take the PSE cold, that is, in the absence of conditions designed to arouse the power motive, achieve *n* Power scores just as high as most persons subjected to conditions of arousal. That is the way their minds normally connect with the social world around them, much in the same way the MBAs felt prompted to think in response to the Kennedy film.

The empirical soundness of this procedure strikes me as especially compelling in light of an event I experienced during the first experiment I conducted with the Winter scoring system. The research participants were MBA students who took the PSE in small groups. On one occasion, four MBAs gathered shortly prior to my arrival in the designated room for taking the PSE. They had just left their evening class. Although only a few minutes had passed before I walked in, they had become embroiled in a heated, acrimonious debate as to the proper interpretation of a business study case they had examined in class. This was more than a case of intellectual disagreement. I had difficulty calming them. The PSE stories they then wrote vastly exceeded the pre-established standard for qualifying as "high" scorers in the forthcoming laboratory experiment scheduled for a few days later. The statistical probability of these scores all occurring at that level under normal circumstances was very slim. The decision, of course, was to exclude them from the actual experiment.

Early Beginnings

The PSE measure of *n* Power that Winter developed derives in part from the Thematic Apperception Test (TAT) originally devised by Henry Murray (1938). The PSE differs markedly from the TAT, however (Winter, 1999). It is more thoroughly grounded in empirical verification procedures. Trained raters analyze written stories by means of a precise and detailed coding system. By contrast, no empirically derived coding system accompanies the traditional TAT. Individual raters evaluate stories based on their own theoretical perspectives and methods of gaining insight. Hence, there can occur a lack of consistency of interpretation across raters. As a projective test, the PSE is predicated largely on the assumption that the stories people write express unconscious motivations. Although scholars attribute the seminal notion of the unconscious to Sigmund Freud, it is interesting to note that without any obvious reference to Freud, the novelist Joseph Conrad (1921) appears to have formulated the same concept:

> ... it is my belief that no man ever understands quite his own artful dodges to escape from the grim shadow of self-knowledge. (p. 64)

Robert Louis Stevenson predated both Freud and Conrad with *Strange Case of Dr. Jekyll and Mr. Hyde*, which was published in 1885 and already contained a rather vivid depiction of the struggle between rational thought and self-control on the one hand and hedonic striving and impulsivity on the other.

Winter (1973) reasoned that the power motive should be associated with occupying positions of office in student organizations in which students can anticipate opportunities to exercise power. He found that officeholders did indeed exhibit high *n* Power scores by comparison with students who did not hold offices in student organizations. He further obtained evidence that college athletes who were varsity letter winners in directly competitive sports (football, basketball, wrestling, hockey, etc.) scored distinctly high by contrast with other students. The man-against-man or team-against-team aspect of these sports in itself provides multiple opportunities for the exercise of power. Indeed, the physical activity that can occur in many of these sports often assumes violent forms. The recognition that comes to varsity athletes of course is well known, as is the realization that this recognition continues beyond the college years. Students who aspired to become teachers also were high in *n* Power. The finding makes obvious sense, as teachers possess abundant opportunity to wield influence over their students and shape in part the kinds of people they become. In sum, *n* Power is related to actions and activities that involve formal social power and personal impact.

Winter and his student associates (Winter, 1973) found that college students high in *n* Power chose as close friends those students who were not well known by other students. The chosen students likely posed minimal threat to those high in *n* Power. They did not compete with them for power and prestige. As persons who were socially "disinherited," they probably were well disposed toward accepting the attention and friendship that the power-motivated students were willing to give them, even if that meant accepting some control over their lives by another person. High-*n*-Power persons, therefore, achieve solidarity within the group and enhance self-esteem in persons of low recognition and status. Power-motivated men, their research further showed, had a preference for unassertive, dependent wives. Overall, *n* Power seems to involve a concern that one not accept much by way of influence from others.

Reliability Issues

Psychometrically minded psychologists (e.g., Entwisle, 1972) have criticized the PSE on grounds that, unlike self-report personality questionnaires, the PSE lacks test–retest reliability. However, the problem may be an artifact deriving from test instructions, which state that the participant should try to write *imaginative* stories. On retesting, the participant may strive so hard to be creatively different from the first occasion that expression of the true motive becomes distorted. An attempt to show oneself as ideationally versatile may overshadow the actual motives that ordinarily shape the writing of PSE stories. When the instructions on retesting state that the participant may now write stories that are similar to *or* different from the ones written on the previous occasion, test–retest reliabilities rise to the .60s (Lundy, 1985; Winter & Stewart, 1977).

In considering the question of internal consistency, it is important to note the distinction between the usual self-report inventory and the PSE. Self-report inventory items such as those measuring introversion/extraversion are closely similar to one another in meaning. With the PSE, this is not so. The various pictures differ in the amount of "pull" they exert for a given need (Carver & Scheier, 2008). When the pictures are similar in the degree to which they suggest power imagery, Cronbach's alpha coefficient is acceptably high, .70 in one study (Fodor, Wick, & Hartsen, 2006).

McAdams (2006) emphasizes a fundamental distinction between motives and traits that goes far to explain why PSE measures of motive strength fail to achieve high levels of test–retest reliability. As the McClelland tradition defines them, motives do not hold absolutely steady over time; they vary in strength. Certain conditions intensify them, others fulfill them. Nevertheless, the strength of a given motive stays within a boundary that characterizes an individual, so that an individual's score at a given time can predict future behavior years later. Traits as measured by self-report remain more consistent even over long periods. Momentary incentives register little effect.

The Distinction Between Implicit and Explicit Motives

The thinking behind use of PSE measures to study motivation is that these measures reflect motivational processes that operate outside a person's conscious awareness. For this reason, McClelland, Koestner, and Weinberger (1989) introduced the term *implicit motives* to describe them. Evidence indicates that PSE measures do not measure *explicit motives* as expressed through self-report questionnaires (deCharms, Morrison, Reitman, & McClelland, 1955; Schultheiss & Brunstein, 2001). The distinction between implicit motives and explicit motives (or traits) is an important one and forms the very basis for use of the PSE as a measure of motive strength.

Writing on the distinction between motives and traits, Winter, John, Stewart, Klohnen, and Duncan (1998) suggested that *motive* (as assessed by the PSE) and *trait* (as measured by self-report questionnaires) reflect conceptually different aspects of motivation but interact with one another in channeling the individual's behavior over the life course. They reasoned that motives involve wishes and goals that often are nonconscious, that is, *implicit*. These wishes and goals do not necessarily attain fulfillment through one's life experience. Traits, Winter et al. defined as "comprised of more-or-less consistent, generalized, intercorrelated clusters of behavior" (p. 233). They channel the ways motives are expressed, essentially acting as a rudder that steers one through the vicissitudes that define human experience, sometimes approaching and sometimes avoiding specific goals according to where the individual fits along the trait dimension.

Studying Radcliffe and Mills college graduates, Winter et al. examined the interactive effects of both the affiliation and power motives, each in combination with measures of the trait introversion/extraversion. Neither motive correlated with introversion/extraversion score but in combination with introversion/extraversion score predicted important outcomes at midlife. As predicted, women high in *n* Affiliation who were also high in extraversion became more involved in volunteer work than did women high in *n* Affiliation but low in extraversion (introverts). Taken by themselves, neither *n* Affiliation nor extraversion correlated with volunteer work. For introverts high in the affiliation motive, volunteer work presumably would bring on too much arousal, whereas extraverts high in the same motive would seek out the social stimulation that volunteer work provides. Also as predicted and by the same line of reasoning, extraverts high in *n* Affiliation were more likely to combine work and family roles than were introverts high in the affiliation motive. Balancing family against work commitments entails much arousal which affiliation-motivated extraverts likely would find totally acceptable. Lastly, affiliation-motivated women low on extraversion (introverts) were more likely to have separated, divorced, or experienced stress in their close relationships than were affiliation-motivated women high in extraversion. Affiliation-motivated introverts, the reasoning goes, should find intimate relationships overarousing, conflictual, and threatening given their preferences for privacy and solitude. That is, there is a conflict between need for closeness (*n* Affiliation) and aversion to overarousal (introversion) that is brought on by close social contact. High *n* Power in combination with extraversion predicted entry into *impact careers* (e.g., teaching, management) for the Radcliffe sample, a finding that makes sense in terms of the channeling hypothesis that Winter et al. put forth. Extraverted women high in power motivation likewise placed greater value on work relationships in their chosen career than did introverted women high on the power motive.

Drinking Behavior

David McClelland and his associates (McClelland, Davis, Kalin, & Wanner, 1972) formulated a theory that high power motivation coupled with a low level of restraining thoughts about power inclines men toward heavy alcoholic beverage consumption. They termed this combination of traits *personal power*. Seligman, Walker, and Rosenhan (2001) describe the known effects of alcohol consumption. Physiologically speaking, alcohol in its short-term effects produces sensations of immediate strength (what some college students at my university aptly term "beer muscles"). Absorbed through the stomach wall directly into the bloodstream, it rapidly increases blood sugar, thereby increasing energy availability. To some degree, the process increases adrenalin flow as well. Vasodilation produces sensations of bodily warmth. The more one drinks (to a certain point), the more the mind becomes suffused with a less inhibited type of thinking about personal dominance, notably, about aggression and exploitative sex.

The theory evolved through a series of studies that the McClelland group conducted in a variety of natural social settings, ostensibly for the purpose of studying the effects of various social situations on fantasy. College undergraduates participated in one of these studies, and MBAs in another. In the college undergraduate study, individual groups consisted of 3–6 members. Half the groups, randomly chosen, drank alcoholic beverages in a party setting, and the other half nonalcoholic drinks. They all wrote PSE stories before the party began, another set to different pictures further into the party, and still another set later on. The research plan included procedures for estimating the amounts of alcohol research participants consumed. PSE analysis disclosed that alcoholic beverage consumption as it progressed did indeed heighten fantasies of personal power (high *n* Power coupled with low inhibition about aggression and exploitative sex). Moreover, the more men showed this combined set of traits in their initial PSE scores, the more alcoholic beverage they consumed. The MBA student study was similar, except that the groups received an invitation to attend a discussion in the living room of an apartment rather than attend a party. Wondering if the results they obtained with college students would apply equally to older men whose drinking habits had become stabilized beyond the youthful exuberance and experimentation that characterize the college population, McClelland and Davis (1972) conducted research at a "working-class" bar where men habitually drank socially in evenings with other men. They wanted to study a group of men whose habits, values, and attitudes likely differed from college students who attend weekend cocktail parties. An advertisement appeared in the local newspaper, specifically mentioning that the study involved the use of alcohol, the telling of a few imaginative stories, and compensation in the amount of $15 (a significant sum at the time). Volunteers reported to an employment agency and provided responses to questionnaires including information as to whether they were light, moderate, or heavy drinkers. Persons who were receiving treatment for alcoholism or who were trying to refrain from drinking did not receive an invitation to participate further.

A few days later, volunteers reported to a local bar at 8:00 and stayed until 9:30. After a few minutes of small talk, one among a number of graduate students in clinical psychology presented four appropriately selected PSE pictures and asked individual participants to tell imaginative stories about each picture, which the graduate student thereupon tape recorded. A waitress took orders for drinks. She recorded what and how much a participant drank. There were no restrictions on what or how many drinks they could order. They were free to do whatever they pleased within the barroom setting. That is, they could talk among themselves, watch television, play pinball, or talk with other customers. At 9:30, they told more stories to a second set of four pictures.

Differences in drinking history proved to be a major determinant in behavioral outcome. Specifically, heavy and moderate drinkers at the second PSE administration showed greater increase in personalized power (unrestrained assertiveness, i.e., high *n* Power coupled with low activity inhibition) than did light drinkers. Men with strong power concerns and low levels of restraint in fantasy, the data seemed to indicate, are the men most likely to be heavy drinkers. In summarizing these and related findings, McClelland and Davis saw in the motivational pattern associated with heavy drinking a special type of power imagery:

> ... a personalized concern in which the world is seen as something of a competitive jungle wherein a man must seek to win out over opponents. Drinking tends to increase generalized power concerns, but particularly personal power concerns which are elevated even more than normal in men with heavy drinking histories. These men, who are already concerned about personal dominance before drinking, are even more concerned after drinking; the inference is that they are using drinking as a means of accentuating their desire to dominate others who would oppose them. They may get direct gratification from thinking about winning out over others in fantasy. (pp. 160–161)

Power Motivation and Ingratiation

Woodrow Wilson was a president whom the psychoanalytically trained political scientists Alexander and Juliette George (1964) characterized as high in power motivation. Woodrow's father, a Presbyterian minister, whom family acquaintances described as harsh in his criticism of young Woodrow, seemed to demand of him standards of deportment and achievement not commonly attained by a boy Woodrow's age. The psychoanalyst Karen Horney (1939) saw in these kinds of circumstances a thwarting of a developing child's need for affection. The consequence, she concluded, is a need for power and prestige, an attempt to demonstrate that one is not to be taken lightly, that one is worthy of notice. Throughout Wilson's career as president of Princeton University, governor of New Jersey, and president of the United States, as well as in his personal life, Wilson showed himself to be especially susceptible to ingratiation, flattery from others that one might expect so intelligent a man as Woodrow Wilson to recognize for its manipulative intent. Colonel Edward House, for example, although he had no formal appointment in the Wilson administration, enjoyed enormous influence with the president. When Wilson delivered an address on a given topic, House would write the president a letter, often extolling the address as the most brilliant statement on that topic ever spoken.

Taking our lead from the George and George biography of Woodrow Wilson, Dana Farrow and I (Fodor & Farrow, 1979) subjected the ingratiation hypothesis to empirical test, using male MBA students as research participants. The format was an industrial simulation experiment in which MBA students who had completed the PSE acted as supervisor in interacting with three supposed workers in the next room who were assembling Tinker Toy models from pictured diagrams, a different model on each of five trials. Communication was via an intercom system. The "workers" were paid actors who had made tape recordings. So as not to interfere with the workers' performance, the experimenter told the student supervisor, communication occurred only at the end of a 5-minute trial. The "supervisor" was to use any and all means at his disposal to motivate the workers toward good performance—exhortations, words of encouragement, threats, and increase or reduction in the amount of pay the workers supposedly received for their participation. The workers, the experimenter further told the MBA student supervisor, were not allowed to respond to the supervisor's comments, lest their response unduly influence the supervisor's ultimate evaluation of them. Otherwise, they were free to make whatever comments to the supervisor they wished, but only at the end of a given trial while waiting for the next to begin. At the end of a trial and hence for each model, the experimenter brought in a card tabulating each worker's number of completed models. Performance always was roughly average according to the performance norms available to the student supervisor (50th percentile give or take a few percentage points). Worker comments were generally neutral and rather meaningless: for example, "You don't mind if we smoke do you?"; "Is it okay if we pull down the shades?" At the end of certain trials in the experimental condition, Man C made ingratiating remarks to the student supervisor: "You know, I really like your approach. I can see you're gonna be a good supervisor"; "Personally, I think you're doin' a great job"; then toward the end, "You've done pretty good." Man C's comments in the control condition were neutral and noningratiating both in content and in emotional tone.

Student supervisors who scored high on the PSE measure of n Power (top third of the overall distribution) evaluated Man C's performance highly when Man C was an ingratiator, more highly than did student supervisors low in power motivation, higher than they evaluated the other workers, and higher than the appraisals high-n-Power supervisors gave the noningrating Man C in the control condition. Table 1.1 displays these results. High-n-Power supervisors also perceived themselves as having influenced the workers more than did low-n-Power supervisors.

These experiments have their humorous moments. I was most eager to meet the gentleman who scored the highest on the PSE n Power measure, so I arranged to conduct the postexperimental interview myself rather than consign the task to my research assistant as was our usual procedure. The hour was late, approaching 9:00 p.m. Friday evening. I asked my research assistant if there was anything out of the ordinary in the session that just ended. He said no there was not ... except for the singing. The gentleman sometimes would turn off the intercom during the ongoing work trials so that the workers in the adjoining soundproof room could not hear him, and he would sing in a loud melodious voice that reverberated down the hallway. Interesting, I thought—certainly

Table 1.1   Mean Performance Evaluations Given the Ingratiating Worker

	Performance	
Level of n Power in Supervisor	Ingratiator	Neutral Worker
High		
M	29.3_a	22.1_b
SD	4.2	4.8
Low		
M	24.2_b	23.0_b
SD	4.9	3.9

Note: Means with differing subscripts differ significantly from each other, $p < .01$.

consistent with the need for recognition aspect of the power motive. I greeted the young man. We shook hands. He was a big guy, built like a football player. I so commented, and yes he had played football as an undergraduate. Nothing else about him seemed out of the ordinary. He was very polite, but he kept looking at his watch. I asked if he had an impending appointment, it being Friday night. He replied that yes he did, that he worked as a bouncer in a local tavern, adding with obvious enthusiasm, "And have I got work to do tonight!"

McAdams, Healy, and Krause (1984) also did an experiment that speaks to the ingratiation theme. They asked college students to describe recent interactions with friends, also listing positive and negative personal characteristics of the people who appeared in these friendship episodes. All participants had previously completed the PSE, which was scored for n Intimacy and n Power. Their findings with respect to n Power strengthen the validity of the n Power construct and the PSE measure for assessing it. High-power individuals, unlike low-power individuals, understood friendships as an opportunity to take on a dominant, controlling role. High-intimacy individuals, by contrast, adopted a listening role in their friendship interactions. In citing reasons behind their friendships, they emphasized themes of trust, self-disclosure, and caring for the others' well-being. With its emphasis on display and expansion of the self, power motivation was negatively related to the friendship understandings that high-intimacy individuals expressed.

The McClelland Model

The theoretical framework within which researchers conceive implicit motives derives in large degree from the McClelland model (McClelland, 1958, 1976, 1985; McClelland, Koestner, & Weinberger, 1989). People vary in how they configure and react to events in their social environment. Specifically, they encounter learned cues, or *nonverbal incentives* (see Chapter 6). These nonverbal incentives set into motion motive dispositions in which the individual enjoys special strength, namely, n Achievement, n Affiliation/Intimacy, or n Power. They signal the opportunity to experience emotionally reinforcing activity relative to a given motive. When the individual encounters a nonverbal incentive that aligns well with the individual's capacity to experience an affective state associated with a motive, the outcome is an emotional "kick" (Woike, 1994), that is, a surge in affect. For the person high in power motivation, the appropriate nonverbal incentive suggests an opportunity to experience feelings of strength, vigor, and energy. As conceived by McClelland, Koestner, and Weinberger (1989), the pleasure the high-n-Power person experiences from registering an impact on others results in the hormonal release of

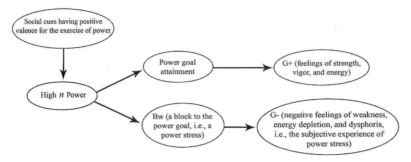

Figure 1.2 Schematic diagram of McClelland's conceptualization of power stress.

norepinephrine, which is a physiological indicator of stress adaptation (cf. McClelland, 1982). Should the power-motivated person not experience the anticipated surge in affect when confronted by an opportunity to exert power, that is, when the power motive is blocked, the result is what McClelland (1976) termed a *power stress*.

The accompanying diagram illustrates the McClelland model. Using Winter's coding symbols, we see the high-power individual reacting to social cues that have positive valence for the exercise of power (i.e., they suggest the opportunity for instrumental activity (I) oriented toward fulfillment of the power need). The need either is successful, thereby resulting in the positive feelings designated as G+; or it is blocked (Bw), eventuating in G−, namely, the negative affect and physiological activation that McClelland defines as power stress. Power stress, in McClelland's analysis, refers both to the thwarting event itself *and* to the reaction to the thwarting event in the high-power person (Fig. 1.2).

Power Stress

McClelland (1976) defined as power stress a social event that simultaneously both arouses and thwarts the power motive. A negative audience reaction to an address by a power-motivated speaker who had intended to create an emotional impact would be an example, as would a thwarted attempt at a committee meeting to persuade others to one's point of view, again if the would-be persuader were high in *n* Power. McClelland saw a similarity between *n* Power and the defining elements researchers had found to characterize persons prone to cardiovascular illness. Most notable among these characteristics were aggression and competitive striving. Supportive of McClelland's view was an experiment by Steele (1973) that showed especially heightened epinephrine output in the urine as a response to a power-arousal manipulation among research participants whose *n* Power scores increased most as a consequence of the arousal manipulation. An achievement-arousal manipulation did not produce the same effect. Epinephrine production is a key element in Selye's (1973) general adaptation syndrome, which when activated repeatedly and to a high degree is thought to increase the likelihood of cardiovascular illness. Among the effects epinephrine secretion produces are increased heart rate, increased blood pressure, and conversion of glycogen from the liver to blood glucose.

McClelland (1979, 1982) hypothesized that power stress can occur in two possible ways. One way is via an internal control mechanism that bottles up anger, assertiveness, and physiological activation—what McClelland termed *activity inhibition*. The bottling-up process constitutes a power stress in power-motivated persons insofar as it denies expression of the power motive. The second way is via social circumstances that block expression of the power motive or present an insurmountable challenge to its expression. Both methods of incurring power stress— internal restraint or a social event that thwarts the power-motivated person's assertive capabilities—checks any attempt to express power and theoretically can result in harmful physiological consequences if experienced many times.

The mere anticipation that others may resist one's power attempts can cause power stress. Harry Truman was one of the presidents whose inaugural address Winter (1987) coded as distinctly high in need for power. David McCullough (1992) describes how in World War I Captain Truman was assigned the role of commander over 194 men. He a third degree Mason and they a defiant and rowdy bunch of Irish Catholics made the leadership challenge especially intimidating. Previous commanders had been unable to handle them. When he first walked out on the parade field, he felt himself to be completely terror stricken, expecting maximal resistance to his authority. McCullough vividly recounts what is known about Truman's inner feelings at the time. Private Edward McKim recalled that the men observing Harry Truman could plainly see that "he was scared to death." Truman's personal recollections express the stress he felt on that occasion:

Harry said . . . he had never been so terrified. He could feel all their eyes on him, feel them sizing him up. "I could just see my hide on the fence, . . . Never on the front or anywhere else have I been so nervous." (p. 117)

As he was to confess long afterward, writing about himself in the third person, "He was so badly scared he couldn't say a word. . ." (p. 117)

At last, he called, "Dismissed!" (p. 117)

In researching the power stress concept, McClelland (1979) focused attention on what he termed the *blocked power motive syndrome* (high power motivation, low need for affiliation, high activity inhibition). Affiliation enters into the equation as an antidote to power stress (McClelland, 1985). People high in the affiliation need tend to seek out the company of others as a means of alleviating stress, talking with them, sharing with them their fears and anxieties. McClelland looked at PSE protocols on record 20 years prior to the time he tested men's blood pressure and found a significant correlation between the blocked power motive syndrome and subsequent high blood pressure. Evidence of the syndrome early in life appears to bear implications for cardiovascular health many years later. Studying a male prison population, McClelland, Davidson, Floor, and Saron (1980) sought to determine whether epinephrine was indeed a response to power stress. Persons with the syndrome who also reported high recent levels of power stress did show high epinephrine concentrations in the urine by contrast with appropriate comparison groups.

Of the two ways that McClelland (1979) saw power stress as likely to occur, he conceded that evidence for the influence of thwarting social events was sparse. To round out the evidence, he expressed a need for experiments that present "strong situational challenges" (p. 189) to the power motive. Following through on McClelland's suggestion, I conducted some industrial simulation experiments with male college students. Situational challenges approximated circumstances that managers who participate in training programs commonly report, namely, hard-to-manage work groups (Fodor, 1984) and seemingly irreconcilable conflict among subordinate managers (Fodor, 1985). In the first experiment, the power stress manipulation consisted of preprogrammed comments from supposed workers in the next room. (Actually the workers were fictitious, the comments playacted for a tape recording.) The comments connoted tension within the work group. The "workers" voiced concern about not meeting the standard, about beating out the competition, about not earning enough money, and fear that they not do well enough to be invited back for an additional experiment. For the power stress manipulation in the second experiment, the "company president" of a hypothetical electronics firm supervised two "managers" each with opposing role scripts, one script exhorting a manager to argue for and the other against the manufacture and marketing of a controversial sun lamp. The experimenter informed the "company president" at the very outset of the experiment that it was his task to resolve any possible conflict among his two managers, guiding the group toward an amicable conclusion, and that his ability to do so was an index of his managerial potential. A debriefing occurred at the end of the session. In both experiments, control groups confronted an absence of power stress. In the first experiment, the "workers" in the control group voiced neutral comments without any hint of tension occurring within the group. In the second experiment, the "managers" in the control group both had role scripts encouraging them to favor manufacture of the sun lamp. High-n-Power participants evinced higher stress reactions than low-n-Power participants in the power stress condition in both experiments and higher stress than all participants in the control condition. Scores on Thayer's (1978) Activation–Deactivation Check List comprised the dependent measure in the first experiment and electromyographic recordings from the forearm extensor muscle in the second. Measures of muscle tension are conceived as an index of physiological arousal (Levenson, 1983).

Noting that the hypothalamic-pituitary-adrenal (HPA) axis responds to psychological stressors by increasing corticosteroid release, Wirth, Welsh, and Schultheiss (2006) hypothesized that high-power individuals are more stressed by a defeat than are low-power individuals and that a defeat should manifest itself in cortisol release. McClelland (1989) likewise stressed the mediating influence that cortisol plays in organizing the general adaptation syndrome. Wirth et al. experimentally induced social defeat in a competitive contest. Participants worked on varying forms of a number tracking test. Half the participants experienced social defeat in this reaction-based cognitive task. The other half experienced social victory, that is, the task was so rigged that they "outperformed" the other participant. The experience of losing the contest against another surely qualifies as a power stress and, as predicted, its occurrence resulted in an increase in salivary cortisol secretion for persons scoring high in power motivation but not in those scoring low.

The process of evaluating a person for employment holds prospects for arousing power stress. As previously noted, power-motivated persons favor as friends and associates persons who are unassuming, unassertive, and disinclined to challenge the power-motivated person's authority. Strong-willed persons, on the other hand, pose a distinct threat to the successful exercise of power. We obtained evidence to confirm this hypothesis (Fodor, Wick, & Hartsen, 2006). In a simulated employment interview, college males imagined themselves as manager to a young man playacting a videotaped interview. He portrayed himself as strong-willed and assertive in one condition, and compliant in another. The research participants who did the evaluating had scored either high or low on the PSE in n Power. As shown in Fig. 1.3, participants scoring high evinced higher electromyographic readings from the corrugator brow (frown) muscle when viewing the strong-willed, assertive candidate than did those scoring low, and higher than all participants who witnessed the compliant candidate. Responses to a scale that measured affect revealed the same pattern for negative affect.

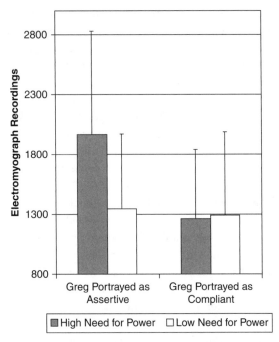

Figure 1.3 Mean EMG recordings from the brow supercilii muscles. Error bars represent standard errors of the mean. (Fodor, Wick, & Hartsen, 2006, p. 605.)

Creativity

McClelland (1964) put forth a theory about creative achievement in science that has a Freudian bent to it. Scientific achievement, he speculated, arises as a sublimation of repressed aggressiveness in childhood, assuming the form of power motivation:

> It is certainly part of the folklore of science that it represents an attempt to *conquer* [italics original] nature, to dominate it and bring it under man's control. Social theorists have noted that the view that man could be more powerful than nature is by no means a common one in history. In fact, the usual belief among peoples of the world, even today, is that nature is more powerful than man ... and that man must somehow placate the gods who control nature. It does not seem too farfetched to assume that it took an unusual psychodynamic situation to create in some men the apparently irrational belief that they could conquer nature. The blocked aggressive needs of a few scientists, diverted toward nature, may well have fulfilled such an important historic function. (pp. 171–172)

> At a more personal level, we have noted that the scientist is intensely analytic in his approach to experience. His response is to freeze the flux of reality, to ask, What is

it?, to take the experience apart and see what makes it tick. It is no mere metaphor to say that the analysis represents a form of aggression. To take something apart is to destroy it in a very real sense. (p. 172)

Implicit in the power motive concept is the notion that a nonverbal incentive may consist of any behavioral opportunity that can result in a surge of positive affect associated with having had impact. Creativity, if its impact can be felt by others, easily qualifies as a nonverbal incentive for the power need. One thinks immediately of James Watson's autobiographical account of how in their quest to understand the molecular structure of DNA, he and Francis Crick were unabashedly driven by a desire to win the Nobel Prize and to be the first to go to press (Watson, 1968). Merton (1973) speaks of the "race for priority" as a major impetus to scientific discovery. Acclaim and recognition most adorn the scientist who is first to publish a scientific discovery. What these writings suggest is that an aspect of power motivation, namely, the desire to have impact (Eff in the Winter coding system) figures into the creative process as it pertains to scientific achievement.

We obtained experimental evidence that appears to support McClelland's (1964, 1975) view that power motivation may indeed result in creative performance (Fodor, 1990; Fodor & Carver, 2000; Fodor & Greenier, 1995). The research strategy required that college student participants at a technological university individually attempt to solve an engineering problem of moderate difficulty, namely, how to keep the classroom windows in an old building from getting so stuck during the winter months that they become difficult to open come spring. The experimenter then "examined" what the participant had written and provided written feedback couched in the language of positive or negative power imagery. Positive feedback informed the participant that the experimenter was impressed and that the participant's proposed solution likely would register a favorable impact on others, notably, members of the engineering and scientific community, essentially causing them to "stand up and take notice." Accompanying this handwritten feedback was a 7-point rating scale that conveyed the same message, that is, how much recognition and visibility the participant's solution was likely to command. The feedback thereby provided was credible because the window frame problem is sufficiently easy that anyone can render a solution that an evaluator might reasonably consider creative, yet the participant might just as likely think a more sophisticated solution possible. The negative feedback condition conveyed an opposite message, signifying that the proposed solution likely would not create much impact. A control condition entailed no experimental feedback.

Positive feedback stated in the language of power imagery enhanced creativity in high-power but not low-power persons, by two different measures: creativity ratings (Amabile, 1983) applied to proposed solutions to a second engineering problem (Fodor, 1990; Fodor & Carver, 2000) and scores on the

Remote Associates Test (RAT) of creativity (Mednick & Mednick, 1967; Fodor & Greenier, 1995), a test which Isen, Daubman, and Nowicki (1987) have shown to be a *state* measure that responds to conditions that instill positive affect. The format of the RAT consists of three words followed by a blank space, requiring that the participant provide in the blank space a word that relates to each of the three words. The following item is an example:

mower   atomic   foreign   _____

The correct answer *power* is a remote, or uncommon, associate of the three stimulus words, far apart from them in semantic space. The RAT has relevance to the study of creativity in science and engineering. Gordon (reported in Mednick & Mednick, 1967) studied scientists and engineers engaged in defense-related research and found that those who scored high on the RAT wrote a greater number of successful research proposals than did those who scored low. Table 1.2 displays the results we obtained with the RAT in one of the studies we did (Fodor & Greenier, 1995).

Negative feedback, phrased in the language of power imagery, produced distinctly low creative outcomes by both of the aforementioned measures in high-power individuals. Measures of positive versus negative affect subsequent to feedback displayed the same pattern, suggesting that creativity and affect levels go hand in hand. The patterns we observed for high-power individuals did not occur in persons scoring low in power motivation, who were relatively unaffected by the feedback they received. What the power-motivated individual perceives as creative success, therefore, appears to manifest itself in both good feeling and creative performance. The experience of failure to register impact through their creative endeavors appears to constitute a power stress in power-motivated persons and to diminish creative performance at least temporarily immediately thereafter. The "sweet smell of success," if it entails recognition and admiration, may well be a guiding motif in the creative life of the power-motivated person, giving sustenance to the power need.

Table 1.2   Remote Associates Test Scores (Fodor & Greenier, 1995, p. 248)

	Positive Feedback	Negative Feedback	No Feedback
High *n* Power			
M	16.4 (n = 22)	10.7 (n = 22)	12.1 (n = 22)
SD	3.8	4.5	3.8
Low *n* Power			
M	12.3 (n = 22)	11.1 (n = 22)	11.6 (n = 22)
SD	3.8	4.6	3.6

Note: From "The power motive, self-affect, and creativity," by E. M. Fodor and K. D. Greenier, 1995, *Journal of Research in Personality*, 29, p. 248.

Other Validity Correlates of *n* Power

There is an abundant research literature to support the construct validity of the PSE measure for *n* Power (McAdams, 2006; Winter, 1996). Much of the discussion in this chapter speaks to the validity of the *n* Power concept and the PSE measure by which it is assessed. As previously mentioned, persons high in the power motive are especially responsive to ingratiation by a subordinate (Fodor & Farrow, 1979). This finding strengthens the construct validity of the PSE measure of *n* Power insofar as it is consistent with Karen Horney's (1937) view that persons needful of power and prestige have experienced a lack of parental affection in their early years. Ingratiation from a subordinate logically compensates for that lack in their lives. Also, members of small groups perceive high-*n*-Power leaders as dominant. Moreover, the presence of a leader high in the power motive appears to inhibit information flow into group discussion (Fodor & Smith, 1982) and reduces feelings of competence in group members (Fodor & Riordin, 1995), presumably because power-motivated persons dominate others and inhibit their self-expression. These findings tie together with the theoretical assumptions that underlie the *n* Power concept.

Mason and Blankenship (1987) studied the relationship between *n* Power and the infliction of physical abuse in intimate relationships. They employed a modified version of the Conflict Tactics scales (Straus, 1979) to measure the amount of psychological and physical abuse college students had inflicted on their partners in the past year. High-*n*-Power men (but not women) inflicted significantly greater abuse on their partners than did low-*n*-Power men. Zurbriggen (2000), correspondingly, obtained positive correlations between *n* Power in men (but not women) and the Coerce and Seduce scales that she administered to test aspects of aggressive sexual behavior.

Further evidence for the validity of implicit measures for *n* Power comes from the finding that *n* Power correlates with frequency of sexual intercourse (McClelland, 1975; Schultheiss, Dargel, & Rohde, 2003; Winter, 1973). Schultheiss et al. (2003) suggest that these findings neatly parallel evidence that social dominance coincides closely with sexual reproduction in other mammalian species. Citing Wilson (1980), they point out that dominance rank among social mammals confers privileged access to mates with a resultant increase in offspring by comparison with mammals of subordinate rank. In humans, the reasoning goes, the implicit power motive (as measured by the PSE) may serve as a marker for actual or desired dominance rank and may be related to reproductive success. Power-motivated individuals show high baseline levels of testosterone, a hormone associated with sexual motivation in both men and women, and they also evince a greater increase in testosterone level when winning a dominance contest than do low-n-Power individuals (Schultheiss, Campbell, & McClelland, 1999; Schultheiss & Rohde, 2002).

Looking to the Future

One can sense an interplay between motivation as measured by the PSE and people's reactions to emotional cues provided by other persons. These cues can serve as nonverbal incentives in relation to n Affiliation and n Power. Consistent with McClelland's (1989) theoretical analysis of the role non-verbal incentives play in activating implicit motives, Schultheiss and Hale (2007) examined how power- and affiliation-motivated individuals oriented toward faces denoting various emotions, specifically, their allocation of attention to the motive-relevant cues inherent in facial expression. They presented participants with faces known to express the emotions of joy, anger, and surprise relative to a neutral expression. Prior research has consistently shown that people can rate facial expressions on the degree to which they reflect dominance (power) and affiliation (e.g., Knutson, 1996). Joyful expressions rate as high on both dominance and affiliation, and anger expressions rate high on dominance but low on affiliation. As regards power motivation, Schultheiss and Hale reasoned that the incentive value of an emotional expression connoting dominance should be *reciprocally* related to the dominance the facial expression displays because such an expression from another signals lack of control by the power-motivated person. Schultheiss and Hale hypothesized, therefore, that facial expressions of high dominance, notably, anger and joy, should figure as *disincentives* in the minds of power-motivated persons, cues they would orient their attention away from. Surprise, as a low-dominance expression, should by contrast serve as an *incentive* for the power-motivated person, giving evidence that the person has produced an impact.

The method by which Schultheiss and Hale tested their predictions was Mogg and Bradley's (1999) dot-probe task. The computer screen presents an emotional and a neutral face side by side. The stimuli then are masked, and a little dot (the probe stimulus) replaces either the emotional or the neutral face just previously seen. How fast the participant orients toward the probe sig-nifies how much the individual's attention was oriented toward the facial stimulus the dot replaces, be it emotional or neutral. The response latency is shorter if the participant's attention was focused on the face that the dot replaces, longer if attention was toward the face that was not replaced by the dot. In line with prediction, the authors found that power-motivated individuals attended to the low-dominance, and therefore, rewarding surprise expression but oriented away from the high-dominance, and therefore aversive, anger and joy facial expressions. These findings were in sharp contrast to what the authors saw in affiliation-motivated participants. The most prominent finding for affiliation-motivated persons was that they showed high vigilance for anger faces, suggesting a sensitivity to interpretational cues signaling rejection.

Exploring the question of emotional reactivity to other persons, we have begun a simulated dating service experiment. College student participants scoring high or low in n Power observe an 8-minute playacted video depicting an interview with an opposite-sexed person who comes across as either assertive or deferentially compliant. Outcome measures consist of electromyographic readings from the brow corrugator (frown) muscle and responses to two different questionnaires that assess affective response. The prediction, of course, is that high-n-Power males, consistent with Winter's early findings, should show an aversive reaction to assertive women, preferring women who are more deferent to the male species. As regards women vis-à-vis men, we anticipate a similar finding, although frankly not with great confidence. There is reported evidence that women factor male dominance into their assessment of a male's desirability to so significant a degree that physical appearance plays less a role in their expressed preference than it does with males evaluating women (cf. Cunninghan, Barbee, & Pike, 1990). The question is: Does n Power moderate women's preference for dominant males?

We can conclude from the foregoing discussion that the n-Power concept is embedded within an intricate and expanding nomological network. What appears to have given sustenance to the concept and kept it alive through the years is its inherently multifaceted nature, which has enabled research scholars to pursue its meaning into realms as diverse as physiology, cognition, group dynamics, creativity, and considerations of mental health. As other writings in the present volume amply demonstrate, n Power also explains important aspects of leadership performance. In summary, the n Power concept has enhanced our understanding of many dimensions of human behavior that without the research the concept has spawned would remain largely unexplained.

References

Amabile, T. M. (1983). *The social psychology of creativity.* New York: Springer-Verlag.

Carver, C. S., & Scheier, M. F. (2008). *Perspectives on personality.* Boston: Allyn & Bacon.

Conrad, J. (1921). *Victory.* New York: Modern Library.

Cunningham, M. R., Barbee, A. P., & Pike, C. L. (1990). What do women want? Facialmetric assessment of multiple motives in the perception of male facial physical attractiveness. *Journal of Personality and Social Psychology, 59,* 61–72.

deCharms, R., Morrison, H. W., Reitman, W. R., & McClelland, D. C. (1955). Behavioral correlates of directly and indirectly measured achievement motivation. In D. C. McClelland (Ed.), *Studies in motivation.* New York: Appleton-Century-Crofts.

Entwisle, D. R. (1972). To dispel fantasies about fantasy-based measures of achievement motivation. *Psychological Bulletin, 77,* 377–391.

Fodor, E. M. (1984). The power motive and reactivity to power stresses. *Journal of Personality and Social Psychology, 47,* 853–859.

Fodor, E. M. (1985). The power motive, group conflict, and physiological arousal. *Journal of Personality and Social Psychology, 49,* 1408–1415.

Fodor, E. M. (1990). The power motive and creativity of solutions to an engineering problem. *Journal of Research in Personality, 24,* 338–354.

Fodor, E. M., & Carver, R. A. (2000). Achievement and power motives, performance feedback, and creativity. *Journal of Research in Personality, 34,* 380–396.

Fodor, E. M., & Farrow, D. L. (1979). The power motive as an influence on the use of power. *Journal of Personality and Social Psychology, 37,* 2091–2097.

Fodor, E. M., & Greenier, K. D. (1995). The power motive, self-affect, and creativity. *Journal of Research in Personality, 29,* 242–252.

Fodor, E. M., & Riordin, J. M. (1995). Leader power motive and group conflict as influences on leader behavior and group member self-affect. *Journal of Research in Personality, 29,* 418–431.

Fodor, E. M., & Smith, T. (1982). The power motive as an influence on group decision making. *Journal of Personality and Social Psychology, 42,* 178–185.

Fodor, E. M., Wick, D. P., & Hartsen, K. M. (2006). The power motive and affective response to assertiveness. *Journal of Research in Personality, 40,* 598–610.

George, A. L., & George, J. L. (1964). *Woodrow Wilson and Colonel House: A personality study.* New York: Dover.

Horney, K. (1937). *The neurotic personality of our time.* New York: Norton.

Isen, A. M., Daubman, K. A., & Nowicki, G. P. (1987). Positive affect facilitates creative problem solving. *Journal of Personality and Social Psychology, 52,* 1122–1131.

Knutson, B. (1996). Facial expressions of emotion influence interpersonal trait inferences. *Journal of Nonverbal Behavior, 20,* 165–182.

Levenson, R. W. (1983). Personality research and psychophysiology: General considerations. *Journal of Research in Personality, 17,* 1–21.

Lundy, A. (1985). The reliability of the Thematic Apperception Test. *Journal of Personality Assessment, 49,* 141–145.

MacLeod, R. B. (1975). *The persistent problems of psychology.* Pittsburgh, PA: Duquesne University Press.

Mason, A., & Blankenship, V. (1987). Power and affiliation motivation, stress, and abuse in intimate relationships. *Journal of Personality and Social Psychology, 52,* 203–210.

McAdams, D. P. (2006). *A new introduction to personality psychology*. Somerset, NJ: John Wiley.

McAdams, D. P., Healy, S., & Krause, S. (1984). Social motives and patterns of friendships. *Journal of Personality and Social Psychology, 47*, 828–838.

McClelland, D. C. (1958). Methods of measuring human motivation. In J. W. Atkinson (Ed.), *Motives in fantasy, action, and society*. Princeton, NJ: Van Nostrand.

McClelland, D. C. (1964). *The roots of consciousness*. Princeton, NJ: Van Nostrand.

McClelland, D. C. (1975). *Power: The inner experience*. New York: John Wiley.

McClelland, D. C. (1976). Sources of stress in the drive for power. In G. Serban (Ed.), *Psychopathology and human adaptation* (pp. 247–270). New York: Plenum Press.

McClelland, D. C. (1979). Inhibited power motivation and high blood pressure in men. *Journal of Abnormal Psychology, 88*, 182–190.

McClelland, D. C. (1982). The need for power, sympathetic activation, and illness. *Motivation and Emotion, 6*, 31–41.

McClelland, D. C. (1985). *Human motivation*. Glenview, IL: Scott, Foresman.

McClelland, D. C. (1989). Motivational factors in health and disease. *American Psychologist, 41*, 675–683.

McClelland, D. C., Davidson, R. J., Floor, E., & Saron, C. (1980). Power motivation, catecholamine secretion, immune function and illness reports. *Journal of Human Stress, 6*, 11–19.

McClelland, D. C., & Davis, W. N. (1972). The influence of unrestrained power concerns on drinking in working-class men. In D. C. McClelland, W. N. Davis, R. Kalin, & E. Wanner (Eds.), *The drinking man* (pp. 142–161). New York: Free Press.

McClelland, D. C., Davis, W. N., Kalin, R., & Wanner, E. (1972). *The drinking man*. New York: Free Press.

McClelland, D. C., Koestner, R., & Weinberger, J. (1989). How do self-attributed and implicit motives differ? *Psychological Review, 96*, 690–702.

McCullough, D. (1992). *Truman*. New York: Simon & Schuster.

Mednick, S. A., & Mednick, M. T. (1967). *Remote Associates Test: Experimenter's manual*. Boston: Houghton Mifflin.

Merton, R. K. (1973). *The sociology of science*. Chicago: University of Chicago Press.

Mogg, K., & Bradley, B. P. (1999). Some methodological issues in assessing attentional biases for threatening faces in anxiety: A replication study using a modified version of the probe detection task. *Behavior Research and Therapy, 37*, 595–604.

Murray, H. A. (1938). *Explorations in personality*. New York: Oxford University Press.

Schultheiss, O. C., & Brunstein, J. C. (2001). Assessment of implicit motives with a research version of the TAT: Picture profiles, gender differences, and relations to other personality measures. *Journal of Personality Assessment, 77*, 71–86.

Schultheiss, O. C., Campbell, K. L., & McClelland, D. C. (1999). Implicit power motivation moderates men's testosterone responses to imagined and real dominance success. *Hormones and Behavior, 36*, 234–241.

Schultheiss, O. C., Dargel, A., & Rohde, W. (2003). Implicit motives and sexual motivation and behavior. *Journal of Research in Personality, 37*, 224–230.

Schultheiss, O. C., & Hale, J. A. (2007). Implicit motives modulate attentional orienting to facial expression of emotion. *Motivation and Emotion, 31*, 13–24.

Schultheiss, O. C., & Rohde, W. (2002). Implicit power motivation predicts men's testosterone changes and implicit learning in a contest situation. *Hormones and Behavior, 41*, 195–202.

Seligman, M. E. P., Walker, E. F., & Rosenhan, D. L. (2001). *Abnormal psychology.* New York: Norton.

Selye, H. (1973). The evolution of the stress concept. *American Scientist, 61*, 672–699.

Steele, R. S. (1973). *The physiological concomitants of psychogenic motive arousal in college males.* Unpublished doctoral dissertation, Harvard University.

Stevenson, R. L. (1885). *Strange case of Dr. Jekyll and Mr. Hyde.* London: Langmans, Green.

Straus, M. A. (1979). Measuring intrafamily conflict and violence: The Conflict Tactics scales. *Journal of Marriage and the Family, 41*, 75–88.

Thayer, R. E. (1978). Factor analytic and reliability studies on the Activation-Deactivation Adjective Check List. *Psychological Reports, 42*, 747–756.

Ullman, J. S. (1972). The need for influence: Development and validation of a measure, and comparison with the need for power. *Genetic Psychology Monographs, 85*, 157–214.

Veroff, J. (1957). Development and validation of a projective measure of power motivation. *Journal of Abnormal Psychology, 54*, 1–8.

Watson, J. D. (1968). *The double helix.* New York: Atheneum.

Wilson, E. O. (1980). *Sociobiology: The abridged edition.* Cambridge, MA: Belknap/Harvard.

Winter, D. G. (1967). Power motivation in thought and action. Unpublished doctoral dissertation, Harvard University.

Winter, D. G. (1973). *The power motive.* New York: Free Press.

Winter, D. G. (1987). Leader appeal, leader performance, and the motive profiles of leaders and followers. *Journal of Personality and Social Psychology, 52*, 196–202.

Winter, D. G. (1992). Power motivation revisited. In C.P. Smith (Ed.), *Motivation and personality: Handbook of thematic content analysis* (pp. 301–310). Cambridge, UK: Cambridge University Press.

Winter, D. G. (1996). *Personality: Analysis and interpretation of lives.* New York: McGraw-Hill.

Winter, D. G. (1999). Linking personality and "scientific" psychology: The development of empirically derived Thematic Apperception Test measures. In L. Geiser & M. I. Stein (Eds.), *Evocative images: The Thematic Apperception Test and the art of projection* (pp. 107–124). Washington, DC : American Psychological Association.

Winter, D. G., John, O. P., Stewart, A. J., Klohnen, E. C., & Duncan, L. E. (1998). Traits and motives: Toward an integration of two traditions in personality research. *Psychological Review, 105*, 230–250.

Winter, D. G., & Stewart, A. J. (1977). Power motive reliability as a function of retest instruction. *Journal of Consulting and Clinical Psychology, 45*, 436–440.

Wirth, M. M., Welsh, K. M., & Schultheiss, O. C. (2006). Salivary cortisol changes in humans after winning or losing a dominance contest depend on implicit power motivation. *Hormones and Behavior, 49*, 346–352.

Woike, B. A. (1994). Vivid recollection as a technique to arouse implicit motive-related affect. *Motivation and Emotion, 18*, 335–349.

Zurbriggen, E. L. (2000). Social motives and cognitive power-sex associations: Predictors of aggressive and sexual behavior. *Journal of Personality and Social Psychology, 78*, 559–581.

Chapter 2

The Achievement Motive: A Review of Theory and Assessment of *n* Achievement, Hope of Success, and Fear of Failure

JOYCE S. PANG
Nanyang Technological University, Singapore

Implicit achievement motivation, often denoted *n* Achievement, refers to a nonconscious and recurrent preference for affectively rewarding experiences related to improving one's performance (Atkinson, 1957). In the following chapter, I will provide a brief and targeted history of the development of the construct of implicit achievement motivation, focusing on the legacy of David McClelland and John Atkinson. The first section highlights the major theoretical and methodological landmarks in achievement motivation research under the McClelland-Atkinson tradition and will cover such topics as measurement, developmental considerations, motivational incentives, and behavioral outcomes. I will also survey some of the major content areas in which implicit achievement motivation researchers have undertaken work in the past. Finally, one of the areas that has not received sufficient attention is the distinction between hope of success (HS) and fear of failure (FF) motivation, particularly in the development of valid measures of these motives, and I end the chapter with a description of and validation data for a new *n* Achievement measure that takes this HS/FF distinction into consideration.

McClelland's Legacy of Achievement Motivation Research

Briefly, David McClelland's legacy is divided into three main areas, the benefits of which extend not only toward *n* Achievement research but also to implicit motivation research in general:

One, his research program influenced a group of researchers with members such as Atkinson, Feather, Koestner, and Winter, who adopted his ideas and research principles so as to develop them further into the full program of work that exists today. For instance, McClelland's (1961) argument that the preferences of *n* Achievement motivated people for activities that involve skill and effort, provide moderate challenge and risk, and present clear performance feedback are more likely to be satisfied in entrepreneurial situations, spawned a formidable body of research on the relationship between *n* Achievement and entrepreneurial behavior and economic productivity (c.f., Collins, Hanges, & Locke, 2004). In addition, Atkinson, a researcher who was directly influenced by McClelland, developed an expectancy- value theory of *n* Achievement that has since led to many productive findings and subsequent theory making about the nature of *n* Achievement (see Cooper, 1983; McClelland, 1987; Schultheiss & Brunstein, 2005).

Two, starting with the publication of *The Achievement Motive* (McClelland, Atkinson, Clark, and Lowell, 1953), McClelland and his colleagues popularized a technique of measuring motivation scientifically, through first experimentally arousing the relevant motive and then developing content coding systems that were based on the effects of motive arousal. McClelland's introduction of these assessment procedures gave researchers ways of measuring *n* Achievement (and other motives) accurately, providing a powerful methodology with which to conduct and evaluate subsequent research. The publication of *The Achievement Motive* also led to a theory about the structure of the achievement-motivated process, which will be described later.

The third accomplishment from McClelland's long history of work is his championship of the distinction between implicit and explicit/self-attributed motivation. McClelland, Koestner, and Weinberger (1989) argued convincingly that these two types of motivation are distinct, each with their own incentives, behavioral outlets, and correlates. The eventual acceptance of the implicit–explicit motive distinction allowed motivation researchers to explain findings that were previously difficult to explain, specifically clarifying many otherwise conflicting characteristics of *n* Achievement.

Thus, I will frame the first part of this literature review around McClelland's three research contributions. I will start with his theoretical concept of *n* Achievement as it is described in *The Achievement Motive* as well as the research and assessment tradition that resulted from this work, chiefly, the development of the theory of *n* Achievement after Atkinson's (1957) expectancy-value theory of *n* Achievement. Finally, I explain why the implicit–explicit distinction calls for a revision of *n* Achievement measures and theory.

The McClelland-Atkinson Assessment Tradition

In the 1930s, Henry Murray and his colleagues developed the Thematic Apperception Test (TAT; Morgan & Murray, 1935) in response to the belief that motive tendencies are unavailable to introspective awareness and need to be assessed through expression in wish-fulfilling fantasies. The development of the TAT technique enabled David McClelland to develop an assessment tool for implicit motives called the Picture Story Exercise (PSE; McClelland, Koestner, & Weinberger, 1989) that was based on the principles of the TAT. The PSE is similar to the TAT in that it requires participants to produce imaginative stories in response to a series of pictures but differs from Morgan and Murray's (1935) original approach in a few important ways (c.f. Pang, Chapter 5).

Importantly, while previous scorers of the TAT relied on a combination of strategies including the individual clinician's expert intuition, consensus between multiple trained raters, and theoretically driven guidelines that were more descriptive than prescriptive (e.g., Bellak, 1975; Cramer, 1991; Shneidman, 1999), McClelland and his colleagues promoted an approach to studying and measuring motivation systematically and scientifically: through first experimentally arousing the relevant motive, and then using content coding systems to measure the differences in PSE protocols (McClelland, Atkinson, Clark, & Lowell, 1953; McClelland, Clark, Roby, & Atkinson, 1949).

In the arousal method, participants would either be exposed to a neutral and controlled setting or to an experimental scenario in which the relevant motive is aroused. Coding categories are then constructed by examining differences found in the imagery of stories written under motive arousal versus those written under neutral conditions.

McClelland, Clark, Roby, and Atkinson (1949) attempted to arouse *n* Achievement in groups of male subjects. Participants were asked to complete a series of tasks that included anagrams, writing, and tests of verbal intelligence, as well as a four-picture PSE. Additionally, participants were exposed to one of three meaningful study conditions:

There was a *Relaxed* group who was instructed that the tests they were completing were devised recently and the data collected was for the purposes of perfecting these tests. In this condition, the experimenters took care to divert attention away from the participants' performance on the tests, thus keeping the need for achievement unaroused.

Conversely, there were two further conditions that led participants to focus their attention on their test performance. The *failure* group received instructions that the tests they were completing were indicative of "a person's general level of intelligence" and "whether or not a person is suited to be a leader." They were also told that they would be able to calculate their scores and find out at once "how well you do in comparison with... [other] students." Then, the experimenter quoted norms for the tests that were so high that practically everyone in the class failed and placed in the lowest quarter of the relevant comparison group (other students at their University).

The *success-failure* group received the same instructions about the tests as the *failure* group did, however, the *success-failure* group were quoted low norms after the first task and then high norms at the end of the last task, thus inducing a taste of success followed by failure.

Content categories were constructed by comparing the PSE protocols of those under *failure* and *success-failure* arousal to the protocols of participants in the *relaxed* condition. Under both the *failure* and the *success-failure* conditions, participants' stories had a greater number of themes about wanting or needing to pursue achievement ("He wants to be a doctor"), of engaging in activities in pursuit of the achievement need ("He is hard at work"), and of having positive or negative feelings in anticipation of either the successful or unsuccessful conclusion of an achievement task ("He is looking forward to the day when he will graduate with honors"; "He is dreading the pending failure").

Based on the themes that emerged, McClelland and his colleagues introduced a useful way of organizing theory regarding *n* Achievement. Although the *n* Achievement coding system was constructed using experimental arousal, its coding categories can be organized into a general sequence of motivated behavior (Fig. 2.1) and is easily explained in this context:

The *n* Achievement behavioral sequence is initiated when the person feels a need (N). The need is represented by an external goal, and the person may anticipate either successful attainment of this goal (Ga+) or she may become

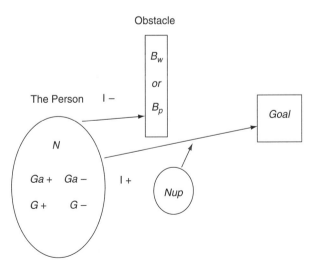

Figure 2.1 Placement of McClelland et al.'s (1953) *n* Achievement scoring categories in a motivation behavior sequence.

frustrated and anticipate nonattainment $(Ga-)$. In order to accomplish her goal, the person has to engage in instrumental activity that is either successful $(I+)$ or not successful $(I-)$. During this process of goal pursuit, the person may either receive assistance (Nup) from others or suffer a hindrance or obstacle that can come from within her person (B_p) or from the world at large (Bw). She may also experience positive $(G+)$ or negative $(G-)$ affect in response to the goal-directed activity and its consequences.

For instance, a gymnast's need (N) to achieve may be represented in a goal of winning a competition. She will engage in instrumental activity $(I+)$ by practicing daily at her routine. During her practice, she may feel encouraged by her progress $(Ga+)$ or become frustrated $(G-)$ because she realizes she has hit a plateau in her training (B_p). If her training pays off and she wins her competition, the gymnast feels happiness and pride $(G+)$ as a result of this accomplishment.

Table 2.1 presents an abbreviated summary of McClelland et al.'s (1953) coding categories. As shown, the n Achievement coding system follows the sequence of motivated behavior presented in Figure 1. The scorer first assesses whether achievement imagery is present in general in the PSE protocols.

Table 2.1   Outline of n Achievement Coding System

Imagery Type	Definition/Criteria
Achievement imagery (AI)	Competition with a standard of excellence through • Competition with a standard • Unique accomplishment • Long-term involvement in an achievement goal
If AI is detected, then score subcategories below:	
Need (N)	Story character states a desire to reach an achievement goal.
Instrumental activity (I)	Overt or mental activity done to reach an achievement goal $(I+)$, if the outcome of the activity is doubtful or unsuccessful, score $(I-)$
Anticipatory goal states (Ga)	Story character experiences past or present, definite or possible goal attainment $(Ga+)$ or frustration or failure $(Ga-)$
Obstacles (B)	When the progress of goal-directed activity is hindered in some way. B_p stands for block within the person; B_w stands for blocks that originate from the world, or the external environment. Only real obstacle, not apparent or imagined ones are scored.
Nurturant press (Nup)	Personal sources in the story aid the story character.
Affective states (G)	Emotions associated with goal attainment, active mastery $(G+)$ or frustration of the goal $(G-)$.
Achievement thema $(Ach\ Th)$	Scored when the achievement imagery is elaborated in such a manner that it becomes the central plot of the story

Source: Adapted from McClelland et al. (1953). This outline is not adequate for scoring purposes.

For instance, if a story is concerned with routine work imagery, then achievement imagery (designated *AI*) is not scored, and no further scoring is carried out. Only after achievement imagery is detected does the scorer proceed to code for the subsidiary coding categories of *N*, *Ga*, *I*, and so forth. The strength of one's achievement motivation is derived from the total score of *n* Achievement motive imagery recorded.

Distinction Between Hope of Success and Fear of Failure Achievement Motivation

In every achievement task—whether it is attaining a personal best, meeting a standard of excellence, or rising to a challenge—there are two possible outcomes: success or failure. Motivated achievement behavior can be categorized as approach tendencies, which are when people are driven to maximize the chances of succeeding at the achievement task, and avoidance tendencies, which are when people are driven to minimize the chances of failing the task. Thus, a distinction has traditionally been made between the active, approach-oriented aspects of *n* Achievement (also named hope of success, or HS) and the anxiety-based, avoidant tendencies of fear of failure (FF).

McClelland's Conditioning Theory of Motivation

In order to understand the effect of HS and FF on achievement behavior and performance, it is important to understand the relationship between learning and motivation. Specifically, McClelland et al. (1953) refer to the role of positive and negative affective change in reinforcing particular behavioral patterns.

In the functional behaviorist tradition, drives are strong internal stimuli that focus the organism's attention on acquiring or maintaining conditions (such as air, food, water) that are necessary for growth and survival. The classic instantiation of this argument is Thorndike's (1911) law of effect, according to which responses are strengthened that lead to rewarding experiences (or, incentives) and responses are weakened that cause unpleasurable or disturbing experiences (or, disincentives).

According to McClelland et al. (1953), *n* Achievement is an acquired drive that is based on a set of instrumental response elements that are directed by their sensory effect. Those behaviors that produce increases in positive affect are seen as naturally rewarding incentives and will be repeated in similar circumstances. Over time, instrumental approach response tendencies become developed; these response tendencies cue anticipated increases in positive affect, are preferred over other responses that are not as closely associated with pleasure, and form the basis of approach motivation.

Conversely, there is a class of behaviors that produces disincentives, notably, responses that produce decreases in positive affect or increases in negative affect as well as those responses that produce decreases in negative affect. In the first two scenarios (reduction of positive affect or increase in negative affect), the antecedent behavior will be less likely to be repeated, while in the third scenario (reduction of negative affect), the behavior is more likely to be repeated. Over time, responses following the third scenario develop into instrumental avoidance response tendencies; these response tendencies cue anticipated decreases in negative affect, are preferred over other responses that are not as closely associated with avoidance of pain, and form the basis of avoidance motivation.

Schultheiss and Brunstein (2005) built on McClelland et al.'s (1953) theory by using learning psychology to highlight some important characteristics of approach and avoidance achievement motivation. They present four possible variations of goal-directed behavior: A person can either display a goal-directed behavior or not (active versus passive responding), and she can either be rewarded or punished (leading to approach or avoidance) as a consequence of the behavior. Thus, four possible modes of goal-directed behavior are: active approach, active avoidance, passive approach, and passive avoidance.

The most straightforward scenario is when a person is in an *active approach* mode, which is when she displays the goal-directed behavior and is rewarded for doing so. The reward increases the likelihood that the person will repeat the goal-directed behavior in the future. On the other hand, the person may also be punished for displaying the goal-directed behavior. In this case, the punishment decreases the likelihood of the goal pursuit, and results in a *passive avoidance* mode, which is when the person avoids punishment by inhibiting goal-directed behavior. In the case when the person is punished for *not* displaying the goal-directed behavior, the punishment has the effect of increasing the likelihood of goal pursuit and results in an *active avoidance* mode, which is when the person executes a goal-directed behavior in order to avoid punishment. Finally, there is the case when a person is rewarded for *not* displaying goal-directed behavior, which results in the passive approach mode. Behavior motivated by the *passive approach* mode—the person is basically being rewarded for doing nothing—is usually rare and difficult to identify with certainty, thus I will not discuss it here.

In the context of achievement motivation, the passive avoidance mode can be interpreted as a fear of success (FS; e.g., Fleming & Horner, 1992). Individuals who score higher on FS learn to avoid negative incentives (e.g., social disapproval or resentment from male colleagues) by inhibiting any achievement-related activity that will lead them closer to goal attainment. A person motivated by FS may have been punished for doing well at an achievement task or for displaying any instrumental activity toward goal attainment; hence, she learns to restrict future goal-directed behavior in order to avoid facing the same punishment. According to Horner and Fleming (1992), the FS motive is scored in PSE protocols whenever there is presence of negative consequences brought about by external forces, when two or more people are involved on an interpersonal level, when there is a relief of tension that comes about without any significant goal-oriented activity, and when there is an absence of instrumental activity. This form of avoidance is also often characterized by a lack of *n* Achievement imagery on PSE protocols (Karabenick, 1977).

In the active approach, or HS, motivational mode, goal-directed behavior is displayed in anticipation of the positive consequences of success. For instance, a novice pianist may successfully tackle a challenging music piece for the first time and be rewarded with praise from her teacher. This makes her more likely to seek out and try to master challenging pieces in the future in order to receive praise. Eventually, the act of mastering challenging music pieces becomes intrinsically rewarding because of the accompanying sense of mastery and self-satisfaction. The HS mode represents the most prototypical notion of achievement-motivated behavior; understandably, measures of HS (Heckhausen, 1991) correlate positively with the original *n* Achievement measure.

In the active avoidance, or FF, motivational mode, the *absence* of goal-directed behavior leads to punishment; goal-directed behavior is displayed in anticipation of negative consequences of failure. Using the above example, a novice pianist may be punished by admonishment or nagging from her teacher whenever she fails to master a difficult piece of music. This causes the pianist to try harder to master the piece in order to avoid hearing the nagging. Subsequently, the act of mastering challenging music pieces becomes intrinsically rewarding because of the sense of relief from any embarrassment, guilt, or shame that accompanies failure to master the pieces. Thus, the person learns to actively pursue a goal in order to avoid the punishment.

Measurement of Hope of Success and Fear of Failure

Because of the hypothesized defensive reasons behind the development of FF, early predictions about FF highlight the role of anxiety in avoidant achievement motivation. Specifically, anxiety is assumed to be the emotional basis of FF, and an achievement-motivated individual with avoidance tendencies engages in achievement behavior in order to minimize her anxiety about impending failure.

Early researchers used a self-report measure of test anxiety in their assessment of fear of failure. The most commonly employed measure was Sarason and Mandler's (1952) Test Anxiety Questionnaire (TAQ). The general procedure was to use the difference between participants' n Achievement scores and their TAQ scores as a measure of FF (thus, FF = TAT n Achievement−TAQ score). Atkinson (1958) and his students developed the Resultant Achievement Motivation (RAM) score, which is obtained by cross-classifying scores on the McClelland et al.'s (1953) n Achievement measure with scores on the TAQ. Specifically, subjects who score above the median in n Achievement and below the median on the TAQ have the greatest RAM scores and are considered to be the most achievement motivated and hope-of-success motivated while those who score below the median in n Achievement and above the median on the TAQ have the lowest RAM scores and are considered to be high in fear of failure.

Atkinson's Expectancy-Value Theory of Motivation

Atkinson's expectancy-value theory of achievement motivation asserts that the tendency to engage in achievement behavior ($T_{succeed}$) is a multiplicative function of motive (M_s), subjective probability (P_s) of succeeding at the task in question, and the incentive value (I_s) of succeeding at that task. Thus, $T_{succeed} = M_s \times P_s \times I_s$.

A basic assumption of Atkinson's theory is that the incentive value of success for a task is directly proportional while the probability of success is inversely proportional to its level of difficulty. Mathematically, the incentive value of a task is defined as one minus the probability of success (thus, $I_s = 1 - P_s$).

A difficult task would carry a high incentive value for success because there is a greater challenge to be mastered. However, the difficult task naturally also carries low probabilities of success. On the other hand, an easy task would carry high probabilities for success but also a low incentive value because the standard of excellence is not challenging enough to be motivationally satisfying. Finally, a moderately difficult task would carry moderate incentive value and moderate probabilities of success. Because the tendency to approach a task is a function of the multiplicative effects of incentive value and probability of success, the preference of achievement-motivated individuals in attempting tasks of varying difficulty approximates an *inverted U-shape* (Fig. 2.2), where tasks of moderate difficulty receive the highest preference and are flanked on both sides by lower preference scores for tasks of lesser and greater difficulty. The model suggests that achievement-motivated people who are high in RAM would be more likely to approach a moderately difficult task than they would be to approach extremely difficult or easy tasks.

Because Atkinson conceived of the avoidance motive as the mirror image of the approach motive, the formula for FF paralleled that of HS. Specifically, the tendency to engage in avoidant achievement behavior is a function of the motive to avoid failure (M_f), the disincentive value of failure (I_f), and the

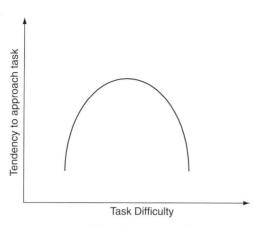

Figure 2.2 Predicted preference for achievement tasks as a function of task difficulty for subjects with high RAM (after Atkinson, 1957).

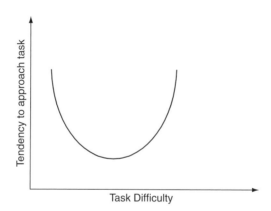

Figure 2.3 Predicted preference for achievement tasks as a function of task difficulty for subjects with low RAM (after Atkinson, 1957).

probability of failing (P_f); thus, $T_{avoid} = M_f \times P_f \times I_f$. Similarly, the disincentive value of failing is inversely related to the probability of failing, mathematically represented as $I_f = 1 - P_f$.

Under Atkinson's model, the preference of FF-motivated individuals in attempting tasks of varying difficulty approximates a *U-shape* (Fig. 2.3), where tasks of moderate difficulty receive the lowest preference and are flanked on both sides by high preference scores for tasks of lesser and greater difficulty. Hence, people motivated by FF would be most likely to avoid tasks of moderate difficulty, just as people motivated by success would be most likely to approach these same tasks.

Table 2.2 illustrates Atkinson's predictions for the tendency to avoid failing as a function of motive strength, disincentive value, and probability of failure.

Table 2.2 Aroused Tendency to Avoid (Tavoid) as a Joint Function of the Motive to Avoid Failure (Mf), Probability of Failure (Pf), and the (Negative) Incentive Value of Failure (If)

Task Difficulty	Low in FF	High in FF
	$M_f \times P_f \times I_f = T_{avoid}$	$M_f \times P_f \times I_f = T_{avoid}$
Hard	$1 \times 0.90 \times 0.10 = 0.09$	$3 \times 0.90 \times 0.10 = 0.27$
Moderate	$1 \times 0.50 \times 0.50 = 0.25$	$3 \times 0.50 \times 0.50 = 0.75$
Easy	$1 \times 0.10 \times 0.90 = 0.09$	$3 \times 0.10 \times 0.90 = 0.27$

The key to this model is that the disincentive value of failure is expected to diminish with the level of difficulty of the task. As shown in Table 2.2, the disincentive should be much greater for failing at an easy task than for failing at a difficult task. However, the probability of failing the task grows relevant to the level of difficulty of the task. Therefore, as a task becomes more difficult, the disincentive value of failure decreases and the probability of failing increases.

Support for the McClelland-Atkinson Model of Achievement Motivation

Atkinson's (1957) expectancy-value theory had a dominating influence on achievement motivation research in the 1960s and 1970s, and the assumptions of his model continue to inform current research. Following Cooper (1983), I briefly describe a nomological network of dependent variables such as task choice and difficulty, persistence, performance, preference for autonomy, and valence that have been commonly studied in relation to Atkinson's theory. Except where mentioned explicitly, n Achievement is measured by the McClelland et al. (1953) PSE-based coding method while HS and FF are measured by Atkinson's (1957) RAM and the PSE-TAQ difference score, respectively.

Task Choice and Task Difficulty

According to Atkinson's model n Achievement–motivated people consistently choose to undertake tasks of moderate difficulty, as opposed to tasks that are too easy or too difficult because moderately difficult tasks provide the maximum opportunity to succeed.

Atkinson's predictions on task difficulty have yielded mixed results. De Charms and Carpenter (1968) found that fifth and sixth grade students who were higher in n Achievement preferred to work at questions of moderate difficulty, compared to students low in n Achievement, who showed no such preference. Atkinson and Litwin (1960) and Litwin (1966) found that subjects with greater RAM chose to throw from moderately long distances in a ring-toss game. Mahone (1960) found that FF (as measured as a difference score between n Achievement and scores on Alpert's 1957 Debilitating Anxiety Scale) was associated with more unrealistic task choices, such as preference for occupations with high discrepancy between one's own ability and the ability that is needed for the occupation. Thus, FF motivated people chose a very "difficult" occupation—which in Atkinson's theory would have a low negative incentive value and a high probability of failure—over a more realistic choice of occupation with moderate incentive value and probability of failure.

However, de Charms and Davé (1965) found contradicting evidence. Their study asked participants to choose distances from which to shoot volleyballs into a basket and used a content-coding measure of HS and FF, instead of RAM. As predicted from Atkinson's formula, participants motivated primarily by FF avoided situations of moderate risk (as calculated by moderate probabilities for making a shot); however, contrary to expectations, subjects motivated primarily by HS also avoided moderate risks. That is, both high HS and high FF groups were taking more extreme risks than low–n Achievement groups. De Charms and Davé's findings that those motivated by HS also avoid moderate risks can be understood in the context of their experimental design and another of their findings. First, the participants did not have prior knowledge of the risk-taking probabilities of the task before they chose the distance to throw their balls from. This may have contributed to their making slightly riskier choices and (at least initially) selecting distances with lower probabilities of success. Additionally, there was an interaction effect of HS and FF, such that subjects with both high FF and high HS are most likely to concentrate their efforts at a point of moderately high risk, or what de Charms and Davé described as a "calculated risk." It seems that a combination of HS and FF leads to results closer to Atkinson's predictions for n Achievement.

De Charms and Davé's results suggest that Atkinson's conception of FF needs to be revised. Since de Charms and Davé (1965), other research on risk taking and task difficulty has contradicted Atkinson's predictions (e.g., Hamilton, 1974). In fact, even in Atkinson and Litwin's (1960) ring-toss study, although subjects with higher FF had a lower preference for moderate distances than subjects motivated by HS, they still preferred moderate to either very high or very low levels of risk. FF-motivated achievement behavior seems to be more complicated than can be predicted by the basic formula of $T = M \times P \times I$.

Atkinson (1957, p. 364) suggests one reason that might explain the preference that FF-motivated people sometimes have for moderately difficult tasks. He makes a distinction between activities that FF-motivated individuals pursue *voluntarily* versus those that they are obligated to perform because they are *constrained* within an achievement situation. In the former case, mounting anxiety about a possible failure outcome may prompt the person to either leave the situation or, if leaving is not an option, perform the task well enough to prevent failing at it. Following Atkinson's argument, the FF-motivated individual who is prevented from escaping an achievement situation will have similar task difficulty and risk preferences as an HS-motivated individual because easy to moderately-difficult tasks have higher chances of success (and lower chances of failure) than extremely difficult tasks.

Persistence

Insofar as a person chooses to perform in an achievement situation, she should also exhibit persistence in that task after failure. Atkinson predicts that HS-motivated individuals will try their hardest and be more likely to persevere after failure when the probability of success is moderate, and people motivated more by FF than by HS should try hardest and persevere at a task when the task is very easy or very difficult.

Atkinson's persistence predictions have received good support from research findings. Feather (1962) reviewed studies testing Atkinson's theory and found that people motivated by HS persist longer after failure when a task is considered easy than when the task is difficult, whereas people motivated by FF persist longer on a more difficult task than on an easy task. Feather's explanation for these variations in persistence highlights the importance of the probability of success. In an easy task, the perceived probability of success is high. However, once a subject fails at the easy task, the task's probability of success becomes lower, thus moving it into the region for medium probability of success. Because, according to Atkinson's formula, HS-motivated people prefer moderately difficult tasks to easy tasks, failure at an easy task will make the task become moderately difficult and thus more attractive to an HS-motivated subject, who will then persist at that task.

Independence and Autonomy

In cases when an extrinsic incentive—such as pleasing the experimenter (French, 1955) or attaining an externally set standard of excellence (McKeachie, 1961)—is provided, n Achievement is either unrelated to or even negatively correlated with performance. It is clear that achievement-motivated people are interested in doing something for *its own sake*, for the intrinsic satisfaction of "doing better."

How does this intrinsic need to do things better become developed in humans? Research and theory have focused mainly on child-rearing practices and parental styles during early childhood; of the extant literature, the findings on age-appropriate independence training are the most consistent and persuasive. Mothers of boys with high n Achievement set high performance standards for their sons at an earlier age and gave more specific directions during an achievement task (Winterbottom, 1958). They are also more warm and affectionate when their sons succeed but more likely to react to poor performance with hostility and disapproval (Rosen & D'Andrade, 1959). Thus, parents who produce highly achievement-motivated boys not only expect more from their sons, but they also encourage the attainment of the higher standards by rewarding progress with praise and warmth and punishing poor performance with social disapproval. Additionally, perhaps as a precursor to the *n* Achievement preference for tasks of moderate difficulty, parents with children who scored high in *n* Achievement presented challenges to their children that were age appropriate, that is, neither too difficult nor too easy for the child's developmental stage (McClelland, 1961; Veroff, 1969).

Why do these parental practices lead to higher *n* Achievement in children, and what kind of incentives do these practices offer that are different from the extrinsic incentives such as money and social validation that have been found in previous studies *not* to arouse *n* Achievement (c.f. French, 1955)? The key lies with McClelland et al.'s (1953) conditioning theory of motivation and the kinds of nonverbal affective reinforcements that parents provide to their children. For children in the preverbal stage, the pleasure that parents express in response to the child's actions is inherently rewarding while the parents' displeasure is inherently punishing. This pleasure or displeasure expressed by the parents often occurs as a result of satisfaction or disappointment at the child's accomplishment of age-appropriate activities (such as grasping, walking) that indicate developmental milestones for the child. Over time, as the children are repeatedly reinforced (by parents) for not relying on anyone else in accomplishing these developmentally challenging skills, the children internalize a standard of performance and develop a self-evaluative sense of pride at the successful outcomes of their own efforts. In addition, they may also learn to associate interference from the outside with failing to master a challenge on their own and the punishment this may entail. The positive affect that occurs as a result of accomplishing a task well eventually becomes intrinsically rewarding and is the basis for *n* Achievement.

Task Performance, Standards of Excellence, Independence, and Autonomy

Since HS is associated positively with persistence and preference for tasks of moderate difficulty, this increased attention and effort is expected to translate into better performance. Hence, HS-motivated individuals are expected to perform best at moderately difficult tasks. In several studies, high *n* Achievement predicted significantly better performance at scrambled word tasks (Lowell, 1952), anagram tasks (Raynor & Entin, 1982), paired associates tasks (Karabenick & Youseff, 1968), and in the classroom (O'Connor, Atkinson, & Horner, 1966).

An interesting finding from Lowell's (1952) study demonstrates that the better performance of achievement-motivated individuals is due to motivation rather than ability. The high–n Achievement and low–n Achievement groups performed similarly at the start of the task; however, the high n Achievement group's performance increased steadily over the course of the task and at a faster rate than the low–n Achievement group. It seems that although superior performance at any achievement task is affected by both ability and determination, n Achievement–motivated people make up for whatever they lack in natural ability with more efficient learning behavior.

However, high achievement motivation does not necessarily translate to good performance in all situations. Among the factors hypothesized to complicate the relationship between achievement motivation and achievement performance are overly high and debilitating levels of motivation, lack of necessary aptitude and ability to carry out achievement tasks, and the presence of extrinsic incentives (c.f. McClelland, 1987). Another important moderator is task difficulty—for instance, when the perceived difficulty of a task is high, students with high RAM performed better than those with low RAM, and when the task is perceived as easy, high RAM actually lowers performance levels (Kukla, 1974). Thus, n Achievement and HS are linked to better performance provided (a) the achievement situation is moderately challenging, (b) the achievement task is within a domain in which the subject has adequate aptitude and proficiency, and (c) the outcome and goals of the task are under the subject's personal control. Spangler (1992) conducted a meta-analysis of achievement motivation studies and found that n Achievement "strongly predicted operant behavior in the presence of activity achievement incentives" (p. 150). In other words, n Achievement predicts better performance on activities that are relatively free from explicit experimenter or external control (e.g., farm and industrial output, professional rank, publications, social behavior occurring under natural conditions), especially when task characteristics that are intrinsically motivating, such as moderate task risk, are present.

The relationship between task performance and FF is more complicated and less well explored. Many motivation researchers (e.g., Covington & Omelich, 1985; Seligman, 1975) have assumed FF to be detrimental to task performance, mainly because of the observation that exposure to failure outcomes increases negative emotional reactions and reduces one's self-efficacy, which in turn weakens one's performance. However, other researchers (e.g., Brunstein and Maier, 2005) have pointed out that while failure may undermine subsequent performance, it also has the likelihood of stimulating it, especially when the individual is given the chance to salvage a threatened goal. However, consistent empirical evidence for FF leading to better or worse performance is sorely lacking.

Valence of Success and Failure

The predictions of Atkinson's theory regarding task choice, task difficulty, and persistence rely on the assumption that *n* Achievement–motivated people, particularly those motivated by HS, place a high incentive value on success, and that those motivated by FF place a high disincentive value on failure. Valence describes the total attractiveness of an outcome, and expectancy-value theory predicts that HS-motivated people should experience more satisfaction (positive valence) after successful achievement outcomes while FF-motivated people should experience more dissatisfaction (negative valence) after failure, when compared to people who are low in *n* Achievement.

However, valence predictions have never received full support. While Atkinson and Litwin's (1960) findings supported the predictions, other research has had difficulty replicating either the predicted relationship between HS and positive emotional valence following success or the hypothesized relationship between FF and negative emotional valence following failure (e.g., Feather, 1967; Karabenick, 1972).

Halisch and Heckhausen (1989) had subjects participate in a stimulus-tracking task where they were given predetermined performance feedback. Participants were then asked to identify a standard for success and failure before the commencement of the task. The study authors calculated valence scores by assessing a participant's level of satisfaction or dissatisfaction with her performance. Specifically, *positive valence gradients* were calculated by asking participants to identify an upper performance threshold beyond which they would experience success, as well as a point on this difficulty scale where they would experience twice the satisfaction in the case of success. In the same fashion, *negative valence gradients* were calculated by asking participants to identify a lower performance threshold below which they would experience failure, as well as a point below the threshold where they would experience twice the dissatisfaction with failure. Notably, this study did not use the RAM measure of HS and FF, but separate PSE-based measures for HS and FF, respectively (Heckhausen, 1963). The authors found that highly motivated participants who received high scores in both HS and FF had steeper positive valence gradients than negative valence gradients; conversely, the participants with lower aggregate motives (i.e., had low scores on either HS or FF, or on both motives) had steeper negative valence gradients than positive valence gradients. Halisch and Heckhausen's results, which were later replicated by Brunstein and Maier (2005) for HS, contradict Atkinson's valence predictions and suggest that those motivated by fear of failure are just as strongly and positively affected emotionally by success as those motivated by hope of success are.

The Importance of Feedback

Finally, another distinctive trait of *n* Achievement–motivated people is their need for performance feedback. French (1958) found participants with high *n* Achievement (measured using a semiprojective test she developed called the Test of Insight) worked more efficiently after performance feedback, and Kagan and Moss (1962) found that boys with high *n* Achievement were more interested in and better at mechanical activities such as carpentry and construction. Theorists have suggested that achievement-motivated individuals prefer mechanical activities such as construction because feedback from these tasks is usually concrete, direct, and immediate (see also Bartmann, 1965; McClelland, 1987). These studies illustrate the attractiveness of performance feedback to achievement-motivated individuals; immediate, consistent, task-centered feedback provides information about how to improve on one's performance, by acting on the feedback.

In more recent work, Fodor and Carver (2000) found that, compared to subjects who did not receive feedback, those with higher PSE-measured *n* Achievement produced more creative performances in response to feedback, regardless of whether the feedback was positive or negative. Brunstein and colleagues found that *n* Achievement assessed by either Heckhausen's (1963) subsystem for HS (Brunstein & Maier, 2005) or by a version of the Implicit Association Test (IAT; Brunstein & Schmitt, 2004; Greenwald, McGhee, & Schwartz, 1998) predicts effortful performance on a mental concentration task, after the receipt of performance feedback.

Summary and Shortcomings of McClelland-Atkinson's Model of *n* Achievement Theory Development

The RAM measure of hope of success (Atkinson, 1958), Heckhausen's (1963) PSE-based content-coding system for HS, and McClelland et al.'s PSE-based content-coding scoring system (1953) for *n* Achievement have generally been treated as the same construct because theoretical and empirical predictions that have been made for either construct have consistently followed Atkinson's model for the approach-oriented achievement motive.

The research findings for HS have generally supported Atkinson's theory regarding *n* Achievement. Specifically, highly HS-motivated individuals prefer, persist in, and perform better in moderately challenging tasks in which they have personal control over the outcome. Valence predictions have received less clear support; it is not clear whether HS-motivated people experience positive affect after they have attained successful achievement outcomes. More importantly, wherever supporting evidence has emerged, valence has been assessed using subjects' self-reported emotional reactions to success and failure. This cardinal criterion of emotional change after a motivationally relevant successful or unsuccessful outcome has never been adequately tested using physiological assessments of affect change—for instance, through facial EMG or through coding of facial emotional expressions (however, see Schultheiss & Hale, 2007, for a study that documents selective orienting responses of *n* Power– and *n* Affiliation–motivated people to certain motivationally relevant facial emotional expressions).

Characteristics of FF-motivated individuals are less well supported. While FF has been linked to more unrealistic task choices and levels of aspiration, FF-motivated people appear more likely to persist after failure at a difficult task than an easy task, and they do not consistently experience greater negative affect after failure than those motivated by HS do (e.g., Halisch & Heckhausen, 1989). In studies that have measured FF using a PSE-based measure rather than RAM, FF-motivated people behave similarly to HS-motivated people, tending to experience greater negative affect after failure and greater positive affect after success compared to low–achievement motivated individuals (Halisch and Heckhausen, 1989) and choosing to make moderately risky decisions (DeCharms and Dave, 1965). These findings suggest that, rather than behaving like someone with low achievement motivation, the person who is motivated by FF is just as likely as to be energized and directed in her achievement behavior as someone motivated by HS.

Development of Assessment Methods

Inadequacy of the RAM Measure for Fear of Failure

The lack of supportive evidence for Atkinson's predictions regarding FF is related to the fact that RAM is neither an adequate nor a valid measure. The lack of an adequate measure of FF has largely been responsible for the reduced emphasis on research conducted on FF relative to the research carried out on HS and *n* Achievement.

Conceptually, levels of test anxiety are neither valid nor appropriate indicators for achievement motivation or fear of failure. Highly anxious subjects with high scores on TAQ perform less well than their less anxious peers on standardized achievement tests (Sarason & Mandler, 1952). This is because the highly test-anxious subjects are afraid of the novel situation that the standardized test represents. However, these highly test-anxious subjects are not necessarily less well performing in all achievement situations. In non-standardized-test settings, for example, in the classroom, when achievement expectations and standards of excellence are informal, clear, and more relaxed, the highly test-anxious subjects actually perform better than less test-anxious subjects (Sarason & Mandler, 1952). Test anxiety is thus a measure of an affective reaction to a very specific achievement setting—standardized tests—it does not represent general achievement need. Furthermore, Sarason and Mandler's (1952) measure is partly indicative of self-perceived ability. Especially in a situation such as a test, demonstrations of competence depend on the performance of a normative reference group. In this situation, individuals with low self-perceived ability expect to do worse than their peers on tasks of moderate difficulty and should therefore avoid such tasks. They might instead choose very easy or very difficult tasks so as to avoid implications of incompetence due to their (self-perceived) low ability. Hence, the behavior of persons with self-perceived low-ability, as measured by their greater test anxiety, is functionally similar to the predicted behavior of persons with high fear of failure. Thus, the use of the TAQ measure as a proxy of FF confuses motivation with self-perceived ability (Nicholls, 1984) or with general negative emotionality and neuroticism (Schmidt & Riniolo, 1999).

Additionally, the employment of a difference score demonstrates a clear theoretical position about the nature of fear of failure. It assumes that the higher one's anxiety is about an achievement situation, the greater their fear of failure is, and the lesser their *n* Achievement will be. Because of the juxtaposition between high TAQ scores and high FF on one hand and low TAQ scores and high *n* Achievement on the other, subjects high in FF are assumed to be less well performing as well as less motivated than those high in *n* Achievement. The main explanation for this belief is that the anxiety that FF-motivated subjects have for failing acts as an inhibitory force that diminishes the need for achievement and hope of success. However, it is important that we make clear the distinction between the individuals with low *n* Achievement on one hand and those with high *n* Achievement and avoidant tendencies on the other. It has never been clearly stated by researchers such as McClelland and Atkinson whether the fear of failure is theoretically or empirically the direct opposite of *n* Achievement, although the TAQ measurement procedure assumes this to be the case.

Additionally, differences scores have been criticized by methodologists and psychometricians (e.g., Cohen & Cohen, 1983; Griffin, Murray, & Gonzalez, 1999) because they inherently create basic conceptual problems. For instance, the TAQ measure obscures possible interactions between HS and FF because the underlying assumption of a difference score is that HS and FF are opposing and mutually exclusive phenomena. More importantly, difference score correlations are actually less informative than the sum of their parts; conclusions derived from difference scores are not easily explained by the individual components of the difference score because a number of underlying models exist, each assigning a different proportion of weights and directionality to each individual component (Griffin, Murray, & Gonzalez, 1999).

Finally, McClelland, Koestner, and Weinberger (1989) introduced the now-accepted idea that self-report measures of achievement motivation and PSE-type measures of *n* Achievement are measuring two fundamentally different types of motives; because of this, the use of difference scores between a self-report scale such as the TAQ and the PSE-based measures such as McClelland et al.'s (1953) *n* Achievement measure is contrived and not psychologically meaningful.

All the studies reviewed above (except Halisch and Heckhausen, 1989, and DeCharms and Dave, 1965) assessed FF using the anxiety questionnaires, thus confounding failure avoidance with self-efficacy. The use of such "contaminated" measures of FF has diminished the validity of evidence for Atkinson's theory regarding FF. Clearly, there is a need to develop measures of FF that are independent from measures of approach achievement motivation and self-efficacy.

The Hostile Press Measure

A measure that sought to address the approach/avoidance distinction without relying on anxiety questionnaires was the Hostile Press (HP) PSE scoring system devised by Birney, Burdick, and Teevan (1969). Just as Atkinson accepted McClelland's original *n* Achievement system as his measure of hope of success, Birney and colleagues did not seek to develop a new HS coding system. Instead, they focused on a technique to measure FF. However, in contrast to Atkinson, who used a self-report measure of test anxiety as a proxy for FF, Birney, Burdick, and Teevan created a PSE-based measure of fear of failure using McClelland and Atkinson's technique of experimental arousal. Birney, Burdick, and Teevan created their coding categories by contrasting stories written by students whose fear of failure was aroused by performing very difficult tasks versus stories written by students in relaxed conditions. The basic arousal design was to have participants complete a task that was so difficult that they were very likely to fail—in one variation, college students were asked to execute a speed-reading task in which sentences were exposed for ever briefer moments of time until the students had to fail; in another, eighth graders were given a very difficult math test. Many of the tasks involved performing in front of a group or an "expert," thus confounding social evaluation anxiety with *n* Achievement and FF.

The resulting coding system was named *Hostile Press* because the stories written either displayed characteristics of being in hostile conditions or cited environmental influences that had to be avoided. However, as Schultheiss and Brunstein (2005) pointed out, the HP system, rather than examining the *motivation* to avoid failure, actually highlights the unwelcome elements in the *environment* that exert a pressure on the person to not fail. This might have been caused by the use of arousal conditions that included an element of social evaluation. If the fear of criticism is taken as a predominant criterion for assessment, then the construct being measured is more likely to represent a fear of social evaluation than the fear of failure per se. Given the very likely possibility that the HP measure is contaminated by one or more motives other than *n* Achievement (such as need to conform), it has not been used much except by those who devised the measure.

McClelland's Continuing Legacy; Building on the McClelland-Atkinson Theory and Assessment Tradition

Since McClelland, Koestner, and Weinberger's (1989) paper and increasingly in recent years, researchers have focused on the distinction between implicit and explicit motivation. Recent research that has respected this distinction between implicit and explicit motivation has added meaningfully to the development of *n* Achievement literature in both theory-building and assessment techniques:

The Role of Feedback—Diagnostic Value or Incentive Value

There is a controversy behind why feedback is rewarding to and continually sought-after by achievement-motivated individuals. Trope (Trope, 1975; Trope & Brickman, 1975; Trope & Neter, 1994) argues that individuals who are achievement motivated value tasks of intermediate difficulty not because they maximize the incentive value of success but because they maximize the informational value of the outcome. His argument is based on the assumption that self-evaluation is an essential goal for achievement-motivated people; tasks of intermediate difficulty maximize the extent to which people can infer their own ability, based on their relative success or failure on a task.

In a series of experiments (e.g., Trope & Ben-Yair, 1982; Trope & Brickman, 1975; Trope & Neter, 1994), Trope arranged for participants to choose between tasks of varying difficulty levels and diagnosticity. He theorized that difficulty levels could be dissociated from diagnosticity of the task. A difficult task would be a task that carried very low percentages of success across all participants while an easy task would carry very high percentages of success across all participants. However, even within tasks of similar difficulty (i.e., with equally high or low percentage of success across participants), the degree of diagnosticity differs according to how well a task differentiates between high performers versus low performers.

In a typical study, Trope and Brickman (1975) administered tests that participants believed were measures of intellectual accomplishment. They were given percentages of successes and failures by high-performing peers as well as percentages of successes and failures by low-performing peers. Trope and Brickman contrasted very difficult and very easy tasks that had high diagnostic value (large difference in success rates between low and high performers) with moderately difficult tasks that had low diagnostic value (comparable rates of success between high and low performers). The authors found that across all difficulty levels, high-diagnosticity tests were preferred over low-diagnosticity tests. However, among tests of equal diagnosticity, easier tests were preferred over more difficult ones. Trope claimed that his findings showed that moderately difficult tasks are selected more frequently by achievement-motivated people mainly because these tasks carry greater informational value for achieving rather than because they carry greater incentive value of success.

There are some criticisms to Trope's conclusions: First, although Trope challenges Atkinson's theory regarding task difficulty preferences for achievement-motivated individuals, he did not typically measure achievement motivation; instead, he assumed that individuals performing an achievement task would already have their achievement motive engaged. When he did measure motivation (e.g., Trope, 1980), he used self-report measures that tap into self-attributed achievement motives. Trope's (1980) finding that self-attributed achievement motivation does not predict people's preferences for tasks actually corroborates McClelland et al.'s (1989) theory that self-attributed motives and implicit motives predict different classes of behavior.

Second, the use of explicit declaration of choice by participants is problematic because such declarative measures are partly based on factors other than motivational drive, such as self-efficacy and demand characteristics (c.f. McClelland, Koestner, & Weinberger, 1989; Schultheiss & Brunstein, 2005). Trope's findings are at best relevant to self-attributed achievement motivation and people's need to make task decisions that maintain their self-consistency. When implicit achievement motivation is studied, incentive value rather than diagnosticity should be the main factor in determining task preference.

Accordingly, more recent research by Brunstein and Meier (2005) has challenged Trope's argument about the value of feedback in n Achievement–motivated behavior. In a sophisticated study, Brunstein and Meier (2005) measured both n and san achievement and asked participants to complete a mental concentration task. They measured participants' performance on the task and asked participants to choose whether they would continue with the task or switch to another task unrelated to achievement. Brunstein and Meier theorized that while task performance is considered a spontaneous behavior that should be energized by implicit motives, task continuation is an example of a choice behavior that should be predicted by self-attributed motivation. Additionally, Brunstein and Meier argued that since implicit achievement motivation is related to self-improvement concerns, *n* Achievement–motivated people should respond more strongly to self-referenced performance feedback (i.e., feedback about how well they are doing now in comparison to how well they were performing previously). Conversely, they argued that because self-attributed Achievement is derived from the self-concept, *san* Achievement–motivated people would react more strongly to norm-referenced feedback (i.e., feedback about how well they are performing in comparison to their peers).

Generally, Brunstein and Maier (2005) point out that when participants received self-referenced feedback, *n* Achievement was linked to task performance but not linked to task continuation (Study 1). Specifically, *n* Achievement was linked to better task performance after exposure to (unfavorable) self-referenced but not to norm-referenced feedback (Study 1). Moreover, *n* Achievement was related to better task performance after exposure to unfavorable norm-referenced feedback only when *san* Achievement was also high (Study 3). Finally, although *san* Achievement was not linked to task performance, it was linked to task continuation after exposure to norm-referenced feedback (Studies 1 and 2) but not to self-referenced feedback (Studies 1 and 2). These findings indicate that *n* Achievement is activated by self-referenced feedback to direct effortful performance but is not activated by norm-referenced feedback. Brunstein and Maier (2005) explain that the interaction that occurred between *n* and *san* Achievement suggests that the *san* Achievement plays a channeling role by directing *n* Achievement energy into better performance when ongoing task pursuits fit normatively defined standards.

Brunstein and Meier's findings clarify Trope's claims about the diagnostic value of feedback. *N* Achievement is related to self-improvement and is aroused by task incentives such as self-referenced feedback, thus it is unconcerned with performance relative to others. Social comparison–related information such as norm-referenced feedback is relatively more useful for people who are motivated by *san* Achievement. Trope's claim—that the value of feedback lies in its ability to provide accurate information for assessment of one's abilities—only applies in a context when a person's ranking vis-à-vis her peers is more significant than her individual performance on the task.

However, because they did not make the distinction between HS and FF, the implications of Brunstein and Meier's findings should extend only to traditional approach-oriented notions of *n* Achievement, that is, HS.

The Heckhausen Assessment Tradition

Heckhausen (1963) expanded on McClelland's and Atkinson's model by developing two independent PSE measures of HS and FF. He corrected two of the major shortcomings of the McClelland et al. (1953) measure. Specifically, he resolved the issue of using mixed self-report (e.g., TAQ) and PSE methods to measure motives and designed a separate measurement procedure for HS and FF, respectively. Heckhausen developed his PSE-based scoring system by reviewing of the protocols of people who either did or did not use defensive goal-setting strategies.

Moreover, Heckhausen built on McClelland et al.' s (1953) scoring system by adopting most of their original *n* Achievement coding categories but defining them separately for HS and FF and adding more relevant coding categories to make the HS/FF distinction the centerpiece of his system. Heckhausen also streamlined the original *n* Achievement categories by dropping some categories (e.g., Nurturant press, or *Nup*) that were relatively infrequent and did not discriminate well between individuals high and low in *n* Achievement. Specifically, Heckhausen retained the original *n* Achievement system themes of *need, instrumental activity, unsuccessful achievement outcomes, positive and negative affect,* and *anticipatory affect,* but discarded categories that were of questionable validity, such as *blocks, successful achievement outcomes,* and *nurturant press.* For instance, imagery-containing references to *blocks* and *nurturant press* could be invoked because of other motives, such as *n* Power and *n* Affiliation. Finally, he added some categories (such as *praise* and *criticism*) that he thought were theoretically relevant to the hope and fear aspects of *n* Achievement. Tables 2.3a and 2.3b present an abbreviated summary of Heckhausen's coding categories for HS and FF, respectively.

Historically, Heckhausen's system has not been used very frequently by McClelland, his colleagues, or other U.S. researchers interested in achievement motivation because Heckhausen's measure was written in German (however, see a recent translation of the system into English by Schultheiss, 2001). Nonetheless, Heckhausen's measure has gained respectability because it is to date the most systematic and comprehensive, theory-driven need achievement scoring system available.

The validity of the system has been displayed in extensive studies conducted in Germany. The FF measure was associated with marked avoidance of tasks of moderate difficulty, thus lending support to Atkinson's expectancy-value model (Schneider, 1978). Research conducted using the Heckhausen system presents a coherent picture of the person motivated by FF. Compared to those who score lower in FF, high-scoring participants tend to recall tasks that they have completed better than those that they have failed to complete, take longer to do their homework, perform worse under time pressure, and perform better after success feedback (Heckhausen, 1980). Taken together, these findings show that FF motivates individuals to work harder, longer, and more carefully than others to ensure that they will not fail at the present task, especially when it is obvious that their hard work will help them avoid the *implications* of failure. That is, FF not only causes individuals to work harder to avoid failure, but it also causes them to dismiss or discount past failures and disrupts their

Table 2.3a   Outline of Heckhausen's Coding System for Hope of Success

Imagery Type	Definition/Criteria
Need for success (NS)	When a story character sets a positively framed achievement goal by using *Positively framed intentions that the goal can be achieved *Wishes and hopes aimed at the achievement goal
Instrumental activity to succeed (IS)	Story character does or will do something that will bring her or him closer to the achievement goal, without relying on others' help
Expectation of success (ES)	Expectations of a story character to succeed in an achievement-related activity
Praise (P)	Whenever a person praises, rewards, or distinguishes somebody else who has worked well or delivered a good performance
Positive Affect (A +)	Positive affective states that occur in an achievement context
Success theme (ST)	At least NS or ES has been scored and no Fear of Failure category has been scored except A - and EF

Source: Adapted from Schultheiss (2001). This outline is not adequate for scoring purposes.

Table 2.3b   Outline of Heckhausen's Coding System for Fear of Failure

Imagery Type	Definition/Criteria
Need to avoid failure (NF)	A story character expresses the need or intention to avoid failure within an achievement context by: *Setting a negatively framed goal *Wishing something is accomplished that will soften a failure *Hesitates to show her or his work for fear of scrutiny or criticism
Instrumental activity to avoid failure (IF)	Story character does, will do, is doing something that will soften or avoid a failure
Expectation of failure (EF)	Expectations of a story character to fail in an achievement-related activity
Criticism (C)	Whenever a person openly criticizes the work, performance, or ability of somebody else
Negative Affect (A −)	Negative affective states that occur in an achievement context
Failure (F)	Whenever achievement-related activities result in a failure or a past failure has not been remedied
Failure theme (FT)	At least NF or F has been scored and no hope of success category has been scored except IS

Source: Adapted from Schultheiss (2001). This outline is not adequate for scoring purposes.

concentration and attention when failure on a present task is possible and impending.

Although Heckhausen developed a very efficient and theoretically sound coding system, there is one major shortcoming in his research. He developed his coding categories through deductive reasoning and literature review instead of using McClelland's recommended procedure of experimentally arousing HS and FF in participants first and then deriving coding categories by observing differences between protocols from the arousal conditions and from the neutral condition.

The method of experimental arousal has an advantage over a theoretically derived coding system because it is based on the actual effects of the motive of interest on fantasy. For this reason, it can be argued that empirically derived coding systems have greater construct validity than theoretically derived coding systems. Heckhausen's method of rational inquiry may have missed out on some content categories that were not obvious to him but would emerge from protocols collected in an experimental arousal condition.

Introducing a Revised Measure of Hope of Success and Fear of Failure

In an effort to correct the shortcomings of previous research in assessing HS and FF, I (Pang, 2006) have built on the McClelland-Atkinson and Heckhausen lines of research by using arousal procedures to develop separate PSE-based measure content-coding systems for HS and FF.

The main goal of this research is to rectify the shortcomings of previous measures by (a) *experimentally arousing HS and FF* in participants in a way that does not prime the affiliation and power motives or the social evaluative element, and (b) developing a PSE-type content-coding system that *focuses on the HS/FF distinction* by constructing separate coding systems for the two orientations.

Previous research (e.g., Brunstein & Meier, 2005; Brunstein & Schmitt, 2004) has demonstrated the effectiveness of self-referenced feedback as an incentive for achievement-motivated individuals. The use of self-referenced feedback as opposed to other- or norm-referenced feedback is based on previous evidence that shows that (a) achievement motivation is only activated in situations where there are intrinsic reasons for succeeding (e.g., Brunstein & Schmitt, 2004), and (b) socially evaluative information tends to arouse other motives such as *n* Affiliation or *n* Power (e.g., Birney, Burdick, & Teevan, 1969). Hence, the general principle of my arousal method was to vary *self-referenced* feedback received by participants in order to increase the salience of either success or failure.

Following the basic premise of McClelland et al.'s (1953) conditioning theory of motivation and Schultheiss and Brunstein's (2005) elaboration of this theory, we would expect people motivated by HS to be in an active-approach mode; hence, they are actively seeking to increase the amount of positive incentives. Thus, in my arousal procedure, participants in an intermittent success" condition were given intermittent positive self-referenced performance feedback (e.g., calculating trial performance and flashing a message on later trials, "You performed significantly better than on your previous trials!") while they executed a mental concentration task. It was expected that intermittent success feedback would arouse HS in participants, who would work harder to improve their performance on subsequent trials in order to receive the positive incentives provided by the encouraging flashing messages.

However, we would expect those people who are motivated by FF to be in an active-avoidant mode; hence, they actively seek to decrease the amount of disincentives. Thus, participants in an "intermittent failure" condition were given intermittent negative self-referenced performance feedback (e.g., "You performed significantly worse than on your previous trials!") during the same task. It was expected that intermittent failure feedback would arouse FF in participants, who would work harder to improve their performance on subsequent trials in order to avoid the disincentives provided by the discouraging flashing messages.

Participants in a neutral condition were not given feedback during the actual task but were told that they would receive some form of feedback on their performance only after having completed the experiment. Thus, these participants would have received no particular positive or negative incentives to improve on their performances.

Table 2.4a represents the coding categories that were developed for HS after analyzing and comparing postarousal protocols in the intermittent success condition with protocols from the neutral condition; Table 2.4b represents coding categories that were developed for FF after analyzing and comparing postarousal protocols in the intermittent failure condition with protocols from the neutral condition.

As an illustration of the different content of the HS and FF scoring systems, the following is an excerpt of a protocol written by a participant in the intermittent success condition that would receive high scores in HS. Wherever they occur, coding categories are indicated in [*italics and square brackets*]:

All the training had built up to this one moment. If Cari could overtake her opponent on the last lap, she could win her country gold. Cari pushed herself as hard as she could, passing those competitors who were becoming more and more tired [*others failed or gave up*]. Although she felt intense pain and exhaustion [*physical strain*], competition was intense and she strove to overtake the person in front of her [competition] while concentrating on her technique [*quality control*]. With the last of her energy [*strong energizing emotion*], Cari pushed herself over the finish line. She had won the Gold medal [*unique accomplishment*].

Table 2.4a   Outline of Pang's (2006) Revised Coding System for Hope of Succ‌

Imagery Type	Definition/Criteria
Positive achievement goal	The story character expresses or experiences an intention (desire, wish, need) to fulfill a positive achievement goal
Strong energizing emotion	A story character experiences positive emotions in the context of an achievement setting that is energizing and/or leads to subsequent achievement-related activity
Quality control	A story character voluntarily engages in self-scrutiny while carrying out a task. The quality of the extra care paid to the task is one of vigilance, defense against potential error or failure
Praise	Whenever a person praises, rewards, or distinguishes somebody else who has worked well or delivered a good performance
Expectation of success	Expectations of a story character to succeed in an achievement-related activity
Compensatory effort	Increased effort or increased resolve to overcome obstacles; persisting with work, despite presence of actual or potential obstacles
Lack of progress	Temporary lack of progress during achievement pursuit; any indication that things are not going as planned
Competition	Detailed description/analysis of the dynamics/intensity of competition
Others' expectation of failure	Other story characters disbelieving, doubtful of protagonist's ability/ potential to fulfill the achievement goal
Physical strain	It is explicitly stated or implied that engaging in the achievement goal entails physical strain
Extreme personal sacrifice	Extreme personal sacrifices made in pursuit of goal, including deprivation or loss of life and limb
Others failed or gave up	A scenario in which others who attempted task either failed or gave up before bringing the task to completion is juxtaposed with that of the main story character who continues on the achievement task.
Success outcome	Achievement goal is fulfilled, over and above simple task completion.
Significant accomplishment	Unique accomplishments; setting a social or achievement precedent, e.g., inventions, discoveries, and cures

Source: Adapted from Pang (2006). This outline is not adequate for scoring purposes.

The following is an excerpt of a protocol written by a participant in the intermittent failure condition that would receive high scores in FF:

Bonnie woke up in Salt Lake City and felt excited about the day's events. Today was the speed skating finals. She arrived early at the venue and mentally prepared herself by visualizing the events that were to come [*preparation and training*]. Race Time. Bonnie is anxious enough she could jump out of her skin. She can't stop thinking about how this has been her life goal [*life dream*], to win the Olympics gold medal. She has been getting up at 5am and training for 10 hours a day for the last six months [*hard work*]. As she skates, Bonnie thinks back to a time when she was unable to compete because she had been injured by a cruel old woman that hit her leg with her walking stick [*obstacle in the environment*]. Bonnie will keep on thinking about this sad event [*distraction*] and will lose the race [*failure outcome*].

Imagery Type	Definition/Criteria
Preparation and training	Physical or mental training and/or preparation that is undertaken in order to bring an achievement goal/task closer to completion/fulfillment
Basic instrumental activity	Engaging in, either in the past, present, or future, activity (whether planned or actual) in order to bring an achievement goal/task closer to completion/fulfillment
Hard work	Includes doing one's best, paying attention, being extra careful with a job, as long as the intention of the extra attention is not to be vigilant in case of error or failure
Positive affect	Distinctly positively valenced emotion that happens as a result of working or of a positive achievement outcome at work
Strong inhibiting emotion	Strong inhibiting emotion, e.g., feeling overwhelmed, that is experienced while pursuing the achievement goal
Quality control by others	Checking up on another story character's progress on the achievement goal
Distraction	Being distracted and/or mentioning concern with distractions while pursuing the achievement goal
Obstacle in the environment	Elements in external environment that cause a disruption in achievement activity and/or prevent achievement goal from being fulfilled
Obstacle within self	Elements within the protagonist that cause a disruption in achievement activity and/or prevent achievement goal from being fulfilled
Expectation of failure	A story character expresses self-doubt (mentally, verbally, or through emotional behavior) that he or she will or could fail in the achievement task/goal. Indications of low self-efficacy are scored.
Life dream	The achievement goal is referred to as a lifelong dream or ambition. The story character undertakes the achievement task because he or she wants to prevent regret in not fulfilling the life dream or because of a feeling of being compelled by this life dream.
Failure outcome	An unsuccessful achievement outcome—the achievement task or goal is not attained. The failure must be explicitly related to some specific achievement goal or task, and not be attributed to some general sense of malaise, disappointment, or misfortune.

Note: Adapted from Pang (2006). This outline is not adequate for scoring purposes.

Interestingly, the revised HS and FF systems included some subcategories that traditionally have not been associated with either motive. Specifically, the revised FF coding system included such subcategories as *instrumental activity*, which are almost identical to subcategories in Heckhausen's system for hope of success, and not fear of failure. Additionally, there are also some content categories that are completely new, which have not been identified by either McClelland or Heckhausen, or which have been given only cursory mention by previous coding systems. Examples of such categories are *competition*[1], and those categories that indicate the costs, either physical or emotional, associated with

Table 2.5   Similarities and Differences between Pang's (2006) Revised Coding System for Hope of Success (HS) and (FF) and Heckhausen's (1963) and McClelland et al.'s (1953) Coding Categories

	Similarities	Additions	Dropped
HS	Positive achievement goal Expectation of success Significant accomplishment Praise	+ Compensatory effort + Competition + Sacrifice/strain + Others failed/gave up + Lack of progress + Success outcome + Quality control by self + Strong energizing emotion + Others' expectation of failure	− Instrumental activity −Nurturant press −Positive affect
FF	Failure Distraction Basic instrumental activity Quality control by others Obstacles Expectation of failure Life ambition/life dream	+ Hard work + Preparation/training + Positive affect + Strong inhibiting emotion	− Criticism − Leaving playing field − Negative affect

pursuing an achievement goal—*physical strain* and *extreme personal sacrifice*. Table 2.5 summarizes the similarities, additions, and subtractions in coding categories between Pang's (2006) revised measure and the coding categories contained in Heckhausen's (1963) and McClelland et al.'s (1953) measures.

Taken together, the subcategories for HS suggest a profile of the prototypical HS-motivated individual as a person who pays greater attention to positive achievement standards as well as to any indications that a positive achievement goal has been obtained (as indicated by the emergence of the themes of *positive achievement goal, successful outcome,* significant *accomplishment,* and *praise*). She assesses the situation for cues about the performance of relevant peers and competitors (*competition, others failed/gave up, others' expectation of failure*) as well as the physical demands of the activity (*strain, sacrifice*). This is an indication that the achievement tasks are evaluated for their potential challenges, which she overcomes by exerting effortful control (*quality control, compensatory effort*) as well as a high level of determination (*strong, energizing emotion*).

Conversely, subcategories for FF depict a person who is focused on negative achievement goals and outcomes, as well as potential obstacles that lead to these negative outcomes (*failure, expectation of failure, obstacles*). This focus on potentially negative outcomes leads to some defensive goal-directed behavior (*quality control*) to the extent that it potentially prevents her from focusing on the goal-directed activity (*distraction*). The goal, although negatively framed, is a personally important one (*life dream*). The combination of a personally meaningful goal and an attentional focus on potentially negative outcomes causes the individual to experience conflicting emotions (*positive emotion, strong inhibiting emotion*) while engaging frenetically in instrumental activity (*basic instrumental activity, hard work, preparation and training*) that is undertaken in order to ensure that the negative outcomes do not come to fruition.

There are some possible reasons for the different themes and patterns of coding categories represented in the present study compared to those found by Heckhausen and McClelland.

First, McClelland et al. (1953) aroused achievement motivation in their participants by suggesting success or failure at a norm-setting task. Specifically, subjects were given the impression that they were completing intelligence and aptitude tests for which norms had already been established and then were quoted norms that were either low enough to arouse a sense of success in most participants, or high enough to arouse a sense of failure in most participants. In contrast, the arousal procedure in the present study was based on an individual's performance on previous trials of the task and was indicative only of speed and accuracy at responding to computer-based visual stimuli, rather than of general leadership abilities. For this reason, the present study may evoke more task-oriented imagery, such as those associated with the costs of engaging in the achievement act, and of intensity of competition—two content categories that are absent in McClelland's coding system.

Furthermore, the participants in McClelland's studies were competing against a pre-established norm, while participants in the present studies were competing against standards set by their own previous performance, which could explain why participants in the present study were more likely to consider the personal costs associated with pursuing an achievement goal.

Second, the coding categories that McClelland et al. (1953) obtained were probably influenced by the fact that they were based on experimental procedures that all involved failure arousal (McClelland, Clark, Roby, & Atkinson, 1949). The emphasis on failure in McClelland et al.'s arousal procedure was a result of their assumption that motivation arises from either physiological or psychological deprivation of condition or object that is necessary for growth and survival. However, while the deprivation principle would apply for basic needs such as hunger and thirst, psychological needs such as achievement motivation tend to possess more complicated origins involving the internalization of social and cultural standards of achievement. Additionally, as illustrated by the conditioning theory of motivation, approach-oriented HS motives develop through conditioning of behavioral-response contingencies for obtaining positive affective experiences. Hence, success is a more obvious positive incentive for those motivated by HS, and experimental conditions designed to arouse HS should also include intermittent success arousal.

Third, the number and type of achievement associations in an imaginative story is partly dependent on the evocative characteristics of the picture cues used in the assessment. Picture cues used in McClelland et al. (1953), Heckhausen (1963), and Pang (2006) were not consistent with each other, and it is possible that certain themes emerged in the revised HS and FF categories because they were strongly associated with certain picture cues. For instance, the picture set in Pang (2006) contained a picture of a figure climbing a snow-covered mountain. The categories *physical strain* and *extreme personal sacrifice* could both have been primed by the mountain climber picture, which may have resonated with the participants in the intermittent-success arousal group in a particular way. Because neither McClelland et al. (1953) nor Heckhausen (1963) used a picture with similar content, there is a valid concern that the differences in resulting imagery may be uniquely elicited by this picture rather than a general effect of motivational arousal. Future work would benefit from an examination of whether and the extent to which themes evoked by common picture cues produce imagery that is idiosyncratic to this set of cues.

Finally, the main difference between the arousal procedure of the present study and the procedure through which Heckhausen (1963) constructed his coding systems is one between empirical and theoretical derivation. Heckhausen's main objective was to construct a measure of theoretically relevant differences between HS and FF. Thus, he ended up with two sets of coding categories that were meaningfully and functionally diametrically opposed. Logically, Heckhausen's HS coding system contained positive goal and goal-relevant imagery, such as *instrumental activity* and *positive affect*, while the FF coding contained negative goal and goal-relevant imagery, such as *expectation of failure*. The fact that *instrumental activity* and *positive affect* are more prevalent in the FF arousal group of the present study while *expectation of failure* is more prevalent in the HS arousal group suggests that fear of failure is not merely a convenient theoretical opposite to hope of success, but that FF is functionally and behaviorally more similar to HS than traditional achievement motivation theory has suggested.

Validation of Pang's (2006) Revised Coding System for HS and FF

The revised coding system was validated in the following ways: (a) HS and FF scores were used to predict decisions on the Iowa Gambling Task (IGT; Bechara et al., 1994), a behavioral measure of risky- and risk-averse decision making, (b) HS and FF scores were correlated with scores on *san* Achievement motivation measures to investigate discriminant validity, (c) convergent and discriminant validity were explored by comparing the scores of the revised HS and FF measure to that of Winter's (1994) coding system for scoring motive imagery in running text, and finally, (d) predictive validity was investigated by using revised-system HS and FF scores to predict performance on a computer-based reaction time task of attention and concentration (adapted from Brickenkamp & Zillmer's, 1998, D2 Test of Attention).

The IGT and Preference for Moderate Risk

As its name suggests, the IGT presents the participant with a gambling scenario in which she makes card choices from four separate decks of playing cards. Two of the card decks are manipulated so that they consistently present opportunities to win large amounts of money but are likely to cause significant monetary losses in the long run (a result of big wins and big losses). On the other hand, the other two decks consistently provide opportunities to win moderate amounts of money and are likely to cause moderate monetary gains in the long run (a result of small wins and small losses).

Typically, a rational participant starts off during the IGT by taking more risky, high-reward bets, thus preferring the disadvantageous, high-win/high-loss decks. By the final block however, most participants tend to develop more risk- and punishment-averse tactics of switching their preference to the more advantageous, small-win/small-losses, decks that possess moderate risk (Denburg, Tranel, & Bechara, 2005). Because it requires participants to choose between options of varying relative risk, the IGT represents a modern version of the kind of risk-taking tasks that Atkinson and others used to test the predictions from the expectancy-value theory about achievement-motivated people's preferences for moderately challenging or moderately risky achievement goals. One key differ- ence between the IGT and say, a ring-toss or a volleyball-dunking game, is that participants have no initial information about the most advantageous strategy at the outset but, through participating in a number of trials, figure out the best strategy intuitively. Nonetheless, Bechara, Damasio, Tranel, and Damasio (1997) found that anticipatory psychophysiological responses occur in partici- pants when they are selecting cards from the advantageous decks even before the participants have conscious awareness of the strategic value of their choices. Thus, the IGT provides a unique opportunity to assess moderate-task preference using a nondeclarative, behavioral measure.

In the present study, HS scores as assessed by the categories in Table 2.4a predicted more risky choice behavior (as indicated by a preference for the riskier, disadvantageous decks) in earlier blocks and more risk-averse choice behavior (as indicated by a preference for moderate risk, more advantageous decks) toward the final blocks of the IGT. This pattern of behavior suggests that HS is related to a hyperrational mode of responding, where highly achieve- ment-motivated participants who have hope of success are more likely than low achievement-motivated participants to engage in behavior that will eventually maximize their monetary gains in the IGT.

On the other hand, participants with greater FF as assessed by the categories in Table 2.4b, were significantly more likely to make more risky, reward-sensitive decisions throughout the entire IGT, suggesting that FF influences early task preference in the same way as HS by encouraging more risky early decision making, although this risky behavior persists for those motivated by FF even after experience with more trials.

The findings of the present study seem to go against the predictions of the expectancy-value model that postulated that people motivated by FF would be most eager to minimize loss and punishment.

The above findings can be more easily explained in the context of the previous study by DeCharms and Davé (1965) that found that high-HS and high-FF groups were associated with taking more extreme risks than low-achievement groups. As previously mentioned, there was an interaction effect of HS and FF, such that subjects with both high fear of failure and high hope of success are most likely to concentrate their efforts at a point of moderately high risk. Consistent with DeCharms and Davé's (1965) findings, participants high in HS and FF are more likely to take moderate to extreme risks in the present study. Left to their own devices, highly achievement-motivated people, whether they are motivated by hope or fear, appear to maximize their satisfaction early on by taking what DeCharms and Davé described as a "calculated risk."

Correlation with Related Explicit and Implicit Motive Measures

The Hope of Success and Fear of Failure scale (HSFF; Schultheiss & Murray, 2002) is a 22-item Likert-type scale with items that are based on Heckhausen's (1963) dimensions of hope of success and fear of failure. In line with previous research showing the lack of convergence between implicit and explicit motive measures, scores on the new PSE scoring system for HS and FF did not display any significant systematic relationship with scores on the self-attributed HS and FF motive measures (see Table 2.6).

Because the Winter scoring system contains simplified versions of the original *n* Achievement (McClelland et al., 1953), *n* Affiliation (Heyns, Veroff, & Atkinson, 1958; McAdams, 1980), and *n* Power (Winter, 1973) coding systems, it can be used to ascertain convergent and divergent validity for the revised coding system for HS and FF. As shown in Table 2.6, convergent and divergent validity was partially demonstrated with postarousal HS scores, which were significantly positively correlated with postarousal Winter *n* Achievement, but not with other Winter system motives. There were no significant correlations between revised-system FF scores and Winter-system *n* Ach, *n* Aff, or *n* Pow scores. These results suggest that the Winter coding system for *n* Achievement is more adept at measuring the active-approach motive disposition of HS than the active-avoidance FF disposition.

Table 2.6   Correlations between Revised Model Postarousal $HS_{revised}$ and $FF_{revised}$ Scores, Winter (1994) n Achievement, n Affiliation, and n Power, and san HS and FF Scores

	Correlations	
Motive/Trait	Revised Model HS	Revised Model FF
n Ach	.38**	.23
n Aff	.06	−.06
n Pow	−.04	.03
HS scale	−.20	−.17
FF scale	.15	.07

Note: $n = 96$, n Ach = need Achievement score, n Pow = need Power score, n Aff = need Affiliation score, HS scale = explicit HS scale, FF = explicit FF scale.
** $p < .01$.

Task Performance

Finally, as evidence of predictive validity, HS and FF scores were correlated with both reaction time and error rates of responding on the D2 Task of Attention (Brickenkamp & Zillmer, 1998). Revised-system HS and FF scores were associated with lower error rates on the D2 task. Specifically, while HS is related to greater accuracy in later trials of the task, FF is related to greater accuracy on earlier trials.

Taken together, the IGT and D2 mental concentration task findings and correlations with related n and san motivation measures suggest that (a) performance feedback is an effective method of arousal HS and FF motivations; (b) dispositional HS and FF are related to moderately risky behavior on the IGT; and (c) functionally, HS and FF are both energizing rather than inhibiting, promoting definite goal-directed behavior such as greater accuracy on the mental concentration task. These findings suggest that both HS and FF are functionally more similar to each other than other theorists (e.g., Atkinson et al., 1960; Heckhausen, 1963) have argued.

Discussion and Future Directions

The development of theory on n Achievement has been intertwined with the development of its instruments and methods. As detailed in this chapter, the methodological conventions have, in turn, affected theoretical conceptions of the motive, particularly in the distinction between hope of success and fear of failure motivation.

Recent theoretical discussion (e.g., Schultheiss & Brunstein, 2005) and empirical work (Brunstein & Meier, 2005; Pang, 2006) has made some interesting advancements from previous notions about achievement motivation, hope-of-success motivation, and fear-of-failure motivation. Specifically, the importance of self-referenced feedback and self-imposed standards of excellence has been highlighted. People motivated by implicit achievement motivation respond to situations that allow them to set their own standards of excellence and perform better when they are working toward and given feedback on their progress in a goal that is personally relevant.

In addition, theoretical developments about the difference between implicit and self-attributed motivation has contributed to awareness of the shortcomings of previous methods of assessing fear-of-failure motivation. The development of better methods of measuring achievement motivation that pay respect to the implicit–explicit motive distinction is important because good measures are the first step toward theory development. For this reason, theory regarding fear of failure has never been fully developed. Specifically, predictions about fear of failure regarding effort, persistence, task choice, task performance, and task valence following Atkinson's expectancy-value theory of motivation have received mottled investigation and support. The revised HS and FF coding systems presented in this chapter represent a first step toward improving theory and measurement of n Achievement. Specifically, when self-referenced rather than norm-referenced feedback is given, people motivated by hope of success and those motivated by fear of failure appear to be functionally more similar than previous theory would expect. Pang's (2006) findings corroborate Halisch and Heckhausen's (1989) study that showed that high HS and FF, as assessed by a PSE-based measure rather than self-reports or the difference score measure, predicted similarly steeper valence gradients for success outcomes than for failure outcomes. This implies that the behavioral similarities between those motivated by HS and FF could be due to the fact that both groups receive equally stronger emotional reinforcements when they obtain positive achievement outcomes.

Much research is needed to clarify the theoretical quandaries and controversies regarding n Achievement, hope of success, and fear of failure. Future work should pay particular attention to (a) ways of arousing n Achievement (perhaps using self-referenced feedback) that do not tap into confounding concepts such as n Power and self-evaluation anxiety, (b) distinguishing between HS and FF in measurement methods in order to achieve greater clarity in mapping out each motive's developmental and behavioral correlates, and (c) validating such measures using behavioral approaches (such as task performance, intuitive decision making, and physiological affect changes), rather than self-report and declarative outcomes.

Author Note

Correspondence concerning this chapter should be addressed to Joyce S. Pang, Division of Psychology, Nanyang Technological University, Singapore 639798, or sent by email to (joycepang@ntu.edu.sg).

Notes

[1] Although *competition with a standard of excellence* is stated as one of the criteria for scoring *n* Achievement–related imagery, it is not elaborated in the subcategories. Hence, in the original McClelland et al. (1953) scoring system, mention of competition would be a criterion for moving on to score subcategories of *need, instrumental activity,* and so on, but does not itself contribute to the motive score. In addition, while *mention of winning or competing with others* is a category in the Winter (1994) integrated system for scoring motive imagery in running text, that category does not specifically include elaboration of degree or intensity of the competition as a criterion for scoring.

References

Atkinson, J. W. (1957). Motivational determinants of risk-taking behavior. *Psychological Review, 64,* 359–372.

Atkinson, J. W. (1958). *Motives in fantasy, action, and society: A method of assessment and study.* Oxford, England: Van Nostrand.

Atkinson, J. W., & Litwin, G. H. (1960). Achievement motive and test anxiety conceived as motive to approach success and motive to avoid failure. *Journal of Abnormal and Social Psychology, 60,* 52.

Bartmann, T. (1965). *Denkerziehung im Programmierten Unterricht.* Munich, Germany: Manz.

Bechara, A., Damasio, A. R., & Damasio, H. (1994). Insensitivity to future consequences following damage to human prefrontal cortex. *Cognition, 50,* 7–15.

Bechara, A., Damasio, H., Tranel, D., & Damasio, A. R. (1997). Deciding advantageously before knowing the advantageous strategy. *Science, 275,* 1293–1294.

Bellak, L. (1975). *The thematic apperception test: The children's apperception test and the senior apperception technique in clinical use* (3rd ed.). New York: Grune & Stratton.

Birney, R. C., Burdick, H., & Teevan, R. C. (1969). *Fear of failure.* NY: Van Nostrand-Reinhold Company.

Brickenkamp, R., & Zillmer. (1998). *d2 Test of Attention.* Seattle, WA: Hogrefe International.

Brunstein, J. C., & Maier, G. W. (2005). Implicit and self-attributed motives to achieve: Two separate but interacting needs. *Journal of Personality and Social Psychology, 89*(2), 205–222.

Brunstein, J. C., & Schmitt, C. H. (2004). Assessing individual differences in achievement motivation with the Implicit Association Test. *Journal of Research in Personality, 38*(6), 536–555.

Cohen, J., & Cohen, P. (1983). *Applied multiple regression/correlation analysis in behavioural sciences.* Hillsdale, NJ: Erlbaum.

Collins, C. J., Hanges, P. J., & Locke, E. A. (2004). The relationship of achievement motivation to entrepreneurial behavior: A meta-analysis. *Human Performance, 17*, 95–117.

Cooper, W. H. (1983). An achievement motivation nomological network. *Journal of Personality and Social Psychology, 44*(4), 841–861.

Covington, M. V., & Omelich, C. L. (1985). Ability and effort valuation among failure-avoiding and failure-accepting students. *Journal of Educational Psychology, 77*, 446–459.

Cramer, P. (1991). Anger and the use of defense mechanisms in college students. *Journal of Personality, 59*, 39–55.

deCharms, R., & Carpenter, V. (1968). Measuring motivation in culturally disadvantaged children. . In H. J. Klausmeirer & G. T. O'Hearn (Eds.), *Research and development toward the improvement of education.* Madison, WI: Educational Research Services.

de Charms, R., & Dave, P. N. (1965). Hope of success, fear of failure, subjective probability, and risk-taking behavior. *Journal of Personality and Social Psychology, 1*, 558–568.

Denburg, N. L., Tranel, D., & Bechara, A. (2005). The ability to decide advantageously declines prematurely in some normal older persons. *Neuropsychologia, 43*, 1099–1106.

Feather, N. T. (1962). The study of persistence. *Psychological Bulletin, 59*, 94–115.

Feather, N. T. (1967). Valence of outcome and expectation of success in relation to task difficulty and perceived locus of control. *Journal of Personality and Social Psychology, 7*, 372–386.

Fleming, J., & Horner, M. S. (1992). The motive to avoid success. In C. P. Smith (Ed.), *Motivation and personality: Handbook of thematic content analysis* (pp. 179–89). New York: Cambridge University Press.

Fodor, E. M., & Carver, R. A. (2000). Achievement and power motives, performance feedback, and creativity. *Journal of Research in Personality, 34*, 380–396.

French, E. G. (1955). Some characteristics of achievement motivation. *Journal of Experimental Psychology, 50*(4), 232–236.

French, E. G. (1958). The interaction of achievement motivation and ability in problem solving success. *Journal of Abnormal & Social Psychology, 57*(3), 306–309.

Greenwald, A. G., McGhee, D. E., & Schwartz, J. L. K. (1998). Measuring individual differences in implicit cognition: The implicit association test. *Journal of Personality and Social Psychology, 74*(6), 1464–1480.

Griffin, D., Murray, S., & Gonzalez, R. (1999). Difference score correlations in relationship research: A conceptual primer. *Personal Relationships. Special issue: Methodological and Data Analytic Advances, 6*, 505–518.

Halisch, F., & Heckhausen, H. (1989). Motive-dependent versus ability-dependent valence functions for success and failure. In F. Halisch & J. H. L. van den Bercken (Eds.), *International perspectives on achievement and task motivation* (pp. 51–67). Lisse, The Netherlands: Swets & Zeitlinger Publishers.

Hamilton, J. O. (1974). Motivation and risk-taking behavior: A test of Atkinson's theory. *Journal of Personality and Social Psychology, 29*, 856–864.

Heckhausen, H. (1963). *Hoffnung und Furcht ub der Leistungsmotivation. [Hope and fear components of achievement motivation.]* Meisenheim am Glam: Anton Hain.

Heckhausen, H. (1980). *Motivation und Handeln.* New York: Spriner-Verlag.

Heckhausen, H. (1991). *Motivation and action.* Berlin, Germany: Springer.

Heyns, R. W., Veroff, J., & Atkinson, J. W. (1958). A scoring manual for the affiliation motive. In J. W. Atkinson (Ed.), *Motives in fantasy, action, and society* (pp. 205–218). Princeton, NJ: Van Nostrand.

Kagan, J., & Moss, H. A. (1962). *Birth to maturity: A study in psychological development.* New York: John Wiley.

Karabenick, S. A. (1972). Valence of success and failure as a function of achievement motives and locus of control. *Journal of Personality and Social Psychology, 21,* 101–110.

Karabenick, S. A. (1977). Fear of success, achievement and affiliation dispositions, and the performance of men and women under individual and competitive conditions. *Journal of Personality, 45,* 117–149.

Karabenick, S. A., & Youseff, Z. I. (1968). Performance as a function of achievement motive level and perceived difficulty. *Journal of Personality & Social Psychology, 10,* 414–419.

Kukla, A. (1974). Performance as a function of resultant achievement motivation (perceived ability) and perceived difficulty. *Journal of Research in Personality, 7,* 374–383.

Litwin, G. H. (1966). Achievement motivation, expectancy of success, and risk-taking behavior. In J. W. Atkinson & N. T. Feather (Eds.), *A theory of achievement motivation.* New York: Wiley.

Lowell, E. L. (1952). The effect of need for achievement on learning and speed of performance. *Journal of Psychology: Interdisciplinary and Applied, 33,* 31–40.

Mahone, C. H. (1960). Fear of failure and unrealistic vocational aspiration. *Journal of Abnormal and Social Psychology, 60,* 253–261.

McAdams, D. P. (1980). A thematic coding system for the intimacy motive. *Journal of Research in Personality, 14,* 413–432.

McClelland, D. C. (1961). *The achieving society.* Princeton, NJ: Van Nostrand.

McClelland, D. C. (1987). *Human motivation.* New York: Cambridge University Press.

McClelland, D. C., Atkinson, J. W., Clark, R. A., & Lowell, E. L. (1953). *The achievement motive.* East Norwalk, CT: Appleton-Century-Crofts.

McClelland, D. C., Clark, R. A., Roby, T. B., & Atkinson, J. W. (1949). The projective expression of needs. IV. The effect of the need for achievement on thematic apperception. *Journal of Experimental Psychology, 39,* 242–255.

McClelland, D. C., Koestner, R., & Weinberger, J. (1989). How do self-attributed and implicit motives differ? *Psychological Review, 96*(4), 690–702.

McKeachie, W. J. (1961). Motivation, teaching methods, and college learning. In M. R. Jones (Ed.), *Nebraska symposium on motivation.* Lincoln, NB: University of Nebraska Press.

Morgan, C. D., & Murray, H. A. (1935). A method for examining fantasies: The Thematic Apperception Test. *Archives of Neurology and Psychiatry, 34,* 289–306.

Nicholls, J. G. (1984). Achievement motivation: Conceptions of ability, subjective experience, task choice, and performance. *Psychological Review, 91,* 328–346.

O'Connor, P. A., Atkinson, J. W., & Horner, M. A. (1966). Motivational implications of ability grouping in schools. In J. W. Atkinson & N. T. Feather (Eds.), *A theory of achievement motivation*. New York: Wiley.

Pang, J. S. (2006). *A revised content-coding measure for hope of success (HS) and fear of failure (FF)*. Unpublished dissertation, University of Michigan, Ann Arbor.

Raynor, J. O., & Entin, E. E. (1982). *Motivation, career striving, and aging.* Washington, DC: Hemisphere.

Rosen, B. C., & D'Andrade, R. (1959). The psychosocial origins of achievement motivation. *Sociometry, 22,* 185–218.

Sarason, S. B., & Mandler, G. (1952). Some correlates of test anxiety. *The Journal of Abnormal and Social Psychology, 47,* 810–817.

Seligman, M. E. P. (1975). *Helplessness: On depression, development, and death.* New York: W. H. Freeman/Times Books/Henry Holt & Co.

Schmidt, L. A., & Riniolo, T. C. (1999). The role of neuroticism in test and social anxiety. *Journal of Social Psychology, 139*(3), 394–395.

Schneider, K. (1978). Atkinson's 'risk preference' model: Should it be revised? *Motivation and Emotion, 2,* 333–344.

Schneidman, E. S. (1999.). The Thematic Apperception Test: A paradise of psychodynamics. In L. Gieser & M. I. Stein (Eds.), *Evocative images: The Thematic Apperception Test and the art of projection* (pp. 87–97). Washington, DC: American Psychological Association.

Schultheiss, O. C. (2001). *Manual for the assessment of hope of success and fear of failure* (English translation of Heckhausen's need Achievement measure). Unpublished instrument, University of Michigan, Ann Arbor.

Schultheiss, O. C., & Brunstein, J. C. (2005). An implicit motive perspective on competence. In A. J. Elliot & C. S. Dweck (Eds.), *Handbook of competence and motivation* (pp. 31–51). New York: Guilford Publications.

Schultheiss, O. C., & Hale, J. A. (2007). Implicit motives modulate attentional orienting to facial expressions of emotion. *Motivation and Emotion, 31,* 13–24.

Schultheiss, O. C., & Murray, T. (2002). *Hope of success/fear of failure questionnaire.* Unpublished instrument, University of Michigan, Ann Arbor.

Spangler, W. D. (1992). Validity of questionnaire and TAT measures of need for achievement: Two meta-analyses. *Psychological Bulletin, 112,* 40–154.

Thorndike, E. L. (1911). *Animal intelligence: Experimental studies.* Lewiston, NY: Macmillan Press.

Trope, Y. (1975). Seeking information about one's own ability as a determinant of choice among tasks. *Journal of Personality and Social Psychology, 32,* 1004–1013.

Trope, Y. (1980). Self-assessment, self-enhancement, and task preference. *Journal of Experimental Social Psychology, 16,* 116–129.

Trope, Y., & Ben-Yair, E. (1982). Task construction and persistence as means for self-assessment of abilities. *Journal of Personality and Social Psychology, 42,* 637–645.

Trope, Y., & Brickman, P. (1975). Difficulty and diagnosticity as determinants of choice among tasks. *Journal of Personality and Social Psychology, 31*(5), 918.

Trope, Y., & Neter, E. (1994). Reconciling competing motives in self-evaluation: The role of self-control in feedback seeking. *Journal of Personality and Social Psychology, 66*(4), 646–657.

Veroff, J. (1969). Social comparison and the development of achievement motivation. In C. P. Smith (Ed.), *Achievement-related motives in children* (pp. 46–101). New York: Russell Sage Foundation.

Winter, D. G. (1973). *Power motive.* New York: Free Press.

Winter, D. G. (1994). *Manual for scoring motive imagery in running text.* Unpublished instrument, University of Michigan, Ann Arbor.

Winter, D. G. (1999). Linking personality and 'scientific' psychology: The development of empirically derived Thematic Apperception Test measures. In L. Gieser & M. I. Stein (Eds.), *Evocative images: The Thematic Apperception Test and the art of projection* (pp. 107–124). Washington, DC: American Psychological Association.

Winterbottom, M. R. (1958). The relation of need for achievement to learning experiences in independence and mastery. In J. W. Atkinson (Ed.), *Motives in fantasy, action, and society.* Princeton, NJ: Van Nostrand.

Chapter 3

The Duality of Affiliative Motivation

JOEL WEINBERGER, TANYA COTLER, AND DANIEL FISHMAN
Adelphi University

The task of this chapter, to review affiliative motivation, is not a straightforward one. In accordance with the other reviews of the major motives in this volume, we focus on implicit motivation. However, unlike the other major implicit motives of power and achievement, there is no single, agreed upon definition of the affiliative motive with standard characteristics. Instead, there are a few such systems and they have important differences. Moreover, two of them (affiliation and intimacy) are often conflated in the literature which, in our view, glosses over, if not distorts, these differences.

In this chapter, we review three affiliative motives: First is the original affiliative motivation, as first described by Heyns, Veroff, and Atkinson (1958). Next is intimacy motivation, as developed by McAdams (1980, 1989), which seems to have supplanted thinking about affiliative motivation to some degree. Later versions of affiliative motivation have combined features of these systems to create affiliative/intimacy motivation (Winter, 1991). We begin by defining and conceptualizing each along with supportive data. We then discuss the conflation of affiliative and intimacy motivation and try to understand recent data in this light. Our thesis is that there is a duality to affiliation motivation that can help make sense of apparently contradictory data related to this motive. Finally, we try to tie it all together and offer suggestions for future work.

Affiliative Motivation

Affiliative motivation (Heynes et al., 1958) is defined as a concern with establishing, maintaining, or restoring a positive emotional relationship with another person or group. Data support the reliability and validity of affiliative motivation (Koestner & McClelland, 1992). Individuals high in affiliative motivation tend to notice social cues and initiate social interactions. Thus, visual cues related to human faces are more salient to affiliatively motivated people (Atkinson & Walker, 1956). They are able to almost effortlessly learn social networks (McClelland, 1985). Affiliative motivation also predicts the initiation of interpersonal interactions (e.g., Lansing & Heyns, 1959).

People high in affiliative motivation also spend their time engaged in affiliative activities or trying to find them. Thus, affiliatively motivated individuals tend to spend as much of their time as they can interacting with others (McClelland, 1985). They are likely to visit friends, make social phone calls, and write letters (Lansing & Heyns, 1959). Their stated career choices tend to be people oriented (Exline, 1960). And when they are not engaged in some social activity, they wish they were (McAdams & Constantian, 1983).

When engaged in social activities, people characterized by high-affiliation motivation tend to do what they can to maintain the good will of their affiliative counterparts (McClelland, 1975). This includes trying to avoid conflict (Exline, 1962). They are sympathetic and accommodating to others (Koestner & McClelland, 1992). They value peace (Rokeach, 1973) and will alter their interpersonal behavior to achieve it (Walker & Heyns, 1962). They try to avoid competitive tasks (Terhune, 1968) and, if they find themselves engaged in such tasks, they tend to do poorly (Karabenik, 1977). This may be partly because they prefer working with friends than with experts (French, 1956), think that goodwill is more important than reason and logic (McClelland, 1975), and ignore competence feedback in favor of feedback related to how well they are getting along with others (French, 1958). When the task is not competitive but related to affiliation, this strategy tends to be successful (Atkinson & Raphelson, 1956; deCharmes, 1957; French, 1956). When the task is competitive, this strategy is maladaptive.

There are health benefits to having high affiliative motivation. McClelland and Jemmott (1980) reported an association between affiliation motivation, as the dominant motive, and lower severity of illness. McClelland, Ross, and Patel (1985) found a relationship between affiliative motivation and salivary immunoglobulin (S-IgA). Level of S-IgA is itself associated with lower incidence of illness, particularly respiratory infections (Jemmott & McClelland, 1988—cited in McClelland, 1989). Jemmott (1987) reviewed other evidence that showed that people high in affiliative motivation have higher S-IgA levels. And McClelland and Kirshnit (1988) showed that experimentally arousing affiliative motivation raised S-IgA levels, thus demonstrating that this relationship is causal.

There is also a dark side to affiliative motivation. It seems to be more about a fear of being alone and/or rejected than about the pleasure of being with others (cf. Boyatzis, 1973). McClelland, Koestner, and Weinberger (1989) reported that the best childhood predictor of adult (age 31) affiliative motivation was the mother ignoring her infant's cries. Clinically and interpersonally, the high-affiliation person is that person we all know whose constant demands for attention, fear of rejection, and interpersonal anxiety drives away the very people he or she is so desperate to connect with. The data lend support to this characterization. People high in affiliation are often unpopular (Atkinson, Heyns, & Veroff, 1954; Crowne & Marlowe, 1964). Byrne (1961) reported that affiliative motivation was associated with social anxiety. Koestner and McClelland (1992) argued that affiliative motivation is best conceptualized as measuring fear of rejection and/or affiliative anxiety.

Mason and Blankenship (1987) provided further data that support the conceptualization of affiliative motivation as having a dark side. They reported that, under stress, uninhibited women high in affiliation motivation were more likely to physically and psychologically abuse their romantic partners than were low affiliatively motivated women. The authors argued that this behavior is motivated by a desperate attempt to maintain the relationship. As such behavior would seem, intuitively, to be likely to engender exactly the opposite effect, an explanation is in order. We would argue that the overwhelming fear of rejection and dependent demands that constitute the negative side of affilia-tive motivation could account for this behavior. A parsimonious explanation is that such relentless and aggressive efforts for closeness and attention is at least partly responsible for the unpopularity of such individuals. This is further supported by Mason and Blankenship's finding that power motivation was not related to abuse by women (as it was for men), indicating that fear of rejection and the need for closeness may be more of a motivating factor than the need for control in these women.

Data on physical health support this negative side to affiliative motivation as well. McClelland (1989) reports a study that found that type I diabetes was characterized by high affiliative motivation and lack of assertiveness. Further, those individuals did not adaptively deal with their illness either physiologically or behaviorally. They showed higher levels of dopamine concentration after affiliative arousal. This is associated with mobilization of more blood sugar from the liver. To compound this problem, they tended to eat more than others when affiliatively aroused and/or stressed. Moreover, this pattern was found to be chronic.

This apparent duality of affiliation motivation seems puzzling. On the one hand, it leads to positive effects, both social and health but, on the other, it results in negative social and health outcomes. We believe that this apparent contradiction is due to a confounding of two factors in affiliative motivation.

This also explains some puzzling findings in recent studies of affiliative motives. We address these issues toward the end of this review.

The reader has probably noticed that many of the references used to illustrate, describe, and support affiliative motivation are quite old. There seem to be no recent citations. The reader would be correct. Affiliative motivation, as originally assessed, seems to have been supplanted by intimacy motivation (to be discussed next) and then both seem to have been superseded by a combination of the two, often termed "affiliation-intimacy" as scored by a system developed by David Winter (1991). In fact, Winter's system seems to have largely replaced all of the original Picture Story Exercise (PSE) systems innovated by McClelland and Atkinson (1948; see Smith, 1992, for a summary of these systems). We discuss these issues after describing the systems and reviewing the data employing the Winter affiliation-intimacy construct.

Intimacy Motivation

Intimacy motivation has been defined as a recurring preference or readiness for experiences of warmth, closeness, and communicative interactions with others (McAdams, 1992). The core experience of intimacy motivation is a noninstrumental sharing of one's inner life—thoughts, feelings, desires, and so forth. (McAdams, 1989). If the intimacy experience is to "work" to gratify intimacy motivation, the other must reciprocate this sharing; it must be mutual. This then results in joy and shared delight in the presence of the other.

People characterized as having high–intimacy motivation show many of the characteristics evidenced by affiliatively motivated individuals. McAdams and Constantian (1983) had participants wear beepers for a week. They were randomly beeped and asked to describe what they were thinking, doing, and experiencing. Individuals high in intimacy motivation spent a significant amount of time engaged in conversations and having interpersonal thoughts. McAdams (1982) reported that high–intimacy motivation individuals viewed their past in interpersonal terms and their futures as centering around warm, communicative relationships with others. McAdams and Powers (1981) had participants put on skits. High-intimacy individuals worked to include all of the group members. They avoided commands, used "we" and "us" rather than "I" and "me," and physically kept themselves close to other members of the group.

One difference between intimacy and affiliative motivation is that intimacy motivation is more focused on close dyadic interactions whereas affiliative motivation is about social contact of any sort. Intimacy-motivated individuals described friendship episodes in dyadic rather than group terms. They also described themselves as listening to and self-disclosing to the other (McAdams, Healy, & Kraus, 1984).

In contrast to affiliatively motivated individuals, intimacy-motivated individuals are pleasant to be around and are happy and well adjusted themselves. They are rated by others as sincere and are not interested in dominance (McAdams, & Powers, 1981). From a young age, children high in intimacy motivation evidence more eye contact, smiling, and laughter in friendly, one-on-one conversations than their low intimacy counterparts (McAdams, Jackson, & Kirshnit, 1984). Fourth- and sixth-grade students high in intimacy motivation were rated by their teachers as more friendly, sincere, cooperative, and popular. This was mirrored by their peers (classmates) who rarely disliked their high-intimacy classmates (McAdams & Losoff, 1984). In adults, intimacy motivation is correlated with the capacity to experience pleasure (Zeldow, Daugherty, & McAdams, 1988). It is also associated with subjective well-being (McAdams & Bryant, 1987). Intimacy motivation has long-term effects in these areas. This makes it seem causally related to such feelings of well-being. McAdams and Vaillant (1982) found that intimacy motivation, assessed when participants were in their early thirties, predicted psychosocial adjustment assessed 17 years later. It also predicted job satisfaction and marital happiness 17 years after it was measured.

Unlike affiliative motivation, intimacy motivation does not seem to have a downside. It leads to positive life outcomes. Intimacy-motivated people are happy and satisfied; others like them. Again, the research is somewhat dated, although not to the same degree as affiliative motivation research. This is probably due to this measure being supplanted by Winter's (1991) affiliation-intimacy measure. We therefore now review more recent research examining affiliation-intimacy. But before doing so, we embark on a brief digression concerning the scoring of motives. We do so because, as stated earlier, we believe that affiliation and intimacy have become somewhat confounded, and the operationalization of these constructs is partially responsible for this confusion. We believe that this brief discussion is relevant to understanding the extant research in this area.

Scoring Implicit Motives

The assumption behind the measurement of implicit motives is that they are inherent in the stories people tell. This idea goes back, at least, to Freud (e.g., 1933/1964), who applied it to his work on dreams and free associations. Murray (Morgan & Murray, 1935; Murray, 1936, 1938) substituted a standardized set of ambiguous pictures for the more spontaneous and unstructured productions Freud patients provided. Scoring of these stories was informal and relied on group consensus. McClelland, Atkinson, and their colleagues (McClelland & Atkinson, 1948; McClelland, Atkinson, Clark, & Lowell, 1953; McClelland, Clark, Roby, & Atkinson, 1949) devised rigorous objective scoring systems to measure the major motives of achievement, affiliation, and power, thereby making them amenable to objective empirical research. The methodology was to arouse the relevant motive, either by finding people in an aroused state (e.g., just having been rejected by a fraternity) or experimentally inducing such a state (e.g., through watching an emotionally arousing film). Aroused individuals and unaroused controls then wrote stories in response to the standard cards. The differences in those stories were then used to devise the relevant systems. (See Winter, 1998, for more detail and an historical context.) The affiliative and intimacy motive measures were created in this way (as were the achievement and power motivation measures).

The PSE scoring system for motives as devised by McClelland, Atkinson, and their colleagues is labor intensive. It is difficult to learn and to implement in a study. It takes 20 hours on average, to become reliable at scoring one motive and, therefore, scorers tend to be proficient at scoring one or two motives at most. Scorers must periodically practice to maintain reliability. This means, practically, that an investigator usually needs two or three reliable scorers to score the three major motives. He or she is therefore dependent on outside resources that may or may not be easily available.[1] Moreover, each story must be scored separately for each motive. As a result, many investigators have been hesitant to conduct this kind of research (cf. Schultheiss & Pang, 2007). Academic incentive systems do not reward this kind of work. Similarly, individuals have been reluctant to spend the time necessary to become expert in a scoring system. So experts are hard to find. This is another disincentive for this kind of research.[2]

Winter (1991) developed a running text scoring system to assess motives in non-PSE texts. The idea was to break the dependence on investigator-administered PSEs and to be able to assess motives "at a distance." That is, Winter wished to develop a means of measuring motives from people's written or spoken productions, whatever their form. He applied his method to speeches, interviews, literary works, letters, and so forth. The motives measured with this method were achievement, power, and affiliation-intimacy. The latter was essentially a combination of the affiliative and intimacy motivation scoring systems. The scores on this measure correlated significantly but not perfectly with the relevant PSE measures (rs = .5-ish). More importantly, for Winter's purposes, the measure worked well. Winter has published a series of papers on political leaders, based on their speeches and other public productions, that are major contributions to our understanding of both personality and leadership (see, e.g., Winter, 2005). The affiliation-intimacy aspect of the measure has a great deal of shared variance with both affiliation and intimacy motivation (it correlates about r = .50 with each). But much of the unique variance of these measures is lost. And that unique variance is central to the point of this chapter.

One, perhaps originally unintended, consequence of Winter's (1991) innovative method is that it has pretty much supplanted traditional PSE measurement of motives. Even research using PSE pictures to assess motives now tend to score the PSEs with Winter's system rather than with the traditional PSE systems. This has occurred for basically two reasons. First, results obtained from Winter's scoring system are related to results obtained using the PSE systems (i.e., are correlated with them). Therefore, they are measuring a similar, if not the same, construct. Perhaps more importantly, it is far less labor-intensive and does not require expertise in several systems. All three motives are scored simultaneously, and a single person has expertise in scoring all, as it is all one system. A perusal of recent research on implicit motives would be hard put to find traditional PSE scoring. Most now use Winter's system.

One consequence of this for the study of affiliative motives is that affiliation and intimacy have been combined into one motive. The differences between them have therefore been folded into a single system. We believe that this has led to some apparently confusing findings. We will use the differences between intimacy and affiliative motivation to attempt to make sense of these findings.

Complicating this picture is another implicit motive system that has a lot in common with the affiliative/intimacy system. This motive has come to be called the oneness motive (OM). Weinberger (1992; Siegel & Weinberger, 1998) conceptualized this motive as a need to become part of, be at one with, or belong to a larger whole. It overlaps with intimacy in that it is largely positive and is most clearly evident in interpersonal relationships. Unlike intimacy (or affiliation) however, OM can also be manifest in noninterpersonal experiences. Any experience in which the person can become part of something outside the self (a larger whole e.g., music, an organization, etc.) can be a oneness experience and be scored for OM. The oneness motive is conceptualized as broader than intimacy in that is encompasses a broader range of experiences than does intimacy. And, it correlates highly with Intimacy Motivation ($r = .50$ or so). Since OM does not score for negative oneness experiences, it does not encompass the dark side of affiliative motivation. (But see Weinberger, 1992, and Siegel and Weinberger, 1998, for a discussion of negative oneness experiences that could possibly be scored in future versions of the OM scoring system.)

Research has shown that OM is related to hypnotizability (Trevouledes, 2003), reduction of symptoms in a behavioral medicine study (Weinberger, 1992), and improvement in psychotherapy (Weinberger, Cotler, & Fishman, this volume). See Weinberger et al. (this volume) for more on the data supporting the existence of this motive. It may therefore represent an overarching system of affiliation/intimacy not restricted to human-to-human interaction or at least another aspect of affiliation/intimacy motivation. Future research will have to determine this.

Yet another complicating factor is an implicit motive scoring system that has recently appeared and may catch on as did Winter's system. It too, seems to conflate affiliation and intimacy. The system is termed the Multi-Motive Grid (MMG; Sokolowski, Schmalt, Langens, & Puca, 2000). The MMG combines a PSE format with self-report in an effort to increase the practicality of measuring implicit motives. As with the traditional PSE motive scoring system, several (14) PSE pictures are presented to participants. Instead of writing stories to these pictures, however, a set of statements appears after each, and the person is asked to endorse or not endorse them. As does the Winter system, this method measures achievement, power, and affiliation. This system, however, retained the negative aspect of affiliation as a separate entity in that it generates a fear of rejection score. To our knowledge, however, results employing the MMG have not yet been compared empirically to either the traditional PSE scoring systems or to Winter's running-text system. This is important because the MMG has a self-report element, and implicit motivation research has traditionally eschewed self-report (McClelland, 1985; Weinberger & McClelland, 1990). This makes findings using this system difficult to interpret and integrate into the existing literature at the moment. It could prove to be a major boon to implicit motivation research if the MMG turns out to capture implicit motivation as well as the other scoring systems (traditional PSE and Winter running text). Specifically, it is relatively accessible, easy to administer, and offers a simpler, less labor intensive scoring system. Future research will determine the usefulness of this system.

Research on Affiliation-Intimacy

Hormone Profiles

Weinberger and McClelland (1990) argued that, ideally, motives would be assessed via physiochemical measurement. There were some promising early studies that showed relationships between affiliation motivation and immune function (McClelland, 1989). Some preliminary work (see McClelland, 1985) showed that affiliation motivation had a dampening effect on noradrenaline release while students were taking an exam. But there was no systematic research on this issue. The future envisioned by Weinberger and McClelland may be arriving now. Schultheiss, Dargel, and Rohde (2003) reported a link between affiliative motivation and progesterone. Schultheiss, Wirth, and Stanton (2004) found that arousing affiliation (through a film) resulted in increased progesterone. The waters were a bit muddied by Wirth and Schultheiss (2006), however. They examined both cortisol (usually associated with stress) and progesterone, while arousing both positive and negative aspects of affiliation motivation using different films. The film designed to arouse the negative aspect of affiliation (fear of rejection) resulted in increased progesterone and cortisol. The film designed to arouse the positive aspect of affiliation (hope for closeness) did not result in increased progesterone and, thereby, apparently failed to replicate the Schultheiss et al. (2004) results.

However, progesterone was related to measured affiliative motivation across the experimental conditions.

It is hard to know what to make of these findings. Progesterone is apparently reliably related to affiliative motivation, but its relationship to affiliative arousal seems less clear. In one study (Schultheiss et al., 2004), it was related to what the authors saw as positive affiliation, but in another, it was only related to the fear of rejection aspect of affiliation (Wirth & Schultheiss, 2006). The films chosen to arouse the affiliation motive may have contributed to the inconsistency in the findings. Affiliative arousal in Schultheiss et al. (2004) was provided by *The Bridges of Madison County*. The plot of this film involves a short-lived, bittersweet love affair. Loneliness and loss are clearly involved in the story. Thus, this film may have aroused the fear of rejection aspect of affiliative motivation at least as much as affiliative hope for closeness. There is no way to know for sure as affiliative anxiety was not assessed, nor was cortisol measured in the Schultheiss et al. (2004) study, but it would explain the apparent discrepancy between these results and those of Wirth and Schultheiss (2006). It may be that progesterone is uniquely tied to the negative aspect of affiliative motivation. Wirth and Schultheiss suggest something of this sort when they wonder whether progesterone released during stress may encourage affiliation as a stress-reducing coping mechanism. Future research needs to tease this out and determine whether our interpretation of the findings makes sense. Whatever the explanation, this finding points to the importance of the social anxiety and fear of rejection aspect of affiliation motivation that, we argue, often tends to be glossed over. This may be a more important aspect of affiliation than researchers realize. It may even have its own hormonal signature.

Autobiographical Memory

Woike and Polo (2001) had people characterized by agentic (power and achievement) or communal (affiliation and intimacy) motivation record their most memorable experiences. They also filled out a Positive Affect and a Negative Affect scale every day for 6 weeks. Woike and Polo found that memories tended to be motive congruent and that communal memories were characterized by integrative themes whereas agentic memories were more differentiated. A second study essentially replicated these findings. This makes sense, as one would expect communal individuals to focus more on connectedness. It also dovetails nicely with McAdams' (1982) finding that intimacy-motivated people tend to see their lives in terms of warm interpersonal connections. This represents the positive side of affiliative motivation.

Woike and Polo (2001) also reported another result, which was not as obvious. In both studies, agentics had higher positive affect and lower negative affect than did communals. This directly contradicts Zeldow, Daugherty, and McAdams (1988), who found a positive correlation between intimacy motivation and the capacity to experience pleasure. This result does not make sense unless the negative aspect of affiliation (which is not present in intimacy motivation) is considered. In addition, although the differences were statistically significant, they were small. This, too, would make sense, as Woike and Polo would be averaging across the positive and negative aspects of affiliation.

Attention to Social Cues

As we mentioned in this paper, early on, Atkinson and Walker (1956) reported that visual cues related to human faces were salient to individuals characterized by affiliative motivation. Building on this finding, Schultheiss et al. (2005) and Schultheiss and Hale (2007) found that not all faces are equal. Individuals characterized by affiliative motivation attended more quickly to an angry face than to a joyful or neutral face. Further, they learned less well when learning was reinforced by a neutral rather than by an angry face. The authors explained these counterintuitive results (why should an angry face grab attention most quickly and be reinforcing?) by suggesting that a neutral face was aversive due to its lack of affectivity. An angry face, on the other hand, may be interpreted as indicating some interest and is therefore less threatening. The finding, in this investigation, that a joyful face was not reinforcing to affiliatively motivated individuals belies this explanation. If the effects of anger are due to its being less threatening than neutrality, would joy not be less threatening, even rewarding? So why is joy not as effective as anger? Another interpretation, in line with our focus on fear of rejection and social anxiety, is that the angry face fulfills the affiliatively motivated person's expectation that he or she will be rejected. The person is quick to recognize a face he or she is chronically primed for and then learns whatever preceded this fulfilled expectation. Our interpretation is buttressed by a recent finding. Schultheiss and Hale (2007) found that affiliatively motivated individuals showed greatest attention to a face depicting rejection. They were also oriented, albeit less so, to a face depicting acceptance. Here are both sides of the affiliative coin. And both attract attention, with rejection grabbing the lion's share. Future research might do well to differentiate between the two kinds of affiliation to see whether they coexist within individuals to roughly equivalent degrees or whether people tend to be characterized by one or the other. We predict the latter, as intimacy motivation seems to be free of this negative quality.

Predictions of Social Behavior and Its Relations to the Rejection Component of Affiliative Motivation

Recall that Mason and Blankenship (1987) found that a relationship between abuse by stressed women toward their romantic partners was related to affiliative motivation. Zurbriggen (2000) used the Winter (1991) scoring system, which combined affiliation and intimacy, to look at aggressive sexual behavior and obtained essentially the same result. Affiliative-intimacy motivation predicted more coercive sexual behaviors in women. This finding puzzled Zurbriggen, as threats and coercion are unlikely to lead to increased intimacy. She cited Mason and Blankenship's finding but did not discuss the negative side of affiliation. We believe that the Zurbriggen (2000) finding is most parsimoniously explained through the dark side of affiliation, which is not emphasized in the Winter affiliative-intimacy system. That is, the person characterized by fear of rejection becomes desperate when faced with social rejection and resorts to any means available, including maladaptive ones, to address the issue. Again, as in the Mason and Blankenship study, power did not relate to these behaviors in women. Thus, the motivation was not control (as it was in men in this study and in the Mason and Blankenship study) but a maladaptive, anxiety ridden, effort to insure that affiliative needs are met.

Finally, in a series of wonderful papers, Winter (e.g., 2002, 2005) has related implicit motives to leadership (mostly presidents of the United States) and to war and peace. He used the running text system he developed (Winter, 1991) to assess implicit motives. We focus on his findings concerning affiliation-intimacy motivation, which, as stated earlier, combines aspects of affiliative and intimacy motivation but tends to be described in terms more related to intimacy motivation. Winter (2002, 2005) found that high affiliative-intimacy motivation could be problematic for a president of the USA because the leader is more concerned with maintaining relationships and not hurting feelings than with achieving goals. He also surrounds himself with like-minded others, which insulates him from views that disagree with his own. This sounds more like affiliation than like intimacy. Recall that affiliatively motivated individuals like to be around supportive others and are more interested in avoiding conflict and maintaining good will than in doing well or succeeding at a task. This is not a prescription for a successful presidency, which requires the advice of experts, a cool rational head, and has conflict built into the job description. A person concerned with maintaining positive relationships over getting the job done could have problems. On the other hand, a president must be able to forge relationships, and one that cannot is also at a disadvantage (Winter, 2005).

Winter's work on war and peace illustrates the complexity of affiliative motivation as well. In a nutshell, war seems to be associated with power motivation whereas peace is associated with affiliative motivation (cf. Rokeach, 1973). Peaceful outcomes seem to involve making concessions, at least in part. This is easier for an affiliatively motivated person to do than for one characterized by high power motivation. To test this hypothesis, Langner and Winter (2001) examined government archives relating to four foreign crises. Two escalated into war and two were peacefully resolved. Diplomatic correspondence revealed that offering concessions (which led to the other side offering its own concessions and ultimately to a peaceful resolution) was positively associated with affiliative-intimacy motivation. This finding was replicated in a laboratory study that asked participants to respond to affiliative (concession-offering) and power (demanding) diplomatic letters. Affiliation-intimacy motivation was related to offering concessions. Additionally, concessions were more likely to be offered by participants when the letters they read also contained them.

It seems that affiliative-intimacy motivation is related to peaceful outcomes. In Langner and Winter's (2001) study, it certainly was. This is undoubtedly a positive side to affiliation. The authors, however, offer a caveat, which we think directly relates to our thesis. They point out that concessions are not always the correct response. Neville Chamberlain offered concessions to Adolph Hitler in order to obtain "peace in our time." What he got instead was World War II. Affiliative motivation is not always adaptive and does not always involve intimacy. A deepening, mutually disclosing relationship is certainly not what governmental negotiations involve. Instead, these negotiations seem motivated by affiliation. On that note, we would like to go beyond the data and speculate a bit. The work of Winter and colleagues involved male leaders. What would happen if the parties or one of the parties to the negotiations were a woman? The works of Mason and Blankenship (1987) and Zurbriggen (2000) suggest that affiliative motivation may not be the best route to peace in this instance. Recall that affiliatively motivated women tended to aggress when under stress. Would the relationship described by Winter be reversed for women? That is, would an affiliatively motivated female leader be more likely to go to war? This is an interesting empirical question and may not be simply an academic one.

Another Research Tradition that Supports the Duality of Affiliation

We believe that our argument would be greatly strengthened if research from a tradition completely independent of the study of implicit affilation assessment showed findings parallel to the ones reviewed above (i.e., duality in the affiliative personality). Such data exist. Bornstein (e.g., 2002, 2005) has found the kind of duality we have described in his study of implicit dependency, as assessed through the Rorschach (Bornstein, Hill, Robinson, Calabrese, & Bowers, 1996). A highly dependent person (the pathological extreme would be dependent personality disorder—American Psychiatric Association, 1994) is described by Bornstein (2005) as alienating others with his or her clinginess and insecurity. He or she is often passive and compliant, trying to curry favor through displays of weakness and vulnerability. However, when stressed, particularly by a threat of a disrupted relationship, the dependent person can become aggressive and do almost anything to avoid being abandoned.

Bornstein (2005) contrasts this with healthy dependency, characterized by mutuality, commitment to others, and positive affect. Substitute affiliation motivation for pathological dependency, and intimacy motivation for healthy dependency and the reader would be hard put to tell the difference between the persons described here and those in the implicit affiliation literature. Thus, our thesis is supported by independent research employing a completely different implicit measure and arising out of a completely different theoretical orientation (clinical psychology). Future research might compare these two kinds of affiliative measures systematically to determine their convergent and divergent validity.

Conclusions

We have argued that affiliative motivation is a double-edged sword. There is a positive aspect to it, characterized by a desire for closeness, pleasure in being with others, and good health (both psychological and physical). It also has a negative aspect, characterized by fear of loss, anxiety about relationships, and poor health (both physical and psychological). The affiliation motive is complex. The positive side is probably best measured through intimacy motivation; the negative through the now rarely used affiliative motivation. Table 3.1 illustrates this duality.

The duality of affiliation helps to explain some apparently anomalous findings in the literature. Progesterone seems more likely to be released when loss is aroused than when togetherness is primed (Wirth & Schultheiss, 2006). Autobiographical memories associated with affiliative motivation tend to be tinged with negative affect (Woike & Polo, 2001). Affiliatively motivated people

Table 3.1   The Duality of Affiliation

	The Bright Side: Intimacy	The Dark Side: Fear of Rejection
Goal	Interpersonal warmth, closeness and reciprocal communication with others	Avoid being alone and/or rejected
Consequences	Close dyadic rrelationships Listens empathically and offers self-disclosures	Clingy and demanding
	Pleasant to be around	Unpopular
	A sense of subjective well-being	Social anxiety
	Marital happiness	Abuse romantic partner (more likely for women than men)
	Lower incidence of illness	More type I diabetes

seem particularly attentive to angry faces, although they also orient to welcoming faces (Schultheiss & Hale, 2007). Women high in affiliation motivation can treat romantic partners aggressively, especially under stress (Mason & Blankenship, 1987) and are even likely to do so when engaged in sex (Zurbriggen, 2000). Leaders need to worry about their power-affiliative balance (Winter, 2002, 2005). And finally, other research traditions, employing different means of assessing implicit processes, report very similar findings (Bornstein, 2002, 2005), thereby supporting the duality of affiliative motivation.

There should be nothing surprising about the duality, complexity, and depth of affiliative motivation. If we can appeal to nonscientific empirical data, the personal experience of any reader who has ever experienced the ups and downs of relationships should confirm the reality of what we have been arguing. There is nothing so joyous and pleasurable as a deep, successful relationship; there is nothing as devastating and sorrowful as the loss of a valued relationship. The arts are filled with testimony to both sides, from uplifting love sonnets to the music of the blues. Our newspapers are filled with stories relating to touching and to pathological efforts to achieve affiliation and intimacy.

William James (1890) argued persuasively that science generally and psychology in particular must begin with and examine phenomenology. And what we find when we examine the phenomenology of affiliation is a stark duality. It leads to our greatest joys and our deepest sorrows. To study and measure only one aspect of our affiliative beings is to do an injustice to the complexity and depth of human affiliative experience.

Notes

1. A personal anecdote may illustrate the problems such an investigator faces. I had a person whom I trusted to score the three major motives. I would periodically contact her to make sure that she was available for scoring of motives. She was not local to put it mildly; she had moved to another country. So this was not straightforward. She was very difficult to get hold of. She then moved again and I had to track her down. I finally lost track of her and now had no one to score my motive protocols. I then relied on my graduate students and those of colleagues conducting similar research. In order to insure their reliability, I would have them score protocols that my original scorer had worked on and then match the scores. This solution was not ideal, as I had to change scorers every couple of years as these people graduated. The students would go on to other things and not be permanent scorers of my protocols. I would then have to train new scorers and make sure they were reliable. My colleagues had to do the same. Eventually, the costs outweighed the benefits, and I cut back my motive work substantially.
2. We do not want to give the impression that we approve of the tendency in psychology to avoid labor-intensive work. In fact, we strongly disapprove of it.

We report it because it is a fact of life in current academic psychology. Most sciences (e.g., biology, physics, chemistry) employ time-consuming analyses and procedures. Social sciences like anthropology also reward careful time-consuming data collection and scoring. Unfortunately, the field of psychology typically does not.

References

American Psychiatric Association. (1994). *Diagnostic and statistical manual of mental disorders (4ᵗʰ ed.)*. Washington, DC: American Psychiatric Publishing, Inc.

Atkinson, J. W., Heyns, R. W., & Veroff, J. (1954). The effect of experimental arousal of the affiliation motive on thematic apperception. *Journal of Abnormal and Social Psychology, 49,* 405–410.

Atkinson, J. W., & Raphelson, A. C. (1956). Individual differences in motivation and behavior in particular situations. *Journal of Personality, 24,* 351–363.

Atkinson, J. W., & Walker, E. W. (1956). The affiliation motive in perceptual sensitivity to faces. *Journal of Abnormal and Personality Psychology, 53,* 38–41.

Bornstein, R. F. (2002). A process dissociation approach to objective-projective test score interrelationships. *Journal of Personality Assessment, 78,* 47–68.

Bornstein, R. F. (2005). The dependent patient: Diagnosis, assessment, and treatment. *Professional Psychology: Research and Practice, 36,* 82–89.

Bornstein, R. F., Hill, E. L., Robinson, K. J., Calabrese, C., & Bowers, K. S. (1996). Internal realiability of Rorschach oral dependency scores. *Educational and Psychological Measurement, 56,* 130–138.

Boyatzis, R. E. (1973). Affiliation motivation. In D. C. McClelland & R. S. Steele (Eds.), *Human motivation: A book of readings* (pp. 252–276). Morristown, NJ: General Learning Press.

Byrne, D. (1961). Anxiety and the experimental arousal of affiliation need. *Journal of Abnormal and Social Psychology, 63,* 660–662.

Crowne, D. P., & Marlowe, D. (1964). *The approval motive.* New York: Wiley.

deCharms, R. (1957). Affiliation motivation and productivity in small groups. *Journal of Abnormal and Social Psychology, 55,* 222–226.

Exline, R. V. (1960). Effects of sex, norms, and affiliation motivation upon accuracy of perception of interpersonal preference. *Journal of Personality, 28,* 397–412.

Exline, R. V. (1962). Need affiliation and initial communication behavior in problem solving groups characterized by low interpersonal visibility. *Psychological Reports, 10,* 79–89.

French, E. G. (1956). Motivation as a variable in work partner selection. *Journal of Abnormal and Social Psychology, 53,* 96–99.

French, E. G. (1958). Effects of the interaction of motivation and feedback on task performance. In J. W. Atkinson (Ed.), *Motives in fantasy, action and society* (pp. 400–408). Princeton, New Jersey: Van Nostrand.

Freud, S. (1933/1964). New introductory lectures on psychoanalysis. In J. Strachey (Ed. and trans.). *The standard edition of the complete works of Sigmund Freud* (Vol. 22, pp. 3–158). London: Hogarth Press.

Heyns, R. W., Veroff, J., & Atkinson, J. W. (1958). A scoring manual for the affilation motive. In J. W. Atkinson (Ed.), *Motives in fantasy, action, and society* (pp. 205–218). Princeton, New Jersey: Van Nostrand.

James, W. (1890). *The principles of psychology (Vol. 1).* New York: Dover Publications.

Jemmott, J. B. (1987). Social motives and susceptibility to disease: Stalking individual differences in health risks. *Journal of Personality, 55,* 267–298.

Karabenick, S. A. (1977). Fear of success, achievement and affiliative dispositions, and the performance of men and women under individual and competitive situations. *Journal of Personality, 45,* 117–149.

Koestner, R., & McClelland, D. C. (1992). The affiliation motive. In D. C. McClelland, J., Veroff, C. P. Smith, & J. W. Atkinson (Eds.). *Motivation and personality: Handbook of thematic content analysis* (pp. 205–210). New York: Cambridge University Press.

Langner, C. A., & Winter, D. G. (2001). The motivational basis of concessions and compromise: Archival and laboratory studies. *Journal of Personality and Social Psychology, 81,* 711–727.

Lansing, J. B., & Heyns, R. W. (1959). Need affiliation and frequency of four types of communication. *Journal of Abnormal and Social Psychology, 58,* 365–372.

Mason, A., & Blankenship, V. (1987). Power and affiliation motivation, stress, and abuse in intimate relationships. *Journal of Personality and Social Psychology, 52,* 203–210.

McAdams, D. P. (1980). A thematic coding system for the intimacy motive. *Journal of Research in Personality, 14,* 413–432.

McAdams, D. P. (1982). Experiences of intimacy and power: Relationships between social motives and autobiographical memory. *Journal of Personality and Social Psychology, 42,* 292–302.

McAdams, D. P. (1989) *Intimacy: The need to be close.* New York: Doubleday.

McAdams, D. P (1992). The intimacy motive. In D. C. McClelland, J. Veroff, C. P. Smith, & J. W. Atkinson (Eds.). *Motivation and personality: Handbook of thematic content analysis* (pp. 224–228). New York: Cambridge University Press.

McAdams, D. P., & Bryant, F. B. (1987). Intimacy motivation and subjective mental health in a nationwide sample. *Journal of Personality, 55,* 395–413.

McAdams, D. P. & Constantian, C. A. (1983). Intimacy and affiliation motives in daily living: An experience sampling analysis. *Journal of Personality and Social Psychology, 45,* 851–861.

McAdams, D. P., Healy, S., & Krause, S. (1984). Social motives and patterns of friendship. *Journal of Personality and Social Psychology, 47,* 828–838.

McAdams, D. P., Jackson, R. J., & Kirshnit, C. (1984). Looking, laughing, and smiling in dyads as a function of intimacy motivation and reciprocity. *Journal of Personality, 52,* 261–273.

McAdams, D. P. & Losoff, M. (1984). Friendship motivation in fourth and sixth graders: A thematic analysis. *Journal of Social and Personal Relationships, 1,* 11–27.

McAdams, D. P. & Powers, J. (1981). Themes of intimacy in behavior and thought. *Journal of Personality and Social Psychology, 40,* 573–587.

McAdams, D. P., & Vaillant, G. E. (1982). Intimacy motivation and psychological adjustment: A longitudinal study. *Journal of Personality Assessment, 46,* 586–593.

McClelland, D. C. (1975). *Power: The inner experience.* New York: Wiley.

McClelland, D. C. (1985). *Human motivation.* GlenviewIL: Scott Foresman.

McClelland, D. C. (1989). Motivational factors in health and disease. *American Psychologist, 44,* 675–683.

McClelland, D. C., & Atkinson, J. W. (1948). Projective expression of needs II: The effect of different intensities of the hunger drive on thematic apperception. *Journal of Experimental Psychology, 38,* 643–658.

McClelland, D. C., Atkinson, J. W., Clark, R. A., & Lowell, E. L. (1953). *The achievement motive.* New York: Appleton-Century-Crofts.

McClelland, D. C., Clark, R. A., Roby, T. B., & Atkinson, J. W. (1949). The projective expression of needs: IV. The effect of need for achievement on thematic apperception. *Journal of Experimental Psychology, 39,* 242–255.

McClelland, D. C. & Jemmott, J. B. (1980). Power motivation, stress, and physical illness. *Journal of Human Stress, 6,* 6–15.

McClelland, D. C., & Kirshnit, C. (1988). The effect of motivational arousal through films on immunoglobulin A. *Psychology and Health, 2,* 31–52.

McClelland, D. C., Koestner, R., & Weinberger, J. (1989). How do self-attributed motives differ? *Psychological Review, 96(4),* 690–702.

McClelland, D. C., Ross, G., & Patel, V. (1985). The effect of an academic examination on salivary norepinephrine and immunoglobulin levels. *Journal of Human Stress, 11,* 52–59.

Morgan, C. D., & Murray, H. H. (1935). A method of investigating fantasies: The thematic apperception test. *Archives of Neurology and Psychiatry, 34,* 289–306.

Murray, H. A. (1936). Basic concepts for a psychology of personality. *Journal of General Psychology, 15,* 241–268.

Murray, H. A. (1938). *Explorations in personality.* Oxford, England: Oxford University Press.

Rokeach, M. (1973). *The nature of human values.* New York: Free Press.

Schultheiss, O. C, Dargel, A., & Rohde, W. (2003). Implicit motives and sexual motivation and behavior. *Journal of Research in Personality, 37,* 224–230.

Schultheiss, O. C., & Hale, J. A. (2007). Implicit motives modulate attentional orienting to facial expressions of emotion. *Motivation and Emotion, 31,* 13–24.

Schultheiss, O. C., & Pang, J. S. (2007). Measuring implicit motives. In R. F. Krueger, R. W. Robins, & R. C. Fraley (Eds.), *Handbook of research methods in personality psychology.* (pp. 322–344). New York, NY: Guilford Press.

Schultheiss, O. C., Pang, J. S., Torges, C. M., Wirth, M. M., Treynor, W., & Derryberry, D. (Eds.) (2005). Perceived facial expressions of emotion as motivational incentives: Evidence from a differential implicit learning paradigm. *Emotion, 5,* 41–54.

Schultheiss, O. C., Wirth, M. M., & Stanton, S. J. (2004). Effects of affiliation and power motivation arousal on salivary progesterone and testosterone. *Hormones and Behavior, 46,* 592–599.

Siegel, P., & Weinberger, J. (1998). Capturing the "mommy and I are one" merger fantasy: The oneness motive. In J. M. Masling & R. F. Bornstein (Eds.) *Empirical perspectives on the psychoanalytic unconscious* (pp. 71–97). Washington, DC: American Psychological Association.

Smith, C. E. (1992). *Motivation and personality: Handbook of thematic content analysis.* New York: Cambridge University Press.

Sokolowski, K., Schmalt, H. D., Langens, T. A., & Puca, R. M. (2000). Assessing achievement, affiliation, and power motives all at once: The Multi Motive Grid (MMG). *Journal of Personality Assessment, 74,* 126–145.

Terhune, K. W. (1968). Motives, situation, and interpersonal conflict within prisoner's dilemma. *Journal of Personality and Social Psychology, 8,* 1–24.

Walker, E. L., & Heyns, R. N. (1962). *An anatomy for conformity.* Englewood Cliffs, NJ: Prentice-Hall.

Weinberger, J. (1992). Demystifying subliminal psychodynamic activation. In R. Bornstein & T. Pittman (Eds.), *Perception without awareness* (pp. 186–203). New York: Guilford.

Weinberger, J., & McClelland, D. C. (1990). Cognitive versus traditional motivational models: Irreconcilable or complementary? In R. M. Sorrentino & E. T. Higgins, (Eds.), *Handbook of motivation and cognition: Foundations of social behavior* (Vol. 2., pp. 562–597). New York: Guilford Press.

Winter, D. G. (1991). Measuring personality at a distance: Development of an integrated system for scoring motives in verbal running text. In A. J. Stewart, J. M. Healy, Jr., & D. J. Ozer (Eds.), *Perspectives in personality: Approaches to understanding lives* (pp. 59–89). London: Jessica Kingsly.

Winter, D. G. (1998). Toward a science of personality psychology: David McClelland's development of empirically derived TAT measures. *History of Psychology, 1,* 130–153.

Winter, D. G. (2002). Motivation and political leadership. In L. O. Valenty & O. Feldman (Eds.), *Political leadership for the new century: Personality and behavior among American leaders* (pp. 27–47). New York: Praeger.

Winter, D. G. (2005). Things I've learned about personality from studying political leaders at a distance. *Journal of Personality, 73,* 557–584.

Wirth, M. M., & Schultheiss, O. C. (2006). Effects of affiliation arousal (hope of closeness) and affiliation stress (fear of rejection) on progesterone and cortisol. *Hormones and Behavior, 50,* 786–795.

Woike, B., & Polo, M. (2001). Motive related memories: Content, structure, and affect. *Journal of Personality, 69,* 391–415.

Zeldow, P. B., Daugherty, S. R., & McAdams, D. P. (1988). Intimacy, power, and psychological well-being in medical students. *Journal of Nervous and Mental Disease, 17,* 82–187.

Zurbriggen, E. L. (2000). Social motives and cognitive power sex associations: Predictors of aggressive sexual behavior. *Journal of Personality and Social Psychology, 78,* 559–581.

Chapter 4

Activity Inhibition

THOMAS A. LANGENS
University of Wuppertal, Wuppertal, Germany

Introduction

A few weeks ago, I invited a friend over for coffee. While I served homemade carrot cake, we chatted about friends we both hadn't seen in a while, about his recent vacation in Israel, and about our jobs. Eventually, there was a brief lull in our conversation, which I tried to keep flowing by saying "so...", intending to have him tell me more about his recent ambition to apply for a challenging job at a big company. He picked up my prompt, only to say "sorry, though it's delicious, I do *not* want another piece of this cake." Being a psychologist, I immediately wondered whether I had just witnessed an instance of the revealing nature of the word *not*, which is so often apparent when people reject an idea no one has alluded to. After all, each of us had already enjoyed a large piece of cake, and since then, there hadn't been any cake offering from my side. True, my prompt ("so...") may have been ambiguous, but given the topics of our conversation, it seemed rather farfetched to me that anybody would have interpreted it as an offering for more cake. So I inquired, "are you *sure* you don't want another piece of cake?" "Well, actually I wouldn't mind," replied my friend, "but I have gained some weight recently, and I really need to stay away from these things if I want to keep in shape." In essence, then, the word *not* indicated two tendencies that were simultaneously present in my friend's mind: a motivational impulse ("this cake surely is delicious; why don't I have another piece or even two?"), which was immediately restrained by a self-prescribed prohibition ("do not indulge in foods that contain excessive amounts of sugar and fat").

Motivational psychologists have been investigating the motivational and emotional significance of using the negation *not* in verbal content for more than 40 years, since McClelland and his colleagues (Kalin, McClelland, & Kahn, 1965; McClelland, Davis, Kalin, & Wanner, 1972) first introduced the notion that spontaneously using the negation *not* in speech or writing indicates a stable tendency to restrain or inhibit motivational impulses, which they termed *activity inhibition* (AI). From then on, AI has been routinely scored not only in the Picture Story Exercise (PSE; McClelland, Koestner, & Weinberger, 1989), but also in other sources of verbal material. Though AI is not an implicit motive, research has found that AI moderates the way implicit motives are expressed in behavior. And more recently, AI has been identified as a disposition that plays a central role in how people regulate negative emotions.

In an effort to illuminate both the origins as well as the consequences of high AI for emotional and motivational processes, this chapter will try to weave together findings accumulated over the past 40 years. It will start out with a brief summary of the history of the concept of AI and its measurement in verbal material, followed by an investigation of the role of AI in the expression of implicit motives and emotion regulation and some speculations about the developmental precursors of AI. Finally, I will outline a model that integrates the various findings on AI, suggesting, in a nutshell, that AI does not neutralize emotional or motivational impulses, but rather leads to their intensification and a delayed and refined expression in behavior.

The History of AI

The concept of activity inhibition (AI) was introduced in the 1960s, when McClelland and his colleagues analyzed folktales collected from native peoples around the world in an attempt to differentiate tribes that were characterized by high levels of alcohol consumption from tribes who refrained from alcohol use (McClelland et al., 1972). In an effort to "get into people's heads," that is, to investigate what people who consume large amounts of alcohol typically think about, McClelland and his colleagues decided to analyze popular folk tales of the cultures that were selected for the study. For each of 44 cultures, a selection of about 10 tales was collected and subjected to a computerized analysis that identified and counted how often certain "tags"—concepts consisting of a group of words that were assumed to be conceptually related (e.g., the tag "fear" consisted of words such as afraid, dread, fright, etc.)—appeared in the text. Initially, this project was designed to test the hypothesis that cultures characterized by high alcohol consumption show evidence of a stronger sub-sistence anxiety or dependency in their folk tales. As it turned out, however, the concept most strongly related to low levels of alcohol consumption was "activity inhibition," a tag that was defined by the negation *not* as well as some other low-frequency words such as *stop* and *catch*. From this finding, McClelland and colleagues concluded that cultures that regularly think in terms of "not doing" something also restrain the impulse to drink large amounts of alcohol. In subsequent research with American participants, McClelland and colleagues conceptually replicated this finding, demonstrating that individuals who frequently use the word *not* in the PSE reported lower consumption of hard liquors (Kalin, McClelland, & Kahn, 1965). Furthermore, experimental studies on the effects of drinking showed that participants who consumed alcohol used the word *not* less often in PSE stories as compared to individuals who did not drink alcohol (McClelland et al., 1972). From this research, McClelland and colleagues concluded that activity inhibition "appears to be a measure of [. . .] stable individual differences in self-restraint [. . .]; that is, it is a general measure of the tendency of the individual to restrain himself on a variety of occasions in a variety of situations" (McClelland et al., 1972, p. 140). As we will see shortly, this conclusion was generally supported by subsequent research. Before I turn to studies that investigated the role of AI in the expression of implicit motives, however, first a few words about the measurement of AI.

Scoring AI in Verbal Material

In contrast to scoring implicit motives like achievement, power, and affiliation, scoring AI is simple and straightforward. A raw score of AI is derived by counting how often a person uses the negation *not* in its full or contracted form in speech or writing. AI can be scored in verbal material of any kind, and indeed has been scored in U.S. presidents' letters, speeches, autobiographies, memoirs, and diaries (Spangler & House, 1991) as well as in letters of CEOs to the stockholders of their companies (Diaz, 1982, as cited in McClelland, 1987). Most typically, though, a measure of AI is derived from the PSE. Coding objectivity is close to perfect (Langens & Stucke, 2005, report kappas ranging from .96 to .98) because disagreements between coders are only due to errors of omission. Raw scores are typically corrected for protocol length either by residualizing raw scores or by expressing raw scores as number of occurrences per 1,000 words. The PSE measure of AI has low to medium internal consistency, with Cronbach's alpha ranging from .30 to .60, depending on the number of pictures employed in a study (Langens & Stucke, 2005; Schultheiss & Brunstein, 2002). Like PSE measures of implicit motives, AI is uncorrelated with self-report measures of personality. Notably, AI is uncorrelated with the Big Five personality traits—extraversion, neuroticism, openness to experiences, agreeableness and conscientiousness—as well as self-report measures of restraint or impulsivity (Pang & Schultheiss, 2005; Schultheiss & Brunstein, 2002). This lack of relationship with self-report is not surprising, given that AI is a *nondeclarative measure* (cf. Schultheiss, 2007) of restraint.

In order to appreciate the significance of the PSE measure of AI, it may be instructive to closely scrutinize how and in which contexts the negation *not* is typically employed in the PSE. The picture cues used to elicit verbal material in the PSE depict at least one and often several persons. Hence, the negation *not* is often employed with respect to a person in the story, for example to negate an *inner state*, such as a thought ("she does not have a lot on her mind"; "he is not planning on working aboard the ship"; "he doesn't think she's stupid"), an emotion ("they are content but not extremely happy"; "he isn't angry"), or a motivational tendency ("not that she is driven by a passion for chemistry in particular"). Also, *not* is often used to state that a character in a story does not pursue or abandons a particular path of action ("they will not do any more races"; "the boxer will not be fighting the man in front of him"; "the girls take the phone number, but do not actually call him"; "Matt isn't pursuing her for a date") or is employed in commands that one character directs at another ("Sandy, don't turn around!"; "C'mon Tom, don't drop her!"). In addition, negations are employed in the PSE in an attempt to define a situation ("the men are competitors, not necessarily opponents"; "it is not a special fight; just another one"; "they are not flawless, but they are entertaining and gripping"). In these latter instances, participants are not negating objective facts about the pictures, but their own subjective associations to the pictures. For example, two persons sitting on a bench by a river can be seen as father and son, siblings, two people who have just met, granddaughter and grandmother, *as well as* a romantic couple. Hence, a participant who states "they are not a couple" is really saying "I thought for a moment they might be a couple, but then I decided to tell a story in which they are not," thus negating his own association to the picture. It is important to note that the negation *not* may be used for other purposes than negating an *inner state*, an *action*, or an *association* ("she does not jump far enough"; "Isn't this great, Emily?"), but these exceptions are a clear minority. In sum, then, it seems safe to conclude that individuals who receive high AI scores typically think in terms of not *thinking*, not *feeling*, not *wanting*, and not *doing* something.

Although there are other negations besides *not* (e.g., no, never), only *not* is scored as an indicator of AI. This decision by McClelland and colleagues (1972) rested on the premise that *not* more than any other negation is employed in directives to regulate one's own or other people's behavior. For this reason, only its full form—and not its contracted form—was originally scored as an indicator of AI, whereas today both forms are scored. Because there is no evidence that lends support to this special status of the negation *not*, we may ask whether other negations may be included to broaden the scoring criteria for AI. To explore this issue, we (Langens et al., 2005) analyzed the transcripts of PSE protocols from over 120 German students and extracted the frequency of the negation *not* and other negations (*nein/no, kein/not a, aber/but, nie/never, nichts/nothing*), as well as tentative words suggesting hypothetical actions (*würde/would, könnte/could, vielleicht/perhaps, möglich/possible, wenn/if, dann/then*) and inclusion words (*mit/with, und/and*). As shown in Figure 4.1, the frequency of using the negation *not* had the highest loading on the first factor of a principal components analysis that also contained loadings from frequency scores of the words *no, not a, but, if,* and *then*. The second factor received loadings from tentative words, including *would, could, maybe* and *possible*. Hence, while people who frequently use *not* also tend to spontaneously employ other negations, using negations in verbal content seems to be independent of tentative words suggesting a possible course of action. Also, except for the inclusion word *and, not* was the word used most frequently in the protocols, and it certainly was the most frequently used negation. In fact, *not* occurred more frequently (8.58 occurrences per 1,000 words) than the three most closely related negations (*no, not a, but*) taken together (6.18 occurrences per 1,000 words). Thus, *not* may rightfully serve as the main indicator of AI. Notably, extending the scoring criterion for AI to other negations increased the internal consistency of the measure. In this sample, Cronbach's alpha rose from .40 to .60 (based on five pictures) when including the three negations most closely related to *not* (no, not a, but). However, it still has to be ascertained that broadening the class of indicators also increases the validity of the measure.

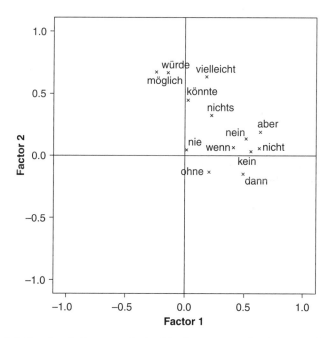

Figure 4.1 Results of a factor analysis of the frequencies of negations and tentative words in PSE protocols in a German sample. (Note: nicht/not; nein/no; kein/not a; aber/but; nie/never; nichts/nothing; würde/would; könnte/could; vielleicht/perhaps; möglich/possible; wenn/if; dann/then; mit/with; und/and; ohne/without).

Activity Inhibition and the Expression of Implicit Motives

Following the initial finding that AI is related to lower levels of alcohol consumption, subsequent studies repeatedly found that the relationship between an implicit motive and some kind of behavioral outlet was stronger for individuals low in AI, suggesting that people high in AI restrain the direct expression of motivational impulses. In the following, studies that found such a moderating effect of AI are presented for each of the big three motives: power, affiliation, and achievement.

AI and Power Motivation

The most comprehensive evidence that AI moderates the way implicit motives are expressed comes from research on power motivation. The power motive has been defined as an enduring and nonconscious capacity to derive pleasure from feeling strong and having impact on other people or the world at large (McClelland, 1975; Schultheiss, 2008; Winter, 1973; see also Chapter 1). There are many ways to have an impact on the world, some of which are long and onerous, while others can be achieved right here and now without great effort or talent. Just think of the Cretan architect Chesiphron, who gained recognition by designing and constructing the Temple of Artemis at Ephesus, one of the Seven Wonders of the World, which was soon to be destroyed by Herostratus, who became famous until today simply by burning down this great achievement of mankind.

As it turns out, both men and women high in *n* Power but low in AI prefer the easy way to gain the pleasure of feeling strong. Men characterized by an *uninhibited* power motive (UPM) are likely to get into arguments, to exert physical violence, to engage in promiscuous sexual activity, and to boast about their sex lives; women with an UPM report getting into arguments more frequently and are more likely to deliberately break things and to slam doors (McClelland, 1975). Hence, individuals with an UPM indulge in actions that provide a direct and impulsive satisfaction of the need to feel strong. In further support of this hypothesis, Schultheiss and Rhode (2002) found increases in testosterone, which is an indicator of the affective reward experienced as a consequence of dominating another person, after winning a dominance contest only among males with an uninhibited power motive. In addition, uninhibited power motivation is related to a preference for vicarious power satisfaction, for example by watching sport events (which show other people succeeding in ritualized dominance contests) and by drinking large amounts of hard liquor (which often instills a feeling of invincibility) (see McClelland, 1975, 1987; McClelland et al., 1972; Winter, 1973).

Quite in contrast, individuals with an *inhibited* power motive (IPM, high *n* Power and high AI) strive to satisfy their need for power by working hard and skillfully to attain some real-world achievement: They excel as managers as well as in other professions (McClelland & Boyatzis, 1982; McClelland & Franz, 1992) and are more likely to hold office in voluntary organizations (Winter, McClelland, & Stewart, 1982). A study by Schultheiss and Brunstein (2002) illustrates the different strategies pursued by individuals with an inhibited or uninhibited power motive in their effort to have an impact on another person. Participants of this study were videotaped while presenting their point of view in a discussion on "experimentation with animals for scientific and commercial purposes" to another person. Later, the tapes were rated for the occurrence of a large variety of behavioral cues, and trained judges rated the overall persuasiveness of the participants. While the prospect of persuading another person of one's own point of view certainly is affectively charged for individuals high in *n* Power, only individuals with an IPM succeeded in actually doing so. They were judged as highly competent and persuasive by the judges, and further analyses revealed that IPM individuals appeared persuasive because they presented their arguments fluently, did not take sides but presented their arguments in a balanced way, and lifted their eyebrows and gestured more in an effort to emphasize their central arguments. Individuals high in power motivation and low in AI may have been equally turned on by the prospect of having the other person accept their point of view, but they failed to employ the sophisticated strategies individuals with an IPM resorted to, instead inserting long pauses of speech, presumably in an attempt to put pressure on the other person.[1]

Spangler and House (1991) tested the hypothesis that the IPM is related to measures of effectiveness among American presidents. While presidents' levels of implicit motives were extracted from presidential first-term inaugural speeches (see Winter, 1987), a measure of AI was derived by counting the frequency of the negation *not* in presidents' letters, speeches, autobiographies, and diaries. Interestingly, this study did not find the expected interaction of *n* Power and AI in predicting several indicators of presidential effectiveness. Rather, there was evidence that AI was directly related to presidents' number of great decisions, perceived greatness, and social and economic performance independently of *n* Power. Thus, AI may be related to social success even in the absence of a strong need for power.

However, there is also evidence that the social success that is so evident among individuals with an IPM comes at the cost of an increased risk for physical illness. High *n* Power combined with high AI has been related to impaired immune system functioning (McClelland, Davidson, & Saron, 1985; McClelland, Floor, Davidson, & Saron, 1980), increased nervous system responsivity (McClelland et al., 1980), and an increased risk for cardiovascular disease and other severe illnesses (McClelland, 1979; McClelland & Jemmott, 1980). The link between IPM and disease seems to be particularly strong if individuals are confronted with high life stress, such as important academic examinations (McClelland & Jemmott, 1980). These findings have been interpreted as showing that individuals high in AI may be less able to regulate negative emotions stemming from stressful situations or unresolved power struggles, an issue I will return to in a later section (see the section below on AI and emotion regulation).

The research summarized so far suggests that power motivation is expressed in impulsive action and vicarious satisfaction among individuals low in AI. In contrast, high levels of AI seem to enable individuals high in n Power to strive for and attain socially acceptable ways of having impact on the world, while at the same time increasing the risk of physical illness. These findings are in accord with McClelland's original conception that AI constrains the *direct* expression of emotional and motivational impulses, while still leaving room for a delayed and refined expression of motivational impulses.

AI and Affiliation Motivation

n Affiliation has been related to both positive, friendly interactions as well as to defensiveness and fear of rejection (Koestner, & McClelland, 1992; Winter, 1996; see also Chapter 3). If activity inhibition is an indicator of motivational restraint, then we would expect both the positive aspects of affiliation motivation as well as its more defensive side to be muted in individuals high in AI. As a general notion, there is evidence that affiliation motivation promotes better health (e.g., McClelland, 1979; McClelland, Alexander, & Marks, 1982), and, more generally, that people who enjoy positive social interaction with their partners, friends, and colleagues typically report better health and manage stressful events more effectively (e.g., Cohen, 1992; Coyne, & Downey, 1991). A study by McClelland and Kirshnit (1988) suggests that the relationship between n Affiliation and better health outcomes may be mediated by responses of the immune system: They found that arousing the affiliation motive by having research participants watch a film of Mother Teresa caring for the poor in the slums of Calcutta led to an increase in salivary immunoglobulin A (S-IgA), the body's first line of defense against upper respiratory infections. Outside the laboratory, however, beneficial effects of affiliation motivation on immune functioning and health seem to occur only in the context of the so-called *relaxed affiliation motive syndrome*, which is characterized by high n Affiliation, low n Power, and, notably, low AI (McClelland, 1989; McClelland & Jemmott, 1980). Because McClelland and his colleagues took a typological approach, there is no way to determine the exact role of AI in this relationship. However, we may speculate that the relaxed affiliation motive syndrome promotes better health because (1) people who have a dominant affiliation motive (n Affiliation $> n$ Power) have the capacity to establish harmonious, reciprocal, and noncompetitive relationships with other people and (2), because of their low AI levels, act on their spontaneous impulses to talk to, approach, or hug other people. In effect, this syndrome may enable people to freely enjoy the positive emotions that are aroused by social interactions, thus fostering all conditions that are necessary for positive effects of social contact to occur. In contrast, a high level of AI may prompt individuals to restrain the impulse to directly engage in close positive interactions with other people and, hence, may undermine the experience of positive emotions aroused by positive social interactions, thus precluding any positive effects of n Affiliation on health and immune functioning.

It is important to note that an inhibited affiliation motive may lead to a refined expression of affiliation motivation in a way similar to the IPM. In the study by Schultheiss and Brunstein (2002) on persuasive communication mentioned above, there was evidence (reported in Schultheiss, 1996) that participants high in n Affiliation and high in AI were strongly committed to the goal of discussing the issue of animal experimentation with another person. Schultheiss (1996) suggested that although the goal was predominantly saturated with incentives for the power motive, individuals with an inhibited affiliation motive responded to the fact that the discussion enabled them to get to know and interact with another person. An analysis of their behavior while they presented their point of view revealed that instead of trying to approach the other person by direct means—for example, by seeking physical proximity or smiling—individuals with an inhibited affiliation motive chose to establish a positive relationship with the other person *indirectly* by presenting even-sided arguments almost everybody could agree to in a calm and self-assured way. In other words, individuals with an inhibited affiliation motive successfully used language to establish positive rapport with another person and succeeded in forming a positive impression in their counterpart, which may have provided a basis for further interaction. Hence, individuals with an inhibited affiliation motive successfully turned a situation that primarily offered incentives for the power motive into a situation that offered a means to satisfy the affiliation motive.

As mentioned above, the affiliation motive seems to carry a large component of fear of rejection, which may explain why individuals high in n Affiliation are defensive when a relationship is impaired or threatened (Winter, 1996; see also Chapter 3). In accord with this conception, there is evidence that n Affiliation combined with high life stress is related to women's reports of inflicting high physical and psychological abuse on partners (Mason & Blankenship, 1987). Notably, though, this relationship is only present among women low in AI and completely absent among women high in AI. Thus, it seems that high AI enables individuals high in n Affiliation to restrain the impulse to lash out verbally or physically at their partners under high stress.

There is even some evidence that high AI restrains the expression of affiliation motivation not only in actual behavior, but possibly also in fantasy. In a sample of over 400 German university students, Schultheiss and Brunstein (2001) found significant negative correlations between AI and affiliation motivation for both men and women (which were not evident in American samples; see Pang & Schultheiss, 2005). In an investigation of daydreaming among German university students that instructed participants to monitor and write down spontaneous fantasies and reveries over a 2-week period (Langens, 1999), there was a significant negative relationship between AI and daydreaming related to close interpersonal relationships (e.g., daydreams related to a significant other). To the extent that fantasy is a precursor for action, these results may suggest that individuals high in AI have learned to restrain affiliative fantasy in an effort to effectively control affiliation-related behavior.

AI and Achievement Motivation

There is little evidence that AI moderates the behavioral expression of n Achievement, which may be defined as a recurrent concern to improve one's skills and do well in comparison to a standard of excellence (McClelland, Atkinson, Clark, & Lowell, 1953; Schultheiss & Brunstein, 2005, see Chapter 2). In particular, there are no studies that suggest that individuals high in n Achievement and high in AI are more (or less) successful in attaining achievement goals than their counterparts low in AI. To account for this lack of moderation, it may be important to note that, in contrast to power and affiliation motivation, n Achievement is typically not expressed in spontaneous or impulsive actions, but rather in long-term involvements within an area of accomplishment (Schultheiss & Brunstein, 2005). Thus, AI may simply be less relevant for the expression of achievement motivation as compared to power and affiliation motivation.

There is, however, some evidence that individuals high in achievement motivation and high in AI may not be able to reap the emotional benefits that result from pursuing achievement goals. Based on the finding that people experience higher levels of emotional well-being if their self-attributed motives and their long-term goals are congruent with their implicit motives (cf. Brunstein, Schultheiss & Grässmann, 1998; see Chapter 12), Langens (2007) investigated whether congruence effects on well-being are present among individuals high in AI. The argument underlying this research runs as follows: In order to gain satisfaction from the pursuit of motive-congruent goals, individuals should have the capacity to enjoy the positive emotions that accompany goal pursuit. Individuals high in AI, however, seem to restrain emotional responses (positive as well as negative) and may thus be less able to derive pleasure and long-term emotional well-being from the pursuit of motive-congruent goals. Two empirical studies yielded evidence that, as expected, congruence of n Achievement and explicit achievement motivation (i.e., *san* Achievement and pursuit of achievement goals) was related to a higher

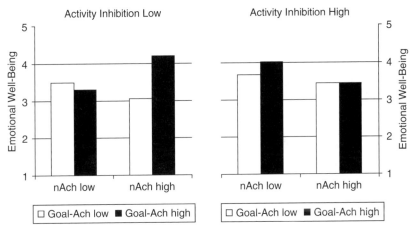

Figure 4.2 Emotional well-being as a function of implicit achievement motivation (PSE achievement) and achievement goal striving for participants high and low in activity inhibition (adapted from Langens, 2007).

emotional well-being only among individuals *low* in AI. For individuals high in AI, congruence of implicit and explicit achievement motivation did not seem to translate into higher emotional well-being (see Fig. 4.2). This effect was independent of perceived progress in goal pursuit, ruling out the alternative explanation that individuals with an inhibited achievement motive may be less successful in attaining congruent goals. In sum, then, while there is no evidence that AI moderates the behavioral expression of achievement motivation, it seems that high AI precludes the positive effects of pursuing motive-congruent goals on subjective emotional well-being.

Activity Inhibition and Emotion Regulation

Right from the conception of AI, McClelland (McClelland, 1975; McClelland et al., 1972) emphasized that individuals high in AI not only restrain motivational impulses, but also inhibit emotional responses. Yet, the role of AI in emotion regulation was rarely investigated in its own right until recently. Instead, research on emotion regulation studied the effects of suppressing behavioral responses to emotionally provocative stimuli as well as the cognitive consequences of suppressing negative mood-relevant thought, mostly without taking individual differences into account. It may be argued that, by asking people to suppress emotional responses or not to think emotional thoughts, these studies investigated AI as a *state* induced by experimental procedures. If this were true, then we may expect individuals who are led to suppress or inhibit emotional responses to behave very much like individuals high in AI not given any special instructions. In the following, I will argue that this speculation is generally supported by empirical findings.

For example, seminal research by Gross and Levenson (1993, 1997) has demonstrated that suppressing behavioral responses to negative emotional stimuli tends to increase physiological arousal. In a typical study, participants were asked to watch an emotionally arousing film (which depicted a horrible accident in a saw mill) and were either instructed to suppress behavioral responses to the film in a way such that outside observers wouldn't notice any emotional expression, or were allowed to watch the movie unconstrained. The authors found that suppressing behavioral responses led to significantly higher sympathetic activation than watching the movie unconstrained. Interestingly, individuals high in AI show similar evidence of increased physiological arousal under stress. Fontana, Rosenberg, Marcus, and Kerns (1987) found that among participants who had to take a performance test, those high in AI showed higher increases in systolic blood pressure than individuals low in AI. Also, Schultheiss (personal communication, February 2008) found elevated cortisol responses in individuals high in activity inhibition who experienced a defeat in a competition with a fellow student. Thus, when confronted with a stressful situation, individuals high in AI show a pattern of physiological responses that is very similar to those of people who are instructed to restrain all behavioral responses. Although this evidence is far from conclusive, it may be reasonable to assume that individuals high in AI habitually suppress behavioral responses to potentially dangerous or aversive situations, which may exacerbate physiological responses to challenging or threatening events.

The cognitive consequences of suppressing mood-relevant thought were investigated by Wegner and colleagues (e.g., Wegner, 1994). Wegner and Smart (1997) have argued that the suppression of a negative mood-relevant thought induces *deep unconscious activation* of that thought. In deep unconscious activation, a thought may not be present in consciousness, but is still highly accessible and subtly influences conscious information processing. For example, deep unconscious activation of a thought (e.g., "I am sad") can bend the meaning of perceptions and other thoughts toward the meaning of the unconsciously activated thought ("this guy looks sad"). Deep unconscious activation of a thought can be measured by indirect indicators of construct accessibility, such as an emotional Stroop task (slower color-naming of the word *sad* as compared to *joy*) or the content of spontaneously generated memories (sad memories come to mind more easily than happy memories). Also, when a thought is activated unconsciously, it has a tendency to spontaneously pop into consciousness (Lane & Wegner, 1995). Typically, then, the suppression of negative mood-relevant thought first induces deep unconscious activation, which eventually causes repeated intrusions of negative thoughts (Wegner, 1994; Wegner & Smart, 1997).

It seems reasonable to assume that individuals high in AI habitually attempt to down-regulate negative emotions by suppressing (i.e., trying not to think about) negative mood-relevant thoughts caused by upsetting or stressful events. If this assumption holds, then we would expect stressful events to have diverging short- and long-term consequences for individuals high in AI. Immediately after suppressing a negative thought, there should be evidence of deep unconscious activation of that thought but no self-report of impaired mood. If a stressful situation persists for a longer time, though, thoughts related to stressful events should intrude regularly into consciousness and may lead to a conscious preoccupation with stress and explicit mood impairment. These predictions were generally confirmed in research by Langens and Stucke (2005), who investigated the role of AI in short- and long-term responses to stressful events. The first study explored the immediate responses to a stressful situation. Participants met in groups of six to eight individuals and were asked to introduce themselves to the group. Then, fear of rejection—which is a potent stressor (Williams, 2007)—was induced in the experimental group by asking participants to pick two people from the group they wanted to work with in upcoming group work and two other people they did not want to work with. The experimenter announced that any participant who was excluded by more than one other participant would not be eligible for the group work, meaning, in plain words, that he or she had been rejected by the group. In the control condition, group participation was determined by the flip of a coin. While still not knowing whether they would take part in the group work or not, partici- pants completed measures of deep unconscious activation of negative mood and conscious mood impairment. For the former, participants were asked to recall six memories of events that happened before age 14 and indicate whether these were happy or sad memories; deep unconscious activation of negative mood was operationalized by the number of sad memories recalled (cf. Weinberger, Kelner, & McClelland, 1997). The largest number of negative childhood memories was recalled by individuals high in AI in the stressful condition. As expected, the same participants did not report any conscious mood impairment, which suggests that individuals high in AI suppressed negative thoughts related to possible exclusion from the group.

The consequences of *persistent* and *prolonged* confrontation with stressful events were investigated in a second study by Langens and Stucke (2005). Students completed questionnaires assessing the number of stressful events they were experiencing (e.g., high work load, financial problems, disagree- ments with friends, etc.) and reported on their mood both at the beginning and in the middle of a semester. Results showed that all participants reported low levels of stress at the beginning of a semester. On average, self-reported stress load increased from the beginning to mid-semester, but this increase was disproportionally larger in students high in AI. Also, it was found that the relationship between stress load and emotional impairment was stronger in students high (as compared to low) in AI. This study suggests that confrontation with persistent stressors leads to a conscious preoccupation with stress and larger emotional impairment in individuals high in AI.

To further investigate the role of AI in emotion regulation, we (Langens & Dorr, 2008) explored the attentional processes triggered by emotionally arousing stimuli. One common strategy to down-regulate negative emotions elicited by emotional stimuli operates by rapidly shifting attention toward emotionally neutral stimuli (e.g., Gross, 2002; Wegner, 1994). For this approach to work, people have to apply a two-tiered strategy: They have to be sensitive to stimuli that trigger an emotional response and, once such stimuli are encountered, have to recruit additional control strategies that direct attention away from them (cf. Baumeister, 1996; Wegner, 1994). We expected such a configuration of attentional processes to be present among participants high in AI. More specifically, we proposed that individuals high (but not those low) in AI can be characterized by (1) a preattentive bias toward emotional stimuli and (2) a tendency to employ effortful control strategies to override automatic responses to highly emotional or threatening stimuli once they are consciously perceived. The presence of such a control process may enable individuals high in AI to rapidly detect emotional stimuli and subsequently minimize their emotional response to them.

To test this hypothesis, we investigated cognitive interference resulting from the presentation of emotional stimuli in a reaction time task. In these studies, participants worked on a visual discrimination task in which they had to respond as quickly as possible to a target stimulus (indicating as quickly as possible whether an arrow presented on a computer screen pointed to the left or to the right). In some trials, schematic faces with neutral, angry, or friendly expressions were presented before the target stimulus appeared. In one condition, faces were presented unmasked for 250 ms and hence fully accessible to conscious awareness. In another condition, 18 stimuli were presented within that 250 ms interval, each for about 16 ms; emotional faces were interspersed in this presentation but were immediately masked so that participants were unable to consciously recognize the faces. Because we assumed individuals high in AI to be characterized by a preattentive bias toward threatening stimuli (angry faces), we expected evidence of cognitive interference (i.e., longer response latencies on the RT task) when angry faces were masked and hence not accessible to conscious awareness. When angry faces were presented unmasked (and hence fully accessible to conscious awareness), however, we expected individuals high in AI to override their preattentive bias by employing effortful control strategies, such as rapidly shifting attention to the task at hand, which should result in facilitation effects (i.e., shorter response latencies).

The results of two experiments generally confirmed our predictions. Participants high in AI showed evidence of cognitive interference when

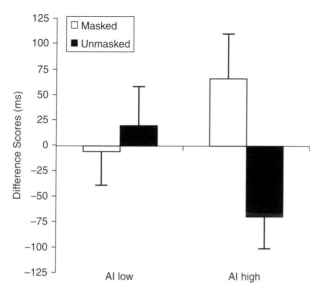

Figure 4.3 Attentional bias for angry faces (relative to no-face control trials) as a function of AI and presentation (masked vs. unmasked presentation). (From Langens & Dorr, 2008, Study 1.)

angry faces were masked, and cognitive facilitation when angry faces were presented unmasked (see Fig. 4.3). This pattern of results emerged for difficult visual discriminations, which could not be solved by habitual and highly routinized response sets (cf. Wentura & Rothermund, 2003), but not for easy discriminations. In contrast, the presentation of angry faces— either masked or unmasked—had no effect on response times for individuals low in AI.

In another study, we (Langens & Dorr, 2006) investigated whether facilitation effects in response to unmasked angry faces are due to an effortful control process rather than an automatic and efficient routine. Research on ego depletion has shown that effortful control is a limited resource that tends to deplete with consistent use (Baumeister, Gailliot, DeWall, & Oaten, 2006; Muraven & Baumeister, 2000). Hence, if individuals high in AI employ effortful control to override an automatic response, then we might expect facilitation effects in response to emotional stimuli to wear off over time. We tested this hypothesis by having participants work on a more demanding reaction time task—naming the color of a circle that was presented on a computer screen—for an extended period of time. The results showed that, early in the experiment, individuals both high and low in AI showed evidence of facilitation following an unmasked presentation of angry faces. As the experiment went on, however, an unmasked presentation of angry faces led to interference effects, but only among individuals high in AI.

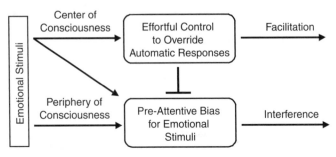

Figure 4.4 A model of attentional control in response to emotional stimuli for individuals high in AI. Emotional stimuli presented in the periphery of consciousness attract attentional capacity and cause a disruption of performance (i.e., interference effects). If emotional stimuli are consciously perceived, then effortful control processes override automatic effects and restore performance. Extended use of effortful control may terminate facilitation effects by way of volitional depletion.

These findings may be interpreted as follows (see Fig. 4.4): Individuals high in AI get distracted by emotional stimuli (such as angry faces) as long as these stimuli are not in the center of conscious awareness. Once consciously identified, emotional stimuli seem to trigger additional effortful control strategies that enable individuals high in AI to ignore emotional stimuli and to concentrate on the "task at hand." When emotional stimuli are presented over extended periods of time, however, cognitive resources to exert attentional control dry up, with the effect that emotional stimuli become highly distractive for individuals high in AI. Note that emotional stimuli had no distracting effect on participants low in AI, which suggests that the control process identified in Figure 4.4 is only instantiated in individuals high in AI.

Taken together, the findings presented in this section give a complex though consistent picture of the immediate and long-term responses of individuals high in AI to threat and stressful events. Even under immediate pressure from threatening or challenging events, individuals high in AI may appear *less* emotional than individuals low in AI to an outside observer: They are unlikely to report any mood impairment and probably behave as controlled and restrained as ever. Physiological responses as well as implicit measures of mood may tell a different story, though, demonstrating high arousal and deep unconscious activation of mood-relevant thought as a response to stressful events. There is some evidence that heightened arousal under challenge may sometimes leak into expressive behavior, as Schultheiss and Brunstein (2002) found higher levels of nonverbal expressiveness (facial and hand gestures) among individuals high in n Power and high in AI when trying to persuade a fellow student. It is only after a prolonged confrontation with stressful events that unconscious activation of negative mood-relevant thought turns into explicit mood impairment and a conscious preoccupation with thoughts related to stressful events.

Further evidence that AI plays an important role in the regulation of negative emotions has recently been obtained by Schultheiss, Riebel, and Jones (2009), who suggested that AI represents a propensity for greater activation of the right hemisphere (RH) than the left hemisphere (LH), particularly in response to stressful stimuli and situations. In a series of four studies, they found that high AI was related to an index of RH activation obtained from a dot-probe task. In this paradigm, a dot is either presented in the left hemifield (projecting to the RH) or in the right hemifield (projecting to the LH), and participants are asked to indicate as quickly as possible in which hemifield the dot appeared. Schultheiss and colleagues consistently found that participants high in AI responded faster to stimuli presented in the left (as compared to the right) hemifield, which points to a greater RH activation. The link between AI and RH activation was even more pronounced when participants were in a negative mood, were confronted with angry faces, or had experienced defeat in a contest. As Schultheiss and colleagues point out, their research has the potential to integrate a wide range of findings on AI. For example, the tendency of individuals high in AI to show increased physiological activation in response to stress (Fontana et al., 1987; Schultheiss & Rohde, 2003) is consistent with the evidence that sympathetic modulation of heart rate and blood pressure are controlled by the RH. Also, the nonverbal expressiveness that is evident among individuals high in AI (Schultheiss & Brunstein, 2002) resonates with the finding that the RH is more strongly involved in nonverbal expression than the left hemisphere. Even the early finding that low AI is linked to high alcohol consumption (McClelland et al., 1972) can be explained by the AI-RH hypothesis because there is evidence that people who abuse alcohol show deficits in RH functioning.

Developmental Precursors of Activity Inhibition

As impressive as the empirical evidence related to AI may seem, it does not answer a crucial question the reader may have raised by now: How can the use of a single word be a valid indicator of incredibly complex processes aimed at restraining emotional and motivational impulses, which seem to involve automatic attentional processes as well as hemispheric activation in response to stress? In order to answer this question, we may get a hint or two by looking at the extensive literature on how children learn to control motivational and emotional impulses.

According to Kopp (1982), children become capable of controlling their behavior by following parental requests in do-contexts (which involve sustaining an unpleasant activity, such as cleaning up toys) as well as don't-contexts (which involve suppressing a prohibited but pleasant activity, e.g., not touching an attractive object). In many languages, the negation *not* is used in firm commands to direct a toddler's behavior in don't-contexts, which may be concerned with child safety (e.g., not touching things that are dangerous, not climbing on furniture, not walking into the street), protection of personal property (not tearing up books, not entering prohibited rooms, not coloring the walls), respect for others (not taking toys away from other children, not being too rough, not interrupting others' conversations), and food and mealtime routines (not playing with food, not leaving table in the middle of meal, not spilling drinks) (see Gralinski & Kopp, 1993).

So how do children acquire the capacity to comply with a caregiver's request to inhibit or cease a highly desirable but inappropriate activity? Initially, parents closely supervise their children's conduct to assure that they conform to the prohibition, reiterating their request ("do not touch the oven!") whenever needed. Gradually, however, regulation shifts to the child while parents increasingly assume the role of remote observers. By 24 months of age, most children learn to follow the rules set by their parents without adult surveillance. Interestingly, Rothbart (1989) argued that behavioral control in don't-contexts precedes successful compliance on do-tasks, and this claim has recently received empirical support. Infants as young as 8 to 10 months are already capable of complying with a caregiver's request not to touch an attractive object, and by 13 to 15 months, toddlers develop the capacity to inhibit a behavior even when the caregiver isn't watching (Kochanska, Coy, & Murray, 2001; Kochanska, Tjebkes, & Forman, 1998). This transition from external to internal control seems to be mediated by developing cognitive and linguistic abilities. More specifically, research has shown that toddlers internalize prohibitions given by a caregiver using self-talk rephrasing the original demands, which is then employed to guide and regulate behavior (Kochanska, & Aksan, 1995; Luria, 1961). As Vygotsky (1978, p. 57) pointed out, children acquire the capacity to voluntarily control their attention and their behavior by transforming an interpersonal process (here: firm requests to stay away from an object or to inhibit an activity) into an intrapersonal one (self-restraint).

Note that such firm commands addressed at the child may foster conditions of nonreward (because the child has to cease a pleasant activity) and possibly threat (because caregivers sometimes imply that disregarding the command will have undesirable consequences). Parental prohibitions may, however, prompt a child to find alternative rewarding activities (e.g., coloring a book or climbing a tree house). Hence, children who are frequently confronted with firm commands to suppress an attractive activity may learn to inhibit spontaneous approach behavior as well as to explore alternative and socially acceptable ways to satisfy their motivational needs.

These findings provide a framework to explain how AI—the tendency to spontaneously use the negation *not* in speech and writing—may develop from early socialization in don't-contexts. Note that the common denominator of all the possible instructions that guide behavior in don't-contexts is the negation *not*, and that children learn to oblige to parental instructions by using self-talk. Hence, adult individuals high in AI may think in terms of not doing, not feeling, and not thinking because they thoroughly internalized parental prohibitions in childhood and continue to employ self-directives containing the negation *not* throughout their life to control their (and possibly other people's) behavior. More than others, they may be capable of restraining spontaneous and impulsive approach behavior (as instigated, for example, by implicit motives) whenever it seems necessary without abandoning the initial motivational impulse. Rather than acting on the spot, they may find a way to come in contact with the desired incentive either by waiting for the right time or by using sophisticated and refined strategies to approach their goals. This latter argument will be further elaborated in the following section.

Integration and Conclusion

The research summarized in this chapter is in accord with the original conceptualization of AI by McClelland and colleagues (1972), who proposed that AI represents a person's inclination to restrain motivational and emotional impulses. However, the evidence collected so far strongly suggests that individuals high in AI are in no way *less* emotional or *less* motivated than those low in AI. Quite in contrast, individuals high in AI respond more emotionally in stressful situations and tend to be more successful in reaching long-term motivational goals. Hence, AI does in no way "neutralize" an aroused emotion or a motivational state. In order to understand the effects of negations on emotional and motivational processes, it may be instructive to address (1) how negations are processed and (2) how negating the expression of a thought, an emotion, or an action tendency may actually increase its initial strength.

First, research by Deutsch, Gawronski, and Strack (2006) suggested that negating is a reflective process that does not become efficient with extended practice. In this research, participants were instructed to indicate as quickly as possible the valence of positive and negative words that were either negated ("no dictator," "no career") or affirmed ("a dictator," "a career"). On average, negating the valence of words took 100 ms longer than affirming their valence, and this difference was independent of amount of practice. Furthermore, although people correctly judge the valence of negated concepts when given time to respond (e.g., "no dictator" is more positive than "no career"), negated positive concepts ("no career") primed responses for positive (rather than negative) targets in an affective priming paradigm, demonstrating that negations are not processed automatically. In short, extracting the valence of a word is an automatic, efficient, and obligatory process, whereas negating its valence is a controlled, effortful, and time-consuming optional process[2].

Second, research by Wegner (1994) has shown that any attempt to control thoughts, emotions, or behavior by giving negated instructions (e.g., "do *not* think of a white bear"; "do *not* feel sad"; "do *not* putt the ball beyond the white line") runs the risk of producing ironic effects, that is, to generate exactly the result an individual is trying to avoid (e.g., constantly thinking about white bears, feeling really sad, over-putting the golf ball; see Wegner, 1994). Like Strack and Deutsch (2004), Wegner (1994) suggests that any attempt to control thoughts, feelings, or actions by giving negated instructions gives rise to two processes, an automatic-affirmative process that represents the to-be-avoided state (e.g., feeling sad) and a controlled process that aims to establish the desired state (e.g., not feeling sad). If the controlled process is weakened—for example, by fatigue or distraction—then the affirmative process directs attention toward stimuli or memories that are congruent with the avoided state, producing ironic effects of mental control.

The models of Strack and Deutsch (2004) and Wegner (1994) can readily be applied to the concept of AI. Let us assume that motivational impulses as well as emotional processes are generally automatic *and* affirmative, whereas negating is generally a reflective and effortful process (cf. Strack & Deutsch, 2004). Applied to the concept of AI, we may then speculate that no matter how often a person has actually successfully restrained a motivational tendency ("Let's not blurt out the good news quite yet") or an emotional impulse ("Do not get upset here") using some sort of subvocal self-instruction, self-restraint will always be an effortful process designed to override an automatic emotional or motivational tendency. Rather than neutralizing an emotion or a motivation, any attempt to negate an emotion or a motivational tendency will instantiate *two* states that are simultaneously present in a person's mind: an automatic affirmative process ("I'd like to blurt out the good news"; "I am upset") and a controlled process aimed at overriding the original automatic process. Although individuals high in AI may successfully restrain the *direct* expression of a motivational or emotional impulse, these impulses can be assumed to persist, gain momentum over time, and shape subjective experience and behavior at some later point. This reasoning is consistent with the evidence that individuals high in AI are more emotional under stress, and it may also be applied to motivational impulses, given the evidence that unexpressed motivational tendencies increase over time (cf. Bargh, Gollwitzer, Lee-Chai, Barndollar, & Trötschel, 2001; Polivy, 1998).

Figure 4.5 presents a model that tries to integrate the diverse lines of evidence presented so far. It assumes that individuals low in AI (see left panel of Fig. 4.5) tend to directly express motivational impulses as well as emotional states. This inclination is associated with costs and benefits. On the positive side, an unrestrained expression of motivational impulses enables an individual to

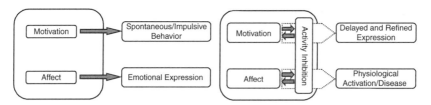

Figure 4.5 An integrated model of emotional and motivational factors in AI. In individuals low in AI (left panel), emotional states and motivational impulses are expressed directly in behavior through routines. Such a direct expression is blocked in individuals high in AI (right panel), leading to an intensification of emotional and motivational states, which are then expressed in flexible, adaptive behavior. As a consequence, individuals high in AI may be more successful socially, while at the same time carrying an increased risk for physical disease.

reap the positive affective consequences of indulging in unrestrained goal-directed behavior, as evidenced, for example, by testosterone increases after a victory in individuals high in *n* Power or positive emotions elicited by pursuing motive-congruent goals (cf. Langens, 2007; Schultheiss and Rhode, 2002). In addition, a free expression of emotional states seems to prevent excessive physiological activation in response to stressors. On the negative side, though, impulsive action may jeopardize the attainment of long-term goals, as indicated by lower levels of social success attained by individuals low in AI.

By way of contrast (see right panel of Fig. 4.5), high levels of AI restrain a direct expression of both motivational states as well as aroused emotions, amplifying these tendencies over time, which may result in a "bottling-up" (cf. Schultheiss & Brunstein, 2002) of motivational and emotional impulses. As far as motivational tendencies are concerned, the research by Schultheiss and colleagues (2009) suggests that conditions of nonreward (i.e., not directly expressing an aroused implicit motive) activate the right hemisphere in individuals high in AI. Goldberg's (2001) model of hemispheric differences states that the RH is involved in developing effective strategies for dealing with *novel* challenges in the environment, which, if successful, are stored as behavioral routines in the left hemisphere (LH). Hence, Schultheiss and colleagues (2009) argue that instead of relying on established behavioral routines, high levels of AI may predispose an individual to acquire new ways of dealing with the environment under conditions of threat, punishment, or nonreward. This inclination may have formed in early childhood as a response to caregivers' repeated demands to cease a desirable activity (which, as noted above, estab-lishes conditions of either nonreward or threat) and find alternative and acceptable ways to satisfy motivational tendencies. This suggestion, speculative as it may be, is entirely consistent with the finding that individuals high in AI are less inclined to approach a desired goal by spontaneous or impulsive behavioral routines (presumably stored in the LH), but rather by employing flexible and sophisticated means of goal pursuit (presumably instigated by the RH). Hence, although initial impulses to approach a goal are restrained, individuals high in AI may ultimately find a delayed or refined way to pursue goal states that satisfy their implicit motives. This tendency to activate the RH under conditions of nonreward may foster the high levels of social success and long-term goal attainment experienced by individuals high in AI.

The tendency of individuals high in AI to restrain emotional states seems to have diverging short- and long-term consequences. Overall, the short-term consequences are generally positive: Individuals high in AI appear calm and composed even when confronted with a stressor (although experiencing high levels of physiological activation) and may initially even manage to put negative thoughts aside. In the long run, however, emotional restraint may cause intrusions of negative mood-relevant thought, leading to conscious mood-impairment and a preoccupation with negative thoughts. In addition, persistent confrontation with stressful events may further increase physiological responses, which may ultimately increase the vulnerability to physical disease among individuals high in AI.

The model in Figure 4.5 suggests that this general conclusion applies to a broad range of motivational impulses (including achievement, power, and affiliation motivation) as well as positive and negative emotions. It is important to note, however, that some elements of this model are better supported by empirical research than others, and this conclusion certainly applies to the restraint of motivational impulses. Up to now, the moderating effects of AI have been tied to specific implicit motives. Recall that social success as well as physical disease have predominantly been linked to the inhibited power motive; the scarce research on the inhibited affiliation motive suggests that high AI is associated with a restrained expression of affiliation motivation, which may nevertheless prompt individuals to employ sophisticated means to establish rapport with another person. An inhibited achievement motive has been linked to an absence of congruence effects on emotional well-being, which suggests that high AI may undermine the emotional benefits of motive-congruent behavior. Although these results are in accord with the general assumption that AI may prompt a delayed and refined expression of motivational tendencies, more research—especially with respect to inhibited achievement motivation—is clearly needed to test the model's validity.

A fairly general picture emerges for the restraint of negative emotions. Here, the empirical findings suggest that high AI is associated with an increased sensitivity for potential threat and life stress, which may over time lead to excessive rumination, distress, and possibly physical disease. So far, the evidence suggests that AI may be conceived as a risk factor for emotional and physical impairment in response to stress; whether or not the combination of high AI and high life stress leads to rumination and physical disease will depend on a variety of additional factors, such as the availability of social support and functional coping strategies. Again, more research is needed to understand how high AI may predispose an individual to experience a high level of distress and disease.

To conclude, this chapter has argued that AI represents a capacity to restrain motivational and emotional impulses that develops as infants learn to control their conduct in response to caregivers' requests and that later in life has important consequences for social success as well as physical health. The research accumulated so far has shown that AI is a fascinating psychological construct that has multiple and complex ramifications for motivational and emotional processes. As such, the concept of AI is clearly worthy of further investigation.

Author Note

Parts of the research summarized in this chapter were supported by Deutsche Forschungsgemeinschaft grant LA 1155/3-1 and LA 1155/4-1.
Please direct correspondence to: Thomas A. Langens, Allgemeine Psychologie II im FB G, University of Wuppertal, Gaußstraße 20, 42097 Wuppertal, Germany. E-mail: langens@uni-wuppertal.de

Notes

1. Notably, these effects were only present when participants took part in a guided imagery exercise in which they visually imagined the ensuing discussion, which was designed to assimilate the experimental task to participants' implicit motives (see Schultheiss & Brunstein, 1999).
2. Note that while individuals high in AI may have automatized the subvocal use of negated self-instructions (which also accounts for the habitual use of the negation *not* in the PSE), the process of restraining motivational and emotional impulses may not automatize and still be experienced as effortful. In other words, initiating restraint may be automatized, while successfully restraining impulses may not.

References

Bargh, J. A., Gollwitzer, P. M., Lee-Chai, A., Barndollar, K., & Trötschel, R. (2001). The automated will: Nonconscious activation and pursuit of behavioral goals. *Journal of Personality and Social Psychology, 81,* 1014–1027.

Baumeister, R. F. (1996). Self-regulation and ego-threat: Motivated cognition, self deception, and destructive goal-setting. In P. M. Gollwitzer & J. A. Bargh (Eds.), *The psychology of action* (pp. 27–47). New York: Guilford.

Baumeister, R. F., Gailliot, M., DeWall, C. N., & Oaten, M. (2006). Self-regulation and personality: How interventions increase regulatory success, and how ego-depletion moderates the effects of traits on behavior. *Journal of Personality, 74,* 1773–1801.

Brunstein, J. C., Schultheiss, O. C., & Grässmann, R. (1998). Personal goals and emotional well-being: The moderating role of motive dispositions. *Journal of Personality and Social Psychology, 75*, 494–508.

Cohen, S. (1992). Stress, social support, and disorder. In H. O. F. Veiel & U. Baumann (Eds.), *The meaning and measurement of social support* (pp. 109–124). New York: Hemisphere.

Coyne, J. C., & Downey, G. (1991). Social factors and psychopathology: Stress, social support, and coping processes. *Annual Review of Psychology, 42*, 401–425.

Deutsch, R., Gawronski, B., & Strack, F. (2006). At the boundaries of automaticity: Negation as reflective operation. *Journal of Personality and Social Psychology, 91*, 385–405.

Fontana, A. F., Rosenberg, R. L., Marcus, J. L., & Kerns, R. D. (1987). Type A behavior pattern, inhibited power motivation, and activity inhibition. *Journal of Personality and Social Psychology, 52*, 177–183.

Goldberg, E. (2001). *The executive brain. Frontal lobes and the civilized mind.* New York: Oxford University Press.

Gralinski, J. H., & Kopp, C. B. (1993). Everyday rules for behavior: Mothers' requests to young children. *Developmental Psychology, 29*, 573–584.

Gross, J. J. (2002). Emotion regulation: Affective, cognitive, and social consequences. *Psychophysiology, 39*, 281–291.

Gross, J. J., & Levenson, R. W. (1993). Emotional suppression: Physiology, self-report, and expressive behavior. *Journal of Personality and Social Psychology, 64*, 970–986.

Gross, J. J., & Levenson, R. W. (1997). Hiding feelings: The acute effects of inhibiting negative and positive emotion. *Journal of Abnormal Psychology, 106*, 95–103.

Kalin, R., McClelland, D. C., & Kahn, M. (1965). The effects of male social drinking. *Journal of Personality and Social Psychology, 1*, 441–452.

Kochanska, G., & Aksan, N. (1995). Mother-child mutually positive affect, the quality of child compliance to requests and prohibitions, and maternal control as correlates of early internalization. *Child Development, 66*, 236–254.

Kochanska, G., Coy, K. C., & Murray, K. T. (2001). The development of self-regulation in the first four years of life. *Child Development, 72*, 1091–1111.

Kochanska, G., Tjebkes, T. L., & Forman, D. R. (1998). Children's emerging regulation of conduct: Restraint, compliance, and internalization from infancy to second year. *Child Development, 69*, 1378–1389.

Koestner, R., & McClelland, D. C. (1992). The affiliation motive. In C. P. Smith (Ed.), *Motivation and personality: Handbook of thematic content analysis* (pp. 205–210). Cambridge, MA: Cambridge University Press.

Kopp, C. B. (1982). The antecedents of self-regulation. *Developmental Psychology, 18*, 199–214.

Lane, J. D., & Wegner, D. M. (1995). The cognitive consequences of secrecy. *Journal of Personality and Social Psychology, 69*, 237–253.

Langens, T. A. (1999). *Activity inhibition and daydreaming.* Unpublished data set, University of Wuppertal, Germany.

Langens, T. A. (2007). Congruence between explicit and implicit motives and emotional well-being: The moderating role of activity inhibition. *Motivation and Emotion, 31*, 49–59.

Langens, T. A., & Dorr, S. (2006). *Ego-depletion following extended exposure to threatening faces in individuals high in activity inhibition.* Unpublished data, University of Wuppertal, Germany.

Langens, T. A., & Dorr, S. (2008). *Attentional bias for emotional faces: The moderating role of activity inhibition.* Unpublished manuscript, University of Wuppertal, Germany.

Langens, T. A., & Stucke, T. S. (2005). Stress and mood: The moderating role of activity inhibition. *Journal of Personality, 73,* 47–78.

Luria, A. R. (1961). *The role of speech in the development of normal and abnormal behavior.* New York: Liveright.

Mason, A., & Blankenship, V. (1987). Power and affiliation motivation, stress, and abuse in intimate relationships. *Journal of Personality and Social Psychology, 52,* 203–210.

McClelland, D. C. (1975). *Power: The inner experience.* New York: Irvington Publishers.

McClelland, D. C. (1979). Inhibited power motivation and high blood pressure in men. *Journal of Abnormal Psychology, 88,* 182–190.

McClelland, D. C. (1987). *Human motivation.* New York: Cambridge University Press.

McClelland, D. C. (1989). Motivational factors in health and disease. *American Psychologist, 44,* 675–683.

McClelland, D. C., Alexander, C., & Marks, E. (1982). The need for power, stress, immune function and illness among male prisoners. *Journal of Abnormal Psychology, 91,* 61–70.

McClelland, D. C., Atkinson, J. W., Clark, R. A., & Lowell, E. L. (1953). *The achievement motive.* New York: Appleton-Century-Crofts.

McClelland, D. C., & Boyatzis, R. E. (1982). Leadership motive pattern and long-term success in management. *Journal of Applied Psychology, 67,* 737–743.

McClelland, D. C., Davidson, R. J., & Saron, C. (1985). Stressed power motivation, sympathetic activation, immune function, and illness. *Advances, 2,* 42–52.

McClelland, D. C., Davis, W. N., Kalin, R., & Wanner, E. (1972). *The drinking man.* New York: Free Press.

McClelland, D. C., Floor, E., Davidson, R. J., & Saron, C. (1980). Stressed power motivation, sympathetic activation, immune function, and illness. *Journal of Human Stress, 6,* 11–19.

McClelland, D. C., & Franz, C. E. (1992). Motivational and other sources of work accomplishments in mid-life: A longitudinal study. *Journal of Personality, 60,* 679–707.

McClelland, D. C., & Jemmott, J. B. (1980). Power motivation, stress and physical illness. *Journal of Human Stress, 6,* 6–15.

McClelland, D. C., & Kirshnit, C. (1988). The effect of motivational arousal through films on salivary immunoglobulin A. *Psychology and Health, 2,* 31–52.

McClelland, D. C., Koestner, R., & Weinberger, J. (1989). How do self-attributed and implicit motives differ? *Psychological Review, 96,* 690–702.

Muraven, M. R., & Baumeister, R. F. (2000). Self-regulation and depletion of limited resources: Does self-control resemble a muscle? *Psychological Bulletin, 126,* 247–259.

Pang, J. S., & Schultheiss, O. C. (2005). Assessing implicit motives in U.S. College students: Effects of picture type and position, gender and ethnicity, and cross-cultural comparisons. *Journal of Personality Assessment, 85,* 280–294.

Polivy, J. (1998). The effects of behavioral inhibition: Integrating internal cues, cognition, behavior, and affect. *Psychological Inquiry, 9,* 181–204.

Rothbart, M. K. (1989). Temperament and development. In G. A. Kohnstamm, J. E. Bates, & M. K. Rothbart (Eds.), *Temperament in childhood* (pp. 187–247). New York: Wiley.

Schultheiss, O. C. (1996). *Imagination, Motivation und Verhalten [Imagery, motivation, and action].* Dissertation, Friedrich-Alexander-Universität Erlangen-Nürnberg.

Schultheiss, O. C. (2007). A memory-systems approach to the classification of personality tests: Comment on Meyer and Kurtz (2006). *Journal of Personality Assessment, 89*(2), 197–201.

Schultheiss, O. C. (2008). Implicit motives. In O. P. John, R. W. Robins, & L. A. Pervin (Eds.), *Handbook of personality: Theory and research,* 3rd ed., (pp. 603–633). New York: Guilford.

Schultheiss, O. C., & Brunstein, J. C. (1999). Goal imagery: Bridging the gap between implicit motives and explicit goals. *Journal of Personality, 67,* 1–38.

Schultheiss, O. C., & Brunstein, J. C. (2001). Assessing implicit motives with a research version of the TAT: Picture profiles, gender differences, and relations to other personality measures. *Journal of Personality Assessment, 77,* 71–86.

Schultheiss, O. C., & Brunstein, J. C. (2002). Inhibited power motivation and persuasive communication: A lens model analysis. *Journal of Personality, 70,* 553–582.

Schultheiss, O. C., & Brunstein, J. C. (2005). An implicit motive perspective on competence. In A. J. Elliot & C. Dweck (Eds.), *Handbook of competence and motivation* (pp. 31–51). New York: Guilford.

Schultheiss, O. C., Riebel, K., & Jones, N. M. (2009). Activity inhibition: A predictor of lateralized brain function during stress? *Neuropsychology, 23,* 392–404.

Schultheiss, O. C., & Rohde, W. (2002). Implicit power motivation predicts men's testosterone changes and implicit learning in a contest situation. *Hormones and Behavior, 41,* 195–202.

Spangler, W. D., & House, R. J. (1991). Presidential effectiveness and the leadership motive profile. *Journal of Personality and Social Psychology, 60,* 439–455.

Strack, F., & Deutsch, R. (2004). Reflective and impulsive determinants of social behavior. *Personality and Social Psychology Review, 8,* 220–247.

Vygotsky, L. S. (1978). *Mind in society: The development of higher psychological processes.* Cambridge, MA: Harvard University Press.

Wegner, D. M. (1994). Ironic processes of mental control. *Psychological Review, 101,* 34–52.

Wegner, D. M., & Smart., L. (1997). Deep cognitive activation: A new approach to the unconscious. *Journal of Consulting and Clinical Psychology, 65,* 984–995.

Weinberger, J., Kelner, S., & McClelland, D. C. (1997). The effects of subliminal symbiotic stimulation on free-response and self-report mood. *Journal of Nervous and Mental Disease, 185,* 599–605.

Wentura, D., & Rothermund, K. (2003). The "meddling-in" of affective information: A general model of automatic evaluation effects. In J. Musch & K. C. Klauer (Eds.), *Psychology of evaluation: Affective processes in cognition and emotion* (pp. 53–86). Mahwah, NJ: Lawrence Erlbaum.

Williams, K. D. (2007). Ostracism. *Annual Review of Psychology, 58,* 425–452.

Winter, D. G. (1973). *The power motive.* New York: Free Press.

Winter, D. G. (1987). Leader appeal, leader performance and the motive profile of leaders and followers: A study of American presidents and elections. *Journal of Personality and Social Psychology, 52,* 196–202.

Winter, D. G. (1996). *Personality.* New York: McGraw-Hill.

Winter, D. G., McClelland, D. C., & Stewart, A. J. (1982). *A new defense of the liberal arts.* San Francisco: Jossey-Bass.

SECTION 2

Assessment of Implicit Motives

Chapter 5

Content Coding Methods in Implicit Motive Assessment: Standards of Measurement and Best Practices for the Picture Story Exercise

JOYCE S. PANG
Nanyang Technological University, Singapore

Thematic content analysis refers to a set of assessment methods where written or oral responses to open-ended questions and naturally occurring narrative material are analyzed in order to reveal complex personality processes such as motivation (e.g., McClelland, Atkinson, Clark, & Lowell, 1953), cognitive complexity (e.g., Suedfeld, Tetlock, & Streufert, 1992), and stereotypes (e.g., Taylor, Lee, & Stern, 1995). The types of content analysis methods are numerous and range from archival analysis (e.g., Winter, 1992) to the thematic analysis of survey responses (Atkinson, 1958).

Although the content-coding method of assessing implicit motives is labor intensive and time consuming, it also possesses the advantage of richness of information. Specifically, the researcher can rescore the same set of protocols for a number of diverse constructs and thus investigate complex personality forces happening at the same time, for example, different motives acting in the same situation. Additionally, researchers are able to measure motives at a distance, thus gaining access to a pool of otherwise unavailable data from subjects, who, for instance, are deceased or live in remote locations. Finally, because the methodology is open ended and nonreactive, researchers are less worried about response sets that commonly occur in self-report methods (c.f., Nisbett & Wilson, 1977).

The goal of this chapter is to inform nonexpert researchers who are interested in assessing implicit motives of the proper and possible uses of content-coding methods. In this chapter, I will reiterate and elaborate on important points from similarly instructional sources on motivational content analysis, such as Schultheiss and Pang (2007) and Smith (1992), as well as provide additional recommendations from previously unpublished data. Specifically, I focus on the Picture Story Exercise (PSE; Koestner & McClelland, 1992) because it is the most widely used method for assessing implicit motives, especially the Big Three motives of *n* Power (the need to have impact on other people), *n* Affiliation (the need to establish and maintain positive relations with others), and *n* Achievement (the need to do things better).

After a discussion of the background of the PSE and two standards of measurement—internal consistency and validity—that have been widely discussed in the evaluation of the PSE as an instrument, the first part of the chapter will introduce various topics such as picture cue selection, administration, coding systems and coder training, data processing, and other pragmatic issues that are relevant to using the PSE in research. In turn, these topics are introduced systematically according to the stages of measurement of pretest, test, posttest, and retest. Readers who are interested in measuring implicit motives with the PSE should be able to embark on such research after reading and carrying out the recommendations contained in this section. The latter part of this chapter discusses the development and choice of picture sets for multi- versus single-motive measurement. This section provides previously unpublished cue strength statistics for a single-motive picture set that "pulls" mainly for *n* Achievement.

Background of the PSE

The PSE is a research version of the Thematic Apperception Test (TAT; Morgan & Murray, 1935), and it is the most widely used tool for measuring implicit motives. It is based on an underlying assumption that needs can be inferred from imaginative material generated in response to sufficiently arousing pictorial, verbal, or textual cues. Accordingly, most nonclinical research on implicit motives use the PSE, which requires participants to write imaginative stories in response to ambiguous picture stimuli that depict people in various "everyday" situations; the imaginative story protocols are then analyzed for motive imagery using experimentally derived coding systems. Researchers have developed and used PSE-based coding systems for a variety of motives on a variety of materials, such as political speeches, diaries, and literary sources (Cramer, 1996; Smith, 1992; Winter, 1994).

Traditional notions of internal consistency are based on the idea that items (or, in the case of the PSE, picture cues) on a test measure related aspects of the same construct and the larger the interitem correlations, the more reliable a test is (Nunnally, 1978). Hence, each item on a trait inventory needs to be sufficiently correlated with other items on the inventory. Internal consistency estimates are suitable tools for evaluating self-report measures such as trait inventories and measures of self-attributed motives (such as Jackson's 1984 Personality Research Form) that tap into people's need to maintain a consistent self-concept. Questions about the typically lower internal consistency of the PSE (around .20 to .50) have been raised in early (Entwisle, 1972) as well as recent critiques (Lilienfeld, Wood, & Garb, 2000).

One reason for the typically low internal consistency coefficients for PSE motive measures is given by a theory about the dynamic and continuous nature of the motivational sequence. According to the dynamics of action theory (DOA; Atkinson & Birch, 1970), a motivational drive sets off a behavioral sequence that culminates in the fulfillment of the underlying need, and the fulfillment of the need acts to decrease the strength of the motivational drive. In other words, the sheer act of expressing a motive reduces its strength or intensity. This decrease in the strength of a motive tendency after that tendency has been expressed is referred to as the consummatory value of the activities/events (Atkinson & Birch, 1970).

Since each PSE cue is assumed to possess consummatory value—a subject's motivation is expressed in the form of motive-relevant imagery in each PSE story—we would expect the motive imagery of pictures that immediately follow motive expression to be decreased; having satisfied her motivational need by responding to one PSE cue, the subject reacts less strongly to the next picture and writes less motive-relevant imagery on the second picture. However, over time, the motivational drive eventually returns to its initial state, thus raising the consummatory value of pictures less immediate in time to the initial motive expression. This waxing and waning nature of the motivational sequence is reflected in the resulting irregularity in the amount of motive imagery in successive PSE stories. Hence, internal consistency estimates may not be suitable tools for assessing PSE motive measures that tap into a dynamic motivational process. Rather, it is the combined motives scores over the entire span of the PSE that should more accurately represent the expression of a person's motive.

However, Tuerlinckx, De Boeck, and Lens (2002) recently tested Atkinson and Birch's theory using models from item response theory and they found no evidence for a consummatory mechanism. Since Atkinson and his colleagues only tested the DOA theory using computer simulations (Atkinson, Bongort, & Price, 1977), there is a need for future studies to empirically test Atkinson and Birch's (1970) widely accepted conventional wisdom about the drive-reducing effect of PSE-measured motives.

Schultheiss and Pang (2007) also pointed out another reason that PSE measures have lower internal consistency. They refer to the issue of *motive extensity*, which is defined as the range of motivationally relevant situations and contexts that are depicted in a given battery of picture cues. There are many situations that could be typically associated with need satisfaction, and these situations are represented in different picture cue settings. For instance, although a courtroom and a boxing ring may be equally obvious settings for *n* Power displays, they arouse themes associated with different aspects of power manifestation (e.g., covert vs. overt, verbal vs. physical).

One important characteristic of motives is the variability of behaviors associated with them. Specifically, motives have no fixed repertoire of instrumental behaviors. Instead, motivated behaviors are very variable, depending on a variety of factors, such as what is required by the immediate situation to achieve the desired incentive, whether there are obstacles to reaching the goal, the intelligence and skills of the person, and the presence of other conflicting motives and desires. For instance, if a person is motivated by *n* Affiliation, she can achieve her goal of establishing friendly relations by doing any of a number of things. Perhaps the person might go to a party to increase the opportunities for being around people. Alternatively, she might stay at home to write letters to her old friends (McAdams & Constantian, 1983). Knowing that someone is affiliation motivated does not increase the likelihood of knowing whether or not the person will express their *n* Affiliation by going out to a party or by staying home to write letters.

This *behavioral variability* in motivated action manifests itself in the PSE partly in the *motive extensity* of PSE picture cues. PSE picture sets frequently depict people in a wide variety of situations. The characters in the picture cues can be seen as acting out various modes of motive consumption and motive expression (e.g., partying versus writing letters). Accordingly, a picture set designed to study *n* Achievement may depict individuals in competitive sporting situations as well as in isolated work environments.

Indeed, McClelland and his colleagues have reasoned that motive extensity in the PSE is an important factor in motive measurement, as motivational strength is not only reflected in the intensity of individual's responses to motivational incentives and cues, but also in the variability and range—the extensity—of cues that elicit a motivational response. According to McClelland (1987), people learn to associate naturally rewarding feelings with situations, events, or behavior that elicit such feelings. Consequently, the more motivated a person is, the greater the range of situations in which she will learn to associate with attaining the naturally pleasurable feeling. The issue of motive extensity has two implications for the internal consistency of the PSE.

First, a PSE measure that contains highly dissimilar pictures would have lower internal consistency but broader validity. Thus, lower internal consistency on the PSE may be partly due to the dissimilarity of different picture cues. A highly motivated person who has developed her motive only in a small range of situations will inject motive imagery unevenly across a set of highly dissimilar pictures. However, another equally highly motivated person who has a more extensive motive will respond to a wider variety of picture cues and will have higher interitem correlations. As Schultheiss and Pang (2007) suggest, there is a problem of bandwidth fidelity, which refers to the trade-off between highly specified, multidimensional, and highly variable assessment of personality constructs on one hand and more simplistic but reliable prediction on the other.

Second, the validity of the PSE can be increased if a researcher carefully chooses a PSE picture set that encompasses a sufficient variety of situations in which the motive can potentially be expressed. Encouragingly, Schultheiss, Liening, and Schad (2008) have recently studied test–retest reliability for handwritten and typed PSEs and found that motive scores show substantial ipsative stability. In other words, participants responded similarly to the same picture cue across testing occasions. The authors' findings corroborate the idea that although the PSE may not necessarily have high interpicture correlations, it still provides reliable and valid readings of motive levels, especially if pictures with similarly motivationally relevant thematic contents are being correlated with each other. This point of sampling a range of motivationally relevant settings to increase PSE extensity will be elaborated on later during the discussion about picture cue selection.

Guide for Using the PSE

Our goal in implementing the PSE methodology is to maximize the validity and reliability of the measure, as well as to minimize the sources of error in assessment. Essentially, we want to make sure that we are measuring the motive of interest, rather than any of its conceptual relatives or artifacts from various demand characteristics. Thus, the researcher should be extra careful to select appropriate picture cues and scoring systems, and to adopt standardized administration instructions and conditions in order to minimize any confounds.

Consequently, the following section provides a step-by-step guide to administering and scoring the PSE. Many of the main points have been covered in detail by Schultheiss and Pang (2007) and Smith (1992, 2000), so I will highlight the important issues here. While Schultheiss and Pang (2007) organized their guide to the PSE around key issues and major questions, such as "Which motives to assess?" and "Which pictures to use?," the step-by-step guide contained in this chapter is organized systematically by the major stages of measurement of pretest, test, posttest and scoring, and retest. Furthermore, while Schultheiss and Pang (2007) offer a greater depth of discussion for certain issues (e.g., on various types of coding systems and test–retest reliability), the range of topics covered here is wider and incorporates all the major points of Schultheiss and Pang's as well as some important points (e.g., regarding administration setting and pretesting of new pictures) that were not dealt with in that chapter.

In Table 5.1, the major standards (internal consistency, validity, and test–retest reliability) and stages of PSE measurement are cross-referenced with citations of relevant sources; the interested reader is referred to these external sources should more detail be desired than is covered in this chapter.

Table 5.1 Factors, Stages, and Standards of Measurement for the Picture Story Exercise (PSE)

Factors		Measurement Standard	Stage of Measurement	Selected References
Administration				
	– Mode of administration (verbal, written, typed)	V, TRR	PRE, T	Blankenship & Zoota, 1998; Schultheiss & Pang, 2007
	– Size of group (individual, group)	V,	PRE, T	Schultheiss & Brunstein, 2001; Schultheiss & Pang, 2007
	– Instructions	V, TRR	PRE, T, RT	Lundy, 1988; Murstein. 1965; Schultheiss & Pang, 2007; Winter & Stewart, 1977
	– Situational factors	V, TRR	PRE, T	Smith, Feld, & Franz, 1992; Veroff, 1992
	– Experimenter characteristics (gender, authority, formality)	V, TRR	PRE, T	Atkinson, 1958; Klinger, 1967; Smith, Feld, & Franz, 1992; Veroff, 1992
Participant characteristics				
	– Social context (culture, race, and gender)	V	PRE, T	Bellak, 1975; Murstein, 1972; Stewart & Chester, 1982
	– Degree of sample heterogeneity	V	PRE, T	Cramer, 1996
	– Recent life changes	V	T, RT	Koestner, Franz, & Hellman, 1991
Data processing and analysis				
	– Data entry format	IR	POST	Schultheiss & Pang, 2007
	– Word count correction	V	POST	Schultheiss & Pang, 2007
	– Selection of scoring scheme	V	SCORE	Schultheiss & Pang, 2007; Smith, 1992
	– Coder training	IR	SCORE	Schultheiss & Pang, 2007
	– Calculating interrater reliability	IR	SCORE	Meyer et al., 2002; Winter, 1994;

Table 5.1 (Continued)

Factors		Measurement Standard	Stage of Measurement	Selected References
Picture cues				
	– Ambiguity	V, IC, TRR	PRE, T	Smith, Feld, & Franz, 1992
	– Universality	V, IC, TRR	PRE, T	Smith, Feld, & Franz, 1992
	– Cue strength	V, IC, TRR	PRE, T	Smith, Feld, & Franz, 1992
	– Content/themes	V, IC, TRR	PRE, T	Langan-Fox & Grant, 2006; Pang & Schultheiss, 2005; Schultheiss & Brunstein, 2005
	– Number of pictures (fatigue, variability in scores, motives being measured)	IC, TRR	PRE, T	Reitman & Atkinson, 1958; Schultheiss & Pang, 2007
	– Picture position	IC	PRE, T	Schultheiss & Pang, 2007
	– Number of motives being measured	V, IC, TRR	PRE, T	Schultheiss & Pang, 2007
	– Gender depicted	V, IC	PRE, T	Worchel, Aaron, & Yates, 1990

Note. Test–retest reliability (TRR); interrater reliability (IR); internal consistency (IC); validity (V); pretesting (PRE); testing (T); retest (RT); posttest (POST); scoring (SCORE)

Pretest

During the pretest stage, the researcher should first be clear about the problem, hypotheses, and goals of the research. This conceptual step is important because it guides the selection of materials such as picture cues and scoring systems. It is also during the pretest stage that the researcher can collect pilot data for the development of new picture sets for motives that are not commonly studied or for which picture sets are not publicly available.

The researcher should also decide if the PSE is the most expedient method of data collection. Smith (2000) suggests that archival or naturally occurring materials such as personal documents, broadcasts, and email exchanges may sometimes be more informative than motive scores from a laboratory-administered PSE; the researcher who is trying to devise cues to measure a heretofore under-studied construct or to use with an unusual population may find that archival and naturally occurring materials provide more meaningful data because these offer greater ecological validity.

Once the researcher has decided to use the PSE, she needs to make a number of other additional decisions during the pretest stage, the main ones being the number, selection, pretesting, and order of presentation of picture cues.

Number of Pictures

Researchers should use picture sets of eight pictures or fewer because longer tests tend to decrease in validity as a result of the effects of fatigue (Reitman & Atkinson, 1958). However, Schultheiss and Pang (2007) have shown that variance of motive scores is inversely related to size of the test battery, so that motive score distributions of picture batteries with fewer than four pictures are considerably skewed to the left. Motive scores start to resemble a normal distribution once a five-picture battery is used. Hence, it is recommended that researchers use between five and eight pictures in a PSE.

Selecting Picture Cues

The selection of PSE cues is based on the principle that evocative images trigger motive-relevant emotions and cognitions. Accordingly, cue selection is a very important topic for valid PSE measurement because picture sets differ in their ability to elicit different motives, their suitability for measuring a single motive versus several motives at once, and in the range of motive-relevant settings that they depict. Among the cue characteristics that a researcher should consider while selecting pictures are cue strength, cue ambiguity, universality, relevance, and extensity.

Cue strength—sometimes referred to as stimulus pull—is the average amount of imagery for a particular motive that is elicited by a picture cue. While some pictures have good cue strength for only one motive, others are capable of eliciting imagery for more than one motive, and still other pictures may elicit very little imagery at all. In order to maximize the effectiveness of the PSE and obtain scores that contain adequate variance, researchers should select pictures that have sufficiently high cue strength for the motive(s) of interest.

Recently, there has been renewed research interest in discovering the cue strength characteristics of commonly used PSE picture cues (Langan-Fox & Grant, 2006; Pang and Schultheiss, 2005; Schultheiss and Brunstein, 2001) for measuring the Big Three motives of *n* Power, *n* Affiliation, and *n* Achievement at once. Table 5.2 presents commonly studied pictures that have been collected from previously published research (Smith, 1992;

Table 5.2 Means and Standard Deviations of Raw Motive Scores by Picture Cue and Country

Picture	*n* Power		*n* Achievement		*n* Affiliation	
	M	*SD*	*M*	*SD*	*M*	*SD*
Women in laboratory						
U.S.[a]	0.77	0.85	1.08	0.93	0.19	0.50
German[b]	0.80	0.84	0.66	0.77	0.19	0.48
Australian students[c]	1.32	1.60	1.66	2.53	0.18	0.63
Australian managers[d]	0.55	1.34	1.91	2.24	0.22	0.60
Ship captain						
U.S.[a]	1.01	0.88	0.14	0.47	0.21	0.53
German[b]	1.16	0.92	0.11	0.37	0.20	0.53
Australian students[c]	1.63	1.71	−0.70	1.01	0.33	0.96
Australian managers[d]	1.08	1.51	−0.88	0.51	0.32	0.84
Couple by river						
U.S.[a]	0.23	0.54	0.00	0.21	2.06	1.07
German[b]	0.43	0.72	0.03	0.17	1.84	1.05
Australian students[c]	0.72	1.26	−0.90	0.58	2.34	1.72
Trapeze artists						
U.S.[a]	0.70	0.79	0.76	0.83	0.49	0.80
German[b]	0.79	0.85	0.78	0.84	0.43	0.71
Australian students[c]	0.99	1.38	1.00	2.44	0.25	0.44
Australian managers[d]	0.51	1.05	0.73	2.18	0.54	1.00
Nightclub scene						
U.S.[a]	0.75	0.82	0.01	0.30	1.32	1.10
German[b]	0.86	0.83	0.09	0.31	1.29	1.08
Boxer						
U.S.[a]	0.79	0.90	1.14	1.06	0.17	0.51

(continued)

Table 5.2 (Continued)

Picture	n Power		n Achievement		n Affiliation	
	M	SD	M	SD	M	SD
Architect at desk						
German[b]	0.22	0.46	0.29	0.55	<u>1.16</u>	<u>0.84</u>
Australian students[c]	0.82	1.32	0.11	2.01	1.09	1.40
Bicycle race						
U.S.[e]	<u>0.95</u>	<u>0.95</u>	<u>1.65</u>	<u>1.08</u>	0.16	0.41
Woman and man arguing						
U.S.[e]	<u>1.70</u>	<u>0.94</u>	0.31	0.66	0.18	0.53
Hooligan attack						
U.S.[e]	<u>2.26</u>	<u>0.95</u>	0.01	0.14	0.15	0.43
Lacrosse duel						
U.S.[e]	0.69	0.84	<u>1.22</u>	<u>0.96</u>	0.16	0.50
Men on ship deck						
U.S.[f]	<u>1.82</u>	<u>1.26</u>	0.48	0.63	0.20	0.51
German[g]	<u>1.14</u>	<u>0.95</u>	0.47	0.73	0.29	0.63
Soldier						
German[g]	<u>0.94</u>	<u>1.01</u>	0.35	0.64	0.17	0.36
Soccer duel						
German[g]	<u>0.74</u>	<u>0.77</u>	<u>1.79</u>	<u>0.81</u>	0.07	0.27
Couple sitting opposite a woman						
U.S.[h]	<u>1.05</u>	<u>0.98</u>	0.40	0.79	<u>0.73</u>	<u>0.90</u>
Girlfriends in café with male approaching						
U.S.[h]	0.53	0.65	0.38	0.76	<u>1.62</u>	<u>1.43</u>
Man and woman with horses and dog						
Australian students[c]	0.61	1.15	−0.63	1.16	1.08	1.55
Conference group: seven men around a table						
Australian managers[d]	1.13	1.55	−0.59	1.12	0.68	1.09

Note. Underlined scores indicate that more than 50% of participants have responded with at least one instance of codable motive imagery to the picture cue. Motive imagery for the U.S. and German samples was scored using Winter's (1994) coding system for scoring motives in running text.

Motive imagery for the Australian samples was scored using McClelland, Atkinson, Clark, & Lowell's (1953) scoring manual for *n* Achievement (scores range from −1 to +11, and mean scores are based on a six-picture set for the student sample and a four-picture set for the manager sample), Heyns, Veroff, & Atkinson's (1958) scoring manual for *n* Affiliation (scores range from 0 to +7), and Winter's (1973) revised scoring manual for *n* Power (scores range from 0 to +11).

[a] From Pang & Schultheiss, 2007 (*n* = 323).
[b] From Schultheiss & Brunstein, 2001 (*n* = 428).
[c] From Langan-Fox & Grant, Study 1, 2006 (*n* = 334).
[d] From Langan-Fox & Grant, Study 2, 2006 (*n* = 213).
[e] From Wirth, Welsh, & Schultheiss, Study 2, 2006 (*n* = 109).
[f] From Schultheiss, Campbell, & McClelland, 1999 (*n* = 42; male participants only).
[g] From Schultheiss & Rohde, 2002 (*n* = 66; male participants only).
[h] From Schultheiss, Wirth, & Stanton, 2004 (*n* = 60).
All picture stimuli are available upon request from the author.

McClelland, 1975; McClelland & Steele, 1972) and their cue strength statistics, as studied by various researchers (e.g., Langan-Fox & Grant, 2006; Pang & Schultheiss, 2005; Schultheiss & Brunstein, 2001).

Generally, a picture cue is designated as having high pull for a motive when it elicits at least one codable image from at least 50% of the participant pool (c.f., Schultheiss & Brunstein, 2001). Researchers interested in measuring all three motives at once are advised to use the data represented in Table 5.2 by selecting pictures with moderately high to high pull for the motive(s) that they are interested in. For instance, as shown in Figure 5.1, *boxer, ship captain, trapeze artists, nightclub,* and *women in laboratory* all qualify as high-pull pictures for *n* Power. A researcher interested in developing a picture set solely for measuring *n* Power should include these five pictures in her picture set. However, if the researcher was interested in measuring only *n* Affiliation, she would use *nightclub* and *bridge* in addition to other pictures that show high to moderately high pull for *n* Affiliation.

Cue ambiguity refers to the ability of a picture to evoke multiple motives (see Smith, Feld, & Franz, 1992, and Murstein, 1972, for a broader discussion of cue ambiguity). Haber & Alpert (1958) suggested that researchers select pictures with low ambiguity, that is, pictures that clearly evoke a particular motive. This is because pictures that are more ambiguous also tend to have lower cue strength compared to less ambiguous pictures. Additionally, according to Haber and Alpert (1958), pictures with low ambiguity and high cue strength

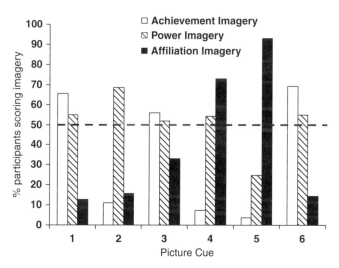

Figure 5.1 Percentage of participants scoring at least one motive image for each picture cue in a multimotive picture set.
Note. N = 323. Data from Pang & Schultheiss (2005). Pictures used in this picture set are: 1 = boxer; 2 = ship captain; 3 = trapeze artists; 4 = nightclub; 5 = bridge; 6 = women in laboratory.

tend to have greater test–retest reliability (r = .59) than pictures with high ambiguity and low cue strength (r = .36).

However, there are also good reasons to ensure that picture cues should have sufficient ambiguity, rather than be overpoweringly representative of a particular motive. First, cue ambiguity ensures an adequate range of scores, thus increasing the variance of the measure and its ability to discriminate between highly motivated and less-motivated participants. If a picture has too low cue ambiguity, then all participants would be prompted by the over-whelming cue strength into inserting certain motive imagery in their stories, resulting in a limited degree of variance in motive scores.

The second reason cue ambiguity is desirable is related to the indirect manner in which implicit motivational intents are expressed in PSE and other free-response assessment formats. Two studies by Clark and Sensibar (1955) are instructive: In the first study, which was conducted in a classroom setting, they showed slides of nude pinup girls to one group of male undergraduates and slides of landscaping and architecture to another group. The stories each of these groups wrote following exposure to the slides were then coded for man-ifest sexual imagery, which included explicit references to sexual acts such as fondling, kissing, and sexual intercourse. Surprisingly, the students exposed to the nude pinup pictures had significantly lower amounts of sexual imagery in their protocols than the students in the landscape condition.

However, when the same study was conducted at a fraternity party, Clark and Sensibar (1955) found different results. The male undergraduates who were shown pictures of nude pinups wrote significantly higher amounts of manifest sexual imagery than students at the same party who saw the landscape slides. Additionally, whether they belonged to the nude pinup or the landscape condi-tion, students at the party wrote significantly more explicit sexual imagery than the students in the classroom administration. Finally, the authors rescored all the protocols from the party and classroom administrations and found that the protocols of students in the nude pinup conditions who had both extremely high *and* extremely low manifest sexual imagery scores also included significantly higher amounts of sexual symbolism (e.g., round objects = breast; long object = penis) than students in either of the landscape-control conditions.

McClelland (1987) has interpreted Clark and Sensibar's study as indicating that some intents—such as sexual arousal—that are typically socially inappropriate cause more anxiety in some settings than in others. In those settings where sexual arousal does not cause anxiety (fraternity party), participants' sexual drives are expressed in both explicit sexual imagery and indirect sexual symbolism. However, in settings where sexual arousal causes anxiety (classroom), participants' sexual drives are expressed more covertly in metaphoric or symbolic imagery.

In addition to McClelland's interpretation, I would like to add another implication of Clark and Sensibar's (1955) findings. The more explicit a picture cue is (e.g., nude pinup girls) in referring to specific motivational intents, the more likely it is to lead to the defense mechanisms seen in Clark and Sensibar's (1955) study. Thus, it is important to vary the content of picture cues so as not to arouse suspicion. This is particularly relevant when one is assessing motives that are expected to arouse anxiety in populations. Hence, a researcher needs to select picture cues that elicit a sufficient amount of ambiguity—so as to provide enough variance in motive scores within a population—while also having a high to moderately high cue strength—so as to effectively evoke the motive(s) of interest.

Another important criterion for selecting picture cues is universality, which is the tendency of pictures to have similar motivational significance to almost all members of a population (Smith, Feld, & Franz, 1992). Universality contributes to the face validity of a picture cue—the picture should clearly evoke certain motivational themes in most members of the population, to the extent that the prototypical response will produce average amounts of motive imagery. By promoting a baseline level of motive imagery, universality allows researchers to more easily observe individual differences in motive tendencies from the variation of motive scores (Atkinson, 1958).

Relevance refers to the ability of pictures to reflect current concerns and experiences of participants. Since the principle behind PSE measurement is that participants will project their predominant wishes, desires, and motives onto the characters in the pictures, the contexts depicted in the picture cues should be representative of current experiences. For this reason, it may be advisable to update pictures that have become out of date with respect to features such as clothes and hairstyles. Additionally, it may not be advisable to use pictures showing characters that are significantly younger than participants, as these pictures may either elicit past recollections of scripted or actual events rather than participants' current motivations (c.f. McClelland et al., 1953).

Generally, pictures used should be representative of common situations in which motives of interest are aroused. For instance, to assess achievement motivation, one might include pictures of work, school, and other performance settings. Furthermore, as discussed earlier, a person's motive can be expressed in a variety of situations. To date, the *extensity* of a picture set has not been studied systematically; however, there have been recommendations by previous motivational researchers (e.g., Schultheiss & Pang, 2007; Smith, 1992) to select picture sets that represent a broad spectrum of motivationally relevant contexts, and situations that have a broader range of validity.

Pretesting New Pictures

Instead of using previously established picture sets (e.g., those mentioned here or contained in Smith, 1992), some researchers may wish to develop and pretest their own picture sets for measuring particular motives. Clearly, this enterprise is labor intensive and time consuming; however, researchers may choose to do so either because they would like to fine-tune pictures to suit particular situations or contexts, or because they are interested in studying some underresearched motives for which cue strength statistics have not previously been published.

During pretest, researchers should include, among new picture cues, commonly used pictures for which cue strength has previously been established, in order to provide a standard of comparison for convergent and divergent validity, and to provide a control in ensuring that the findings on cue strength of the new pictures are not due to some spurious artifacts of the experimental condition or some other extraneous factor.

Pretest pictures may come from a variety of media outlets, such as print and television advertisements, newspapers, and magazines, and even screenshots from films that are of sufficient resolution quality to be presented clearly. There are a number of pointers that the researcher can follow in identifying suitable pretest pictures:

1. Pictures included in the pretest battery should depict one or more persons engaging in or preparing to engage in instrumental behavior related to the motive. The researcher should also apply the criteria of cue strength, ambiguity, universality, relevance, and extensity during the selection of cues for pretesting.

2. Conduct thematic searches for usable pictures by considering prevailing theory about the motive or construct in question. For instance, when looking for cues for the n Achievement picture set described in the latter part of this chapter, I typed in search terms such as "workplace," "competition," "achieve," and "excellence" into an Internet search engine. These search terms were arrived at after careful perusal of the available literature on achievement motivation and after prolonged reflection of the contexts and situations through which the achievement-motivated process, as described in *The Achievement Motive* (McClelland, Atkinson, Clark, & Lowell, 1953), is expressed.

3. To increase motive extensity, broaden the pretest picture set to include pictures that depict as many motive-relevant behaviors and situations as possible. For instance, pictures for which cue strength statistics have previously been published and that appear to arouse related motives can be included in pretest battery. Thus, for the n Achievement picture set, I included in the pretest battery pictures that were used by Heckhausen (1963) to develop his scoring system for hope of success and fear of failure motivation. Additionally, include pictures that depict motive-relevant contexts that may not have been represented in commonly available picture cues. For instance, some pictures in the n Achievement pretest battery also depicted individuals in competitive group sporting event settings, such as skating and soccer.

4. Favor contemporary sources of pictures over dated ones and contexts that are familiar but not so well known as to evoke scripted responses.

Additionally, pictures that showcase famous events and/or persons should not be used, since there is the danger that participants will inject historical, biographical, or general knowledge about these people and events into their stories rather than writing an imaginative account. For instance, I once pretested a picture with a distinguished-looking lady in Victorian attire holding a test tube. This picture cue was quickly excluded from future testing because nearly every story written in response to it made some reference to Marie Curie and radiation poisoning.

5. In order to increase the generalizability of the pictures across different participant samples (e.g., across different genders, age groups, races, social strata, etc.), select pictures that are either sufficiently light on detail as to be relatively ambiguous, or that do not depict recognizably extreme samples (e.g., characters in the pictures are neither very young nor very old).

The pretest administration procedure and conditions should be as similar to the main testing conditions as possible. In other words, researchers should try to exert minimum social, instructional, and time pressure on participants. Similarly, although there may eventually be a sizeable number of pictures included in the pretest battery, the number of picture cues presented to each participant in pretest conditions should be limited to the number that would be presented to each participant in actual test conditions (i.e., between 5 and 8). Although this means that each participant in the pretest may not view all the pictures that are being pretested, it is preferable to compromising the validity of data due to the effects of fatigue. The number of participants required in a pretest is small (about 20–30 per cue).

Once protocols from the pretested pictures have been collected and coded using the same coding system that will be used in the actual study, the researcher should select picture cues while bearing in mind the principles of ambiguity, cue strength, universality, relevance, and test extensity. For single-motive measurement, the main issue is making sure that there is sufficient pull for the motive in question. Thus, pictures selected for single-motive measurement should demonstrate high cue strength for the motive of interest. However, for multimotive measurement, the balance between ambiguity and cue strength is more important. Picture cues selected for multimotive picture sets will naturally have greater cue ambiguity, which brings down cue strength. For this reason, it is advisable when administering a multimotive picture set to either choose a picture set containing pictures that all possess moderate to high cue strength for several motives, or to alternate picture cues of high cue strength for one motive with picture cues of high cue strength for another motive.

Picture Order and Placement

Pang and Schultheiss (2005) have explored the influence of picture position on motive scores and found that varying a picture's position in a sequence of pictures has little effect on total amounts of n Power, n Affiliation, and n Achievement imagery obtained for that picture cue. In general, picture order effects are minimal, especially if picture order can be randomized across participants. However, if picture serial position cannot be randomized, Smith, Feld, and Franz (1992) recommend that pictures with low and high pull for a given motive should be alternated within a battery of pictures. Their recommendation is based on the rationale that a picture cue with high cue strength will decrease the consummatory value of subsequent picture cues. The alternating of high- with low-pull pictures mimics the waxing and waning motivational process and increases overall validity of the instrument. In the same way, pictures with similar thematic contexts (e.g., showing competitive situations; showing potential disruption of familial relations) should be alternated with pictures with dissimilar contexts.

Test

During the test stage, care must be taken to ensure that all PSE administration conditions are standardized. If possible, coders can start to be trained in the coding system of choice since the coders will require sufficient time to achieve satisfactory intercoder agreement with practice or pilot materials, and—in the case of multiple coders—with each other. Among the various administration conditions that the researcher should pay attention to, are the setting and experimenter characteristics, mode of administration (group vs. individual; handwritten versus typed), instructions, and participant characteristics.

Administration Setting

The main aim of PSE administration is to exert as little pressure as possible on participants. For this reason, situational factors such as locality, mood of surrounding atmosphere, experimenters, instructions, and timing and tone of the experiment should be standardized as much as possible and presented in a way that does not exert too much social or time pressure on participants. Hence, experimenters should be as inconspicuous as possible, avoid referring to the PSE as a "test," and avoid openly using a stopwatch or any kind of time-tracking device (c.f. Lundy, 1988; Murstein, 1965).

Because of the assumed sensitivity of motives to situational incentives, the PSE should be administered before other components of the experiment, that is, mood induction or any other experimental manipulation (Lundy, 1988; Veroff, 1992).

The PSE can be administered individually or in small groups of fewer than eight participants (c.f., Schultheiss & Brunstein, 2001). Although previous research suggests that both individual and group testing produce similar motive scores (Lindzey & Heinemann, 1955), Schultheiss and Brunstein

(2001) showed that groups larger than eight are not optimal because the presence of others starts to become more obvious to the participant and may prompt social evaluative and/or affiliative concerns. While limiting group size makes it easier to control for potential interactions (either between participants or between the experimenter and participants) that may have unintended motive-arousing effects, individual testing is also not desirable because it is difficult to establish the same testing situation and rapport between the participant and the experimenter for all participants.

One way out of this dilemma is to use personal computers for the presentation of PSE instructions and picture stimuli and the recording of responses. Blankenship and Zoota (1998) utilized computerized administration and compared typed responses with handwritten ones. They found no significant differences in motive imagery between the two data collection formats. Similar findings were also reported by Schultheiss, Liening, and Schad (2008), who recommended the use of computer-based PSE administration for future research on implicit motives. Where computer administration is not possible, experimenter-administered PSE sessions can be conducted quite effectively—based on personal experience and research convention, sessions with 4–8 participants allows the experimenter to interact with participants in a way that avoids most of the problems posed by too large or too small groups.

Instructions

Lundy (1988) showed the importance of instructions in ensuring that an administration setting has neutral connotations for participants. When instructions provided an ego threat, emphasized that the TAT was a personality measure, or stressed the importance of following rules and instructions carefully, resulting motive scores failed to correlate with criterion measures. Thus, care must be taken to ensure that instructions are as neutral and nonthreatening as possible because nonneutral instructions elicit less valid motive scores.

The following instructions, adapted from Schultheiss and Pang (2007), have been used successfully in numerous studies. They are standard instructions that have been compiled from various sources (Atkinson, 1958; Lundy, 1988; Smith, 1992) and may either be spoken by an experimenter, printed on an instruction page and distributed to each participant, or displayed on a computer screen:

PICTURE STORY EXERCISE
In the Picture Story Exercise, your task is to write a complete story about each of a series of [number of] pictures—an imaginative story with a beginning, a middle, and an end. Try to portray who the people in each picture are, what they are feeling,

thinking, and wishing for. Try to tell what led to the situation depicted in each picture and how everything will turn out in the end.

On your desk are [number of pictures] sheets of paper for you to write your stories on. They are labeled PSE 1 through PSE [number of pictures] . . . In the upper left hand corner of each writing sheet there are some guiding questions— these . . . are only guides to writing your story. You do not need to answer them specifically.

Each picture will be presented for 10 seconds. After that, please write whatever story that comes to mind. Don't worry about grammar, spelling, or punctuation— they are of no concern here. You will have about 5 minutes for each story. I will tell you when there are 20 seconds remaining and when it is time to move on to the next picture.

The guiding questions referred to in the above instructions are printed at the top left hand corner of every writing page (c.f. Schultheiss & Pang, 2007):

What is happening? Who are the people?
What happened before?
What are the people thinking about and feeling?
What do they want?
What will happen next?

In a typical PSE administration, after participants have read or been given the abovementioned general instructions, they are allowed to view each PSE picture for between 10–15 seconds, after which they are prompted to start writing. Participants should not be allowed to refer back to the picture after they have started writing because constant reference encourages stories that contain purely descriptive elements of a picture rather than imaginative material. Generally, the writing time allocated to each picture is 5 minutes— participants are alerted when they have about 20–30 seconds remaining and then asked to move on to the next picture at the end of 5 minutes. If researchers wish to test more pictures within the same overall time frame, writing time can be shortened to 4 minutes per picture without dramatically sacrificing the resulting amount of codable material. Additionally, Schultheiss, Liening, and Schad (2008) found that people generally produce about 30% more material when typing their responses, so writing time per story in computer administrations can be reduced to 4 minutes without substantially compromising amount of codable data.

Blankenship and Zoota (1998) recommend that researchers should not set a time limit during individual computer administration, since participants vary in their typing abilities; however, in group settings, researchers may find it easier to standardize administration conditions if they set a time limit, even for computer administrations. In experimenter-administered studies, the experimenter can monitor and be sensitive to the writing speed of all participants in the group, perhaps encouraging the group to move on to the next picture, sometimes even before the allotted time of 5 minutes is up, if all participants have clearly finished writing.

For computer administrations, researchers may use a detectable but low-key message to prompt participants to move on to the next phase in the PSE. For instance, Schultheiss and Pang (2007) recommend pairing a blinking message such as "Please finish your story and press the [previously specified] key to move on to the next picture" with a short beep every 10 seconds in order to remind participants to move on to the next picture. Another pre-caution that should be taken during computer administrations is to program the software to allow participants to move on to the next picture only after enough time (e.g., 4 min) has elapsed for them to produce enough story material.

Participant Gender Considerations

Prior research has shown that different samples are differentially responsive to different picture cues (e.g., Bellak, 1975). Accordingly, researchers have been interested in whether the validity of the PSE can be increased by tailoring it to the population of interest. For instance, researchers typically use either gender-balanced picture sets or different pictures for males and females (Smith, Feld, & Franz, 1992).

Previous research studying whether different PSE pictures pull for different stories as a function of the participant's sex has confounded participant sex with sex of persons depicted in the picture cue (Worchel, Aaron, & Yates, 1990). Stewart and Chester (1982), in their comprehensive review of research on the question of sex differences in PSE stories, concluded that research conducted over the 25 years that they surveyed was inconclusive about gender differences in n Affiliation. Chusmir (1983, 1985) conducted a study in which male and female subjects were given a picture set that was balanced for sex. The results indicated that sex of the pictures had no significant main or interaction effects for scores on n Achievement or n Power, although cues that depicted female characters produced higher n Affiliation scores than cues that depicted male characters, and this effect was greater for women than for men. Some recent work has either found no significant gender differences for n Achievement, n Power, or n Affiliation (e.g., Langan-Fox & Grant, 2006; Tuerlinckx, De Boeck, & Lens, 2002) or significantly higher n Affiliation scores in women's protocols (Pang & Schultheiss, 2005; Schultheiss & Brunstein, 2001). The pattern of findings suggests that participant and picture gender may affect, if anything, n Affiliation scores, albeit not consistently so. Thus, although women generally write more than men do and their affiliation scores are slightly higher (Pang & Schultheiss, 2005; Schultheiss & Brunstein, 2001), no other motive differences exist between men and women.

Posttest

During the posttest stage, identifying information should be removed from protocols before they are coded. Additionally, coders should score material only after having obtained sufficient interrater reliability with practice materials of the chosen scoring system, and they should at minimum be blind to the study conditions in which participants are in, if not to the study hypotheses. Blind coding reduces coder biases, which may compromise validity.

Other major considerations during the posttest stage have to do with processing of protocols to prepare for coding, the selection of a suitable coding system and training coders to the selected system, and the calculation and reporting of interrater reliability.

Protocol Transcription and Processing

Ideally, handwritten entries should be transcribed in order to increase accuracy of coding and ease of data storage and sharing. If the protocols cannot be transcribed, then coders should make their markings on photocopies rather than originals. This precaution of preserving the originals allows future reanalyses or recoding without the danger of leaving coding marks that will bias future coders.

In preparation for scoring, all identifying information about the participant and experimental condition should be removed from the protocols, in order to preserve the participant's anonymity as well as to prevent the "halo effect," which happens when the coder may have formed impressions about the participant during the process of scoring that influence the future scoring of subsequent, ambiguous responses. In order to prevent the halo effect, the coder may wish to score stories randomly either within or across participants. However, I would recommend against following Smith, Feld, and Franz's (1992) suggestion that the coder score all stories for one cue before moving on to all stories for another cue, as my personal experience is that this strategy increases the likelihood of *scorer drift*, which is the tendency of forming implicit rules-of-thumb after continuously scoring many stories with similar content. Scorer drift is minimized by scoring stories by participant instead of by cue, particularly if picture cue sequence is randomized within participants.

At this point, it may be necessary to drop certain participants who either display low verbal fluency or whose stories clearly reflect a lack of cooperation. Specifically, stories with fewer than 30 words have been found to be unscorable and should thus be excluded (c.f. Walker & Atkinson, 1958). Additionally, through an initial reading of the protocols and experiment logs, it may become obvious to the coder when a participant has clearly misunderstood the task, or is uncooperative. For instance, an uncooperative subject might intentionally include rampant verbal insults, violent or facetious imagery, or nonsensical storylines, or they may repeatedly and explicitly state their disdain for the story writing task. These uncooperative participants should be dropped from coding and further analyses. However, if numerous participants in a sample show lack of cooperation, the researcher should investigate whether there was some problem with the data collection procedures (e.g., a disturbing public event, an overly directive experimenter) and whether the entire group's data should be discarded.

Coding Systems

There are numerous content coding systems available to the interested researcher. The most commonly used coding systems are for n Achievement, n Affiliation, n Intimacy, and n Power. These coding systems are summarized in more detail in Schultheiss and Pang (2007), and their full versions are compiled in Smith (1992).

Briefly, these coding systems share two common traits. First, all of these systems were constructed through the examination of differences in story themes in experimentally manipulated or naturally occurring groups that differ in degrees in strength of a given motive. Second, the subcategories in these systems all follow a general framework for a hypothetical sequence of motivated behavior. Specifically, the motivated behavioral sequence is initiated when the person or persons experiences a *need* and then engages in goal-directed *instrumental activity* in order to fulfill this need. This instrumental behavior could result in either *positive or negative affect* as well as *positive or negative goal anticipation*, depending on either successful or unsuccessful goal progress. A scoring decision is first made for the absence or presence of motive-relevant imagery before moving on to score subcategories; typically, one point is awarded for the presence of each category or subcategory and each category or subcategory can only be scored once per story.

For instance, in the n Achievement scoring system (McClelland, Atkinson, Clark, & Lowell, 1953), stories are scored for achievement-related imagery if there is a mention of *competition with a standard of excellence*. Having scored presence of achievement-related imagery, the coder then goes on to score for subcategories of *need, instrumental activity, positive and negative anticipatory goal states, blocks to goal progress, positive or negative affect, achievement thema* (a weighting category given when the achievement imagery is the central theme of the story).

Similarly, in the n Affiliation scoring system (Heyns, Veroff, & Atkinson, 1958), n Affiliation–related imagery is scored whenever there is concern for establishing, maintaining, or restoring positive relations with others. Once the n Affiliation imagery is scored, the coder goes on to look for subcategories that are similar to those for n Achievement, for example, *need, instrumental activity*, and so forth.

In the *n* Intimacy scoring system (McAdams, 1980), the coder first decides if there is *n* Intimacy–related imagery by looking out for either dialogue or any verbal or nonverbal exchange between story characters. After scoring for the presence of *n* Intimacy imagery, subcategories such as *psychological growth and coping* and *time- or space-transcending quality of a relationship* can be scored.

In the *n* Power scoring system (Winter, 1973), the coder scores *n* Power–related imagery whenever a story character is concerned about having an impact on other people. Once *n* Power content is identified, then subcategories such as *prestige of actor* and *stated need for power* can be scored.

Finally, Winter's (1994) *Manual for Scoring Motive Imagery in Running Text* distills the four coding systems described above into its major coding categories only. Winter's (1994) integrated system is popular with researchers because it is an abbreviated version and hence less time consuming to learn and to use. The integrated system also combines *n* Affiliation and *n* Intimacy into a single conjoint category because of the presumed theoretical overlap between the two concepts (see Chapter 3 "The Duality of Affiliative Motivation").

When selecting a coding system, the researcher should consider the complexity and the conceptual background of the system. Some systems are similar conceptually but may differ in complexity (e.g., original *n* Achievement system and the *n* Achievement subsystem of the Winter system for running text). There will be a trade-off between complexity and construct validity on one hand and interrater reliability on the other. The less complicated system will be easier to learn and achieve greater levels of interrater reliability, but the more complicated system will include a more comprehensive and differentiated representation of the construct.

Coder Training

Before coding any of the study materials, the coder needs to spend sufficient time reading the coding definitions and categories associated with each coding system. Practice materials consisting of sample protocols and "expert" coding answer keys are usually provided with each coding manual. The amount of practice required depends on the size and complexity of the coding system. Generally, novice coders should undergo at least 12 hours of scoring practice material before moving on to scoring any PSE protocols (c.f. Smith, Feld, & Franz, 1992). In the event that coders fail to achieve at least 85% agreement with coding materials, even though they have completed all available practice materials in the coding manual, they should reread the coding manual carefully and rescore practice materials (restarting with the earliest practice stories) until the 85% criterion is reached.

An efficient way of improving accuracy of coding is to encourage coders to construct a "crib" sheet during training, to which each coder should refer liberally during the actual coding stage. This document—preferably not more than two pages long to maintain ease of reference—represents a condensation of the coding system and contains the main points, definitions, and descriptions of each coding category, as well as exceptions, examples, and other important coding conventions that the coder has discovered from experience. By referring liberally to this customized crib sheet during coding, the coder will find it easier to remain faithful to coding categories and thus minimize scorer drift.

Coding

It is very important to make coding decisions based on information available in the data only, and not from inference. It is equally important that the coder should be able to justify every coding decision by noting which coding category an image falls under; an image that does not fall into any coding category should not be scored, no matter how obvious a manifestation of the motive it may seem to the coder. It is recommended that coders err on the side of caution and refrain from scoring any imagery that is marginal. When coding, a useful maxim is, "When in doubt, leave it out."

Another method for reducing coding errors is to enter motive scores at as fine-grained a level as possible. Specifically, reliability is improved when motive scores are entered at the subcategory level rather than the category level because coders are forced to refer explicitly to each subcategory when making coding decisions. Thus, for the *n* Achievement coding system, coders should enter scores for *need*, *instrumental activity*, *goal State*, and so on.

Once motive scores are entered, researchers should check for outliers, examine score distributions to total scores for each motive, and make adjustments using statistical transformations to correct any scores that do not conform to a normal distribution.

If motive scores correlate with protocol length, they should be subjected to word count correction before being used together with other variables in data analysis. There are two ways of correcting for word count. A simple method is to multiply the total motive score by 1,000 and then divide the result by the total word count for each participant. The resulting score can be easily interpreted as motive images per 1,000 words. While image per 1,000 words is readily interpretable and allows for easy between-sample comparisons, this correction method sometimes creates artifacts because the resulting motive scores are not necessarily 0-correlated with word count. Thus, researchers who use this method should always check again for the variance overlap between corrected motive scores and total word count. Another commonly used word count correction method is to residualize motive scores for word count and use the resulting residuals in subsequent analyses. However, while this method is effective at removing the influence of verbal fluency on motive scores, the residualized motives scores are not as easily interpreted and will not be directly comparable between different samples and studies.

If there is more than one coder, an adequate degree of agreement (at least 85%) must be obtained between the coders before scoring of raw data can commence. Coders should score stories from a pilot study or, in lieu of that, from a small subset of stories from the actual study in order to establish interrater agreement before going on to score stories from the rest of the respondents. This is because there are some coding conventions that may be idiosyncratic to each study and that have to be agreed through discussion between the coders. Coding discrepancies should be resolved through consensus, in the view of establishing coding guidelines that are specific to the idiosyncrasies of the particular participant sample but that are still consistent with the coding categories of the scoring manual. Once coders have established the requisite 85% reliability with each other, however, they should score the remaining protocols independently, without discussion or collaboration.

Typically, most participants produce stories around 100 words in length, and an experienced coder will need 2–5 min to score a PSE story; hence a typical study with six-picture protocols from 100 participants will take between 20 and 50 hours to code (with additional time needed to review the scores and to enter scores into the data spreadsheet).

Interrater Reliability Reporting

In published work, an index of interrater agreement between two or more independent coders should be reported. There are a number of methods to determine interrater reliability: Spearman's rank correlation, index of concordance, and the intraclass correlation coefficient. Specifically, the index of concordance between two coders, A and B, is calculated by using the following formula:

$$(2 \times \text{agreements on motive imagery})/(\text{total motive imagery score for coder A} + \text{total motive imagery score for coder B}).$$

The intraclass correlation coefficient (ICC) is a chance-corrected reliability coefficient for continuous data that is equivalent to kappa under appropriate conditions (Meyer et al., 2002). The one-way random effects ICC is especially desirable as a measure of interrater reliability because it calculates correlations between observations that do not have an obvious order (i.e., who is "rater 1" and "rater 2" is irrelevant). The one-way random effects ICC is calculated by the following formula:

$$[\text{MS (between coder)} - \text{MS (within coders)}]/[\text{MS (between coders)} + \text{MS (within coders)}].$$

Retest

As previously noted, if a researcher is interested in stability and change in motive scores, a second PSE will be administered to participants in the retest stage. The retest stage is largely similar to the test stage with the exception of a slight modification in the instructions to participants should the same picture cues be used in subsequent sessions. As with the test stage, administration conditions should be neutral and standardized so as to minimize the influence of demand characteristics.

Researchers have previously recommended some strategies for modifying retest instructions so as to improve test–retest reliability (Reumann, 1982; Winter & Stewart, 1977). Winter and Stewart (1977) found that test–retest reliability coefficients for *n* Power after one week were relatively high when participants were either given explicit instruction to write the same story that they had at the previous testing ($r = .61$) or when they were told not to worry about the degree of similarity between the two sets of stories ($r = .58$). In contrast, participants asked to write a different story in the second testing session had significantly lower test–retest reliability coefficients of $.27$.

The authors concluded that during retesting, participants feel the pressure to be original in their storytelling; when instruction is given to ignore the similarity between their stories in both sessions, test–retest reliability increased. For this reason, researchers have since recommended that retest instructions should include a statement that assures participants that they are not expected to produce stories that are different from those in a previous PSE testing session (Schultheiss & Pang, 2007):

> You may remember seeing some of these pictures before. If you do, feel free to react to them as you did before, or differently, depending on how you feel now. In other words, tell the story the picture makes you think of now, whether or not it is the same as the one you told last time.

Additionally, in a meta-analysis of published and unpublished data from studies employing empirically derived coding systems and standardized PSE administration conditions, Schultheiss and Pang (2007) showed that average motive stability coefficients are $.71$ for a 1-day retest interval, remain fairly high at $.52$ for a 1-month interval, and drop to $.25$ if the retest interval is extended to 10 years. These levels of retest stability are adequate over time and show a rate of decrease that is similar to that found for self-report trait measures (e.g., Schuerger, Zarrella, & Hotz, 1989).

Introducing an n Achievement Picture Set

Using the abovementioned procedures for pretesting new picture cues, I pre-tested a set of 11 picture cues selected specially for measuring *n* Achievement in three different samples (total $\underline{N}$ = 81) of American college-aged students. Of these pictures, *director*, *man-at-desk*, and *workers* were obtained from Heckhausen (1963), *women in laboratory* is a well-used picture that was originally used by McClelland and his associates in developing practice sets for their scoring system (c.f., Smith & Franz, 1992), and the other pictures come from numerous print and media searches. All the pictures were scored for n Power, n Affiliation, and n Achievement using Winter's (1994) manual for scoring motive imagery in running text. Table 5.3 presents average motive scores for all three motives, organized by picture cue.

As shown in Figure 5.2, six pictures—*women in laboratory, skaters, pianist, footballers (soccer duel), chemist,* and *gymnast*—with low cue ambiguity and moderately high to high cue strength were eventually chosen to become part of this n Achievement picture set. These six pictures had high pull for n Achievement, with the percentage of participants having at least one instance of n Achievement imagery per story ranging from 54% to over 90%. Additionally, in each of these six pictures, n Achievement scores were higher than compared to the other two motives.

While cue strength relates to the intensity of the motive evoked by a picture, picture set extensity relates to the ability of a picture set to depict different motive-relevant situations. The six pictures in the n Achievement picture set illustrate motive-relevant behavior in at least three distinct contexts: in competition, at work, and during sports and leisure, thus demonstrating the picture set's degree of motive extensity.

Table 5.3   Means and Standard Deviations of Motive Scores by Picture Cue

Picture	n Power		n Achievement		n Affiliation	
	M	SD	M	SD	M	SD
Director[a]	0.36	0.60	0.57	0.74	0.04	0.20
Gymnast	0.39	0.57	1.82	1.34	0.04	0.12
Mountain climber	0.11	0.32	0.48	0.69	0.46	0.66
Soccer duel	0.41	0.63	1.56	1.02	0.24	0.75
Man-at-desk[a]	0.25	0.59	0.29	0.53	0.18	0.39
Pianist	0.46	0.67	0.69	0.70	0.37	0.60
Auto mechanics	0.33	0.61	0.54	0.82	0.46	0.84
Workers[b]	0.33	0.64	0.30	0.57	0.41	0.60
Skaters	0.22	0.50	1.74	0.87	0.48	0.80
Women in laboratory[b]	0.57	0.86	0.69	0.72	0.31	0.58
Chemist	0.22	0.50	0.76	0.81	0.30	0.58

Note. N = 81. Underlined motive scores indicate that more than 50% of participants have responded with at least one instance of codable motive imagery to the picture cue.
[a] From Heckhausen, 1963.
[b] From Smith, 1992.
All picture stimuli are available upon request from the author.

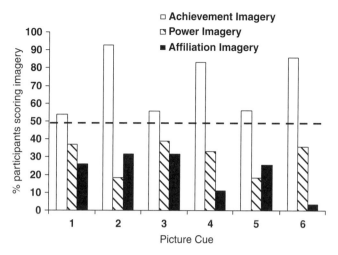

Figure 5.2 Percentage of participants scoring at least one motive image for each picture cue in a single-motive picture set.
Note. N = 81. Pictures used in this picture set are: 1 = women in laboratory; 2 = skaters; 3 = pianist; 4 = soccer duel; 5 = chemist; 6 = gymnast.

Summary

This step-by-step guide offers a systematic description of different aspects of preparing, administering, scoring, and processing PSE data. Some important points such as picture set extensity and administration conditions have been highlighted because these elements are easily standardized, but if they are not standardized, they can greatly affect the reliability and validity of the data. By following this guide, the interested researcher should be able to successfully carry out PSE-based motivational research. Additionally, this chapter provides recommendations for developing motive-specific picture sets and gives *n* Achievement, *n* Power, and *n* Affiliation cue strength statistics for numerous commonly used picture cues as well as cue strength statistics for a dedicated *n* Achievement picture set.

The reader may wonder whether it is worth it to undergo so much preparation and careful handling to administer the PSE. As Veroff (1992) argues, the PSE enables us to have richer data to study how different life experiences affect motivational striving in different ways. Also, the conceptual motivational process folded into the measure combined with the coherent storyline of PSE protocols ensures that we can test general propositions about the nature of motives, especially how motives are resolved over the life span and immediate time frame. By means of content analysis, large amounts of qualitative information can be reduced to smaller and more manageable forms of representation of quantitative categories, frequencies, and ratings. Finally, as McClelland et al. (1989) have shown, PSE and other related measures are capable of assessing implicit motivation into which self-report measures are unable to tap.

Moreover, as recent empirical work reviewed in this chapter has shown, it is possible to improve the reliability and validity of the instrument by reducing errors in data collection, ensuring adequate scorer training, developing standardized and neutral experimental conditions, and creating new picture cues that efficiently tap into the motive(s) of interest. Nonetheless, more research is needed to investigate other important issues. Some ideas for future work include: producing validation of picture sets by testing the ability of motive scores derived from the sets to predict motive-relevant behavior; embarking on more systematic investigations of the gender difference issue as well as the issue of participant gender–cue gender interactions; and customizing the PSE method to investigate more and other motives (e.g., sex, hunger).

The PSE is a complex instrument to learn and to use. However, based on personal experience and review of recent literature, steep learning curves have not prevented the discovery of meaningful findings. Given the significant advantages of using the PSE, our goal for using this rich instrument is to maximize sources of validity and minimize any sources of error. It is hoped that this chapter has contributed to the effort for better measurement of implicit motives and that researchers will continue to develop and refine the instrument toward this cause.

Author Note

All picture stimuli described in this chapter are available on request from the author. Correspondence concerning this chapter should be addressed to Joyce S. Pang, Division of Psychology, Nanyang Technological University, Singapore 639798, or sent by e-mail to joycepang@ntu.edu.sg.

References

Atkinson, J. W. (1958). *Motives in fantasy, action, and society: A method of assessment and study.* Oxford, England: Van Nostrand.

Atkinson, J. W., & Birch, D. (1970). *The dynamics of action.* New York: Wiley.

Atkinson, J. W., Bongort, K., & Price, L. H. (1977). Explorations using computer simulation to comprehend thematic apperceptive measurement of motivation. *Motivation and Emotion, 1,* 1–27.

Bellak, L. (1975). *The Thematic Apperception Test, the Children's Apperception Test and the Senior Apperception Technique in clinical use.* New York: Grune & Stratton.

Blankenship, V., & Zoota, A. L. (1998). Comparing power imagery in TATs written by hand or on the computer. *Behavior Research Methods, Instruments & Computers, 30(3),* 441–448.

Chusmir, L. H. (1983). Male-oriented vs. balanced-as-to-sex thematic apperception tests. *Journal of Personality Assessment, 47*, 29–35.

Chusmir, L. H. (1985). Motivation of managers: Is gender a factor? *Psychology of Women Quarterly, 9*, 153–159.

Clark, R. A., & Sensibar, M. R. (1955). The relationship between symbolic and manifest projections of sexuality with some incidental correlates. *The Journal of Abnormal and Social Psychology, 50*, 327–334.

Cramer, P. (1996). *Storytelling, narrative, and the Thematic Apperception Test.* New York: Guilford Publications.

Entwisle, D. R. (1972). To dispel fantasies about fantasy-based measures of achievement motivation. *Psychological Bulletin, 77*, 377–391.

Haber, R. N., & Alpert, R. (1958). The role of situation and picture cues in projective measurement of the achievement motive. In J. W. Atkinson (Ed.), *Motives in fantasy, action, and society* (pp. 644–663). New York: Van Nostrand.

Heckhausen, H. (1963). *Hoffnung und Furcht in der Leistungsmotivation [Hope and fear components of achievement motivation]* Meisenheim am Glam, Germany: Anton Hain.

Heyns, R. W., Veroff, J., & Atkinson, J. W. (1958). A scoring manual for the affiliation motive. In J. W. Atkinson (Ed.), *Motives in fantasy, action, and society* (pp. 205–218). Princeton, NJ: Van Nostrand.

Jackson, D. N. (1984). Personality Research Form (3rd ed.). Port Huron, Saginaw, MI: Sigma Assessment Systems, Inc.

Koestner, R., & McClelland, D. C. (1992). The affiliation motive. In C. P. Smith (Ed.), *Motivation and personality: Handbook of thematic content analysis* (pp. 205–210). New York: Cambridge University Press.

Langan-Fox, J., & Grant, S. (2006). The Thematic Apperception Test: Toward a standard measure of the Big Three motives. *Journal of Personality Assessment, 87*(3), 277–291.

Lilienfeld, S. O., Wood, J. M., & Garb, H. N. (2000). The scientific status of projective techniques. *Psychological Science in the Public Interest, 1*(2), 27–66.

Lindzey, G., & Heinemann, S. H. (1955). Thematic Apperception Test: Individual and group administration. *Journal of Personality and Social Psychology, 24*, 34–55.

Lundy, A. (1988). Instructional set and Thematic Apperception Test validity. *Journal of Personality Assessment, 52*, 309–320.

McAdams, D. P. (1980). A thematic coding system for the intimacy motive. *Journal of Research in Personality, 14*(4), 413–443.

McAdams, D. P., & Constantian, C. A. (1983). Intimacy and affiliation motives in daily living: An experience sampling analysis. *Journal of Personality and Social Psychology, 45*(4), 851–861.

McClelland, D. C. (1975). *Power: The inner experience.* New York: Irvington.

McClelland, D. C. (1987). *Human motivation.* New York: Cambridge University Press.

McClelland, D. C., Atkinson, J. W., Clark, R. A., & Lowell, E. L. (1953). *The achievement motive.* East Norwalk, CT: Appleton-Century-Crofts.

McClelland, D. C., Koestner, R., & Weinberger, J. (1989). How do self-attributed and implicit motives differ? *Psychological Review, 96*(4), 690–702.

McClelland, D. C., & Steele, R. S. (1972). *Motivation workshops.* New York: General Learning Press.

Meyer, G. J., Hilsenroth, M. J., Baxter, D., Exner, J. E., Fowler, J. C., Piers, C. C., et al. (2002). An examination of interrater reliability for scoring the Rorschach, comprehensive system in eight data sets. *Journal of Personality Assessment, 78,* 219–274.

Morgan, C. D., & Murray, H. A. (1935). A method for examining fantasies: The Thematic Apperception Test. *Archives of Neurology and Psychiatry, 34,* 289–306.

Murstein, B. I. (1965). Projection of hostility on the TAT as a function of stimulus, background, and personality variables. *Journal of Consulting Psychology, 29*(1), 43–48.

Nisbett, R. E., & Wilson, T. D. (1977). Telling more than we can know: Verbal reports on mental processes. *Psychological Review 84,* 231–259.

Nunnally, J. C. (1978). *Psychometric theory.* New York: McGraw-Hill.

Pang, J. S., & Schultheiss, O. C. (2005). Assessing implicit motives in U.S. college students: Effects of picture type and position, gender and ethnicity, and cross-cultural comparisons. *Journal of Personality Assessment, 85,* 280–294.

Reuman, D. A. (1982). Ipsative behavioural variability and the quality of thematic apperceptive measurement of the achievement motive. *Journal of Personality and Social Psychology, 43,* 1098–1110.

Schuerger, J. M., Zarrella, K. L., & Hotz, A. S. (1989). Factors that influence the temporal stability of personality by questionnaire. *Journal of Personality and Social Psychology, 56*(5), 777–783.

Schultheiss, O. C., & Brunstein, J. C. (2001). Assessment of implicit motives with a research version of the TAT: Picture profiles, gender differences, and relations to other personality measures. *Journal of Personality Assessment, 77*(1), 71–86.

Schultheiss, O. C., & Brunstein, J. C. (2005). An implicit motive perspective on competence. In A. J. Elliot & C. S. Dweck (Eds.), *Handbook of competence and motivation* (pp. 31–51). New York: Guilford Publications.

Schultheiss, O. C., Campbell, K. L., & McClelland, D. C. (1999). Implicit power motivation moderates men's testosterone responses to imagined and real dominance success. *Hormones and Behavior, 36*(3), 234–241.

Schultheiss, O. C., Liening, S., & Schad, D. (2008). The reliability of a Picture Story Exercise measure of implicit motives: Estimates of internal consistency retest reliability, and ipsative stability. *Journal of Research in Personality, 42,* 1560–1571.

Schultheiss, O. C., & Pang, J. S. (2007). Measuring implicit motives. In R. W. Robins, R. C. Fraley, & R. F. Krueger (Eds.), *Handbook of research methods in personality psychology* (pp. 322–344). New York: Guilford Press.

Schultheiss, O. C., Pang, J. S., Robins, R. W., Fraley, R. C., & Krueger, R. F. (2007). Measuring implicit motives. In *Handbook of research methods in personality psychology* (pp. 322–344). New York, NY US: Guilford Press.

Schultheiss, O. C., & Rohde, W. (2002). Implicit power motivation predicts men's testosterone changes and implicit learning in a contest situation. *Hormones and Behavior, 41*(2), 195–202.

Schultheiss, O. C., Wirth, M. M., & Stanton, S. J. (2004). Effects of affiliation and power motivation arousal on salivary progesterone and testosterone. *Hormones and Behavior, 46*(5), 592–599.

Smith, C. P. (Ed.). (1992). *Motivation and personality: Handbook of thematic content analysis.* Cambridge [England]; New York: Cambridge University Press.

Smith, C. P. (2000). Content analysis and narrative analysis. In H. T. Reis & C. M. Judd (Eds.), *Handbook of research methods in social and personality psychology* (pp. 313–335). New York: Cambridge University Press.

Smith, C. P., Feld, S. C., & Franz, C. E. (1992). Methodological considerations: steps in research employing content analysis systems. In C. P. Smith (Ed.), *Motivation and personality: Handbook of thematic content analysis* (pp. 515–536). Cambridge, England: Cambridge University Press.

Smith, C. P., & Franz, C. E. (1992). Appendix I: Practice materials for learning the scoring systems. In C. P. Smith (Ed.), *Motivation and personality: Handbook of thematic content analysis* (pp. 537–630). New York: Cambridge University Press.

Stewart, A. J., & Chester, N. L. (1982). Sex differences in human social motives: Achievement, affiliation, and power. In A. J. Stewart (Ed.), *Motivation and society* (pp. 172–218). San Francisco: Jossey-Bass.

Suedfeld, P., Tetlock, P. E., & Streufert, S. (1992). Conceptual/integrative complexity. In C. P. Smith (Ed.), *Motivation and personality: Handbook of thematic content analysis* (pp. 393–400). New York: Cambridge University Press.

Taylor, C. R., Lee, J. Y., & Stern, B. B. (1995). Portrayals of African, Hispanic, and Asian Americans in magazine advertising. *American Behavioural Scientist, 38,* 608–621.

Tuerlinckx, F., De Boeck, P., & Lens, W. (2002). Measuring needs with the Thematic Apperception Test: A psychometric study. *Journal of Personality and Social Psychology, 82*(3), 448–461.

Veroff, J. (1992). Thematic apperceptive methods in survey research. In C. P. Smith (Ed.), *Motivation and personality: Handbook of thematic content analysis* (pp. 100–109). New York: Cambridge University Press.

Walker, E. L., & Atkinson, J. W. (1958). The expression of fear related motivation in thematic apperception as a function of proximity to an atomic explosion. In J. W. Atkinson (Ed.), *Motives in fantasy, action, and society* (pp. 143–159). Princeton, NJ: Van Nostrand.

Winter, D. G. (1973). *The power motive.* New York: Free Press.

Winter, D. G. (1992). Content analysis of archival materials, personal documents, and everyday verbal productions. In C. P. Smith (Ed.), *Motivation and personality: Handbook of thematic content analysis.* New York: Cambridge University Press.

Winter, D. G. (1994). *Manual for scoring motive imagery in running text.* Unpublished instrument, University of Michigan, Ann Arbor.

Winter, D. G., & Stewart, A. J. (1977). Power motive reliability as a function of retest instructions. *Journal of Consulting and Clinical Psychology, 45,* 436–440.

Wirth, M. M., Welsh, K. M., & Schultheiss, O. C. (2006). Salivary cortisol changes in humans after winning or losing a dominance contest depend on implicit power motivation. *Hormones and Behavior, 49*(3), 346–352.

Worchel, F. T., Aaron, L. L., & Yates, D. F. (1990). Gender bias on the Thematic Apperception Test. *Journal of Personality Assessment, 55,* 593–602.

Chapter 6

Assessing Individual Differences in Achievement Motivation with the Implicit Association Test: Predictive Validity of a Chronometric Measure of the Self-Concept "Me = Successful"

JOACHIM C. BRUNSTEIN AND CLEMENS H. SCHMITT
Justus-Liebig University

But the key to progress in science lies not only in theoretical clarification, but also in adequate measurement.

—David C. McClelland (1987, p. 588)

Introduction

Since its beginnings, the systematic exploration of human motive dispositions has been inspired by the idea that people have no or only little insight into the motivational basis of their personality. Although the origins of this idea can be traced back throughout the history of psychology to the work of Freud (1904) and Murray (1938), it was David C. McClelland, John W. Atkinson, and their associates (see, for instance, McClelland, Clark, Roby, & Atkinson, 1949) who transformed it into a concise theoretical framework and developed a measurement device that enabled researchers to investigate in detail how motives interact with environmental incentives to drive and direct goal-directed behavior. McClelland (1958) generally distrusted the validity of introspective methodologies but felt especially skeptical about the possibility of inferring motivational preferences from self-report instruments. Instead, he assumed that motivational dispositions operate outside of a person's conscious awareness and exert their influence on behavior without a great deal of self-reflective thought.

Among the first attempts to assess motivational processes of which the person is not aware were projective techniques, such as the Thematic Apperception Test (TAT) developed by Murray (1943) to infer latent desires and needs from coding the content of imaginative stories written to ambiguous pictures. During the past six decades, this story-based or thematic procedure has gradually been refined by many researchers and still continues to be the primary source of information today's generation of motivation psychologists relies on to assess the structure and strength of psychological motives. The impact that the TAT had on the development of motivation psychology can hardly be overestimated when one considers the wealth of ideas and the richness of evidences that have been inspired by this assessment instrument. However, as with any measurement approach that relies on only one single assessment tool, the question should be raised whether test scores derived from the TAT truly inform researchers about the essential features of the motive of interest or reflect, at least up to a certain extent, method-specific qualities of the chosen instrument (see Tuerlinckx, De Boeck, & Lens, 2002). Clearly, to explore the structure and process underlying a mental construct, it is more informative and reliable if researchers have two (or more) different methods of measurement on hand.

In the past decade, there has been a resurgence of interest in the exploration and measurement of implicit personality components, and theorists representing a broad spectrum of research on individual differences have contributed to this endeavor. Yet the methods of measurement used for this purpose markedly differ from the laborious work of coding TAT protocols for the presence of motive-relevant thought. Instead, it has become popular to use chronometric procedures (or measures of response latencies) to draw inferences about hidden aspects of personality and associated implicit social (and self-related) cognitions.

Analogous to the TAT approach, the development of this modern generation of *indirect* assessment tools (as opposed to the *direct* measure of personality attributes with self-report methods) is inspired by the idea that measures of individual differences constructed from reaction-time-based measures will account for differences in behavioral outcome variables that cannot be explained by introspective methods. And similar to early versions of the TAT, many exemplars of this novel approach are still in their infancy and, thus, have to struggle with a number of teething troubles, such as psychometric inadequacies and shortcomings in criterion validity (see Bosson, Swann, & Pennebaker, 2000, for a discussion of this issue in the domain of self-esteem research). Remarkably, however, there appears to be at least one exception from this rule: the Implicit Association Test (IAT) introduced by Greenwald, McGhee, and Schwartz (1998) to assess the strengths of associations among a variety of mental concepts. Due to its psychometric integrity as well as its respectable predictive validity (see Greenwald, Poehlman, Uhlmann, & Banaji,2009), since its publication the IAT has increasingly attracted the attention of many researchers who intend to expand the study of individual differences to the realm of implicit personality processes.

In this chapter we will explore potential links between thematic and chronometric methods of measuring motives. Our discussion of this issue will focus on TAT and IAT methods and contrast them with self-report measures of motivation. To make our line of argument fairly simple and concise, we will narrow, right from the beginning, the focus of our consideration on the domain of achievement motivation. To be more concrete, in this chapter we intend to accomplish three things: (1) to demonstrate that current theorizing in the field of implicit motives can benefit from an exchange of ideas with several important lines of social cognitive research on the automatic nature of motivational concerns; (2) to exemplify that procedures designed to manipulate and assess implicit social cognitions (e.g., priming procedures and the IAT) can provide many important insights into how implicit motives work and translate into goal-directed action; (3) to describe in summary form several studies from our lab examining the predictive validity of an IAT for assessing individual differences in achievement motivation. To start with, we will briefly reflect on the beginnings of motive measurement.

Implicit Motives

Thematic Assessment of Need for Achievement

Recognizing the need for an empirically justified measure of human motivation, McClelland, Atkinson, and their associates began in the late 1940s to develop an assessment procedure for gathering useful information about people's motivational states and enduring preferences. In so doing, they combined the clinical insight that a hidden desire is often expressed in a person's free-associative thoughts with a rigorous experimental procedure for the arousal of specific needs, such as the "need for food," which can easily be induced by temporary food deprivation (McClelland & Atkinson, 1948). Adopting Murray's (1943) TAT procedure, McClelland and Atkinson sought to capture the effects of experimentally manipulated motivations on people's associative thoughts by asking their research participants to write imaginative stories about stimuli depicting one or more people in a variety of ambiguous situations. In this way, they discovered that the experimental arousal of a certain motive (e.g., the hunger motive) was regularly reflected in an increase in the frequency of motive-related thought contents (e.g., imagery about food seeking).

Encouraged by these results, McClelland and Atkinson extended their procedure to investigate a different type of motive, one that Murray (1938) had already described in his conceptual analysis of psychogenic (or acquired) needs as one of the prime movers of human behavior: the "need for achievement" or motive for doing a thing really well and surpassing standards of excellence. In their analysis of this overarching concern for efficiency and competence, McClelland and Atkinson made an observation that laid the foundation for the development of an individual difference measure of achievement motivation. The critical observation was that even in the absence of any external source of stimulation (e.g., a prior experience with success or failure), many, but by far not all, participants still produced in their stories a considerable number of achievement-related imageries, so as if they were regularly in a state of arousal with respect to achievement-related needs. This observation was followed by a period of intensive work on the standardization of the test taking procedure, the choice of adequate pictures for eliciting stories about achievement, and the construction of a scoring system for coding the content of stories as to the presence of achievement-related motive imagery.

In 1953, McClelland, Atkinson, Clark, and Lowell published the results of their inquiry in "*The Achievement Motive*," a landmark monograph that should have, in retrospect, a sustainable effect on the development of the entire discipline of motivation psychology. In this publication, the authors introduced their newly developed thought-sampling device, nowadays called the Picture Story Exercise (PSE; see McClelland, Koestner, & Weinberger, 1989), as a diagnostic tool for the assessment of the strength of need for achievement (or "*n*Ach"), and individual differences thereof, and reported evidence of its validity in predicting a rich diversity of achievement-related criteria. The PSE methodology was soon applied to other kinds of motivation, such as the need for power and the need for affiliation, and thereby became a standard procedure for the measurement of social motive dispositions.

Motives in an Implicit Mode of Functioning

Three decades later, motivation researchers using the PSE had gathered a wealth of information about the principles underlying motive–behavior relations as observed in a variety of laboratory experiments and real-life settings. In 1987, McClelland integrated the existing body of evidence in a text book published as *Human Motivation*. Yet, at this time, many motivation researchers had already turned their attention away from the unconscious nature of motivational processes and dispositions and had started, instead, to focus on cognitively more elaborated constructs, such as self-appraisals, causal explanations, and cognitive needs for self-evaluation (see Kukla, 1978; Patten & White, 1977; Trope, 1975; Weiner, 1974). Individual differences in the outcomes of such self-reflective activities (e.g., attributions of one's successes and failures) were generally found to be better predicted by direct measures of self-reported motives than by motives indirectly inferred from content coding methods. At the same time, an increasing number of researchers (e.g., Entwisle, 1972) questioned the psychometric integrity of the PSE as reflected in the low internal consistency among stories from which motive scores are obtained (but see Atkinson, 1981; and Schultheiss, Liening, & Schad, 2008, for a consideration of reliability issues involved in the PSE from the perspective of motivation theory). Indeed, the frequently observed lack of correlation between thematic and self-report measures of nominally similar motivations (see also Mayer, Faber, & Xu, 2007; Schultheiss & Brunstein, 2001; Spangler, 1992) was now attributed by many researchers to a measurement error problem inherent in the PSE.

In an influential article, McClelland et al. (1989) took a different point of view (see also Weinberger & McClelland, 1990). They postulated that the lack of convergence among self-reported and PSE-derived motives cannot be explained by a lack of reliability or validity of one or the other type of instrument but reflects the fact that the two types of measures tap two different kinds of motives. They recommended that thematically coded motives be referred to as implicit needs because people do not describe themselves as having a particular motive, whereas self-report motives should better be termed explicit or self-attributed needs because they indicate the view people have of their own motives.

McClelland et al. (1989; see also Koestner & McClelland, 1990; Koestner, Weinberger, & McClelland, 1991) reviewed investigations demonstrating that the two kinds of motives are differently involved in the prediction of behavior (see also Spangler, 1992, for a meta-analytic review). Drawing primarily on findings reported in the achievement motivation literature, McClelland and colleagues presented two main arguments to bolster their idea that within a given content domain, "dual motives" operate on a person's behavior, each leaving its unique marks in a distinct class of outcome variables. First, they argued that the implicit, or PSE-assessed, motive to achieve energizes *spontaneous* impulses to act (e.g., energetic persistence in effort-sensitive tasks), whereas the explicit, or self-report, motive to achieve is most directly expressed in *deliberate* choice behavior (e.g., an explicitly stated preference for difficult tasks). Second, they suggested that the implicit motive is aroused through *intrinsic* incentives inherent to performing an activity (e.g., overcoming challenges), whereas the explicit motive is more apt to be stimulated through the presence of *social-extrinsic* incentives (e.g., an explicitly stated demand for doing something well).

The term implicit motive, as introduced by McClelland et al. (1989), denotes at least three meanings: Implicit motives are assumed to be (a) represented in the cognitive unconscious, so that people are often unaware of what propels their overt behavior; (b) triggered automatically by environmental incentives without any need for self-reflection and conscious decision making; and (c) expressed in spontaneous behaviors, the enactment of which requires only little conscious effort. Hence, the motivational sequence described by McClelland et al. (1989; see also Weinberger & McClelland, 1990), from the arousal of motives to the enactment of relevant behavior, does not involve at any point in the chain an act of will or need for conscious attention.

Automaticity of Motivational Preferences

Auto-Motives

McClelland et al.'s (1989) ideas about how implicit motives work bear some resemblance to what social psychologists have reported, since the late 1970's (cf. Higgins, Rholes, & Jones, 1977), to be characteristic of a good deal of social information processing: the attention-free nature of mental processes that link environmental information with judgmental reactions and social behavior (for an overview, see Bargh, 2007). One important lesson learned from research on implicit social cognitions is that social knowledge structures stored in memory can be activated unobtrusively by appropriate (supraliminal and subliminal) external stimuli and can then proceed to influence a person's perception, evaluation, motivation, and behavior in a nonconscious manner (i.e., without the person's knowledge of this influence).

It was John A. Bargh (1990) who transferred this idea of *automaticity* from social cognitive psychology to motivation research and framed it there in a model of auto-motives. By "auto-motive" Bargh means that similar to perceptual and evaluative judgments (e.g., in person perception and impression formation studies), goals, intentions, and many other kinds of motivations can all be "primed" and activated temporarily to create an internal state of readiness, with the effect that people enact goal-directed activities without knowing what has put these activities into motion. Hence, Bargh's thought-provoking idea claims that people often engage in goal-directed action without consciously intending to do so.

Bargh and Gollwitzer (1994; see also Bargh & Barndollar, 1996; Bargh, Gollwitzer, Lee-Chai, Barndollar, & Trötschel, 2001) reported a number of experiments illustrating how this idea can contribute to our understanding of motivated behavior. In one study, participants were first primed either with achievement-related words or with affiliation-related words embedded in a scrambled sentence test and were then placed in a mixed-motive situation where they could either pursue the achievement-related goal of solving some further word search puzzles or switch to the affiliation-related goal of interacting with a partner (actually a confederate) who allegedly had done not very well in previous attempts to solve the puzzles. Participants primed with achievement in the initial phase of the experiment worked harder and found more words in the second phase of the experiment than participants primed with affiliation. In the debriefing procedure, Bargh and Gollwitzer observed that no participant showed any awareness of the potential influence of the priming manipulation on his or her subsequent performance in the mixed-motive situation.

To draw an analogy between motivational effects produced by priming procedures and motivational effects elicited by chronic motives, Bargh and Gollwitzer (1994) integrated in a second experiment a number of individual difference measures (among others the PSE) for the assessment of achievement- and affiliation-related motives. Replicating the findings obtained from the above experiment, participants primed with achievement performed better at the word search puzzles than those primed with affiliation, but only on the early trials of the experimental task. On the later trials, the priming effect gradually diminished, and the chronic motives began to dominate and predict participants' preferences (i.e., whether a participant continued to concentrate on the word search task or began to interact with the confederate).

This latter finding is particularly important because it suggests that chronic motives produce their (long-term) effects on a person's behavior analogous to experimentally generated (short-term) motivations that translate into goal-directed action without any conscious intention on the actor's part. Chronic motives can originate, as Bargh (1990) speculated, from the frequent experience that a specific state of motivation is consistently associated with certain environmental features. In the presence of such features, the respective motivation is automatically activated by very fast cognitive activities and then proceeds to translate into certain patterns of behavior that, too, can become automatized over time (especially when the respective activity has often led to the gratification of the activated motive). In effect, the entire process of motivation, from the activation of a chronic motive to the enactment of motive-related action, can essentially become nonconscious.

Although Bargh's (1990) model of auto-motives shares many important features with McClelland's (1987) "neo-instinctive" model of implicit motives (for a full description of this model, see Weinberger & McClelland, 1990), the strategy of investigation Bargh and Gollwitzer (1994) chose to draw an analogy between the functioning of primed and chronic motivations has found only little imitation in research on implicit motives (but see Siegel & Weinberger, 1998; Woike, 1995). Conversely, individual differences in personal motivations are often treated in social cognitive experiments as if they would represent a negligible source of random error variance (but see Cesario, Plaks, & Higgins, 2006).

Recently, however, Perugini and Prestwich (2007) have assigned individual difference variables a key role in Bargh's (1990) auto-motive model. For this purpose, they added to Bargh's model a so-called "gatekeeper" authority representing individual differences in automatic evaluations and motivational tendencies. Due to their implicit nature, these preferences are assumed to be able to modulate cognitive activities elicited by priming manipulations and thereby determine what kind of behavior will follow from the priming procedure. In keeping with this view, Perugini and associates found (as reported in Perugini & Prestwich, 2007) that implicit altruism (assessed with the IAT procedure described below) moderated the effects a subliminal priming procedure had on spontaneous helping behavior. Individual differences in (implicit) altruism predicted helping under condition of priming, whereas the priming manipulation itself had no main effect on helping. It thus appears, as Perugini and Prestwich concluded, that cognitive activities induced by a priming manipulation are linked to the enactment of behavior lined up with the primed concept only when a person's personal motivation is consistent with the respective behavior. Notably, the gatekeeper exercises this authority in the execution of goal-directed behavior *without* any need to leave the preferred mode of implicit functioning and switch to a conscious mode of self-controlled behavior regulation. This research nicely illustrates that individual differences in motivational preferences (and further types of automatic evaluations) can smoothly be integrated into models of social information processing.

Sequential Priming of Evaluative Distinctions

Before we turn to the IAT, it should be noted that priming procedures can be used not only to manipulate transitory mental states (or very fast cognitive activities) originating from recent experiences but also to assess the strength of chronic associations between mental representations, across which automatic activation spreads (e.g., the connection between an attitude object and its evaluation). Sequential or affective priming procedures are particularly instructive for this purpose (see Bargh & Chartrand, 2000). For instance, in a widely used paradigm developed by Fazio, Sanbonmatsu, Powell, and Kardes (1986), the presentation of the prime (e.g., exemplars of an attitude object) is followed by an evaluative decision task where the respondent is asked to react to positive and negative words by pressing as quickly as possible one of two buttons, one labeled "good" and the other one labeled "bad". If the preceding priming procedure speeds up reactions to positive words and slows down reactions to negative words in the categorization task, it is concluded that a respondent has a positive attitude towards the prime object. The automatic (vs. controlled) nature of the respective association can be determined by varying the delay or "stimulus onset asynchrony" between prime and target presentation (see Neely, 1977). If the time gap is too short to allow for a strategic response and the prime still affects a person's speed of responding in categorizing the target, then the prime and the target can be said to be associated automatically.

Fazio, Jackson, Dunton, and Williams (1995) reported a study in which they derived from this procedure an unobtrusive measure of individual differences in the implicit attitude towards African Americans and then used this measure to predict people's prejudicial behavior. By assessing the degree of automatic affective associations of African-American faces (the prime) with positive and negative adjectives, Fazio et al. constructed a reaction time–based measure of implicit prejudicial beliefs. Participants scoring high on this measure of racial prejudice were found to behave in a less friendly manner when they later interacted with an African-American experimenter, whereas a self-report measure of racial attitudes failed to predict the negativity of participants' behavioral reactions to the "Black" target.

Although attitudes and motives differ from each other with respect to the focal construct of interest, they share many important features with respect to the (implicit) nature of the cognitive processes that are supposed to mediate their behavioral influences (see Wilson, Lindsey, & Schooler, 2000, for a detailed discussion of these parallels[1]). One might therefore speculate that reaction time–based measures of implicit social cognitions can also be used to tap individual differences in implicit motives. For instance, in the domain of achievement, investigators could present as prime stimuli either pictorial (e.g., PSE-type scenes of achievement behavior) or verbal material (e.g., achievement-related trait adjectives) representing achievement-oriented concerns and then infer from subjects' reactions to affectively polarized words the implicit affective evaluation of this specific motivational concern. Unfortunately, an obstacle to this assessment strategy is the modest reliability of individual differences derived from affective priming effects (see Banse, 2001). It must thus be left up to future research if these reliability problems can be resolved effectively so that affective priming indices can be used for the analysis of individual differences in affectively tinged implicit motives.

The Implicit Association Test

Recently, several theorists have begun to explore implicit personality processes by using a different chronometric tool, the Implicit Association Test (IAT) developed by Greenwald et al. (1998) as a procedure to assess automatic evaluative distinctions. The IAT relies on a reaction time methodology that bypasses self-deception and impression management strategies evident in self-report instruments. For this reason, it has become very popular to use this assessment tool to tap implicit sources of attitudes and prejudices people are either unwilling (due to presentation concerns) or unable (due to introspective limits) to reveal in subjective accounts (Greenwald et al., 2002). Remarkably, in a number studies, the IAT was adapted to measuring individual differences in self-esteem (Greenwald & Farnham, 2000) and self-concepts of personality, such as shyness (Asendorpf, Banse, & Mücke, 2002) and anxiety (Egloff & Schmukle, 2002).

The development of the IAT was almost entirely unaffected by past and present research on the implicit/explicit distinction as established by D. C. McClelland. Yet, in two original publications, one dealing with achievement orientation (Brunstein & Schmitt, 2004) and another one dealing with power and intimacy motivations (Sheldon, King, Houser-Marko, Osbaldiston, & Gunz, 2007), and in one theoretical analysis pleading for an integration of direct and indirect methods of motive measurement, especially in the context of organizational settings (Bing, LeBreton, Davison, Migetz, & James, 2007), the IAT methodology was hailed as a potential candidate for the chronometric assessment of motivational preferences that are unavailable for conscious self-report.

Measurement Procedure and Operating Principles in the IAT

IAT measures are designed to tap individual differences in the mental organization of social knowledge structures (think, for instance, of a gender stereotype) whose concept nodes are interconnected by links differing in associative strength (Greenwald et al., 2002). The IAT examines the associative strength between two concepts by combining a pair of target categories (e.g., male vs. female) with a supposedly associated pair of attribute categories (e.g., math vs. arts) (for an IAT assessing math–gender stereotypes, see Nosek, Banaji, & Greenwald, 2002). In two categorization tasks, target and attribute concepts are presented either in an association-compatible or in an association-incompatible manner. The IAT procedure obliges the respondent to rapidly sort stimuli representing the four concepts into just two response categories mapped onto the right-hand and left-hand button of a two-key response panel. The basic principle of the IAT procedure is that it should be easier for people to categorize two concepts using the same response key if the concepts are strongly associated (e.g., male + math / female + arts) than if they are only weakly associated or opposed (e.g., male + arts / female + math).

For instance, to measure self-esteem, Greenwald and Farnham (2000) devised an IAT that assesses automatic associations of self- versus other-related words (target categories) with pleasant versus unpleasant words (attribute categories). In this computerized test, category labels (me vs. not me; pleasant vs. unpleasant) are displayed in the upper right and upper left corner of a monitor. Exemplars of the bipolar target concept and the bipolar attribute concept appear sequentially in the middle of the screen. The IAT procedure involves five steps represented by five consecutive test blocks. During the first two blocks, participants learn to sort exemplars of the bipolar target concept (Block 1) and the bipolar attribute dimension (Block 2) into their superordinate categories by pressing one of two buttons mapped to these categories. In Block 3, respondents are then asked to sort together (by pressing one of the two keys) self-related and pleasant words and to do the same with other-related and unpleasant words (by pressing the second key). In Block 4 the spatial location for either the target or attribute concept is switched. Block 5 is similar to Block 3 but uses the reversed key assignments practiced in Block 4, such that self-related and unpleasant words share one key and other-related and pleasant words, the second key. The difference in the mean reaction times between the two combined categorization tasks presented in Blocks 3 and 5 represents the IAT effect. To the extent that respondents more strongly associate the self with pleasant words, relative to the reverse pairings, they are manifesting high self-esteem.[2]

The mechanisms underlying the IAT are still an issue of much debate (see Fazio & Olson, 2003). Several researchers have offered a number of thoughtful explanations detailing the exact nature of the cognitive processes driving subjects' IAT reactions, especially during the critical test blocks (e.g., task set switching, see Klauer & Mierke, 2005; shift in response criteria, see Brendl, Markman, & Messner, 2001; figure–ground asymmetry, see Rothermund & Wentura, 2001). Generally, however, IAT measures are presumed to rely on processes that are implicit or automatic in the sense that they are expressed without any intention or control on the part of the respondent. In keeping with this notion, existing evidence (see Nosek, Greenwald, & Banaji, 2007) suggests that it is not easy to fake the IAT; that IAT measures are relatively unaffected by presentation biases; and that a good deal of information provided by the IAT is not available for self-reports.

The IAT assesses individual differences in implicit person variables (e.g., attitudes and self-concepts) with a satisfactory degree of reliability. Internal consistency coefficients mostly exceed the critical value of .70 but often reach levels of .80 and above (Banse, Seise, & Zerbes, 2001; Schmukle & Egloff, 2004). The test–retest reliability of IAT measures is lower (mean $r = .56$) and depends only a little upon the length of retesting intervals (Egloff, Schwerdtfeger, & Schmukle, 2005). Although nominally similar IAT and self-report measures have mostly been found to be positively correlated (Banse et al., 2001), they often share only little common variance (Karpinski & Hilton, 2001). In a meta-analysis of IAT and self-report correlations obtained from numerous content domains, Hofmann, Gawronski, Gschwendner, Le, and Schmitt (2005) found a mean r of .24.

In the recent past, IAT researchers have generated a growing body of evidence suggesting that IAT measures significantly add to the predictive validity of self-report instruments by explaining incremental portions of variance in relevant behavior criteria (e.g., observer ratings of anxious behavior; see Egloff & Schmukle, 2002). Other studies suggest that parallel IAT and self-report measures are dissociable in the sense that they are linked to distinct classes of behavioral variables. Most notably, Asendorpf et al. (2002) reported that a shyness IAT uniquely predicted spontaneous behavioral expressions of shyness (e.g., tenseness of body posture) whereas explicit self-ratings of shyness best predicted controlled shy behavior (e.g., speech duration in a shyness-inducing social interaction situation). Unfortunately, in-depth analyses of IAT-behavior relations, such as the one conducted by Asendorpf and associates, are still a rarity in the IAT literature (but see Perugini, 2005).

Measuring Implicit Achievement Orientation with the IAT

Hence, available evidence suggests that IATs and self-report tests of nominally similar person variables tap unique sources of variance and provide distinctive information for the prediction of relevant behavioral criteria. This pattern of findings struck us as bearing strong resemblance to that evident in the motivation literature reviewed by McClelland et al. (1989). We therefore speculated that the IAT methodology might be suitable to tap self-related representations of motivational orientations that operate on a person's behavior in an implicit mode of functioning. As noted in the introduction of this chapter, in our pursuit of this idea we chose to focus on the domain of achievement behavior.

Within the context of our present research, we use the term "achievement orientation" to denote general representations of the self as being successful in the pursuit of achievement-related goals (i.e., goals that imply a sense of mastery and self-improvement relative to some standard of excellence). In doing so, we agree with the view most directly spelled out by Koestner and McClelland (1990) but shared as well by many other scholars of achievement motivation (see Covington & Omelich, 1979; Meyer, 1987; Moulton, 1974; Nicholls, 1984; Schultheiss & Brunstein, 2005; Shrable, & Moulton, 1968) that the achievement motive can essentially be understood as an "intrinsic competence motive." By using the IAT methodology, we therefore sought to assess the strength of associative links connecting the self with attributes of achievement-related competence (i.e., motivationally significant person characteristics that connote a sense of ambition and efficiency in the pursuit of achievement-relevant goals). And in keeping with the implicit/explicit framework outlined by McClelland et al. 1989), we (tentatively) supposed that a good deal of the associative network representing a person's self-concept of competence resides in the cognitive unconscious and may therefore not permit accurate assessment by subjective accounts.

To construct the five categorization tasks involved in the IAT, we chose *successful* versus *not successful* as attribute labels and *me* versus *others* as target labels. Self-related (I, me, myself, mine) and other-related items (they, them, their, theirs) were adopted from previous IAT studies (Nosek et al., 2002). We used *successful* versus *not successful* as attribute labels because these categories strongly connote competent accomplishments within achievement-oriented contexts. Attribute items were inspired by standard questionnaire measures of achievement motivation as well as content coding categories listed in manuals for scoring achievement-related motive imagery in PSEs. We selected success-related adjectives according to the criterion that they should capture a sense of both ambitiousness (ambitious, curious, persistent, diligent) and efficiency (efficient, competent, successful, inventive) in the enactment of achievement-oriented pursuits. Not-successful items (idle, uninterested, sluggish, distractible, incompetent, unsuccessful, inefficient, unimaginative) were phrased in terms of antonyms of the success-related items.[3]

Figure 6.1 displays the structure of the resulting instrument (for further details, see Brunstein & Schmitt, 2004). Block 1 requires respondents to categorize self- and other-related items into *me* (right-hand key press) and *other* categories (left-hand key press). Block 2 requires them to distinguish *successful* (right key) and *not-successful*-meaning items (left key). In Block 3, respondents sort items into two combined categories: Items related to *me* and *successful* require a response of the right key; items related to *others* and *not successful* a response of the left key. As compared with Block 2, assignments of *successful* and *not-successful* items to the right and left answer keys are reversed in Block 4. Similar to Block 3, both categorization tasks are again combined in Block 5, but this time participants are required to respond to *me* and *not successful* items by pressing the right key and to *other* and *successful* items by pressing the left key, respectively. Before participants work on the critical trials in Blocks 3 and 5, they are presented with a number of practice trials.

In all of the studies reported in this chapter, we transformed response time latencies by a reciprocal transformation (see Fazio, 1990) into speed of responding before we calculated a respondent's IAT score. Accordingly, the IAT effect was computed by subtracting the mean of the reciprocal latencies in Block 5 from the mean of the reciprocal latencies in Block 3. Different from other conventional measures of the IAT effect (see Greenwald, Nosek, & Banaji, 2003), in our own investigations the reciprocal transformation yielded the only IAT measure that was unrelated to individual differences in general response

Block	1	2	3	4	5
Task description	Target discrimination	Attribute discrimination	Initial combined task	Reversed attribute discrimination	Reversed combined task
Category labels	● Me / Others ●	● successful / not successful ●	● Me successful / Others not successful ●	● not successful / successful ●	● Me not successful / Others successful ●
Sample stimuli	○ I / Me / They / Them ○	○ ambitious / competent / idle / inefficient ○	○ I ambitious / They inefficient ○	○ inefficient idle / competent ambitious ○	○ I inefficient / They ambitious ○
Trials	24	48	32 + 128	48	32 + 128

Figure 6.1 Implicit Association Test (IAT) for the assessment of individual differences in achievement orientation. From Brunstein & Schmitt (2004. p. 552). Copyright by *Journal of Research in Personality* (reprinted with permission).

Note. Black circles indicate assignment of category labels to left and right answer keys. Open circles indicate correct responses. The schematic description of the IAT is adapted from "Measuring individual differences in implicit cognition: The Implicit Association Test," by A. G. Greenwald, D. E. McGhee, and J. L. K. Schwartz, 1998, *Journal of Personality and Social Psychology, 74.* p. 1465.

speed (a positive correlation of this kind would pose a serious threat to the internal validity of achievement experiments that often use speeded tests as criterion variables).

In the studies reported below, the internal reliability of the IAT score was $alpha > .78$.[4] Brunstein and Schmitt (2004) reported the 1-week test–retest correlation for the achievement orientation IAT to be .56, a value quite comparable with the stability coefficients obtained in other IAT experiments (Egloff et al., 2005). In a sample of 41 college students, the achievement orientation IAT was administered to respondents in conjunction with Greenwald and Farnham's (2000) IAT for measuring implicit self-esteem. The intertest correlation among the two IAT effects was .26 (see Brunstein & Schmitt, 2004). In one further investigation, we jointly administered to 122 college students the achievement orientation IAT and Egloff and Schmukle's (2002) IAT for measuring anxiety. The correlation among the two IAT effects was −.28. As Mierke and Klauer (2003) reported, modest to medium-sized correlations among different IATs primarily reflect method-specific variance in the IAT. Accordingly, the aforementioned correlations document that the achievement orientation IAT has a respectable degree of discriminant validity relative to other IAT measures of implicit personality variables. To complete this report of preliminary analyses, it should be noted that, quite different from self-report measures of achievement motivation, in neither of our investigations did the IAT measure significantly covary with self-presentation measures (e.g., self-deception and social desirability).

Predictive Validity of the Achievement Orientation IAT

In the four experiments reported in this section, we examined whether the achievement orientation IAT would qualify as a measure of implicit achievement tendencies according to criteria spelled out in achievement motivation theory.

In the first two experiments, we examined whether the IAT would predict effective coping with challenges. In Experiment 1 (published in Brunstein & Schmitt, 2004), we analyzed whether individuals scoring high on IAT-assessed achievement orientation would try to give their best and surpass their own achievements in a mental concentration test that involved a personal performance standard. In Experiment 2, we administered in varying degrees of difficulty a memory task and examined the capacity of the achievement orientation IAT to predict variations in physiological arousal during task performance. In both experiments, we also assessed subjective accounts of task involvement. This procedure enabled us to compare the validity of the achievement orientation IAT with that of self-reported needs for achievement in predicting objective versus subjective criteria of task engagement.

In two further experiments, we adopted (Experiment 3) and elaborated (Experiment 4) McClelland's idea that implicit and explicit motives for achievement are often expressed in different kinds of behavior. As noted, McClelland et al. (1989) hypothesized that the implicit motive to achieve drives spontaneous efforts to succeed, whereas the self-attributed achievement motive better predicts cognitive choices and task-related preferences. To examine this "dichotomic validity theorem" (Heckhausen, 1986), we related indirect (IAT) and direct (self-report) tests of achievement motivation to energetic and decisional aspects of achievement behavior. In doing so, we intended to test whether IAT-assessed and self-reported motives would account for distinguishable aspects of achievement-oriented behavior.

One further aim of our research was to explore whether IAT-based and PSE-based motive scores would converge in predicting similar patterns of criterion behaviors. Although IATs and PSEs involve quite different strategies of assessment, we speculated that they might tap, at least up to a certain extent, interrelated features of (implicit) achievement concerns. To address this issue, we added to the personality measures administered in Experiments 2, 3, and 4 a story-based test of need for achievement (no such test was administered in Experiment 1). In each of these experiments, we used Heckhausen's (1963; see also Heckhausen, Schmalt, & Schneider, 1985) scoring system to code PSE protocols for the presence of success-related motive imagery (for an English translation of Heckhausen's scoring manual, see Schultheiss, 2001).

Concern with a Standard of Excellence

Our first experiment (Brunstein & Schmitt, 2004) was designed to assess whether the achievement orientation IAT would capture and reflect the core or essence of what is meant when motivation researchers refer to the term *achievement*. According to McClelland et al. (1953), the motive to achieve can be defined as a recurrent concern for surpassing standards of excellence. This definition implies the view that individuals with a strong achievement motive feel attuned to situations that give them feedback on how well they are doing. In contrast, the same highly achievement-motivated individuals are less attracted to situations where there is no standard of comparison to evaluate the quality of one's performance. Seeking challenges (as, for instance, by tackling a task where the outcome of one's effort is uncertain) and seeking feedback (as, for instance, by searching information that documents the development of one's performance) thus constitute two interrelated features inherent in all kinds of behavior driven by the human need to excel and surpass one's previous achievements (Breckler & Greenwald, 1986; Brunstein & Heckhausen, 2008).

In our first test of the predictive validity of the achievement orientation IAT, we thus contrasted an experimental condition rich in achievement-related incentives with a control condition where such incentives were absent. At the beginning of the experiment, 88 college students first completed the achievement orientation IAT and then filled out a checklist consisting of the same self-descriptive adjectives as those displayed as attribute items in the IAT (ambitious, persistent, etc.). In this way, we derived from the same kind of test material both an indirect (implicit achievement orientation) and a direct measure (explicit achievement orientation) for the assessment of individual differences in the strength of achievement tendencies.

After they had completed the two personality tests, all students were asked to work on a computerized task adapted from Brickenkamp and Zillmer's (1998) d2 Test of Attention. The task required the respondent to indicate, by pressing one of two response keys, whether a stimulus presented on the computer monitor represented a "d" having two dashes or whether it represented a different type of symbol (e.g., a "d" having more or less than two dashes). Effective performance on this task requires a great deal of mental effort, making it a suitable tool to assess the influence of motivational variables (Brunstein & Gollwitzer, 1996; Brunstein & Maier, 2005). We organized the presentation of the stimulus material in a number of 18 consecutive blocks, with each block consisting of 40 stimuli (d2s and non-d2s).

In the achievement-relevant condition, participants received feedback after each test block indicating whether they had, or had not, surpassed the best performance they had reached in any of the previous blocks. This information served to establish a personal standard of excellence enabling the participants to monitor the development of their performance over the course of the experimental task. The presence of a "top performance" (or new personal best) was indicated on the computer screen by the appearance of a plus sign; its absence was indicated by a minus sign. Independent of their true performance, all feedback students were presented with an equal number of plus and minus signs. We used this procedure to ensure that feedback participants would learn during the test task that performance improvements were by no means a guarantee. Control (or no feedback) participants did not receive any information as to the development of their performance.

To obtain a criterion reflecting how much effort a student had put in this mental concentration test, we determined her or his speed of responding during the experimental phase with a pre-experimental measure of performance speed covaried out (participants did not receive feedback during the pre-experimental phase). To obtain a declarative measure of achievement behavior, all participants were asked to indicate on a number of postexperimental rating scales how much they had enjoyed working on the test task.

Findings were as follows: First, despite the similarity of the test materials administered in the two achievement measures, IAT-assessed and self-reported achievement orientations turned out to be uncorrelated ($r = -.07$). This lack of correlation could not be attributed to a lack of reliability of either of the two tests (*alpha* > .80, for each test). Second, as reflected in significant interactive relationships between experimental condition and motivational dispositions, both achievement orientation measures (IAT and self-ratings) were highly responsive to the presence (vs. absence) of feedback. In the no-feedback situation, neither of the two individual difference measures predicted either of the two dependent variables. In contrast, in the feedback condition, each of the two measures selectively predicted a specific criterion reflecting students' task involvement. Self-reported achievement orientation did not predict task performance, but IAT-assessed achievement orientation did. The higher students scored on the IAT, the faster they responded during the test phase (see Fig. 6.2, Panel A). In the same (feedback) condition, the self-report scale but not the IAT was positively related to postexperimental ratings of task enjoyment. Students who described themselves as achievers were more likely than other participants to report that they had enjoyed working on the test task (see Fig. 6.2, Panel B).

Hence, when students received information about how well they were doing, the IAT predicted how hard they tried to improve their task performance, whereas the self-report scale better predicted students' appraisals of how much they had liked performing the test task. As noted, no comparable effects emerged among no-feedback participants. However, relative to the feedback condition, the absence of feedback in the control condition was reflected in both a lower speed of responding and a lower level of task enjoyment.

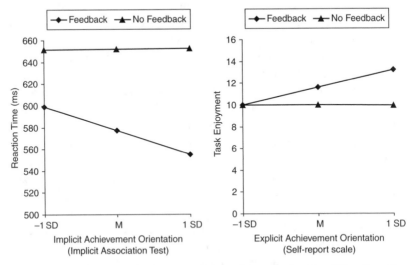

Figure 6.2 Task performance (Panel A) and task enjoyment (Panel B) as functions of feedback condition and achievement orientation tests. From Brunstein & Schmitt (2004, pp. 547–548). Copyright by *Journal of Research in Personality* (reprinted with permission).

Effort Expenditure and Sympathetic Arousal

In our second experiment, we investigated the validity of the achievement orientation IAT with respect to one further idea integral to achievement motivation theory. In his model of risk-taking behavior, Atkinson (1957, 1964) postulated that the strength of the tendency to achieve depends primarily upon two influences: the level of difficulty associated with a given task and the strength of the need for achievement (or motive to succeed) carried by the individual. Specifically, Atkinson postulated that the tendency to achieve would be stronger when (a) a task is perceived to be one of intermediate difficulty rather than when it is perceived to be very easy or impossible; and (b) the motive to achieve is strong rather than when this motive is weak. Combining these two assumptions in one multiplicative Motive × Difficulty function, Atkinson predicted a substantial difference in the tendency to achieve attributable to differences in the strength of the achievement motive only when a task is perceived to be moderately difficult (i.e., when the probability of success and failure is the same). From the logic of this theorem, Atkinson concluded that (a) the tendency to achieve would be an inverted U-shaped function of task difficulty and (b) the strength of the motive to achieve would determine the peak or maximum value of this quadratic function.

Motivation researchers who tested this idea (and extensions of it addressing the influence of the failure avoidance motive) mostly used as achievement criteria measures of task choice, goal setting, and level of aspiration (for an overview, see Brunstein & Heckhausen, 2008). Yet, inherent in Atkinson's line of theorizing was the view that the tendency to achieve would be reflected in a person's task-related effort to reach the goal of mastering a given challenge.

Effort, or mental energy, can be assessed with many different methods. For many years, effort reports have been one of the methods widely used in achievement studies. Yet effort expenditure can (and should) be assessed more unobtrusively, as Brehm (see Brehm & Self, 1989) and Wright (see Wright and Kirby, 2001) pointed out in their theory of motivational intensity. Based on pioneering work by Obrist (1981), these researchers predicted and found that activity in the sympathetic branch of the autonomous nervous system varies with the intensity of effort a person exerts when performing a cognitive challenge. Because sympathetic activity is reflected in cardiovascular (CV) reactions, but especially in systolic changes in blood pressure (SBP), measuring CV outcomes provides a reliable method of assessing the degree of mental effort a person exerts during task performance (for a discussion of the sensitivity of different CV outcomes to variations in effort, see Wright & Kirby, 2001).

In the present experiment, we tested the validity of the achievement orientation IAT, relative to thematic and self-report measures of need for achievement, by examining its capability of moderating the relation between effort and difficulty as specified by Atkinson. For this purpose, we presented, in the sequence listed here, the following individual differences measures to 54 college students: a four-picture version of the PSE, representing a thematic measure of the implicit motive to achieve; the achievement orientation IAT, representing a reaction time–based measure of supposedly the same, or a similar (implicit) motive; and a German translation of Mehrabian's (1969) Achievement Risk Preference Scale (MARPS), representing a self-report measure of individual differences in achievement motivation.

In a repeated measure, within-subjects design, all participants were administered three memory tasks consisting of the same kind of stimuli but differing from each other with respect to the degree of difficulty involved in the given task. On each task, participants were first presented with a list of meaningless letter strings, each consisting of four letters (e.g., N-C-T-F), and then asked to recall the *entire* list of strings after a couple of minutes. In order of presentation, students were presented with a list comprising 4 (easy task), 7 (intermediate difficulty task), and 20 (extremely difficult or "impossible" task) letter strings.

To assess the intensity of task engagement, we measured both SBP reactions and self-reported effort intentions regarding each of the three successive tasks presented during the experimental phase. Using a multiple-baseline design, we monitored for each participant SBP levels prior to and during each task with an apparatus using oscillometry as the assessment method. To create a measure of SBP reactivity, we subtracted from averaged baseline SBP values the mean of three SBP scores collected during task performance (these difference scores were unrelated to baseline SBP scores). In addition, immediately before they started working on each task, the participants were asked to rate how much effort they would intend to expend during the performance phase.

To analyze SBP change scores, we used a repeated-measures analysis of variance approach. When task difficulty was used as a within-subjects predictor, this analysis resulted in a curve (see Fig. 6.3, Panel A) supporting Atkinson's (1957, 1964) prediction. As reflected in a significant quadratic trend, systolic reactivity increased from the easy task to the intermediate difficulty task but relapsed when participants performed the extremely difficult (or impossible) task. We then analyzed whether this observed difficulty–effort relation would be qualified by any of the individual difference measures. PSE and IAT were significantly interrelated ($r = .33$), but each of them was statistically independent of self-reported achievement motivation (MARPS). Different from the questionnaire scale, both PSE-assessed and IAT-assessed motivations significantly moderated the effect that variations in task difficulty had on the intensity of SBP reactions. As Panels B and C in Figure 6.3 illustrate, the two indirect motivation tests yielded similar patterns of results: High and low scorers on these tests markedly differed from each other with respect to

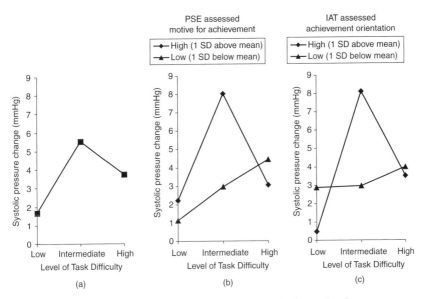

PSE assessed
motive for achievement

→ High (1 SD above mean)
→ Low (1 SD below mean)

IAT assessed
achievement orientation

→ High (1 SD above mean)
→ Low (1 SD below mean)

Figure 6.3 Systolic reactivity as a function of task difficulty and indirect achievement motivation tests (PSE = Picture Story Exercise; IAT = Implicit Association Test).

their SBP reactions only at the intermediate level of task difficulty ($r = .39$, for the PSE and the IAT, respectively).

Ratings of intended effort were analyzed in the same fashion. Similar to SBP, self-reported effort reached its peak on the medium-difficulty task. Despite this similarity, for each of the three memory tasks, ratings of intended effort were unrelated to SBP reactivity ($rs < .10$). Moreover, neither the PSE nor the IAT predicted students' effort intentions. In contrast, the achievement motivation questionnaire (MARPS) qualified the effect that variations in task difficulty had on intended effort. Relative to low scorers, students scoring high on this instrument indicated that they would intend to expend more effort at the moderately difficult task ($r = .42$). No such difference emerged for the easy or the extremely difficult tasks.

Hence, this study yielded three results: First, the achievement orientation IAT and the PSE measure of need for achievement were equally useful in predicting a physiological measure of effort intensity at a level of task difficulty that normally creates an optimal challenge for success-motivated individuals. Second, at the same (intermediate) level of task difficulty, students with a strong self-attributed motive to achieve intended to put more effort in the given task than students with a weak self-attributed need for achievement. In contrast, neither the IAT nor the PSE predicted effort reports. Third, the two indirect motive measures (PSE und IAT) were modestly interrelated but showed no significant correlation with self-reported achievement motivation (MARPS).

Task Choice and Task Performance

In two further experiments, we drew on McClelland et al.'s (1989) idea that implicit and self-attributed motives for achievement predict different classes of behavior (see Experiment 3) but added to this idea the notion that, at least under certain conditions, the two motives may take only different routes (namely, a direct vs. a self-controlled route) to fuel the same kind of behavior (see Experiment 4).

As we explained in greater detail elsewhere (see Brunstein & Maier, 2005), the implicit motive for achievement can be considered as an *energizer* of activities aimed at performing a task more effectively whereas the self-attributed achievement motive operates as a *decision maker* that influences people's choice behavior in accordance with conscious self-beliefs (e.g., the view a person has of her own motives). Proceeding on this view, in Experiment 3 we examined the prognostic capacity of indirect (PSE and IAT) and direct motive tests (self-report) in the prediction of effort-related and choice-related aspects of achievement motivation. Ninety-nine college students were presented with a thematic (PSE), a chronometric (IAT), and a self-report measure (MARPS) of achievement tendencies. Because the criterion variables assessed in this study required the participants to process and understand verbal material, we added to our assessment battery a standardized test of verbal fluency (this measure enabled us to control all of our predictions for individual differences in relevant cognitive abilities). One week after they had completed these tests, all participants were presented with two kinds of test tasks: one task served to assess participants' effectiveness in solving a number of word-finding puzzles (task performance); the other one served to assess their preference for working on hard, relative to easy, verbal analogy items.

The first task consisted of four word-finding puzzles. Each puzzle required a participant to identify in a letter matrix a number of nouns denominating specific exemplars of a certain class of real-world objects (e.g., certain kinds of fruits). The nouns appeared in the rows, in the columns, and in the diagonal axes of the letter matrixes. Most nouns were written in the natural, forward direction of written language (e.g., P E A C H) but others were reversed and had to be decoded from backward (e.g., M U L P). Pilot work indicated that participants working on these tasks found the word-finding activity to be quite absorbing and demanding. The criterion measure was the number of words correctly identified in the letter matrixes.

The second task consisted of verbal analogies drawn from the lower and upper third of the normatively defined level of difficulty of a standardized test of intelligence. The analogies were divided into two test pools. Students were informed that the first pool would consist of relatively difficult problems whereas the second pool would comprise relatively easy problems, as specified in the test norms. After they had been presented with a few sample tasks, participants were asked to choose by their own a total of 12 analogy problems from among the two test pools. The number of analogies chosen from the pool of difficult tasks provided the task choice criterion.

The two indirect achievement motivation tests (PSE and IAT) were significantly interrelated ($r = .27$), but each of these tests was statistically independent of questionnaire-assessed need for achievement ($rs = .0$). The two criterion variables (task performance at the word finding puzzles and task choice at the verbal analogy problems) were uncorrelated ($r = .0$). We thus submitted measures of task performance and task choice to two separate regression analyses. The three achievement motivation tests and the test of verbal ability were entered simultaneously as predictors into the regression equations. In this way, we were able to determine the unique relationship between each predictor and the specific criterion of interest. For the sake of simplicity, we will illustrate the results obtained from these analyses by reporting partial correlation coefficients.

First, a high degree of verbal fluency significantly predicted both a greater number of nouns correctly identified in the letter matrixes (partial $r = .34$) and a stronger preference for difficult, relative to easy, tasks in the verbal analogies test (partial $r = .23$). Second, both IAT-assessed (partial $r = .21$) and PSE-assessed (partial $r = .20$) achievement motivations uniquely predicted how well students did on the word-finding puzzles. Students scoring high on these tests outperformed students scoring low on these tests. In contrast, neither the PSE nor the IAT predicted participants' task choice behavior. Third, the achievement motivation questionnaire (MARPS) yielded a complementary pattern of results. The questionnaire failed to account for differences in word-finding performance. Yet students who described themselves as achievers chose a greater number of analogies from the difficult item pool than students who ascribed to themselves a weak sense of achievement (partial $r = .26$).

These findings nicely fit the idea that implicit and explicit tendencies to achieve are differently involved the prediction of energetic and decisional aspects of achievement-relevant behavior. Implicit motivation measures (PSE and IAT) uniquely predicted variations in task performance that could not be accounted for by differences in cognitive abilities. And the measure of self-attributed need for achievement (MARPS) was a unique predictor of achievement choices as reflected in a (stronger) preference for working on difficult tasks. Hence, in terms of its predictive validity, the IAT shared many important features with the PSE but markedly differed from the achievement motivation questionnaire.

As noted, the two achievement criteria (effort and choice) assessed in Experiment 3 were statistically independent of each other. At first glance, this lack of correlation may raise serious concerns about the existence of a nomological network integrating choice-related and effort-related criteria in one and the same achievement theory (see also Cooper, 1983; Kuhl, 1984). Yet, it should be acknowledged that in the above experiment, two isolated tasks were used to assess the aforementioned criteria. One might therefore speculate that decisional and energetic aspects of achievement are more closely interrelated when choice and performance motivations are assessed within one and the same task situation. Evidence corroborating this view comes from Locke and Latham's (1990, 2002) research on goal-setting behavior. According to these researchers, goals motivate people to exert effort up to a point or level of difficulty aspired to by the individual. Accordingly, a basic tenet of goal setting theory is that relative to easy goals, difficult goals are more effective in mobilizing effort. As Locke and Latham reported, this postulate has been supported by a wealth of evidence from laboratory experiments and real-life field studies.

In Experiment 4, we thus expanded our analysis of motive–behavior relations to integrate goal setting as a potential mediator intervening between motivational preferences and task achievements. In doing so, we considered goal setting as a cognitive regulator of effort, enabling people to optimize their achievements through the pursuit of self-set standards or reference points. Because people with a strong explicit need for achievement prefer difficult tasks relative to easy ones, we expected this group of individuals to set more difficult goals than any other group of individuals. If this is true, active engagement in goal setting activities should establish a link between a person's explicit need for achievement and her or his task performance. In contrast, as McClelland et al. (1989) stated, implicit motives operate on behavior mostly without any awareness on the actor's part. In keeping with this view, the implicit need to achieve has seldom been found to influence volitional choices, levels of aspiration, and related measures of explicitly stated preferences and evaluations (see Koestner et al., 1991). We therefore did *not* expect implicit achievement tendencies to use, or have access to, this deliberate mechanism of self-control.

To examine these ideas, we administered to 92 college students the same kind of motivation tests as described above (PSE, IAT, MARPS). One week after they had completed these tests, we invited the participants to come back to the lab and work on a speeded test designed to examine their skills of concentrating on a given task. The test task required each participant to solve a large number of very easy math problems (2 + 3 = ?). The test material was organized in 12 blocks (or test columns) presented to the participants in paper-and-pencil format. At each block, the performance criterion was the number of tasks a participant was able to solve within 20 seconds. Because all test columns were imprinted on one sheet of paper, students could easily monitor their achievements, and changes thereof, across the columns.

Different from the above experiment, participants of the present experiment were explicitly instructed to engage in goal setting activity during the performance phase. The first block served to assess students' "pretest" performance. Then, through Blocks 2 to 12, students were explicitly told to indicate on their test forms how many tasks they would aspire to solve in the test column to follow. To obtain a measure of goal setting, we counted the number of blocks where a student had raised her or his level of aspiration above the maximum score she or he had set at any of the previous blocks. Different from the absolute level of goal difficulty, this relative criterion of goal setting was unrelated to students' pretest performance (i.e., the level of performance they had reached before they engaged in the goal-setting activity).

Similar to the above results, PSE and IAT were significantly correlated ($r = .25$), but each of these two tests was unrelated to self-assessed achievement motivation (MARPS). With pretest performance covaried out, *each* of the three motive measures was positively related to students' performance throughout the test phase (partial $r = .31$, $.27$, and $.28$ for IAT, PSE, and MARPS, respectively). Hence, different from Experiment 3, in the present experiment self-reported need for achievement *was* a reliable predictor of task performance.

What happened when we included in our analysis goal setting as a potential mediator of the observed motive–performance relations? To answer this question, we computed a path model, the results of which are depicted in Figure 6.4. In keeping with goal setting theory, the number of increases in the maximum level of goal difficulty turned out to be a positive predictor of performance on the test task. Moreover, self-reported achievement motivation (MARPS) reliably predicted how often a student had raised his or her goal level up to a new maximum score. Indeed, this criterion of goal setting fully accounted for the effect the self-attributed achievement motive had on students' test performance. Hence, in this experiment, a strong explicit motive for achievement

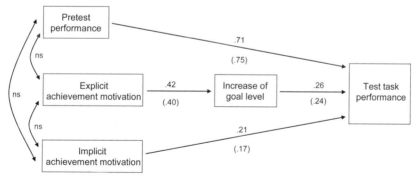

Figure 6.4 Path diagram illustrating the relationships among achievement motivation tests, goal-setting behavior, and test task performance. Explicit achievement motivation was assessed with a self-report scale. Implicit achievement motivation was assessed with the Implicit Association Test (path coefficients depicted above arrows) and with the Picture Story Exercise (path coefficients depicted in parentheses below arrows), respectively. Depicted are statistically significant path coefficients ($ps < .05$).

indirectly translated into better task performance, mainly through its influence (or direct path) on self-set standards. In contrast, no matter how implicit tendencies to achieve had been assessed (with the PSE or the IAT, respectively), goal setting was unrelated to the strength of these tendencies. For this reason, goal setting was also unable to explain the performance effects associated with the two indirect motive tests. Instead, the associated effects were quite direct and remained fully intact with differences in goal setting covaried out.

Discussion

Which general conclusions can be drawn from the reported results? According to McClelland (1987), a motive drives, orients, and selects behavior, and any presumed measure of a certain motive should satisfy these criteria to be considered a valid indicator of individual differences in motive strength. Koestner et al. (1991, p. 63) further elaborated this view by arguing that the implicit motive for achievement "is most likely to be energized and regulated by factors *intrinsic* to the process of performing an activity." The reported findings suggest that the IAT measure of achievement orientation is able to tap the kind of energetic impetus typical of the motive described by McClelland and Koestner. Relative to low scorers, high scorers on the IAT measure tried harder to surpass an internal standard of excellence (Experiment 1), showed a higher level of sympathetic activation while working on a task where success was uncertain (Experiment 2), and generally performed better at effort-sensitive tasks that required a great deal of mental effort (Experiments 3 and 4). Hence, in the presence of achievement-related incentives (some standard of excellence, a moderate risk of failing, or any other kind of cognitive challenge), participants scoring high on the IAT were more likely than other participants to try hard and put forth high levels of effort throughout ongoing task pursuits.

The pattern of intertest correlations that we obtained from the administration of multiple instruments for the assessment of individual differences in achievement motivation was a bit more complex but generally supported the view that the IAT procedure assesses implicit features of achievement-oriented concerns. In all of the reported investigations, the IAT was unrelated to both trait-like and state-like measures of self-attributed achievement motivation. In contrast, although IAT and PSE shared little common variance (less than 10%), the intertest correlation between these two instruments was positive and statistically significant in each of the three investigations where they had jointly been administered. This finding deserves attention because PSE-assessed achievement needs (or motives to succeed) have seldom been found to correlate substantially with *any* other individual difference measure of achievement motivation (see Brunstein & Heckhausen, 2008; Spangler, 1992). Here, we can only speculate whether motivationally significant implicit cognitions can become activated by stimuli depicted on PSE cards so that they are able to intrude the stream of imaginative behavior from which fantasy stories are drawn. Most interesting, however, was the finding that the two indirect motive tests (IAT and PSE) yielded similar patterns of criterion validity coefficients. Both instruments reliably predicted behavioral and physiological manifestations of task engagement but failed to account for explicit declarations of achievement-congruent self-views.

Despite these parallels in the predictive validity of IAT and PSE, it would be premature to conclude that these two tests assess essentially the same kind of motive. Their intertest correlations ($r \leq .33$) were by far too modest to justify this view. Furthermore, although IAT and PSE predicted similar, or even the same, behavioral criteria, each measure accounted for a unique portion of variance in the predicted variables.[5] From our view, it is still speculative but more appropriate to interpret these findings as suggesting that IAT-assessed and PSE-assessed achievement tendencies reflect important but distinct features of the implicit need for doing something well. In a sense, this view is similar to Heckhausen's (1977) earlier idea that (the implicit) need for achievement embodies a multiplicity of cognitive and affective preferences (the predilection for competing with internal standards, the capacity of experiencing pride after success, etc.) that interact with certain situational influences to drive and shape a person's behavior. To the extent that this is true, it should no longer be assumed that a summary test score derived from a single (and more or less idiosyncratic) assessment tool can portray the entire whole architecture or complex anatomy of the implicit achievement motive. Nor should one expect that measures assessing one or two specific features of this multifaceted psychological construct will be likely to share substantial portions of overlapping variance (although they should correlate with each other at least up to a certain degree). Like Heckhausen, we thus believe that a multivariate assessment strategy is most useful and imperative to paint a more complete picture of the human need to achieve. Our findings suggest that whatever kind of measures one may choose to administer for this purpose, the IAT procedure deserves to be included among them.

Conclusion

From six decades of research on human motives, we have learned a great deal about the quality and functioning of motivational preferences of which people are not aware. Per definition, these preferences are not available for self-report methods but can only be inferred indirectly from less obtrusive procedures. To explore individual differences in the strength of certain motive dispositions, such as the need to achieve, for quite some time motivation researchers have relied on the story-based approach established by D. C. McClelland and J. W. Atkinson. Recently, however, proponents of personality research and social psychology have started a new endeavor to construct from response latency measures test scores representing individual differences in implicit social cognitions. The respective mental concepts are assumed to be represented in an associative network, where they are interconnected by very fast cognitive processes, and implicit self-related cognitions can be considered an important part of this network. Although this novel approach to the study of individual differences is still complicated by a number of difficulties, one of the strengths evident in the IAT is that this test procedure enables researchers to assess with high accuracy (and with taking as little time as possible) personality components that are unavailable for introspective methodologies.

The above evidence suggests that the IAT procedure can easily be adapted by researchers who would like to assess individual differences in the strength of motivational orientations. In our examination of the predictive validity of an IAT constructed for the assessment of individual differences in achievement motivation, we found that this newly developed instrument (a) showed virtually no overlap with self-reported achievement motives, (b) significantly related to the traditional PSE measure of need for achievement, and (c) produced a pattern of criterion validity coefficients that nicely fit the implicit/explicit framework outlined by D. C. McClelland. Further research is needed to scrutinize the construct validity of this IAT measure and to test the predictive validity of related IATs across different domains of motivational engagement. Still, we believe that the IAT, and related procedures of inferring individual differences from chronometric assessment tools, can strengthen the methodological foundation of contemporary research on implicit motives.

Author Note

Parts of the research summarized in this chapter were supported by Deutsche Forschungsgemeinschaft grants BR 1056/8-1 and 8-2.

Notes

1. One important parallel between McClelland et al.'s (1989) motivation model and Wilson et al.'s (2000) attitude model is that both models assume that implicit and explicit measures of individual differences represent two qualitatively *different* aspects of personality. Implicit and explicit personality systems (e.g., attitudinal or motive systems) coexist in memory, each operating on a person's behavior according to its own, unique principles. In contrast, other theorists (see Fazio & Olson, 2003) assume that implicit and explicit measures refer to essentially the *same* person attributes (e.g., a specific attitude). Discordance (or a lack of correlation) between the two kinds of measures is explained by the operation of deliberative thoughts (e.g., a cost-benefit analysis of the enactment

of certain types of behavior) that influence a person's responses to explicit, but not to implicit, measures. One important implication of this latter view is that implicit and explicit measures are expected to converge when either the opportunity or the motivation to deliberate is low (see Fazio & Towles-Schwen, 1999). Which of these two theoretical perspectives (a dual-system approach or a single-system/two-measures approach) is more adequate to account for the variety of findings reported in the implicit/explicit literature is still an issue of much debate among personality researchers and social psychologists (cf. Deutsch & Strack, 2006; Greenwald et al., 2002; Strack & Deutsch, 2004).

2. In more recent descriptions of the IAT, practice trials that commonly precede the combined categorization tasks presented in Blocks 3 and 5 are enumerated as separate blocks that are to be included in a scoring algorithm denoted as D-score by Greenwald, Nosek, and Banaji (2003). For the sake of simplicity, in this chapter, we will describe the IAT procedure in terms of the five essential steps necessary to obtain a measure of the IAT effect.

3. From Heckhausen's (1977) achievement motive theory, we derived one further (theoretical) principle guiding the selection of attribute items. According to Heckhausen, the achievement motive can be understood as a weighting disposition that augments (or attenuates) the influence of incentive-related and expectancy-related information (e.g., information about a task's difficulty) on a person's inclination to engage and persist in achievement-related endeavors. Because we have more fully elaborated this principle elsewhere (Brunstein & Schmitt, 2004), we do not delve further into it. It should be noted, however, that one-half of the attribute items (e.g., ambitious, curious) served to address incentive-related aspects of achievement-oriented concerns, whereas the other half of attribute items (e.g., efficient and successful) was chosen to address a sense of self-confidence in achievement-oriented pursuits.

4. To test the reliability of the (reciprocal) IAT score, we split the two combined tasks into four consecutive blocks each consisting of 32 trials. Accordingly, coefficient alpha was computed across four test "items."

5. Even the highest degree of convergence in the predictive validity of IAT and PSE would not guarantee the identity of the assessed motive. Construct validation methodologies, such as exploratory and confirmatory factor analyses, are more appropriate to address this issue. From our own experience with exploratory factor analyses, it is all but not too difficult to show that PSE and IAT load on a common "implicit motive" factor, whereas measures of self-report motives generally load on a second "explicit motive" factor. Unfortunately, the relatively low correlation among IAT-assessed and PSE-assessed motivations makes it much more difficult, or even impossible, to map these two tests to the same latent variable in confirmatory factor analyses. This should not come as too much of a surprise because a fair amount of redundancy in measurement is an important prerequisite of latent variables analysis, and IAT and PSE clearly lack this redundancy. Another reason why we hesitate to draw a firm conclusion about the factorial structure of indirect motive tests is that we found in our own data sets that correlations among IAT-assessed and PSE-assessed achievement motivations can markedly differ across different subsamples. For instance, in the

majority of our studies, PSE/IAT correlations were higher for men (up to a maximum level of .50) than for women (mostly below the value of .20). Unfortunately, we are still far from an adequate understanding of such moderating influences (for a detailed discussion of related issues, see Chapter 11 in the present volume).

References

Asendorpf, J. B., Banse, R., & Mücke, D. (2002). Double dissociation between implicit and explicit personality self-concept: The case of shy behavior. *Journal of Personality and Social Psychology, 83,* 380–393.

Atkinson, J. W. (1957). Motivational determinants of risk taking behavior. *Psychological Review, 64,* 359–372.

Atkinson, J. W. (1964). *An introduction to motivation.* Princeton, NJ: Van Nostrand.

Atkinson, J. W. (1981). Studying personality in the context of an advanced motivational psychology. *American Psychologist, 36,* 117–128.

Banse, R. (2001). Affective priming with liked and disliked persons: Prime visibility determines congruency and incongruency effects. *Cognition and Emotion, 15,* 501–520.

Banse, R., Seise, J., & Zerbes, N. (2001). Implicit attitudes towards homosexuality: Reliability, validity, and controllability of the IAT. *Zeitschrift für Experimentelle Psychologie, 48,* 145–160.

Bargh, J. A. (1990). Auto-motives. Preconscious determinants of thought and behavior. In E. T Higgins & R. M. Sorrentino (Eds.), *Handbook of motivation and cognition: Foundations of social behavior* (Vol. 2, pp. 93–130). New York: Guilford.

Bargh, J. A. (Ed.). (2007). *Social psychology and the unconscious: The automaticity of higher mental processes.* New York: Psychology Press.

Bargh, J. A., & Barndollar, K. (1996). Automaticity in action: The unconscious as repository of chronic goals and motivation. In P. M. Gollwitzer & J. A. Bargh (Eds.), *The psychology of action: Linking cognition and motivation to behavior* (pp. 457–481). New York: Guilford.

Bargh, J. A., & Chartrand, T. L. (2000). The mind in the middle: A practical guide to priming and automaticity research. In H. T. Reis & C. M. Judd (Eds.), *Handbook of research methods in social and personality psychology* (pp. 253–285). New York: Cambridge University Press.

Bargh, J. A., & Gollwitzer, P. M. (1994). Environmental control of goal-directed action: Automatic and strategic contingencies between situations and behavior. In W. Spaulding (Ed.), *Nebraska Symposium on Motivation: Vol. 41. Integrative views of motivation, cognition, and emotion* (pp. 71–124). Lincoln, NB: University of Nebraska Press.

Bargh, J. A., Gollwitzer, P. M., Lee-Chai, A., Barndollar, K., & Trötschel, R. (2001). The automated will: Nonconscious activation and pursuit of behavioral goals. *Journal of Personality and Social Psychology, 81,* 1014–1027.

Bing, M. N., LeBreton, J. M., Davison, H. K., Migetz, D. Z., & James, L. R. (2007). Integrating implicit and explicit social cognitions for enhanced personality assessment: A general framework for choosing measurement and statistical methods. *Organizational Research Methods, 10,* 136–179.

Bosson, J. K., Swann, W. B., Pennebaker, J. W. (2000). Stalking the perfect measure of implicit self-esteem: The blind men and the elephant revisited? *Journal of Personality and Social Psychology, 79,* 631–643.

Breckler, S. J., & Greenwald, A. G. (1986). Motivational facets of the self. In R. M. Sorrentino & E. T. Higgins (Eds.), *Handbook of motivation and cognition* (pp. 145–164). New York: Guilford.

Brehm, J. W., & Self, E. (1989). The intensity of motivation. In M. R. Rosenzweig & L. W. Porter (Eds.), *Annual review of psychology, 40,* 109-131. Palo Alto, CA: Annual Reviews, Inc.

Brendl, C. M., Markman, A. B., & Messner, C. (2001). How do indirect measures of evaluation work? Evaluating the inference of prejudice in the Implicit Association Test. *Journal of Personality and Social Psychology, 81,* 760–773.

Brickenkamp, R., & Zillmer, E. (1998). *d2 Test of Attention.* Seattle, WA: Hogrefe International.

Brunstein, J. C., & Gollwitzer, P. M. (1996). Effects of failure on subsequent performance: The importance of self-defining goals. *Journal of Personality and Social Psychology, 70,* 395–407.

Brunstein, J. C., & Heckhausen, H. (2008). Achievement motivation. In J. Heckhausen & H. Heckhausen (Eds.), *Motivation and action* (pp. 137–183). New York: Cambridge University Press.

Brunstein, J. C., & Maier, G. W. (2005). Implicit and self-attributed motives to achieve: Two separate but interacting needs. *Journal of Personality and Social Psychology, 89,* 205–222.

Brunstein, J. C., & Schmitt, C. H. (2004). Assessing individual differences in achievement motivation with the Implicit Association Test. *Journal of Research in Personality, 38,* 536–555.

Cesario, J., Plaks, J. E., & Higgins, E. T. (2006). Automatic social behavior as motivated preparation to interact. *Journal of Personality and Social Psychology, 90,* 893–910.

Cooper, W. H. (1983). An achievement motivation nomological network. *Journal of Personality and Social Psychology, 44,* 841–861.

Covington, M. V., & Omelich, C. L. (1979). Are causal attributions causal? A path analysis of the cognitive model of achievement motivation. *Journal of Personality and Social Psychology, 37,* 1487–1504.

Deutsch, R., & Strack, F. (2006). Duality models in social psychology: From dual processes to interacting systems. *Psychological Inquiry, 17,* 166–172.

Egloff, B., & Schmukle, S. C. (2002). Predictive validity of an Implicit Association Test for assessing anxiety. *Journal of Personality and Social Psychology, 83,* 1441–1455.

Egloff, B., Schwerdtfeger, A., & Schmukle, S. C. (2005). Temporal stability of the Implicit Association Test – anxiety. *Journal of Personality Assessment, 84,* 82–88.

Entwisle, D. R. (1972). To dispel fantasies about fantasy-based measures of achievement motivation. *Psychological Bulletin, 77*, 377–391.

Fazio, R. H. (1990). A practical guide to the use of response latency in social psychological research. In C. Hendrick & M. S. Clark (Eds.), *Research methods in personality and social psychology* (Vol. 11, pp. 74–97). Newbury Park, CA: Sage.

Fazio, R. H., Jackson, J. R., Dunton, B. C., & Williams, C. J. (1995). Variability in automatic activation as an unobtrusive measure of racial attitudes. A bona fide pipeline? *Journal of Personality and Social Psychology, 69*, 1013–1027.

Fazio, R. H., & Olson, M. A. (2003). Implicit measures in social cognition research: Their meaning and use. *Annual Review of Psychology, 54*, 297–327.

Fazio, R. H., Sanbonmatsu, D. M., Powell, M. C., & Kardes, F. R. (1986). On the automatic activation of attitudes. *Journal of Personality and Social Psychology, 50*, 229–238.

Fazio, R. H., & Towles-Schwen, T. (1999). The MODE model of attitude-behavior processes. In S. Chaiken & Y. Trope (Eds.), *Dual process theories in social psychology* (pp. 97–116). New York: Guilford.

Freud, S. (1904). *The psychopathology of everyday life*. London: Ernest Benn.

Greenwald, A. G., Banaji, M. R., Rudman, L. A., Farnham, S. D., Nosek, B. A., & Mellot, D. S. (2002). A unified theory of implicit attitudes, stereotypes, self-esteem, and self-concept. *Psychological Review, 109*, 3–25.

Greenwald, A. G., & Farnham, S. D. (2000). Using the Implicit Association Test to measure self-esteem and self-concept. *Journal of Personality and Social Psychology, 79*, 1022–1038.

Greenwald, A. G., McGhee, D. E., & Schwartz, J. L. K. (1998). Measuring individual differences in implicit cognition: The implicit association test. *Journal of Personality and Social Psychology, 74*, 1464–1480.

Greenwald, A. G., Nosek, B. A., & Banaji, M. R. (2003). Understanding and using the Implicit Association Test I. An improved scoring algorithm. *Journal of Personality and Social Psychology, 85*, 197–216.

Greenwald, A. G., Poehlman, T. A., Uhlmann, E. L., & Banaji, M. R. (2009). Understanding and using the Implicit Association Test: III. Meta-analysis of predictive validity. *Journal of Personality and Social Psychology, 97*, 17–41.

Heckhausen, H. (1963). *Hoffnung und Furcht in der Leistungsmotivation* [Hope and fear in achievement motivation]. Meisenheim, Germany: Verlag Anton Hain.

Heckhausen, H. (1977). Achievement motivation and its constructs. *Motivation and Emotion, 1*, 283–329.

Heckhausen, H. (1986). Why some time out might benefit achievement motivation research. In J. H. L. van den Bercken, E. E. J. De Bruyn, & T. C. M. Bergen (Eds.), *Achievement and task motivation* (pp. 7–39). Lisse, The Netherlands: Swets & Zeitlinger.

Heckhausen, H., Schmalt, H.-D., & Schneider, K. (1985). *Achievement motivation in perspective*. San Diego, CA: Academic Press.

Higgins, E. T., Rholes, W. S., & Jones, C. R. (1977). Category accessibility and impression formation. *Journal of Experimental Social Psychology, 13*, 141–154.

Hofmann, W., Gawronski, B., Gschwendner, T., Le, H., & Schmitt, M. (2005). A meta-analysis on the correlation between the Implicit Association Test and explicit self-report measures. *Personality and Social Psychology Bulletin, 31,* 1369–1385.

Karpinski, A., & Hilton, J. L. (2001). Attitudes and the Implicit Association Test. *Journal of Personality and Social Psychology, 81,* 774–788.

Klauer, K. C., & Mierke, J. (2005). Task-set inertia, attitude accessibility, and compatibility-order effects: New evidence for a task-set switching account of the Implicit Association Test effect. *Personality and Social Psychology Bulletin, 31,* 208–217.

Koestner, R., & McClelland, D. C. (1990). Perspectives on competence motivation. In L. Pervin (Ed.), *Handbook of personality theory and research* (pp. 527–548). New York: Guilford.

Koestner, R., Weinberger, J., & McClelland, D. C. (1991). Task-intrinsic and social-extrinsic sources of arousal for motives assessed in fantasy and self-report. *Journal of Personality, 59,* 57–82.

Kukla, A. (1978). An attributional theory of choice. *Advances in Experimental Social Psychology, 11,* 113–144.

Locke, E. A., & Latham, G. P. (1990). *A theory of goal setting and task performance.* Englewood Cliffs, NJ: Prentice Hall.

Locke, E. A., & Latham, G. P. (2002). Building a practically useful theory of goal setting and task motivation: A 35-year odyssey. *American Psychologist, 57,* 705–717.

Kuhl, J. (1984). Motivational aspects of achievement motivation and learned helplessness: Toward a comprehensive theory of action control. In B. A. Maher & W. B. Maher (Eds.), *Progress in experimental personality research* (Vol. 13, pp. 99–171). New York: Academic Press.

McClelland, D. C. (1958). Methods of measuring human motivation. In J. W. Atkinson (Ed.), *Motives in fantasy, action, and society* (pp. 7–45). Princeton, NJ: Van Nostrand.

McClelland, D. C. (1987). *Human motivation.* New York: Cambridge University Press.

McClelland, D. C., & Atkinson, J. W. (1948). The projective expression of needs: I. The effects of different intensities of the hunger drive on perception. *Journal of Personality, 25,* 205–222.

McClelland, D. C., Atkinson, J. W., Clark, R. A., & Lowell, E. L. (1953). *The achievement motive.* New York: Appleton-Century-Crofts.

McClelland, D. C., Clark, R. A., Roby, T. B., & Atkinson, J. W. (1949). The effect of need for achievement on thematic apperception. *Journal of Experimental Psychology, 37,* 242–255.

McClelland, D. C., Koestner, R., & Weinberger, J. (1989). How do self-attributed and implicit motives differ? *Psychological Review, 96,* 690–702.

Mayer, J. D., Faber, M. A., & Xu, X. (2007). Seventy-five years of motivation measures (1930–2005): A descriptive analysis. *Motivation and Emotion, 31,* 83–103.

Mehrabian, A. (1969). Measures of achieving tendency. *Educational and Psychological Measurement, 29,* 445–451.

Meyer, W.-U. (1987). Perceived ability and achievement-related behavior. In F. Halisch & J. Kuhl (Eds.), *Motivation, intention, and volition* (pp. 73–86). Berlin, Germany: Springer Verlag.

Mierke, J., & Klauer, K. C. (2003). Method-specific variance in the Implicit Association Test. *Journal of Personality and Social Psychology, 85,* 1180–1192.

Moulton, R. W. (1974). Motivational implications of individual differences in competence. In J. W. Atkinson & J. O. Raynor (Eds.), *Motivation and achievement* (pp. 77–82). Washington, DC: Winston.

Murray, H. A. (1938). *Explorations in personality.* New York: Oxford University Press.

Murray, H. A. (1943). *Thematic Apperceptive Test Manual.* Cambridge, MA: Harvard University Press.

Neely, J. H. (1977). Semantic priming and retrieval from lexical memory: Roles of inhibitionless spreading activation and limited-capacity attention. *Journal of Experimental Psychology: General, 106,* 226–245.

Nicholls, J. G. (1984). Achievement motivation: Conceptions of ability, subjective experience, task choice, and performance. *Psychological Review, 91,* 328–346.

Nosek, B. A., Banaji, M. R., & Greenwald, A. G. (2002). Math = male, me = female, therefore math ≠ me. *Journal of Personality and Social Psychology, 83,* 44–59.

Nosek, B. A., Greenwald, A. G., & Banaji, M. R. (2007). The Implicit Association Test at age 7: A methodological and conceptual review. In J. A. Bargh (Ed.), *Automatic processes in social thinking and behavior* (pp. 265–292). New York: Psychology Press.

Obrist, P. A. (1981). *Cardiovascular psychophysiology: A perspective.* New York: Plenum.

Patten, R. L., & White, L. A. (1977). Independent effect of achievement motivation and overt attribution on achievement behavior. *Motivation and Emotion, 1,* 39–59.

Perugini, M. (2005). Predictive models of implicit and explicit attitudes. *British Journal of Social Psychology, 44,* 29–45.

Perugini, M., & Prestwich, A. (2007). The gatekeeper: Individual differences are key in the chain from perception to behavior. *European Journal of Personality, 21,* 303–317.

Rothermund, K., & Wentura, D. (2001). Figure-ground asymmetries in the implicit association test (IAT). *Zeitschrift für Experimentelle Psychologie, 48,* 94–106.

Schmukle, S. C., & Egloff, B. (2004). Does the Implicit Association Test for assessing anxiety measure trait and state variance? *European Journal of Personality, 18,* 483–494.

Schultheiss, O. C. (2001). *Manual for the assessment of hope of success and fear of failure* (English translation of Heckhausen's need Achievement measure). Unpublished scoring manual. University of Michigan, Ann Arbor.

Schultheiss, O. C., & Brunstein, J. C. (2001). Assessment of implicit motives with a research version of the TAT: Picture profiles, gender differences, and relations to other personality measures. *Journal of Personality Assessment, 77,* 71–86.

Schultheiss, O. C., & Brunstein, J. C. (2005). An implicit motive perspective on competence motivation. In A. J. Elliot & C. S. Dweck (Eds.), *Handbook of competence and motivation* (pp. 31–51). New York: Guilford.

Schultheiss, O. C., Liening, S., & Schad, D. (2008). The reliability of a Picture Story Exercise measure of implicit motives: Estimates of internal consistency, retest reliability, and ipsative stability. *Journal of Research in Personality, 42,* 1560–1571.

Sheldon, K. M., King, L. A., Houser-Marko, L., Osbaldiston, R., & Gunz, A. (2007). Comparing IAT and TAT measures of power versus intimacy motivation. *European Journal of Personality, 21,* 263–280.

Shrable, K., & Moulton, R. W. (1968). Achievement fantasy as a function of variations in self-rated competence. *Perceptual and Motor Skills, 27,* 515–528.

Siegel, P., & Weinberger, J. (1998). Capturing the "Mommy and I Are One" merger fantasy: The oneness motive. In R. Bornstein & J. Masling (Eds.), *Empirical perspectives on the psychoanalytic unconscious* (pp. 71–97). Washington, DC: APA Press.

Spangler, W. D. (1992). Validity of questionnaire and TAT measures of need for achievement: Two meta-analyses. *Psychological Bulletin, 112,* 140–154.

Strack, F., & Deutsch, R. (2004). Reflective and impulsive determinants of social behavior. *Personality and Social Psychology Review, 8,* 220–247.

Trope, Y. (1975). Seeking information about one's own ability as a determinant of choice among tasks. *Journal of Personality and Social Psychology, 32,* 1004–1013.

Tuerlinckx, F., De Boeck, P., & Lens, W. (2002). Measuring needs with the Thematic Apperception Test: A psychometric study. *Journal of Personality and Social Psychology, 82,* 448–461.

Weinberger, J., & McClelland, D. C. (1990). Cognitive versus traditional motivational models: Irreconcilable or complementary? In E. T. Higgins & R. M. Sorrentino (Eds.), *Handbook of motivation and cognition: Foundations of social behavior* (Vol. 2, pp. 562–597). New York: Guilford.

Weiner, B. (1974). *Achievement motivation and attribution theory.* Morristown, NJ: General Learning.

Wilson, T., Lindsey, S., & Schooler, T. Y. (2000). A model of dual attitudes. *Psychological Review, 107,* 101–126.

Woike, B. A. (1995). Most memorable experiences: Evidence for a link between implicit and explicit motives and social cognitive processes in everyday life. *Journal of Personality and Social Psychology, 67,* 142–150.

Wright, R. A., & Kirby, L. D. (2001). Effort determination of cardiovascular response: An integrative analysis with applications in social psychology. In M. P. Zanna (Ed.), *Advances in experimental social psychology* (Vol. 33, pp. 256–307). San Diego, CA: Academic Press.

Chapter 7

Computer-Based Modeling, Assessment, and Coding of Implicit Motives

VIRGINIA BLANKENSHIP
Northern Arizona University, Flagstaff

Alread the computer has had a tremendous impact on the study of implicit motives, and the future will bring more ways to use the computer and the Internet to collect and analyze data to further our understanding of human motivation. In this c\hapter I will discuss four ways that the computer can be used in research on implicit motives: (1) for modeling the dynamics of implicit motives and their resultant actions, (2) for presenting task-based measures of implicit motives, (3) for writing Picture Story Exercise (PSE) stories and for studying implicit motives reflected in online materials such as chat rooms; and (4) for coding implicit motives in PSE stories. First I will review the Atkinson and Birch (1970) dynamics of action theory as a basis for developing task-based measures of implicit motives.

Computer-Based Modeling of Implicit Motives

In their distinction between implicit and self-attributed motives, McClelland, Koestner, and Weinberger (1989) proposed that implicit motives "are aroused by affective experiences intrinsic to an activity and not by explicit references to unmet goals" (p. 698). Thus, persons with high need for achievement will not necessarily know that they are motivated by competing with others or by pursuing long-term involvement in a career. McClelland et al. conceived of the implicit motive as leading to an activity that provided an incentive for that

186

motive. In line with McClelland (1980), they characterized implicit motives as predictive of spontaneous behavior over time.

The Atkinson and Birch (1970) dynamics of action provides a model for predicting which activity will be expressed in spontaneous behavior over time based on the strength of implicit motives. The dynamics of action focuses on a stream of behavior, the surface of which is determined by underlying forces analogous to ebb and flow. The stream of behavior changes through time as the result of forces internal to the person and incentives from the environment.

The dynamics of action theory has been translated into a computer simulation model with graphical output (Blankenship, Tumlinson, & Sims, 1995; Bongort, 1975; Selzer, 1973; Selzer & Sawusch, 1974) in which every behavior is represented by a line that rises and falls through time. The line for each behavior represents the resultant action tendency, defined as the action tendency minus the negaction tendency (defined below and in Table 7.1). Among the available behaviors, the highest resultant action tendency is expressed in behavior. Each alternative activity has an instigating force that causes the action tendency to rise over time. If the behavior is being expressed in action, a consummatory force[1] decreases the action tendency and the line goes down. Inhibitory forces are tied to sources of anxiety or threats surrounding the activity and result in negative action (or negaction) tendencies. It takes time for these negaction tendencies to stabilize. During that time the line representing the resultant action tendency goes down, but then eventually it turns in a positive direction. The net effect of a large inhibitory force is to delay initiation of an activity.

Changes in behavior are represented in the simulation when the line corresponding to the highest action tendency of the currently ongoing behavior crosses (or is crossed by) another line representing another behavior. A common way a change in behavior occurs is when the first behavior has stabilized and is represented by a flat line parallel to the X-axis. As the new behavior gains in strength from its instigating force, it crosses the line and becomes the dominant and new ongoing behavior. A second common change in behavior occurs when the first ongoing behavior is decreasing in value because the effect of its consummatory force is larger than the effect of its instigating force. As the resultant action tendency descends, it crosses the line representing the new behavior. For more examples of changes in behavior see Atkinson and Birch (1974), p. 272.

Another important assumption of the dynamics of action is that a tendency, once aroused, will persist until it is satisfied (expressed in behavior or decreased through substitute activity). Dependent variables that can be predicted using the model include latency (time to initiate the activity), persistence (how long the behavior lasts before a change to another behavior), and percentage time spent in one activity (as compared to the entire time period). See Table 7.1 for a brief summary of the dynamics of action concepts.

Table 7.1   Dynamics of Action Concepts with Definitions, Symbols Used in Formulating Equations, and Coordinating Definitions in the Achievement Motivation Setting

Dynamics of Action Concept	Definition	Symbol	Coordinating Definition in Achievement Setting
Action tendency	The momentary amount of positive tendency to do something	T	The momentary amount of positive tendency to achieve
Instigating force	Rate of increase of the action tendency for each unit of time	F	Related to the motive to approach success and the subje-ctive probability of success: $F_s = M_s \times P_s \times (1 - P_s)$
Negaction tendency	The momentary amount of negative tendency not to do something	N	The momentary amount of negative tendency not to achieve
Inhibitory force	The rate of increase in negaction tendency for each unit of time	I	Related to the motive to avoid failure and the subjective probability of success: $I_f = M_f \times P_s \times (1 - P_s)$
Resultant action tendency	At each point in time the action tendency minus the negaction tendency	T_R	At each point in time the action tendency minus the negaction tendency
Consummatory value	A coefficient that determines how strong the consummatory force will be	c	A coefficient that determines how strong the consummatory force will be. It is assumed that the consummatory value of success is greater than the consummatory value of failure: $c_s > c_f$
Consummatory Force	Decreases the action tendency for an ongoing behavior that is dominant or compatible with the dominant behavior – determined by $c \times T_R$	C	Decreases the action tendency for an achievement behavior that is dominant—determined by $c \times T_R$
Resistance value	A coefficient that determines the rate at which the negaction tendency is dissipated	r	A coefficient that determines the rate at which the negaction tendency is dissipated. It is assumed that the resistance value of success is greater than the resistance value of failure: $r_s > r_f$
Force of Resistance	Decreases the negaction tendency at all times, whether the behavior is dominant or not— determined by $r \times N$	R	Decreases the negaction tendency at all times, whether the behavior is dominant or not—determined by $r \times N$

Although the dynamics of action is a general model applicable to all types of behaviors, the first uses of the model were within the field of achievement motivation. Atkinson, Bongort, and Price (1977) simulated time spent thinking about achievement within the PSE. The focus of their study was to demonstrate that an implicit measure of need for achievement could be construct valid even though the internal consistency of the test was low. They produced 25 simulations of 18 to 30 hypothetical participants of varying levels of achievement motivation who thought about achievement as they "wrote" five or six stories to pictures of varying cue strength (incentive values). The hypothetical participants were high, medium, or low in achievement motivation, as reflected in their instigating forces to think about achievement. Three alternative activities incompatible with thinking about achievement provided the context in which percent of time spent thinking about achievement was calculated. Selective attention, the tendency to be influenced by competing environmental cues or incentives for alternative activities, was varied among the simulations. Also varied was the consummatory value, the turning-off value of thinking about achievement. Inhibitory forces, which would be related to fear of failure, were not included in these simulations.

Atkinson et al. (1977) then identified the percentage of hypothetical participants (who had been assigned high, medium, or low levels of instigating forces representing their achievement motives) who were correctly identified as high, medium, or low based on the percentage of time spent thinking about achievement as derived from the simulations. In 24 of the 25 simulations, 75% to 100% of the participants were correctly categorized. In the 25th simulation, only 60% were correctly identified. Coefficient alpha, the measure of internal consistency and reliability from classical test theory, was computed using percentage time spent out of 100 units for each of the five or six pictures. For the 25 simulations, coefficient alphas ranged from −.18 to .97. Atkinson et al. argued that the dynamics of action demonstrates that the PSE is a valid measure of achievement motivation because simulated participants were correctly categorized as high, medium, or low in assigned achievement motivation, even though the reliability of the simulated test results (coefficient alpha) was relatively low.

The Dynamics of Achievement Action

The first use of the dynamics of action computer simulation was to simulate hypothetical participants thinking about achievement (Atkinson et al, 1977), but quickly the simulation was used to develop hypotheses about what actual participants would do in actual achievement settings. Kuhl and Blankenship (1979a) focused on "behavioral change in a constant environment" (p. 141) and explored how the risk preferences of participants with higher motives to approach success rather than to avoid failure would change through time. Classic achievement motivation theory, as developed by Atkinson and Feather (1966), was an episodic theory that predicted what a participant would do at a particular time. Within this model, a change in risk preference would only come about if the participant changed his/her perception of the subjective probability of success as a result of success and/or failure outcomes. The dynamics of achievement motivation moved beyond that episodic focus to explain how risk preference could change even after the environment and subjective probability of success had stabilized.

Constructing hypotheses using the dynamics of action model required coordinating definitions tying the implicit motive to approach success to the instigating force to achieve (see Table 7.1). Specifically, the instigating force to engage in an achievement task was defined as a multiplicative function of the motive to approach success and the subjective probability of success at each difficulty level. The inhibitory force was defined using the motive to avoid failure and the subjective probability of success. Kuhl and Blankenship also related the consummatory value of performing an achievement task to the success or failure outcome, proposing that the consummatory value of success was greater than the consummatory value of failure.

In a study with 77 participants, Kuhl and Blankenship (1979b) provided evidence supporting the dynamic approach to achievement behavior. Specifically, in the free choice condition, participants chose from among five difficulty levels of an achievement-oriented perceptual reasoning task with success/failure outcomes. Five stacks of 50 puzzles each were placed in front of the participants. Each stack was clearly labeled with the probability of success: .1 (very difficult), .3 (difficult), .5 (intermediate), .7 (easy), and .9 (very easy). Participants were free to choose from among the five difficulty levels for 50 trials. Male participants with the motive to approach success (M_s as measured by the TAT/PSE) higher than the motive to avoid failure (M_f as measured by the Mandler & Sarason 1952 Test Anxiety Questionnaire)[2] initially chose the intermediate level of difficulty with a probability of success of .5 (as predicted by traditional achievement motivation theory). Contrary to traditional achievement motivation theory, however, and in concert with the dynamics of action model, they moved to more difficult tasks over time. This movement to more difficult tasks over time was explained as a function of the greater consummatory value of success than of failure, bringing about the cessation of the intermediate task and the movement to more difficult tasks, with fewer success outcomes.

In a review of nine studies in which participants had 10 to 15 choices among nine difficulty levels of a psychomotor task in which they pushed a steel ball through a gap of nine different widths on a table, Schneider and Posse (1982) found the same pattern of choices to increasingly more difficult tasks. They were able to model this sequence of risk choices with a computer program using two simple rules: move to a more difficult task after success and stay at the same level following failure. This cognitive strategy results in the same pattern of choices as the more dynamic explanation presented by Kuhl and Blankenship (1979a, 1979b).

To explore the relationship between consummatory value and task difficulty, Blankenship (1982) generated hypotheses predicting latency to initiate an achievement task and persistence at the achievement task. The use of time measures such as latency and persistence, instead of risk preference, takes advantage of the focus of the dynamics of action model on the stream of behavior and on when and for how long a behavior is expressed in action. Blankenship generated computer simulations of two activities, one achievement task and one nonachievement activity, where the only difference between simulations was the level of consummatory value. When the instigating forces were held constant, a higher consummatory value resulted in shorter time (persistence) at the achievement task.

In this experiment, 61 male participants with high implicit achievement motive (as measured by the PSE) started rating how funny jokes were that were presented on a computer. When they wished, they could play a target-shooting game. Approximately half were randomly assigned to play at the easy level ($P_s = .7$), and the other half were assigned to play at the difficult level ($P_s = .3$). Because the instigating force of an achievement task is equal to the motive to succeed (M_s) times the probability of success (P_s) times the incentive value of success (I_s), and because I_s is assumed to be inversely related to P_s ($I_s = 1 - P_s$), the instigating forces for these two tasks [$M_s \times P_s \times (1 - P_s)$] would be equal. In the simulations of the experimental situation, the latency to initiate the target-shooting achievement game was the same for these two groups. However, participants assigned the achievement task with the greater consummatory value would persist at the task for a shorter amount of time. The rate of success was held constant for the two groups at .5. Even though they received the same amount of successes (50%), the subjective probabilities reported by the two groups were significantly different, indicating they perceived the tasks to be easy (if assigned the $P_s = .7$ level) and difficult (if randomly assigned the $P_s = .3$ level). Although time to initiate the achievement task was the same for the two groups, persistence at the target-shooting game was not. Participants assigned the easy task (n = 29) persisted a median of 6.75 minutes whereas participants assigned the difficult target-shooting game (n = 32) persisted a median of 9.38 minutes, a highly significant difference. The dynamics of action was used to simulate the results with the consummatory value of success at the easy task higher than the consummatory value of success at the difficult task.

Based on these early results, Blankenship (1987) developed a computer-based behavioral measure of achievement motivation drawing from Lewin's level of aspiration theory (Lewin, Dembo, Festinger, & Sears, 1944), traditional achievement motivation theory (Atkinson, 1957; Atkinson & Feather, 1966), and the dynamics of action (Atkinson & Birch, 1970). Participants in the first experiment of this study made 21 choices among three difficulty levels (easy, intermediate, and difficult) of a target-shooting task. Using Lewin's concept of atypical shifts (the choice of an easier task following success or the choice of a more difficult task following failure) and based on previous research by Moulton (1965), those participants who made more atypical shifts were categorized as low in resultant achievement motivation (low RAM) whereas those who made fewer or no atypical shifts were categorized as high RAM. Littig (1963) had shown that high RAM participants were less responsive to point incentives than those with low RAM. Blankenship offered points on half of the trails and no points on the other half. Participants who took higher risks on trails with points were put into the low RAM category, and those who did not differentiate based on point incentives were put into the high RAM category.

Hypotheses derived from the dynamics of action were based on computer simulations of four types of individuals: (1) high RAM—those with high instigating force to approach achievement (F_s) and low inhibitory force from low fear of failure (I_f); (2) low RAM—those with low instigating force to achieve and high inhibitory force from high fear of failure (low F_s and high I_f); (3) F_s and I_f both high; and (4) F_s and I_f both low. Figure 7.1 shows the four graphs that result from these simulations. In all cases the high forces are three times the low forces. The panels represent the predicted latency to the achievement task for participants with high RAM (Panel 1) and low RAM (Panel 4) and those with equal instigating and inhibitory force—both high (Panel 2) and both low (Panel 3).

The vertical axis on the graphs in Figure 7.1 represents the resultant tendency strength of the activities (action tendency minus negative or negaction tendency), and the horizontal axis represent passing time. Each of the four panels represents four activities, watching a color design on a computer (represented by the initial dominant activity that is a flat line highest among the alternatives in each graph at 200 units of tendency strength), and three difficulty levels (easy, intermediate, and difficult) of a target-shooting game. Table 7.2 lists the time predictions for the four simulations, listing latency to the achievement task and percentage time spent at the four activities for 500 time units. Based on these simulations, it was predicted that participants who make fewer atypical shifts and who are less responsive to incentives (high RAM: high F_s and low I_f, Panel 1) were expected to have shorter latency to the achievement task and to spend a larger percentage of time at the intermediate task. Participants who make more atypical shifts and who are more responsive to incentives were expected to have the longest latency to the achievement task and to spend the most time watching the color design (low RAM: low F_s and high I_f, Panel 4).

Participants in Experiment 1 (Blankenship, 1987) returned a week later and began watching a color design. They were told that three levels (easy,

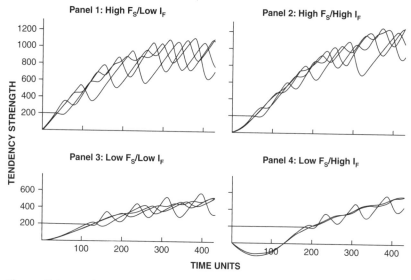

Figure 7.1 Simulations of activity choices among one nonachievement task (represented by flat line with initial tendency strength of 200) and three levels (easy, intermediate, and difficult) of the achievement task for individuals with motive to succeed greater than motive to avoid failure (Panel 1); motive to succeed equal to motive to avoid failure, both high (Panel 2); motive to succeed equal to motive to avoid failure, both low (Panel 3); and motive to succeed less than motive to avoid failure (Panel 4). (In each panel, the first positively sloped line to cross the flat line represents the intermediate level of the achievement task.) Copyright © 1987 by the American Psychological Association. Reproduced with permission. The official citation that should be used in referencing this material is Blankenship, V. (1987). A computer-based measure of resultant achievement motivation. *Journal of Personality and Social Psychology*, 53, 361–372.

intermediate, and difficult) of the target-shooting task were available and that they were free to choose from among the activities. The computer kept track of their choices for 15 minutes. Based on their choices the previous week, 23 participants were put in the high-RAM category (low number of atypical shifts

Table 7.2 Predictions Based on Dynamics of Action simulations of 500 Time Units, Corresponding to Figure 7.1

Forces		Latency to Achievement Task (Time Units)	Percent of Time Spent (After Achievement Task Initiated)			
F_s	I_f		Color	Easy	Intermediate	Difficult
High	Low	33.2	22.7	19.8	31.7	25.8
High	High	52.8	17.8	25.9	29.6	26.8
Low	Low	110.5	35.8	16.7	23.8	23.8
Low	High	184.4	32.6	19.6	27.1	20.7

Note: F_s = Instigating force to achieve success; I_f = inhibitory force to avoid failure.

and low responsiveness to incentives), and 23 participants were put in the low-RAM category (high number of atypical shifts and high responsiveness to incentives). In support of the dynamics of action and the research hypothesis, the two groups did not differ significantly on their latency to the achievement tasks, but low-RAM subjects spent significantly more time on the nonachievement task throughout the 15-minute testing period (M = 19.9%) than high-RAM participants (M = 8.4%).

In Experiment 2 test–retest reliability of the atypical shift and responsiveness to incentives measures of RAM were addressed. The atypical shift implicit measure of RAM was found to be more reliable than the responsiveness to point incentives indicator. However, due to the problem of nonshifters in Experiment 2 (i.e., participants who stayed at the same level of difficulty regardless of success or failure) Blankenship, changed the focus in Experiment 3 to number of *typical* shifts, meaning that participants with high RAM were assumed to make more typical shifts, choosing an easier task following failure and choosing a more difficult task following success.

In Experiment 3 of this study (Blankenship, 1987), the choices available on the computer were changed to focus more explicitly on latency to the achievement task instead of choice among achievement task difficulty levels. In the first session of Experiment 3, 59 participants were given 21 trials with free choice among five difficulty levels of the target-shooting game. High-RAM participants were those who made six or more *typical* shifts, and low-RAM participants made five or fewer *typical* shifts. They returned a week later and participated in a test of the dynamic effect of situational anxiety in which approximately one-third of the participants experienced a simulated computer breakdown to create anxiety. This experiment was conducted on an Apple II+ microcomputer, and these participants were not suspicious when the computer screen went blank and they had to go outside into the hall to get the research assistant to come and help them. An "interruption" control group was instructed to go outside the room and get the research assistant to enter a code number, to control for the effects of a break in the activity comparable to the computer breakdown but without the increased anxiety. A "no interruption" control group went directly to the testing session with no interruption.

In this experiment, participants began watching a color design on the computer screen, and at any time they could choose to rate jokes (a nonachievement task) or play the intermediate level (P_s = .5) of the target-shooting game. These three task choices were chosen to take full advantage of latency measures to the achievement task. In contrast to the task choices in Experiment 1 of this study, where participants watched a color design and then chose from among three difficulty levels of the achievement task, a nonachievement task (rating jokes) was available in Experiment 3 so that when subjects tired of the color design (which was fairly uninteresting in those early days), they could delay playing the target-shooting game by reading and rating jokes. The inclusion of a second alternative, nonachievement-related activity was important to allow for differences in implicit motives to reveal themselves in the time spent on the achievement task. The computer kept track of latency to the achievement task. Based on computer simulations of the dynamics of action, it was predicted that participants with low RAM, based on fewer typical shifts, would take longer to go to the target-shooting game if they had experienced a computer breakdown, an anxiety-provoking experience, than if they had not. The results confirmed this hypothesis; participants in the breakdown condition with low RAM took 406 seconds on average to begin playing the achievement game whereas high RAM participants in the breakdown condition took just 174 seconds on average to begin the target-shooting game.

The way that inhibitory forces work in the dynamics of action may be one of the most important contributions of the theory to the study of implicit motives. Lewin (1946) conceptualized conflicts as situations where approximately equal forces are acting on the person in opposite directions. The approach-avoidance conflict involves one goal with both positive and negative valences (attraction and repulsion). A person in an approach-avoidance conflict sees the goal as more attractive from farther away and more repulsive or frightening when the goal is nearer. The end result of an approach–avoidance conflict is for the person to be stuck at a safe distance from the goal, where the attracting and repelling forces are equal. In Lewin's example of a little boy who is both attracted by the ocean and repelled by the fearsome waves, the child is left on shore going back and forth toward the water and away from the waves when they come crashing into shore. In the dynamics of action, negative action tendencies that result from inhibitory forces (e.g., anxiety produced by ocean waves or by a computer breakdown) are eventually overcome because of the force of resistance—it just takes longer for that to happen for participants with low RAM. In the case of the little boy at the beach, the dynamics of action predicts that he will eventually go into the water; it will just take an inhibited, anxious child longer than an uninhibited, nonanxious child.

In a study comparing the traditional risk preference approach to achievement motivation (Atkinson, 1957; Atkinson & Feather, 1966) and the Atkinson and Birch (1970) dynamics of achievement activity, Blankenship (1992) again used the computer-based measure of achievement motivation utilizing Lewin's concept of atypical shifts. Participants in this study worked on the computer at two different times, one week apart. During the first session they made 21 choices among five difficulty levels (very easy, easy, intermediate, difficult, and very difficult) of a target-shooting game. Based on their sequence of choices, they were categorized as high in resultant achievement motivation (high RAM) if they made zero or just one atypical shift during that sequence. They were categorized as low RAM if they made two or more atypical shifts.

The focus of this study was on persistence at the achievement task. Participants began watching a color design and could choose to rate jokes on their funniness or play one of five levels of the target-shooting task. Thus, each participant had three activities available: watching the color design, rating jokes, or playing one assigned level of the target-shooting game. There were nine conditions, and the 309 participants were randomly assigned to one. In the first set of three of the conditions, approximately one-third of the participants were assigned to the very easy, easy, or intermediate levels with nominal success rates of 9/10, 7/10, and 5/10. The actual success rates for all three levels were 7/10. In the second set of three of the conditions, approximately one-third of the participants were assigned to the easy, intermediate, or difficult levels of the game with nominal success rates of 7/10, 5/10, and 3/10, but all received actual success rates of 5/10. Finally, in the last set of three of the conditions, approximately one third of the participants were randomly assigned to the intermediate, difficult, or most difficult level with nominal success rates of 5/10, 3/10, and 1/10, but all received actual success rates of 3/10. Approximately 33 participants were in each of the nine groups, and approximately half of each group was high RAM and half was low RAM based on number of atypical shifts the week before. Results from the three conditions where participants received 5/10 successes were strongly supportive of the dynamics-of-action predictions that those participants with high RAM will persist longer at an achievement task than those with low RAM, especially at the intermediate level of task difficulty. High-RAM participants (n = 42) persisted longer at the target-shooting task when the success rate was their theoretically preferred 5/10 (M = 437 seconds) than low-RAM participants (n = 38, M = 259 seconds).

Generally, the experimental evidence is supportive of a dynamics-of-action approach to achievement behavior. Lens, Lacante, Vansteenkiste, and Herrera (2005) applied the dynamics of action to understand how competing activities get in the way of student success. They proposed that "in order to understand why some students persist in their studying and others give up more easily, it is not only important to look at these students' level or strength of motivation for studying, but also to consider the number and strength of competing action alternatives such as playing, sport, going to the movies, watching TV, or working in order to make some money" (p. 277). In two studies of the amount of time students spent in leisure activities and in working, they found that students who spent 1-4 hours per week relaxing were more successful at passing their examinations than those who had no leisure or 4 or more hours a week of leisure. The results of competing time spent working was more straightforward; the more time students spent working, the lower their study motivation and the poorer their academic achievement. Their results indicate that it is important to consider competing activities but that the nature of those activities, whether relaxing or stressful, is also important.

The Dynamics of Action and Other Implicit Motives

Coordinating definitions linking the dynamics-of-action concepts of instigation and inhibition to implicit measurement of the motive to approach success and self-attributed measurement of test anxiety or fear of failure, respectively, have allowed researchers to generate hypotheses regarding latency to achievement tasks and persistence at those tasks. Coordinating definitions linking other motives to the dynamics of action have not been pursued yet, but Wirth and Schultheiss (2006) have conceptualized hope of closeness as an arousal factor and fear of rejection as a stress factor in affiliation motivation, a distinction they have traced to Boyatzis (1973).

In an analysis of intimate partner violence, Finkel (2007) distinguishes between impelling forces that lead to violence and inhibiting forces that keep violence from occurring. Impelling forces include having learned violent behaviors toward an intimate partner by having watched one's parents fight. Certainly, aggressive cues in the current situation and anger are impelling forces that can lead to a higher tendency to strike out. Inhibiting forces include cultural attitudes about the inappropriateness of intimate violence, self-control, or fear of injury to oneself. This dynamic model of intimate partner violence has much in common with the dynamics-of-action concepts of instigating force and inhibitory force, and applying implicit motives to create testable hypotheses would be a valuable goal. For example, Atkinson and Birch (1974) describe the implications of an action tendency being "bottled up" by the force of resistance that accumulates as a result of the inhibitory force and cues in the environment of threat and punishment. The action tendency to engage in a socially proscribed behavior, such as violence against an intimate partner, could be building up after weeks of direct provocation and/or imagined slights. Because the force of resistance was stronger than the action tendency, the behavior would not be expressed. However, according to Atkinson and Birch, "a person who is inhibited about aggressive behavior will literally become much more angry than a less inhibited person by the time he finally initiates an aggressive reaction to a frustrating incident" (p. 299). This is because, by the time the action tendency has overcome the force of resistance, it has become substantially stronger. Additionally, if the source of inhibition is taken away (e.g., the person is away from family and friends who condemn aggression), the bottled up action tendency will be expressed in behavior at a much higher level of intensity. These dynamics-of-action processes can be a source for explaining aggression that occurs with no obvious triggering event in the immediate environment.

Collecting PSE Stories and Other Verbal
Material by Computer and Online

By using the computer for writing PSE stories researchers save time because they do not have to transcribe stories for coding. Online assessment increases the reach of research on implicit motives to other parts of the world (c.f. Gosling, Vazire, Srivastava, & John, 2004), wherever computers and Internet access are available. Clariana and Wallace (2002) have identified a number of factors that should be taken into account when comparing the results of computer-based and paper-based testing. A fair comparison requires that important character-istics, such as the ability to see what one has already written, be made as similar as possible between the two modes of testing. Blankenship and Zoota (1998) compared the amount of power imagery in stories written by hand and those written on the computer under timed and untimed conditions in a laboratory setting. In a crossed design with 120 participants, 60 wrote five PSE stories to pictures on the computer and 60 wrote the stories by hand. Half of each group was timed and given 5 minutes to write each story; the other half was not timed. The same pictures were used in all conditions, and computer-based and paper-based measures both allowed participants to see what they had pre-viously written in each story but did not allow them to go back to look at previous completed stories. Stories were scored for power imagery using Winter's (1973) system, and the number of words produced in each story was calculated. As expected, participants wrote significantly more words in the untimed conditions (M = 127.61, SD = 46.19, n = 60) than in the timed conditions (M = 105.41, SD = 29.65, n = 60). But contrary to expectations, there were no differences in total amount of power imagery for five stories (raw scores) in computer-written versus handwritten conditions (M = 10.45, SD = 5.58, n = 60 versus M = 10.63, SD = 6.04, n = 60, respectively) or in timed versus untimed conditions (M = 10.43, SD = 5.44, n = 60 versus M = 10.65, SD = 6.16, n = 60, respectively). Blankenship and Zoota noted that partici-pants in the timed, computer-written condition reported that they felt rushed; therefore, they recommend that when the PSE is presented on the computer, participants not be timed.

Kraut et al. (2004) discussed the implications of collecting data online, and researchers who are content-coding non-PSE materials and mining the Internet to study implicit motives should consult these guidelines. The distinc-tion between private and public behavior as it relates to the protection of human subjects and the need for informed consent is an important concept to keep in mind when taking text from chat rooms and support groups that have open access to users of the Internet. Respecting the privacy of members of support groups designed for people who share a medical condition is particu-larly important and Kraut et al. warn that the identity of quoted text can be tracked with search engines, letting others identify the source of quotes that were meant to be anonymous contributions to chat rooms.

Naglieri et al. (2004) provided further guidance for testing online. Most research with implicit motives has the goal of exploring the relationship among variables, as opposed to psychological assessment of an individual; thus, online assessment is appropriate when proper attention is given to validity and reliability. Gosling et al. (2004) explored six preconceptions held about Internet collection of data. They compared Internet versus traditional modes of gathering data using the Big Five Inventory and found that Internet samples did not report more maladjustment and were motivated to take the test seriously, and that the findings based on data gathered on the Internet are comparable to those from traditional methods. Although the sample of Internet participants is not representative of the population as a whole, diversity of Internet samples is quite high and often higher than most published studies, which depend on college students as participants. The problem of participants filling out the online questionnaire multiple times can be partially controlled by checking IP addresses and eliminating repeat data from the same address. The question of how PSE stories collected on the Internet compare with stories that are handwritten or collected on the computer in a laboratory setting deserves more study using comparisons similar to those used by Gosling et al. The feasibility of coding thousands of stories collected over the Internet will probably be delayed until a computer-based method of coding the stories is refined.

Using the Computer to Code PSE Stories

Nacos et al. (1991) recognized that "the coding of large volumes of text is a very labor intensive, time consuming, tiresome, and costly task" (p. 112), and combined forces to see whether a computer-based system could cut down on these costs while maintaining the accuracy desired. They compared human-coded and computer-coded analyses of news reports on topics such as defense spending. The computer coding used a filtering method, and the initial pass was to search online databases and compile relevant stories. The computer program looked for instances in the text where three target concepts, "America," "defense," and "spending" or their synonyms (e.g., "United States," "military," expenditures"), were found within a few words of each other. When these instances were found, the text within 50 words of these target concepts was stored for analysis. Assigning meaning to the target text necessitated the development of dictionaries of words associated with key concepts that indicated "pro," "con," or "neutral" attitudes toward defense spending. Although the two human coders agreed 87% of the time on the three categories, the computer and the human coders agreed only about 50% of the categories. Nacos et al. concluded that the reliability of the computer is "minimally adequate for purposes of aggregating large numbers of these scores in order to track changes in media content over time" (p. 119). This level of reliability would be considered totally inadequate for the coding of implicit motives in PSE stories. Nacos et al. attributed part of their lack of convergence between the human coding and the computer coding to a lack of personal involvement of the human coders in devising the program for computer coding. "With hindsight, we are convinced that the researchers who establish the text analysis objectives must be closely involved in all steps of the successive filtration method, especially in the establishment of the search words, the dictionaries, and the rules as well as in the testing of the rules by scoring sample paragraphs" (p. 124).

To compare the verbal content of free speech samples and of TAT stories, Schnurr, Rosenberg, and Oxman (1992) used the Dartmouth Adaptations of the General Inquirer (Smith, 1968) program for content analysis. The General Inquirer's original dictionary was based on the Bales interaction process, but later dictionaries included Lasswell's values and Osgood's semantic differentials (Krippendorff, 2004). Schnurr et al. used the third version of the Harvard Psychosociological Dictionary developed by Stone, Dunphy, Smith, and Ogilvie (1966). Participants produced speech samples to four TAT cards from the Morgan and Murray (1938) set and also talked about any topic that they wanted for 5 minutes (free speech sample). The content analysis program assigned words to one of 55 categories describing first-order themes such as self, roles, actions, and feelings. If applicable, a word was also assigned to one of 28 second-order categories such as overstate or understate. There were mean differences in frequency of responses in 58 first- and second-order categories between TAT responses and free speech samples. Additionally, the TAT content profiles were more highly related to individual differences in depression, for example, than the free speech profiles, leading Schnurr, et al. to conclude that the TAT is a better source of speech samples.

Hogenraad (2005) used a Motive Dictionary and content analysis software (PROTAN, developed by Hogenraad, Daubies, & Bestgen (1995), to examine McClelland's (1975) theory about the gap between power and affiliation motives in public discourse and subsequent wars. McClelland proposed that the imperial motivation pattern, in which the power motive is high and the affiliation motive is low, creates reform movements that make war possible. Hogenraad used PROTAN and the Motive Dictionary to code for power words, such as ambition, invade, captive, and weak, and for affiliation words, such as family, thoughtful, accompany, and sweetheart. He analyzed fictional materials and political speeches, especially those of George W. Bush and Tony Blair in the 19 months prior to the 2003 invasion of Iraq. In support of McClelland's theory, the gap between power words and affiliation words increased during that time leading up to the Iraq war as evidenced by speeches given by both leaders.

Another word-based content analysis program is the Linguistic Inquiry and Word Count (LIWC) program developed by Pennebaker and Francis (1999). Pennebaker and King (1999) demonstrated the reliability and validity of this program for detecting linguistic styles evidenced in the words people use to write about a variety of subjects, from journals produced by substance abuse inpatients to research abstracts of elite social psychologists to writing assignments of college students. Like earlier content analysis programs, the LIWC categorizes individual words; however, it differs from previous programs by scoring a word into numerous categories. For example, the word "cried" is scored into "four word categories: sadness, negative emotion, overall affect, and past-tense verb" (Pennebaker & King, p. 1298). In developing the LIWC program, Pennebaker and Francis collected words in targeted categories such as emotional words and had three judges independently rate words for inclusion in the various dictionaries. Words were added or excluded if at least two of the three judges agreed. The process was refined through psychometric procedures that led to the deletion of some categories and the addition of others. The current version of the LIWC application, LIWC2007, is the third version and handles multiple language files and allows users to develop their own dictionaries (Pennebaker, Chung, Ireland, Gonzales, & Booth, 2007).

Although Pennebaker and King doubt that a word count strategy could replace the use of human raters of TAT/PSE stories, their analysis of five TAT stories written by 79 volunteers from a psychology class provides some intriguing results, especially with regard to the acquired need for achievement. Human ratings of achievement imagery were negatively correlated with linguistic style factors termed Immediacy and Rationalization and positively correlated with The Social Past. Immediacy is composed of more references to the first-person singular, to discrepancies (e.g., would, should, could), and to use of the present tense and fewer instances of articles and words of six or more letters. Thus, participants who scored higher on achievement imagery as coded by human raters made fewer references to the first-person singular and had more words of six or more letters. Rationalization includes more words indicating insight (e.g., understand, realize) and causation (e.g., because, realize) and fewer negative emotions. Thus, the stories of those participants with high achievement imagery scores had fewer insight and causation words and more negative emotions. The Social Past factor contains more past-tense and social words (e.g., friends, family) and fewer present-tense and positive-emotion words. Thus, the stories of those who scored high on achievement imagery would contain more past tense and social words and fewer instances of positive emotions.

Pennebaker and King performed a regression analysis predicting the average of two indicators of achievement-related preferences: (1) whether participants preferred having their grade based on their own work or based on their work relative to others and (2) whether they were interested in teaching themselves computer-related tasks of intermediate difficulty. An LIWC indicator that reflected the linguistic styles related to achievement, as outlined above, was related to the achievement-related preference score over and above the contribution of the TAT measure of achievement imagery. Pennebaker and King point out that this result is striking, especially "given that the LIWC domains were never designed to tap any of the motivational states associated with the TAT" (p. 1308).

The Macintosh version of LIWC2007 allows for searching for phrases in addition to individual words. This expanded facility may allow for its use in the development of PSE coding systems that will have high reliability and convergent validity with human coding systems. For example, the revised method for coding achievement imagery (Blankenship et al., 2006) has three defining categories and seven subcategories that are coded. The defining category, Standard of Excellence, is coded when the story contains statements such as "wants to win," "wants to succeed," or "wants to overcome obstacles." Variants of these statements, using "want," "wanted," and "wanting" would capture a large number of achievement stories. Because the LIWC2007 allows for coding words and phrases into multiple categories, these same statements would count as Stated Need, one of the subcategories for coding achievement imagery. Flags could also be constructed to warn the researcher that a story with the phrase "wants to win," for example, might not be achievement oriented if it also contained the word "lottery." Human coders could review flagged stories to make sure that the story is indeed about achievement and not about luck.

Although the process of constructing the dictionaries would be labor intensive, once the scoring system were refined, PSE stories could be scored in a much more efficient manner, and the necessity to keep training new coders (typically undergraduates who soon move on) would be eliminated. Also, data entry would be automatic, saving time and eliminating data entry errors. The possibilities are exciting to contemplate.

Other Issues Related to Assessment of Implicit Motives

Blankenship and Zoota (1998) also addressed the issue of low internal consistency of the PSE by coding the four paragraphs that are written in response to questions that are used to elicit PSE stories. The four guiding questions are: (1) What is happening? Who are the persons? (2) What has led up to this situation? That is, what has happened in the past? (3) What is being thought? What is wanted? By whom? (4) What will happen? What will be done? In a study comparing handwritten and computer-written PSE stories given under timed and untimed conditions, 120 participants wrote five stories each to pictures known to elicit power imagery. The stories were coded for power imagery using the coding method developed by Winter (1973). Categories and subcategories of power imagery were assigned to the paragraphs in which they were scored, and 20 scores were entered for each participant (four paragraphs $\times$ 5 stories). The four scores were summed to provide a total score for each story. Cronbach's alpha was .46 when five scores (one for each story) were used to compute internal consistency reliability; it increased to .65 when 20 scores (one for each of the four paragraphs of the five stories) were used to compute Cronbach's alpha. Blankenship and Zoota recommended that the four paragraphs of the PSE be used as the units (or items) on the implicit measure.

Blankenship et al. (2006) extended the focus on the four paragraphs that are produced when participants write stories to pictures in response to the four guiding questions for achievement imagery. In a study using the Rasch (1980) model of measurement as executed by a computer program that analyzes multiple dimensions or facets of the measure (FACETS, Linacre, 2005), they explored the psychometric characteristics of pictures developed to measure achievement imagery. New pictures were tested showing two or more people in achievement situations. In Experiments 1 and 2 of the study, six strong achievement pictures were identified: two people jogging, three people performing surgery, two people in a laboratory, a group at graduation, two people climbing a mountain, and five people skydiving. In Experiment 3 these six pictures and four more showing a single individual (studying, swimming, star-watching, and kayaking) were tested. In response to the four standard guiding questions listed above, 201 participants wrote PSE stories to six pictures, each person receiving a random sample of the 10 pictures.

Expert coders scored the 1206 stories by paragraphs using a revised scoring method developed in the study. In all cases the scores for the paragraphs ranged from 0 to 4 categories or subcategories. The data were analyzed using FACETS, a multifaceted Rasch model, with three facets, participants, pictures, and the four guiding questions. The scores (0–4) fit a partial credit model, in that stories were given points in a way similar to how teachers might score an essay as covering 0 to 4 points required on an exam. The FACETS analysis reports the personal separation reliability, which is "the Rasch equivalent of the KR-20 or Cronbach Alpha 'test reliability' statistic, i.e., the ratio of 'True variance' to 'Observed variance' for the elements of the facet. . . . High (near 1.0) person and item reliabilities are preferred" (Linacre, 2008). For this sample of 1206 stories, the person separation reliability was .75. Blankenship et al. (2006) concluded that the PSE can be improved when the psychometric characteristics of the pictures are examined and pictures are chosen that provide an appropriate range of difficulty, from easy pictures with a higher probability of eliciting achievement imagery to difficult pictures that have a weaker "pull" for achievement imagery. Additionally, they recommend that the PSE be coded by paragraphs to provide more "items" on the test and to allow for full use of the rich categories and subcategories of achievement imagery.

Conclusion

The computer is a powerful tool that has already had a tremendous impact on research in all fields, and especially in psychology. PSE stories can be captured on computers in the laboratory or through the Internet using survey programs, expanding the reach of data collection and preparing the way for computer-based or computer-assisted coding of implicit motives. The Internet contains a wealth of narrative text that can be mined for reflections of implicit motives on blogs, in chat rooms, and in public documents posted and archived on various websites.

The dynamics of action (Atkinson & Birch, 1970) has much to offer the field of implicit motives. With its focus on time measures (i.e., latency, persistence, percentage time spent), it challenges researchers to change their thinking and construct coordinating definitions to apply the theory beyond achievement applications to affiliation, intimacy, and power situations. Wirth and Schultheiss (2006) have conceptualized hope of closeness as an arousal factor and fear of rejection as a stress factor in affiliation situations. Making coordinating definitions of hope of closeness as an instigating force and fear of rejection as an inhibitory force is the starting point for simulations that could make time-oriented predictions of affiliative behaviors. These predictions can then be tested in laboratory studies or in applied settings (cf. Lens et al., 2005).

So far coordinating definitions have matched hope concepts (e.g., hope of success) with an instigating force and fear concepts (e.g., fear of failure) with an inhibitory force. However, an inhibitory force does not have to be caused by fear; it is anything that would delay the initiation of the target behavior. Within McClelland's imperial motivation pattern, the power motive is related positively to war, and the affiliation motive is related negatively to war when it comes to predicting reform movements. By conceptualizing the power motive as an instigating force and the affiliation motive as an inhibitory force with regard to reform movements, hypotheses could be generated that focus not only on whether war occurs or not, but also how long it takes a country with high-power and low-affiliation motives to engage in war as compared to a country with high-power and high-affiliation motives.

Of course there is much more to be done in the achievement domain as well. To date there have been no studies to test whether the computer-based behavioral measure of RAM, based on Lewin's concept of atypical shifts, converges with the PSE measure of achievement motive. Now that the PSE has been improved with updated and stronger picture cues, a test of convergence with behavioral measures is needed.

The development of a computer-based coding system for implicit motives would greatly facilitate research in the field. Recent advances in computer content-coding systems should be explored with the hope that laborious human training and coding of stories can be minimal, focusing just on flagged stories that appear to have troubling content that may violate the assumptions of established coding systems.

It is an exciting time to be affiliated with the field of implicit motives. There is much to achieve using the power of the computer to further our goals.

Notes

1. The term "consummatory" has a long history that can be traced to Sherrington (1906). The distinction between appetitive behaviors and consummatory behaviors has been controversial (cf. Ball & Balthazart, 2007; Sachs, 2007, 2008). Atkinson and Birch (1970) specifically avoided that distinction by assuming that "all activities, the ones customarily referred to as instrumental, as well as the ones customarily referred to as consummatory produce consummatory force" (p. 15).

2. The use of the PSE, an implicit measure of the motive to approach success, and the Test Anxiety Questionnaire, a self-attributed measure of the motive to avoid failure, was standard practice in achievement motivation research in the United States prior to the clear distinction between the two motive measures made by McClelland, Koestner, and Weinberger in 1989.

References

Atkinson, J. W. (1957). Motivational determinants of risk-taking behavior. *Psychological Review, 64*, 359–372.

Atkinson, J. W., & Birch, D. (1970). *The dynamics of action.* New York: Wiley.

Atkinson, J. W., & Birch, D. (1974). The dynamics of achievement-oriented activity. In J. W. Atkinson & J. O. Raynor (Eds.), *Motivation and achievement* (pp. 271–325). Washington, DC: V. H. Winston & Sons.

Atkinson, J. W., Bongort, K., & Price, L. H. (1977). Explorations using computer simulation to comprehend thematic apperceptive measurement of motivation. *Motivation and Emotion, 1*(1), 1–27.

Atkinson, J. W., & Feather, N. T. (1966). *A theory of achievement motivation.* New York: Wiley.

Ball, G. F., & Balthazart, J. (2007). How useful is the appetitive and consummatory distinction for our understanding of the neuroendocrine control of sexual behavior? *Hormones and Behavior, 53*, 307–311.

Blankenship, V. (1982). The relationship between consummatory value of success and achievement task difficulty. *Journal of Personality and Social Psychology, 42*, 911–924.

Blankenship, V. (1987). A computer-based measure of resultant achievement motivation. *Journal of Personality and Social Psychology, 53*, 361–372.

Blankenship, V. (1992). Individual differences in resultant achievement motivation and latency to and persistence at an achievement task. *Motivation and Emotion, 16*, 35–63.

Blankenship, V., Tumlinson, J., & Sims, M. A. (1995). A STELLA-II teaching simulation of the dynamics of action model. *Behavior Research Methods, Instruments and Computers, 27*(2), 244–250.

Blankenship, V., Vega, C. M., Ramos, E., Romero, K., Warren, K., Keenan, K., Barton, V., Vasquez, J. R., & Sullivan, A. (2006). Using the multifaceted Rasch model to improve the TAT/PSE measure of need for achievement. *Journal of Personality Assessment, 86*(1), 100–114.

Blankenship, V., & Zoota, A. L. (1998). Comparing power imagery in TATs written by hand or on the computer and computing reliability. *Behavior Research Methods, Instruments, and Computers, 30*, 441–448.

Bongort, K. (1975). Most recent revision of computer program for dynamics of action. Unpublished computer program, University of Michigan, Ann Arbor.

Boyatzis, R. E. (1973). Affiliation motivation. In D. C. Mc Clelland & R. S. Steele (Eds.) *Human motivation: A book of readings* (pp. 253–276). Morristown, NJ: General Learning Press..

Clariana, R., & Wallace, P. (2002). Paper-based versus computer-based assessment: Key factors associated with the test mode effect. *British Journal of Educational Technology, 33*(5), 593–602.

Finkel, E. J. (2007). Impelling and inhibiting forces in the perpetration of intimate partner violence. *Review of General Psychology, 11*(2), 193–207.

Gosling, S. D., Vazire, S., Srivastava, S., & John, O. P. (2004). Should we trust web-based studies? A comparative analysis of six preconceptions about Internet questionnaires. *American Psychologist, 59*(2), 93–104.

Hogenraad, R. (2005). What the words of war can tell us about the risk of war. *Journal of Peace Psychology, 11*(2), 137–151.

Hogenraad, R., Daubies, C., & Bestgen, Y. (1995). Une théorie et une méthode générale d'analyse textuelle assistée par ordinateur. Le système PROTAN (PROTocol Analyzer) (Version March 2, 1995). Luvain-la-Neuve, Belgium: Psychology Department, Catholic University of Louvain. http://www.psor.ucl.ac.be/protan/protanae.html

Kraut, R., Olson, J., Banaji, M, Bruckman, A., Cohen, J., & Couper, M. (2004). Psychological research online: Report of the Board of Scientific Affairs Advisory Group. *American Psychologist, 59*(2), 105–117.

Krippendorff, K. (2004). *Content analysis: An introduction to its methodology.* Thousand Oaks, CA: Sage Publications.

Kuhl, J., & Blankenship, V. (1979a). The dynamic theory of achievement motivation: From episodic to dynamic thinking. *Psychological Review, 86*(2), 141–151.

Kuhl, J., & Blankenship, V. (1979b). Behavioral change in a constant environment: Shift to more difficult tasks with constant probability of success. *Journal of Personality and Social Psychology, 37*(4), 551–563.

Lens, W., Lacante, M., Vansteenkiste, M., & Herrera, D. (2005). Study persistence and academic achievement as a function of the type of competing tendencies. *European Journal of Psychology of Education, 20*(3), 275–287.

Lewin, K. (1946). Behavior and development as a function of the total situation. Reprinted in Dorwin Cartwright (Ed.), *Field theory in social science: Selected theoretical papers* (1951). New York, NY: Harper & Rowe, Publishers, Inc., pp. 238–303.

Lewin, K., Dembo, T., Festinger, L., & Sears, P. S. (1944). Level of aspiration. In. J. M. Hunt (Ed.), *Personality and the behavior disorders* (pp. 333–378). New York: Roland.

Linacre, J. M. (2005). *A user's guide to Facets: Rasch-model computer programs.* Retrieved May 15, 2005 from www.winsteps.com

Linacre, J. M. (2008). *A user's guide to Facets: Rasch-model computer programs.* Program Manual 3.63.0. Retrieved May 12, 2008 from http://www.winsteps.com/facetman/index.htm?reliability.htm

Littig, L. W. (1963). Effects of motivation on probability preferences. *Journal of Personality, 31,* 417–427.

Mandler, G., & Sarason, S. B. (1952). A study of anxiety and learning. *Journal of Abnormal and Social Psychology, 47,* 166–173.

McClelland, D. C. (1975). *Power: The inner experience.* New York: Irvington Publishers.

McClelland, D. C. (1980). Motive dispositions: The merits of operant and respondent measures. In L. Wheeler (Ed.), *Review of personality and social psychology* (Vol. 2, pp. 10–41). Beverly Hills, CA: Sage.

McClelland, D. C., Koestner, R., & Weinberger, J. (1989). How do self-attributed and implicit motives differ? *Psychological Review, 96*(4), 690–702.

Morgan, C. D., & Murray, H. A. (1938). Thematic Apperception Test. In H. A. Murray (Ed.) *Explorations in personality* (pp. 530–545). New York: Oxford University Press.

Moulton, R. W. (1965). Effects of success and failure on level of aspiration as related to achievement motives. *Journal of Personality and Social Psychology, 1,* 399–406.

Nacos, B. L., Shapiro, R. Y., Young, J. T., Fan, D. P., Kjellstrand, T., & McCaa, C. (1991). Content analysis of news reports: Comparing human coding and a computer-assisted method. *Communication, 12,* 111–128.

Naglieri, J. A., Drasgow, F., Schmit, M., Handler, L., Prifitera, A., Margolis, A., & Velasquez, R. (2004). Psychological testing on the Internet: New problems, old issues. *American Psychologist, 59*(3), 150–162.

Pennebaker, J. W., Chung, C. K., Ireland, M., Gonzales, A., & Booth, R. J. (2007). *The development and psychometric properties of LIWC2007.* Austin, TX: LIWC, Inc.

Pennebaker, J. W., & Francis, M. E. (1999). *Linguistic inquiry and word count: LIWC.* Mahwah, NJ: Erlbaum.

Pennebaker, J. W., & King, L. A. (1999). Linguistic styles: Language use as an individual difference. *Journal of Personality and Social Psychology, 77*(6), 1296–1312.

Rasch, G. (1980). *Probabilistic models for some intelligence and attainment tests.* Chicago, IL: The University of Chicago Press.

Sachs, B. D. (2007). A contextual definition of male sexual arousal. *Hormones and Behavior, 51*, 569–578.

Sachs, B. D. (2008). The appetitive-consummatory distinction: Is this 100-year-old baby worth saving? Reply to Ball and Balthazart. *Hormones and Behavior, 53*, 315–318.

Schneider, K., & Posse, N. (1982). Risk taking in achievement-oriented situations: Do people really maximize affect or competence information? *Motivation and Emotion, 6*(3), 259–271.

Schnurr, P. P., Rosenberg, S. D., & Oxman, T. E. (1992). Comparison of TAT and free speech techniques for eliciting source material in computerized content analysis. *Journal of Personality Assessment, 58*(2), 311–325.

Seltzer, R. A. (1973). Simulation of the dynamics of action. *Psychological Reports, 32*, 859–872.

Seltzer, R. A., & Sawusch, J. R. (1974). Computer program written to simulate the dynamics of action. In J. W. Atkinson & J. O. Raynor (Eds.), *Motivation and achievement* (pp. 411–423). Washington, DC: W. H. Winston.

Sherrington, C. S. (1906). *The integrative action of the nervous system.* New York: Charles Scribner's Sons.

Smith, M. S. (1968). The computer and the TAT. *Journal of School Psychology, 6*(3), 206–214.

Stone, P. J., Dunphy, D. C., Smith, M. S., & Ogilvie, D. M. (1966). *The General Inquirer: A computer approach to content analysis.* Cambridge, MA: MIT Press.

Winter, D. G. (1973). *The power motive.* New York: Free Press.

Wirth, M. M., & Schultheiss, O. C. (2006). Effects of affiliation arousal (hope of closeness) and affiliation stress (fear of rejection) on progesterone and cortisol. *Hormones and Behavior, 50*, 786–795.

SECTION 3

Basic Concepts and Processes

Chapter 8

Learning and Memory Correlates of Implicit Motives

MICHAEL BENDER
Tilburg University

BARBARA A. WOIKE
Barnard College, Columbia University

Humans cannot respond equally to all stimuli in their social environment with the same degree of attention, strength, or persistence. Motivation is one factor that guides us in choosing which tasks to pursue, where to take a closer look, and what to keep in mind. But personality differences may not fully explain why and how individuals allocate their resources differently in varying situations. For example, a memory about a past success may come more easily during a job interview, while the memories of the last vacation with friends may be recalled more easily while sitting and chatting in a bar. In this chapter we aim to shed some light on the relationship between an individual's implicit motive dispositions and situational factors that work in concert to influence memory, in particular the processes of attention, learning, and recall.

First, an outline of how the perspective on the relationship of cognitive factors and implicit motivation has changed over the years is presented. In general, two theoretical perspectives can be distinguished: the view of motivation as primarily affective with only nonconscious representation (e.g., McClelland, 1987), and the view of motivation as a cognitive phenomenon in which people are aware and can accurately report their goals (e.g., Carver & Scheier, 1981). However, approaching motivation exclusively from a cognitive perspective (e.g., causal attributions, Weiner, 1980) is not sufficient; a substantial amount of effects can only be explained by the assumption of an implicit motive disposition (McClelland, 1987). A closer scrutiny of the interface between cognition and motivation can foster the understanding of the motivation–action sequence and can help explain how motive-related behavior comes about (Dweck & Wortman, 1982; Trope, 1975). To that end, we will offer a general model of information processing to integrate past findings on how implicit motivation relates to basic and complex cognitive processes in the stages of orientation to, attention to, and encoding of motive-relevant stimuli, as well as rehearsal and organization of such stimuli and their retrieval.

Individuals are assumed to direct their attention to stimuli in their environment that match their motive disposition, and that, accordingly, performance for incentive cues is improved relative to neutral stimuli. Findings of various empirical studies are presented to substantiate this assumption (Atkinson & Walker, 1958; McClelland & Liberman, 1949; Schultheiss & Hale, 2007).

Furthermore, studies indicate that implicit motives may not only guide the attention toward salient stimuli, but they also appear to influence the manner of encoding new information into memory. Findings from controlled recognition tasks (Woike, Lavezzary, & Barsky, 2001) highlight the regulatory role of implicit motivation in encoding new information and the facilitation of access to recently acquired knowledge.

The types of experiences that are reported reflect the motive disposition of the individual (McAdams, 1982), with agentic individuals reporting peak experiences about successes, and communal individuals writing about connectedness in their autobiographical accounts. In addition, a number of studies (Woike, Gershkovich, Piorkowski, & Polo, 1999; Woike & Polo, 2001) demonstrated that not only the content but also the structural organization of memories typically matches an individual's predominant implicit motivation: Agentic individuals use more elements of distinction to narrate a memory concerned with competition, while communal individuals structure their memories about cooperation with elements of connectedness. The type of experiences that are sought may differ between individuals, and may be rooted in the ontogenetic development of implicit motivation. Because the childhood contexts in which such a development takes place may vary, we suggest including a cultural perspective on individual differences to more fully understand the variation of implicit motivation and its influence on cognitive processes.

Implicit Motives and Cognition in a Contextual Perspective

Over the past two decades, evidence has been accumulating in many areas of psychology in favor of multiple system approaches to cognitive processing including learning and memory (e.g., Kihlstrom, 1990; Schacter,

1987; Tulving, 1985), attention and perception (e.g., Greenwald, Klinger, & Schuh, 1995; Posner, 2004), social cognition (e.g., Bargh, 1989; Hill, Lewicki, Czyzewska, & Boss, 1989; Tversky & Kahneman, 1983), creativity and problem solving (e.g., Dorfman, Shames, & Kihlstrom, 1996), as well as personality (Epstein, 1994). These models share the assumption that cognitive processing occurs at both conscious and less or nonconscious levels of awareness. This rationale can easily be applied to the investigation of the relationship between implicit motivation and memory. Implicit motives reflect a desire for pleasure derived from affective learning experiences and can thereby be associated with intrinsic incentives. As such, they may be linked to cognitive processes that automatically influence behavior without conscious effort, which may allow the individual to (re-)experience specific affective experiences linked to learning experiences in childhood. In this phase, children learn to associate affect with certain stimuli or behavior according to principles of Pavlovian or instrumental conditioning, as well as other learning processes. The close link between implicit motivation and affect is most likely a result of these ontogenetic learning experiences (see also Schultheiss, 2008).

In contrast, explicit motivation relies heavily on information stored in the self-knowledge system (Conway and Pleydell-Pearce, 2000), which reflects explicitly learned, well-articulated goals and values, and is linked to conscious goal setting, including the formulation of plans and rules for behavior that correspond to the self-concept. The explicit system therefore involves highly elaborated networks of knowledge about the self and one's values and does not develop ontogenetically until sufficient cognitive resources are available. Thus, the implicit and explicit motivational systems seem to parallel dual cognitive processing models that have a differential emphasis on conscious versus non-conscious processing and affect versus cognition.

Both the explicit and implicit motivational system influence behavior and direct it towards the pursuit of specific goals (McClelland, 1987), but they are linked to different types of behavior (deCharms, Morrison, Reitman, & McClelland, 1955; McClelland, 1980). Implicit motives, which respond to natural, contextual incentives, are better suited to predict long-term behavioral trends (e.g., McAdams & Vaillant, 1982; McClelland & Pilon, 1983), while self-attributed motives are best suited to predict behaviors occurring in well-structured situations that are rich in social incentives and require a cognitive decision on the course of action (e.g., Ajzen & Fishbein, 1970; Patten & White, 1977). In other words, being implicitly motivated for achievement predicts a long-term interest and pleasure in challenging tasks, while being explicitly motivated for achievement is a good indicator of assigning importance to and studying extensively for an exam.

Due to such specific characteristics, it is not surprising that implicit and explicit motives are differentially linked to responsiveness to incentive cues.

Differences in the encoding, organization, and retrieval of memories can be understood through an identification of the link between the motives that people bring to a specific situation and the aspects of those events that relate to their motives (Woike, 2008). Following the classic Person × Situation framework originally proposed by Lewin (1935), and its more recent versions (e.g., Krahe, 1992), researchers can better understand why some experiences are remembered and some are forgotten. For instance, McClelland and colleagues (McClelland, Koestner, & Weinberger, 1989) have argued that implicit motives respond to task-intrinsic incentives like the affective enjoyment of working on a challenging task in the case of achievement motivation. Following this line of argumentation, recent research suggests that implicit motives are more likely to respond to affective stimuli like nonverbal cues than to verbal-symbolic stimuli (Klinger, 1967; Schultheiss, 2001; Schultheiss & Brunstein, 1999).

Explicit motives, on the other hand, respond to social extrinsic incentives, that is, to salient external demands and social norms as reflected in, for instance, an experimenter's explicit instruction. This means that a person who scores high in the self-attributed need for achievement (*san* Achievement) should be particularly sensitive to instructions highlighting the importance of excellent performance on a task (a demand) or how well others have done on a similar task (a social norm). And indeed, Brunstein and Hoyer (2002) could demonstrate that individuals with a strong *san* Achievement pay attention to norm-referenced (but not self-referenced) information when making an explicit decision about whether to continue an achievement-related task, or not. This confirms past research, in which procedural stimuli like the experimental setting have been used to elicit the affiliation motive (Atkinson, Heyns, & Veroff, 1958).

To conclude, implicit and explicit motivation represent two distinct motivational systems that develop at different stages in childhood and through different mechanisms, respond differently to environmental stimuli, and have different predictive validity for different types of behavior—including cognition. In the following, we will summarize some of the most important findings on the relationship between implicit motivation and cognition.

General Model of Information Processing

In general, implicit motives like *n* Achievement, *n* Power, and *n* Affiliation facilitate the memory performance on motive-related content (McClelland, 1984). Most of the studies investigating such effects focus on the change in performance associated with different experimental settings and attribute changes to enhanced cognitive processing of motive-related stimuli (e.g., Woike, 2008). Such changes are assumed to take place during all stages of general information processing; they facilitate the orientation to motive-relevant stimuli and improve encoding of such stimuli in a way that makes retrieval more likely in a situation that matches the motive.

Implicit motives do not exert a consciously accessible influence on cognitive processes, and, among other mechanisms, Pavlovian conditioning is considered to represent the developmental core of implicit motivation (cf. McClelland, Atkinson, Clark, & Lowell, 1953), as it represents the learning history of cues that have become associated with affective experiences. Ultimately, an individual seeks out hedonically charged stimuli and experiences while negotiating learning experiences of reward and punishment. Studies investigating this link support this notion, finding that individuals generally approach motive-congruent and avoid motive-incongruent stimuli (e.g., Schultheiss & Hale, 2007).

Research on the link between instrumental conditioning and implicit motivation reveals that individuals who associate a task with a previously experienced situation characterized by a motive-relevant reward perform better in such tasks (Teitelbaum, 1966). In other words, reinforcement of motive-relevant behavior increases the probability of further motive-relevant behavior. More recently, Schultheiss and colleagues (Schultheiss & Rohde, 2002; Schultheiss et al., 2005) demonstrated the link between instrumental conditioning and implicit motivation by finding that individuals high in *n* Power performed better on a visuomotor sequence task after winning an experimentally induced dominance contest, and performed worse after losing such a contest.

Such findings highlight the role implicit motivation plays for nondeclarative memories. Nondeclarative memories (Squire, 2004) are consciously not accessible, include learning capacities that can be measured in performance tests, procedural learning (habits, skills, instrumental learning), Pavlovian conditioning (in particular the association of events and emotions), priming memory (recent exposure to stimuli facilitates their later identification), and nonassociative learning (including reflexes, habituation, sensitization). Declarative memory is defined as memory content that can be accessed consciously, from the recollection of facts (semantic memory) to the recall of events and life stories (episodic and autobiographical memory).

Although the influence of implicit motivation on cognitive processes may not be easily articulated by a person, its impact may not be limited to nondeclarative content. In the following sections, we will summarize findings along the stages of general information processing, showing that both declarative and nondeclarative memory systems are influenced by implicit motives.

A comprehensive model on how motivation, both implicit and explicit, shapes cognition has yet to be formulated. The most recent model on episodic and autobiographical memory formulated by Conway and Pleydell-Pearce (2000) partially addresses the influence of motivation on information

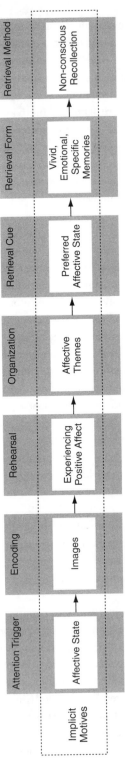

Figure 8.1 Implicit motives and the general information processing model.

processing. In this model, Conway and Pleydell-Pearce describe memories as transitory mental constructions within the self-memory system (SMS), which contains both an autobiographical knowledge base as well as current goals of the working self-concept (Markus & Wurf, 1986). Such goals in the SMS are a frame of reference for autobiographical memories, that is, they generate retrieval models to guide search processes for autobiographical information (DeSteno & Salovey, 1997).

The model proposed by Conway and Pleydell-Pearce (2000) has been found to be valuable in explaining the crucial links between the self and memory. But it does not differentiate between motivational and nonmotivational personality constructs, nor does it differentiate between conscious (self-attributed) and nonconscious (implicit) motives and goals. Past research has shown that a differentiation of these personality constructs can help explain different mnemonic information-processing strategies, especially implicit and explicit motivational systems (Woike, 2008). To develop a more comprehensive understanding of how motivational dispositions influence memory, both motivational systems and their relationship to cognitive processes must be considered, not only explicit goals and the self-concept.

According to McClelland (1987), implicit motives play an important role in the orientation, direction, and selection of attention to environmental stimuli. More precisely, an individual should attend to motive-relevant stimuli more often than to motive-irrelevant stimuli. If that is the case, this increased attention should also lead to a greater probability of encoding motive-related information. Initial percepts may be encoded into images and narratives (rather than translated into cognitively elaborated self-schema), thereby preserving a vivid perceptual image of the experience, similar to flashbulb memories. Flashbulb memories are memories of personally significant events, or events of national or international importance, and are unlike other autobiographical memories due to their high emotional intensity, vivid details, and long-term retention (Brown & Kulik, 1977). Due to the association of motive-relevant stimuli with intrinsic incentives, it is then, in turn, more likely that motive-relevant information is rehearsed more often, in order to experience the affect that is associated with these experiences as a reward (Woike, 1994b). Rehearsal may be facilitated by experiencing events or situations that match implicit motives and, in turn, again increases the likelihood of later activation. Because such experiences are vividly encoded with rich details, reconstructed memories should contain a great deal of event-specific knowledge (ESK; Conway & Pleydell-Pearce, 2000). Finally, in contexts in which the individual is experiencing affective or motivational arousal that is congruent with the memory, the motive-relevant memory should be more readily retrieved as compared to neutral conditions. Each aspect of the general information-processing model will be discussed in more detail in the following (for an overview, see Fig. 8.1).

Attention

It has been proposed very early that the association of specific contextual stimuli with implicit motives through learning experiences results in a readiness to attend to incentive cues in the future (Craig, 1918), and such connections are assumed to reflect an evolutionary evolved inheritance (Lang, Bradley, & Cuthbert, 1999).

Support for the impact of implicit motivation on attention can be found in an early study by McClelland and Liberman (1949), who found that n Achievement (assessed with a PSE) was related to the recognition threshold for achievement-related words presented to the individual such that n Achievement facilitated recognition of achievement-related stimuli. However, arguments have been raised that this relationship could merely represent an artifact of verbal learning. In other words, motive-related words previously written down in the imaginative stories of the PSE may have lowered the threshold for the recognition of motive-related words in the subsequent task (Farber, 1955). This, however, seems unlikely, because the very same relationship could be obtained with a signal detection task that is not susceptible to such verbal habits: Atkinson and Walker (1958) conducted a recognition task, in which participants saw faces presented almost subliminally. Faces have been chosen as an affiliative stimulus, because facial expressions represent an important aspect of interpersonal behavior by conveying information about emotional states and interpersonal intentions (see also Knutson, 1996; Hess, Blairy, & Kleck, 2000). Atkinson and Walker (1958) found that individuals high in affiliation performed better in recognizing faces than individuals low in affiliation. In this psychophysical recognition task, participants indicated the presence of stimuli (faces vs. neutral stimuli) in their field of vision by writing down a symbol, thereby ruling out any confounding effects of mere verbal learning.

In a recent study, Schultheiss and Hale (2007) could differentiate the attentive focus exhibited by individuals high in n Affiliation and n Power in a dot-probe task (see also Mogg, Philippot, & Bradley, 2004). High-power individuals, compared to low-power individuals, oriented their attention toward low-dominance facial expressions (surprise), and away from high-dominance facial expressions (joy, anger). These effects clearly demonstrate a heightened sensitivity to motive-relevant cues, and that implicit motives are particularly attuned to the information processing of nonverbal stimuli (see Klinger, 1967; McClelland et al., 1989; Schultheiss, 2001, see also Brunstein & Hoyer, 2002, for motive effects on a vigilance task).

In a very related way, Goschke and Kuhl (1993) demonstrated that participants recognized words related to prospective actions faster if participants were instructed to actually carry out the specific action themselves (compared to being carried out by the experimenter). The study by Goschke and Kuhl (1993) served as the basis for a recent approach on the relationship between implicit motives and cognitive processing: Kazen and Kuhl (2005) investigated the influence of motivation on the performance in Stroop tasks, which are excellent tasks to assess executive attention. In Stroop tasks, participants are presented with words that are presented in a color different from the word's semantic meaning (e.g., the word "red" is presented in the color "blue," Stroop, 1935). Incongruent combinations are typically accompanied by a strong interference because the conflicting color indications require a considerable amount of attentive focus. Kazen and Kuhl (2005) could show a reduction of Stroop interference when participants were presented with primes that were motive relevant (in this case, n Achievement). In other words, participants experienced less interference, and thus performed better, when the task's characteristics (i.e., the prime word) matched their motive disposition. Thus, attentive focus (see also Chapter 13) facilitated performance only in an achievement situation, and only if the participant was motivated for n Achievement.

On the basis of such findings, it becomes apparent that implicit motivation indeed orients the individual toward motive-relevant cues in the environment, supporting the relationship postulated by McClelland (1987).

Encoding and Organization

After attention is directed toward a stimulus, information about the stimulus is encoded into the existing knowledge base. In Conway and Pleydell Pearce's (2000) model, explicit values, preferences and the self represent a frame of reference to organize mental representations into the self-memory system (SMS). Although encoding and organization are by definition distinct stages in information processing, it is difficult to draw a precise line between the two, because new information is always encoded into the network of pre-existing existing knowledge.

What further complicates the description of encoding and organization as separate stages is that, for example, studies investigating autobiographical memory typically focus on narrative data. Thus, such studies only inspect the differences in the actual memory performance (i.e., the differences that have been recalled). However, individual differences are not necessarily restricted to this final stage of information processing—differences occur as soon as an individual orients her/his attention toward a motive-relevant stimulus. Studies only assessing recall performance are therefore not appropriate to investigate differences in encoding and organization of memories. Especially with regard to narrative data, differences in the structure and content of recalled information may not only reflect mnemonic differences, but also differences in the life history or writing style of participants.

Woike, Lavezzary, and Barsky (2001) used an experimental encoding paradigm to test the hypothesis that implicit motives modulate accessibility of autobiographical motive-related knowledge. Participants were presented with vignettes that were controlled for their structural characteristics regarding their cognitive complexity (Woike, 1994a). Cognitive complexity consists of two main components; differentiating elements, which refer to contrasting aspects in a narrative (e.g., "better", "unlike", etc.), and elements of integration, which refer to interrelationships and connections between aspects (e.g., "similar", "same"; see also Schroder, Driver, & Streufert, 1967; Suedfeld, Tetlock, & Streufert, 1992; Woike, 1997). While perceiving differences represents a more self-focused structure, and is thus linked to agentic implicit motives like n Achievement and n Power, a narrative structure rich in the perception of similarities and dynamics points to a more social use, which is linked to communal motives like n Affiliation (for a functional perspective, see also Bender & Chasiotis, in press; Chasiotis, Bender, Kiessling, & Hofer, in press). In their experiments, Woike and colleagues (2001) controlled input for elements of differentiation and integration, which allowed for an investigation of how individuals differing in their implicit motive disposition subsequently retrieve these stimuli. Individuals first read a vignette about a soccer team; one version emphasized competition and winning, and another version emphasized cooperation and teamwork. After a retention interval, participants completed a written recognition task, asking them to identify elements of the vignette. As expected, individuals high in agentic implicit motivation, who read the competitive vignette, had fewer errors in identifying statements of differentiation, while individuals with a communal motive orientation who read the cooperative vignette had fewer errors in recognizing integrated statements. In addition, implicit motives were experimentally primed to test the generalizability of these effects: The same pattern was obtained in two further experiments, one written and one computerized. This means that the manner in which information is presented can help or hinder later performance in a recognition task. Only information that is presented, and therefore encoded, in a motive-congruent structure facilitates later recognition.

Rehearsal

People may rehearse episodes of their life for various reasons, from re-experiencing the affect that is associated with the event to finding new solutions to old problems, or to share a memory with someone to establish an emotional bond. In general, the importance of the re-experience of the affective quality of a motive-related memory enhances the likelihood of rehearsal to occur.

Several researchers have addressed the specific functions of memories and the reasons why individuals may want to rehearse and retrieve memories (for an overview, see Bluck, 2003), and the benefits of such a functional approach had been addressed quite early (Baddeley, 1988; Bartlett, 1932; Neisser, 1988; Robinson &Swanson, 1990). However, only a few studies have investigated these functions empirically (e.g., Bluck, Alea, Habermas, & Rubin, 2005;

Hyman & Faries, 1992; Pasupathi, Lucas, & Coombs, 2002). The functions can generally be distinguished between interpersonal functions (social) and intrapersonal functions (self, directive, see Bluck, 2003; Bluck & Alea, 2002; Bluck, Alea, Habermas, & Rubin, 2005; Pillemer, 1992; Robinson & Swanson, 1990). Indirectly, some findings point toward a motivated rehearsal of autobiographical memories. For example, Alea and Bluck (2007) report that autobiographical recall served the function of maintaining intimacy in romantic relationships. In their study (Alea & Bluck, 2007), young and older adults recalled either autobiographical relationship events or fictional relationship vignettes, and indicated intimacy scores (warmth, closeness) before and after recollection. Bluck and Alea (2007) found that recalling autobiographical events enhanced the perception of some intimacy aspects, and that the personal significance of the reported autobiographical memory was the best predictor of warmth and closeness in the relationship. Although it is not clear whether the measure for intimacy reflects implicit or self-attributed intimacy, it seems likely that an implicit mechanism is at least partly responsible for the findings: If an individual is driven by a specific implicit motive, it becomes more likely that he or she will seek out experiences that are congruent with this motive. This, in turn, will again increase the probability of future motive-relevant behavior, facilitated by the rewarding hedonic quality associated with the event. Individuals seeking out such experiences may also fulfill their need of re-experiencing the associated affective pleasure by rehearsing similar events.

Retrieval

Very early, experimental psychologists (e.g., Bartlett, 1932) assumed that an important factor in an individual's reconstruction of memory was her or his attitudes and motives toward the recalled event. Accordingly, personality was perceived of as a frame of reference for recall processes (see also Markus, 1977), a view that is still prominent (DeSteno & Salovey, 1997; Singer & Salovey, 1993). In the following, we will outline the effects of implicit motivation on the retrieval of episodic and autobiographic memory. In particular, we will provide evidence (a) that supports the notion that implicit motives serve as a frame of reference for the content of recalled events, (b) that helps shed light on why some individuals recall interrupted tasks better than others, (c) for an influence of implicit motives on the structure of recalled memories, and (d) on how neurophysiological studies corroborate results from social and cognitive psychology.

Implicit Motives Determine What Is Remembered

Numerous narrative studies, in which individuals write accounts of their past experiences in story form, offer support for the influence of implicit motivation on the content of autobiographical reconstruction. In particular, agentic and communal implicit motives are linked to the themes of autobiographical narratives: When individuals are asked to describe an emotionally involving life experience (or peak experience, McAdams, 1982) the content of this experience typically matches their predominant motive disposition. Individuals with strong implicit achievement or power motives (agency) are more likely to recall experiences about achievement, dominance, self-mastery, or losing face, whereas individuals with strong implicit intimacy (communal) motives are more likely to recall experiences pertaining to love, friendship, or social rejection (McAdams, 1982, McAdams, Hoffman, Mansfield, & Day, 1996; Woike 1994a, 1994b, 1995; Woike, Gershkovich, Piorkowski, & Polo, 1999). For example, McAdams (1982) could show that individuals high in the need for power recalled more autobiographical peak experiences with a strong power theme. Positive correlations were found between implicit power motivation scores (assessed with PSEs) and the power themes found in narratives of peak experiences and emotionally satisfying experiences, as well as between intimacy scores and intimacy themes in the experiences. These correlations could not be found for less personally meaningful or affectively neutral experiences. Further specifying these findings, Woike (1994b) found that agentic and communal implicit motivations of participants are reflected in narratives about affective experiences, but not neutral experiences. Supporting this notion, McAdams and colleagues (McAdams, Hoffmann, Mansfield, & Day, 1996) found that implicit scores of agency and communion were correlated with agentic and communal themes, respectively, in narratives of significant autobiographical scenes, including peak experiences, turning points, and earliest memories.

Woike et al. (1994a) also found that agentic and communal individuals recalled more emotional experiences related to their implicit motives. Specifically, participants were asked to recall events in which they felt three positive emotions (happiness, pride, and relief) and three negative emotions (anger, sadness, and fear). Participants recalled experiences with motive-congruent themes for the happy and angry memories. Agentic individuals recalled experiences of success and recognition for the happy memory and experiences of loss of face through betrayal for the angry memory. Communal individuals, on the other hand, recalled experiences of love and friendship for the happy memory and experiences of betrayal through a violation of trust for the angry memory. Most participants, regardless of their motivation, recalled an agentic event (e.g., scholastic achievement) for the pride memory and recalled a communal experience (e.g., loss of a loved one) for the sad memory. The content of the relief and fear memories was mixed, some not pertaining to agency and communion at all. For instance, many of the fear memories were about personal safety. The findings are in line with McClelland's (1987) assertion that implicit motives are related to specific affective states, not affective states in general, and highlight the importance of the link between implicit motivation and personally involving, affective auto-biographical memories.

Data from longitudinal diary studies reveal the same pattern in daily recorded experiences (Woike, 1995; Woike & Polo, 2001). For instance, Woike (1995) conducted two studies to investigate the relationship of implicit motives and explicit motives to daily reported most memorable experiences (MMEs). Participants completed implicit and explicit measures of agentic and communal motives and recorded their MMEs for 60 days. In Study 1, implicit motives were expected to be related to affective MMEs associated with the implicit motive, whereas explicit motives were expected to be related to routine MMEs corresponding to subjects' self-descriptions and values. To test the hypotheses, the content of the MMEs was analyzed for affective and routine daily experiences that corresponded to the task (agentic) and social (communal) domains. Results supported the predictions in both areas. For example, people high in *n* Achievement recalled more emotional experiences about achievement, such as feeling excited to have done well on a test, and people high in *n* Intimacy recalled emotional experiences about interpersonal relationships such as feeling good after talking with one's best friend. By contrast, the stronger an individual's self-attributed motive, the more routine experiences were recalled, such that higher *san* Achievement related to the recall of more experiences about routine achievement tasks (e.g., writing a term paper), and higher *san* Intimacy related to the recall of more experiences about routine social activities (e.g., meeting friends). In a second study, implicit and explicit motives were primed in either domain (Woike, 1995). Implicit primes were vivid recollection tasks, while explicit primes were open-ended self-descriptions. Participants were then asked to recall the first 12 MMEs that immediately came to mind. These MMEs were scored as routine or affective experiences related to each domain. The results showed that individuals recalled more prime-relevant MMEs in each of the priming conditions. The findings suggest that the two different motivational systems are related to the encoding of different experiences. It appears that the motive type (agentic or communal) is related to the content of what is remembered, that is, whether it is a task-related or social experience, and the level of motivation (implicit or explicit) is related to whether it is remembered as an emotional memory or a routine experience. In these studies there were many more routine experiences than emotional ones. The mundane nature of these routine experiences and their multitude suggests that they may not be remembered as discrete experiences, but rather may be combined as general events.

Woike, Mcleod, and Goggin (2003) conducted two studies to test the hypothesis that the implicit–explicit motivational systems are linked differentially to accessibility of autobiographical memories. In both studies, participants completed implicit and explicit measures of achievement and intimacy/

affiliation motivation. In Study 1, they recalled an emotional and a self-descriptive memory. In both domains, implicit motive scores were higher when motivational content was present in the emotional memory. When motivational content was present in the self-descriptive memory, explicit motive scores were higher in both domains. In Study 2, participants recalled four autobiographical memories (two agentic, two communal) that were then categorized as specific or general events. Implicit motive scores were higher for participants who recalled specific agentic and specific communal events. Explicit motive scores were higher for participants who recalled general achievement events, but not general communal events. Findings suggest that implicit motives are linked to accessibility of specific and emotionally involving experiences, whereas explicit motives are linked more strongly to accessibility of specific and general memories that correspond to a conscious representation of self.

To some degree, this influence is not completely limited to affective experiences: In a study by McAdams and McClelland (1983), participants were presented with a story containing an equal number of power- and intimacy-related elements, as well as a fixed number of neutral elements. In a standardized recall situation, individuals high in the need for power recalled more power facts relative to neutral facts than individuals low in the need for power. Similarly, McClelland and colleagues (McClelland, Davidson, Saron, & Floor, 1980) found evidence for selective recall. In a learning task, individuals high in the need for power outperform those low in the need for power when power-related material is concerned. Common to these studies is, however, that simply being motivated for a specific motive may not suffice to exhibit an increased performance. Instead it is the correspondence with the salient motive constellation and the stimulus material that determines the effect. Put differently, a person who is motivated for *n* Achievement may not feel prompted to excel at a task if this task is not achievement related. Only if an individual's motivation and situational cues are aligned can superior performance be expected. Following this line of thought, Woike, Bender and Besner (in press) showed that implicit motives interact with arousal states that facilitate not only selective encoding and recall, but also effort and speed in memory performance. In one experiment, participants responded to a vivid recall procedure that either prompted them to provide an achievement-related autobiographical memory, or an everyday, routine experience. After that, they were presented with a word list containing an equal number of achievement-related and neutral stimuli. It was found that the combination of arousal state (neutral or achievement-related initial memory) and implicit motivation (*n* Achievement) predicted the performance during the recall phase for achievement words. Individuals high in *n* Achievement, in an achievement context, recalled more achievement-related words than other participants. In a further experiment, it was found that people motivated for *n*

Achievement not only recall more achievement-related words in a motive-arousing context, but they do so faster. This finding on reaction time is a demonstration that an interaction of motivation and situation specifically affects the retrieval of motive-relevant memory content.

Recall of Interrupted Tasks

The Zeigarnik effect represents the observation that people remember interrupted tasks better than completed ones (Zeigarnik, 1967). It has been found, however, that individuals may differ in the number of interrupted tasks recalled, and it has been suggested that individual differences in implicit motives may help explain why (McClelland et al., 1953). McClelland and colleagues (1953) found that individuals high in *n* Achievement recalled more interrupted tasks than individuals low in implicit achievement. This, however, only holds true if the structure of the task suggests the importance of doing well, or, put differently, if the context is achievement related. Similarly, Atkinson (1953) suggests that it depends on the context whether individuals high or low in *n* Achievement remember more incomplete or completed tasks. People high in *n* Achievement (with a high hope for success) recall more incomplete tasks after being instructed that completion of the task will signify success than when the importance of the task is decreased (Atkinson, 1953). The reverse relationship holds true for individuals low in achievement: When trying to avoid failure, they recall more completed tasks in an achievement situation and more incomplete tasks when the importance of success is decreased. Thus, the context determines whether more interrupted tasks are recalled. These findings are in accordance with Weiner's (1965) results that individuals high in achievement resume incomplete tasks after receiving feedback that they were about to fail, while individuals low in achievement only resumed tasks after they were about to succeed.

Implicit Motives Determine the Ways in Which Events Are Remembered

The link between implicit motivation and information processing may not only be limited to the issue of what is remembered, or how much is remembered—implicit motives may also play an important role in shaping how memories are remembered. It has been theorized that implicit motives may be linked to procedures that allow the individual to (re-)experience the intrinsic pleasure of motive-related affect by seeking out the stimulus, or executing the behavior that is associated with previous learning experiences. Such selecting procedures should play a role in the organization of emotional experiences, vivid memories, and event-specific knowledge that are thematically associated with a given implicit motive. The memories relating to such experiences should be organized and then recalled in a way that facilitates re-experiencing the pleasure associated with the implicit motive (Woike, 1994b). Accordingly, the structure of the narratives should be different across motives, as it serves different purposes.

For example, the experience of agency includes independently striving toward achievement (*n* Achievement), as well as being distinct from another person, or having power over others (*n* Power). In contrast, the experience of communion revolves around being close and connected to others (e.g., *n* Intimacy). Woike (1994a) reasoned that implicit agentic motivation may be related to perceiving motive-relevant information in terms of differences, distinctions, and contrasts, whereas implicit communal motivation may be related to perceiving experiences in terms of similarities, links, and interrelationships. Such functionally different structures of organizing motive-related knowledge may allow individuals to experience intrinsic pleasure that is either related to feeling distinct from others or feeling connected to others. A narrative scoring system to investigate these structural differences was developed by expanding upon the existing literature on cognitive complexity (see Woike & Aronoff, 1992, for details). Cognitive complexity, as a structural feature of narratives, comprises two important ways of organizing information: Differentiation refers to the number of different and contrasting aspects (e.g., "better", "unlike", etc.), and integration refers to the number of interrelationships and connections between aspects (e.g., "similar", "same"; Woike, 1997). Both processes reflect basic narrative elements and are often assumed to operate together (Schroder et al., 1967; Suedfeld et al., 1992). However, differentiation and integration are conceptually and operationally very different. Differentiation involves perceiving differences and opposition through relative comparisons and restrictions, whereas integration involves perceiving similarity, connection, interdependence, and congruity.

In situations in which their concerns become salient, agentic people may use differentiation to attain their goals. For example, individuals concerned with reaching a standard of excellence (*n* Achievement) may engage in making many distinctions and comparisons between themselves and others, or against external standards and demands. An individual may achieve greater impact and control by imposing restrictions on information presented to others and by being alert to the restrictions and conditions imposed on incoming information. Thus, perceiving oneself, others, and events as differentiated may help agentic people satisfy their needs to be autonomous, competitive, and dominating in the social world. They should therefore be particularly likely to use differentiation in social situations related to intrinsic agentic incentives.

On the other hand, structuring information in an integrated way may facilitate the satisfaction of communal needs and thus should be more likely found in individuals motivated for communion. The perception of similarities and connections between the individual and others may help communal individuals feel a greater sense of belonging. In social situations that allow for such perceptions, individuals motivated for communion should be particularly likely to use more integration.

It has to be stressed that differentiation and integration as structural elements are not synonymous with agentic and communal motives. It is possible that individuals choose to structure narratives about agentic and communal topics in either a predominantly differentiated or integrated way or even using both ways equally. In situations that are relevant to an individual's motive, however, the individual is more likely to use structural elements that match the motive in order to experience the associated affect.

Woike (1994a) tested this relationship by asking individuals with either a strong power (an aspect of agency) or intimacy motive to recall an important, emotionally involving personal experience. One group of the participants was then asked to form an impression of two people engaged in a power-related task, while the other participants were to form an impression of two people in an intimacy setting. In other words, participants were presented with a (potentially) motive-matching condition. When in this motive-relevant condition, participants formed more differentiated or integrated impressions of the other people depending on their motive. That is, the power-motivated individuals formed impressions with more distinctions, contrasts, and comparisons in the power-related task, whereas the intimacy-motivated individuals formed their impression with more similarities, links, and interrelationships in the intimacy-related task.

Woike and colleagues (Woike et al., 1999) conducted a series of studies to further investigate this influence of implicit motivation on the structure of autobiographical narratives. They found that individuals with strong agentic motives recalled more memories about agentic experiences and used more differentiation in doing so, while those with strong communal motives recalled more memories about communal experiences and used more integration in doing so. Similarly, Woike and Polo (2001) found that the way individuals organize memories of daily events is also related to their implicit motives. Individuals with strong agentic motives organize their daily memories in a differentiated manner, whereas individuals with strong communal motives organize their daily memories in an integrated way. Thus, it appears that motive-related memories are structured differently and in ways that may allow individuals to feel their preferred affective state.

These results suggest that motives do not only influence the accessibility of autobiographical memories, but that they also shape how this information is reconstructed during recall. Individuals concerned with implicit needs for agency (n Power, n Achievement) focus on differences, and individuals concerned with communion (n Intimacy) focus on similarities in organizing information. These findings seem to suggest that motive-linked organizational strategies may facilitate the memory construction process, that is, individuals with a specific motive disposition (e.g., n Communion) may rely on structural indices (e.g., similarities and links) to guide their search process. Without such organizational cues, it may take more time to arrive at a motive-related memory.

Biopsychological Findings on Implicit Motives and Cognition

It has been previously shown that the arousal of implicit motives releases hormones that enhance memory performance for motive-related content (McClelland, 1987). For example, arousal of n Power has been associated with an increase in epinephrine and norepinephrine (McClelland et al., 1980; McClelland, Ross, & Patel, 1985). There is evidence that norepinephrine increases performance for memory tasks of motive-related material: Subjects high in n Power (and low in n Affiliation) and 3-methoxy-4-hydroxyphenyl-glycol (MHPG), an index of brain norepinephrine turnover, showed superior performance in recall of power-related words in a free recall task to that of individuals who were low in the need for power and MHPG (McClelland, Maddocks, & McAdams, 1985). Similarly, McClelland and colleagues (1980) found that individuals high in n Power, who showed more central norepinehrine turnover, learned power-related paired associates faster than other individuals. These findings show the extent to which power-related stimulation has aroused the catecholamine-based norepinephrine-related reward system and offer evidence for a specific link between n Power arousal and the release of hormones associated with enhanced memory performance.

McClelland (1995) could also show that individuals whose n Achievement had been aroused, and who were to recall elements of a complex story, showed physiological signs of enhanced memory, indicated by the amount of water secreted through the kidneys as urine, which was taken as an indicator for Arginine vasopressin (AVP). This hormone enhances memory performance in humans and animals (McGaugh, 1990), and also acts as an antidiuretic hormone. The greater the decrease in urine flow (i.e., presumably the more AVP is released), the better the recall of participants who were aroused for n Achievement. McClelland (1995) argues that the achievement arousal leads to the release of AVP, which in turn has facilitated achievement-related retention and performance. It has to be noted that these effects were found particularly for individuals high in n Achievement in a situation that matched their motive constellation. It was not found for individuals low in n Achievement and/or in high-achievement individuals in a no-arousal control condition.

Furthermore, it has been shown in animals that injection of vasopressin in the posttraining phase of a learning procedure improves memory (de Wied, 1984). Treating human subjects with vasopressin parallels these effects, improving retention (Beckwith, Petros, Betgloff, & Staebler, 1987; Hamburger-Bar, Eisenberg, & Belmaker, 1987). The specificity of the relationship between AVD and memory performance is striking and can be understood in the light of studies on desmopression acetate (DDAVP), an analogue of AVD that can be applied intranasally. DDAVP improves recall of important aspects of a task more than secondary details (see Beckwith et al., 1987; Jennings, Nebes, & Reynolds, 1986). One limitation of such studies is the generally small sample size, which does not always allow for generalizable interpretations. As well, some results hold true only for men, not women, which has been attributed to a lack of control of the menstrual cycle (see Beckwith, Till, & Schneider, 1984).

Similarly, Schultheiss & Rohde (2002) found that the need for power was a predictor of testosterone elevation when an individual's activity inhibition (i.e., impulse control) was low. Among such individuals, the need for power predicted implicit learning after a victory and was a negative predictor of implicit learning after a defeat. On top of that, increases in testosterone are associated with increased implicit learning (for individuals low in activity inhibition). Such gains in implicit learning were mediated by increases in testosterone. In a recent study, Schultheiss and colleagues (Schultheiss et al., 2005) further investigated the relationship of n Power and learning: In both men and women, power motivation predicted enhanced learning in visuomotor sequences after victory, and impaired learning after a defeat. Among male participants, power motivation was associated with testosterone increases after victory, and decreases after defeat. The negative effect of power motivation on learning was mediated by levels of testosterone. However, findings on women's performance are less clear, with n Power predicting testosterone increases after defeat, not victory.

On the basis of these studies, it becomes clear that some hormonal markers/ neurotransmitters are associated with the influence of implicit motivation on memory performance. However, during which stage of information processing this influence takes place is not always differentiated and clearly warrants further investigation. Nevertheless, biopsychological studies of the link between cognition and implicit motivation further solidify that implicit motives influence cognitive performance.

Extending the Contextual Approach: Culture and Memory

Situational and Developmental Context

The findings summarized in this chapter document how implicit motives influence cognition, and they highlight how a situational perspective can enhance our understanding of such effects: Investigating situational factors can help us understand why individuals show enhanced (or decreased) cognitive performance only in settings rich in motive-relevant cues.

In the last part of this chapter, we would like to continue further on this path, which can lead us to a more global perspective on the impact that situation may have on the expression and formation of implicit motivation, and thus ultimately their influence on cognition. We summarized research indicating that individuals differ in their response to situational stimuli. While a person motivated for *n* Achievement may respond to incentives related to notions of mastery, goal characteristics, and rewards in his or her environment, another person driven by *n* Intimacy may be less aroused by the very same stimuli. Therefore, individuals with a specific motive orientation may actively seek out environments that match their motives and satisfy their needs, thereby creating contexts for themselves that are rich in specific, motive-related incentives. These contexts are then—to some degree—characteristic of their motive orientation, as well as many other individual factors like social strata, education, preferences, and beliefs about the world in general. Such contexts therefore transcend the boundaries of specific situations described in a Person × Situation approach (Krahe, 1992).

Stable contexts may then, in turn, serve as a developmental environment. Rosen and D'Andrade (1959) report evidence in line with this notion. They observed interactions between 9- to 11-year-old boys and their parents in a lab setting, finding that parents of high-achievement boys were more likely than parents of low-achievement boys to set challenging goals for their son, to have a higher regard for his problem-solving competence, and, in the case of mothers, to be directive, to reward good performance with affection, but also to punish poor performance with hostility and disapproval. This finding corroborates the assumption that when a child associates pleasure with certain types of behavior (e.g., achieving a goal), it becomes more likely that the child will seek out the same or similar behaviors in the future, in pursuit of a (re-) experience of that pleasurable affective state (Woike, 1994b).

Naturally, this pursuit of pleasure is shaped during the early, preverbal stages, in particular by parental caregivers who help children learn to interpret the world, their lives, and how to reminisce about their own past. Parents may differ in the way they facilitate the acquisition of such skills, and in the importance they assign to them. As well, such socialization goals and styles can vary across cultures. A growing body of literature documents substantial cultural differences in parental goals and pratices (Keller & Greenfield, 2000). To address such differences, the component model of parenting postulated by Keller (2006) differentiates between the styles of interaction that parents from different cultural contexts engage in with their children. For example, Keller (2006) suggests that face-to-face interactions (often found in U.S.-American contexts) between the child and a caregiver promote the development of a more independent self-construal because the child is learning quickly to perceive of itself as a separate and distinct individual. In contrast, parenting behaviors involving more body contact (often found in African or Asian contexts), increase a sense of belonging and may at the same time blur the distinctiveness of the motivational states of the child and mother (or any other significant caregiver interacting with the child).

It can therefore be expected that socialization practices shape the expression and formation of implicit motivation that vary in their focus on the self (e.g., *n* Achievement and *n* Power) and others (e.g., *n* Intimacy). A very early study by McClelland and colleagues (1953) provides support for the interaction between implicit motives (*n* Achievement) and childhood context. In a case study, they reported that a pronounced achievement motive was linked to a focus on mastery and independence in parental socialization practices. Such practices included encouraging children to eat by themselves, early toilet training, or children learning to dress themselves. These findings suggest that a socialization context emphasizing early independence, self-reliance, and acquisition and mastery of skills may lead to a strong need for achievement. Further research by McClelland and Pilon (1983) focused in more detail on the importance of child rearing in later life, finding that a strict parental style of toilet training, focusing on mastery and independence, was on average more likely to lead to high *n* Achievement scores in adulthood. Similar results were obtained in a study with German preschoolers (Heckhausen and Kemmler, 1957). Findings from a study by Rosen (1962) suggests that these relationships are not an epiphenomenon of one culture. Rosen (1962) reported that Brazilian mothers emphasized self-reliance, autonomy, and achievement in child rearing to a lesser degree than U.S.-American mothers, and drew on this cultural difference to explain the lower *n* Achievement score of Brazilian boys. Taken together, the literature therefore suggests that an emphasis on mastery and autonomy is related to a pronounced *n* Achievement. But even with a renewed interest in studying implicit motivation in culturally diverse settings (Chasiotis, Hofer, & Campos, 2006; Hofer, Busch, Bender, Lee, & Hagemeyer, in press; Hofer, Chasiotis, Friedlmeier, Busch, & Campos, 2005), studies on motives other than achievement are still scarce (see Chapter 15).

In summary, apart from the situation that may provide immediate incentives to act in a motive-consistent fashion, the individual's developmental, and thus cultural, context allows us to gain a better understanding of the formation of implicit motives. A focus on independence or interdependence in differing cultural contexts is likely to be associated with a pronounced agentic (*n* Achievement / *n* Power) or communal need (*n* Affiliation), respectively. In turn, individual differences in implicit motivation may help explain a portion of the variance in cognitive processes observed across cultural settings. One such cognitive area that has received a lot of interest across different cultural contexts is autobiographical memory.

Implicit Motives, Cultural Context, and Autobiographical Memory

Cultural Differences in Autobiographical Memory

A key result of research on autobiographical memory is that individual differences in recall originate in early socialization. Such differences are rooted in the coconstruction of a child's past with her or his parents, which is considered to take place after a child's implicit motivation has formed in the preverbal stages (Chasiotis et al., in press). Two major styles in parent–child conversations have been identified, a normative, and an elaborative reminiscing style (Reese & Fivush, 1993). Mullen and Yi (1995) investigated naturally occurring conversations of mother–child dyads (3-year-old children), and found that Caucasian (Western) dyads were more likely to cast the child as the central character of a story, to talk about the child's feelings and thoughts, and to make many references to personal attributes. Such an elaborated style of reminiscing is contrasted with a normative approach to joint remembering in Korean mother-child dyads, who emphasized behavioral expectations and social roles to a greater extent than did Caucasian (Western) mothers (Mullen & Yi, 1995). This pattern was replicated in a study of Chinese and Euro-American mother–child dyads (3-year olds; Wang, 2001a; see also Wang, Leichtman, & Davies, 2000). These findings of differential conversational styles in mother–child dyads are complemented by differences in the structure and content of memories that 4- and 6-year old children recall on their own (Han, Leichtman, & Wang, 1998). Han and colleagues (1998) found that Euro-American children's memories, compared with Korean and Chinese children's memories, included more references to specific past events, more references to internal states and evaluations, and more mentioning of themselves relative to others. Results of both studies (Mullen & Yi, 1995; Wang, 2001a) are mirrored in a study with 6-year olds (Wang & Leichtman, 2000), in which Chinese children showed greater orientation toward social engagement, concern with moral correctness, and more situational detail than American children (see also Miller, Wiley, Fung, & Liang, 1997; Wang, 2004).

These cultural differences are expected to "become larger and more stable among older children" (Wang, 2004, p.5), indicating increased differences in adult autobiographical recall across cultures (Pillemer, 1998). Indeed, adults' autobiographical recall shows similar differences: Caucasian Americans have more detailed memories, with themselves as the central characters, whereas Chinese individuals had rather general memories, with a strong group orientation (Wang, 2001b). Furthermore, in four studies by Mullen (1994), Caucasian participants reported a significantly earlier memory than Asian individuals, consistent with findings by Wang (2001b). These findings were extended to a sample from Africa (Cameroon) which, compared to a German sample, showed a later age of first memory (Bender & Chasiotis, in press).

But why do individuals reminisce differently, and why do parents engage in different forms of scaffolding behavior? Until recently, this question was usually answered by referring to different cultures as the driving force behind such differences. However, this may merely serve as a description, a placeholder or a label for the observed differences, because being "Chinese" is not an explanation in itself. In cross-cultural research, one is strongly advised to investigate contextual variables to help identify what exactly constitutes such cultural differences (Poortinga, van de Vijver, Joe, & van de Koppel, 1987). Following this line of argumentation, Bender and Chasiotis (in press) suggested that moving away from labels such as "Western," and understanding cultural differences in the light of individual differences like implicit motives and different ontogenetic contexts (e.g., number of siblings), will result in a functional perspective that can help "peel the onion" called culture (Poortinga et al., 1987).

Contextual and Individual Differences

Building on the theory on independence and interdependence formulated by Markus and Kitayama (1991), Kağitçibaşi (1996) further differentiated socio-cultural orientation (or self-construal) into the orthogonal dimensions of interpersonal distance (separateness–relatedness) and agency (autonomy—heteronomy; see Kağitçibaşi, 1996). The end poles of these dimensions define independence as the combination of autonomy and separateness. Kağitçibaşi (1996) suggests that the prototypical combinations of these dimensions (e.g., interdependence, independence) are adaptive in different cultural contexts. The prototypical interdependent sociocultural orientation (heteronomy/relatedness) is regarded as adaptive in rather rural contexts with populations of lower socioeconomic and educational status (cf. Keller et al., 2004) because intergenerational interdependence is necessary for the family's livelihood: Children often contribute to the family's economy and provide a security net for their aging parents (Kağitçibaşi, 2005). From an evolutionary perspective, independence in this context is not functional because an independent child may leave the family and look after her/his own self-interest when she/he is grown (see also Keller, 2003; Keller et al., 2004; Greenfield, 1994; Greenfield, Keller, Fuligni, & Maynard, 2003; Kağitçibaşi, 1996, 2005). This is contrasted with the prototypical independent context that can be found in affluent, educated, middle-class, nuclear families (typical especially for Western countries; Kağitçibaşi, 1996). With alternatives for old-age support, economic dependence on offspring is often not considered necessary or even desirable. Children are therefore raised to be independent and self-sufficient, fostering a sense of separateness and uniqueness (Kağitçibaşi, 2005).

These different contexts therefore have different implications for the family structure and thus the immediate context of socialization that is assumed to shape a multitude of variables like self-construal (Kağitçibaşi, 1996, 2005)—including implicit motivation (see Fig. 8.2). In a context in which close-knit families and interdependencies between generations are adaptive, it is more likely that children have better opportunities to be provided with contextual incentives that reinforce their affiliative needs. In contrast, contexts that put special emphasis on independence, being singled out, and treating the child as an individual (see also Keller, 2003; Keller et al., 2004) are more likely to be

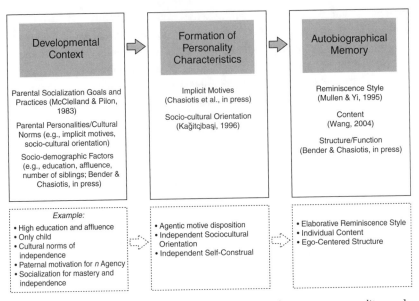

Figure 8.2 Basic relationships between developmental context, personality, and autobiographical memory.

rich in incentives and affective experiences that relate to agentic implicit motivation (for a similar argument, see Markus & Kitayama, 1991).

The investigation of these cultural relationships still has to overcome several obstacles, including methodological complications (Van de Vijver, 2000; see also Chapter 15), and the need for a closer investigation of the conceptual equivalence of definitions of motives across cultures. Nevertheless, there is some evidence pointing toward the described direction. For example, Bender and Chasiotis (in press) showed that having a large number of siblings predicts having a structurally more interdependent memory, both across and within cultural contexts (Cameroon, Germany, People's Republic of China; see Fig. 8.2). Furthermore, Chasiotis and colleagues (in press) could show that in a sample of German and Cameroonian preschoolers, implicit motivation was related to autobiographical memory, in both cultures. In particular, Chasiotis and colleagues found that an independent mode of implicit motivation (e.g., striving for status, n Power) was related to a self-focused structure of autobiographical memories. This finding is in agreement with research from intracultural studies, in which Woike and colleagues found that individuals with a high implicit communal motivation make more use of integration to structure their autobiographical recall (social focus), whereas individuals exhibiting a highly agentic implicit motive make more use of differentiation to structure their memories (self-focus; Woike et al., 1999, 2001, 2003).

Implicit motives, which develop preverbally, and thus ontogenetically earlier than autobiographical memory, may therefore act as a facilitator in the socialization process. Repeatedly, implicit motives have been shown to act as a selective filter for encoding and retrieval of autobiographical knowledge (Woike et al., 1999, 2001). An interdependent implicit motive orientation may thus facilitate the recall of social memories (with an integrative structure and a focus on others), while an independent motive constellation may be more apt to increase self-related memories (with a differentiated structure and the own person as the main character; see Bender & Chasiotis, in press, and see Fig. 8.2). If that is the case, implicit motives may also act as a vehicle that serves as a guiding frame of reference throughout the life course and may thus help explain why differences in reminiscence styles not only persist into adulthood, but are also believed to become even larger (Wang, 2004).

In this section, we outlined a new approach to the interaction between situational factors and implicit motivation. By shifting toward a focus on more general, enduring differences in contexts in which implicit motivation develops, we hope to have opened an avenue to more fully understand the impact of implicit motivation on cognitive behavior like autobiographical recall. Through an identification of the specific sociodemographic and developmental contexts (not just their cultural labels) and implicit motivation (as an individual difference), it may be possible not only to describe, but also to explain, the emergence of differences in autobiographical memory. Individuals that grow up in prototypical independent contexts rich in affective experiences relating to an agentic, self-focused implicit motivation should be more likely to develop an autobiographical reminiscence style that revolves around self-focused themes and structures than individuals growing up in prototypical interdependent contexts.

Conclusion

We find evidence that implicit motives influence cognitive performance during each stage of information processing, from the perception of a stimulus to its recall. In line with McClelland's early contention, implicit motives orient, direct, and select behavior (e.g., McClelland, 1987). This entails that people automatically attend to stimuli in the social environment that carry incentives linked to their implicit motives, especially nonverbal cues and incentives (Schultheiss, 2008). Perceptual images are more likely to be encoded if the images evoke motive-related affect. The information is not elaborated or worked over cognitively to fit the self-concept but remains as a vivid perceptual image of the experience preserved in memory similar to a flashbulb memory (Brown & Kulik, 1977). Once these images are encoded, they may be rehearsed often because through rehearsal the person can re-experience the pleasure associated with the implicit motive (Woike, 1994b). And, because these experiences are encoded with rich imagery, the retrieved memories contain a great deal of vividness. Motive-relevant memories are more readily retrieved under conditions of motive arousal in which the person is in a motive-arousing state of engagement than under neutral conditions. These memories are emotional, vivid, and unique. Studies on autobiographical narratives, encoding and retrieval of recently acquired knowledge, and controlled autobiographical memory retrieval offer a great deal of evidence that implicit motives influence the encoding and recall of autobiographical events related to the motives that are emotional and specific via organizational strategies that facilitate the attainment of the desired affective end state.

We have detailed support for the effects of implicit motivation on the various stages of information processing. However, studies concerned with implicit motives and memory mostly investigate the effect of implicit motives on the retrieval of motive-relevant material. This does not necessarily imply that such effects are actually linked to implicit motivation during the retrieval phase. For example, for some effects, it might be possible to assume that implicit motives may have played a much larger role in the preceding phases of information processing (e.g., motivated rehearsal). Therefore, more studies are needed to more clearly differentiate how and when implicit motives exert their influence on the stages of information processing.

To conclude, this chapter provided a comprehensive overview on the influence of implicit motives on cognition, with a special focus on the role of situational factors that interact with implicit motivational states. It has become apparent that a multidisciplinary model for the relationship of implicit motives to learning and memory is clearly needed to advance our understanding of how implicit motivation shapes the way people think, reminisce, and behave. Such a model would not only need to account for findings from research in motivation and cognition, but should also incorporate advances in developmental and cross-cultural psychology. Identifying situational, and contextual (cultural) effects on the expression and formation of implicit motivation not only will advance our theoretical understanding of how motivation relates to cognition, but can also promote a true understanding of cultural differences.

References

Ajzen, I., & Fishbein, M. (1970). The prediction of behavior from attitudinal and normative variables. *Journal of Experimental Social Psychology, 6,* 466–487.

Alea, N., & Bluck, S. (2007). I'll keep you in mind: The intimacy function of autobiographical memory. *Applied Cognitive Psychology, 21,* 1091–1111.

Atkinson, J. W. (1953). The achievement motive and recall of interrupted and completed tasks. *Journal of Experimental Psychology, 46,* 381–390.

Atkinson, J. W., Heyns, R. W., & Veroff, J. (1958). The effect of experimental arousal of the affiliation motive on thematic apperception. In J. W. Atkinson (Ed.), *Motives in fantasy, action, and society: A method of assessment and study* (pp. 95–104). Princeton, NJ: Van Nostrand.

Atkinson, J. W., & Walker, E. L. (1958). The affiliation motive and perceptual sensitivity to faces. In J. W. Atkinson (Ed.), *Motives in fantasy, action, and society: A method of assessment and study* (pp. 360–366). Princeton, NJ: Van Nostrand.

Baddeley, A. D. (1987). But what the hell is it for? In M. M. Gruneberg, P. E. Morris, & R. N. Sykes (Eds.), *Practical aspects of memory. Vol. 1: Memory in everyday life* (pp. 3–18). Chichester: Wiley.

Bargh, J. A. (1989). Conditional automaticity: Varieties of automatic influence in social perception and cognition. In J. S. Uleman & J. A. Bargh (Eds.), *Unintended thought* (pp. 3–51). New York: Guilford Press.

Bartlett, F. C. (1932). *Remembering: An experimental and social study.* Cambridge: Cambridge University Press.

Beckwith, B. E., Petros, T. V., Bergloff, P. J., & Staebler, R. J. (1987). Vasopressin analogue (DDAVP) facilitates recall of narrative prose. *Behavioral Neuroscience, 103,* 429–432.

Beckwith, B. E., Till, R. E., & Schneider, V. (1984). Vasopressin analog (DDAVP) improves memory in human males. *Peptides, 11,* 473–476.

Bender, M. & Chasiotis, A. (in press). Number of siblings explains cultural differences in autobiographical memory in PR China, Cameroon and Germany. *Journal of Cross-Cultural Psychology.*

Bluck, S. (2003). Autobiographical memory: Exploring its functions in everyday life. *Memory, 11,* 113–124.

Bluck, S., & Alea, N. (2002). Exploring the functions of autobiographical memory: Why do I remember the autumn? In J. D. Webster & B. K. Haight (Eds.), *Critical advances in reminiscence work: From theory to application* (pp. 61–75). New York, NY: Springer Publishing Co.

Bluck, S., Alea, N., Habermas, T., & Rubin, D. C. (2005). A TALE of three functions: The self-reported uses of autobiographical memory. *Social Cognition, 23,* 89–115.

Brown, R., & Kulik, J. (1977). Flashbulb memories. *Cognition, 5,* 73–99.

Brunstein, J. C., & Hoyer, S. (2002). Implizites und explizites Leistungsstreben: Befunde zur Unabhängigkeit zweier Motivationssysteme [Implicit versus explicit achievement strivings: Empirical evidence of the independence of two motivational systems]. *Zeitschrift für Pädagogische Psychologie, 16,* 51–62.

Carver, C. S., & Scheier, M. F. (1981). *Attention and self-regulation: A control theory approach to human behavior.* New York: Springer-Verlag.

Chasiotis, A., Bender, M., Kiessling, F., & Hofer, J. (in press). On the emergence of the independent self: Cognitive complexity in autobiographical memory as a mediator of false belief understanding and sociocultural motive orientation in Cameroonian and German preschoolers. *Journal of Cross-Cultural Psychology.*

Chasiotis, A., Hofer, J., & Campos, D. (2006). When does liking children lead to parenthood? Younger siblings, implicit prosocial power motivation, and explicit love for children predict parenthood across cultures. *Journal of Cultural and Evolutionary Psychology, 4*(2), 95–123.

Conway, M. A., & Pleydell-Pearce, C. W. (2000). The construction of autobiographical memories in the self-memory system. *Psychological Review, 107* (2), 261–288.

Craig, W. (1918). Appetites and aversions as constituents of instincts. *Biological Bulletin of Woods Hole, 34,* 91–107.

deCharms, R., Morrison, H. W., Reitman, W., & McClelland, D. C. (1955). Behavioral correlates of directly and indirectly measured achievement motivation. In D. C. McClelland (Ed.), *Studies in motivation* (pp. 414–423). New York: Appleton-Century-Crofts.

DeSteno, D., & Salovey, P. (1997). Structural dynamism in the concept of self: A flexible model for a malleable concept. *Review of General Psychology, 1*(4), 389–409.

De Wied, D. (1984). Neurophysiological hormone influences on learning and memory processes. In G. Lynch, J. L. McGaugh, & N. M. Weinberger (Eds.), *Neurobiology of learning and memory* (pp. 289–312). New York: Guilford Press.

Dorfman, J., Shames, V. A., & Kihlstrom, J. F. (1996). Intuition, incubation, and insight: Implicit cognition in problem solving. In G. D. M. Underwood (Ed.), *Implicit cognition* (pp. 257–296). Oxford: The Oxford University Press.

Dweck, C. S., & Wortman, C. B. (1982). Learned helplessness, anxiety, and achievement motivation: Neglected parallels in cognitive, affective, and coping responses. In H. W. Krohne & L. Laux (Eds.), *Achievement, stress, and anxiety.* (pp. 93–125). Washington, DC: Hemisphere.

Epstein, S. (1994). Integration of the cognitive and the psychodynamic unconscious. *American Psychologist, 49,* 709–724.

Farber, I. E. (1955). The role of motivation in verbal learning and performance. *Psychological Bulletin, 52,* 311–327.

French, E.G. (1955). Some characteristics of achievement motivation. *Journal of Experimental Psychology, 50,* 232–236.

Goschke, T., & Kuhl, J. (1993). Representation of intentions: Persisting activation in memory. *Journal of Experimental Psychology: Learning, Memory, and Cognition, 19,* 1211–1226.

Greenfield, P. M. (1994). Independence and interdependence as developmental scripts: Implications for theory, research and practice. In P. M. Greenfield & R. R. Cocking (Eds.), *Cross-cultural roots of minority child development.* (pp. 1–40). Hillsdale, NJ: Lawrence Erlbaum Associates.

Greenfield, P. M., Keller, H., Fuligni, A. & Maynard, A. (2003). Cultural pathways through universal development. Annual Review of Psychology, 54, 461–490.

Greenwald, A. G., Klinger, M. R., & Liu, T. J. (1989). Unconscious processing of dichoptically masked words. *Memory and Cognition, 17,* 35–47.

Greenwald, A. G., Klinger, M. R., & Schuh, E. S. (1995). Activation by marginally perceptible ("subliminal") stimuli: Dissociation of unconscious from conscious cognition. *Journal of Experimental Psychology, 124,* 22–42.

Hamburger-Bar, R., Eisenberg, J., & Belmaker, R. H. (1987). Animal and clinical studies of vasopression after drinking in dehydrated humans. *American Journal of Physiology, 247,* R968–R971.

Han, J. J., Leichtman, M. D., & Wang, Q. (1998). Autobiographical memory in Korean, Chinese, and American children. *Developmental Psychology, 34*(4), 701–713.

Heckhausen, H., & Kemmler, L. (1957). Entstehungsbedingungen der kindlichen Selbstaendigkeit. Der Einfluss der muetterlichen Selbstaendigkeitserziehung auf die soziale Schulreife der Soehne [Developmental factors for children's autonomy. The influence of autonomy socialization on school aptitude]. Zeitschrift fur Experimentelle und angewandte Psychologie, 4, 603–622.

Hess, U., Blairy, S., & Kleck, R. E. (2000). The influence of facial emotion displays, gender, and ethnicity on judgments of dominance and affiliation. *Journal of Nonverbal Behavior, 24*, 265–283.

Hill, T., Lewicki, P., Czyzewska, M., & Boss, A. (1989). Self-perpetuating development of encoding biases in person perception. *Journal of Personality and Social Psychology, 57*, 373–387.

Hofer, J., Busch, H., Bender, M., Lee, M., & Hagemeyer, B. (in press). Arousal of achievement motivation among student samples in three different cultural contexts: Self and social standards of evaluation. *Journal of Cross-Cultural Psychology*.

Hofer, J., Chasiotis, A., Friedlmeier, W., Busch, H., & Campos, D. (2005). The measurement of implicit motives in three cultures: Power and affiliation in Cameroon, Costa Rica, and Germany. *Journal of Cross-Cultural Psychology, 36*, 689–716.

Hyman, I. E., & Faries, J. M. (1992). The functions of autobiographical memory. In M. A. Conway, D. C. Rubin, H. Spinnler, & W. A. Wagenaar (Eds.), *Theoretical perspectives on autobiographical memory* (pp. 207–221). Dordrecht: Kluwer.

Jennings, J. R., Nebes, R. D., & Reynolds, C. F., III (1986). Vasopressin peptide (DDAVP) may narrow the focus of attention in normal elderly. *Psychiatry Research, 17*, 31–39.

Kağitçibaşi, C. (1996). The autonomous-relational self: A new synthesis. *European Psychologist, 1*, 180–186.

Kağitçibaşi, C. (2005). Autonomy and relatedness in cultural context: Implications for self and family. *Journal of Cross-Cultural Psychology, 36*, 1–20.

Kazen, M., & Kuhl, J. (2005). Intention memory and achievement motivation: Volitional facilitation and inhibition as a function of affective contents of need-related stimuli. *Journal of Personality and Social Psychology, 89*(3), 426–448.

Keller, H. (2003). Socialization for competence: Cultural models of infancy. *Human Development, 46*, 288–311.

Keller, H. (2006). *Cultures of infancy.* Mahwah, NJ: Erlbaum.

Keller, H., & Greenfield, P. M. (2000). History and future development in cross-cultural psychology. *Journal of Cross-Cultural Psychology, 31*, 52–62.

Keller, H., Yovsi, R. D., Borke, J., Kärtner, J., Jensen, H., & Papaligoura, Z. (2004). Developmental consequences of early parenting experiences: Self regulation and self recognition in three cultural communities. *Child Development, 75*(6), 1745–1760.

Kihlstrom, J. F. (1990). The psychological unconscious. In L. A. Pervin (Ed.), *Handbook of personality: Theory and Research* (pp. 445–464). New York: The Guilford Press.

Klinger, E. (1967). Modeling effects on achievement imagery. *Journal of Personality and Social Psychology, 7*, 49–62.

Knutson, B. (1996). Facial expressions of emotion influence interpersonal trait inferences. *Journal of Nonverbal Behavior, 20,* 165–182.

Krahe, B. (1992). *Personality and social psychology.* London: Sage Publications.

Lang, P. J., Bradley, M. M., & Cuthbert, B. N. (1997). Motivated attention: Affect, activation, and action. In P. J. Lang, R. F. Simons, & M. T. Balaban (Eds.), *Attention and orienting: Sensory and motivational processes* (pp. 97–135). Mahwah, NJ: Lawrence Erlbaum Associates.

Lewin, Kurt (1935). *A dynamic theory of personality: Selected papers.* New York: McGraw-Hill.

Markus, H. (1977). Self-schemata and processing information about the self. *Journal of Personality and Social Psychology, 35,* 63–78.

Markus, H. R., & Kitayama, S. (1991). Culture and the self: Implications for cognition, emotion, and motivation. *Psychological Review, 98*(2), 224–253.

Markus, H., & Wurf, E. (1986). The dynamic self-concept: A social psychological perspective. *Annual Review of Psychology, 38,* 299–337.

McAdams, D. P. (1982). Experiences of intimacy and power: Relationships between social motives and autobiographical memory. *Journal of Personality and Social Psychology, 42,* 292–302.

McAdams, D. P., Hoffman, B. J., Mansfield, E. D., & Day, R. (1996). Themes of agency and communion in significant autobiographical scenes. *Journal of Personality, 64,* 339–377.

McAdams, D. P., & McClelland, D. C. (1983). *Social motives and memory.* Unpublished manuscript, Harvard University, Cambridge, MA.

McAdams, D. P., & Vaillant, G. E. (1982). Intimacy motivation and psychosocial adjustment: A longitudinal study. *Journal of Personality Assessment, 46,* 586–593.

McClelland, D. C. (1953). *The achieving society.* New York: Appleton.

McClelland, D. C. (1980). Motive dispositions. The merits of operant and respondent measures. In L. Wheeler (Ed.), *Review of personality and social psychology* (Vol. 1, pp. 10–41). Beverly Hills, CA: Sage.

McClelland, D. C. (1984). *Motives, personality, and society. Selected papers.* New York: Praeger.

McClelland, D. C. (1987). *Human motivation.* New York: Cambridge University Press.

McClelland, D. C. (1995). Achievement motivation in relation to achievement-related recall, performance, and urine flow, a marker associated with release of vasopressin. *Motivation and Emotion, 19,* 59–76.

McClelland, D. C., Atkinson, J. W., Clark, R. A., & Lowell, E. L. (1953). *The achievement motive.* New York: Appleton-Century-Crofts.

McClelland, D. C., Davidson, R., Saron, C., & Floor, E. (1980). The need for power, brain norepinephrine turnover and learning. *Biological Psychology, 10,* 93–102.

McClelland, D. C., Koestner, R., & Weinberger, J. (1989). How do self-attributed and implicit motives differ? *Psychological Review, 96,* 690–702.

McClelland, D. C., & Liberman, A. M. (1949). The effect of need for achievement on recognition of need-related words. *Journal of Personality, 18,* 236–251.

McClelland, D. C., Maddocks, J. A., & McAdams, D. P. (1985). The need for power, brain norepinephrine turnover, and memory. *Motivation and Emotion, 9*, 1–9.

McClelland, D. C., Patel, V., Stier, D., & Brown, D. (1987). The relationship of affiliative arousal to dopamine release. *Motivation and Emotion, 11*, 51–66.

McClelland, D. C., & Pilon, D. A. (1983). Sources of adult motives in patterns of parent behavior in early childhood. *Journal of Personality and Social Psychology, 44*, 564–574.

McClelland, D. C., Ross, G., & Patel, V. (1985). The effect of an academic examination on salivary norepinephrine and immunoglobulin levels. *Journal of Human Stress, 11*, 52–59.

McGaugh, J. L. (1990). Significance and remembrance: The role of neuromodulatory systems. *Psychological Science, 1*, 15–25.

Miller, P. J., Wiley, A., Fung, H., & Liang, C. (1997). Personal storytelling as a medium of socialization in Chinese and American families. *Child Development, 68*, 557–568.

Mogg K., Phillippot, P., & Bradley, B. P. (2004). Selective attention to angry faces in clinical social phobia. *Journal of Abnormal Psychology, 113*, 160–165.

Mullen, M. K. (1994). Earliest recollections of childhood: A demographic analysis. *Cognition, 52*, 55–79.

Mullen, M. K., & Yi, S. (1995). The cultural context of talk about the past: Implications for the development of autobiographical memory. *Cognitive Development, 10*, 407-419.

Neisser, U. (1988). Five kinds of self-knowledge. *Philosophical Psychology, 1*, 35–59.

Pasupathi, M., Lucas, S., & Coombs, A. (2002). Conversational functions of autobiographical remembering: Long-married couples talk about conflicts and pleasant topics. *Discourse Processes, 34*, 163–192.

Patten, R. L., & White, L. A. (1977). Independent effects of achievement behavior. *Motivation and Emotion, 1*, 39–59.

Pillemer, D. B. (1992). Remembering personal circumstances: A functional analysis. In E. Winograd & U. Neisser (Eds.), *Affect and accuracy in recall: Studies of "flashbulb" memories* (Emory symposia in cognition 4th ed., pp. 236–264). New York: Cambridge University Press.

Pillemer, D. B. (1998). *Momentous events, vivid memories.* Harvard University Press, Cambridge, MA.

Poortinga, Y. H., van de Vijver, F. J. R, Joe, R. C., & van de Koppel, J. M. H. (1987). Peeling the onion called culture: A synopsis. In C. Kağitçibaşi (Ed.), *Growth and progress in cross-cultural psychology* (pp. 22–34). Berwyn, PA: Swets North America.

Posner, M. I. (2004). *Cognitive neuroscience of attention.* New York: Guilford

Reese, E., & Fivush, R. (1993). Parental styles of talking about the past. *Developmental Psychology, 29*(3), 596–606.

Robinson, J. A., & Swanson, K. L. (1990). Autobiographical memory: The next phase [Special Issue: Applying cognitive psychology in the 1990s]. *Applied Cognitive Psychology, 4*, 321–335.

Rosen, B. C. (1962). Socialization and achievement motivation in Brazil. *American Sociological Review, 7*, 612–624.

Rosen, B. C., & D'Andrade, R. (1959). The psychosocial origins of achievement motivation. *Sociometry, 22*, 185–218.

Schacter, D. L. (1987). Implicit memory: History and current status. *Journal of Experimental Psychology: Learning, Memory, & Cognition, 13*, 501–518.

Schroder, H. M., Driver, M. J., & Streufert, S. (1967). *Human information processing.* New York: Holt, Rinehart, & Winston.

Schultheiss, O. C. (2001). An information processing account of implicit motive arousal. In M. L. Maehr & P. Pintrich (Eds.), *Advances in motivation and achievement. Vol. 12: New directions in measures and methods* (pp. 1–41). Greenwich, CT: JAI Press.

Schultheiss, O. C. (2008). Implicit motives. In O. P. John, R. W. Robins, & L. A. Pervin (Eds.), *Handbook of personality: Theory and research* (3rd ed., pp. 603–633). New York: Guilford.

Schultheiss, O. C., & Brunstein, J. C. (1999). Goal imagery: Bridging the gap between implicit motives and explicit goals. *Journal of Personality, 67*, 1–38.

Schultheiss, O. C., & Hale, J. A. (2007). Implicit motives modulate attentional orienting to perceived facial expressions of emotion. *Motivation and Emotion, 31*(1), 13–24.

Schultheiss, O. C., & Rohde, W. (2002). Implicit power motivation predicts men's testosterone changes and implicit learning in a contest situation. *Hormones and Behavior, 41*, 195–202.

Schultheiss, O. C., Wirth, M. M., Torges, C. M., Pang, J. S., Villacorta, M. A., & Welsh, K. M. (2005). Effects of implicit power motivation on men's and women's implicit learning and testosterone changes after social victory or defeat. *Journal of Personality and Social Psychology, 88*(1), 174–188.

Singer, J. A., & Salovey P. (1993). *The remembered self: Emotion and memory in personality.* New York: The Free Press.

Squire, L. R. (2004). Memory systems of the brain: A brief history and current perspective. *Neurobiology of Learning and Memory, 82*, 171–177.

Stroop, J. R. (1935). Studies of interference in serial verbal reactions. *Journal of Experimental Psychology, 18*, 643–662.

Suedfeld, P., Tetlock, P. E., & Streufert, S. (1992). Conceptual/integrative complexity. In C. Smith (Ed.), *Handbook of thematic analysis* (pp. 401–418). Cambridge, England: Cambridge University Press.

Teitelbaum, P. (1966). The use of operant methods in the assessment and control of motivational states. In W. K. Honig (Ed.), *Operant behavior: Areas of research and application* (pp. 565–608). New York: Appleton-Century-Crofts.

Trope, Y. (1975), "Seeking information about one's own ability as a determinant of choice among tasks," *Journal of Personality and Social Psychology, 32*, 1004–1013.

Tulving, E. (1985). How many memory systems are there? *American Psychologist, 40*, 385–398.

Tversky, A., & Kahneman, D. (1983). Extensional versus intuitive reasoning: The conjunction fallacy in probability judgment. *Psychological Review, 90*, 293–315.

Van de Vijver, F. J. R. (2000). The nature of bias. In R. H. Dana (Ed.), *Handbook of cross-cultural and multicultural personality assessment* (pp. 87–106). Mahwah, NJ: Lawrence Erlbaum.

Wang, Q. (2001a). "Did you have fun?" American and Chinese mother-child conversations about shared emotional experiences. *Cognitive Development, 16*, 693–715.

Wang, Q. (2001b). Culture effects on adult's earliest childhood recollection and self-description: Implications for the relation between memory and self. *Journal of Personality and Social Psychology, 81*, 220–223.

Wang, Q. (2004). The emergence of cultural self-constructs: Autobiographical memory and self-description in European American and Chinese children. *Developmental Psychology, 40*, 3–15.

Wang, Q., & Leichtman, M. D. (2000). Same beginnings, different stories: A comparison of American and Chinese children's narratives. *Child Development, 71*, 1329–1347.

Wang, Q., Leichtman, M. D., & Davies, K. I. (2000). Sharing memories and telling stories: American and Chinese mothers and their 3-year-olds. *Memory, 8*, 159–178.

Weiner, B. (1965). Need achievement and the resumption of incompleted tasks. *Journal of Personality and Social Psychology, 1*, 165–168.

Weiner, B. (1980). *Human motivation*. New York: Holt, Rinehart & Winston.

Woike, B. A. (1994a). The use of differentiation and integration processes: Empirical studies of "separate" and "connected" ways of thinking. *Journal of Personality & Social Psychology, 67*(1), 142–150.

Woike, B. A. (1994b). Vivid recollection as a technique to arouse implicit motive-related affect. *Motivation & Emotion, 18*(4), 335–349.

Woike, B. A. (1995). Most memorable experiences: Evidence of a link between implicit and explicit motives and social cognitive processes in everyday life. *Journal of Personality and Social Psychology, 68*, 1081–1091.

Woike, B. A. (1997). Categories of cognitive complexity: A scoring manual. Technical document, Barnard College, Columbia University, New York, NY.

Woike, B. A. (2008). A functional framework for the influence of implicit and explicit motives on autobiographical memory. *Personality and Social Psychology Review, 12*(2), 99–117.

Woike, B. A., & Aronoff, J. (1992). Antecedents of complex social cognitions. *Journal of Personality & Social Psychology, 63*(1), 97–104.

Woike, B. A., Bender, M., & Besner, N. (2009). Implicit motivational states influence memory: Evidence for incidental learning in personality. *Journal of Research in Personality, 43*(1), 39–48.

Woike, B. A., Gershkovich, I., Piorkowski, R., & Polo, M. (1999). The role of motives in the content and structure of autobiographical memory. *Journal of Personality and Social Psychology, 76*, 600–612.

Woike, B. A., Lavezzary, E., & Barsky, J. (2001). The influence of implicit motives on memory processes. *Journal of Personality & Social Psychology, 81*(5), 935–945.

Woike, B., Macleod, S., & Goggin, M. (2003). Implicit and explicit motives influence accessibility to different autobiographical knowledge. *Personality & Social Psychology Bulletin, 29*(8), 1046–1055.

Woike, B. A., & Polo, M. (2001). Motive-related memories: Content, structure and affect. *Journal of Personality, 69*(3), 391–415.

Zeigarnik, B. (1967). On finished and unfinished tasks. In W. D. Ellis (Ed.), *A sourcebook of Gestalt psychology*. New York: Humanities Press.

Chapter 9

Properties of Motive-Specific Incentives

STEVEN J. STANTON
Duke University

JULIE L. HALL
University of Michigan

OLIVER C. SCHULTHEISS
Friedrich-Alexander University

Overview

Over the past 50 years, motivation theorists have generally agreed that implicit motives represent capacities to experience specific classes of incentives as rewarding (see Atkinson, 1957; McClelland, 1987; Schultheiss, 2008). Thus, individuals high in the need for achievement (*n* Achievement) find pleasure in mastering challenging tasks; individuals high in the need for power (*n* Power) get a kick out of having impact on others; and individuals high in the need for affiliation (*n* Affiliation) enjoy having close, harmonious contact with others. An important consequence of implicit motives' capacity to affectively charge incentives is that they orient attention and energize and select behaviors aimed at attaining these incentives (McClelland, 1987).

However, despite the nominal importance theorists have ascribed to motive-specific incentives, their exact properties have remained strangely undefined in the past. We believe that this state of affairs has hindered theoretical and empirical advances in the field because a key ingredient for a more thorough understanding of motives, what they are and how they operate, has been missing. This has led to a somewhat insular existence of motive research outside of mainstream personality psychology, social psychology, and biopsychology, the three disciplines traditionally most concerned with motivation. At the same time, the relative lack of precision inherent in the definitions of motives and particularly their incentives has led to a Babylonic proliferation of motive measures and theories that often do not share much except the name with the original concepts and measures developed by McClelland and colleagues (see McClelland, Koestner, & Weinberger, 1989, for a discussion of this issue). Neither development was apt to move research on implicit motives forward in great and confident strides. As deplorable as this outcome may be, we suggest it can be revised to a large extent by going back to the incentive concept at the core of implicit motive research and defining and testing it rigorously.

In the present chapter, we aim to move in this direction by tracing in the first half the conceptualization of motive-specific incentives from their origin in McClelland, Atkinson, Clark and Lowell's (1953) pioneering work on the achievement motive through its metamorphoses in the work of McClelland and his associates (McClelland, 1980; McClelland et al., 1989) to the information-processing account of implicit motivation formulated by Schultheiss (2001, 2008). In the second half of the chapter, we will present a motivational field theory of motivational incentives, proposing that nonverbal social signals, specifically facial expressions of emotion, function as incentives for implicit motives. We will argue that nonverbal signals indicating the sender's dominance versus submission represent incentives for power-motivated individuals and that nonverbal signals indicating the sender's friendliness versus hostility represent incentives for affiliation-motivated individuals. We will review studies in support of this model and also discuss emerging evidence for a role of nonverbal social signals in achievement motivation arousal.

Conceptual Accounts of Motive-Specific Incentives

Conditioned Incentives: The McClelland et al. (1953) Affect-Redintegration Model

In *The Achievement Motive*, the culmination of several years of research on the development, validation, and conceptual grounding of a measure of the need to achieve, McClelland et al. (1953) provided a first speculative sketch of what kinds of incentives implicit motives respond to. They defined the achievement motive as a concern with meeting or surpassing a standard of excellence when dealing with a task. They developed the original *n* Achievement measure by manipulating the motivational state of research participants (e.g., by having them succeed or fail at challenging anagram tasks or giving them no feedback at all about their performance) and then having participants write imaginative stories about pictures showing people in achievement-related situations. Stories were then scrutinized for differences between motivational-arousal conditions, and the coding system for *n* Achievement was thus developed. The picture story measure of *n* Achievement turned out to be a good predictor of task performance when the task was challenging and provided immediate feedback about how well participants did (e.g., because a given problem could be solved or not). In contrast, tasks that either provided no challenge or were much too difficult to be solved or on which participants could not tell how well they were doing did not elicit superior performance in individuals high in *n* Achievement.

To account for the way *n* Achievement selectively enhanced performance on challenging tasks (but not easy or difficult tasks), McClelland et al. (1953) developed the affect-redintegration model of motivation. According to this model, people learn to associate specific cues with a subsequent change in affect. In the case of *n* Achievement, the cue is the perception of a challenging task, and the subsequent affective change is the pleasure of solving it. Thus, the prospect of pleasure triggered by the moderate difficulty inherent in a task becomes the incentive for achievement-motivated individuals to work hard on challenging tasks. However, the theory was not limited to *n* Achievement but was designed by McClelland et al. (1953) to account for other motives, such as *n* Power or *n* Affiliation, too.

McClelland et al.'s (1953) theory of motivation went far beyond the then prevailing motivational theories based on drive reduction and is much closer to the incentive accounts of motivation (e.g., Bindra, 1978; Toates, 1986) that would eventually replace them. Like these more modern theories, the affect-redintegration model presents a Pavlovian-conditioning account of motivational incentives: A motive-specific incentive is a cue (e.g., task difficulty) that reliably predicts a rewarding affective state (e.g., the pleasure of mastery). As a consequence, the cue itself takes on affective meaning, which, in the case of *n* Achievement, can even turn the negative connotations associated with task difficulty into something positive and desirable because it portends better things to come (for a modern version of this line of reasoning, see Eisenberger's 1992 theory of learned industriousness).

Despite its conceptual rigor, the affect-redintegration model of achievement motivation—like several other promising concepts introduced in McClelland et al.'s 1953 volume—had only very limited impact on subsequent research. Direct empirical tests of the validity of the model were not conducted by McClelland, Atkinson, and their associates, owing perhaps to the lack of suitable testing paradigms for the assessment of Pavlovian conditioning in humans at the time the model was introduced. The first direct test for a relationship between implicit motives and Pavlovian conditioning was eventually conducted more than 50 years later (Stanton, Wirth, & Schultheiss, 2006; see below). Moreover, no systematic effort was made in subsequent research to apply it to other domains of motivation, despite its explicit designation as a general model of motivation. Finally, the model did not specify what sorts of cues were particularly suitable for arousing a motive. Although the authors used nonverbal cues from animal experiments as examples throughout much of their presentation of the theory, they presented verbal cues in most of their studies to arouse the achievement motive. However, whether these verbal cues were actually the effective ingredients of the experimental manipulations is somewhat doubtful, as we will discuss below.

After the affect-redintegration model was introduced, interest in the development of new and better conceptual accounts of motivational arousal languished for several decades. This does not imply that no new theories were developed in the field—Atkinson's (1957) risk-taking theory of achievement motivation is probably the most famous and influential example. But these were theories about particular motives and what factors they interact with, not overarching accounts of motives and their mode of operation. Still, the seeds for such a theory were already laid in the 1953 volume. Several case studies presented toward the end of "The Achievement Motive" revealed what would become a hallmark of motives assessed with the PSE: Achievement scores derived from picture stories failed to correlate with the level of achievement motivation that the individuals tested for these case studies ascribed to themselves on a questionnaire. They also failed to correlate with the judgments of clinical psychologists and psychiatrists acquainted with these individuals. McClelland et al. (1953) concluded from this "that people's perception of achievement motivation and achievement motivation itself are two different things" (p. 327).

A classic study by deCharms, Morrison, Reitman, and McClelland (1955) underscored the fundamental validity of this insight. n Achievement as assessed with the PSE not only failed to correlate with achievement motivation measured per self-report, but the PSE and self-report measures also predicted different types of behavior: PSE-based achievement scores predicted actual performance on an anagram task, but not judgments of art or other people, whereas self-reported achievement motivation predicted such judgments, but not anagram performance. Despite the findings of this study, no further attempts were made to translate the insights gained from this type of research into a general model of (implicit) motivation. With hindsight, this is unfortunate, because the lack of systematic differentiation between motivation assessed per PSE versus motivation assessed per self-report led to a long turf war between proponents of the PSE and researchers using questionnaire measures of motivation, with each side arguing that the other measure lacked validity because it did not correlate with one's own measure and did not predict the same behavioral phenomena (e.g., Entwisle, 1972; Lilienfeld, Wood, & Garb, 2000; McClelland, 1980).

McClelland, Koestner, and Weinberger's (1989) Dual-Systems Model of Motivation

McClelland (1980) made a first attempt to transcend this state of affairs by arguing that motives as assessed by the PSE are good at predicting spontaneously occurring or *operant* behavior, particularly over extended periods of time, whereas motives assessed by questionnaire are good at predicting immediate choices in response to specific, identifiable social stimuli and demands (*respondent* behavior). Moreover, PSE-based motive measures do not predict respondent measures well, and questionnaire-based motive measures perform poorly when predicting operant behavior.

McClelland et al. (1989; see also Weinberger & McClelland, 1990) extended and refined McClelland's (1980) distinction between PSE- and questionnaire-based measures of motivation. Adopting the distinction between implicit and explicit processes from research on learning and memory (e.g., Schachter, 1987), they introduced the term *implicit motive* for motivational needs assessed with the PSE and *explicit (or self-attributed) motive* for needs assessed per self-report. They also introduced domain-specific incentives as a key moderator of the effects of implicit and explicit motives on operant and respondent outcomes. Specifically, the presence of task-intrinsic incentives, that is, aspects of a task that are inherently rewarding for individuals high in a given motive, represents a necessary prerequisite for implicit motives to become aroused and to affect operant behavior. Conversely, the presence of social-extrinsic incentives, that is, social rewards, explicit instructions, and demands, is a necessary condition for explicit motives to become activated and influence respondent behaviors. McClelland et al. (1989) also argued that social-extrinsic incentives should not be arousing for implicit motives and task-intrinsic incentives should not be arousing for explicit motives.

Although the supporting evidence presented by McClelland et al. (1989) was not particularly straightforward, concurrent and subsequent research by other scholars corroborated the fundamental heuristic validity of their two-level motive × incentive × behavior model of motivation. For instance, Brunstein and Hoyer (2002; see also Schultheiss & Brunstein, 2005, for an English description of this study and its findings) predicted and found that participants with a high implicit achievement motive, relative to those low in this motive, respond to task performance feedback (task-intrinsic incentive) by increasing their actual performance on an attention task (operant behavior). Participants with a high explicit achievement motive, in contrast, responded to information about how well they were doing vis-à-vis other participants (social-extrinsic incentive) by choosing whether to continue the task or do something else (respondent behavior). Notably, participants' implicit achievement motive neither responded to social-extrinsic incentives, nor did it predict the choice to continue the task. Conversely, participants' explicit achievement motive was not influenced by task performance feedback and did not predict actual task performance. For the domain of *n* Achievement, these findings were replicated and extended by Brunstein and Schmitt (2004) and Brunstein and Maier (2005). Parallel findings have also been obtained for the domain of power motivation (Koestner, Weinberger, & McClelland, 1991) and intimacy motivation (Craig, Koestner, & Zuroff, 1994). Furthermore, a meta-analysis by Spangler (1992) indicates that across studies, the predictive validity of PSE and self-report measures of achievement motivation depends on incentive type (task-intrinsic and social-extrinsic) and outcome measure (operant versus respondent). The direction of these effects was as predicted by the McClelland et al. (1989) model.

McClelland et al. (1989) also offered some speculative explanations as to why implicit and explicit motives respond to different types of incentives and influence different kinds of behavioral outcomes. They argued that implicit motives are shaped by ontogenetically early, prelinguistic, affectively toned learning experiences, whereas explicit motives are based on verbal learning of rules, demands, and expectations later in life. They also proposed that implicit motives are rooted in brain structures dedicated to automatic emotional processing whereas explicit motives are represented in cortical areas subserving explicit memory and the voluntary regulation of behavior.

While McClelland et al.'s (1989) dual-systems model of motivation represented a considerable step forward on the way toward a comprehensive model of implicit motives (and the explicit needs and goals that they need to be contrasted with), it lacked precise concepts and definitions and was therefore ill-suited for the derivation of testable hypotheses that went beyond an impressionistic understanding of how implicit motives operate. Schultheiss (2001) highlighted several problems and inconsistencies of the model. Chief among them is the lack of a clear-cut definition of what task-intrinsic incentives actually are. McClelland et al. (1989) stated that for individuals high in an implicit motive, "the primary incentive for carrying out the activity is the activity itself" (pp. 695 & 696); thus, the incentive is somehow embedded in the very behavior one wants to predict. If taken at face value, this framing of the term "task-intrinsic incentive" would lead to a circular conundrum:

"Why is Bob so good at this task?"
"Because it contains task-intrinsic incentives."
"How do you know that?"
"Because Bob performs this task so well."

However, for *n* Achievement, McClelland et al. (1989) identified some additional aspects of achievement tasks that made them attractive for high-achievement individuals, such as medium difficulty and task feedback. Obviously, such task characteristics can be measured and thus used to determine independently whether a task contains task-intrinsic incentives (see Spangler's 1992 coding of studies for achievement incentives). For *n* Power and *n* Affiliation, the nature of task-intrinsic incentives remained ill defined, though.

One reason for this is that McClelland et al.'s (1989) definition of social-extrinsic incentives as social rewards, prompts, expectations, and demands is problematic. The definition fits well with research on *n* Achievement, where a wealth of studies has shown that such incentives are good for activating explicit achievement concerns, but not for arousing implicit achievement motivation. Schultheiss (2001) pointed out that as soon as it is applied to other motives, the definition of social-extrinsic incentives runs into problems because social rewards such as smiles and laughter can be powerful incentives for the social motives *n* Power and *n* Affiliation, and they are not necessarily embedded in the activity that a person performs to reap such rewards.

The problems with the definition of task-intrinsic and social-extrinsic incentives become obvious when clear-cut research hypotheses need to be derived. For instance, Koestner et al. (1991) aimed to validate the McClelland et al. (1989) model by assessing implicit and explicit levels of power motivation in the prediction of behavior. Although they were able to independently conceptualize and manipulate social-extrinsic incentives and the assessment of respondent behavior in the domain of explicit power motivation, they were unable to do so for implicit power motivation: Presentation of a pictorial social intelligence test served as a task-intrinsic incentive, and performance on it as a measure of operant behavior (see our previous discussion of the circularity issue), but the presence of task-intrinsic incentives was not manipulated. Even more strikingly, McClelland and colleagues sometimes used the very same instructions to arouse an implicit motive in one study and an explicit motive in another (see Schultheiss, 2001, for an example), which further underscores the lack of precision and hence usefulness of the incentive concepts presented by McClelland et al. (1989). As Schultheiss (2001) succinctly stated, "what cannot be pinpointed cannot be manipulated, either" (p. 5).

Yet another problem of the McClelland et al. (1989) model is the distinction between operant and respondent types of behavior. These terms date back to an earlier era in psychology when behaviorist concepts dominated research on learning and motivation. However, behaviorism has long been replaced by more sophisticated and complex models of learning and behavior (see, for instance, Mazur, 1998). Moreover, the way in which McClelland et al. (1989) defined and used the terms *operant* and *respondent* is ambiguous and does not dovetail easily with empirical findings. *Operant* referred to spontaneous behavioral trends, and McClelland (1980) even stated that the term characterizes behavior that occurs in the absence of clearly identifiable stimuli. But this contradicts earlier research that had documented reliable effects of tangible stimuli and situational features on motives, such as the facilitating effects of feedback, autonomy, and tasks of medium difficulty on the performance of achievement-motivated individuals (e.g., McClelland, 1987). Clearly, implicit motives do respond to identifiable stimuli, and this effect is manifested in behavior!

Conversely, in McClelland et al.'s (1989) model, *respondent* is reserved for immediate choice behaviors. But what, exactly, is an immediate choice? The preference of achievement-motivated individuals for tasks of medium difficulty over low- or high-difficulty tasks, a classic validity criterion for implicit achievement motivation (Atkinson, 1957)? Or the choice between continuing on one task or switching to another, which is predicted by explicit achievement motivation (Brunstein & Maier, 2005)? McClelland (1980) was perhaps a bit clearer in his use of the term when he cited the process of filling out a personality questionnaire as an example for respondent behavior. So what he had in mind was choice behavior in which a person declares something to be true or not true with respect to her or his own sense of self. This is very different from, for instance, the split-second choices a car driver has to make to evade a sudden obstacle on the road. Thus, describing respondent behaviors as "choice behaviors" does not get one much further toward a robust, testable concept.

Still, the McClelland et al. (1989) model represented an important and heuristically fruitful advancement over earlier theories because it distinguished for the first time on two separate levels between the predictive motive construct, the incentive that activates a motive, and the behavior that is ultimately emitted or influenced by the motive × incentive interaction. The model thus acknowledged the existence of two separate ways to conceptualize human motivation, one in which humans have conscious values, beliefs, and goals that guide their actions and one in which humans are driven by unconscious needs that affect behavioral outcomes, and integrated them into one over-arching framework. McClelland et al. (1989) also pointed out that the independent operation of two qualitatively different forms of motivation in humans may cause between-systems friction and psychological problems, a prediction that has received considerable attention by researchers in recent years.

Schultheiss's (2001, 2008) Two-Level Information-Processing Model of Motivation

Schultheiss (2001, 2008) presented a model that retained the two-level motive × incentive × behavior framework of motivation as originally introduced by McClelland et al. (1989), but that defined the differences between incentives and behaviors on both levels of motivation more precisely and in better alignment with current concepts and findings from cognitive psychology and neuroscience (see Fig. 9.1). It also introduced a mechanism, referential processing, by which the implicit and explicit levels of motivation can dissociate or be brought into alignment.

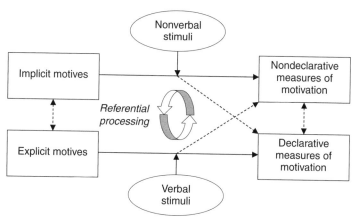

Figure 9.1 Information processing model of implicit and explicit motivation (solid lines, significant correlation/influence; dashed lines, no significant correlation/influence). Adapted with permission from Schultheiss, O. C. (2008). Implicit motives. In O. P. John, R. W. Robins, & L. A. Pervin (Eds.), *Handbook of personality: Theory and research* (3rd ed., pp. 603–633). New York: Guilford.

Based on work by Paivio (1986, 1991) and other proponents of multiple-coding accounts of cognition, learning, and memory (e.g., Poldrack & Foerde, 2008; Squire, 2004), Schultheiss proposed that the crucial difference between incentives that implicit motives respond to and those that explicit motives respond to is that the former are perceived and represented nonverbally and the latter in a verbal-symbolic format. This hypothesis is supported by several lines of research. Klinger (1967) observed that individuals respond with increases in affiliation or achievement motivation expressed in the PSE to watching an affiliation-oriented or achievement-oriented experimenter, even when they could not hear his verbal instructions. Moreover, Schultheiss and Brunstein (1999, 2002) demonstrated that experimenters who assigned and described a power-related goal verbally to their participants failed to arouse participants' power motive. Only after participants had had an opportunity to translate the verbally assigned goal into an experiential format through a goal imagery exercise did their power motive predict goal commitment and task performance. Finally, as we will discuss in more detail below, facial expressions of emotion are particularly salient nonverbal cues for implicit motives. Facial signals of friendliness and hostility interact with individuals' implicit affiliation motive, and facial signals of dominance and submission interact with individuals' implicit power motive to shape attentional orienting and instrumental learning (Schultheiss & Hale, 2007; Schultheiss, Pang, et al., 2005).

The hypothesis that implicit motives respond preferentially to nonverbal incentives is also compatible with the previously mentioned finding that one and the same verbal instruction appears to arouse implicit motives in one study and explicit motives in another: In all likelihood, in the former case it was not the experimenter's verbal instructions that activated the implicit motive but rather, as Klinger's (1967) findings suggest, the experimenter's nonverbal demeanor and perhaps also paralinguistic factors such as tone and modulation of voice. Since nonverbal aspects of an experimenter's behavior were never seen as a potential source of motive arousal in work other than Klinger's (1967), researchers have never paid much attention to, controlled for, or reported them in the method sections of their papers. However, differences in experimenters' nonverbal behavior could be a key factor for explaining inconsistencies in findings obtained in past research on implicit motives.

According to Schultheiss (2001), explicit motives preferentially respond to verbally-framed incentives such as instructions that highlight a task as an opportunity to achieve (e.g., "Students who perform well at this task also shine academically") or to affiliate (e.g., "For this task it is important that you get to know the other participants well and work together with them"). A study by Brunstein and Gollwitzer (1996, Study 1) illustrates this point. Participants with a strong explicit commitment to become a medical doctor were administered a judgment task that was presented as a sensitive indicator of their future success as a physician. Half of all participants were given negative feedback on this task, whereas the other half received no feedback. Afterwards, participants worked on an attention task that the experimenter either described as a completely unrelated task or as another indicator of participants' medical talents. This mere difference of words was sufficient to make participants who had been frustrated on the first task outperform all others (task related to medical ability) or perform worse than all others (unrelated task condition) on the second task.

Schultheiss (2001, 2008) also replaced McClelland et al.'s (1989) distinction between operant and respondent behavioral indicators of implicit and explicit motives with concepts that are more closely aligned with current theorizing and research on learning and memory (see also Schultheiss, 2007a). He argued that implicit motives preferentially predict *nondeclarative measures of motivation*, that is, behavior that represents the output of the brain's nondeclarative systems for regulating behavior (such as procedural learning, Pavlovian conditioning, emotional expression), including autonomous nervous system changes and hormone release (see Rolls, 1999; Squire, 2004). Explicit motives, in contrast, preferentially influence *declarative measures of motivation*, that is, the self-referenced judgments, decisions, preferences, and so forth, that people spontaneously state or declare when prompted. These are closely tied to the brain's systems for episodic and semantic memory, verbally-based executive functions, and the left hemisphere's capacity to rationalize and interpret one's own and others' behavior (see Gazzaniga,1985; Luria & Homskaya, 1964; Rolls, 1999; Squire, 2004).

The declarative/nondeclarative distinction of criterion measures of explicit and implicit motives is consistent with and encompasses virtually all research using the respondent/operant distinction, including the studies we previously used to illustrate McClelland et al.'s (1989) model. But it goes beyond this distinction by allowing both types of behavioral correlates of implicit and explicit motives to be influenced by specifiable stimuli. Brain systems dedicated to nondeclarative forms of learning and behavior respond to, and can be tested with, clearly specifiable stimuli, although these typically have to be nonverbal. And brain systems dedicated to declarative forms of learning and behavioral regulation respond to other, typically verbal-symbolic classes of stimuli. By steering closer to current theory and research in cognitive psychology and the neurosciences, the declarative/nondeclarative distinction allows researchers to pinpoint the processes through which implicit motives influence behavior, the brain systems involved, and the testing paradigms that are particularly suitable to detect motive effects on behavior.

For instance, Schultheiss, Wirth, et al. (2005) hypothesized that *n* Power should predict instrumental learning that is reinforced by social victory and defeat. A vast body of literature attests to the striatum's critical role in instrumental learning, and a well-established measure of striatal function in humans is Nissen and Bullemer's (1987) visuomotor learning task (Curran, 1998). This task requires participants to respond to complex, but repeating sequences of stars on different locations of the computer screen with a pattern of key presses mapped onto the stimulus locations. Because participants show improvements on the sequence that can be attributed to learning in the absence of an intention to learn and an awareness of the pattern inherent in the task, the Nissen and Bullemer task is also called a measure of *implicit* or *procedural learning* and fits squarely in the nondeclarative domain in Squire's (2004) taxonomy of learning and memory.

Schultheiss, Wirth, et al. (2005) had pairs of participants go through ten 1-min rounds on a visuomotor learning task and experimentally varied the outcome such that the winner won eight and the loser only two rounds. Implicit learning gains on the task were assessed after the contest was over. Among winners, individuals high in *n* Power had the largest implicit learning gains and individuals low in *n* Power had the smallest, suggesting that a victory over an opponent was positively reinforcing for high-power participants. Among losers, the pattern was reversed, with high-power individuals showing the smallest gains, suggesting that a defeat was particularly punishing for them.

Notably, *n* Power effects on implicit learning gains in this study and in a previous one (Schultheiss & Rohde, 2002) were mediated by parallel changes in the steroid hormone testosterone, another nondeclarative indicator of motivational processes. And perhaps equally notably, *n* Power did not predict satisfaction with the contest outcome, which was assessed with a mood adjective list and thus represents a declarative measure of motivation.

The results of the Schultheiss, Wirth, et al. (2005) studies and those reported by Schultheiss and Rohde (2002) thus provide evidence that n Power influences procedural learning contingent on power-relevant incentives. Because procedural learning is closely tied to striatal function, these findings suggest that n Power (and perhaps other motives, too) recruits, and is represented in part by, the striatum, a critical structure for behavioral learning and incentive processing. Recent research using brain imaging supports this hypothesis: Relative to low-power individuals, high-power individuals show greater activation of anterior parts of the striatum in response to angry faces (Schultheiss et al., 2008; see also below).

This example illustrates the usefulness of the declarative/nondeclarative distinction and the cognitive neuroscience work it was derived from for modeling and testing the effects of implicit motives on behavior. They also show that using well-established measures and concepts from cognitive psychology and the neurosciences is heuristically extremely fruitful because they immediately link implicit motives to a rich nomological network of findings, correlates, and substrates associated with these measures. For instance, the link between n Power, implicit learning, and striatal function described above would suggest that the need for power is compromised when striatal function is impaired (as in Parkinson's or Huntington's disease; Kolb & Whishaw, 2003) or that the independence between implicit and explicit measures of power motivation may reflect, in part, the mutually inhibitory effects of striatal and neocortical control over behavior (Poldrack et al., 2001).

We acknowledge that under specific circumstances, the mapping of implicit motives onto nondeclarative measures and explicit motives onto declarative measures may not be mutually exclusive. For instance, explicit motivational functions such as verbally mediated self-regulatory strategies may exert a transient influence on specific nondeclarative measures of motivation, such as performance speed, even in the absence of, or in conflict with, implicit motives. However, we would expect this top-down control of motivated behavior to differ from the bottom-up behavioral regulation exerted by motives by being more short-lived and to incur considerable costs in the form of self-regulatory depletions on subsequent tasks (see Muraven & Baumeister, 2000). Implicit motives, in contrast, should be characterized by longer-lasting and less defatigable effects on motivated performance. As another case in point, Woike (2008) has shown that implicit motives influence episodic memory, which according to Schultheiss's (2008) model would represent a declarative measure of motivation. However, Woike (2008) also points out that this effect of motives on episodic memory is only present for affectively charged episodes of daily lives, not for mundane, affectively cold events. Her research is thus consistent with neurobiological accounts of memory that demonstrate strong modulatory effects of the amygdala, a key structure for nondeclarative emotional processing, on the hippocampus, which is part of the declarative memory system supporting episodic memory (e.g., McGaugh, 2002). Clearly, further work is needed to carefully delineate under which specific circumstances implicit motives can influence declarative measures and explicit motives non-declarative measures of motivation.

We finally turn to *referential processing* between verbal and nonverbal representations, the mechanism through which incentives processed by one motivational system can be translated into the representational format of the other. Work by Paivio (1986; Paivio, Clark, Digdon, & Bons, 1989) and Bucci (1984, 2002) illustrates how verbal representations can be translated into nonverbal representations (e.g., creating the mental image of a cow in response to the word cow) and vice versa (e.g., retrieving the proper verbal label for an object or a color). However, compared to processing information in its native format (i.e., linking words to other words or associating different nonverbal percepts and representations with each other), converting information from one representational format into the other requires additional processing steps and thus extra time and effort. The ease and speed with which referential processing can occur depends on situational factors, that is, having the opportunity to devote one's cognitive resources to translating words into images and vice versa, as well as individual factors, that is, having the skills and cognitive resources to quickly move back and forth between nonverbal representations and verbal symbols (also termed *referential competence*).

Schultheiss (2001, 2008) hypothesized that heightened referential processing could facilitate the translation of verbal incentives into a nonverbal representation format that is accessible to implicit motives and, by the same token, aid the quick verbal representation of nonverbal affective responses triggered by implicit motives and thus promote conscious awareness of one's preferences and distastes. The previously mentioned studies by Schultheiss and Brunstein (1999, 2002) corroborate these assumptions: Individuals who had imagined a verbally assigned goal committed to and enacted the goal in congruence with their implicit motives, whereas goal commitment and enactment were independent of individuals' implicit motives in the absence of an opportunity to translate the verbal goal description into mental images. These findings have been replicated by Job and Brandstätter (2009).

Schultheiss, Patalakh, Rawolle Liening, & MacInnes (2009) recently found evidence for an influence of individual differences in referential competence on the degree to which individuals' goal commitments match their implicit motives. Using a simple color-naming task adapted from Bucci (1984), Schultheiss et al. (2009) first assessed the latency difference between participants' reading of color words (e.g., "red," "blue," "green," "yellow") and naming of color patches (i.e., monochromatic squares in red, blue, green, etc). On average, participants took about 80 ms longer for naming color patches than for reading color words, a finding that is consistent with

Paivio's (1986) prediction that referential processing across representational domains involves more processing steps than within-domain processing. However, participants also had large interindividual differences in referential competence, with some showing virtually no slowing down on color naming whereas others named colors with an average delay of up to 200 ms relative to the reading of color words. These differences in referential competence were related to the level of congruence between individuals' goals and their implicit motives across the domains of power, achievement, and affiliation: Participants with high referential competence had significantly lower absolute z-score discrepancies between their commitment levels and their motive scores than participants with low referential competence. This finding is consistent with the notion that referential competence promotes congruence between the implicit and the explicit motivational systems. Still, further work is necessary to clearly establish that referential competence plays a causal role in the choice of motive-congruent goals or, more generally, the ability to consciously access and represent one's implicit motivational needs.

Summary

As our review of conceptual accounts of implicit motivation indicates, motivational theories in the McClelland-Atkinson tradition have from the very start been characterized by the idea that motivational processes may elude conscious introspection and therefore need to be assessed through means other than self-report (see also Murray, 1938). They have also been characterized by the fundamental tenet of motivation research: Behavior is the result of the interplay between a motivational need and a suitable incentive (Schultheiss, Kordik, Kullmann, Rawolle, & Rösch, 2009). Beyond these commonalities, each model has contributed valuable insights into the operation of implicit motives and therefore also into the ways that explicit motives are different from implicit motives. McClelland et al.'s (1953) affect-redintegration model introduced the idea that implicit motives are characterized by Pavlovian-conditioned associations between incentive cues and the affective change or outcome that they reliably predict. McClelland et al.'s (1989) dual-systems model of motivation considerably extended earlier models of motivation by emphasizing that implicit and explicit motives respond to different kinds of incentives and influence different kinds of behavior. Schultheiss's (2001, 2008) information-processing model suggests that implicit motives process nonverbal types of incentives whereas explicit motives are tied to the verbal-symbolic representation of incentives, that nonverbal and verbal representations can be aligned through the process of referential processing, and that implicit motives shape nondeclarative behavior (including physiological changes) and explicit motives shape declarative behavior.

Taking the Nonverbal-Processing Hypothesis Further: A Motivational Field Theory Model of Facial Expressions As Nonverbal Incentives

A central claim of Schultheiss's (2001, 2008) information-processing model of motivation is that implicit motives respond to specifiable nonverbal incentives. Recently, Schultheiss and colleagues have put this hypothesis to the test by exploring the role of facial expressions of emotion (FEE) as motivational incentives for the perceiver (Schultheiss & Hale, 2007; Schultheiss, Pang, et al., 2005; Schultheiss et al., 2008; Stanton et al., 2006; Wirth & Schultheiss, 2007).

FEEs are particularly good candidates for testing the nonverbal-processing hypothesis because the face is arguably the most significant and salient source of social information for humans, and emotional expressions that occur during social interactions between sender and perceiver carry information about the sender's intentions vis-à-vis the perceiver as well as the perceiver's effect on the sender (e.g., Argyle, 1975; Eibl-Eibesfeldt, 1995; Keltner & Haidt, 1999). FEEs are frequently classified and assessed with regard to their valence and arousal, that is, how pleasant or unpleasant or how arousing versus calming they appear to the perceiver (e.g., Johnsen, Thayer, & Hugdahl, 1995). We contend, however, that this view of FEEs and their functions is too shortsighted and obscures more fundamental functions of FEEs. What is the point, for instance, of having just one pleasant FEE (joy), but several unpleasant ones (e.g., anger, disgust, fear, contempt, sadness)? And can the joy face really be an unambiguously positive stimulus when bared teeth are a primate's way of showing off his or her weapons (Eibl-Eibesfeldt, 1995)? Clearly, something more is going on than emotional expression for the sake of merely expressing one's pleasant and unpleasant emotions.

In recent years, conceptual and empirical work has started to examine the role of FEEs as devices for regulating people's interpersonal behavior. Keltner (Keltner, Ekman, Gonzaga, & Beer, 2003; Keltner & Haidt, 1999) has argued that specific FEEs in an interaction partner can act as rewards that people will work for or punishments that they will try to avoid. Knutson (1996) and Hess, Blairy, and Kleck (2000) showed that perceivers can readily judge FEEs with regard to how much they signal friendliness versus hostility and dominance versus submission. For instance, in both studies joy faces were judged to express dominance and friendliness alike, whereas anger was seen as a hostile dominance signal.

In the motivational field theory (MFT) of FEEs we present here, we extend on this line of work and integrate it with the interpersonal field approach to personality. The basic premise of interpersonal field theory is that people elicit and constrain each other's behavior (Wiggins & Trobst, 1999). Behavior is seen as intrinsically determined by the interdependent relationship between two people, never just as the effect of only one individual's personality. Interpersonal behavior can be described by two fundamental dimensions that are orthogonal to each other and form a circumplex (see Fig. 9.2): dominance (also variously called agency, power, mastery, or assertion) and affiliation (also called communion, love, intimacy). These dimensions entail different behavior-regulating principles. Dominance behavior is characterized by *complementarity*; that is, if one interactant asserts his or her dominance, this automatically forces the other interactant into the submissive role. And vice versa: Taking a submissive stance toward another person puts that person in a dominant position. Affiliation behavior, in contrast, is characterized by the principle of *reciprocity*. The friendlier one interactant behaves, the friendlier the other will respond. Conversely, cold detachment and hostility in one person will elicit hostile behavior in the other.

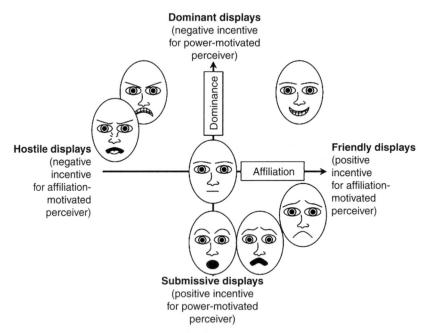

Figure 9.2 Motivational field theory circumplex model of the incentive value of nonverbal signals of emotion. Expressions of anger, disgust, and joy signal high dominance, and expressions of surprise, fear, and sadness signal low dominance. Expressions of anger and disgust signal low affiliation, and expressions of joy, sadness, and fear signal high affiliation. The extent to which these expressions then represent a positive or a negative incentive depends on the perceiver's needs for power and affiliation.

In MFT, we add to these basic assumptions a motivational perspective, which owes a large debt to one of the pioneers of interpersonal field theory, Harry Stack Sullivan (1953). Specifically, we extend interpersonal field theory by three hypotheses that guide our theorizing and research on the role of FEEs as motivational incentives.

1. The Sender's Aroused Motivational Need Determines the Nonverbal Signal He or She Sends

A person whose affiliation motive has been aroused is likely to send friendly affiliative signals, such as looking and smiling at the interaction partner. Likewise, a person high in *n* Power who perceives a dominance challenge may frown or look outright angry, speak in a loud voice, and perhaps close in on the challenger. However, which signal is sent depends not only on the sender's motive but also on the context in which the motive is aroused. For instance, high-affiliation individuals who are faced with the task of arguing against another's point of view—who essentially have to keep or increase their distance from another person—can also show a frown (Schultheiss, 1996). They are also known to become downright prickly and hostile if they perceive another person as being too dissimilar to themselves (Winter, 1996), a finding that is very much in line with the notion that hostile behavior represents the pole opposite of friendliness on the affiliation axis of interpersonal behavior. Thus, there is not necessarily a static one-to-one relationship between implicit motivational needs and specific nonverbal signals.

2. The Incentive Value of Nonverbal Signals for the Perceiver Depends on Their Location on the Dominance/Affiliation Circumplex

In line with the complementary nature of behavior revolving around dominance, MFT predicts that a sender's dominance signal acts as a disincentive for the perceiver, forcing her or him to either passively adopt a submissive stance in the interaction or to actively fight against the sender's assertion of dominance. Conversely, a sender's signal of low dominance or submission is an incentive for the perceiver, allowing her or him to take a dominant position in the interaction. For the affiliation dimension, behavior is ruled by the principle of symmetry: friendly signals are incentives for the perceiver, whereas hostile signals are disincentives. Thus, MFT explains the behavioral patterns between interactants based on the motivational properties of signals sent on the dominance and the affiliation axis of interpersonal behavior.

3. The Incentive Value of Nonverbal Signals
Depends on Perceivers' Implicit Motives

The degree to which submissive and affiliative signals are positively reinforcing and dominant and hostile signals are aversive is not only a function of the signal itself, but also of the motivational needs of the perceiver. This position of MFT reflects Sullivan's (1953) early insight that one person's need satisfaction depends on the cooperation and complementary motivational states of another person. Thus, for a person who gets a kick out of being dominant herself or himself (i.e., a person high in *n* Power), another's dominance signal is much more aversive and another's submissive signal much more rewarding than for a person who doesn't care for dominance at all. Likewise, for a person who cherishes intimacy and close, friendly relations with others (i.e., a person high in *n* Affiliation), friendly nonverbal signals are more rewarding, and hostile signals more punishing, than for a person who lacks the capacity for finding pleasure in affiliative closeness.

It is readily apparent that these three predictions of MFT correspond to a basic *sender → signal → receiver* model of social communication that can be chopped up for research purposes into a *sender → signal* and a *signal → receiver* component. However, the model can also be tested as a whole using a Brunswickian lens model approach (see, for instance, Schultheiss & Brunstein, 2002). Moreover, by adding a recursive component, it can be used to study the complex back-and-forth in social interactions in which the receiver of a signal subsequently sends a signal that impinges on the former sender, who now becomes the receiver, which in turn elicits a response from her or him, etc., etc.

In the following, we will apply the *signal → receiver* component of MFT to the analysis of FEEs as motivational incentives. In so doing, we proceed on the assumption that FEEs can be located on the circumplex represented by the axes "dominance" and "affiliation," as has been suggested by Knutson's (1996) and Hess et al.'s (2000) work. Figure 9.2 provides an overview of the hypothesized positions of seven fundamental FEEs—joy, sadness, fear, surprise, disgust, anger, and neutral—on the circumplex. We will first discuss the conceptual and empirical reasons for placing each FEE on the circumplex and then review research that illustrates the interplay between perceivers' implicit motives and the incentive value inherent in FEEs.

Neutral Expression

Neutral expressions generally do not hold positive or negative incentive value for perceivers. They are not dominant or friendly, nor do they signal submission or hostility. They therefore represent meaningful control stimuli in experiments examining the effects of FEEs on the perceiver. One caveat is in order, however: Some research suggests that neutral expressions can be viewed as slightly negative (e.g., Lee, Kang, Park, Kim, & An, 2008). From the perspective of implicit motives, we would expect this to be particularly the case for power-motivated perceivers, whose overarching goal is to gain dominance by having impact on others. A neutral expression directed at the perceiver signals that the perceiver has no impact on the sender, a state of affairs that should be unsatisfactory to the high-power individual.

Joy

Research participants rate joy faces as high on affiliation and dominance (Hess et al., 2000; Knutson, 1996). This suggests that the facial expression of joy represents a positive incentive for individuals high in *n* Affiliation, but a disincentive for individuals high in *n* Power. The latter prediction is also consistent with the hypothesis that baring one's teeth in a grin represents a display of weapons among primates. A lot may depend on context factors, however. For instance, a smile by a member of the opposite sex may be interpreted as less dominant and more affiliative than a smile displayed by a member of one's own sex, and thus by a potential competitor for attention from the other sex. The exact meaning of a smile may also depend on whether it is displayed with a lifted chin (= high-dominance signal; see Tracy & Robins, 2004) or as a "sheepish" smile indicating shame, with a slightly lowered head and gaze directed away from the observer (= low-dominance signal; see Keltner, 1995). In general, however, and other factors notwithstanding, expressions of joy have ambiguous incentive properties: positive from the perspective of the affiliation-motivated perceiver, negative from the perspective of the power-motivated perceiver.

Sadness

In placing the FEE of sadness on the circumplex, we follow the frequently made argument that sadness and crying represent appeals for help and thus for the restoration or utilization of close relationships with others (see Barr-Zisowitz, 2000, for a discussion of this issue). The sad face is therefore primarily a positive affiliation incentive. However, sadness also communicates that the sender is not in charge of her or his situation and perhaps even that the person she or he is looking at may be the source of this deprivation of control. For this reason, the sad face also represents a slightly positive incentive for the power-motivated perceiver.

Fear

Fear directed at the perceiver is a highly ambiguous emotional signal. Many theorists interpret it as a communication of imminent danger (e.g., Öhman, 2002). But what is the source of the danger? Most emotion researchers use fear-face stimuli to invoke a state of fear in the observer, too, an effect that is plausible to the extent that FEEs tend to elicit similar FEEs in the perceiver and thus may make him or her experience the same emotion as the sender (Lakin & Chartrand, 2003). But that does not explain why the sender is looking at the perceiver in the first place. Part of it may be an appeal for help, similar to the sad face, only more intense and calling for immediate action. We think that this explanation has some plausibility, and we therefore place the fear face slightly on the positive incentive side of the affiliation dimension. However, we also think that a fear expression directed at the perceiver suggests to the perceiver *that the sender fears the perceiver*, that perhaps the moment before the perceiver has done something to profoundly intimidate the sender. This is a scenario that may happen relatively frequently in childhood, when a child learns that he can have power over other children by threatening them, but which can also occur in adolescence and even in adulthood, such as in situations of bullying or spousal abuse. For that reason, and also because fear is a defensive, withdrawal-oriented emotion, we place the fear FEE at the lower end of the dominance dimension, where it becomes a positive incentive for the power-motivated perceiver.

Surprise

Surprise is displayed when the surprisee's expectations have been violated (Camras et al., 2002). In the case of a social interaction, such a violation is likely to have been committed, either verbally or nonverbally, by the person to whom the sender directs the surprised expression. Thus, surprise can reflect a power differential between sender's and perceiver's control over the interaction, with the surpriser having power over the surprised (cf. Conway, DiFazio, & Mayman, 1999). We therefore place the surprise expression at the low end of the dominance dimension. Because surprise communicates neither a clear appeal for succor to the sender, nor does it signal hostility, it is located on the neutral midpoint of the affiliation dimension.

Disgust

Although the most basic function of disgust is the withdrawal from, or expulsion of, contaminated substances (see, for instance, Berridge, 2000), in humans the disgust face represents a strong signal of moral or social rejection (Rozin, Haidt, & McCauley, 2000). We therefore categorize it as a clear affiliation disincentive and place it on the low end of the affiliation dimension. However, the open expression of rejection toward another person also signals the sender's superiority over the perceiver, whereas a lower-ranking person would tend to inhibit such expressions toward the perceiver (Conway et al., 1999; Tiedens, 2001). Thus, a side effect of expressing disgust toward another person is that the sender signals her or his dominance, which should make this expression a negative incentive for power-motivated perceivers.

Anger

Anger directed at the perceiver represents a threat to the perceiver and thereby also signals the sender's claim to dominance in the relationship. This function of the anger expression has been amply documented in humans and primates (Eibl-Eibesfeldt, 1995) and places anger at the high end of the dominance dimension. Anger also suggests a rejection of the perceiver, which makes this expression an affiliation disincentive. However, anger is more ambiguous in this regard than disgust, which signals outright rejection of the person this expression is directed at. Anger, in contrast, does not necessarily signify the final dissolution of a relationship; rather, it is a signal that the relationship is in trouble, and the outcome of the conflict can go either way: reconciliation or repulsion. Therefore, anger is expected to be a moderately negative, but salient affiliation incentive.

Moderators of Signal → Perceiver Effects

Our overview of incentive effects of FEEs on the perceiver presents only a first approximation to the true state of affairs. As we have already pointed out, the *perceiver's motives* play a crucial role in whether an FEE can actually have motivational impact on her or him and whether the FEE acts as an incentive or disincentive. A perceiver low in power and affiliation motivation, for instance, will have no particularly strong response to a joy face, whereas a perceiver high in *n* Affiliation may feel attracted to it, a perceiver high in *n* Power may feel repelled by it, and a perceiver high in both motives may have conflicted feelings about it. Thus, we argue that *the incentive value of a face lies neither in the face nor in the perceiver alone, but rather in the interaction between the specific expression displayed in the sender's face and the motivational needs of the perceiver.*

Another critical moderator of an FEE's incentive value is, in people with heterosexual preferences, *the perceiver's gender vis-à-vis the sender's gender,* particularly from the perspective of intrasexual and intersexual competition (see Wilson, 1980). We suggest that perceivers should be particularly sensitive to the dominance dimension of FEEs displayed by a member of their own gender because dominance needs to be established within one's gender first if one wants to attract the attention of the other gender. Conversely, perceivers should be particularly sensitive to the affiliation dimension of FEEs signaled by a member of the other gender because FEEs high or low in affiliation incentive value reflect the likelihood of the perceiver getting closer to the opposite-sex sender. Of course, we expect these hypothesized gender effects to be compounded by the motivational needs of the perceiver: power-motivated individuals should be most sensitive to dominance signals of a same-sex sender, affiliation-motivated individuals (particularly if they are high in intimacy motivation, the love dimension of the need to affiliate) should be most sensitive to affiliation signals of sender from the other sex.

A third critical moderator of signal → perceiver effects is *head orientation and/ or gaze direction* (e.g., Adams & Kleck, 2005). A joy expression flashed at the perceiver has a very different meaning from a joy expression that the perceiver happens to observe but that is directed at someone else. In the former case, the affiliative and dominance-related meaning of joy is directly relevant for the perceiver's relationship with the sender; in the latter case, it is not. Accordingly, we would generally expect FEEs directed at someone else to represent weaker incentives than facial expressions directed at the perceiver.

Finally, the *strength of the emotional signal conveyed in an FEE* determines how a motivated perceiver will respond to it. Consider the case of anger. A full anger display—furrowed brow, glaring eyes, bared teeth—represents a clear-cut high-dominance and low-affiliation signal and, as we pointed out before, will be aversive for power- and affiliation-motivated perceivers. But what if the expression appears only fleetingly on the face (e.g., as a so-called microexpression; see Ekman & O'Sullivan, 1991) or in a much milder form, barely different from a neutral expression? Research suggests that eliciting low-level anger in others—teasing—may actually have positive incentive qualities for the perceiver (Keltner, Young, Heerey, Oemig, & Monarch, 1998), particularly if he or she has a strong need to dominate others. A study by Wirth and Schultheiss (2007) revealed that individuals high in testosterone, a hormonal marker of *n* Power (see Schultheiss, 2007b; Stanton & Schultheiss, 2009), showed enhanced instrumental learning of behavior that was reinforced with 12 ms displays of anger faces. This effect did not occur when the anger faces were shown for longer durations. It is important to recall in this context that power-motivated individuals are characterized by a need to have emotional impact on others, a need that could in principle be satisfied by any FEE, as long as it does not threaten the perceiver's need for dominance. Thus, a low-intensity or very short dominance display can actually have positive incentive qualities for the power-motivated perceiver because it does not represent an open dominance challenge as a full-fledged anger display would. It is noteworthy, too, that lower-ranking individuals typically restrain or inhibit their negative emotional displays toward a higher-ranking individual (e.g., Conway et al., 1999). For this reason, an inhibited anger expression, if detected and recognized as such, may represent a validation and reinforcement of the perceiver's own claim to dominance. This example illustrates that the incentive value of a given FEE for the perceiver's motivational needs can be related in a nonlinear fashion to the FEE's intensity.

Our discussion of moderators of *signal* → *perceiver* effects has highlighted what we consider the most critical factors that influence the interpretation of

FEEs from a motivational point of view. It is not exhaustive. Other factors, such as sender attractiveness, or the age and ethnicity of sender and perceiver, are likely to influence the effect of FEEs on the perceiver, too, and therefore deserve to be explored conceptually and empirically in future work.

Empirical Findings in Support of MFT

Early evidence suggesting that emotions could be construed as motivational incentives emerged from the previously described study by Klinger (1967) and from another study by Atkinson and Walker (1958). In the already described study by Klinger (1967), nonverbal aspects of the experimenter's behavior by themselves were already fully effective at arousing participants' n Achievement and n Affiliation. However, the specific cues that elicited these effects (i.e., whether it was the experimenter's facial expression, body language, or a combination of both) were not studied. Atkinson and Walker (1958) reported that individuals with higher n Affiliation levels were more perceptually sensitive to facial stimuli, but not to neutral control stimuli (i.e., pictures of home furnishings). This study therefore provides the first specific clue that, from the perspective of the implicit motivational needs of the perceiver, faces represent a special class of stimuli.

Several recent studies provide more specific corroborating evidence for MFT. Schultheiss, Pang, Torges, Wirth, and Treynor (2005) tested the incentive value of FEEs as a function of individuals' implicit motives, using an implicit learning task that measured the extent to which participants learned a behavior that was followed by an FEE. The FEE thus acted as an operant reward or punishment, depending on the person's implicit motives. Schultheiss and colleagues found that power-motivated individuals showed enhanced learning of visuomotor sequences that were followed by the low-dominance surprise expression and impaired by the high-dominance joy expression (see Fig. 9.3). In line with the hypothesized moderating effect of sender and perceiver gender, these effects emerged only for FEEs displayed by a same-sex sender. Anger faces, another high-dominance signal, led to general learning impairments in power-motivated participants, regardless of the match between perceivers' and senders' gender. Effects of n Affiliation on learning responses to FEEs were less pronounced. The hypothesized incentive effect of joy faces for affiliation-motivated individuals could not be detected, and anger (affiliation disincentive) had complex effects on affiliation-motivated participants' learning that were primarily due to impaired learning in response to neutral faces relative to emotional faces.

Schultheiss and Hale (2007) further explored motivational incentive effects of FEEs by measuring how much participants attended to FEEs. Using a dot-probe task to assess attentional orienting to emotional versus neutral faces presented for very short durations (between 12 and 231 ms), they found that

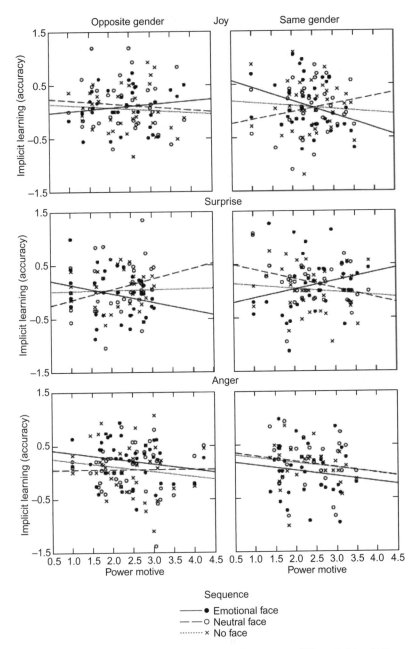

Figure 9.3 Effects of facial expressions as reinforcers in a differential implicit learning task during extinction. Solid lines, sequences were reinforced with emotional face; dashed lines, sequences were reinforced with neutral face; dotted lines, sequences were not reinforced with face stimuli. Adapted with permission from Schultheiss, O. C., Pang, J. S., Torges, C. M., Wirth, M. M., & Treynor, W. (2005). Perceived facial expressions of emotion as motivational incentives: Evidence from a differential implicit learning paradigm. *Emotion*, 5(1), 41–54.

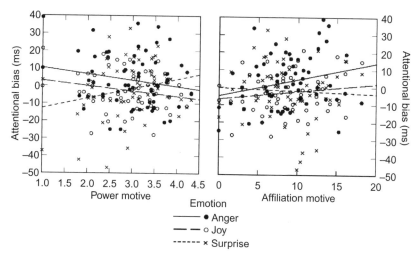

Figure 9.4 Effects of facial expressions and implicit motives on attentional orienting in a dot-probe task. Positive bias scores, attentional orienting toward emotional face; negative scores, attentional orienting towards neutral face. Illustration of data reported by Schultheiss & Hale (2007, Study 2).

individuals' motivational needs influenced how much attention they allocated to anger, joy and surprise expressions (see Fig. 9.4). Across two studies, power-motivated participants attended toward the low-dominance surprise expression, but away from the high-dominance anger and joy (Study 2 only) expressions. Affiliation-motivated individuals attended toward angry faces, but were again indifferent to joy faces. One explanation for the lacking effects of joy faces on affiliation-motivated individuals in this study and the previously described study by Schultheiss et al. (2005) may be the use of a content coding system (Winter, 1994) that may have captured only the fear-of-rejection component of affiliation motivation, but not the hope-for closeness or love component, which presumably would make individuals more sensitive to positive affiliation incentives.

Stanton, Wirth, and Schultheiss (2006) extended research on the attention-grabbing effects of motivational incentives by demonstrating that Pavlovian-conditioned predictors of FEEs influence the allocation of attention similar to actual FEEs. They found that high-power individuals orient their attention away from conditioned stimuli (CS) that predicted the presentation of high-dominance FEEs (anger and joy faces). The incentive value of the FEE had been transferred to the CS, and the CS alone became sufficient to shape attentional orienting. Incidentally, this research also provided empirical support for McClelland et al.'s (1953) affect-redintegration model by demonstrating that implicit motives respond to conditioned cues that predict an affectively charged outcome.

Finally, in a study using functional magnetic resonance imaging, Schultheiss et al. (2008) tested effects of individuals' *n* Power, high-dominance anger faces, and low-dominance surprise faces on activation of brain areas involved in motivation and incentive processing. Relative to participants low in power motivation, power-motivated participants showed more activation of the anterior caudate, the insula, and the lateral orbitofrontal cortex in response to angry faces. They also had greater insula activation in response to surprised expressions.

Taken together, these studies provide encouraging support for the hypothesis that implicit motives respond to nonverbal incentives in general and specifically for the main tenet of MFT that the incentive value of facial expression is a joint function of the specific emotion displayed and the motivational needs of the perceiver. Research findings are particularly strong for *n* Power, whereas results for *n* Affiliation are limited and only in partial agreement with the predictions of MFT. However, this may be due to the limited validity of the *n* Affiliation measure used in the studies reviewed above. Switching to a more suitable measure of the need to bond, such as McAdams's (1992) *n* Intimacy coding system, may yield findings more consistent with MFT in future research.

The Role of n Achievement

What about the role of *n* Achievement in the perception of FEEs? *n* Achievement represents a motivational dimension that is independent of *n* Power and *n* Affiliation and therefore cannot be readily fit into the same interpersonal field framework that these two motives, due to their profoundly social nature, naturally occupy. After all, *n* Achievement represents a need to do well on tasks, not with people. Nevertheless, it is interesting to note that the achievement motive has its origins in early childhood learning experiences that deal with the autonomous mastery of challenges and that are reinforced by parents' praise for successful mastery, and rejection and punishment for failing to master challenges (cf. McClelland & Pilon, 1983; Rosen & d'Andrade, 1959; Winterbottom, 1958). Thus, while the achievement motive may later be expressed in nonsocial life domains, its roots are social, and it therefore appears plausible that achievement-motivated individuals remain sensitive to social signals of emotion beyond the initial training that gave rise to their need to achieve.

Suggestive evidence in support of this conjecture comes from a reanalysis of data collected by Schultheiss and Hale (2007). When we scored participants' PSEs for *n* Achievement in Schultheiss and Hale's (2007) Study 2, we found that higher levels in this motive were associated with more attentional orienting toward joy faces ($r = .29$, $p < .05$). In an earlier pilot study on the effects of motives on attentional orienting to faces, Schultheiss and Hale (unpublished data) found that individuals high in *n* Achievement oriented attention away from female faces showing anger ($r = -.38$, $p < .01$, $N = 61$) and that this effect was stronger for very short face presentation durations (12 ms, 23 ms) than for longer presentations (up to 370 ms). Evidence that high-achievement individuals may be sensitive to facial expressions also comes from a study by Riebel (2004; $N = 60$), who found that n Achievement predicted attentional orienting toward emotional (fear, sadness, disgust, contempt) faces presented for 12 ms ($r = .42$, $p < .001$), but attentional orienting away from such faces and toward neutral faces when they were presented for 231 ms ($r = -.28$, $p < .05$).

The specific significance of these findings is presently unclear because attentional orienting is not a straightforward measure of the rewarding and aversive qualities of a stimulus, only its overall motivational salience. Using instrumental-learning paradigms in future studies may provide more straightforward answers in this regard. Also, the difference between very short and longer FEE presentations for achievement-motivated perceivers is puzzling. Does it suggest that individuals high in n Achievement are highly sensitive to even the minutest of facial expressions, but tend to shut out others' emotions if they become too intense? And how exactly are these effects of FEEs on achievement-motivated perceivers related to their need to master challenging tasks on their own? Are the effects related to the early childhood socialization of achievement-motivated individuals? We think that these are intriguing questions that may provide important new impulses to research on n Achievement.

Future Directions

As we have indicated previously, our discussion of the implications of MFT and all supporting research so far have focused on the *signal → perceiver* portion of MFT. We have not touched on the role of motivation in the *sender → signal* path of the communication model underlying MFT or the more complex predictions for dynamic interpersonal behavior that would result if the entire *sender → signal → perceiver* model were taken into account. After all, the signal a person perceives from a sender may be the harvest of what she or he sowed as the sender of another signal just the moment before. Although charting out these aspects of MFT in depth is beyond the scope of this chapter, their consideration in future research is likely to provide important insights into implicit motivation and the dynamics of interpersonal behavior.

For instance, we have already pointed out that power-motivated individuals are keen on having an emotional impact on others. But if showing an emotion is an acknowledgment of another's impact on oneself, how do power-motivated persons handle the display of their own emotions? We would predict that in general, they would try to show a "poker face" and be reluctant to show any emotion at all. If they cannot avoid expressing an emotion, then joy may be the

FEE of choice because it signals relaxed, nonaggressive dominance and thus states a claim to other dominance seekers without necessarily eliciting a dominance struggle as the anger face would. Another advantage of the joy FEE is that it may serve to bring all affiliation-motivated perceivers on the side of the sender, an effect that could help power-motivated individuals rally support for their claim to dominance. Clearly, however, joy is also expressed by senders high in the need for affiliation, and in this case not for the sake of appearing dominant, but for making and keeping friends.

This example illustrates the complexities emerging from a motivational analysis of the factors that determine the presentation of an FEE. It also highlights the need to search for and pinpoint subtle differences in the presentation of FEEs (e.g., How does the joy expression displayed by a power-motivated sender differ from the joy expression displayed by an affiliation-motivated sender?) as well as the contexts in which individuals with specific motivational needs typically display an FEE (e.g., In what kinds of social situations are power-motivated or affiliation-motivated individuals more likely to smile?).

Because MFT is a theory of the general role of emotional signals in motivation and interpersonal behavior, we think that it might also be fruitful to apply the principles and hypotheses we have sketched out here to other nonverbal communication channels. Clearly, power or affiliation is not only communicated by FEEs, but also by vocal characteristics, body language, and the dynamic interplay of different nonverbal channels (see, for instance, Schultheiss & Brunstein, 2002). We believe that the systematic exploration of these issues presents a rich, fascinating, and fruitful field for future research.

Conclusion

In this chapter, we have chronicled the history of incentive concepts in research on implicit motives, starting with the general mechanism of charging stimuli with incentive value (McClelland et al., 1953), moving on to dual-systems approaches (McClelland et al., 1989), and all the way to the most recent (but likely not the last) conceptualization that emphasizes the nonverbal nature of implicit motive incentives (Schultheiss, 2001, 2008). By presenting MFT, a spin-off of classic interpersonal field theories, we have also tried to illustrate how a careful analysis and conceptualization of motivational incentives can lead to clear-cut predictions about which stimuli should be rewarding or aversive for specific implicit motives and why. It is our hope that the arguments and hypotheses laid out in this chapter will help other researchers conduct rigorous and systematic research on implicit motives based on sound and testable principles and concepts. It turns out that implicit motivational incentives *can* be pinpointed, after all, and we believe that this insight is critical for further substantive advances in experimental research on implicit motives.

Author Notes

We thank Andreas G. Rösch for comments and suggestions on an earlier version of this chapter.

Parts of the research summarized in this chapter were supported by Deutsche Forschungsmeinschaft grants SCHU 1210/1_2, 1-3, and 2-2, NIMH grant 1 R03 MH63069-01, NSF grant BCS 0444301, and a Rackham Predoctoral Fellowship.

References

Adams, R. B., Jr., & Kleck, R. E. (2005). Effects of direct and averted gaze on the perception of facially communicated emotion. *Emotion, 5*(1), 3–11.

Argyle, M. (1975). Non-verbal communication in human social interaction. In R. A. Hinde (Ed.), *Non-verbal communication* (pp. 243–269). Cambridge, UK: Cambridge University Press.

Atkinson, J. W. (1957). Motivational determinants of risk-taking behavior. *Psychological Review, 64*, 359–372.

Atkinson, J. W., & Walker, E. L. (1958). The affiliation motive and perceptual sensitivity to faces. In J. W. Atkinson (Ed.), *Motives in fantasy, action, and society: A method of assessment and study* (pp. 360–366). Princeton, NJ: Van Nostrand.

Barr-Zisowitz, C. (2000). "Sadness"—is there such a thing? In M. Lewis & J. M. Haviland-Jones (Eds.), *Handbook of emotions* (2nd ed., pp. 607–622). New York: Guilford.

Berridge, K. C. (2000). Measuring hedonic impact in animals and infants: Microstructure of affective taste reactivity patterns. *Neuroscience and Biobehavioral Reviews, 24*(2), 173–198.

Bindra, D. (1978). How adaptive behavior is produced: A perceptual-motivational alternative to response-reinforcement. *Behavioral and Brain Sciences, 1*, 41–91.

Brunstein, J. C., & Gollwitzer, P. M. (1996). Effects of failure on subsequent performance: The importance of self-defining goals. *Journal of Personality and Social Psychology, 70*, 395–407.

Brunstein, J. C., & Hoyer, S. (2002). Implizites und explizites Leistungsstreben: Befunde zur Unabhängigkeit zweier Motivationssysteme [Implicit versus explicit achievement strivings: Empirical evidence of the independence of two motivational systems]. *Zeitschrift fur Pädagogische Psychologie, 16*, 51–62.

Brunstein, J. C., & Maier, G. W. (2005). Implicit and self-attributed motives to achieve: Two separate but interacting needs. *Journal of Personality and Social Psychology, 89*(2), 205–222.

Brunstein, J. C., & Schmitt, C. H. (2004). Assessing individual differences in achievement motivation with the Implicit Association Test. *Journal of Research in Personality, 38*(6), 536–555.

Bucci, W. (1984). Linking words and things: Basic processes and individual variation. *Cognition, 17*, 137–153.

Bucci, W. (2002). The referential process, consciousness, and the sense of self. *Psychoanalytic Inquiry, 22,* 766–793.

Camras, L. A., Meng, Z., Ujiie, T., Dharamsi, S., Miyake, K., Oster, H., et al. (2002). Observing emotion in infants: Facial expression, body behavior, and rater judgments of responses to an expectancy-violating event. *Emotion, 2*(2), 179–193.

Conway, M., Di Fazio, R., & Mayman, S. (1999). Judging others' emotions as a function of the others' status. *Social Psychology Quarterly, 62,* 291–305.

Craig, J. A., Koestner, R., & Zuroff, D. C. (1994). Implicit and self-attributed intimacy motivation. *Journal of Social and Personal Relationships, 11,* 491–507.

Curran, T. (1998). Implicit sequence learning from a cognitive neuroscience perspective: What, how, and where? In M. A. Stadler & P. A. Frensch (Eds.), *Handbook of implicit learning* (pp. 365–399). Thousand Oaks, CA: Sage.

deCharms, R., Morrison, H. W., Reitman, W., & McClelland, D. C. (1955). Behavioral correlates of directly and indirectly measured achievement motivation. In D. C. McClelland (Ed.), *Studies in motivation* (pp. 414–423). New York: Appleton-Century-Crofts.

Eibl-Eibesfeldt, I. (1995). *Die Biologie des menschlichen Verhaltens: Grundriß der Humanethologie [The biology of human behavior: Principles of human ethology]* (3rd ed.). Munich, Germany: Piper.

Eisenberger, R. (1992). Learned industriousness. *Psychological Review, 99,* 248–267.

Ekman, P., & O'Sullivan, M. (1991). Who can catch a liar? *American Psychologist, 46,* 913–920.

Entwisle, D. R. (1972). To dispel fantasies about fantasy-based measures of achievement motivation. *Psychological Bulletin, 77,* 377–391.

Gazzaniga, M. S. (1985). *The social brain: Discovering the networks of the mind.* New York: Basic Books.

Hess, U., Blairy, S., & Kleck, R. E. (2000). The influence of facial emotion displays, gender, and ethnicity on judgments of dominance and affiliation. *Journal of Nonverbal Behavior, 24,* 265–283.

Job, V., & Brandstätter, V. (2009). Get a taste of your goals: Promoting motive-goal congruence through affect-focus goal fantasy. *Journal of Personality, 77,* 1527–1560.

Johnsen, B. H., Thayer, J. F., & Hugdahl, K. (1995). Affective judgment of the Ekman faces: A dimensional approach. *Journal of Psychophysiology, 9,* 193–202.

Keltner, D. (1995). Signs of appeasement: Evidence for the distinct displays of embarrassment, amusement, and shame. *Journal of Personality and Social Psychology, 68,* 441–454.

Keltner, D., Ekman, P., Gonzaga, G. C., & Beer, J. (2003). Facial expression of emotion. In R. J. Davidson, K. R. Scherer, & H. H. Goldsmith (Eds.), *Handbook of affective sciences* (pp. 433–456). New York: Oxford University Press.

Keltner, D., & Haidt, J. (1999). Social functions of emotions at four levels of analysis. *Cognition and Emotion, 13,* 505–521.

Keltner, D., Young, R. C., Heerey, E. A., Oemig, C., & Monarch, N. D. (1998). Teasing in hierarchical and intimate relations. *Journal of Personality and Social Psychology, 75*(5), 1231–1247.

Klinger, E. (1967). Modeling effects on achievement imagery. *Journal of Personality and Social Psychology, 7,* 49–62.

Knutson, B. (1996). Facial expressions of emotion influence interpersonal trait inferences. *Journal of Nonverbal Behavior, 20,* 165–182.

Koestner, R., Weinberger, J., & McClelland, D. C. (1991). Task-intrinsic and social-extrinsic sources of arousal for motives assessed in fantasy and self-report. *Journal of Personality, 59,* 57–82.

Kolb, B., & Whishaw, I. Q. (2003). *Fundamentals of human neuropsychology* (5th ed.). New York: Worth.

Lakin, J. L., & Chartrand, T. L. (2003). Using nonconscious behavioral mimicry to create affiliation and rapport. *Psychological Science, 14*(4), 334–339.

Lee, E., Kang, J. I., Park, I. H., Kim, J. J., & An, S. K. (2008). Is a neutral face really evaluated as being emotionally neutral? *Psychiatry Research, 157*(1–3), 77–85.

Lilienfeld, S. O., Wood, J. E., & Garb, H. N. (2000). The scientific status of projective techniques. *Psychological Science in the Public Interest, 1,* 27–66.

Luria, A. R., & Homskaya, E. D. (1964). Disturbances in the regulative role of speech with frontal lobe lesions. In J. M. Warren & K. Akert (Eds.), *The frontal grabular cortex and behavior* (pp. 353–371). New York: McGraw-Hill.

Mazur, J. E. (1998). *Learning and behavior* (4th ed.). Upper Saddle River, NJ: Prentice Hall.

McAdams, D. P. (1992). The intimacy motive. In C. P. Smith (Ed.), *Motivation and personality: Handbook of thematic content analysis* (pp. 224–228). New York: Cambridge University Press.

McClelland, D. C. (1980). Motive dispositions. The merits of operant and respondent measures. In L. Wheeler (Ed.), *Review of personality and social psychology* (Vol. 1, pp. 10–41). Beverly Hills, CA: Sage.

McClelland, D. C. (1987). *Human motivation.* New York: Cambridge University Press.

McClelland, D. C., Atkinson, J. W., Clark, R. A., & Lowell, E. L. (1953). *The achievement motive.* New York: Appleton-Century-Crofts.

McClelland, D. C., Koestner, R., & Weinberger, J. (1989). How do self-attributed and implicit motives differ? *Psychological Review, 96,* 690–702.

McClelland, D. C., & Pilon, D. A. (1983). Sources of adult motives in patterns of parent behavior in early childhood. *Journal of Personality and Social Psychology, 44,* 564–574.

McGaugh, J. L. (2002). Memory consolidation and the amygdala: A systems perspective. *Trends in Neurosciences, 25*(9), 456.

Muraven, M., & Baumeister, R. F. (2000). Self-regulation and depletion of limited resources: Does self-control resemble a muscle? *Psychological Bulletin, 126*(2), 247–259.

Murray, H. A. (1938). *Explorations in personality.* New York: Oxford University Press.

Nissen, M. J., & Bullemer, P. (1987). Attentional requirements of learning: Evidence from performance measures. *Cognitive Psychology, 19,* 1–32.

Öhman, A. (2002). Automaticity and the amygdala: Nonconscious responses to emotional faces. *Current Directions in Psychological Science, 11,* 62–66.

Paivio, A. (1986). *Mental representations. A dual coding approach.* New York: Oxford University Press.

Paivio, A. (1991). Dual coding theory: Retrospect and current status. *Canadian Journal of Psychology, 45,* 255–287.

Paivio, A., Clark, J. M., Digdon, N., & Bons, T. (1989). Referential processing: Reciprocity and correlates of naming and imaging. *Memory & Cognition, 17*(2), 163–174.

Poldrack, R. A., Clark, J., Pare-Blagoev, E. J., Shohamy, D., Creso Moyano, J., Myers, C., et al. (2001). Interactive memory systems in the human brain. *Nature, 414*(6863), 546–550.

Poldrack, R. A., & Foerde, K. (2008). Category learning and the memory systems debate. *Neuroscience and Biobehavioral Reviews, 32*(2), 197–205.

Riebel, K. (2004). *Implicit motives modulate attentional orienting to facial expressions of fear, disgust, contempt, and sadness.* Unpublished diploma thesis, Johannes-Gutenberg University, Mainz, Germany.

Rolls, E. T. (1999). *The brain and emotion.* Oxford, UK: Oxford University Press.

Rosen, B. C., & D'Andrade, R. (1959). The psychological origins of the achievement motive. *Sociometry, 22,* 185–218.

Rozin, P., Haidt, J., & McCauley, C. R. (2000). Disgust. In M. Lewis & J. M. Haviland-Jones (Eds.), *Handbook of emotions* (2nd ed., pp. 637–653). New York: Guilford.

Schacter, D. L. (1987). Implicit memory: History and current status. *Journal of Experimental Psychology Learning, Memory, and Cognition, 13,* 501–518.

Schultheiss, O. C. (2001). An information processing account of implicit motive arousal. In M. L. Maehr & P. Pintrich (Eds.), *Advances in motivation and achievement. Vol. 12: New directions in measures and methods* (pp. 1–41). Greenwich, CT: JAI Press.

Schultheiss, O. C. (2007a). A memory-systems approach to the classification of personality tests: Comment on Meyer and Kurtz (2006). *Journal of Personality Assessment, 89*(2), 197–201.

Schultheiss, O. C. (2007b). A biobehavioral model of implicit power motivation arousal, reward and frustration. In E. Harmon-Jones & P. Winkielman (Eds.), *Social neuroscience: Integrating biological and psychological explanations of social behavior* (pp. 176–196). New York: Guilford.

Schultheiss, O. C. (2008). Implicit motives. In O. P. John, R. W. Robins, & L. A. Pervin (Eds.), *Handbook of personality: Theory and research* (3rd ed., pp. 603–633). New York: Guilford.

Schultheiss, O. C., & Brunstein, J. C. (1999). Goal imagery: Bridging the gap between implicit motives and explicit goals. *Journal of Personality, 67,* 1–38.

Schultheiss, O. C., & Brunstein, J. C. (2002). Inhibited power motivation and persuasive communication: A lens model analysis. *Journal of Personality, 70,* 553–582.

Schultheiss, O. C., & Brunstein, J. C. (2005). An implicit motive perspective on competence. In A. J. Elliot & C. Dweck (Eds.), *Handbook of competence and motivation* (pp. 31–51). New York: Guilford.

Schultheiss, O. C., & Hale, J. A. (2007). Implicit motives modulate attentional orienting to perceived facial expressions of emotion. *Motivation and Emotion, 31*(1), 13–24.

Schultheiss, O. C., Kordik, A., Kullmann, J. S., Rawolle, M., & Rösch, A. G. (2009). Motivation as a natural linchpin between person and situation. *Journal of Research in Personality, 43,* 268–269.

Schultheiss, O. C., Liening, S., MacInnes, J. J., Patalakh, M., & Rawolle, M. (2009). *Referential competence predicts congruence between implicit motives and explicit goals.* Manuscript in preparation, Friedrich-Alexander University, Erlangen, Germany.

Schultheiss, O. C., Pang, J. S., Torges, C. M., Wirth, M. M., & Treynor, W. (2005). Perceived facial expressions of emotion as motivational incentives: Evidence from a differential implicit learning paradigm. *Emotion, 5*(1), 41–54.

Schultheiss, O. C., & Rohde, W. (2002). Implicit power motivation predicts men's testosterone changes and implicit learning in a contest situation. *Hormones and Behavior, 41,* 195–202.

Schultheiss, O. C., Wirth, M. M., Torges, C. M., Pang, J. S., Villacorta, M. A., & Welsh, K. M. (2005). Effects of implicit power motivation on men's and women's implicit learning and testosterone changes after social victory or defeat. *Journal of Personality and Social Psychology, 88*(1), 174–188.

Schultheiss, O. C., Wirth, M. M., Waugh, C. E., Stanton, S. J., Meier, E., & Reuter-Lorenz, P. (2008). Exploring the motivational brain: Effects of implicit power motivation on brain activation in response to facial expressions of emotion. *Social Cognitive and Affective Neuroscience, 3,* 333–343.

Spangler, W. D. (1992). Validity of questionnaire and TAT measures of need for achievement: Two meta-analyses. *Psychological Bulletin, 112,* 140–154.

Squire, L. R. (2004). Memory systems of the brain: A brief history and current perspective. *Neurobiology of Learning and Memory, 82*(3), 171–177.

Stanton, S. J., & Schultheiss, O. C. (2009). The hormonal correlates of implicit power motivation. *Journal of Research in Personality, 43,* 942–949.

Stanton, S. J., Wirth, M. M., & Schultheiss, O. C. (2006, January). *Effects of perceivers' implicit power motivation on attentional orienting to Pavlovian-conditioned cues of anger and joy.* Paper presented at the Society for Personality and Social Psychology, Palm Springs, CA.

Sullivan, H. S. (1953). *The interpersonal theory of psychiatry.* New York: Norton.

Tiedens, L. Z. (2001). Anger and advancement versus sadness and subjugation: The effect of negative emotion expressions on social status conferral. *Journal of Personality and Social Psychology, 80,* 86–94.

Toates, F. (1986). *Motivational systems.* Cambridge, UK: Cambridge University Press.

Tracy, J. L., & Robins, R. W. (2004). Show your pride: Evidence for a discrete emotion expression. *Psychological Science, 15,* 194–197.

Weinberger, J., & McClelland, D. C. (1990). Cognitive versus traditional motivational models: Irreconcilable or complementary? In E. T. Higgins & R. M. Sorrentino (Eds.), *Handbook of motivation and cognition: Foundations of social behavior* (Vol. 2, pp. 562–597). New York: Guilford Press.

Wiggins, J. S., & Trobst, K. K. (1999). The fields of interpersonal behavior. In L. A. Pervin & O. P. John (Eds.), *Handbook of personality: Theory and research* (2nd ed., pp. 653–670). New York: Guilford.

Wilson, E. O. (1980). *Sociobiology: The abridged edition.* Cambridge, MA: Belknap/ Harvard.

Winter, D. G. (1994). *Manual for scoring motive imagery in running text* (4th ed.). Unpublished manuscript, Department of Psychology, University of Michigan, Ann Arbor.

Winter, D. G. (1996). *Personality: Analysis and interpretation of lives.* New York: McGraw-Hill.

Winterbottom, M. R. (1958). The relation of need for achievement to learning experiences in independence and mastery. In J. W. Atkinson (Ed.), *Motives in fantasy, action, and society: A method of assessment and study* (pp. 453–478). Princeton, NJ: Van Nostrand.

Wirth, M. M., & Schultheiss, O. C. (2007). Basal testosterone moderates responses to anger faces in humans. *Physiology and Behavior, 90*(2–3), 496–505.

Woike, B. A. (2008). A functional framework for the influence of implicit and explicit motives on autobiographical memory. *Personality and Social Psychology Review, 12*(2), 99–117.

Chapter 10
Biopsychological and Neural Processes of Implicit Motivation

JULIE L. HALL
University of Michigan

STEVEN J. STANTON
Duke University

OLIVER C. SCHULTHEISS
Friedrich-Alexander University

Introduction

Virtually all mammalian and many nonmammalian species share fundamental evolutionarily preserved motivational systems that propel them toward the formation of attachments with their kin to ensure safety and protection (i.e., affiliation). In addition, they are also propelled by a need to move upward in the dominance hierarchy to obtain more resources and mating opportunities (i.e., power). As a result, animals and humans share similar biopsychological and neural systems that facilitate affiliation-motivated and power-motivated behavior (Schultheiss & Wirth, 2008). For example, the gonadal steroid hormone testosterone promotes power-motivated and dominant behavior across species (Monaghan & Glickman, 1992). On the other hand, the peptide hormone oxytocin promotes affiliative and attachment behavior across species (Insel & Young, 2001). In comparison to power and affiliation motivation, relatively less is known about the hormonal and neural mechanisms involved in achievement motivation and whether the need for achievement is universal across species or a species-specific motive.

In the first part of this chapter, we will review the hormonal aspects of implicit motives and their role in immune system functioning and health. We will summarize and integrate the existing research on power motivation and the release of the hormones testosterone, epinephrine, norepinephrine, and cortisol within the framework of a psychoneuroendocrine model of power motivation; discuss its applicability to male and female power motivation; and examine its validity in the context of research on the effects of stressed power motivation on health. Next, we will review past and current research on the hormonal and health correlates of affiliation motivation with a particular focus on recent findings of the role of progesterone and cortisol in affiliation motivation, and discuss links between research on the neuroendocrine and health aspects of affiliation motivation and the literature implicating oxytocin in social bonding and stress buffering. Finally, we will also review evidence for a hormonal basis of achievement motivation, focusing on the role of arginine vasopressin in the cognitive and behavioral correlates of this motive.

In the second part of the chapter, we will describe a core motivational brain circuit consisting of the amygdala, striatum, and orbitofrontal cortex, which we hypothesize to be critically involved in implicit motivation. We will present fMRI research findings in which several of these structures have been found to be more activated in power-motivated and achievement-motivated individuals and less activated in affiliation-motivated individuals. In closing, we will discuss parallels between the functional dissociation of the core motivational brain circuit and brain structures involved in conscious goal setting and action regulation on the one hand, and the lack of overlap between implicit motives and explicit goals and needs on the other.

Biopsychological Processes of Implicit Motivation

Power Motivation and Sympathetic Nervous System Activation

Power motivation has consistently been linked to activation of the sympathetic nervous system, a branch of the autonomic nervous system that becomes more active during times of stress (McClelland, 1982). Power-motivated individuals respond to experimental arousal of the power motive and social dominance challenges with increases in salivary and urinary metabolites of epinephrine and norepinephrine, two catecholamines that are released by the sympathetic nervous system in response to stressors (McClelland, Davidson, & Saron, 1985; McClelland, Floor, Davidson, & Saron, 1980; McClelland, Ross, & Patel, 1985; Steele, 1973, reported in McClelland, 1987). In addition, they also respond with increases in blood pressure (Fontana, Rosenberg, Marcus, & Kerns, 1987) and muscle tone (Fodor, 1985).

For example, Steele (1973) compared participants whose power motive had been aroused through the presentation of inspirational speeches with participants in achievement-arousal and control conditions. Steele found that power-arousal participants had significantly higher postarousal power motive scores than control and achievement-arousal participants. Furthermore, postarousal power motive scores were positively correlated with increases in epinephrine ($r = .71$) and norepinephrine ($r = .66$) in power-arousal participants. By contrast, changes in sympathetic catecholamines after the experimental manipulation were not significantly associated with power motive scores in control and achievement-arousal participants. These results suggest that experimental arousal of the power motive is uniquely associated with an enhanced response in the sympathetic nervous system as reflected by increases in epinephrine and norepinephrine.

McClelland and colleagues (1980, 1985) have found further support for an association between power motivation and greater sympathetic nervous system activation. McClelland and colleagues (1980) found that power-motivated college males who experienced frequent power challenges in their daily lives and were unable to spontaneously express power-related impulses showed above average epinephrine excretion rates in urine. In a later study, McClelland, Ross, and Patel (1985) collected saliva samples in college students immediately after an important midterm exam, 105 minutes later, and several days after the exam to obtain a baseline measure. The power stress of the exam was associated with an increase in norepinephrine, and this increase was greater for students whose power motive was stronger than their affiliation motive in comparison to students whose affiliation motive was stronger than their power motive. These findings provide additional support for the theory that power motivation, in combination with power-arousing situations and cues, predicts sympathetic nervous system activation and catecholamine release.

Power Motivation and Testosterone

Power motivation has also been linked with the gonadal steroid testosterone (Dabbs, Hopper, & Jurkovic, 1990; Schultheiss, Campbell, & McClelland, 1999; Schultheiss, Dargel, & Rohde, 2003; Schultheiss & Rohde, 2002; Schultheiss et al., 2005). In both humans and animals, high testosterone levels have been associated with dominance, social success, enhanced libido, assertiveness, and violent behavior (Albert, Jonik, & Walsh, 1992; Carter, 1992; Mazur & Booth, 1998; Monaghan & Glickman, 1992). In many primates, dominant males show transient testosterone increases in response to dominance challenges (Bernstein, Gordon, & Rose, 1983; Mazur, 1985; Sapolsky, 1987). Human males respond with testosterone increases to victory and testosterone decreases to defeat in social dominance contests, including tennis matches, chess tournaments, and even games of chance against another person (reviewed in Mazur & Booth, 1998).

The relationship between dominance and testosterone is less consistent for women whose testosterone levels are about one-fourth to one-sixth of those found in men (Dabbs, 1990; Mazur & Booth, 1998). However, research suggests that testosterone is also crucial for female dominance. For example, elevated testosterone levels in women lead to increased attention and heightened physiological responses to angry faces (van Honk et al., 1999, 2001). Furthermore, women with high testosterone levels occupy higher occupational positions compared to women with low testosterone levels (Dabbs, Alford, & Fielden, 1998; Purifoy & Koopmans, 1979). In addition, high testosterone levels have also been associated with high rank in the prison hierarchy and a history of unprovoked aggression among female prisoners (Dabbs & Hargrove, 1997; Dabbs, Ruback, Frady, Hopper, & Sgoutas, 1988).

Subjectively, high testosterone levels are associated with feelings of vigor and activation (Dabbs, Strong, & Milun, 1997; Sherwin, 1988). Research also suggests that testosterone has significant antidepressant effects for men with very low or absent endogenous testosterone production (Rabkin, Wagner, & Rabkin, 1996). However, at above-average doses, testosterone can lead to addiction (Pope & Katz, 1994). Consistent with testosterone's addictive properties, animal studies provide evidence for a reinforcing role of testosterone. Systemically or locally administered testosterone increases dopamine transmission in the nucleus accumbens (Packard, Schroeder, & Alexander, 1998), a core structure in the brain's incentive motivation system (Cardinal, Parkinson, Hall, & Everitt, 2002). Administration of testosterone has also been shown to reinforce behavior in conditioned-place-preference paradigms (Alexander, Packard, & Hines, 1994; Wood, Johnson, Chu, Schad, & Self, 2004). Furthermore, testosterone-induced conditioned place preference can be abolished by the concomitant administration of dopamine antagonists (Packard et al., 1998; Schroeder & Packard, 2000). Accumbens-mediated reinforcing effects of testosterone are particularly pronounced after testosterone has been metabolized to 3α-androstanediol (Frye, Rhodes, Rosellini, & Svare, 2002).

Research in our laboratory has found a slight positive association between basal testosterone levels and implicit power motivation (Schultheiss et al., 1999, 2003, 2005; Schultheiss & Rohde, 2002), particularly in males. In a study using an experimental motive arousal design, Schultheiss, Wirth, and Stanton (2004) found that a movie depicting the aggressive pursuit of dominance (i.e., The Godfather II) elicited increases in power motivation in both men and women. In addition, testosterone levels increased in men with high basal testosterone levels. However, no testosterone changes occurred in women regardless of their basal testosterone levels. For participants in the power-arousal group, testosterone changes correlated substantially with changes in power motive scores among men, but not women. While these findings may suggest that power motivation and arousal of the power motive are not specifically associated with testosterone in women, it is also conceivable that the relatively higher measurement error for the comparatively low testosterone levels in women and the smaller magnitude of situation-induced testosterone changes in women may mask a more substantial positive association between testosterone and power motivation in women.

Research conducted in our laboratory also suggests that both the anticipation of success and actual success outcomes during social dominance contests lead to transient testosterone increases in power-motivated men (Schultheiss et al., 1999, 2005; Schultheiss & Rohde, 2002). During the social dominance contests, same-sex pairs competed on several rounds of an implicit learning task that required them to learn a complex visuomotor pattern in a paper-and-pencil task (Schultheiss & Rohde, 2002) or on a computer screen (Schultheiss et al., 2005). The outcome of the contests was experimentally manipulated: one participant in each pair was randomly assigned to be the winner and the other to be the loser. Participants' motivational dispositions and personality were assessed with the Picture Story Exercise (PSE) and self-report questionnaires prior to the contest. Salivary testosterone levels and self-reported affect were assessed before and after the contest. Instrumental learning was assessed by learning gains on the implicit learning task after the contest. Notably, participants had no conscious intention to acquire the visuomotor sequence featured on the implicit learning task, nor did they become aware of the fact that they had learned anything in the first place. Thus, learning was implicit in the sense that it happened automatically and was not mediated by declarative processes (e.g., through explicit memory and self-instruction).

Across three studies conducted with male college students in the United States and Germany, Schultheiss and colleagues (Schultheiss et al., 1999, 2005; Schultheiss & Rohde, 2002) consistently found that power motivation predicted testosterone increases among winners and testosterone decreases among losers. By contrast, social dominance contests led to transient testosterone increases regardless of contest outcome in women (Schultheiss et al., 2005; Study 2). This testosterone increase was particularly strong in power-motivated losers immediately after the contest whereas power-motivated winners showed only a very slight and nonsignificant testosterone increase at this time.

In contrast to the gender differences seen in hormonal responses to experimentally manipulated social victory and defeat, power motivation predicted contest-outcome effects on instrumental learning in the same manner and magnitude in men and women. In both men and women, power motivation predicted enhanced instrumental learning (i.e., sequence execution accuracy) among winners and impaired instrumental learning among losers (Schultheiss et al., 2005). These results replicate findings from an earlier study obtained by Schultheiss and Rohde (2002) in a German sample of male college students. Together these studies provide strong evidence for a moderating role of implicit power motivation on instrumental learning of behavior that has impact on others (i.e., beating one's opponent on a contest) and the inhibition of behavior that leads to the frustration of the need for impact (i.e., being beaten by one's opponent on a contest).

Consistent with the reinforcing effects of testosterone observed in the animal literature, Schultheiss and colleagues (Schultheiss & Rohde, 2002; Schultheiss et al., 2005) also found that men's testosterone changes after a social dominance contest were associated with instrumental learning and statistically mediated the effect of power motivation on instrumental learning. In their study, Schultheiss and Rohde (2002) found that among male power-motivated winners, testosterone increases transmitted the boosting effect of power motivation on instrumental learning. In addition, Schultheiss et al. (2005) found that testosterone decreases mediated the negative effect of power motivation on instrumental learning in male power-motivated losers.

However, Schultheiss and colleagues (2005) did not find any evidence for a reinforcing effect of testosterone on instrumental learning in women. In fact, higher postcontest testosterone levels showed a negative association with speed of visuomotor pattern execution on the implicit learning task, which is inconsistent with a role of testosterone in reinforcement. The lack of evidence for a reinforcing effect of testosterone on instrumental learning in women does not rule out priming effects of testosterone on power-motivated behaviors. Animal studies show that testosterone lowers the threshold for aggressive behavior in males and females (Albert et al., 1992), and research conducted in our laboratory suggests that a priming role of testosterone on female assertiveness also exists in humans (Schultheiss et al., 2005). Consistent with the hypothesis that testosterone primes self-assertion in women, Schultheiss (2007) reports that in the Schultheiss et al. (2005) study, female losers with the strongest postcontest testosterone increases also showed the greatest power imagery increases in response to a postcontest PSE picture suggesting aggression (e.g., a woman with an angry face and bared teeth), but not to nonaggressive PSE pictures. Thus, while elevated testosterone levels after a social defeat do not seem to reinforce instrumental learning in women, they are associated with what seems to be a compensatory need to assert oneself in a forceful manner.

Stressed Power Motivation and Cortisol

While testosterone appears to scale the reward value of social dominance contest outcomes in men and may subserve a general power-motivation-enhancing function in women, recent evidence points to a role of cortisol in stressed power motivation in both men and women. Cortisol is released by the adrenal gland during uncontrollable stress and induces the body to shunt available energy into coping with the stressor. While cortisol is not consistently related to declarative measures of negative affect and stress (Dickerson & Kemeny, 2004), it increases reliably during social stressors such as the Trier Social Stress Test (TSST; Kirschbaum, Pirke, & Hellhammer, 1993) and is chronically elevated in depressed individuals (Rothschild, 2003). Wirth, Welsh, and Schultheiss (2006) analyzed saliva samples for cortisol levels collected during social dominance contests in a male German sample and a mixed-sex U.S. sample. In both samples, power motivation predicted changes in salivary cortisol levels after winning or losing a dominance contest. Power motivation was associated with increased cortisol levels after a defeat and decreased cortisol levels after a victory. These findings suggest that losing a social dominance contest is particularly stressful for high-power individuals whereas winning a social dominance contest reduces stress levels.

In several studies, stressed power motivation has been associated with impaired immune system functioning and health (Jemmott, 1987; McClelland, 1989). During academic examinations, high-power students compared to low-power students show elevated and prolonged sympathetic stress activation and decreased levels of salivary immunoglobulin A (s-IgA), a measure of B-cell immune function (Jemmott et al., 1983; McClelland et al.,1985). Similarly, McClelland, Alexander, & Marks (1982) found that male prisoners with high levels of power motivation and self-reported stress showed the highest levels of illness and the lowest concentrations of s-IgA compared to high-power, low-stress, and low-power groups.

Stressed power motivation is also associated with decreased natural killer cell activity (Jemmott et al., 1990). As a consequence of depressed immune system functioning, individuals high in power motivation and power stress are more likely than low-power individuals to report more frequent and severe illnesses (McClelland & Jemmott, 1980; McClelland et al., 1980, 1982, 1985). Although the specific mechanism underlying the relationship between stressed power motivation and impaired immune function is unclear, McClelland and colleagues (1980, 1985) suggest that the immunosuppressive effects of chronic sympathetic activity may make individuals characterized by this syndrome more susceptible to illness. Additionally, Wirth and colleagues (2006) propose that another mechanism underlying this relationship may be greater or chronically elevated cortisol levels. It is important to note that high levels of power motivation in combination with low power stress and success in power-related efforts have been found to predict low levels of physical symptoms and overall good health (McClelland, 1989), which suggests that power motivation is not associated with a general vulnerability for impaired immune function or illness.

Psychoneuroendocrine Model of Power Motivation

The observed changes in sympathetic catecholamines, testosterone, and cortisol in response to arousal of the power motive and outcomes during social dominance contests represent the operation of a functionally integrated neuroendocrine mechanism that subserves dominance motivation in males (Sapolsky, 1987; Schultheiss, 2007; see Fig. 10.1). Sympathetic catecholamines cause general changes in physiology that prepare the body for physical activity in response to stress (i.e., fight-or-flight response). They have fast, stimulating effects on testosterone release from the gonads, and they are typically released

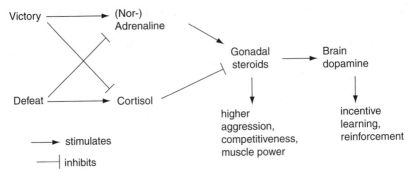

Figure 10.1 Biobehavioral model of endocrine responses to victory and defeat during a dominance contest in individuals high in *n* Power. High–*n* Power winners respond with greater sympathetic activation (catecholamine release) than cortisol release, which stimulates the release of gonadal steroids (testosterone in men, estradiol in women) that facilitate dominant behavior and are involved in brain reinforcement processes. In high–*n* Power losers, the cortisol response outweighs sympathetic activation, resulting in a net inhibition of gonadal steroid release and therefore transiently less competitiveness and behavioral reinforcement. Based on Schultheiss (2007) and Stanton & Schultheiss (2007).

in situations in which the individual can actively cope with the stressor, such as beating an opponent in a social dominance contest (Sapolsky, 1987). Testosterone further aids active coping by increasing energy supply to the muscles (Tsai & Sapolsky, 1996) and lowering the threshold for aggressive behavior through its actions on the brain (Albert et al., 1992).

By contrast, cortisol is released by the adrenal gland during situations in which the individual is exposed to an uncontrollable stressor (e.g., social defeat, being subjected to another's dominance; Sapolsky, 2002). Cortisol inhibits testosterone release from the gonads (Sapolsky, 1987), thereby lowering the individual's inclination to engage in further, potentially costly and fruitless dominance battles. According to Sapolsky's (1987) balance model of testosterone release, testosterone increases in male power-motivated winners of a social dominance contest represent the net effect of relatively greater sympathetic catecholamine release throughout a surmountable challenge, whereas testosterone decreases in male power-motivated losers represent the net effect of relatively greater cortisol release during and after a confrontation that overtaxes the individual's capabilities and ends in a defeat.

Although testosterone is known to be positively associated with violence, aggression, and dominance in females (Dabbs, Ruback, Frady, Hopper, & Sgoutas, 1988; van Honk et al., 2001), the mechanisms underlying this relationship and the precise role of the contest-induced testosterone increases observed in power-motivated women are still not well characterized. In addition, it remains to be determined whether contest-induced testosterone increases lead to long-term increases in power motivation and, conversely, whether contest-induced testosterone decreases lead to long-term reductions in power motivation, as predicted by models of reciprocal effects of dominance behavior and testosterone (Mazur, 1985; Oyegbile & Marler, 2005).

Estradiol and Female Power Motivation

Recent research suggests that estradiol plays an important role in women's need for dominance (Stanton & Schultheiss, 2007). Behaviorally, estradiol has been linked to increases in women's efforts to impress and attract a mate (Grammer, Renninger, & Fischer, 2004; Haselton, Mortezaie, Pillsworth, Bleske-Rechek, & Frederick, 2007) in addition to sexual activity (Adams, Gold, & Burt, 1978; Udry & Morris, 1968). Research on female rats indicates that estradiol enhances dopamine release and sensorimotor functioning in the striatum (Hu & Becker, 2003). In addition, there is also evidence that estradiol plays a role in reward and reinforcement mediated by the mesolimbic dopamine system (Bless, McGinnis, Mitchell, Hartwell, & Mitchell, 1997; Russo et al., 2003).

Stanton and Schultheiss (2007) found that estradiol in women may serve a similar role in power motivation as testosterone in men. During social dominance contests, estradiol changes in women varied as a function of power motivation and contest outcomes. Estradiol levels increased in power-motivated winners—an effect that was still evident 24 hours after the contest—whereas they decreased in power-motivated losers. Although the mechanism through which these rapid and sustained estradiol changes come about still needs to be clarified, these findings mirror the testosterone changes seen in power-motivated men as a result of social dominance contest outcomes.

Biopsychological Correlates of Implicit Affiliation Motivation

Whereas power motivation is strongly associated with sympathetic nervous system activation, which prepares the body for action, affiliation motivation is correlated with indices of parasympathetic nervous system activity, which returns the body to a state of rest and recovery (Jemmott, 1987; McClelland, 1989). Individuals high in affiliation at age 30 have lower blood pressure at age 50 compared to low-affiliation individuals (McClelland, 1979). They also show better immune system function (e.g., increases in s-IgA) during stressful situations, such as academic examinations (Jemmott et al., 1983; McClelland et al., 1985). In the absence of stressors, high-affiliation individuals show greater natural killer cell activity than individuals low in affiliation motivation (Jemmott et al., 1990), and they also respond with greater s-IgA increases to positive affiliation arousal through films (McClelland & Kirshnit, 1988). Experimental arousal of affiliation motivation also leads to increases in dopamine concentration levels in saliva and plasma (McClelland, Patel, Stier, &

Brown, 1987). As a result of its association with parasympathetic nervous system activity and immune system function, affiliation motivation may have protective and beneficial effects on health (Jemmott, 1987; McClelland, 1989; McClelland & Jemmott, 1980), particularly if it is coupled with low levels of stress or activity inhibition, indicating left-hemispheric engagement during stress (Schultheiss, Riebel, & Jones, 2009; Wittling, 1995).

Research also indicates links between implicit affiliation motivation and the steroid hormone progesterone. Women using oral contraceptives, which contain progesterone, have higher levels of affiliation motivation than men or normally cycling women (Schultheiss, Dargel, & Rohde, 2003). In addition, higher levels of affiliation motivation are preceded by greater increases of progesterone in the course of women's menstrual cycles (Schultheiss et al., 2003). Furthermore, Schultheiss and colleagues (2004) found that experimental arousal of affiliation motivation, but not power motivation, led to increases in progesterone levels in both women and men (Fig. 10.2; for related findings linking social bonding to progesterone release, see also Brown et al., 2009). Schultheiss et al. (2004) speculated that the observed changes in progesterone may reflect the ovarian action of oxytocin, a hormone implicated in attachment and affiliative behavior in both animals and humans (Insel & Young, 2001; Uvnäs-Moberg, 1998).

Following up on this research, Wirth and Schultheiss (2006) found a connection between implicit affiliation motivation and progesterone. Using film

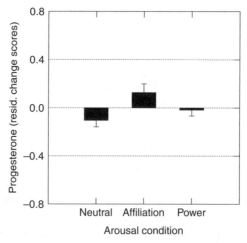

Figure 10.2 Effects of motivational arousal through 30-min movie excerpts on postmovie salivary progesterone levels, residualized for premovie progesterone. Participants who had watched an affiliation-arousing movie (*Bridges of Madison County*) had higher postmovie progesterone than participants who had watched a neutral movie (Amazon documentary) or a power-arousing movie (*The Godfather II*). Adapted with permission from Schultheiss, O. C., Wirth, M. M., & Stanton, S. J. (2004). Effects of affiliation and power motivation arousal on salivary progesterone and testosterone. *Hormones and Behavior, 46*(5), 592–599.

segments containing approach- or avoidance-oriented affiliation themes, they found that progesterone covaried positively with affiliation motivation, and baseline affiliation motivation predicted progesterone increases during avoidance-oriented affiliation arousal. Based on these findings, Wirth and Schultheiss (2006) suggested that progesterone may exert anxiolytic effects in the brain and may therefore help down-regulate "fight-or-flight" stress responses and promote "tend-and-befriend" affiliative behavior (Taylor et al., 2000). This interpretation is consistent with high-affiliation individuals' better stress resistance (McClelland, 1989) and with the observation that affiliative behavior increases during threat (Gump & Kulik, 1997; Schachter, 1959). Thus, Wirth and Schultheiss (2006) argue for a bidirectional relationship between affiliation motivation and progesterone, in which a strong affiliation motive leads to increased progesterone release, particularly during stress, and high levels of progesterone in turn facilitate affiliation motivation.

Biopsychological Correlates of Implicit Achievement Motivation

The biopsychological systems involved in achievement motivation have received considerably less attention despite the fact that intriguing clues to the existence of such a foundation emerged from the beginning of achievement motivation research. For example, Mücher and Heckhausen (1962) found that higher levels of achievement motivation correlated strongly ($r = .65$) with leg muscle tone during rest. In addition, Mueller and colleagues (Mueller & Beimann, 1969; Mueller, Kasl, Brooks, & Cobb, 1970) reported that men with high levels of uric acid, a risk factor for gout, have higher levels of hope for success, the approach component of the achievement motive, and lower levels of fear of failure, the avoidance component of the achievement motive, compared to men with normal uric acid levels. Finally, Bäumler (1975; cf. Schultheiss & Brunstein, 2005) showed that administration of a drug that increases dopaminergic transmission leads to increases in hope for success, whereas administration of a drug that decreases dopaminergic transmission leads to decreases in both hope for success and fear of failure. These findings suggest that achievement motivation is mediated in part by a neurotransmitter system whose role in various types of incentive seeking (e.g., food, sex, affiliation) has been thoroughly studied in primates and other mammals (see Panksepp, 1998). Unfortunately, the suggestive links of achievement motivation to muscle tone, uric acid concentration, and dopamine levels in the brain have not been further investigated.

The relationship between achievement motivation and urine excretion has been explored somewhat more systematically. After observing in two previous studies that high achievement motivation was associated with low-volume urine samples collected from research participants (McClelland et al., 1980, 1985; reported in McClelland, 1995), McClelland (1995) experimentally tested the notion that high levels of achievement motivation lead to low urine excretion. McClelland (1995) found that participants' baseline achievement motive scores predicted low urine sample volume after achievement arousal, but not in a neutral control condition. Moreover, in the arousal condition, achievement motivation predicted better recall for achievement-related material on a memory test, and better recall was negatively correlated with urine sample volume. McClelland (1995) attributed these effects to the release of the peptide hormone arginine vasopressin, which promotes water retention in the body and episodic memory processes in the brain (cf. Beckwith, Petros, Bergloff, & Staebler, 1987; Stricker & Verbalis, 2002). However, arginine vasopressin levels in individuals varying in achievement motivation have not yet been directly measured or manipulated, and thus the link between achievement motivation and arginine vasopressin remains to be determined.

To summarize, a large body of evidence indicates that implicit motives are closely linked to hormone release and related physiological processes. The evidence is particularly compelling for the power motive, which has been linked to stress responses, immune system function impairment, and testosterone release; moderately substantial for the affiliation motive, which is involved in enhanced immune system functioning and progesterone release; and suggestive for the achievement motive, which may be functionally related to the body's fluid retention processes and central dopamine release. The regulation of these endocrine, immunological, and physiological processes by the hypothalamus and other regions of the "emotional brain" (LeDoux, 1996) is well known. Therefore, we will next turn to the evidence linking implicit motives to brain regions critically involved in motivational processes.

Neural Processes of Implicit Motivation

Core Motivational Brain Circuit

Evidence from affective neuroscience reveals a network of core motivational brain structures dedicated to the analysis of a stimulus for emotional content and the preparation of motivated action toward or away from the stimulus (for reviews, see Cardinal, Parkinson, Hall, & Everitt, 2002; LeDoux, 1996, 2002; Panksepp, 1998; Rolls, 1999; Schultheiss & Wirth, 2008). The core motivational brain circuit (Fig. 10.3) includes the amygdala, striatum, and orbitofrontal cortex (OFC) in addition to structures with direct connections to and from these regions (e.g., hypothalamus, insula). These core motivational structures receive highly processed and integrated information through association cortices and send their output to the motor cortex for the regulation of behavior and to the hypothalamus for the regulation of autonomic responses, including the release of hormones.

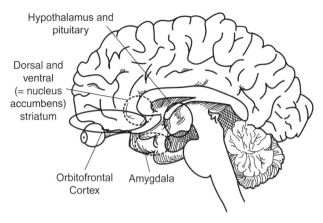

Figure 10.3. Sagittal cut of the brain at the midline, with approximate locations of key structures of the motivational brain. Closed circles represent structures fully or partly visible in a sagittal cut; dashed circles represent structures that are hidden from view in a sagittal cut. The amygdala is hidden inside the frontal pole of the temporal lobe; the striatum lies at the front of the subcortical forebrain, with its tail extending to more posterior regions. Modified from Schultheiss, O. C., & Wirth, M. M. (2008). Biopsychological aspects of motivation. In J. Heckhausen & H. Heckhausen (Eds.), *Motivation and action* (2nd ed., pp. 247–271). New York: Cambridge University Press.

A growing body of evidence indicates that activity in the core motivational brain circuit occurs largely outside of conscious awareness and guides implicit motivational responses to incentives whereas other brain areas (e.g., dorsolateral prefrontal cortex, cortical areas involved in language) are dedicated to the explicit regulation of goal-directed behavior (see Berridge, 1996; LeDoux, 1996, 2002; Rolls, 1999). LeDoux (2002) has therefore suggested that the implicit motive construct proposed by McClelland and colleagues is closely tied to activity in the core motivational brain circuit. To test this hypothesis, our laboratory conducted an fMRI study to investigate how individual differences in implicit motivation influence brain activation in the core motivational brain circuit in response to social dominance cues (Hall et al., 2007; Hall, Wirth, Waugh, Stanton, & Schultheiss, in preparation; Schultheiss et al., 2008). We focused our region of interest analyses on the amygdala, striatum, and orbitofrontal cortex.

Amygdala

The amygdala is an almond-shaped structure located deep within the medial temporal lobes of the brain in higher vertebrates. It is considered part of the limbic system and plays a primary role in the generation of emotional reactions and the memory of emotional cues. The amygdala can be considered a motivational "homing-in" device that allows individuals to adjust their physiological states and overt behavior in response to cues that predict the occurrence of unconditioned rewards and punishers (Schultheiss & Wirth, 2008). Such cues are learned through Pavlovian conditioning, a process that enables an organism to make emotional and motivational responses to previously neutral stimuli that have become associated with rewards and punishers.

The amygdala consists of two important structures, the central nucleus and basolateral nucleus, which allow it to mediate the organism's emotional and motivational responses to motivationally charged stimuli. The central nucleus influences *emotional reactions* mediated by the hypothalamus and brainstem. It sends impulses to the hypothalamus, which activates the sympathetic nervous system (e.g., skin conductance, heart rate, blood pressure, pupil dilation) and the release of stress hormones, such as cortisol. The central nucleus also connects to the brainstem, which is involved in autonomic reflexes and the release of neurotransmitters, such as norepinephrine, through which it increases arousal and vigilance. By contrast, the basolateral nucleus of the amygdala connects to the ventral striatum to influence *motivated behavior*. Animals with central nucleus lesions are still able to show motivated behavior but fail to exhibit emotional reactions to the stimulus. On the other hand, animals with basolateral nucleus lesions show impairments on motivational action, but their emotional reactions to the stimulus remain intact (Killcross, Robbins, & Everitt, 1997).

Early research on rhesus monkeys provided insights into the function of the amygdala. As early as 1888, researchers found that rhesus monkeys with lesions in the temporal cortex, including the amygdala, had considerable social and emotional deficits (Brown and Schafer, 1888). Klüver and Bucy (1939) later showed that lesions in the anterior temporal lobe produced behavioral abnormalities characterized by overreaction to objects, hypoemotionality, loss of fear, hypersexuality, and hyperorality, a condition that was later named Klüver-Bucy syndrome. Klüver and Bucy (1939, p. 984) described what they observed in one monkey: "The [. . .] monkey shows a strong tendency to approach animate and inanimate objects without hesitation. This tendency appears even in the presence of objects which previously called forth avoidance reactions, extreme excitement and other forms of emotional response." Thus, amygdala damage leads to an inability to assess the motivational value of an object from a distance ("psychic blindness" or, perhaps more aptly, emotional blindness). As a result, the monkey must get in direct contact with the object in order to assess its hedonic significance.

Recent research using functional magnetic resonance imaging (fMRI) has provided explanations concerning the function of the amygdala in humans. The amygdala appears to play a critical role in the recognition and processing of facial expressions of emotion (FEEs), particularly those involving negative emotions such as fear, anger, and sadness (Adolphs, 2002). In an early fMRI study, Whalen and colleagues (1998) found that the amygdala was activated in response to fearful faces even in the absence of explicit knowledge that the stimuli were presented. However, in animals and humans, the amygdala is also involved in motivated responses to stimuli predicting reward (Baxter & Murray, 2002).

Striatum

The striatum plays a critical role in the acquisition, execution, and invigoration of behavior that is instrumental for incentive attainment (e.g., Rolls, 1999; Schultz, Tremblay, & Hollerman, 2000). The striatum is divided into two sections: the dorsal part consisting of the caudate nucleus and putamen, and the ventral part consisting of the nucleus accumbens. While most research has focused on the role of the ventral striatum in motivation, studies conducted on both primates and humans suggest that the motivational functions of the striatum also extend to its dorsal part, particularly the caudate nucleus (Apicella, Ljungberg, Scarnati, & Schultz, 1991).

The dorsal striatum is critically involved in the acquisition of complex stimulus–response sequences, as evidenced by its involvement in implicit visuomotor learning in humans (Seger, 2006). It also supports the execution of instrumental behavior in response to incentive cues. For example, the desire to punish a cheater on an economic exchange game and the actual severity of the punishment applied are associated with neural activation in the right anterior caudate (de Quervain et al., 2004). These results suggest that the caudate is involved in the anticipated reward value of aggressive acts.

Furthermore, research indicates that the functions of the dorsal striatum are not limited to antagonistic forms of motivation. For example, the presentation of food stimuli to food-deprived participants was associated with increased activation in the caudate nucleus (Volkow et al., 2002). In addition, right anterior caudate activation can be observed in individuals in the early stages of romantic love when they see pictures of their loved one (Aron et al., 2005). Thus, the dorsal striatum seems to mediate the acquisition and execution of both appetitive and aversive forms of instrumental behavior.

On the other hand, the ventral portion of the striatum, the nucleus accumbens, is particularly involved in tagging unpredicted reward cues and invigorating instrumental behavior in response to these cues. This effect is mediated by dopamine release in the nucleus accumbens, which modulates the effects of input from the amygdala and OFC on motor output such that higher dopamine levels augment the likelihood that the incentive cue will be acted upon (Schultz, 1998). Conceptually, one can think of the nucleus accumbens as contributing a "Go and get it!" impulse to the motivational process that invigorates behavior in response to incentive cues (Berridge, 1996; Ikemoto & Panksepp, 1999).

While lesioning the nucleus accumbens or blocking dopamine transmission in the nucleus accumbens abolishes vigorous approach behavior to reward, the following processes remain intact: the capacity for motor behavior, affective responding to the reward mediated by the OFC, and conditioned emotional reactions to reward cues mediated by the amygdala (Berridge, 1996; Everitt, 1990; Ikemoto & Panksepp, 1999). These findings suggest that the greater availability of dopamine in the nucleus accumbens can be equated specifically with a stronger "magnetic pull" of incentives on instrumental behavior (Schultheiss & Wirth, 2008).

Orbitofrontal Cortex

The orbitofrontal cortex (OFC) is the ventral part of the prefrontal cortex that rests directly above the orbits of the eyes and receives projections from the amygdala and mesolimbic dopamine system. It also receives highly processed olfactory, visual, auditory, and somatosensory information from the medio-dorsal thalamus. Because of its role in emotion and reward, the OFC is often considered part of the limbic system. A considerable research literature indicates that the OFC is involved in sensory integration, the representation of the affective value of reinforcers, as well as decision making and expectation (Kringelbach, 2005). The OFC is also thought to play a specific role in regulating planning behavior associated with sensitivity to reward and punishment (Bechara, Damasio, Damasio, & Anderson, 1994). The proposed functions of the OFC are supported by corroborating evidence from research in rodents, nonhuman primates, human studies of healthy individuals, and neuropsychology studies of individuals with damage to the OFC.

Research indicates that the reward value, the expected reward value, and even the subjective pleasantness of a broad array of primary and conditioned reinforcers (e.g., food, monetary gains and losses, FEEs) are represented in the OFC (Kringelbach, 2005; Rolls, 1999, 2000). Furthermore, research indicates that different types of reinforcers are represented by anatomically distinct areas of the OFC (reviewed in Rolls, 2000, 2004). A large meta-analysis of existing fMRI studies demonstrated that activity in medial parts of the OFC is related to the monitoring, learning, and memory of the reward value of reinforcers, whereas activity in lateral parts of the OFC is related to the evaluation of punishers, which may lead to a change in ongoing behavior (Kringelbach & Rolls, 2004).

For example, O'Doherty and colleagues (2001) found that monetary punishment was associated with activation of the lateral OFC while monetary reward was associated with activation of the medial OFC. In addition, the presentation of happy faces is associated with medial OFC activation (Monk et al., 2003). On the other hand, the presentation of angry faces is associated with lateral OFC activation (Blair, Morris, Frith, Perrett, & Dolan, 1999). These findings support the assertion that the medial OFC represents the reward value of reinforcers whereas activity in the lateral OFC is related to the evaluation of punishers that require a change in ongoing behavior (Kringelbach & Rolls, 2004).

A second important feature of the OFC is that it responds to reward based on the motivational needs of the organism. For example, monkeys show strong activation in the OFC to food when hungry, but they show little OFC activation when fed to satiety. The decrease in OFC activation is directly proportional to the animals' decreasing willingness to have another bite (Rolls, Sienkiewicz, & Yaxley, 1989). In addition, the OFC is also one of the most potent sites of brain self-stimulation, which suggests that activation of the OFC is pleasurable (Rolls, 1999). However, the likelihood of OFC self-stimulation depends on the motivational state of the organism. Hungry animals show vigorous self-stimulation of OFC sites related to food reward whereas satiated animals do not (Mora, Avrith, Phillips, & Rolls, 1979).

Additional Motivational Brain Regions

While the amygdala, striatum, and OFC constitute what we have termed the core motivational brain circuit, other brain areas are also important in motivational processes. For example, the hypothalamus has bidirectional projections to the core motivational brain circuit and contributes, for instance, information about the organism's current need state. It is also important in regulating the body's autonomic and endocrine responses to incentives (Panksepp, 1998; Rolls, 1999). Some researchers have argued for motivational functions of association cortex structures, which feed information about incentives and contexts to the core motivational brain circuit (cf. Fig. 10.3). More specifically, Damasio (1994) has proposed that the insula and related associative cortices provide somatosensory information (i.e., "gut" feelings) about the affective qualities of incentives and thus inform individuals' motivated cognitions, decision making, and actions.

Core Motivational Brain Circuit: Evidence from Neuroimaging Research

Research conducted in our laboratory provides the first evidence that individual differences in implicit motivation predict activation in the motivational brain circuit we have just described (Hall et al., 2007, in preparation; Schultheiss et al., 2008). Using an fMRI design, 24 participants viewed blocks of social cues signaling high dominance (i.e., angry faces) alternating with blocks of neutral faces during an oddball-task condition (surprised faces were also shown as low-dominance cues but will not be discussed here; see Schultheiss et al., 2008, for further details). Twelve individuals high in power motivation and twelve individuals low in power motivation were selected to participate based on their power motivation scores assessed with a Picture Story Exercise (PSE; McClelland et al., 1989) during a screening session. For the presentation of the following findings, we also coded PSEs for affiliation and achievement motivation. While in the scanner, participants viewed blocks of color pictures of individuals with either an angry or neutral facial expression followed by a white fixation cross. During the oddball task, participants were instructed to indicate with a button press whether an "X" appeared on the screen instead of the fixation cross.

Our results[1] show that while implicit power motivation and implicit achievement motivation are associated with greater activation in the core motivational brain circuit (amygdala, insula, caudate, nucleus accumbens, OFC), implicit affiliation motivation is associated with activation only in the amygdala and deactivation in the insula, caudate, nucleus accumbens, and OFC. Scatterplots of the correlations between participants' motive z-scores and brain activation changes in response to angry versus neutral faces, along with the peak voxel coordinates, are shown in Figure 10.4.

As predicted, individual differences in implicit power motivation moderated brain activation in the core motivational brain circuit in response to FEEs signaling another person's anger. This pattern of activation is consistent with previous research in our laboratory indicating that angry faces are motivationally significant for power-motivated individuals (Schultheiss & Hale, 2007; Schultheiss, Pang, Torges, Wirth, & Treynor, 2005). Schultheiss and Hale (2007) have argued that angry facial expressions signal a challenge to the perceiver. For power-motivated perceivers, they represent a negative incentive and prompt behavior aimed at reasserting one's own claim to dominance. Thus, it is not surprising that power-motivated individuals show activation in areas of the brain associated with the preparation and invigoration of motivated action.

Significantly less research has been conducted on achievement motivation and FEEs as motivational incentives. Similar to power motivation, achievement motivation was also associated with greater activation in the core motivational brain circuit in response to angry versus neutral facial expressions in our study. Because the independent mastery of challenging tasks is at the core of achievement motivation and failure to deal with challenges autonomously is associated with parents' negative emotions in the socialization history of achievement-motivated individuals (e.g., Rosen & D'Andrade, 1959), we speculate that angry faces serve as a conditioned cue to which achievement-motivated individuals respond with active avoidance. That is, they have learned to escape others' anger by engaging in behavior aimed at mastering a challenge, resulting in approach-related behavior and activation in the core motivational brain circuit.

Angry facial expressions also have aversive properties for affiliation-motivated individuals, although for a different reason: They represent a threat to the affiliation-motivated individual's need to have secure and harmonious relationships with others. As several authors have pointed out (e.g., Boyatzis, 1973; Schultheiss & Hale, 2007; see also chapter 3), the affiliation motive is

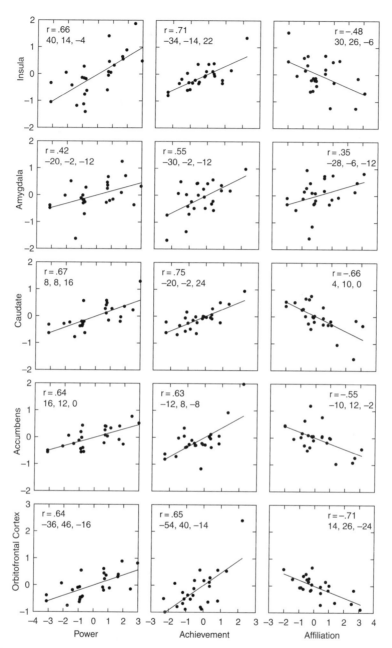

Figure 10.4. Effects of implicit motives (z-scores) on brain activation changes (peak voxels) in response to angry versus neutral faces in the insula, amygdala, caudate, nucleus accumbens, and orbitofrontal cortex. Results represent peak activation voxels from significant region-of-interest analyses. Correlation coefficients ≥ .39 are significant at p < .05; correlation coefficients ≥ .50 are significant at p < .01. The numbers given below each correlation coefficient represent x, y, and z coordinates in the brain space of the Montreal Neurological Institute. Based in part on Hall et al. (in preparation) and Schultheiss et al. (2008).

characterized by a strong fear of rejection component, which makes affiliation-motivated individuals particularly sensitive for social signals that suggest rejection. The anger face is, of course, a cardinal signal of rejection, and it is therefore not surprising that high-affiliation individuals show brain activation patterns in response to this stimulus that differ markedly from those of low-affiliation individuals. It is interesting to note, though, that while they show signs of heightened emotional sensitivity to this FEE (increased amygdala response), the behavior-generating structures of the motivational brain (caudate, accumbens) show reduced activation. This perhaps suggests that affiliation-motivated individuals react with passive avoidance to emotionally highly aversive nonverbal signals of rejection. Alternatively, affiliation-motivated individuals may be responding to angry facial expressions with increases in progesterone and oxytocin, which may have deactivating effects on brain regions involved in core motivational processes. Clearly, further research is needed to resolve this issue.

In conclusion, our findings provide support for the original idea proposed by McClelland and colleagues (1989) that implicit motives are mediated predominantly by subcortical brain structures subserving motivation. They also support LeDoux's (2002) argument for a nonconscious motivational system that drives behavior in response to incentives and operates independently from a cortical system involved in the explicit regulation of behavior.

Conclusions and Future Directions

To summarize, research on the behavioral endocrinology of motives indicates that power motivation is strongly associated with sympathetic nervous system activation whereas affiliation motivation is associated with indices of parasympathetic nervous system activity. Power motivation is associated with higher basal testosterone levels and testosterone changes during social dominance contests as a function of victory or defeat in men. Recent research suggests that estradiol in women may serve a similar role in power motivation as testosterone in men. Power motivation predicts enhanced instrumental learning in both men and women. Furthermore, stressed power motivation has been associated with cortisol increases and impaired immune system functioning. By contrast, affiliation motivation is associated with resistance to illness and better immune system functioning, which may be linked to progesterone levels. The hormonal correlates of achievement motivation have not been systematically explored so far, although tantalizing clues exist that this may present a rewarding field for future research.

Affective neuroscience research suggests that the implicit motive construct may be closely tied to activity in motivational brain structures, including the amygdala, insula, caudate, nucleus accumbens, and OFC. Neuroimaging evidence from our laboratory reveals that power-motivated and achievement-motivated individuals show increased activation in the core motivational brain circuit in response to social cues signaling dominance whereas affiliation-motivated individuals show deactivation in all of these regions with the exception of the amygdala. Thus, the biopsychological roots of implicit motives have been well documented in research examining the associations between implicit motives, hormones, and immune system functioning. In addition, these connections are starting to be confirmed and further explored with fMRI research investigating the neural substrates of implicit motives.

A systematic exploration of the brain areas and functions involved in implicit and explicit forms of motivation represents a highly overdue and in all likelihood very fruitful next step for motivation research. Studies already indicate that implicit and explicit systems involved in emotional processing and motivated action compete with and suppress each other (e.g., Ochsner, Bunge, Griss, & Gabrieli, 2002; Lieberman et al., 2007; Poldrack et al., 2001). And several theorists of the biopsychology of motivation recognize the necessity to distinguish between brain systems dedicated to conscious, goal-directed forms of action and nonconscious, automatic forms of striving for incentives (e.g., Berridge & Robinson, 2003; LeDoux, 2002; Rolls, 1999). We believe that bringing implicit motive research into the affective neuroscience arena might be mutually beneficial to both fields. Work on implicit motives, particularly on how they contrast and interact with explicit motives and goals, can inform neuroscience research on the motivational and volitional wellsprings of action. Findings from cognitive and affective neuroscience can help motivation researchers better understand how and why implicit and explicit levels of motivation can exist independently and often be in conflict with each other.

Author Notes

Parts of the research summarized in this chapter were supported by Deutsche Forschungsmeinschaft grants SCHU 1210/1_2, 1-3, and 2-2, NIMH grant 1 R03 MH63069-01, and NSF grant BCS 0444301.

Preparation of this chapter was supported by an NSF Graduate Research Fellowship awarded to Julie L. Hall.

Note

1. In contrast to the results reported in Schultheiss et al. (2008), who employed relatively rigorous significance thresholding for the presentation of their results, we used more lenient criteria for small-volume regions of interest like the nucleus accumbens and the amygdala ($p < .05$, uncorrected), for the findings we present here.

References

Adams, D. B., Gold, A. R., & Burt, A. D. (1978). Rise in female-initiated sexual activity at ovulation and its suppression by oral contraceptives. *New England Journal of Medicine, 299*(21), 1145–1150.

Adolphs, R. (2002). Recognizing emotion from facial expressions: Psychological and neurological mechanisms. *Behavioral and Cognitive Neuroscience Reviews, 1,* 21–61.

Albert, D. J., Jonik, R. H., & Walsh, M. L. (1992). Hormone-dependent aggression in male and female rats: Experiential, hormonal, and neural foundations. *Neuroscience and Biobehavioral Reviews, 16(2),* 177–192.

Alexander, G. M., Packard, M. G., & Hines, M. (1994). Testosterone has rewarding affective properties in male rats: Implications for the biological basis of sexual motivation. *Behavioral Neuroscience, 108,* 424–428.

Apicella, P., Ljungberg, T., Scarnati, E., & Schultz, W. (1991). Responses to reward in monkey dorsal and ventral striatum. *Experimental Brain Research, 85*(3), 491–500.

Aron, A., Fisher, H., Mashek, D. J., Strong, G., Li, H., & Brown, L. L. (2005). Reward, motivation, and emotion systems associated with early-stage intense romantic love. *Journal of Neurophysiology, 94*(1), 327–337.

Baxter, M. G., & Murray, E. A. (2002). The amygdala and reward. *Nature Reviews: Neuroscience, 3*(7), 563–573.

Bäumler, G. (1975). Beeinflussung der Leistungsmotivation durch Psychopharmaka: I. Die 4 bildthematischen Hauptvariablen [The effects of psychoactive drugs on achievement motivation: I. The four motivation scales]. *Zeitschrift für experimentelle und angewandte Psychologie, 22,* 1–14.

Bechara, A., Damasio, A. R., Damasio, H., & Anderson, S. W. (1994). Insensitivity to future consequences following damage to human prefrontal cortex. *Cognition, 50,* 7–15.

Beckwith, B. E., Petros, T. V., Bergloff, P. J., & Staebler, R. J. (1987). Vasopressin analogue (DDAVP) facilitates recall of narrative prose. *Behavioral Neuroscience, 101*(3), 429–432.

Bernstein, I. S., Gordon, T. P., & Rose, R. M. (1983). The interaction of hormones, behavior, and social context in nonhuman primates. In B. B. Svare (Ed.), *Hormones and aggressive behavior* (pp. 535–561). New York: Plenum.

Berridge, K. C. (1996). Food reward: Brain substrates of wanting and liking. *Neuroscience and Biobehavioral Reviews, 20,* 1–25.

Berridge, K. C., & Robinson, T. E. (2003). Parsing reward. *Trends in Neurosciences, 26*(9), 507–513.

Blair, R. J., Morris, J. S., Frith, C. D., Perrett, D. I., & Dolan, R. J. (1999). Dissociable neural responses to facial expressions of sadness and anger. *Brain, 122*(Pt. 5), 883–893.

Bless, E. P., McGinnis, K. A., Mitchell, A. L., Hartwell, A., & Mitchell, J. B. (1997). The effects of gonadal steroids on brain stimulation reward in female rats. *Behavioural Brain Research, 82*(2), 235–244.

Boyatzis, R. E. (1973). Affiliation motivation. In D. C. McClelland & R. S. Steele (Eds.), *Human motivation—A book of readings* (pp. 252–276). Morristown, NJ: General Learning Corporation.

Brown, S. L., Fredrickson, B. L., Wirth, M. M., Poulin, M. J., Meier, E. A., Heaphy, E. D., et al. (2009). Social closeness increases salivary progesterone in humans. *Hormones and Behavior, 56*, 108–111.

Brown, S., & Shafer, E. (1888). An investigation into the functions of the occipital and temporal lobes of the monkey's brain. *Philosophical Transactions of the Royal Society of London: Biological Sciences, 179*, 303–327.

Cardinal, R. N., Parkinson, J. A., Hall, J., & Everitt, B. J. (2002). Emotion and motivation: The role of the amygdala, ventral striatum, and prefrontal cortex. *Neuroscience & Biobehavioral Reviews, 26*, 321–352.

Carter, C. S. (1992). Hormonal influences on human sexual behavior. In J. B. Becker, S. M. Breedlove, & D. Crews (Eds.), *Behavioral endocrinology* (pp. 131–142). Cambridge, MA: MIT Press.

Dabbs, J. M. (1990). Salivary testosterone measurements: Reliability across hours, days, and weeks. *Physiology and Behavior, 48*, 83–86.

Dabbs, J. M., Alford, E. C., & Fielden, J. A. (1998). Trial lawyers and testosterone: Blue-collar talent in a white-collar world. *Journal of Applied Social Psychology, 28*, 84–94.

Dabbs, J. M., & Hargrove, M. F. (1997). Age, testosterone, and behavior among female prison inmates. *Psychosomatic Medicine, 59*, 477–480.

Dabbs, J. M., Hopper, C. H., & Jurkovic, G. J. (1990). Testosterone and personality among college students and military veterans. *Personality and Individual Differences, 11*, 1263–1269.

Dabbs, J. M., Ruback, R. B., Frady, R. L., Hopper, C. H., & Sgoutas, D. S. (1988). Saliva testosterone and criminal violence among women. *Personality and Individual Differences, 9*, 269–275.

Dabbs, J. M., Strong, R., & Milun, R. (1997). Exploring the mind of testosterone: A beeper study. *Journal of Research in Personality, 31*, 577–587.

Damasio, A. R. (1994). *Descartes' error: Emotion, reason, and the human brain.* London: Papermac.

de Quervain, D. J.-F., Fischbacher, U., Treyer, V., Schellhammer, M., Schnyder, U., Buck, A., et al. (2004). The neural basis of altruistic punishment. *Science, 305*(5688), 1254–1258.

Dickerson, S. S., & Kemeny, M. E. (2004). Acute stressors and cortisol responses: a theoretical integration and synthesis of laboratory research. *Psychological Bulletin, 130*(3), 355–391.

Everitt, B. J. (1990). Sexual motivation: A neural and behavioural analysis of the mechanisms underlying appetitive and copulatory responses of male rats. *Neuroscience and Biobehavioral Reviews, 14*(2), 217–232.

Fodor, E. M. (1985). The power motive, group conflict, and physiological arousal. *Journal of Personality and Social Psychology, 49*, 1408–1415.

Fontana, A. F., Rosenberg, R. L., Marcus, J. L., & Kerns, R. D. (1987). Type A behavior pattern, inhibited power motivation, and activity inhibition. *Journal of Personality and Social Psychology, 52*, 177–183.

Frye, C. A., Rhodes, M. E., Rosellini, R., & Svare, B. (2002). The nucleus accumbens as a site of action for rewarding properties of testosterone and its 5α-reduced metabolites. *Pharmacology, Biochemistry and Behavior, 74*, 119–127.

Grammer, K., Renninger, L., & Fischer, B. (2004). Disco clothing, female sexual motivation, and relationship status: Is she dressed to impress? *Journal of Sex Research, 41*(1), 66–74.

Gump, B. B., & Kulik, J. A. (1997). Stress, affiliation, and emotional contagion. *Journal of Personality and Social Psychology, 72*(2), 305–319.

Hall, J. L., Waugh, C. E., Stanton, S. J., Wirth, M. M., Reuter-Lorenz, P. A., & Schultheiss, O. C. (2007). Implicit motivation in the brain: The role of implicit power and affiliation motivation on neural responses to angry facial expressions of emotion. *Psychophysiology, 44*, S45.

Hall, J. L., Wirth, M. M., Waugh, C. E., Stanton, S. J., & Schultheiss, O. C. (in preparation). Individual differences in affiliation motivation and neural reactivity to angry facial expressions of emotion.

Haselton, M. G., Mortezaie, M., Pillsworth, E. G., Bleske-Rechek, A., & Frederick, D. A. (2007). Ovulatory shifts in human female ornamentation: Near ovulation, women dress to impress. *Hormones and Behavior, 51*, 693–699.

Hu, M., & Becker, J. B. (2003). Effects of sex and estrogen on behavioral sensitization to cocaine in rats. *Journal of Neuroscience, 23*(2), 693–699.

Ikemoto, S., & Panksepp, J. (1999). The role of nucleus accumbens dopamine in motivated behavior: A unifying interpretation with special reference to reward-seeking. *Brain Research Reviews, 31*(1), 6–41.

Insel, T. R., & Young, L. J. (2001). The neurobiology of attachment. *Nature Reviews: Neuroscience, 2*(2), 129–136.

Jemmott, J. B. (1987). Social motives and susceptibility to disease: Stalking individual differences in health risks. *Journal of Personality, 55*(2), 267–298.

Jemmott, J. B., Borysenko, J. Z., Borysenko, M., McClelland, D. C., Chapman, R., Meyer, D., et al. (1983). Academic stress, power motivation, and decrease in secretion rate of salivary secretory immunoglobulin A. *Lancet, 8339*, 1400–1402.

Jemmott, J. B., Hellman, C., McClelland, D. C., Locke, S. E., Kraus, L., Williams, R. M., et al. (1990). Motivational syndromes associated with natural killer cell activity. *Journal of Behavioral Medicine, 13*, 53–73.

Killcross, S., Robbins, T. W., & Everitt, B. J. (1997). Different types of fear-conditioned behaviour mediated by separate nuclei within amygdala. *Nature, 388*(6640), 377–380.

Kirschbaum, C., Pirke, K. M., & Hellhammer, D. H. (1993). The Trier Social Stress Test: A tool for investigating psychobiological stress responses in a laboratory setting. *Neuropsychobiology, 28*, 76–81.

Klüver, H., & Bucy, P. C. (1939). Preliminary analysis of functions of the temporal lobes in monkeys. *Archives of Neurology and Psychiatry, 42*, 979–1000.

Kringelbach, M. L. (2005). The human orbitofrontal cortex: Linking reward to hedonic experience. *Nature Reviews: Neuroscience, 6*(9), 691–702.

Kringelbach, M. L., & Rolls, E. T. (2004). The functional neuroanatomy of the human orbitofrontal cortex: Evidence from neuroimaging and neuropsychology. *Progress in Neurobiology, 72*, 341–372.

LeDoux, J. E. (1996). *The emotional brain.* New York: Simon & Schuster.

LeDoux, J. E. (2002). *The synaptic self.* New York, NY: Viking.

Lieberman, M. D., Eisenberger, N. I., Crockett, M. J., Tom, S. M., Pfeifer, J. H., & Way, B. M. (2007). Putting feelings into words: Affect labeling disrupts amygdala activity in response to affective stimuli. *Psychological Science, 18*(5), 421–428.

Mazur, A. (1985). A biosocial model of status in face-to-face primate groups. *Social Forces, 64,* 377–402.

Mazur, A., & Booth, A. (1998). Testosterone and dominance in men. *Behavioral and Brain Sciences, 21,* 353–397.

McClelland, D. C. (1979). Inhibited power motivation and high blood pressure in men. *Journal of Abnormal Psychology, 88,* 182–190.

McClelland, D. C. (1982). The need for power, sympathetic activation, and illness. *Motivation and Emotion, 6,* 31–41.

McClelland, D. C. (1987). *Human motivation.* New York: Cambridge University Press.

McClelland, D. C. (1989). Motivational factors in health and disease. *American Psychologist, 44,* 675–683.

McClelland, D. C. (1995). Achievement motivation in relation to achievement-related recall, performance, and urine flow, a marker associated with release of vasopressin. *Motivation and Emotion, 19,* 59–76.

McClelland, D. C., Alexander, C., & Marks, E. (1982). The need for power, stress, immune function, and illness among male prisoners. *Journal of Abnormal Psychology, 91,* 61–70.

McClelland, D. C., Davidson, R. J., & Saron, C. (1985). Stressed power motivation, sympathetic activation, immune function, and illness. *Advances, 2,* 42–52.

McClelland, D. C., Floor, E., Davidson, R. J., & Saron, C. (1980). Stressed power motivation, sympathetic activation, immune function, and illness. *Journal of Human Stress, 6,* 11–19.

McClelland, D. C., & Jemmott, J. B. (1980). Power motivation, stress and physical illness. *Journal of Human Stress, 6,* 6–15.

McClelland, D. C., & Kirshnit, C. (1988). The effect of motivational arousal through films on salivary immunoglobulin A. *Psychology and Health, 2,* 31–52.

McClelland, D. C., Koestner, R., & Weinberger, J. (1989). How do self-attributed and implicit motives differ? *Psychological Review, 96,* 690–702.

McClelland, D. C., Patel, V., Stier, D., & Brown, D. (1987). The relationship of affiliative arousal to dopamine release. *Motivation and Emotion, 11,* 51–66.

McClelland, D. C., Ross, G., & Patel, V. (1985). The effect of an academic examination on salivary norepinephrine and immunoglobulin levels. *Journal of Human Stress, 11,* 52–59.

Monaghan, E. P., & Glickman, S. E. (1992). Hormones and aggressive behavior. In J. B. Becker, S. M. Breedlove, & D. Crews (Eds.), *Behavioral endocrinology* (pp. 261–285). Cambridge, MA: MIT Press.

Monk, C. S., McClure, E. B., Nelson, E. E., Zarahn, E., Bilder, R. M., Leibenluft, E., et al. (2003). Adolescent immaturity in attention-related brain engagement to emotional facial expressions. *NeuroImage, 20*(1), 420–428.

Mora, F., Avrith, D. B., Phillips, A. G., & Rolls, E. T. (1979). Effects of satiety on self-stimulation of the orbitofrontal cortex in the rhesus monkey. *Neuroscience Letters, 13*(2), 141–145.

Mücher, H. P., & Heckhausen, H. (1962). Influence of mental activity and achievement motivation on skeletal muscle tonus. *Perceptual and Motor Skills, 14,* 217–218.

Mueller, E. F., & Beimann, M. (1969). Die Beziehung der Harnsäure zu Testwerten der nach Heckhausen gemessenen Leistungsmotivation [Relationship between uric acid and Heckhausen's measure of achievement motivation]. *Zeitschrift für Experimentelle und Angewandte Psychologie, 16(2),* 295–306.

Mueller, E. F., Kasl, S. V., Brooks, G. W., & Cobb, S. (1970). Psychosocial correlates of serum urate levels. *Psychological Bulletin, 73*(4), 238–257.

Ochsner, K. N., Bunge, S. A., Gross, J. J., & Gabrieli, J. D. (2002). Rethinking feelings: An FMRI study of the cognitive regulation of emotion. *Journal of Cognitive Neuroscience, 14*(8), 1215–1229.

O'Doherty, J., Kringelbach, M. L., Rolls, E. T., Hornak, J., & Andrews, C. (2001). Abstract reward and punishment representations in the human orbitofrontal cortex. *Nature Neuroscience, 4*(1), 95–102.

Oyegbile, T. O., & Marler, C. A. (2005). Winning fights elevates testosterone levels in California mice and enhances future ability to win fights. *Hormones and Behavior, 48*(3), 259–267.

Packard, M. G., Schroeder, J. P., & Alexander, G. M. (1998). Expression of testosterone conditioned place preference is blocked by peripheral or intra-accumbens injection of alpha-flupenthixol. *Hormones and Behavior, 34*(1), 39–47.

Panksepp, J. (1998). *Affective neuroscience: The foundations of human and animal emotions.* New York: Oxford University Press.

Poldrack, R. A., Clark, J., Pare-Blagoev, E. J., Shohamy, D., Creso Moyano, J., Myers, C., et al. (2001). Interactive memory systems in the human brain. *Nature, 414*(6863), 546–550.

Pope, H. G., & Katz, D. L. (1994). Psychiatric and medical effects of anabolic-androgenic steroid use. *Archives of General Psychiatry, 51,* 375–382.

Purifoy, F. E., & Koopmans, L. H. (1979). Androstenione, testosterone, and free testosterone concentration in women of various occupations. *Social Biology, 26,* 179–188.

Rabkin, J. G., Wagner, G., & Rabkin, R. (1996). Testosterone replacement therapy in HIV illness. *General Hospital Psychiatry, 17,* 37–42.

Rolls, E. T. (1999). *The brain and emotion.* Oxford, UK: Oxford University Press.

Rolls, E. T. (2000). The orbitofrontal cortex and reward. *Cerebral Cortex, 10*(3), 284–294.

Rolls, E. T. (2004). The functions of the orbitofrontal cortex. *Brain and Cognition, 55*(1), 11–29.

Rolls, E. T., Sienkiewicz, Z. J., & Yaxley, S. (1989). Hunger modulates the responses to gustatory stimuli of single neurons in the caudolateral orbitofrontal cortex of the macaque monkey. *European Journal of Neuroscience, 1*(1), 53–60.

Rosen, B. C., & D'Andrade, R. (1959). The psychological origins of the achievement motive. *Sociometry, 22*, 185–218.

Rothschild, A. J. (2003). The hypothalamic-pituitary-adrenal axis and psychiatric illness. In O. M. Wolkowitz & A. J. Rothschild (Eds.), *Psychoneuroendocrinology: The scientific basis of clinical practice* (pp. 139–163). Arlington, VA: American Psychiatric Publishing, Inc.

Russo, S. J., Festa, E. D., Fabian, S. J., Gazi, F. M., Kraish, M., Jenab, S., et al. (2003). Gonadal hormones differentially modulate cocaine-induced conditioned place preference in male and female rats. *Neuroscience, 120*(2), 523–533.

Sapolsky, R. M. (1987). Stress, social status, and reproductive physiology in free-living baboons. In D. Crews (Ed.), *Psychobiology and reproductive behavior: An evolutionary perspective* (pp. 291–322). Englewood Cliffs, NJ: Prentice-Hall.

Sapolsky, R. M. (2002). Endocrinology of the stress-response. In J. B. Becker, S. M. Breedlove, & D. Crews (Eds.), *Behavioral endocrinology* (2nd ed., pp. 409–450). Cambridge, MA: MIT Press.

Schachter, S. (1959). *The psychology of affiliation.* Stanford, CA: Stanford University Press.

Schroeder, J. P., & Packard, M. G. (2000). Role of dopamine receptor subtypes in the acquisition of a testosterone conditioned place preference in rats. *Neuroscience Letters, 282*(1–2), 17–20.

Schultheiss, O. C. (2007). A biobehavioral model of implicit power motivation arousal, reward and frustration. In E. Harmon-Jones & P. Winkielman (Eds.), *Social neuroscience: Integrating biological and psychological explanations of social behavior* (pp. 176–196). New York: Guilford.

Schultheiss, O. C., & Brunstein, J. C. (2005). An implicit motive perspective on competence. In A. J. Elliot & C. Dweck (Eds.), *Handbook of competence and motivation* (pp. 31–51). New York: Guilford.

Schultheiss, O. C., Campbell, K. L., & McClelland, D. C. (1999). Implicit power motivation moderates men's testosterone responses to imagined and real dominance success. *Hormones and Behavior, 36*(3), 234–241.

Schultheiss, O. C., Dargel, A., & Rohde, W. (2003). Implicit motives and gonadal steroid hormones: Effects of menstrual cycle phase, oral contraceptive use, and relationship status. *Hormones and Behavior, 43*, 293–301.

Schultheiss, O. C., & Hale, J. A. (2007). Implicit motives modulate attentional orienting to perceived facial expressions of emotion. *Motivation and Emotion, 31*(1), 13–24.

Schultheiss, O. C., Pang, J. S., Torges, C. M., Wirth, M. M., & Treynor, W. (2005). Perceived facial expressions of emotions as motivational incentives: Evidence from a differential implicit learning paradigm. *Emotion, 5*, 41–54.

Schultheiss, O. C., Riebel, K., & Jones, N. M. (2009). Activity inhibition: A predictor of lateralized brain function during stress? *Neuropsychology, 23*, 392–404.

Schultheiss, O. C., & Rohde, W. (2002). Implicit power motivation predicts men's testosterone changes and implicit learning in a contest situation. *Hormones and Behavior, 41*, 195–202.

Schultheiss, O. C., & Wirth, M. M. (2008). Biopsychological aspects of motivation. In J. Heckhausen & H. Heckhausen (Eds.), *Motivation and action* (2nd ed., pp. 247–271). New York: Cambridge University Press.

Schultheiss, O. C., Wirth, M. M., & Stanton, S. J. (2004). Effects of affiliation and power motivation arousal on salivary progesterone and testosterone. *Hormones and Behavior, 46*(5), 592–599.

Schultheiss, O. C., Wirth, M. M., Torges, C. M., Pang, J. S., Villacorta, M. A., & Welsh, K. M. (2005). Effects of implicit power motivation on men's and women's implicit learning and testosterone changes after social victory or defeat. *Journal of Personality and Social Psychology, 88*(1), 174–188.

Schultheiss, O. C., Wirth, M. M., Waugh, C. E., Stanton, S. J., Meier, E., & Reuter-Lorenz, P. (2008). Exploring the motivational brain: Effects of implicit power motivation on brain activation in response to facial expressions of emotion. *Social Cognitive and Affective Neuroscience, 3*, 333–343.

Schultz, W. (1998). Predictive reward signal of dopamine neurons. *Journal of Neurophysiology, 80*(1), 1–27.

Schultz, W., Tremblay, L., & Hollerman, J. R. (2000). Reward processing in primate orbitofrontal cortex and basal ganglia. *Cerebral Cortex, 10*(3), 272–284.

Seger, C. A. (2006). The basal ganglia in human learning. *Neuroscientist, 12*(4), 285–290.

Sherwin, B. B. (1988). A comparative analysis of the role of androgen in human male and female sexual behavior: Behavioral specificity, critical thresholds, and sensitivity. *Psychobiology, 16*, 416–425.

Stanton, S. J., & Schultheiss, O. C. (2007). Basal and dynamic relationships between implicit power motivation and estradiol in women. *Hormones and Behavior, 52*(5), 571–580.

Steele, R. S. (1973). *The physiological concomitants of psychogenic motive arousal in college males.* Unpublished dissertation thesis, Harvard University, Boston, MA.

Stricker, E. M., & Verbalis, J. G. (2002). Hormones and ingestive behaviors. In J. B. Becker, S. M. Breedlove, & D. Crews (Eds.), *Behavioral endocrinology* (2nd ed., pp. 451–473). Cambridge, MA: MIT Press.

Taylor, S. E., Klein, L. C., Lewis, B. P., Gruenewald, T. L., Gurung, R. A., & Updegraff, J. A. (2000). Biobehavioral responses to stress in females: Tend-and-befriend, not fight-or-flight. *Psychological Review, 107*(3), 411–429.

Tsai, L. W., & Sapolsky, R. M. (1996). Rapid stimulatory effects of testosterone upon myotubule metabolism and sugar transport, as assessed by silicon microphysiometry. *Aggressive Behavior, 22*, 357–364.

Udry, J. R., & Morris, N. M. (1968). Distribution of coitus in the menstrual cycle. *Nature, 220*(167), 593–596.

Uvnäs-Moberg, K. (1998). Oxytocin may mediate the benefits of positive social interaction and emotions. *Psychoneuroendocrinology, 23*(8), 819–835.

van Honk, J., Tuiten, A., Hermans, E., Putman, P., Koppeschaar, H., Thijssen, J., et al. (2001). A single administration of testosterone induces cardiac accelerative responses to angry faces in healthy young women. *Behavioral Neuroscience, 115*(1), 238–242.

van Honk, J., Tuiten, A., Verbaten, R., van den Hout, M., Koppeschaar, H., Thijssen, J., et al. (1999). Correlations among salivary testosterone, mood, and selective attention to threat in humans. *Hormones and Behavior, 36*(1), 17–24.

Volkow, N. D., Wang, G. J., Fowler, J. S., Logan, J., Jayne, M., Franceschi, D., et al. (2002). "Nonhedonic" food motivation in humans involves dopamine in the dorsal striatum and methylphenidate amplifies this effect. *Synapse, 44*(3), 175–180.

Whalen, P. J., Rauch, S. L., Etcoff, N. L., McInerney, S. C., Lee, M. B., & Jenike, M. A. (1998). Masked presentations of emotional facial expressions modulate amygdala activity without explicit knowledge. *Journal of Neuroscience, 18*(1), 411–418.

Wirth, M. M., & Schultheiss, O. C. (2006). Effects of affiliation arousal (hope of closeness) and affiliation stress (fear of rejection) on progesterone and cortisol. *Hormones and Behavior, 50*, 786–795.

Wirth, M. M., Welsh, K. M., & Schultheiss, O. C. (2006). Salivary cortisol changes in humans after winning or losing a dominance contest depend on implicit power motivation. *Hormones and Behavior, 49*(3), 346–352.

Wittling, W. (1995). Brain asymmetry in the control of autonomic-physiologic activity. In R. J. Davidson & K. Hugdahl (Eds.), *Brain asymmetry* (pp. 305–357). Cambridge, MA: MIT Press.

Wood, R. I., Johnson, L. R., Chu, L., Schad, C., & Self, D. W. (2004). Testosterone reinforcement: Intravenous and intracerebroventricular self-administration in male rats and hamsters. *Psychopharmacology (Berlin), 171*(3), 298–305.

Chapter 11
Factors That Influence the Relation Between Implicit and Explicit Motives: A General Implicit–Explicit Congruence Framework

TODD M. THRASH, SCOTT E. CASSIDY[1], LAURA A. MARUSKIN
College of William and Mary

ANDREW J. ELLIOT
University of Rochester

Issues of discrepancy and conflict between unconscious and conscious motives are among the oldest topics in psychology (Whyte, 1978) but have only recently become the subject of rigorous empirical investigation. In contemporary research, a motive, whether "unconscious" (implicit) or "conscious" (explicit), refers to a predisposition to approach a particular class of incentives, such as achievement, affiliation, or power, or to avoid a particular class of threats, such as failure, rejection, or domination by others. According to most theorists, *implicit motives* develop early in life through preverbal, affect-based associative learning, respond to task-based or experiential incentives, predict spontaneous behavior trends, and are introspectively inaccessible. *Explicit motives*, in contrast, develop later through verbally mediated learning, are responsive to social-extrinsic or verbal-symbolic incentives, predict deliberate choices, and are accessible in the form of consciously articulated values (McClelland, Koestner, & Weinberger, 1989; McClelland & Pilon, 1983; Schultheiss, 2001a; Thrash & Elliot, 2002). Because individuals are presumed not to know the level of their implicit motives, these motives are assessed indirectly, most often using a Picture Story Exercise (PSE). In this method, participants view a series of pictures and write the stories that spontaneously come to mind. The level of a given implicit motive is coded based on the thematic content of the stories. Explicit motives, because they are consciously accessible, are assessed with self-report questionnaires.

It is well-established that implicit and explicit motives representing the same content domain (e.g., achievement) tend to be uncorrelated or weakly positively correlated across individuals (McClelland et al., 1989; Thrash & Elliot, 2002). For instance, Spangler's (1992) meta-analysis showed that the correlation between implicit and explicit need for achievement (nAch) was $r = .09$, a significant but weak effect. To illustrate the implications of this finding, we have generated data representing 26 hypothetical individuals, such that the implicit–explicit correlation is $r = .09$, and we have plotted these data in Figure 11.1a. The weak correlation reflects the fact that the data points are scattered and are not summarized well by a straight line. Accordingly, individuals differ markedly in the extent to which they exhibit *motive congruence*—that is, consistency in the levels of an implicit motive and the corresponding explicit motive. As illustrated in Figure 11.1b, which shows the same data points as Figure 11.1a, individuals who are relatively congruent are those whose standing on one motive is similar to their standing on the other (after standardization of scores); these individuals fall near the diagonal from the lower left corner to the upper right corner (open circles). Conversely, individuals who are relatively incongruent are those whose standing on one motive is dissimilar to their standing on the other; these individuals fall near the upper left corner or lower right corner (closed circles).

Motive incongruence is generally considered to be an undesirable condition. An individual with a strong explicit nAch and a weak implicit nAch may consciously desire achievement and yet may lack a spontaneous inclination to work hard. Conversely, an individual with a strong implicit nAch and a weak explicit nAch may have a spontaneous inclination to achieve and yet may fail to proactively organize his or her life pursuits in a way that makes effective use of this source of motivation. In light of these portraits of incongruent individuals, it is not surprising that incongruence has been found to lead to a variety of negative outcomes, including decrements in emotional well-being and life satisfaction

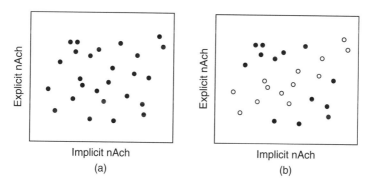

Figure 11.1 Chart (a) illustrates a correlation of r = .09 between implicit need for achievement (nAch) and explicit nAch. The same data are plotted in (b), which distinguishes relatively congruent individuals (open circles) from relatively incongruent individuals (closed circles).

(Baumann, Kaschel, & Kuhl, 2005; Kehr, 2004a; for related research on motive-goal congruence, see Brunstein, Schultheiss, & Grässmann, 1998; Hofer & Chasiotis, 2003). Well-being and other consequences of incongruence are discussed in greater detail in Chapter 12 of this volume. In the present chapter, we review the empirical literature on factors that have been posited to predict or influence motive congruence. In addition, we provide a conceptual framework that may organize past research and guide future research, and we identify new directions for the conceptualization of congruence and for integration with other research literatures.

Empirical Research on Motive Congruence

As an organizational framework, Thrash and Elliot (2002) identified three classes of factors that may influence motive congruence: (a) motive characteristics (e.g., domain or valence), (b) methodological factors, and (c) substantive moderating variables. The first set of factors has not yet been examined systematically, but researchers have begun to investigate the latter two sets of factors. In the following, we provide an overview of this empirical literature.

Methodological Factors

Thrash, Elliot, and Schultheiss (2007) argued that the correlation between implicit and explicit nAch may have been underestimated in past research (as noted, $r = .09$) because implicit and explicit measures had not been designed to correspond directly in content (cf. Ajzen & Fishbein, 1977). Consistent with this argument, Thrash et al. found that three existing measures of explicit nAch were unrelated to implicit nAch, as assessed using Schultheiss's (2001b) translation of Heckhausen's (1963) coding system for hope for success (r ranged from .00 to .02). In contrast, a new measure of explicit nAch (Schultheiss & Murray, 2002), with item content that directly corresponds to the categories of Heckhausen's coding system, was found to be significantly related to implicit nAch ($r = .17$, $p < .05$). This study establishes correspondence of content as a methodological factor that influences implicit–explicit correlations. Moreover, it indicates that implicit and explicit motives may not be as independent as previous research has suggested.

Substantive Moderating Variables

The correlation between an implicit motive and the corresponding explicit motive does not fully characterize the relationship between them. A correlation coefficient reveals the extent to which one motive varies linearly as a function

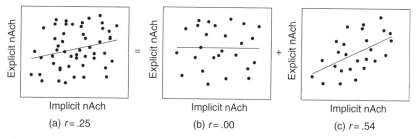

Figure 11.2 Chart (a) illustrates a correlation of r = .25. The sample in (a) is decomposed into subsamples for which r = .00 (b) and r = .54 (c). The plotted lines are the best-fitting lines based on least-squares regression.

of the other, but it does not provide information about nonlinear effects, including quadratic (curvilinear) effects and moderated effects (interactions). Moderation exists when the implicit–explicit relationship varies systematically as a function of a third variable, called a *moderator*.

To make the concept of moderation concrete, imagine that the true correlation between implicit and explicit nAch, once all possible methodological and measurement problems are eliminated, is $r = .25$. This scenario is illustrated in Figure 11.2a with data from a hypothetical sample of 52 individuals. One might take the relatively weak correlation as evidence that implicit and explicit motivational systems are largely independent, such that efficacious integrative mechanisms do not exist or are not operative. However, consider the possibility that this correlation is the net result of combining two or more distinct groups—across which the implicit–explicit correlation differs—into one sample. A correlation of r = .25 could arise, for instance, from combining one group ($N = 26$) in which the correlation is $r = .00$ (as plotted in Figure 11.2b) and a second group ($N = 26$) in which the correlation is $r = .54$ (as plotted in Figure 11.2c). Thus, it is possible that efficacious integrative mechanisms exist but are only operative among certain segments of the population. In contrast to the independence perspective (e.g., McClelland, 1987), this perspective motivates a search for moderating variables that discriminate such segments of the population.[2] Substantively important moderating variables have been the subject of several recent investigations, as summarized in Table 11.1. We begin by reviewing studies of implicit and explicit motives, and we then turn to studies of related constructs (e.g., explicit goals rather than explicit motives).

Thrash and Elliot (2002) examined the moderating role of *self-determination*, which refers to self-regulation based on one's core interests and values (Deci & Ryan, 2002). Thrash and Elliot argued that self-determination may reflect, at least in part, the development of explicit values that are well aligned with one's more deeply grounded implicit motivational tendencies. As predicted, trait self-determination interacted with implicit nAch in the prediction of explicit nAch, such that implicit nAch was a robust predictor of

Table 11.1 Summary of Studies of Predictors of Implicit–Explicit Motive Congruence

Study	Implicit Construct	Explicit Construct	Predictor Variable	Relation to Congruence
Studies That Examined Methodological Factors				
Thrash, Cassidy, Maruskin, & Elliot (2008)[a]	nAch	nAch	Reliability of measurement	+
Thrash, Elliot, & Schultheiss (2007)	nAch	nAch	Correspondence of content	+
Studies That Examined Substantive Moderating Variables				
Baumann, Kaschel, & Kuhl (2005)	nAch	nAch, achievement goal variables	State orientation × stress	−
Brunstein (2001)	Agency, communion	Agency, communion	State orientation	−
Hofer, Busch, Bond, Kärtner, Kiessling, & Law (in press)	nAch	Importance of Achievement goals	self-determination	+
Hofer, Busch, Chasiotis, & Kiessling (2006)	nAff	nAff	Identity achievement	+
	nAff	nAff	Identity foreclosure	−
	nAff	nAff	Identity diffusion	*ns*
	nAff	nAff	Identity moratorium	*ns*

Table 11.1 (Continued)

Study	Implicit Construct	Explicit Construct	Predictor Variable	Relation to Congruence
Kehr (2004)	MMG nAch, nAff, nPow	nAch, nAff, nPow	Volitional strength	+
Schultheiss & Brunstein (1999)	nPow	Goal commitment	Use of goal imagery	+
	nAff	Goal commitment	Use of goal imagery	+
Thrash & Elliot (2002)	nAch	nAch	Self-determination	+
	FF	FF	Self-determination	ns
Thrash, Elliot, & Schultheiss (2007)	nAch	nAch	Private body consciousness	+
	nAch	nAch	Self-monitoring	−
	nAch	nAch	Preference for consistency	+

Note: ns = not significant; MMG = Multi-Motive Grid; nAch = need for achievement; nAff = need for affiliation; FF = fear of failure; nPow = need for power. This table excludes well-being correlates of congruence. All implicit constructs were assessed by PSE except where noted. All explicit constructs were assessed by self-report.
[a] Thrash, Cassidy, Maruskin, & Elliot (2009) is the present chapter. The Thrash et al. (2009) finding is reported below.

313

explicit nAch among individuals high in self-determination ($r = .40, p < .01$) but failed to predict explicit nAch among individuals low in self-determination ($r = -.07$, ns). Extending these findings, Hofer et al. (in press) reported that self-determination moderated congruence in culturally diverse samples from Germany, Cameroon, and Hong Kong.

Thrash et al. (2007) examined three additional candidate moderators, again in the achievement domain: private body consciousness, self-monitoring, and preference for consistency. *Private body consciousness* refers to a sensitivity to internal bodily processes (Miller, Murphy, & Buss, 1981). Thrash et al. argued that individuals higher in private body consciousness may be more congruent because implicit motive arousal is embodied and may be perceptible via interoception (bodily feedback). *Self-monitoring* refers to a tendency to monitor the social environment and adjust one's behavior or attitudes accordingly (Snyder & Gangestad, 1986). Self-monitoring was posited to impede congruence because values internalized from the social environment are less likely to correspond to one's implicit motives than are internally generated values. *Preference for consistency*, finally, refers to a tendency to seek consistency among cognitions (Cialdini, Trost, & Newsom, 1995). Preference for consistency was expected to predict greater congruence because individuals higher in this trait would be more motivated to reconcile discrepancies between an explicit motive and any rudimentary knowledge of the corresponding implicit motive. Results showed that, as expected, all three traits functioned as moderators, such that implicit and explicit nAch were correlated among individuals high (but not low) in private body consciousness and preference for consistency, and low (but not high) in self-monitoring. Moreover, each trait had a unique moderating effect, suggesting that multiple, distinct processes are responsible for motive congruence. These findings are consistent with the self-determination findings reported above. Indeed, self-access, resistance to heteronomous influences, and personality integration—which parallel the three moderators examined by Thrash et al. (2007)—are all core aspects of what it means to be self-determined (Deci & Ryan, 1985).

Hofer, Busch, Chasiotis, and Kiessling (2006) linked congruence between implicit and explicit need for affiliation (nAff) to identity development (Marcia, 1966). Individuals higher in the status of *identity achievement*, who have committed themselves to an identity following a period of exploration or crisis, were found to be more congruent. In addition, individuals higher in the status of *foreclosure*, who have committed themselves to an identity internalized from the social environment, without having undergone a period of exploration or crisis, were found to be less congruent. These findings are similar in theme to the self-determination and self-monitoring findings reported above, suggesting that the portrait of the congruent individual is similar across the achievement and affiliation domains.

In related research, Kehr (2004a) investigated congruence between motives as assessed by the Multi-Motive Grid (MMG; Sokolowski, Schmalt, Langens, &

Puca, 2000) and explicit self-report. The MMG is a semiprojective measure that shares features with both implicit and explicit measures. A composite index of incongruence based on three motive domains—achievement, affiliation, and power—was negatively related to concurrent and subsequent volitional strength. These findings are consistent with Kehr's (2004b) compensatory model, which holds that volitional resources must be recruited to overcome conflicts caused by motive incongruence.

In research on congruence between implicit motives and explicit goals, Schultheiss and Brunstein (1999) found that implicit motives predicted commitment to assigned goals only when participants were first given the opportunity to use imagery to envision goal pursuit and attainment. These theorists argued that the use of imagery allows individuals to represent their goals in a perception-like modality that makes contact with the experientially based implicit motivational system; imagery thus provides a bridge between implicit motives and explicit goals. Because explicit goals are closely associated with explicit motives, this research suggests that imagery may also play a role in the promotion of motive congruence.

Brunstein (2001) linked motive–goal congruence to action orientation (versus state orientation), which refers to an ability to generate positive affect or reduce negative affect in the face of demands or stressors. A match in content between implicit motives and personal goals was related to greater goal commitment among individuals who were more action oriented. More recently, Baumann et al. (2005) proposed that state orientation represents a vulnerability factor, rather than a direct cause, of incongruence. These researchers reported that state orientation interacted with stress to predict incongruence between implicit and explicit nAch and between implicit nAch and personal goals, such that state orientation predicted incongruence under conditions of high but not low stress.

These studies of moderating factors provide additional evidence, beyond that of the methodological study described above, that implicit and explicit motives are not statistically independent. The fact that a variety of theoretically meaningful moderator variables has been documented indicates that the correlations between implicit and explicit motives are not weak because there is little systematic relationship between them. Instead, they are weak because implicit and explicit motives tend to be related only among certain segments of the population or under certain conditions.

A General Implicit–Explicit Congruence Framework

Above, we drew on Thrash and Elliot's (2002) organizational framework, in which three classes of influences on motive congruence were identified: motive characteristics, methodological factors, and substantive moderator variables. We now present a more detailed organizational framework, shown in Figure 11.3, with the aims of facilitating organization of the growing literature on motive congruence, identifying gaps in extant theory and research, and facilitating integration with related literatures. We focus on implications of the framework for ways in which methodological factors and substantive moderating variables may influence implicit–explicit correlations for a given motive pair (e.g., implicit and explicit nAch). However, the framework is also useful for theorizing about ways in which motive characteristics influence congruence because one or more of the processes identified in our framework may be posited to differ depending on the type of motive (e.g., a given pathway may be present for implicit and explicit nAch but absent for implicit and explicit fear of failure [FF]). The framework itself is not intended to represent a particular theoretical perspective. Instead, it is based on a general structural equation model (SEM) and provides a "shell" that

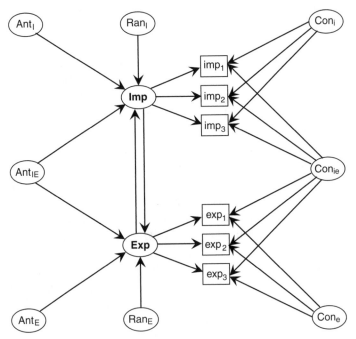

Figure 11.3 A general implicit–explicit congruence framework. Imp = implicit motive; Exp = explicit motive; Ant_{IE} = common antecedent of the implicit and explicit motives; Ant_I = antecedent of the implicit motive but not the explicit motive; Ant_E = antecedent of the explicit motive but not the implicit motive; Ran_I = random error influencing the implicit motive; Ran_E = random error influencing the explicit motive; imp_1–imp_3 = observed indicators of the implicit motive; exp_1–exp_3 = observed indicators of the explicit motive; Con_{ie} = confound common to the indicators of the implicit and explicit motives; Con_i = confound present in the indicators of the implicit motive but not the indicators of the explicit motive; Con_e = confound present in the indicators of the explicit motive but not the indicators of the implicit motive.

may be infused with content from a variety of theoretical perspectives. The fact that we draw on SEM does not imply that SEM must be used to analyze motive congruence data; regardless, SEM provides a useful heuristic for understanding the various routes through which a correlation between two variables may come about.

The premise of our framework is that the correlation between a given measure of an implicit motive and a given measure of the corresponding explicit motive may be decomposed into several distinct sources of covariance; accordingly, the issue of moderating factors may be explicated most precisely if moderators are conceptualized or modeled as influencing particular sources of covariance. In the following, we identify the various elements of the model in Figure 11.3. Imp and Exp refer to latent (unmeasured) variables representing a given implicit motive (e.g., implicit nAch) and the corresponding explicit motive (e.g., explicit nAch), respectively; these latent variables may be viewed as representing the abstract, hypothetical constructs that are the subject of motivational theories.[3] The paths between Imp and Exp represent possible bidirectional influences of the implicit and explicit motives on one another. The two motives may have common antecedents, as represented by Ant_{IE}, and unique antecedents, as represented by Ant_I and Ant_E. Imp and Exp are also influenced by a variety of unidentifiable influences that comprise random error terms, Ran_I and Ran_E. Individuals' levels of each motive are posited to be reflected in scores on one or more observed (measured) variables or indicators, which are represented by imp_1, imp_2, imp_3, exp_1, exp_2, and exp_3. Imp and Exp are not the only influences on the observed variables. The observed indicators of Imp and Exp may be influenced by confounds (systematic error) common to both implicit and explicit measures, as represented by Con_{ie}, and by confounds unique to implicit or explicit measures, as represented by Con_i and Con_e. Each observed variable is also influenced by a uniqueness (not shown), which includes random measurement error and systematic error that is specific to that indicator. Whereas Imp and Exp refer to specific constructs, Ant_{IE}, Ant_I, Ant_E, Con_{ie}, Con_i, and Con_e are intended to stand in for potentially large numbers of identifiable influences.

The correlation between a given indicator of Imp and a given indicator of Exp is potentially multiply determined. The observed correlation is a function of a number of pathways or sources of covariance (Kline, 2005), the most important of which are listed in Table 11.2. Table 11.2 also decomposes each pathway into separate structural and measurement components. Structural components concern relations among latent variables, whereas measurement components concern relations between latent and observed variables (Anderson & Gerbing, 1988). We use the distinction between structural and measurement components as the foundation for distinguishing substantive and methodological considerations. The structural components identified in the first three rows of Table 11.2 represent three distinct sources of covariation between underlying implicit and explicit motive constructs. Implicit and

Table 11.2 Primary Pathways Linking Observed Indicators of Implicit and Explicit Motives

Full Pathway	Structural Component	Measurement Component
observed imp ← latent Imp → latent Exp → observed exp	latent Imp → latent Exp	latent Imp → observed imp, latent Exp → observed exp
observed exp ← latent Exp → latent Imp → observed imp	latent Exp → latent Imp	latent Imp → observed imp, latent Exp → observed exp
observed exp ← latent Exp ← latent Ant$_{IE}$ → latent Imp → observed imp	latent Exp ← latent Ant$_{IE}$ → latent Imp	latent Imp → observed imp, latent Exp → observed exp
observed imp ← latent Con$_{Ie}$ → observed exp	N/A	observed imp ← latent Con$_{Ie}$ → observed exp

Note: Imp = implicit motive; Exp = explicit motive; imp = observed indicator of the implicit motive; exp = observed indicator of the explicit motive; Ant$_{IE}$ = common antecedent of the implicit and explicit motives; Con$_{Ie}$ = confound common to the indicators of the implicit and explicit motives.

explicit motive constructs may be related because (a) the implicit motive influences the explicit motive, (b) the explicit motive influences the implicit motive, or (c) a common antecedent influences the implicit and explicit motives. We recommend that substantive hypotheses target one or more of these sources of covariance. For instance, one may posit the existence of one of these effects (e.g., the implicit motive influences the explicit motive); one may posit the presence of mediating processes (e.g., the implicit motive influences process M, which in turn influences the explicit motive); and one may posit that the magnitude or direction of a given effect differs as a function of one or more moderator variables (e.g., the implicit motive influences the explicit motive within developmental context X but not Y). In contrast, the measurement model, which links latent variables to observed variables, provides a context for positing a diverse set of influences that are generally regarded as methodological rather than substantive.

It is important not to confuse the issues of whether implicit and explicit *variables* are related and whether particular *individuals* are congruent. Some individuals would be expected to have similar levels of implicit and explicit motives even if no factors operate to produce a correlation between these variables across individuals. Specifically, unique antecedents (Ant_I and Ant_E) and unique random factors (Ran_I and Ran_E) would be expected to produce similar levels of implicit and explicit motives in some individuals (e.g., those near the diagonal running from the lower left corner to the upper right corner in Figure 11.2b) and dissimilar levels in others (those in the upper left corner or lower right corner). Thus, although effects of Ant_I, Ant_E, Ran_I, and Ran_E are not among the sources of covariance that may produce an implicit–explicit correlation, they may nevertheless result in implicit–explicit congruence within particular individuals.

The Addition of Content to the General Framework

We now begin the task of adding content to the general framework outlined above. We turn first to methodological considerations and then discuss the three substantive sources of covariance between underlying implicit and explicit latent constructs.

Methodological Influences

There are a variety of ways in which methodological factors may influence the association between observed implicit and explicit motive variables. We discuss three such factors. First is the issue of convergent and discriminant validity of the observed variables. Do multiple measures of a given motive (e.g., imp_1, imp_2, and imp$_3$) converge as indicators of the same factor (Imp), and are the implicit and explicit factors (Imp and Exp) distinct? Are more than two factors necessary to account for the relations among measures? Unfortunately, these issues, particularly the issue of convergent validity of alternative indicators of a given implicit motive, have rarely been investigated. It is unclear, for instance, whether PSE (e.g., Smith, 1992) and IAT (Implicit Association Test; Brunstein & Schmitt, 2004) measures of implicit nAch are related and would cohere in a factor analysis. In a study in which power-versus-intimacy motives were assessed by PSE, IAT, and questionnaire, the measures that converged most strongly were the PSE and questionnaire measures (Sheldon, King, Houser-Marko, Osbaldiston, & Gunz, 2007), a finding that is inconsistent with an implicit–explicit factor structure (see also King, 1995). Moreover, the PSE methodology alone may yield multiple implicit motive factors depending on which pictures are used and whether specific content categories are modeled as separate indicators.[4] Future multimethod, factor analytic research is likely to yield new insights into the structure of motives and may lead to the conclusion that the implicit–explicit distinction is inadequate or not sufficiently differentiated. Issues of convergent and discriminant validity have direct implications for conclusions about motive congruence. If, for instance, multiple implicit nAch constructs exist, then conclusions about the correlation between implicit and explicit nAch may differ depending which implicit nAch is operationalized in a given study.

Second, to the extent that observed variables are confounded with extraneous sources of systematic variance, observed implicit–explicit correlations are subject to positive or negative bias. Podsakoff, MacKenzie, Lee, and Podsakoff (2003) reviewed the literature on sources of method variance and offered recommendations for avoiding and removing them. As depicted by Con$_{ie}$ in Figure 11.3, some method effects could potentially influence both implicit and explicit motive scores. Some characteristics of the experimenter, for instance, may influence responses on both types of measures (Klinger, 1967). As depicted by Con$_i$ and Con$_e$, other method effects may be specific to one motive or the other. Many types of poor correspondence (e.g., Thrash et al., 2007) are instances in which one motive measure (or both) is confounded with content peripheral to the core construct.

Social desirability, the tendency to present oneself as having desirable characteristics, is generally presumed to influence responses on explicit but not implicit measures (but see Paulhus, 1998, regarding nonconscious aspects of social desirability). The confounding of explicit measures with social desirability has long been argued to be a reason for poor congruence (e.g., Murray, 1938), but this variable has not yet been the subject of empirical research in the motive congruence literature. We should note that we have characterized social desirability as an example of Con$_e$, an influence on observed variables (a methodological issue) rather than as an example of Ant$_E$, an influence on the underlying latent explicit motive (a substantive issue). However, it is possible that a social desirability motive influences the explicit motive per se. Without the structural-measurement model distinction present in our framework, these two possibilities are easily blurred. We also note that nuance is needed when deriving predictions about social desirability or other confounding variables. If a bias led all participants to distort their responses (on either motive measure or both) in the same direction and to the same degree, then implicit–explicit correlations would not be affected. Of greater concern are differential effects across individuals, which may arise, for instance, from ceiling effects on rating scales or individual differences in social desirability (Paulhus, Bruce, & Trapnell, 1995).

In all motive studies that have been reported to date, the implicit and explicit motive constructs have been confounded with their associated measurement techniques. For instance, in a typical motive congruence study, the implicit motive (Imp) is assessed by PSE (Con_I), and the explicit motive (Exp) is assessed by questionnaire (Con_E). Ideally, this type of confound would be avoided by employing the same, multiple methods to assess the implicit and explicit motives. Each source of method variance could then be modeled and removed using a contemporary multitrait-multimethod (MTMM; Campbell & Fiske, 1959) analytic strategy, such as confirmatory factor analysis (Brown, 2006).

This ideal poses a thorny problem for motive researchers because the cognitive processes associated with responding to PSEs and questionnaires have generally been viewed as being intrinsic to the types of motives that they assess (e.g., see McClelland's, 1980, distinction between operant and respondent measures and Schultheiss's, 2007, distinction between nondeclarative and declarative measures). Indeed, it was in part the repeated failure of questionnaire and PSE measures to converge that led researchers to conclude that different motive constructs underlie the two methodologies. We note, however, that dissociations between constructs and methods have been achieved in some implicit–explicit literatures (e.g., Jaccoby, Yonelinas, & Jennings, 1997) and may be possible in the motive literature as well. For instance, it is possible, in theory (see below) if not in practice, that individuals would be able to report their level of implicit nAch if they understood exactly what is meant by an implicit need to achieve and how it differs from an explicit need to achieve. Indeed, some of the strongest PSE–questionnaire correlations reported to date were from two studies by Sherwood (1966), in which participants were asked to rate themselves on implicit nAch or implicit nAff after in-depth instruction about implicit motive theory. These findings raise the intriguing possibility that Sherwood had succeeded in measuring implicit motives by self-report, although the reported observed correlations alone do not warrant firm conclusions. Self-ratings of brief descriptions of motives, in the absence of in-depth instruction, have been found to be unrelated to PSE measures (King, 1995). If using the same multiple methods proves impossible, it is nevertheless possible to model and remove implicit- and explicit-specific method variance (see Nosek & Smyth,

2007, for an example in the IAT literature) if certain assumptions are made (e.g., that these method effects are uncorrelated; Conway, Lievens, Scullen, & Lance, 2004).

Third, if random measurement error is not removed from the indicator(s) of each construct, then the correlation between the underlying constructs is likely to be underestimated (Reuman, Alwin, & Veroff, 1984). This problem occurs when only a single indicator of each construct is available and, to a lesser extent, when responses to multiple indicators (e.g., items on a questionnaire, or scores from individual PSE stories) are summed or averaged to create a single composite observed variable. In order to gauge the magnitude of this problem, we reanalyzed data from Thrash et al. (2007). In that article, implicit–explicit correlations were based on observed variables. Specifically, the index of implicit nAch was a composite of scores derived from each of five stories, and the matched-content and non-matched-content indexes of explicit nAch were composites formed by summing across items from a given questionnaire.

We report here the results of two new confirmatory factor analyses (CFAs). In the first analysis, five implicit nAch scores based on the individual stories were used as separate indicators of an implicit nAch latent variable, and the three non-matched-content measures of explicit nAch were used as separate indicators of a non-matched-content explicit nAch latent variable. The resulting correlation between these non-matched-content latent variables was $r = .07$, $p = .62$. Consistent with the findings of Thrash et al. (2007), this correlation is nonsignificant, but as expected it is stronger than the correlations based on observed variables (as reported above, r ranged from .00 to .02 for the three non-matched explicit nAch measures). More importantly, in our second analysis, the five implicit nAch scores from the individual stories again were used as indicators of an implicit nAch latent variable, and the 10 items from the matched-content explicit nAch measure were used as indicators of a matched-content explicit nAch latent variable. The resulting correlation between these matched-content latent variables was $r = .38$, $p = .006$. This correlation is substantially larger than the correlation based on observed variables (as reported above, $r = .17$). Indeed, the adjustment for attenuation through analysis of latent rather than observed variables resulted in a 5-fold increase ($.38^2/.17^2 = 5.00$) in the percentage of shared variance. This finding provides striking evidence that unreliability of observed variables—even of composites based on multiple indicators—attenuates the implicit–explicit correlation. Moreover, it implies that past studies may have underestimated the true correlation between implicit and explicit motives, not only because of imperfect correspondence of content, but also because CFA or other means of disattenuation have rarely been employed.[5]

Most of the methodological factors discussed above concern ways in which imperfect measurement leads to bias in estimating the correlation between underlying implicit and explicit motive constructs. In most but not all cases, problems of measurement would be expected to lead to an underestimation of the true correlation between implicit and explicit motives. The emerging evidence that implicit and explicit nAch (or other motives) are not statistically independent should not be viewed as a threat to their discriminant validity, because discriminant validity rests on the presence of unique variance rather than the absence of shared variance. Indeed, efforts to improve the reliability and validity of motive instruments would be expected not only to increase the correlation of the two motives with one another, but also to increase the correlations of each with the criterion variables that discriminate them. In the next three sections, we turn to the three classes of substantive influences on the implicit–explicit relationship.

Processes Through Which an Implicit Motive May Influence an Explicit Motive

As noted, one substantive reason that implicit and explicit motives may be related is that the implicit motive may influence the explicit motive. Bringing the explicit motive into alignment with the implicit motive is generally viewed as, or assumed to be, the primary means through which congruence is achieved (e.g., Schultheiss & Brunstein, 1999; Thrash & Elliot, 2002). Freud (1933/1965) summed up the goal of therapy with the statement, "where id was, there ego shall be" (p. 80). Murray (1938) argued, "one of the steps in the development of personality is that of becoming conscious of what is unconscious" (p. 114).

In delineating possible routes through which implicit motives may influence explicit motives, we begin by drawing on Freud (1909/1989), who identified three roads to the unconscious: free association, interpretation of dreams, and analysis of parapraxes (i.e., "faulty and haphazard actions" (p. 33), such as slips of the tongue. Perhaps less important than these techniques per se are the common themes that link them. Each involves observation of thoughts, affects, and behaviors that result from automatic associative processes, followed by careful interpretation and inference about underlying motivational processes. We believe that these are fundamentally important processes, and we refer to them as *access* and *interpretation*, respectively.

The fact that implicit motives cannot be readily accessed was one of McClelland's primary explanations of poor correspondence between implicit and explicit motives (Thrash et al., 2007). Because the associative networks that comprise implicit motives, and implicit constructs more generally, are not directly accessible to introspection, access is necessarily indirect (Wilson & Dunn, 2004). Trying to gain direct introspective access to an implicit motive would be like turning on a light in the attic in order to see what is in the basement. However, it is plausible that the various effects of implicit motive activation (e.g., thoughts, affects, and behavior) bear the fingerprints of the implicit motive lurking in the basement.

Thoughts, affects, and behavior tend to be multiply determined; they may be influenced by a variety of factors, including explicit motives, and therefore may not provide direct readouts of a given implicit motive (Elliot & Church, 1997; Frenkel-Brunswik, 1942; Thrash & Hurst, 2008). Successful access therefore hinges on accessing information that is distinctively diagnostic of an implicit motive. Most extant theory and research in the motive congruence literature appear to emphasize means of accessing diagnostic information. For instance, Thrash et al. (2007) argued that bodily arousal may be more informative than thoughts and feelings because implicit motives are closely tied to the physiological state of the body and explicit motives are not. Schultheiss and Brunstein's (1999) research suggests that use of imagery provides a means of testing whether goal pursuit will arouse one's implicit motives. Baumann et al.'s (2005) finding that state-oriented individuals became incongruent under stress was posited to reflect poor access to the extensive (nondeclarative) memory system, of which implicit motives were posited to be a part.

Other sources of diagnostic information may exist, beyond those previously examined in the motive congruence literature (see Wilson & Dunn, 2004, for a review of access-related processes more generally). Brunstein et al. (1998) found that progress toward personal goals predicts emotional well-being only when the goal is consistent with one's implicit motives; thus, one's emotional response to goal progress is a source of information about one's implicit motives. Self-observation (Bem, 1972), observation of one's own behavior, may provide diagnostic information, particularly if one attends to long-term behavioral trends (McClelland et al., 1989) and incorporates introspective information about whether the behaviors stem from intentions (which reflect explicit processes) or automatic processes (which reflect implicit processes). Feedback from others may be diagnostic, particularly when it contradicts one's existing self-image (Murray, 1938). Indeed, the observer's external frame of reference is well suited for detecting some effects of implicit processes, such as facial expressions or other nonverbal behaviors. Attention to one's thoughts may also be diagnostic if one distinguishes automatic from controlled thoughts. A mindful, observant perspective on one's thought processes (Brown & Ryan, 2003; Gendlin, 1981) is likely to be beneficial.

As a corollary to the argument that distinctively diagnostic forms of information gathering are critical, we propose that relatively undifferentiated forms of data gathering, as reflected in constructs such as self-awareness (Duval & Wicklund, 1972), private self-consciousness (Fenigstein, Scheier, & Buss, 1975), and reflection (Trapnell & Campbell, 1999), are less likely to promote congruence. Consistent with this proposal, Thrash et al. (2007) found that, whereas private body consciousness moderated implicit–explicit congruence, private self-consciousness did not. Moreover, the moderating effect of private body consciousness remained significant when the (nonsignificant) moderating effect of private self-consciousness was controlled.

Once diagnostic information is accessed, it must be interpreted. For instance, bodily arousal requires interpretation and labeling based, at least in part, on the context in which it occurs (Schachter & Singer, 1962). Opportunities for error abound. Arousal of implicit nAch by an achievement cue could be misattributed to a power cue, or it could be properly attributed to the achievement cue but misinterpreted as FF. Moreover, the interpretation must be sufficiently differentiated to exploit the diagnosticity of the informational input. We suspect that difficulty in differentiating and interpreting one's motivational states stems in part from an impoverished lexicon—at least in English, if not in all languages—related to implicit processes (see Schultheiss, 2001a, for a possible evolutionary basis). "Wanting," for instance, can denote anything from a felt (but disavowed) desire for the candy bar before one's eyes to an unfelt (but avowed) attitude toward peace in a foreign nation. Furthermore, we speculate that individuals with alexithymia, who have difficulty identifying and describing their feelings and bodily states (Taylor & Bagby, 2000), are prone to motive incongruence.

Another hypothesis for future research is that interpretation is most successful when grounded in "multimethod" self-analysis that is based, for instance, on information gathered through imagery, interoception, reactions to goal progress, and self-observation. Much as a researcher cannot measure an implicit motive well without converging evidence based on its various manifestations, an individual is unlikely to draw a veridical inference if he or she relies on a single indicator, which is fallible and multiply determined. Indeed, interpreting one's own motivational traits is analogous to what personality researchers do when they measure (access) a variety of indicators and then determine the underlying factor structure. Like the researcher, the person must decide (a) how many motivational constructs to "extract" (as in exploratory factor analysis) or "specify" (as in confirmatory factor analysis), (b) how strongly each indicator "loads" on its factor for optimal weighting, (c) whether particular indicators "cross-load," such that they reflect more than one motivational construct, (d) how to label the motivational constructs based on the weightings, and (e) whether the model provides an adequate summary of the data. The factor analysis metaphor illustrates that the task of interpreting one's motivations is complex, and therefore the benefits of a multimethod self-analysis may depend on whether the individual has an adequate strategy for self-analysis. We speculate that unconscious thought, which occurs when conscious attention is turned elsewhere (Dijksterhuis, 2004), is more likely than conscious self-analysis to result in a veridical interpretation (see also Wilson, 2002). Unconscious thought tends to lead to better judgments when the task is complex and when many types of information must be organized, weighted, and integrated into a summary judgment (Dijksterhuis, 2006).

Access and interpretation are posited to result in an explicit, declarative representation of the implicit motive, such as "I have [or lack] a spontaneous inclination to achieve." Although they are explicit, such representations may be distinguished from explicit values (e.g., "It is [or is not] important to me to achieve"), which, in our view, represent the conceptual core of explicit motives.[6] Whether explicit representations of implicit motives influence one's explicit motives is not a given, but rather depends on the result of a third process, which we call *reconciliation*. During reconciliation, the representation of the implicit motive must be reconciled with other sources of values (Ant_E), including values or expectations internalized from the social environment. We posit that reconciliation is more likely to result in congruence to the extent that the process is independent of controlling or determining influences. For instance, the finding that self-monitoring moderates congruence (Thrash et al., 2007) is theorized to reflect the fact that high self-monitors base their explicit motives more on others' expectations than on their own representations of implicit motives.

Finally, we note that reconciliation requires not only the freedom, but also the motivation, to use knowledge of implicit motives as the basis for one's explicit motives. The finding that preference for consistency moderates congruence (Thrash et al., 2007) is posited to reflect the fact that individuals high in this trait are more motivated to minimize dissonance between representations of implicit motives and other sources of values. Given that implicit motives are difficult to change, individuals are presumed to try to bring their values into alignment with their representations of implicit motives. We further posit that the reconciliation process may be invigorated in some cases by inspiration (Thrash & Elliot, 2003, 2004), particularly when unconscious interpretation processes produce an insight about the nature of one's core self. Inspiration has been shown to lead to greater self-determination (Thrash & Elliot, 2003) but has not yet been linked empirically to motive congruence. We also note that humanistic theories posit an actualizing tendency or organismic integration process (Deci & Ryan, 1985; Rogers, 1959; Sheldon, Arndt, & Houser-Marko, 2003), an inherent tendency of living organisms to move in the direction of greater differentiation and integration within supportive environments; this process may be viewed as an underlying motivation in all individuals and is likely to promote motive congruence (Thrash & Elliot, 2002).

Although motive congruence is widely regarded as a desirable and well being–promoting condition, we believe that reconciliation sometimes results in desirable outcomes in which motive congruence is compromised. Our position is based on psychoanalytic and existential writings. In particular, Freud (1909/1989) argued that the individual has three healthy options after bringing unconscious material into awareness: accept it, reject it, or sublimate it. These ideas may be interpreted in terms of contemporary theory with little distortion of Freud's original theorizing. We interpret *acceptance* as the attainment of motive congruence; one uses the strength of the implicit motive as a foundation for the development of one's explicit values. We interpret *rejection* as an informed and nondefensive decision not to embrace the strength of an implicit motive as the basis of one's conscious values. In many instances, rejection may be a reasonable and healthy response, particularly when an implicit approach motive is weak (in which case compensatory explicit strivings may be needed) or when an implicit avoidance motive is strong. Sublimation—we prefer the term *rechanneling*, which has less conceptual baggage—may be interpreted as a self-regulation strategy in which one rechannels implicit motive energy so that it serves one's explicit motives. An example is the rechanneling of energy from implicit FF toward pursuit of a positively valenced performance approach goal (Elliot & McGregor, 1999; Thrash & Elliot, 2002), thereby facilitating satisfaction of explicit nAch. Rechanneling may be a more desirable outcome than rejection, given that implicit motive energy is put to effective use.

Although the access-interpretation-reconciliation model described above represents a rational sequential process, it is possible that access and interpretation are in some cases achieved through an iterative process of compatibility testing. Lacking easy access to implicit motives, a child or adolescent may experiment with explicit values, either systematically or through a blind trial-and-error process. This type of experimentation corresponds to the moratorium stage that has been theorized to precede identity achievement and motive congruence (Hofer et al., 2006). Those explicit values and goals that are compatible with the individual's implicit motives, and therefore are emotionally rewarding (Brunstein et al., 1998), may then be selected and retained through a basic reinforcement mechanism or a cognitively complex (e.g., expectancy valence) evaluation process (Atkinson, 1957; Berridge & Robinson, 2003). In this model, access is attained in roundabout fashion through compatibility testing, and the problem of interpretation is largely bypassed, given that an explicit value is adopted tentatively prior to compatibility testing. This iterative model is an example of a selection theory, as are theories of natural selection (Darwin, 1859/1964), reinforcement of operant responses (Skinner, 1938), and selective retention of creative cognitions (Campbell, 1960). This iterative process, although inefficient, may be a viable pathway to congruence for individuals who lack the knowledge or skills necessary to undergo a more direct access-interpretation sequence.

Processes Through Which an Explicit Motive May Influence an Implicit Motive

A second substantive reason that implicit and explicit motives may be related is that the explicit motive may influence the implicit motive. An obstacle to translation in this direction is that implicit motives cannot be controlled directly or easily. As LeDoux (2002) noted, "Our brain has not evolved to the point where the new systems that make complex thinking possible can easily control the old systems that give rise to our base needs and motives, and emotional reactions" (p. 323).

By the time that explicit motives have developed, the implicit motive system may be particularly resistant to change. McClelland (1951) theorized that early, preverbal learning is uniquely capable of producing the strong, generalized, and persistent associative networks that make up implicit motives. However, McClelland (1965) later suggested that it is possible, but difficult, to change an implicit motive in an adult through systematic training. Research on motive modification programs has suggested that change is indeed possible, at least to a limited degree (Heckhausen & Krug, 1982; Miron & McClelland, 1979; see also Chapter 18 of this volume). In the following, we identify three factors that are likely to play important roles in bringing an implicit motive into alignment with an explicit motive. We focus on the case of increasing the strength of an implicit motive and then comment briefly on the case of decreasing the strength of an implicit motive.

First, and most fundamentally, strengthening an implicit motive may require strengthening incentive–affect associations. McClelland (1987) argued that the natural incentives that underlie implicit motives, such as "doing something better" in the case of implicit nAch, naturally elicit pleasurable affective states ("reward"). However, an individual may not associate pleasure with doing well if he or she has had few experiences of success. Accordingly, we posit that more frequent contact with a natural incentive may enhance the affective associative core of an implicit motive. Increasing the duration of gratification—for instance, by *savoring* the pleasant affect (Bryant & Veroff, 2007)—may also be beneficial. Finally, reward from the social environment, such as praise for one's successes, may bolster the affective component of a motive (Winterbottom, 1958), although social reinforcement, if perceived as manipulative, may create a separate and competing extrinsic motive (Deci, Koestner, & Ryan, 1999). Moreover, given that each major implicit motive system appears to have a distinguishable physiological reward substrate (e.g., hormone profile; McClelland, 1995; Schultheiss et al., 2005), efforts to experience the unique rewards of natural incentives may be preferable to seeking the more generic currency of social reinforcement.

No matter how strong one's association between pleasure and the incentive that elicits it, an implicit motive is not present unless the incentive has become associated with cues that signal the presence of the incentive and the opportunity for gratification (McClelland, 1987). The requisite learning is a form of Pavlovian conditioning (Domjan, 2005) and is similar to emotional or evaluative conditioning (De Houwer, Thomas, & Baeyens, 2001). The diversity of cues capable of triggering an anticipatory motivational state determines the *extensity* of the motive (McClelland, Atkinson, Clark, & Lowell, 1953) and may influence the extent to which the incentive becomes a general and recurrent concern. Extensity may in turn promote motive intensity or strength because greater extensity increases the likelihood that multiple cues will arouse the motive simultaneously. Although extensity may be promoted most readily by early learning in which fine discriminations of stimuli are not yet possible (McClelland, 1951), we posit that, later in life, efforts to seek a given incentive across diverse life contexts may promote extensity and motive strength. For instance, striving to be an excellent parent or spouse may result in arousal of nAch by social cues (Thrash & Elliot, 2001).

The first two processes described above involve strengthening the affective and motivational aspects of a motive. The third important process is the elaboration of cognitive aspects of the associative network, such as those that facilitate transformation of an aroused motivational state into flexible instrumental behaviors and, in turn, motive gratification. Apparently for pragmatic reasons, elaboration of cognitive aspects of the associative network was central to McClelland's (1965) achievement motivation training programs, which consisted largely of teaching individuals to imitate the thinking style of individuals high in implicit nAch (e.g., thinking in terms of competition with standards of excellence, instrumental activity, and anticipation of affect) and of teaching individuals to select cognitive strategies that have been linked to implicit nAch in empirical research (e.g., choice of tasks of intermediate difficulty). Specific cognitive processes, such as realistic goal setting and choice of particular attributions for success and failure, have been found to be important ingredients of the motive training programs later developed in Germany (Heckhausen & Krug, 1982). The hierarchical model of approach–avoidance motivation (Elliot, 2006; Elliot & Church, 1997; Thrash & Hurst, 2008) also suggests that cognitive processes—specifically, the types of goals that one pursues—are important links between motive arousal and motive gratification. Although contemporary motive researchers tend to view cognitive constructs, such as attributions and goals, as distinct from motive constructs (but see Thrash & Elliot's, 2001, discussion of *goal complexes*), cognitive factors may, at a minimum, enhance the efficiency with which motives are aroused or translated into action. Moreover, enhancing motive-relevant cognitions may strengthen motives indirectly by facilitating contact with natural incentives.

For some individuals, achieving congruence requires weakening rather than strengthening an implicit motive. The three factors discussed in connection with strengthening an implicit motive are also relevant here. For instance, it may be possible to weaken an implicit avoidance motive by (a) using emotion regulation strategies (Gross, 2007) to ameliorate motive-relevant affects, (b) promoting extinction of Pavlovian associations by increasing exposure to feared stimuli (Mowrer, 1939), and (c) replacing avoidance goals with approach goals (Elliot & Friedman, 2007). Whether these strategies are effective in producing change in motives and whether such change is stable remain to be explored.

Common Antecedents of Implicit and Explicit Motives

Often overlooked is the fact that the correlation between implicit and explicit motives may be influenced by a third variable that influences, directly or indirectly, both motive variables. Sperry, Gazzaniga, and Bogen (1969) presented an argument that supports the possibility of common antecedents, although they were concerned with incongruence between cerebral hemispheres, rather than between motive systems:

> [T]he fact that these two separate mental spheres have only one body so they always frequent the same places, meet the same people, see and do the same things all the time and thus are bound to have a great overlap of common, almost identical, experience. The unity of the eyeball as well as the conjugate movements of the eyes causes both hemispheres to automatically center on, focus on, and hence probably attend to, the same items in the visual field all the time. (p. 286)

Similarly, because implicit and explicit motives are nested within individuals, it is likely that at least some of a given individual's experiences (or genes, for that matter) may have an impact on both motives and therefore may create an implicit–explicit correlation. However, to the extent that implicit and explicit motivational systems are attuned to different aspects of the environment, one's experiences may not be as unitary and as conducive to congruence as one would presume. For instance, a parent who extols the value of success without facilitating effectance experiences, or who fails to express authentic emotion when praising a child's successes, may be speaking to the explicit but not the implicit nAch system. Accordingly, as McClelland and his colleagues have argued (e.g., McClelland & Pilon, 1983), motive incongruence may be traced in part to discrepancies across those aspects of the social environment that promote development of the implicit and explicit motive systems. Indeed, a preponderance of unique rather than common developmental antecedents, together with poor access to implicit motives, were McClelland's primary explanations of poor correspondence between implicit and explicit motives (Thrash et al., 2007).

Although implicit and explicit motives may have primarily unique rather than common antecedents, we presume that some antecedent variables are more relevant to a particular motive domain than to the implicit or explicit motive in particular. For instance, it is possible that a childhood home environment rich in achievement opportunities or affordances (e.g., one in which musical instruments, sporting equipment, books, and puzzles are amply present) may be conducive to the development of both implicit and explicit nAch. An enriched environment provides a context for both the experiential learning that underlies implicit motives and the verbally based training that underlies explicit motives, whereas an impoverished environment would provide less opportunity for either form of socialization.

Integration with Related Literatures

The literature on motive congruence has parallels in a number of other literatures within and beyond psychology. In this section, we draw connections between our framework and a number of literatures that have developed largely independently of the motive congruence literature.

Psychoanalysis

Although we have drawn on several of Freud's ideas in the presentation of our framework, we have not yet addressed the possible role of defense mechanisms, which occupy a central position in psychoanalysis. Interest in defense mechanisms waned dramatically with the decline of psychoanalysis, and recourse to defense mechanisms generally is not necessary to explain unconscious processes (Kihlstrom, 1990; Wilson, 2002). Nevertheless, defenses may contribute to incongruence, particularly in the case of avoidance motives (Thrash & Hurst, 2008). Advances in the conceptualization and assessment of defenses (Baumeister, Dale, & Sommer, 1998; Cramer, 2006; Egloff & Krohne, 1996; Nesse & Lloyd, 1992; Vaillant, 2000) provide a contemporary foundation for research. From the perspective offered by our framework, defenses are particularly relevant to the translation of implicit motives into explicit motives. Various defenses may be relevant for different reasons. For instance, repression, if it exists, may interfere with access to implicit motives; projection, reaction formation, and self-esteem maintenance may lead to misinterpretation; and suppression and compartmentalization may preclude adequate reconciliation.

Cognitive Psychology

Bucci (1997) gave new life to some psychoanalytic principles (and sealed the coffin of others) by grounding them in the contemporary memory literature. A similar integration may benefit the motive literature. Several theorists have drawn a parallel between implicit and explicit motives, on the one hand, and memory systems (e.g., nondeclarative and declarative), on the other (Baumann et al., 2005; Kuhl, 2000; Schultheiss, 2001a; for an alternative perspective, see Westen, Weinberger, & Bradley, 2007). Our misgivings about whether a two-factor, implicit–explicit structure adequately represents the motive conceptual space parallel debates about the adequacy of a two-system organization of memory. Squire (2004) proposed a hierarchical model of memory systems, in which declarative and nondeclarative systems each consist of several subsystems, some of which are further differentiated. Schultheiss (2007) argued that Squire's model may provide a useful framework for categorizing personality instruments. We note, in addition, that memory system organization may provide a foundation for a differentiated model of the factorial structure of implicit and explicit motive constructs. In addition, memory researchers' increasing attention to interrelationships among memory systems (Kim & Baxter, 2001) parallels a similar trend in the motive literature and is likely to provide new insights into the nature of the implicit–explicit motive interface.

Social Cognition

The issue of implicit–explicit motive incongruence is analogous to the issue of dissociation between implicit and explicit components of attitudes, stereotypes, and self-esteem. Unfortunately, there has been little cross-talk between the motive congruence literature and these social cognition literatures (for exceptions, see Brunstein & Schmitt, 2004; Greenwald & Banaji, 1995; Thrash et al., 2007; Wilson & Dunn, 2004).

Within the social cognition literature, the model that is most similar to our general framework is that outlined by Hofmann, Gschwendner, Nosek, and Schmitt (2005). Hofmann et al. (2005) identified five classes of factors that influence the degree of consistency between implicit and explicit measures: "[1] *translation* between implicit and explicit representations, [2] additional *information integration* for explicit representations, [3] properties of *explicit assessment*, [4] properties of *implicit assessment*, and [5] research *design factors* such as sampling selectivity and measurement correspondence" (p. 344). Parallels between models may be identified. Translation corresponds to the paths between the latent Imp and Exp variables in our framework. Information integration is similar to reconciliation (of explicit representations of Imp with Ant_E) within our framework. Explicit and implicit assessment correspond to aspects of our measurement model linking latent variables (Imp and Exp) to observed indicators (each imp and exp). Finally, we have outlined several design factors, including measurement correspondence, which in our framework represents an issue of confounded measurement (Con_i or Con_e). Unique aspects of our framework include the formal mapping of processes onto a SEM model, a distinction between association of variables and congruence of persons, and an emphasis on processes other than translation through which congruence may emerge (e.g., common antecedents, random influences). Hofmann et al.'s model also makes a number of important contributions that deserve the attention of motive congruence researchers.

Neuroscience

Several prominent neuroscientists have described dual routes to action that parallel the distinction between implicit and explicit motives (Berridge & Robinson, 2003; LeDoux, 2002; Rolls, 2007). Berridge and Robinson (2003), for instance, distinguished *"wanting"* and *cognitive incentives*, which correspond to implicit and explicit motivation, respectively. "Wanting," which refers to an associatively cued desire that is not necessarily consciously represented, is characterized most centrally by mesolimbic dopamine neurotransmission, with the involvement of the nucleus accumbens, amygdala, basal forebrain, and cortex. Pursuit of cognitive incentives, which are subjectively desired and intended to be acquired through goal pursuit, requires little involvement of mesolimbic dopamine systems and instead depends heavily on orbitofrontal and insular cortical regions. Berridge and Robinson suggested that "wanting" and cognitive incentive expectations generally act in concert but diverge under some conditions. Among explicit constructs, Berridge (2007) distinguished conscious, secondary processing of "wanting" from the conscious processing involved in the pursuit of cognitive incentives. These two explicit constructs correspond, respectively, to what we have called explicit representations of implicit motives and explicit motives.

LeDoux (2002) argued that we *are* our synapses. Congruence within personality may therefore be viewed as a problem of plasticity and integration of neural systems. LeDoux summarized a set of principles from neuroscience that are pertinent to congruence in general and implicit–explicit congruence in particular. These include (a) parallel plasticity or integration resulting from synchronous activation of distinct networks; (b) coordination of plasticity through modulators, chemicals that are released broadly throughout the brain in response to a significant event; (c) the cross-modality integration of information within hierarchically organized convergence zones; (d) the top-down influence of thoughts and intentions on parallel plasticity; and (e) the capacity of emotion to coordinate diverse brain functions. Again, we are seeing a shift from an emphasis on independence of systems to an emphasis on coordination and integration of systems.

Design Issues

Next we discuss several general research design issues that do not fall within the purview of our variable-based framework, but that nevertheless have important implications for interpretation of findings of motive congruence studies.

Statistical Power

We caution that interactions among measured (as opposed to manipulated) variables, such as motives and trait moderator variables, are difficult to detect due to the shape of their natural distributions (Cohen, Cohen, West, & Aiken, 2003; McClelland & Judd, 1993). If the interacting variables are bivariate normally distributed, then most cases fall near the center of the two-dimensional predictor space, resulting in naturally small effect sizes and low power. By comparison, in a traditional 2×2 experiment, researchers exploit the ability to control the independent variables by making manipulations as potent as possible, such that individuals are assigned only to the "four corners" of the predictor space. The efficiency of this design results in large effect sizes and a high degree of statistical power. In order to detect an interaction, a correlational study requires approximately 20 times as many participants as an experimental study (McClelland & Judd, 1993). Given that a half-century elapsed between the first indications that implicit and explicit nAch are only weakly related (de Charms, Morrison, Reitman, & McClelland, 1955; McClelland et al., 1953) and the documentation of a variable that moderates their association (Thrash & Elliot, 2002; see also Brunstein, 2001; Schultheiss & Brunstein, 1999), we wonder how many otherwise well-conceived studies have been "file drawered" in the interim due to inefficient designs and low power.

Correlation and Causality

Two notes of caution about correlation and causality are needed. One is familiar to most researchers: *correlation does not imply causality.* Our framework makes clear the fact that a correlation between implicit and explicit motives may not reflect a causal process; it may be due, for instance, to common antecedents or methodological factors. Moreover, if an implicit–explicit correlation (or a specific source of variance that underlies it) is found to be moderated by a particular variable (e.g., self-monitoring), then the moderator may be regarded, loosely speaking, as merely a "correlate" of congruence. The moderator may be related to congruence because (a) it is a cause of congruence, (b) it is an effect of congruence, (c) congruence and the moderator are products of a common antecedent, or (d) they are products of a common confound.

Two methodological approaches hold the most promise for drawing causal inference: experiments and naturalistic longitudinal designs. The experimental method, which is based on manipulation and random assignment to condition, provides the most direct evidence of causality. A limitation of the experimental method in the study of motive congruence is that neither an implicit motive nor an explicit motive, if conceptualized as an independent variable, is subject to manipulation; it is difficult to impose personality change and unethical to do so by random assignment. Moreover, neither an implicit motive nor an explicit motive, if treated as a dependent variable, is subject to short-term change; most short-term change that is documented is likely to reflect error variance or change in temporary states, rather than change in the underlying disposition. Although implicit and explicit motives per se are not amenable to strict experimental research, state arousal of implicit motivation and commitment to temporary explicit goals are more amenable to manipulation and short-term change. Accordingly, these constructs may be treated as (imperfect) proxies for their dispositional counterparts, or as objects of study in their own right. Some antecedents and moderators are also subject to manipulation (e.g., Baumann et al., 2005; Schultheiss & Brunstein, 1999).

The factors that *can* produce congruence between implicit and explicit states, contingent upon their manipulation in a laboratory study, may or may not be the factors that *tend to* produce motive congruence in the absence of intervention. The latter issue is best examined using naturalistic longitudinal methods. Reasonably strong evidence of causality may be obtained using carefully designed studies, such as cross-lagged longitudinal designs with statistical control of known and suspected confounds.

Our second note of caution challenges conventional wisdom (e.g., Campbell & Stanley, 1963): *Lack of correlation does not imply lack of causality* (Bollen, 1989). We offer six examples of reasons that an effect of an implicit motive on an explicit motive could be accompanied by a lack of correlation between them. First, as emphasized above, inadequate reliability, validity, or power could obscure a true causal effect. Second, given that causality is distributed across time rather than instantaneous, a causal effect that has a nonnegligible temporal lag may be underestimated or undetected if the variables are assessed concurrently. Third, a positive effect of an implicit motive on an explicit motive could be offset by a negative effect in the opposite direction. Fourth, a common antecedent that has opposite effects on the implicit and explicit motives could suppress a correlation between them. Fifth, if the effect of the implicit motive on the explicit motive is curvilinear (e.g., an inverse-U-shaped function), then the positive and negative effects at different ranges of the implicit motive would offset one another and could result in no overall correlation. Finally, if the effect of the implicit motive on the explicit motive is negative at one pole of a moderator and positive at the other—Freud's concept of reaction formation comes to mind—then the positive and negative correlations again would offset one another and could result in no overall correlation. Of course, some of these possibilities are highly speculative, but they highlight the fact that the absence of a correlation is subject to a variety of interpretations.

New Directions in the Conceptualization of Motive Congruence

Conceptual issues related to the meaning of "congruence" have received little attention in the motive congruence literature. In the following, we point to some new directions in the conceptualization of congruence.

Congruence Versus Integration

At the beginning of this chapter, we noted that a congruent individual has comparable levels of implicit and explicit motives. This definition is consistent with the label "congruence," which implies equality. We now introduce the related concept of *integration*, which we define as unity of structure and coordination of function (see also Deci & Ryan, 1991; Rogers, 1959). Because we have not defined it in operational terms, integration may be more difficult to assess and investigate than congruence; nevertheless, we believe that it is important not to conflate the simple mathematical concept of equality with the more elusive, more complex, and ultimately more important issue of harmony and unity in personality. We presume that congruence and integration often go hand in hand. However, these constructs are dissociated in cases of unintegrated congruence and integrated incongruence.

Unintegrated congruence is a condition in which an individual has comparable levels of implicit and explicit motives; however, this congruence is attributable to factors exogenous to the person. For instance, unintegrated congruence is promoted when implicit and explicit motives are influenced by common antecedents (Ant_{IE}) that are exogenous to the person, as when a parent is consistent across verbal and nonverbal socialization practices. In addition, the independence of Ran_I and Ran_E implies that some individuals (e.g., those near the positively sloped diagonal in Figure 2b) will be congruent by chance. Similarly, the independence of Ant_I and Ant_E suggests that some individuals will be congruent due to the whims of identifiable deterministic influences—fate, one might say. We posit that such fortuitous cases of congruence are less stable and conducive to well-being than are cases of congruence attained at least in part through an endogenous integrative process, such as the gaining of self-insight.

Integrated incongruence is a condition in which an individual has discrepant levels of implicit and explicit motives; yet, the implicit and explicit motives have structural contact and are functionally coordinated. Integrated incongruence is posited to arise, for instance, if a veridical interpretation of an implicit motive is followed nondefensively by what we have termed rejection or rechanneling. For instance, one could be well integrated if one mindfully chooses to develop a strong explicit motive as compensation for weak implicit motivation. We posit that such instances of incongruence are not as detrimental to well-being as are cases of incongruence that result from lack of contact or coordination between the motivational systems. These ideas await future research.

Individual Differences in Normative, Temporal, and Configural Congruence

We now bring attention to an issue that often goes under the radar in the motive congruence literature and beyond: the question of whether two variables that are correlated cannot be posed meaningfully without specifying the *units of analysis* across which the variables may or may not covary. Implicit in our discussion so far, and in the motive literature more generally, is that persons represent the units of analysis. However, other units are possible, such as occasions (distributed across time), classrooms, or countries. In principle, an implicit–explicit correlation may be quite different depending on which units are examined (Nezlek, 2001), and moderating variables may also differ. We posit that three units of analysis are particularly relevant to the issue of motive congruence: persons, occasions, and motive contents.

With *persons* as the units of analysis, an implicit–explicit correlation indicates that the implicit and explicit motives vary together as one moves from individual to individual. If a substantive variable functions as a moderator, then it specifies subgroups (e.g., individuals at particular levels of a trait) across which the person-to-person implicit–explicit correlation differs. The moderator thus identifies individuals who are "congruent"—but congruent in a specific sense. These are individuals whose *normative* standing on one motive corresponds to his or her normative standing on the other.

With *occasions* as the units of analysis, an implicit–explicit correlation indicates that the implicit and explicit motives, or their state analogues, vary together across time for a given individual. This correlation may be different for different individuals. Some moderators may reside at the occasion level; for instance, there may be a weekend or Blue Monday effect (Thrash, 2007), such that one's implicit and explicit motives vary together during some parts of the week but not others. In addition, given that goal imagery has been found to influence temporary motive–goal congruence (Schultheiss & Brunstein, 1999), variance in an individual's use of imagery may account for variance in congruence across time. Other moderators may reside at the person level; for instance, individuals higher in mindfulness, who are more aware of what is happening in the present, may display greater implicit–explicit covariation across time (Brown & Ryan, 2003). The person-level moderator thus identifies individuals who are "congruent"— but congruent in a specific sense. These are individuals with greater *temporal* coordination of implicit and explicit processes; on occasions when their explicit motivation is strong, their implicit motivation is also strong.

With *motive contents* as the units of analysis, an implicit–explicit correlation indicates that the implicit and explicit scores vary together as one moves, within a given individual, from one type of motive to another (e.g., nAch, nAff, need for power [nPow], FF, fear of rejection [FR], and fear of power [FP]). This correlation may be different for different individuals (or at different points in time). Some moderators may reside at the motive content level; for instance, implicit and explicit motive profiles may be more similar for avoidance motives than for approach motives. Other moderators may reside at the person level; for instance, individuals with a higher level of identity achievement (Marcia, 1966) may value most strongly the domains for which they have the strongest implicit motivation. Once again, the person-level moderator identifies individuals who are "congruent"—but congruent in a specific sense. These are individuals with greater *configural* congruence; the content domains that are the most important to the individual are the content domains for which he or she has the strongest implicit motivation. McClelland (1992) argued that an individual's implicit motive profile or configuration (e.g., whether implicit nPow is stronger than implicit nAff) carries important information; it follows that the similarity of one's implicit motive profile to one's explicit motive profile may carry important information as well.

The fact that individual differences in congruence may be defined in terms of any of a variety of units of analysis raises many questions for future research. For instance, to what extent are normative, temporal, and configural congruence correlated across individuals? Do various personality characteristics or developmental contexts distinctively influence particular types of congruence? Does each type of congruence account for unique variance in outcomes? We posit that temporal and configural congruence may be more fundamental psychologically than is normative congruence. Indeed, if one were to discover that one is normatively incongruent—for instance, if one's implicit nAch were in the 80th percentile and one's explicit nAch were in the 40th percentile— would this necessarily be cause for alarm? Perhaps one places insufficient value on achievement; alternatively, it is possible that one's peer group places inordinate value on achievement, a very real possibility with some undergraduate samples. In contrast, if one does not pursue explicit goals when one is implicitly motivated (temporal incongruence) or if one values most strongly the activities for which one is least implicitly motivated (configural incongruence), then incongruence resides unambiguously within the person.

Conclusion

Having identified a variety of processes that may influence motive congruence, we close this chapter by posing a critical and classic question: Why are so many individuals incongruent, in the normative sense? Our general framework shows that a three-part substantive explanation is required. We suspect that (a) implicit motives have only modest impact on explicit motives because the odds are high that at least one of the three key processes—access, interpretation, and reconciliation—will break down; (b) explicit motives have little impact on implicit motives, because implicit motives are difficult to change; and (c) implicit and explicit motives have few common antecedents because stimulus inputs are often themselves incongruent across the modalities that influence the implicit and explicit motive systems. In addition, our discussion of correlation and causality raises the possibility that one or more processes that promote congruence are operative but are offset or suppressed by factors that promote incongruence.

On a more optimistic note, there are reasonable grounds for challenging the very premise of the question. Here are three: (a) evidence that implicit and explicit motives are largely uncorrelated rests on somewhat crude (but improving) measurement instruments, measurement models, and analytic tools; (b) one may have a high degree of temporal or configural congruence in spite of normative incongruence; and (c) one may be well integrated in spite of motive incongruence, as when one chooses rejection or rechanneling in the service of a form of congruence other than—maybe better than—motive congruence. For instance, one may seek "homonomy" (Angyal, 1958) with one's social group or with life goals that are intrinsically worthy of pursuit, even if they do not "fit" one's implicit motives. We hope that our framework will guide researchers to new answers regarding the reasons for incongruence, and that dissemination of such knowledge will itself become a force for change in the direction of greater congruence and integration.

Notes

1. Scott Cassidy is now at The Pennsylvania State University.
2. Apparently for the sake of consistency with his argument that implicit and explicit motives are statistically independent, McClelland (1987) downplayed the importance of characteristics that discriminate such segments of the population: "When occasional correlations appear between [implicit and explicit motives], they are the product of a peculiar set of circumstances related to the particular group being tested" (p. 521). However, the existence of such moderating factors, peculiar or not, is inconsistent with statistical independence. Unfortunately, McClelland did not identify for the reader the moderating factors to which he referred.
3. In practice, latent variables do not correspond perfectly to theoretical constructs.
4. It is not yet clear what type of measurement model best characterizes the internal structure of an implicit motive as assessed by PSE. PSE indicators differ along two dimensions, story (e.g., first, second) and coding category (e.g., instrumental activity, anticipation of success), and therefore the optimal modeling strategy would take both sources of variance into account. In addition, there are a variety of possibilities for how to model the relations between indicators and latent constructs. Examples include (a) standard "effect indicator" CFA models (in which the latent construct is modeled as the common cause of its indicators), (b) second-order effect indicator CFA models (which include a superordinate implicit motive latent variable [e.g., nAch], multiple subordinate implicit motive latent variables [e.g., sports nAch, classroom nAch, and work nAch], and observed indicators), and (c) "causal indicator" CFA models (in which each indicator is modeled as a cause of the latent construct). We see strengths and weaknesses of each as a measurement model for implicit motives, but discussion of these issues is beyond the scope of the present chapter.
5. Of course, reliability of measurement influences not only estimates of the implicit–explicit association, but also estimates of moderation effects and the ability to detect them. For instance, Thrash et al. (2007, endnote 3) found that moderation effects were consistently significant when a composite of four indicators of explicit nAch was used. When a single indicator was used, all effects were in the expected direction, but only 50% of the effects were statistically significant.

6. Researchers generally have not made a distinction between explicit values and explicit representations of implicit motives. The conflation of these concepts is reflected in the fact that the terms "explicit motive" and "self-attributed motive" tend to be used interchangeably. Whereas an explicit value *provides reason* to act, an explicit representation of an implicit motive is an *inference or attribution of the reason* for acting. Although explicit representations of implicit motives have important implications for motivation and action, as attribution theory suggests, only explicit values are consistent with the label "motive" in our view.

References

Ajzen, I., & Fishbein, M. (1977). Attitude-behavior relations: A theoretical analysis and review of empirical research. *Psychological Bulletin, 84,* 888–918.

Anderson, J. C., & Gerbing, D. W. (1988). Structural equation modeling in practice: A review and recommended two-step approach. *Psychological Bulletin, 103,* 411–423.

Angyal, A. (1958). *Foundations for a science of personality.* Cambridge, MA: Harvard University Press.

Atkinson, J. W. (1957). Motivational determinants of risk-taking behavior. *Psychological Review, 64,* 359–372.

Baumann, N., Kaschel, R., & Kuhl, J. (2005). Striving for unwanted goals: Stress-dependent discrepancies between explicit and implicit achievement motives reduce subjective well-being and increase psychosomatic symptoms. *Journal of Personality and Social Psychology, 89,* 781–799.

Baumeister, R. F., Dale, K., & Sommer, K. L. (1998). Freudian defense mechanisms and empirical findings in modern social psychology: Reaction formation, projection, displacement, undoing, isolation, sublimation, and denial. *Journal of Personality, 66,* 1081–1124.

Bem, D. J. (1972). Self-perception theory. In L. Berkowitz (Ed.), *Advances in experimental social psychology* (Vol. 6, pp. 1–62). New York: Academic Press.

Berridge, K. C. (2007). The debate over dopamine's role in reward: The case for incentive salience. *Psychopharmacology, 191,* 391–431.

Berridge, K. C., & Robinson, T. E. (2003). Parsing reward. *Trends in Neurosciences, 26,* 507–513.

Bollen, K. A. (1989). *Structural equations with latent variables.* New York: Wiley.

Brown, K. W., & Ryan, R. M. (2003). The benefits of being present: Mindfulness and its role in psychological well-being. *Journal of Personality and Social Psychology, 84,* 822–848.

Brown, T. A. (2006). *Confirmatory factor analysis for applied research.* New York: Guilford Press.

Brunstein, J. C. (2001). Persönliche Ziele und Handlungs-versus Lageorientierung: Wer bindet sich an realistische und bedürfniskongruente Ziele? [Personal goals and action versus state orientation: Who builds a commitment to realistic and need congruent goals?]. *Zeitschrift für Differentielle und Diagnostische Psychologie, 22,* 1–12.

Brunstein, J. C., & Schmitt, C. H. (2004). Assessing individual differences in achievement motivation with the Implicit Association Test. *Journal of Research in Personality, 38*, 536–555.

Brunstein, J. C., Schultheiss, O. C., & Grässmann, R. (1998). Personal goals and emotional well-being: The moderating role of motive dispositions. *Journal of Personality and Social Psychology, 75*, 494–508.

Bryant, F. B., & Veroff, J. (2007). *Savoring: A new model of positive experience.* Mahwah, NJ: Lawrence Erlbaum Associates.

Bucci, W. (1997). *Psychoanalysis and cognitive science: A multiple code theory.* New York: Guilford Press.

Campbell, D. T. (1960). Blind variation and selective retention in creative thought as in other knowledge processes. *Psychological Review, 67*, 380–400.

Campbell, D. T., & Fiske, D. W. (1959). Convergent and discriminant validity by the multitrait-multimethod matrix. *Psychological Bulletin, 56*, 81–105.

Campbell, D. T., & Stanley, J. C. (1963). *Experimental and quasi-experimental designs for research.* Chicago: Rand McNally.

Cialdini, R. B., Trost, M. R., & Newsom, J. T. (1995). Preference for consistency: The development of a valid measure and the discovery of surprising behavioral implications. *Journal of Personality and Social Psychology, 69*, 318–328.

Cohen, J., Cohen, P., West, S. G., & Aiken, L. S. (2003). *Applied multiple regression/ correlation analysis for the behavioral sciences* (3rd ed.). Mahwah, NJ: Lawrence Erlbaum Associates.

Conway, J. M., Lievens, F., Scullen, S. E., & Lance, C. E. (2004). Bias in the correlated uniqueness model for MTMM data. *Structural Equation Modeling, 11*, 535–559.

Cramer, P. (2006). *Protecting the self: Defense mechanisms in action.* New York: Guilford Press.

Darwin, C. (1859/1964). *On the origin of species.* Cambridge, MA: Harvard University Press.

de Charms, R., Morrison, H. W., Reitman, W., & McClelland, D. C. (1955). Behavioral correlates of directly and indirectly measured achievement motivation. In D. C. McClelland (Ed.), *Studies in motivation* (pp. 414–423). New York: Appleton-Century-Crofts.

Deci, E. L., Koestner, R., & Ryan, R. M. (1999). A meta-analytic review of experiments examining the effects of extrinsic rewards on intrinsic motivation. *Psychological Bulletin, 125*, 627–668.

Deci, E. L., & Ryan, R. M. (1985). *Intrinsic motivation and self-determination in human behavior.* New York: Plenum.

Deci, E. L., & Ryan, R. M. (1991). A motivational approach to self: Integration in personality. In R. Dienstbier (Ed.), *Nebraska Symposium on Motivation: Vol. 38. Perspectives on motivation* (pp. 237–288). Lincoln, NE: University of Nebraska Press.

Deci, D. E., & Ryan, R. M. (Eds.) (2002). *Handbook of self-determination research.* Rochester, NY: University of Rochester Press.

De Houwer, J., Thomas, S., & Baeyens, F. (2001). Associative learning of likes and dislikes: A review of 25 years of research on human evaluative conditioning. *Psychological Bulletin, 127*, 853–869.

Dijksterhuis, A. (2004). Think different: The merits of unconscious thought in preference development and decision making. *Journal of Personality and Social Psychology, 87,* 586–598.

Dijksterhuis, A. (2006). A theory of unconscious thought. *Perspectives on Psychological Science, 1,* 95–109.

Domjan, M. (2005). Pavlovian conditioning: A functional perspective. *Annual Review of Psychology, 56,* 179–206.

Duval, S., & Wicklund, R. A. (1972). *A theory of objective self-awareness.* New York: Academic Press.

Egloff, B., & Krohne, H. W. (1996). Repressive emotional discreteness after failure. *Journal of Personality and Social Psychology, 70,* 1318–1326.

Elliot, A. J. (2006). The hierarchical model of approach-avoidance motivation. *Motivation and Emotion, 30,* 111–116.

Elliot, A. J., & Church, M. A. (1997). A hierarchical model of approach and avoidance achievement motivation. *Journal of Personality and Social Psychology, 72,* 218–232.

Elliot, A. J., & Friedman, R. (2007). Approach-avoidance: A central characteristic of personal goals. In B. R. Little, K. Salmela-Aro, & S. D. Phillips (Eds.), *Personal project pursuit: Goals, action, and human flourishing* (pp. 97–118). Mahwah, NJ: Lawrence Erlbaum Associates.

Elliot, A. J., & McGregor, H. A. (1999). Test anxiety and the hierarchical model of approach and avoidance achievement motivation. *Journal of Personality and Social Psychology, 76,* 628–644.

Fenigstein, A., Scheier, M. F., & Buss, A. H. (1975). Public and private self-consciousness: Assessment and theory. *Journal of Consulting and Clinical Psychology, 43,* 522–527.

Frenkel-Brunswik, E. (1942). Motivation and behavior. *Genetic Psychology Monographs, 26,* 121–265.

Freud, S. (1909/1989). *Five lectures on psycho-analysis: The standard edition.* New York: Norton & Co.

Freud, S. (1933/1965). *New introductory lectures on psychoanalysis.* New York: Norton & Co.

Gendlin, E. T. (1981). *Focusing* (2nd ed.). New York: Bantam.

Greenwald, A. G., & Banaji, M. R. (1995). Implicit social cognition: Attitudes, self-esteem, and stereotypes. *Psychological Review, 102,* 4–27.

Gross, J. J. (2007). *Handbook of emotion regulation.* New York: Guilford Press.

Heckhausen, H. (1963). *Hoffnung und Furcht in der Leistungsmotivation [Hope and fear components of achievement motivation].* Meisenheim am Glan, Germany: Anton Hain.

Heckhausen, H., & Krug, S. (1982). Motive modification. In A. J. Stewart (Ed.), *Motivation and society: A volume in honor of David C. McClelland* (pp. 274–318). San Francisco: Jossey-Bass.

Hofer, J., Busch, H., Bond, M. H., Kärtner, J., Kiessling, F., & Law, R. (in press). Is self-determined functioning a universal prerequisite for motive-goal congruence? Examining the domain of achievement in three cultures. *Journal of Personality.*

Hofer, J., Busch, H., Chasiotis, A., & Kiessling, F. (2006). Motive congruence and interpersonal identity status. *Journal of Personality, 74,* 511–541.

Hofer, J., & Chasiotis, A. (2003). Congruence of life goals and implicit motives as predictors of life satisfaction: Cross-cultural implications of a study of Zambian male adolescents. *Motivation and Emotion, 27,* 251–272.

Hofmann, W., Gschwendner, T., Nosek, B. A., & Schmitt, M. (2005). What moderates implicit-explicit consistency? *European Review of Social Psychology, 16,* 335–390.

Jaccoby, L. L., Yonelinas, A. P., & Jennings, J. M. (1997). The relation between conscious and unconscious (automatic) influences: A declaration of independence. In J. D. Cohen & J. W. Schooler (Eds.), *Scientific approaches to consciousness* (pp. 13–27). Mahwah, NJ: Lawrence Erlbaum Associates.

Kehr, H. M. (2004a). Implicit/explicit motive discrepancies and volitional depletion among managers. *Personality and Social Psychology Bulletin, 30,* 315–327.

Kehr, H. M. (2004b). Integrating implicit motives, explicit motives, and perceived abilities: The compensatory model of work motivation and volition. *Academy of Management Review, 29,* 479–499.

Kihlstrom, J. F. (1990). The psychological unconscious. In L. A. Pervin (Ed.), *Handbook of personality: Theory and research* (pp. 445–464). New York: Guilford Press.

Kim, J. J., & Baxter, M. G. (2001). Multiple brain memory systems: The whole does not equal the sum of its parts. *Trends in Neuroscience, 24,* 324–330.

King, L. A. (1995). Wishes, motives, goals, and personal memories: Relations of measures of human motivation. *Journal of Personality, 63,* 985–1007.

Kline, R. B. (2005). *Principles and practice of structural equation modeling* (2nd ed.). New York: Guilford Press.

Klinger, E. (1967). Modeling effects on achievement imagery. *Journal of Personality and Social Psychology, 7,* 49–62.

Kuhl, J. (2000). A functional-design approach to motivation and volition: The dynamics of personality systems interactions. In M. Boekaerts, P. R. Pintrich, & M. Zeidner (Eds.), *Self-regulation: Directions and challenges for future research* (pp. 111–169). New York: Academic Press.

LeDoux, J. (2002). *The synaptic self: How our brains become who we are.* New York: Viking.

Marcia, J. E. (1966). Development and validation of ego identity status. *Journal of Personality and Social Psychology, 3,* 551–558.

McClelland, D. C. (1951). *Personality.* New York: Sloane.

McClelland, D. C. (1965). Toward a theory of motive acquisition. *American Psychologist, 20,* 321–333.

McClelland, D. C. (1980). Motive dispositions. The merits of operant and respondent measures. In L. Wheeler (Ed.), *Review of personality and social psychology* (Vol. 1, pp. 10–41). Beverly Hills, CA: Sage.

McClelland, D. C. (1987). *Human motivation.* Cambridge, UK: Cambridge University Press.

McClelland, D. C. (1992). Motivational configurations. In C. P. Smith (Ed.), *Motivation and personality: Handbook of thematic content analysis* (pp. 87–99). Cambridge, UK: Cambridge University Press.

McClelland, D. C. (1995). Achievement motivation in relation to achievement-related recall, performance, and urine flow, a marker associated with release of vasopressin. *Motivation and Emotion, 19,* 59–76.

McClelland, D. C., Atkinson, J. W., Clark, R. A., & Lowell, E. L. (1953). *The achievement motive.* New York: Appleton-Century-Crofts.

McClelland, D. C., Koestner, R., & Weinberger, J. (1989). How do self-attributed and implicit motives differ? *Psychological Review, 96,* 690–702.

McClelland, D. C., & Pilon, D. A. (1983). Sources of adult motives in patterns of parent behavior in early childhood. *Journal of Personality and Social Psychology, 44,* 564–574.

McClelland, G. H., & Judd, C. M. (1993). Statistical difficulties of detecting interactions and moderator effects. *Psychological Bulletin, 114,* 376–390.

Miller, L. C., Murphy, R., & Buss, A. H. (1981). Consciousness of body: Private and public. *Journal of Personality and Social Psychology, 41,* 397–406.

Miron, D., & McClelland, D. C. (1979). The impact of achievement motivation training on small businesses. *California Management Review, 21,* 13–28.

Mowrer, O. H. (1939). A stimulus-response analysis of anxiety and its role as a reinforcing agent. *Psychological Review, 46,* 553–565.

Murray, H. A. (1938). *Explorations in personality.* New York: Oxford University Press.

Nesse, R. M., & Lloyd, A. T. (1992). The evolution of psychodynamic mechanisms. In J. H. Barkow, L. Cosmides, & J. Tooby (Eds.), *The adapted mind: Evolutionary psychology and the generation of culture* (pp. 601–624). New York: Oxford University Press.

Nezlek, J. B. (2001). Multilevel random coefficient analyses of event and interval contingent data in social and personality psychology research. *Personality and Social Psychology Bulletin, 27,* 771–785.

Nosek, B. A., & Smyth, F. L. (2007). A multitrait-multimethod validation of the Implicit Association Test. *Experimental Psychology, 54,* 14–29.

Paulhus, D. L. (1998). *Paulhus Deception Scales (PDS): The balanced inventory of desirable responding—7: User's manual.* North Tonawanda, NY: Multi-Health Systems.

Paulhus, D. L., Bruce, M. N., & Trapnell, P. D. (1995). Effects of self-presentation strategies on personality profiles and their structure. *Personality and Social Psychology Bulletin, 21,* 100–108.

Podsakoff, P. M., MacKenzie, S. B., Lee, J.-Y., & Podsakoff, N. P. (2003). Common method biases in behavioral research: A critical review of the literature and recommended remedies. *Journal of Applied Psychology, 88,* 879–903.

Reuman, D. A., Alwin, D. F., & Veroff, J. (1984). Assessing the validity of the achievement motive in the presence of random measurement error. *Journal of Personality and Social Psychology, 47,* 1347–1362.

Rogers, C. R. (1959). A theory of therapy, personality, and interpersonal relationships, as developed in the client-centered framework. In S. Koch (Ed.), *Psychology: A study of a science: Vol. 3. Formulations of the person and the social context* (pp. 184–215). New York: McGraw-Hill.

Rolls, E. T. (2007). The affective neuroscience of consciousness: Higher-order syntactic thoughts, dual routes to emotion and action, and consciousness. In P. Zelazo, M. Moscovitch, & E. Thompson (Eds.), *The Cambridge handbook of consciousness* (pp. 831–859). New York: Cambridge University Press.

Schachter, S., & Singer, J. E. (1962). Cognitive, social and physiological determinants of emotional state. *Psychological Review, 69,* 379–399.

Schultheiss, O. C. (2001a). An information processing account of implicit motive arousal. In M. L. Maehr & P. Pintrich (Eds.), *Advances in motivation and achievement* (Vol. 12, pp. 1–41). Greenwich, CT: JAI.

Schultheiss, O. C. (2001b). *Manual for the assessment of hope of success and fear of failure* (English translation of Heckhausen's need for achievement measure). Unpublished manuscript, Department of Psychology, University of Michigan, Ann Arbor.

Schultheiss, O. C. (2007). A memory-systems approach to the classification of personality tests: Comment on Meyer and Kurtz (2006). *Journal of Personality Assessment*, *89*, 197–201.

Schultheiss, O. C., & Brunstein, J. C. (1999). Goal imagery: Bridging the gap between implicit motives and explicit goals. *Journal of Personality*, *67*, 1–38.

Schultheiss, O. C., & Murray, T. (2002). *Hope of success/fear of failure questionnaire.* Ann Arbor, MI: University of Michigan, Department of Psychology.

Schultheiss, O. C., Wirth, M. M., Torges, C. M., Pang, J. S., Villacorta, M. A., & Welsh, K. M. (2005). Effects of implicit power motivation on men's and women's implicit learning and testosterone changes after social victory or defeat. *Journal of Personality and Social Psychology*, *88*, 174–188.

Sheldon, K. M., Arndt, J., & Houser-Marko, L. (2003). In search of the organismic valuing process: The human tendency to move towards beneficial goals. *Journal of Personality*, *71*, 835–869.

Sheldon, K. M., King, L. A., Houser-Marko, L., Osbaldiston, R., & Gunz, A. (2007). Comparing IAT and TAT measures of power versus intimacy motivation. *European Journal of Personality*, *21*, 263–280.

Sherwood, J. J. (1966). Self-report and projective measures of achievement and affiliation. *Journal of Consulting Psychology*, *30*, 329–337.

Skinner, B. F. (1938). *The behavior of organisms: An experimental analysis.* New York: Appleton-Century.

Smith, C. P. (Ed.) (1992). *Motivation and personality: Handbook of thematic content analysis.* Cambridge, UK: Cambridge University Press.

Snyder, M., & Gangestad, S. (1986). On the nature of self-monitoring: Matters of assessment, matters of validity. *Journal of Personality and Social Psychology*, *51*, 125–139.

Sokolowski, K., Schmalt, H.-D., Langens, T. A., & Puca, R. M. (2000). Assessing achievement, affiliation, and power motives all at once: The Multi-Motive Grid (MMG). *Journal of Personality Assessment*, *74*, 126–145.

Spangler, W. D. (1992). Validity of questionnaire and TAT measures of need for achievement: Two meta-analyses. *Psychological Bulletin*, *112*, 140–154.

Sperry R. W., Gazzaniga, M. S., & Bogen, J. E. (1969). Interhemispheric relationships: The neocortical commissures: Syndromes of hemisphere disconnection. In P. J. Vinken & G. W. Bruyn (Eds.), *Handbook of clinical neurology* (Vol. 4, pp. 273–290). Amsterdam: North Holland Publishing.

Squire, L. R. (2004). Memory systems of the brain: A brief history and current perspective. *Neurobiology of Learning and Memory*, *82*, 171–177.

Taylor, G. J., & Bagby, R. M. (2000) An overview of the alexithymia construct. In R. Bar-On & J. D. A. Parker (Eds.), *The handbook of emotional intelligence* (pp. 40–67). San Francisco: Jossey-Bass.

Thrash, T. M. (2007). Differentiation of the distributions of inspiration and positive affect across days of the week: An application of logistic multilevel modeling. In A. D. Ong & M. Van Dulmen (Eds.), *Oxford handbook of methods in positive psychology* (pp. 515–529). New York: Oxford University Press.

Thrash, T. M., & Elliot, A. J. (2001). Delimiting and integrating achievement motive and goal constructs. In A. Efklides, J. Kuhl, & R. M. Sorrentino (Eds.), *Trends and prospects in motivation research* (pp. 3–21). Boston: Kluwer.

Thrash, T. M., & Elliot, A. J. (2002). Implicit and self-attributed achievement motives: Concordance and predictive validity. *Journal of Personality, 70,* 729–755.

Thrash, T. M., & Elliot, A. J. (2003). Inspiration as a psychological construct. *Journal of Personality and Social Psychology, 84,* 871–889.

Thrash, T. M., & Elliot, A. J. (2004). Inspiration: Core characteristics, component processes, antecedents, and function. *Journal of Personality and Social Psychology, 87,* 957–973.

Thrash, T. M., Elliot, A. J., & Schultheiss, O. C. (2007). Methodological and dispositional predictors of congruence between implicit and explicit need for achievement. *Personality and Social Psychology Bulletin, 33,* 961–974.

Thrash, T. M., & Hurst, A. L. (2008). Approach and avoidance motivation in the achievement domain: Integrating achievement motive and achievement goal traditions. In A. J. Elliot (Ed.), *Handbook of approach and avoidance motivation* (pp. 215–231). New York: LEA.

Trapnell, P. D., & Campbell, J. D. (1999). Private self-consciousness and the five-factor model of personality: Distinguishing rumination from reflection. *Journal of Personality and Social Psychology, 76,* 284–304.

Vaillant, G. E. (2000). Adaptive mental mechanisms: Their role in a positive psychology. *American Psychologist, 55,* 89–98.

Westen, D., Weinberger, J., & Bradley, R. (2007). Motivation, decision making, and consciousness: From psychodynamics to subliminal priming and emotional constraint satisfaction. In P. D. Zelazo, M. Moscovitch, & E. Thompson (Eds.), *The Cambridge handbook of consciousness* (pp. 673–702). New York: Cambridge University Press.

Whyte, L. L. (1978). *The unconscious before Freud.* New York: St. Martin's Press.

Wilson, T. D. (2002). *Strangers to ourselves: Discovering the adaptive unconscious.* Cambridge, MA: Harvard University Press.

Wilson, T. D., & Dunn, E. W. (2004). Self-knowledge: Its limits, value, and potential for improvement. *Annual Review of Psychology, 55,* 493–518.

Winterbottom, M. R. (1958). The relation of need for achievement to learning experiences in independence and mastery. In J. W. Atkinson (Ed.), *Motives in fantasy, action, and society: A method of assessment and study* (pp. 453–478). Princeton, NJ: Van Nostrand.

Chapter 12

Implicit Motives and Explicit Goals: The Role of Motivational Congruence in Emotional Well-Being

JOACHIM C. BRUNSTEIN
Department of Psychology
Justus-Liebig University

Introduction

Telic theories of well-being rest on the idea that a sense of happiness and satisfaction can be achieved when people successfully strive for desired end states (Diener, 1984; Diener, Suh, Lucas, & Smith, 1999). Integral to telic theories is thus the view that how happy or satisfied a person generally feels depends on what this person is trying to do in life and how successful he or she is in doing it (Brickman & Coates, 1987; Cantor & Sanderson, 1999). The basic idea is that individuals use desired ends as reference standards to evaluate the status of their ongoing pursuits (Emmons, 1996). Hedonic reactions generated by the affect system are sensitive to discrepancies detected in this comparison process. Individuals feel pleased when they are making good progress toward desired outcomes but react negatively when they perceive that they are falling short of what they have sought to attain (for a more detailed discussion and theoretical elaboration of this idea, see Carver & Scheier, 1998; Diener & Lucas, 2000; Hsee & Abelson, 1991).

From the perspective of motivation theory, Brunstein, Schultheiss, and Grässmann (1998) argued that the desired ends that are involved in well-being experiences can be traced back to mainly two motivational sources: (a) broadly defined motives that reside in the cognitive unconscious but propel individuals toward the attainment of incentives intimately tied to desired states of need fulfillment (think, for instance, of a person who has a strong need to achieve and, thus, seeks pleasure from mastering challenges); and (b) relatively more specific, consciously represented goals individuals set and pursue in an effort to furnish their daily activities with a sense of inner coherence and personal meaning (think, for instance, of a student who has entered college and thus is trying to make new friends and get good grades at academic exams; see McGregor & Little, 1998).

Goal achievement and *motive satisfaction* have often been considered in the motivation literature (see below) to refer to two different levels of abstraction within a hierarchically ordered motivation system. Motives and goals are considered to be related in the sense that underlying motives lead to specific goals the person is aware of and can translate into elaborated plans, which serve to furnish the particular structures and resources goal strivers need to enact their self-chosen endeavours. From this view, motives and goals are closely interconnected and both belong to one and the same, unitary motivation system. Motives influence the formation of goals and thereby the enactment of goal-directed behavior; goals in turn instantiate motives and thereby personalize fundamental needs that seek their behavioral outlets within the affordances and constraints inherent in a person's life context (see Emmons, 1997).

Recent evidence, however, suggests that this cognitive-behavioral transformation of broadly defined motives into more specific aims does *not* automatically happen in the natural dynamics of goal formation processes. Some people may be able, at least at certain moments in life, to generate goals that nicely fit their motives and concretize the expression of needs in goal-directed activities; others, however, are less successful in this respect, frequently forming commitments that have little relation to the preferences represented by their motives.

Right at the beginning of this chapter, let me be clear that this variation in the strength of motive–goal relations can hardly be detected when motives (e.g., the need to achieve) are simply equated with self-attributed needs ("I want to be successful") and motivational self-views ("Me as an achievement-oriented person") that are part of a person's self-knowledge. Superordinate life goals of this sort are closely tied to their multifaceted derivates (e.g., a person's more specific goals and plans) and, like them, can be assessed with self-report instruments (e.g., Pöhlmann & Brunstein, 1997). This situation changes, however, when researchers seek to address the specific functional characteristics of psychological motives (see Schultheiss, 2001) by inferring the strength of a particular need from relatively unconstrained, imaginative thoughts respondents produce in response to motive-eliciting pictures akin to Murray's (1943) Thematic Apperception Test. It is thus important to note that the majority of studies I will review were inspired by the phenomenon that subjective goals assessed with self-report inventories show no or only little overlap with motives assessed with Picture Story Exercise (PSE) methods, and that I will therefore focus in this chapter on research using this latter method for assessing the strength of psychological motives (for a review of different motivational approaches to subjective well-being, see Diener & Lucas, 2000; and Ryan & Deci, 2001).

In doing so, I will propose that McClelland, Koestner, and Weinberger's (1989) distinction between implicit and explicit motivational systems is particularly instructive to understand the observed lack of convergence between PSE-derived motives and self-reported strivings. Remarkably, during the 1990s, a number of goal theorists (see Brunstein et al., 1998; Cantor & Blanton, 1996; King, 1995) adopted this distinction and postulated that implicit motives and subjective intentions do *not* belong to the same underlying system but represent two qualitatively different modes of motivational functioning: one being associated with the effortless pursuit of pleasurable incentives a person seeks to attain without any need for self-reflection, and the other one being associated with the laborious work of accomplishing self-generated goals representing what a person considers to be meaningful and seeks to attain in certain life domains.

One important implication of this theoretical distinction is that individuals may differ greatly with respect to their ability of achieving a sense of harmony between what they consciously intend to do (the realm of explicit goal pursuits) and what they nonconsciously would like to do (the realm of implicit motives) in life. A second implication is that differing degrees of *motivational congruence*, defined as the extent to which self-chosen goals thematically correspond with strong motives, may be reflected in how people experience the affective quality of their lives (McClelland et al., 1989).

In this chapter, I will review research highlighting the importance of the concept of motivational congruence in the prediction of affective experiences of well-being. Although motives and goals show little overlap, I will argue that they often interact, such that they synergistically influence people's moods. Generally, I will propose that a high degree of congruence between the two motivational systems is a key prerequisite for high emotional well-being. More specifically, however, I will suggest that motivational congruence is not enough to guarantee happiness. Instead, I will argue that the same kind of motive disposition that makes the pursuit of a specific goal particularly pleasurable can easily revert its influence to become a source of distress if an ongoing pursuit is blocked through obstacles. Before I consider these issues in greater detail, however, I will briefly summarize the basic premises underlying the concept of motivational congruence.

Implicit Motives and Explicit (Personal) Goals

The core idea of McClelland et al.'s (McClelland et al., 1989; Weinberger & McClelland, 1990) model of *dual motives* is that two different motivational systems coexist within the individual: The first system is termed *implicit* because it is hypothesized to be based on affective preferences that operate on a person's behavior outside of his or her conscious awareness. The second system is referred to as *explicit* because it is cognitively based and essentially reflects the view people have of their own wishes, goals, and intentions.

Implicit Motives

According to Weinberger and McClelland (1990), the functioning of the implicit motivational system can roughly be described as follows: On a personal level, a limited number of motives (e.g., the motives for achievement, power, affiliation, and intimacy) constitute the pillars of this system. Each motive is hypothesized to be based upon a relatively enduring preference for a broadly defined class of affectively charged incentives (e.g., doing a thing better; having impact upon others; doing things together with others; being engaged in affectionate relationships). The consummation of a motive-specific incentive automatically releases a pleasant affect (e.g., feeling proud, strong, secure, and comfortable), which too is specific to the respective motive or need.

Implicit motives are automatically activated when environmental cues signal the availability of a motive-specific incentive. Motive arousal is expressed in anticipatory affective states, which provide a glimpse of the pleasant affect associated with the desired incentive (hope of success, for instance, is the anticipation of taking pride from success in mastering a challenge). According to McClelland (1987), an aroused motive drives, orients, and selects behavior directed at the attainment of the desired incentive. Because approach tendencies elicited in this way trigger immediate responses and spontaneous acts, motive-supported behavior needs little conscious effort (think, for instance, of an achievement-motivated person who immediately reacts to negative feedback by increasing his or her task-related effort without any need to switch from a procedural mode into a deliberative mode of effort regulation; see Brunstein & Maier, 2005).

Because motives are assumed to be represented in the unconscious, individuals are assumed to be unaware of their motives and, accordingly, unable to accurately report on their own motives if they are explicitly requested to do so (by filling out, for instance, a forced-choice questionnaire administered to them by an experimenter). Instead, as it is evident in the many chapters of this book, motivation researchers who try to understand the functioning of implicit motives prefer more indirect methods, and primarily the thematic analysis of Picture Story Test material, for assessing the strength of a particular motive. Variations in motive strength as inferred from the thematic contents evident in respondents' PSE protocols are then interpreted in terms of individual differences in people's capacity of getting satisfaction from seeking a particular type of incentive (for an empirical test of this notion in the area of achievement motivation, see Brunstein & Maier, 2005).

Inherent in the line of theorizing put forth by McClelland (1987) is the view that experiences of emotional involvement and personal satisfaction emerge from person–environment transactions that first arouse and then fulfill a person's particular motives. Drawing on this view, Brunstein et al. (1998) posited that "positive well-being emotions, such as feeling happy and pleased, should follow from a person's engagement in behavior projects and activities that offer opportunities to satisfy motives" and continued to argue that "a person should feel dissatisfied if a strong motive cannot be gratified or is put under stress" (p. 494).

Unfortunately, only a few studies have directly examined the notion that the satisfaction of motives is reflected in people's well-being emotions. Motivation researchers using the PSE procedure for assessing the strength of particular motives have never put too much emphasis on the analysis of *subjective* feeling states but relied in their examination of how motives interact with the affect system on more *objective* indicators (e.g., physiological and hormonal correlates of positive and negative affect) reflecting how people react to the fulfillment or frustration of important needs (e.g., needs for power and affiliation) on a psycho-physiological level of functioning (cf. Jemmott, 1987; Schultheiss, 2007).

A few exceptions should be noted, however. McClelland and Jemmott (1980) reported that power-motivated individuals (i.e., respondents whose PSE stories were saturated with power-related motive imagery), responded to motive-relevant stressful events with more affective and physical symptoms than individuals scoring low in power. McAdams and Bryant (1987) found that women whose intimacy motive was strong (PSE) generally felt happier in life than women whose intimacy motive was weak. However, intimacy-motivated women who lacked opportunities for intimacy in their daily lives reported less satisfaction and experienced more uncertainty than women low in intimacy motivation. Although these studies focused primarily on experiences of ill-being, rather than of well-being, their findings were generally in accord with the idea that the (dis-)satisfaction of motives can be gauged by asking respondents to report how they generally feel.

Explicit (Personal) Goals

The goals people set for themselves and seek to attain in different areas of life constitute a crucial part of what Weinberger and McClelland (1990) termed the explicit motivational system. Although this system hosts a multiplicity of interrelated constructs, such as a person's self-concepts, cognitive beliefs, and personal values, subjective goals and behavioral intentions represent its dynamic components. To put it metaphorically, these "self-"generated motivators are the explicit system's propelling forces that link a person's self-views to the enactment of future-oriented goals and plans. Self-generated (or *personal*) goals are part of a person's self-related knowledge (here: a person's declarative knowledge about what she or he intends to do and who she or he wants to become in the future). As such, they are verbally represented, expressed in linguistic or other symbolic terms, and accessible to introspective methods.

Traditionally, motivation researchers and developmental psychologists agree that it is much healthier for individuals to generate their own personal goals than to adopt, without closer examination, the goals other people, or society as a whole, would like them to pursue (Kuhl, 1992; Lerner & Busch-Rossnagel, 1981; Ryan, Sheldon, Kasser, & Deci, 1996). However, personal-goal setting can be a burdensome task, requiring the individual to engage in a rather lengthy process of deliberative thought (see Gollwitzer, 1993). In this process, individuals carefully weigh their own wishes, interests, and desires against the expectations, constraints, and demands inherent in their social life situations. In order to set goals that are both desirable and feasible, individuals often ponder on a number of alternatives, reflect on the pros and cons associated with a potential goal, and carefully examine if a specific pursuit would match or contradict their life plans. Sooner or later, progress in this highly self-reflective process demands a decision to select and act on a given goal, as Gollwitzer (1993; Achtziger & Gollwitzer, 2008) argued with reference to the so-called Rubicon model of action phases (see also Heckhausen, 1991). Personal-goal setting is thus not just a product of internal and external influences, but also implies an act of choice and self-commitment.

But even after crossing the Rubicon, the really hard work still needs to be done (see Gollwitzer, 1999). In order to materialize their commitments, people translate their goals into behavioral plans and associated instrumental activities, selectively choose environments that facilitate goal enactment, monitor progress toward goal attainment, and modify their strategies and plans in response to goal-relevant feedback information. Goal obstacles may further complicate the route toward goal attainment, requiring individuals to expend extra effort and develop more efficient plans to fulfill their commitments in the face of adversities. Hence, when people start to realize their self-chosen goals, success is anything but granted. Many goals that are important are also troublesome (McGregor & Little, 1998) and thus, as Cantor and Blanton (1996) stated, "simply cannot be attained without considerable self-regulation and effort" (p. 339).

On the positive side, however, having goals and being able to work on them in a wide array of situations enables individuals to furnish their daily activities with a sense of agency and personal meaning (Klinger, 1977; Wessman & Ricks, 1966). Indeed, there is considerable evidence to suggest that a sense of goal directedness represents a major source of well-being in people's lives (see Brunstein et al., 1999; Emmons, 1996; Sheldon, 2002). In the majority of studies addressing this issue, respondents were asked first to describe their personal goals in different life domains and then to assess them according to a number of attributes. Framed in a *personal-goal model of emotional well-being* (see Fig. 12.1; the dashed line will be explained below), Brunstein and

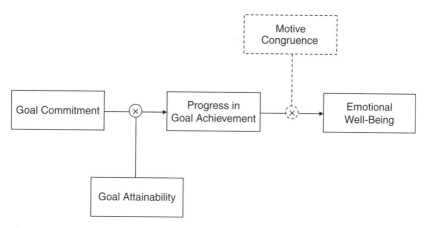

Figure 12.1 Personal-goal model of emotional well-being (see Brunstein, 1993) and its extension (indicated by the dashed lines) by the concept of motivational congruence (see Brunstein, Schultheiss, & Grässmann, 1998).

colleagues (Brunstein 1993; Brunstein, Dangelmayer, & Schultheiss, 1996; Maier & Brunstein, 2001) predicted and found that three goal-appraisal dimensions are particularly important to account for individual differences in affective and judgmental measures of well-being: goal commitment, goal attainability, and progress in goal achievement.

Following the logic of this model, people are most likely to reach high levels of well-being when they perceive that they succeed in realizing their commitments. High rates of progress in goal achievement give rise to elated moods (e.g., feeling happy and pleased) whereas low rates of progress are reflected in dejected moods. One further prediction of this model is that in order to succeed in the pursuit of a given goal, two conditions have to be met: (a) Individuals must feel strongly committed to their personal goals (e.g., identify themselves with their goals and feel an urgent need to enact them). (b) Individuals' life situations must offer favorable opportunities (e.g., enough time to implement personal goals; social support of personal goals; and personal control over goal-related outcomes) to attain these goals.

If each of these two conditions is met, people are likely to make substantial progress toward their goals, and this experience, in turn, gives rise to pleasant moods. In contrast, when people pursue goals under poor conditions, they will be likely to suffer from feelings of disappointment, especially if they are, and remain, strongly committed to their stressful pursuits (for a detailed discussion of how disengagement from unrealistic goals may prevent individuals from chronic states of dissatisfaction, see Wrosch, Scheier, Miller, Schulz, & Carver, 2003). Unfavorable conditions to attain personal goals can dramatically impair goal progress and thereby lead to negative well-being emotions. In comparison, a lack of goal commitment may also have adverse effects on goal progress but relatively less dramatic effects on well-being emotions. The reason for this is that the strength of goal commitment determines the extent to which well-being experiences depend on the pursuit of personal goals. For a review of empirical evidence corroborating the validity of these propositions in different domains of satisfaction (e.g., job satisfaction and marital satisfaction), the reader is referred to the overview given in Brunstein et al. (1999).

Conceptual and Empirical Relationships Between Motives and Goals

To recapitulate, explicit (personal) goals differ from implicit motives in at least three important respects: (a) Whereas implicit motives involve enduring preferences for broadly defined classes of incentives that are available in a wide array of situations, self-generated goals constitute more narrowly defined motivators that indicate what a person is consciously trying to do within a specific life domain. (b) In contrast to the spontaneous pursuit of implicit motives, the accomplishment of self-chosen objectives mostly requires considerable effort and self-control. (c) Explicit (personal) goals are stored in a person's memory for future intentions and, thus, can be assessed with self-report methods. In contrast, due to introspective limits, the affective preferences underlying motive dispositions are inaccessible to subjective awareness. Indirect assessment tools, such as the PSE procedure, are more adequate to determine the strength of particular motives.

Despite these differences, motives and goals have often been described in the motivation literature as two closely interrelated constructs. Both Lewin (1926) and Murray (1938) assumed that specific goals typically derive from super-ordinate needs. Goals are chosen to meet these motives or needs and link them to the execution of goal-directed activities. In the same vein, Nuttin (1984) argued that goal setting results from an urge to elaborate a higher-order need, "seeking its behavioral outlet at the cognitive level of functioning" (p. 152). Extending on this idea, Wurf and Markus (1991) suggested that it is through a process of "personalizing motivation" that a broadly defined motive is translated into more concrete, idiosyncratic concerns. Which particular type of goal (e.g., improving one's motor skills in playing tennis, or exercising one's conversation skills in a foreign language) a person adopts from a class of functionally equivalent goals (here: achievement-related goals) depends on what Weinberger and McClelland (1990) described as further ingredients, or definitional characteristics, of the explicit motivational system (e.g., a person's consciously held self-beliefs) as well as the affordances and constraints inherent in a person's social environment.

All of these ideas may be considered as variations of one and the same motif: Self-generated goals represent "personalized outlets" or "idiosyncratic instantiations" of underlying motives (see Emmons, 1996). What is added to a vaguely defined motive in the goal-construction process is the specificity of contextual features, the integration of life experiences, the consideration of societal expectations, and the development of cognitive plans, all of which serve to furnish the particular structures and resources that channel the expression of motives in coherent patterns of goal-directed behavior.

Remarkably, this intuitively plausible view has received little support from correlational research in which participants completed implicit *and* explicit measures of motivation. In these studies, written protocols of self-descriptive goal reports were coded for the presence (vs. absence) of the same motivational themes as those typically used to assess the strength of particular motives with the PSE method (cf. Emmons & King, 1992). In this way, it was determined if the themes and concerns (power, achievement, intimacy, and affiliation) a respondent had expressed in the PSE were, or were not, reflected in the themes and concerns the same respondent had described as being characteristic of his or her self-articulated strivings.

Investigators who adopted this procedure found only moderate (Emmons & McAdams, 1991) or no significant correlations (Brunstein, Lautenschlager, Nawroth, Pöhlmann, & Schultheiss, 1995; King, 1995) between implicit and explicit measures of nominally similar motivations (and the studies reported below provide further evidence for this lack of convergence between motive-based and goal-based assessments of motivational concerns). For instance, King (1995) found significant correlations among different measures of explicit motivations (among others: a measure of self-reported goal strivings) both within and across specific motivational domains, yet relative independence between PSE-type assessments and self-report measures within the same motivational domain.

From a methodological point of view, this finding is quite surprising because the conjoint content coding analysis of PSE protocols and self-reported goal strivings might have established a source of common method variance, which is generally assumed to exaggerate, rather than underestimate, the true relationship between two constructs (here: motives and goals within a given motivational domain). Independence between implicit and explicit motive measures despite highly similar assessment methods was also observed by Schultheiss, Yankova, Dirlikov, and Schad (2009). In this study, a self-report measure employing the same picture stimuli as the PSE and items that were derived from the content coding categories used in the assessment of motive imagery failed to show substantial convergent validity with a PSE measure of implicit motives.

From the theoretical perspective outlined by McClelland et al. (1989), the lack of convergence between PSE-derived motives and declarative statements of motivation and goal striving observed in the above studies might appear less amazing, however. Self-reported goals were significantly related to self-attributed needs and self-rated preferences, measures that have been known for long time to be unrelated to PSE motives (McClelland, 1951, 1980; see also Schultheiss & Brunstein, 2001). Consistent with these earlier findings, the results of the reviewed studies show that motivational tendencies surfacing out of the stream of imaginative thoughts (PSE-derived motives) can, but need not, be mirrored in the intentions and plans people attribute to themselves and describe as being characteristic of what they want to achieve in life (self-reported goals).

Motivational Congruence and Emotional Well-Being

The Motivational-Congruence Hypothesis

Drawing on these findings, Brunstein et al. (1995) speculated that varying degrees of motivational congruence might be reflected in individual differences in affective experiences of well-being. Brunstein et al. hypothesized that within a given domain of motivation (e.g., achievement), the strength of the respective motive (here: the implicit need to achieve) determines the extent to which a person gets satisfaction from thematically related goal strivings (here: a person's achievement-related goals).[1]

To be more specific, Brunstein et al. (1995) built their research on three arguments: (a) Motive satisfaction is reflected in general feelings of well-being. (b) When goals are furnished with incentives thematically related to strong motives, they are suitable for satisfying motives and can thereby promote experiences of positive well-being. In comparison, goals unrelated to motives have relatively little influence on people's feelings and moods. (c) Individuals differ with respect to the extent to which their consciously selected goals are thematically congruent with their predominant motives.

From this line of argument, it follows that individual differences in motivational congruence will be reflected in individual differences in feeling of well-being. People who are involved in goals that thematically correspond with their implicit preferences should display higher levels of well-being than individuals who are preoccupied with motive-incongruent concerns. Brunstein et al. (1995) termed this idea as the "motivational congruence" hypothesis, which essentially states that implicit motives moderate the influence of explicit-goal pursuits on people's emotional well-being.

Initial Test of the Motivational-Congruence Hypothesis

In a sample of college students, Brunstein et al. (1995) classified both motives and goals in terms of Bakan's (1966) distinction between *agency* and *communion* as two fundamental but often incommensurable modalities of human life.

According to Bakan, agency denotes a concern for autonomy, self-assertion, and mastery experiences whereas communion is expressed in a concern for forming friendly and warm relationships with others. Based on this distinction, Brunstein et al. (1995) categorized motivational themes of power and achievement as agentic concerns and classified affiliation- and intimacy-related concerns as communal strivings. Implicit needs for agency (power and achievement) and communion (affiliation and intimacy) were assessed with a PSE, which was coded using Winter's (1991) running-text integrated scoring system. A related scoring key was used to code the content of students' self-reported goals for the presence of agentic and communal concerns. As noted above, in neither of the two striving areas, were PSE-assessed motives significantly correlated with goal reports. To explore the affective consequences of varying degrees of fit between implicit motives and self-reported goals, Brunstein et al. (1995) administered a mood adjective checklist designed to assess students' current emotional well-being. These data were analyzed with a moderated multiple regression equation that included a Motive Strength × Goal Striving term to represent within each striving area (agency and communion) the interactive effect of the two motivation measures on students' mood.

In each of the two striving areas, the multiplicative relationship between PSE-assessed motive strength and the intensity of self-reported strivings predicted individual differences in students' well-being above and beyond the first-order effects of motive and goal measures. Greater involvement in motive-congruent goals (see Fig. 12.2) was generally associated with higher levels of well-being. For instance, among students with a strong communal motive, striving for communion-oriented goals was reflected in enhanced mood (see Panel A). Correspondingly, among students with a strong agentic motive, striving for agentic goals was positively related to well-being (see Panel B).

These results lent preliminary support to the idea that active engagement in motive-congruent goals promotes positive well-being. Remarkably, however, the regression analyses yielded one further result: Students who were strongly involved in goals that did not fit their motives (communal goals for students with a predominant agentic motive and agentic goals for students with a strong communal motive) reported relatively low levels of well-being. This finding suggests that motive-incongruent goals are not as affectively neutral as Brunstein et al. (1995) initially expected them to be but may lead to detrimental effects on the affective quality of people's lives. Clearly, this finding needs further clarification and will be discussed in later sections.

Cross-Cultural Evidence

Further evidence of the validity of the motivational-congruence hypothesis comes from research conducted by Hofer and colleagues (Hofer, Busch, Chasiotis, & Kiessling, 2006; Hofer, Busch, & Kiessling, 2008; Hofer &

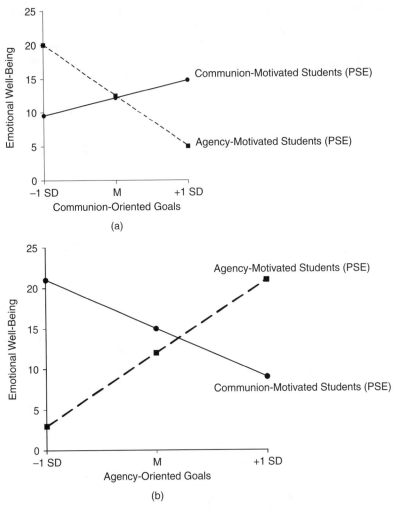

Figure 12.2 Emotional well-being as a function of type of goal striving. Regression slopes for students with predominant agentic and communal motives (PSE = Picture Story Exercise). Adapted from Brunstein, Lautenschlager, Nawroth, Pöhlmann, and Schultheiss (1995, p. 7).

Chasiotis, 2003; Hofer, Chasiotis, & Campos, 2006). These researchers investigated in various cultures and populations how implicit and explicit sources of motivation jointly influence well-being and psychological adjustment (e.g., life satisfaction and experiences of need fulfillment). In samples recruited from African (Zambia, Cameroon) and Latin-American (Costa Rica) countries, Hofer and his associates replicated the finding originally identified in European and American samples that implicit motives assessed with PSE tests do not correlate with their self-reported counterparts (e.g., explicit goals and value orientations). Furthermore, across Western and nonWestern cultures,

Hofer and colleagues consistently found that the alignment of implicit motives on the one hand and explicit values and life goals on the other hand was associated with enhanced well-being whereas discrepancies between implicit motives and explicit goals were negatively related to well-being.

Similar to Brunstein et al. (1995), Hofer and associates established this evidence by showing that PSE-assessed motives statistically interact with self-reported strivings in the prediction of individual differences in well-being. This finding underscores the idea that achieving a high degree of harmony between one's implicit and explicit preferences is associated with high levels of well-being. It also suggests that this idea describes a human universal that can be observed across different cultural settings.

Goal Achievement and Motive Satisfaction

To further advance the idea that motive dispositions play an important role in people's emotional life, Brunstein et al. (1998) integrated the concept of motivational congruence into a model originally developed by Brunstein (1993) to explain how personal goals are involved in the prediction of well-being. As noted above (see "Explicit (Personal) Goals" section), this model was built on three assumptions (see Fig. 12.1): (a) People reach high levels of well-being when they perceive that they are succeeding in their ongoing pursuits. Progress in goal achievement is thus considered an immediate precursor of well-being. (b) To achieve high rates of progress, individuals need both a strong sense of commitment to their personal goals and favorable conditions to attain these goals. (c) Goal commitment and goal attainability are thus considered distal predictors of well-being.

The new element Brunstein et al. (1998) added to this model was that not all goals are equally effective in producing well-being effects. Extending on the motivational-congruence hypothesis, they hypothesized that goals carrying motive-relevant incentives are more effective in this respect than goals unrelated to strong motives. Brunstein et al. therefore concluded that experiences with success and failure in the pursuit of personal goals should have strong well-being effects only if a given goal qualifies for the satisfaction of motives. The rationale underlying this notion is as follows:

If self-generated goals are furnished with motive-relevant incentives, a person who makes good progress on such a goal has many contacts with affectively charged incentives, leading to repeated pleasure responses. The intensity of these responses corresponds to the strength of the gratified motive. Hence, if a goal is congruent with a particular motive, the affective consequences of goal success are augmented up to an extent determined by the strength of this motive. The same rationale can be used to predict how individuals react to a perceived lack of progress in goal achievement. In this situation, the strength of the relevant motive determines the extent to which a person feels dissatisfied and distressed in response to this frustrating experience. In contrast, if personal goals do not offer opportunities to satisfy an underlying need and, thus, are disconnected from the affective impetus associated with strong motives, well-being will not be increased by goal success, but neither will it be negatively affected by setbacks during goal pursuit.

Phrased in statistical terms, the core of this *goal-achievement/motive-satisfaction* (or in an acronym: GAMeS) hypothesis is that the intensity of the affective consequences of goal-related successes and failures is contingent upon (or moderated by) the strength of implicit motives. The intensity is high when goals are backed up by strong motives but low when goals are irrelevant to the satisfaction of motives. In Figure 12.1, the addition of this proposition to Brunstein's (1993) original model is signified by the dashed line and the multiplication sign between goal progress and motive congruence. The latter symbol is to signify that the Goal Progress × Motive Congruence interaction term is considered to be a unique predictor of well-being above and beyond the first-order effect of progress in goal achievement.

An Initial Test of the GAMeS Hypothesis

To examine the GAMeS hypothesis, Brunstein et al. (1998, Study 1) assessed both implicit motives and explicit goals in a sample of college students. Implicit needs for agency (power and achievement) and communion (affiliation and intimacy) were measured with a PSE. Within the same strivings areas, personal goals and associated perceptions of progress were assessed with a personal-goal inventory. Daily mood reports were collected over 2 weeks and then averaged for each participant to obtain an aggregate measure of students' daily emotional well-being. The predictions were as follows: (a) Among participants with a predominant need for agency (i.e., students scoring high in power- and achievement-related needs but relatively low in affiliative and intimacy-related needs), emotional well-being is highly sensitive to variations in agentic-goal progress. (b) Correspondingly, among participants with an unambiguous need for communion (i.e., individuals whose needs for affiliation and intimacy are much stronger than their motives for achievement and power), feelings of well-being are especially sensitive to variations in communal goal progress.

Results of moderated multiple regression analyses revealed that in both striving areas, students' predominant motives combined with their perceptions of goal progress to account for significant portions of variance in daily experiences of well-being. For students with a relatively strong agentic need, greater progress at communal goals did *not* translate into positive well-being, but greater progress at agentic goals did. Correspondingly, for communion-motivated students, greater progress at agentic goals was not reflected in enhanced well-being but communal-goal progress was. These findings also imply that a lack of progress at motive-congruent goals led to subsequent decreases in well-being. In contrast to the marked effects of low or high progress on motive-congruent goals, goals unrelated to students' predominant motives had virtually no effect on their emotional well-being, regardless of how much progress a participant made in realizing his or her self-chosen objectives.

Taken together, these findings show that the motivational-congruence hypothesis spelled out by Brunstein et al. (1995; see above) offers, at best, a rough approximation to the principles that determine how implicit motives interact with explicit goals to shape people's well-being experiences. Active engagement in motive-congruent goals is not enough to guarantee happiness. Rather, when people set goals in line with their motives but fail to accomplish their commitments, they will be likely to display future deficits in well-being.

Testing an Extended Version of the GAMeS Hypothesis

In a follow-up study, Brunstein et al. (1998, Study 2) expanded their analysis of how motive–goal relationships are involved in well-being experiences to the antecedents of progress in goal achievement (see Fig. 12.1). Brunstein et al. (1998) postulated that the interaction between goal commitment and goal attainability accounts for individual differences in emotional well-being only in the domain of motive-congruent goals, but not in the domain of motive-incongruent goals.

To understand the logic of this postulate, think, for instance, of individuals who are high in the implicit need for agency. According to Brunstein et al. (1998), these individuals are likely to reach high levels of well-being if they (a) feel strongly committed to agentic goals and (b) experience favorable conditions to attain these goals. If these two conditions are met, agency-motivated individuals are likely to make good progress in accomplishing motive-congruent (i.e., agentic) goals and this experience in turn translates into pleasant moods. Conversely, if agency-motivated individuals experience poor conditions to attain agentic goals, they are likely to fail in realizing their objectives, even if they feel strongly committed to achieve them. In this case, a person's agentic need is aroused through the presence of motive-relevant goal incentives but frustrated by setbacks to attain these incentives. This experience, in turn, gives rise to unpleasant moods. In contrast, because goals that are unrelated to a person's motives are assumed to have little impact on well-being emotions, agency-motivated individuals should be largely insensitive to variations in both commitment to and attainability of communal goals. The same rationale can be used to predict the well-being of individuals who have a strong communal motive.

To test the validity of these ideas, Brunstein et al. (1998, Study 2) carried out a semester-long research project with college students. At the beginning of a new term, students' implicit needs for agency and communion were assessed with the PSE, and they were also asked to report the agentic and communal

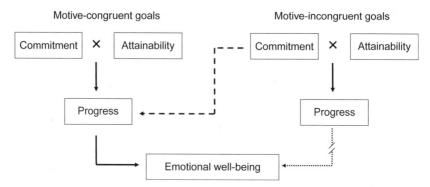

Figure 12.3 Emotional well-being as a function of motive congruence and goal striving attributes: schematic representation of findings reported by Brunstein, Schultheiss, & Grässmann (1998, Study 2). Straight arrows indicate a positive relationship between variables. The dashed arrow indicates a negative relationship between commitment to motive-incongruent goals and progress at motive-congruent goals. The disconnected dotted arrow indicates a lack of significant relationship between goal progress and well-being after controlling for motivational incongruence of goal pursuits.

goals they would pursue over the course of the term. Students rated each goal on measures of goal commitment, attainability, and progress. The dependent variable of interest—students' affective well-being—was measured twice, in the initial phase and in the final phase of the term.

Figure 12.3 provides a schematic overview of the findings obtained from this study. With initial well-being covaried out, students' well-being in the final semester phase was reliably predicted by the interactive relationship between goal commitment and goal attainability and implicit motive dispositions. Throughout the course of the semester, students with a predominant need for agency reached high levels of well-being if they were strongly committed to agentic goals and perceived the conditions to attain these goals to be favorable. Correspondingly, among students with a strong communal motive, an increase in well-being from the initial phase to the final phase of the term was observed if they felt strongly committed to communal goals and experienced favorable conditions to attain these goals.

This pattern of findings was fully in accord with the predictions specified by Brunstein et al. (1998): In conjunction with a strong sense of commitment to motive-congruent goals, favorable conditions to attain these goals were associated with enhanced well-being. In contrast, in both groups of participants (i.e., agency-motivated students and communion-motivated students), poor conditions to attain motive-congruent goals led to subsequent decreases in well-being. This latter finding illustrates that it is only under certain conditions that motive-congruent goals promote people's affective well-being (i.e., when strong commitments to motive-congruent goals combine with favorable conditions to attain these goals).

A different result emerged from the analysis of motive-incongruent pursuits, defined as agentic goals for communion-motivated students and communal goals for agency-motivated students. A strong sense of commitment to motive-incongruent goals led to a decline in well-being during the course of the semester (see the dashed arrow in Fig. 12.3). This finding is reminiscent of the observation reported by Brunstein et al. (1995): People who are strongly involved in motive-incongruent goals appear to be prone to impaired moods. At first glance, this finding runs counter to the idea that motive-incongruent goals have little impact on feelings of well-being.

A meditational analysis integrating measures of goal progress, which had been collected in this study several times during the semester, helped to clarify this issue. In accord with the GAMeS hypothesis, progress at motive-incongruent goals did *not* predict feelings of well-being (in Fig. 12.3 this finding is represented by the disrupted arrow, a symbol that serves to signify that goal progress is unable to predict well-being when goals are decoupled from strong motives), yet progress at motive-congruent goals did. Moreover, within the domain of motive-congruent goals, both goal commitment and goal attainability were positively related to progress in goal achievement, a finding corroborating one further prediction derived from the personal-goal model of well-being.[2] In contrast, high commitment to *motive-incongruent* goals turned out to be a negative predictor of progress at *motive-congruent* goals and thus, as noted above, was associated with decreased well-being.

This latter meditational finding indicates that the greater the strength of students' commitment to motive-incongruent goals, the lower the progress they achieved in the pursuit of motive-congruent pursuits. From this finding one may conclude, as Brunstein et al. (1998) did, that high investments in the pursuit of motive-incongruent goals may keep individuals from accomplishing motive-congruent pursuits and thereby result in a lack of motive satisfaction, which in turn translates into feelings of disappointment and dejection. This finding is important because it provides an explanation for why incongruent goal pursuits may have adverse effects on people's well-being: Active involvement in motive-incongruent goals can have undesired side-effects on the pursuit of motive-congruent goals and thereby indirectly impair people's well-being.

"Hot" and "Cold" Modes of Goal Pursuit

Schultheiss, Jones, Davis, & Kley (2008) further advanced this line of argument by drawing a contrast between *hot* and *cold* goal pursuits. For Schultheiss and associates, goals are hot if they are supported by strong motives and thus have the capacity to influence people's feelings. In contrast, cold pursuits have little impact on well-being experiences because they are not supported by strong motives. Schultheiss et al. (2008) postulated that although hot (i.e., motive-supported) goals may often promote experiences of *motivational gratification* by providing "opportunity structures that allow people to experience emotional highs through consummation of affectively charged incentives" (p. 972), the same goals also have the potential to "set up a person for *motivational frustration*, if his or her efforts to promote the goal and take advantage of opportunities to do so are frequently thwarted" (p. 972). According to the logic of this argument, the pursuit of motive-congruent goals can be described as a double-edged sword that may cut both ways into a person's emotional life, depending on how well she or he is doing in attaining a desired outcome. In contrast, as Schultheiss et al. noted, goals that are decoupled from strong motives should have less dramatic effects on people's emotions, regardless of whether a person succeeds or fails in realizing these affectively cold goal strivings.

To examine these hypotheses, Schultheiss et al. (2008) administered a PSE test to two student samples and then computed across different motivational domains (power, achievement, affiliation) each respondent's total motive score in an attempt to determine the overall capacity of the implicit motive system. Students' personal goals were assessed with conventional self-report procedures. In both studies, these investigators found that the Goal Progress × Implicit Motives interaction term was a reliable predictor of affective well-being, which was assessed with a mood adjective checklist. Follow-up analyses revealed that high rates of goal progress translated into high well-being only among students endowed with strong implicit motives. In addition, Schultheiss et al. found that this interaction effect generalized to a clinical measure of depression. Among students who failed to materialize their commitments, those scoring high in implicit motives reported a greater number of depressive symptoms than students who also were unsuccessful but scored low on implicit motives. This latter finding suggests that the affect system is relatively insensitive to failure episodes occurring in the pursuit of motive-incongruent goals.

One further result of this study deserves comment. Among students *low* in goal commitment, Schultheiss et al. (2008) found that strong implicit motives facilitated progress toward goal attainment. Remarkably, no such effect was observed among students who felt strongly committed to their goals. This finding suggests that the influence of implicit motives on explicit-goal pursuits is not restricted to the realm of affective reactions generated in response to goal-related outcomes. Rather, implicit motives appear to intervene much earlier in the motivation sequence by stimulating activities instrumental to goal accomplishment. This, however, happens only when goal pursuits are *not* controlled by an effortful mode of self-regulation induced by a strong goal commitment. Preliminary support for this interpretation comes from another finding reported by Schultheiss et al. (2008, Study 2): In the absence of a strong sense of commitment, strong implicit motives were associated with less goal rumination, defined as mental preoccupation with ongoing goal pursuits. This finding suggests that implicit motives facilitate goal enactment only in situations where an effortful mode of goal pursuit is "turned off" and, thus, unable to control the smooth implementation of behavioral preferences propelled by implicit motives.

Conclusions and Future Directions

Conclusions

The findings reviewed in this chapter are consistent with the view that people's behavior and experiences are influenced by two separate motivational systems (see McClelland et al., 1989; Weinberger & McClelland, 1990): an implicit motivation system that orients a person's behavior toward the attainment of affectively charged incentives and an explicit motivation system that is built on human's capacity to determine their own activities through the pursuit of future-oriented goals. Although the two systems may often exist side by side, the research reported in this chapter shows that they frequently interact to jointly influence people's feelings and moods in daily life.

Implicit motives automatically react to incentives associated with pleasant affect and spontaneously energize behavior directed at desired states of need fulfillment. Individuals differ greatly with respect to their preferences for seeking particular types of incentives, and these differences are reflected in the strength of specific motives. In contrast, personal goals are part of the explicit motivation system. Personal-goal setting usually involves a lengthy process of conscious deliberation and eventually leads to a decision to act on a selected goal. Although the choices individuals make when they commit themselves to goals may partly reflect their implicit needs, seeking pleasure and hedonic fulfillment is not the primary motive for establishing personal goals. Accordingly, although some of the goals individuals choose to pursue may be built on incentives permitting the expression of motives, individuals frequently commit themselves to goals that do not fit their motives.

One key finding of the line of research reviewed in this chapter is that PSE-assessed motives do not correlate with self-reported goals in terms of thematic content. A second key finding is that even when individuals focus on the pursuit of cognitively elaborated goals, the implicit motivational system is not overridden but remains active in the sense that the strength of implicit motives moderates the influence of successful or unsuccessful goal pursuits on individuals' feelings and moods. Implicit motives may therefore be conceived of as emotional weighting dispositions that determine the extent to which the successful pursuit of personally valued goals leads to experiences of positive well-being. In accord with this interpretation, the studies reviewed in this chapter yielded converging evidence that the affective consequences of explicit goal pursuits are not exclusively or even originally produced within the boundaries of the explicit motivational system. Rather, they also reflect the extent to which a given goal is attuned to the implicit motive system.

In the above investigations, it was consistently found that that the pursuit and fulfillment of motive-congruent goals, but not of incongruent goals, promoted experiences of positive well-being. Yet several of these investigations (Brunstein et al., 1998, Studies 1 and 2; and Schultheiss et al., 2008, Studies 1 and 2) also found that the ability of implicit motives to augment affective reactions to goal-relevant outcomes is not restricted to successful goal pursuits; it applies as well to less successful strivings. More specifically, the studies reported by Brunstein et al. (1998) and Schultheiss et al. (2008) agreed in the observation that people who experience a lack of progress at motive-congruent goals are particularly prone to dejected moods and symptoms of depression (and this observation is bolstered by further evidence suggesting that the internal inhibition of the expression of motives in goal-directed behavior has adverse effects on people's mood; see Langens, 2007).

The finding that implicit motives may facilitate, at least under certain conditions, the enactment of consciously selected goals is thus a promising result of the research reported by Schultheiss et al. (2008). Here, however, a cautionary word seems warranted. Even if goals are supported by strong motives, careful planning of goal-directed action remains a task of high priority, preventing individuals from all too easily losing personal control over goal pursuits that will have strong effects on their feelings and moods. This is one further argument why individuals may benefit from integrating the affective resources integral to the implicit motive system with the effortful-strategic capabilities of the explicit goal pursuit system to regulate affect and behavior effectively and in a self-determined fashion.

Future Directions

The findings reviewed above point to a number of potentially fruitful areas for future research. Before closing, I will sketch out three issues that I believe are particularly important to advance our understanding of how the two motivational systems interact with each other to shape people's experiences and behavior.

First, it is important to clarify the exact meaning of the concept of motive *incongruence*. In this chapter, I used this concept as a summary term to denote an entire family of goals sharing one important feature: They do *not* fit a person's motives. Yet, on closer examination, individual members of this family turn out to differ greatly from each other. Some goals that are classified as motive-incongruent may simply be ill-suited or irrelevant to the satisfaction of motives; yet, as Brunstein et al. (1998) found, they may still absorb mental resources a person would need to succeed at motive-congruent strivings. Other members of this family may lack motive-relevant incentives but can easily be refurnished with opportunities for satisfying motives (think, for instance, of an affiliation-motivated student who is going to take an exam but decides to do her preparations together with friends; see also Schultheiss et al., 2008). Still other members of this family may be fully at odds with a person's enduring needs or operate as self-generated *antineeds*, the expression of which directly contradicts the preferences underlying implicit motives (think, for instance, of a manager who is high in affiliation but feels the urge to sack employees in an effort to save his company from insolvency).

When motives and goals are at odds with each other, goal-related successes must be considered Pyrrhic victories, as I stated elsewhere (Brunstein, 2008). Each step the person takes on the ladder to success runs counter to her own inner needs, turning progress in goal achievement into an aversive experience associated with the dissatisfaction (or violation) of strong motives. Baumann, Kaschel, and Kuhl (2005) reported that "unwanted goals" of this sort operate as "hidden stressors" in the mental machinery where they can produce adverse effects on people's health and well-being. Clearly, to improve our understanding of *when* and *how* consciously selected goals interfere with the expression of motives, it would be useful to break down the heterogeneous category of motive-incongruent pursuits into a number of more homogeneous subcategories along the lines I sketched out above. This procedure should enable researchers to make more accurate predictions as to the influences certain types of motive-incongruent goals have on people's well-being and psychological adjustment.

Second, it would be quite useful to identify procedures helping people reduce the gap between implicit and explicit motives. A logical first step in this direction is to bring the phenomenon of interest (motivational congruence) under experimental control. Proceeding in this direction, Schultheiss and Brunstein (1999; see also Schultheiss, 2001) posited that *goal imagery*, defined as the perception-like mental simulation of the pursuit and attainment of a potential goal, serves as a means of connecting goal setting activities to implicit motives. Drawing on earlier work of Epstein (1994), Schultheiss and Brunstein (1999) argued that the functioning of implicit motives is much better suited to an *experiential* than to a *verbal-symbolic* form of information processing. They therefore hypothesized that implicit motives can only affect the formulation of consciously selected intentions if a goal is translated from its original linguistic format into an experiental format. Goal imagery is ideally suited for this purpose, as Schultheiss and Brunstein found in two investigations with student participants. In an experimenter-guided exercise, one group of participants was led through a guided imagery during which the group vividly imagined the pursuit and attainment of a goal previously assigned by the experimenter (e.g., a power or affiliation goal). After completing the guided imagery exercise, participants only felt committed to the goal if it corresponded with their implicit motives (e.g., with their PSE needs for power and affiliation). A second group of students, who were assigned the same goal but did not engage in a goal imagery exercise, displayed no systematic relationship between the strength of implicit motives and the strength of their goal commitment. Moreover, a second study showed that goal imagery participants were more successful in achieving a motive-congruent goal than control group participants.

In a similar vein, Job and Brandstätter (2009) argued that emotion-focused fantasies about prospective goal pursuits are particularly useful to bridge the gap between implicit motives and consciously selected goals. More specifically, Job and Brandstätter posited that goal-related fantasies that are saturated with emotion-focused imagery helps individuals realize how pursuing and attaining a specific goal will affect them emotionally. In accord with this idea, Job and Brandstätter found that students who were led to engage in emotion-focused fantasies subsequently adopted and committed themselves to goals that were attuned to their PSE-assessed motives. These data illustrate that goal imagery is a promising tool to link implicit motives to consciously selected goals. Further research is needed to scrutinize whether goal imagery interventions not only reduce discrepancies between implicit and explicit motivations but also promote, in effect, experiences of positive well-being.

Third, seen from a broader perspective, further research is needed to expand the analysis of interactive relationships between implicit and explicit motivational systems to other fields of motivation research. For instance, Brunstein and Maier (2005) reported that in the domain of achievement-motivated behavior, implicit and explicit needs to achieve frequently work together, such that "individuals who are high in both motives have an edge in achieving a desired outcome (or preventing an undesired one)" (p. 219). Winter, John, Stewart, Klohnen, and Duncan (1998) theorized that personality traits (e.g., extroversion, which contains self-attributed needs for both power and affiliation) channel the expression of (implicit) motives (e.g., power- and affiliation-related needs) and thereby determine the specific way in which a motive is translated into goal-directed behavior. In a longitudinal research project with women, Winter et al. found that the joint effects of traits (assessed with a personality inventory) and motives (assessed with a PSE test) reliably predicted important life outcomes (e.g. relationship and career success). In the same vein, Bornstein (1998) and Bing, LeBreton, Davison, Migetz, and James (2007) suggested that to advance our understanding of how implicit motives interact with their explicit counterparts, it might be particularly instructive to investigate the behavioral correlates of certain kinds of personality prototypes. Within a specific domain of motivational involvement (e.g., dependency-related needs or achievement-oriented strivings), these prototypes may be identified by crossing high and low conditions of implicit and explicit motivations, yielding a four-category schema to which a researcher may add a fifth "center cell" representing individuals who are at the average level both on implicit and explicit motives (see Bing et al., 2007). By adopting this typological approach, future researchers should be able not only to paint a more complete picture of the specific patterns of behavior associated with different motivational configurations, but also to investigate in greater detail how continuities (e.g., when both kinds of motives are strong) and discontinuities (e.g., when a strong implicit motive combines with a weak explicit motive, and vice versa) in the motivational basis of personality relate to important outcome variables (see Bornstein, 2002).

To conclude, the research reviewed in this chapter supports McClelland et al.'s (1989) claim that although implicit and explicit motivations are functionally independent, they can work in tandem to jointly influence people's experiences and behavior. Subjective experiences of well-being constitute an area of research where such interactive effects have regularly been observed, yielding a coherent pattern of results that can be replicated in different samples and cultures. The examination of implicit–explicit interactions is certainly a challenge for every motivation theorist who seeks to understand how multiple components of personality interact with each other, get into conflict with one another, or coact in harmony to influence certain kinds of outcome criteria. However, an understanding of the interplay between implicit and explicit motivational systems is not only an important theoretical issue. As the research reviewed in this chapter demonstrates, it has important practical implications for how people evaluate the emotional quality of their lives.

Author Note

Parts of the research summarized in this chapter were supported by Deutsche Forschungsgemeinschaft grants BR 1056/2-1, 3-1, and 9-1.

Notes

1. It should be noted that this idea can be traced back to Atkinson's (1957) claim that individual differences in the strength of a given motive (e.g., the need to succeed) essentially describe variations in people's capacity of experiencing certain types of pleasant affect. For instance, according to Atkinson, the need to achieve is reflected in the extent to which a person takes pride from success and enjoys the mastery of challenges.
2. For motive-incongruent goals, the joint effect of goal commitment and goal attainability on progress in goal achievement was also significant, indicating that motives had no significant effect on goal progress in this study (but see below).

References

Achtziger, A., & Gollwitzer, P. M. (2008). Motivation and volition in the course of action. In J. Heckhausen & H. Heckhausen (Eds.), *Motivation and action* (pp. 272–295). New York: Cambridge University Press.

Atkinson, J. W. (1957). Motivational determinants of risk taking behavior. *Psychological Review, 64,* 359–372.

Bakan, D. (1966). *The duality of human existence.* Chicago: Rand McNally.

Baumann, N., Kaschel, R., & Kuhl, J. (2007). Striving for unwanted goals: Stress-dependent discrepancies between explicit and implicit achievement motives reduce subjective well-being and increase psychosomatic symptoms. *Journal of Personality and Social Psychology, 89,* 781–799.

Bing, M. N., LeBreton, J. M., Davison, H. K., Migetz, D. Z., & James, L. R. (2007). Integrating implicit and explicit social cognitions for enhanced personality assessment: A general framework for choosing measurement and statistical methods. *Organizational Research Methods, 10,* 136–179.

Bornstein, R. F. (1998). Implicit and self-attributed dependency strivings: Differential relationships to laboratory and field measures of help seeking. *Journal of Personality and Social Psychology, 75,* 778–787.

Bornstein, R. F. (2002). A process dissociation approach to objective-projective test score interrelationships. *Journal of Personality Assessment, 78,* 47–68.

Brickman, P., & Coates, D. (1987). Commitment and mental health. In P. Brickman (Ed.), *Commitment, conflict, and caring* (pp. 222–309). Englewood Cliffs, NJ: Prentice-Hall.

Brunstein, J. C. (1993). Personal goals and subjective well-being: A longitudinal study. *Journal of Personality and Social Psychology, 65,* 1061–1070.

Brunstein, J. C. (2008). Implicit and explicit motives. In J. Heckhausen & H. Heckhausen (Eds.), *Motivation and action* (pp. 227–246). New York: Cambridge University Press.

Brunstein, J. C., Dangelmayer, G., & Schultheiss, O. C. (1996). Personal goals and social support in close relationships: Effects on relationship mood and marital satisfaction. *Journal of Personality and Social Psychology, 71,* 1006–1019.

Brunstein, J. C., Lautenschlager, U., Nawroth, B., Pöhlmann, K., & Schultheiss, O. C. (1995). Persönliche Anliegen, soziale Motive und emotionales Wohlbefinden [Personal goals, social motives, and emotional well-being]. *Zeitschrift für Differentielle und Diagnostische Psychologie, 16,* 1–10.

Brunstein, J. C., & Maier, G. W. (2005). Implicit and self-attributed motives to achieve: Two separate but interacting needs. *Journal of Personality and Social Psychology, 89,* 205–222.

Brunstein, J. C., Schultheiss, O. C., & Grässmann, R. (1998). Personal goals and emotional well-being: The moderating role of motive dispositions. *Journal of Personality and Social Psychology, 75,* 494–508.

Brunstein, J. C., Schultheiss, O. C., & Maier, G. W. (1999). The pursuit of personal goals: A motivational approach to well-being and life adjustment. In J. Brandtstädter & R. M. Lerner (Eds.), *Action and self-development: Theory and research through the life span* (pp. 169–196). New York: Sage.

Cantor, N., & Blanton, H. (1996). Effortful pursuit of personal goals in daily life. In P. M. Gollwitzer & J. A. Bargh (Eds.), *The psychology of action: Linking cognition and motivation to behavior* (pp. 338–359). New York: Guilford.

Cantor, N., & Sanderson, C. A. (1999). Life task participation and well-being: The importance of taking part in daily life. In D. Kahneman, E. Diener, & N. Schwarz (Eds.), *Well-being: The foundations of hedonic psychology* (pp. 230–243). New York: Russell Sage Foundation.

Carver, C. S., & Scheier, M. F. (1998). *On the self-regulation of behavior*. New York: Cambridge University Press.

Diener, E. (1984). Subjective well-being. *Psychological Bulletin, 95*, 542–575.

Diener, E., & Lucas, R. E. (2000). Explaining differences in societal levels of happiness: Relative standards, need fulfillment, culture, and evaluation theory. *Journal of Happiness Studies, 1*, 41–78.

Diener, E., Suh, M. E., Lucas, R. E., & Smith, H. L. (1999). Subjective well-being: Three decades of progress. *Psychological Bulletin, 125*, 276–302.

Emmons, R. A. (1996). Striving and feeling: Personal goals and subjective well-being. In P. M. Gollwitzer & J. A. Bargh (Eds.), *The psychology of action: Linking motivation and cognition to behavior* (pp. 313–337). New York: Guilford.

Emmons, R. A. (1997). Motives and goals. In R. Hogan, J. Johnson, & S. Brigges (Eds.), *Handbook of personality psychology* (pp. 485–512). San Diego, CA: Academic Press.

Emmons, R. A., & King, L. (1992). Thematic analysis, experience sampling, and personal goals. In C. P. Smith (Ed.), *Motivation and personality: Handbook of thematic content analysis* (pp. 73–86). New York: Cambridge University Press.

Emmons, R. A., & McAdams, D. P. (1991). Personal strivings and motive dispositions: Exploring the links. *Personality and Social Psychology Bulletin, 17*, 648–654.

Epstein, S. (1994). Integration of the cognitive and the psychodynamic unconscious. *American Psychologist, 49*, 709–724.

Gollwitzer, P. M. (1993). Goal achievement: The role of intentions. In W. Stroebe & M. Hewstone (Eds.), *European review of social psychology* (Vol. 4, pp. 141–185). Chichester, England: Wiley.

Gollwitzer, P. M. (1999). Implementation intentions: Strong effects of simple plans. *American Psychologist, 54*, 493–503.

Heckhausen, H. (1991). *Motivation and action*. New York: Springer.

Hofer, J., Busch, H., Chasiotis, A., & Kiessling, F. (2006). Motive congruence and interpersonal identity status. *Journal of Personality, 74*, 511–541.

Hofer, J., Busch, H., & Kiessling, F. (2008). Individual pathways to life satisfaction: The significance of traits and motives. *Journal of Happiness Studies, 9*, 503–520.

Hofer, J., & Chasiotis, A. (2003). Congruence of life goals and implicit motives as predictors of life satisfaction: Cross-cultural implications of a study of Zambian male adolescents. *Motivation and Emotion, 27*, 251–272.

Hofer, J., Chasiotis, A., & Campos, D. (2006). Congruence between social values and implicit motives: Effects on life satisfaction across three cultures. *European Journal of Personality, 20*, 305–324.

Hsee, C. K, & Abelson, R. P. (1991). Velocity relations: Satisfaction as a function of the first derivate of outcome over time. *Journal of Personality and Social Psychology, 60,* 341–347.

Jemmott, J. B. (1987). Social motives and susceptibility to disease: Stalking individual differences in health risks. *Journal of Personality, 55,* 267–298.

Job, V., & Brandstätter, V. (2009). Get a taste of your goals: Promoting motive-goal congruence through affect-focus goal fantasy. *Journal of Personality, 77,* 1527–1560.

King, L. A. (1995). Wishes, motives, goals, and personal memories: Relations of measures of human motivation. *Journal of Personality, 63,* 985–1007.

Klinger, E. (1977). *Meaning and void: Inner experience and the incentives in people's lives.* Minneapolis, MN: University of Minnesota Press.

Kuhl, J. (1992). A theory of self-regulation: Action versus state orientation, self-discrimination, and some applications. *Applied Psychology: An International Review, 41,* 97–129.

Langens, T. A. (2007). Congruence between implicit and explicit motives and emotional well-being: The moderating role of activity inhibition. *Motivation and Emotion, 31,* 49–59.

Lerner, R. M., & Busch-Rossnagel, N. A. (1981). *Individuals as producers of their own development: A life-span perspective.* New York: Academic Press.

Lewin, K. (1926). *Vorsatz, Wille und Bedürfnis* [Intention, will, and need]. Psychologische Forschung, 7, 330–385.

Maier, G. W., & Brunstein, J. C. (2001). The role of personal work goals in newcomers' job satisfaction and organizational commitment: A longitudinal analysis. *Journal of Applied Psychology, 86,* 1034–1042.

McAdams, D. P., & Bryant, F. B. (1987). Intimacy motivation and subjective mental health in a nationwide sample. *Journal of Personality, 55,* 395–413.

McClelland, D. C. (1951). *Personality.* New York: Holt, Rinehart, and Winston.

McClelland, D. C. (1980). Motive dispositions: The merits of operant and respondent measures. In L. Wheeler (Ed.), *Review of personality and social psychology* (Vol. 1, pp. 10–41). Beverly Hills, CA: Sage.

McClelland, D. C. (1987). *Human motivation.* New York: Cambridge University Press.

McClelland, D. C., & Jemmott, J. B. (1980). Power motivation, stress and physical illness. *Journal of Human Stress, 6,* 6–15.

McClelland, D. C., Koestner, R., & Weinberger, J. (1989). How do self-attributed and implicit motives differ? *Psychological Review, 96,* 690–702.

McGregor, I., & Little, B. R. (1998). Personal projects, happiness, and meaning: On doing well and being yourself. *Journal of Personality and Social Psychology, 74,* 494–512.

Murray, H. A. (1938). *Explorations in personality.* New York: Oxford University Press.

Murray, H. A. (1943). *Thematic Apperceptive Test manual.* Cambridge, MA: Harvard University Press.

Nuttin, J. (1984). *Motivation, planning, and action.* Hillsdale, NJ: Erlbaum.

Pöhlmann, K., & Brunstein, J. C. (1997). GOALS: Ein Fragebogen zur Messung von Lebenszielen [GOALS: A questionnaire for assessing life goals]. *Diagnostica, 43*, 103–119.

Ryan, R. M., & Deci, E. L. (2001). On happiness and human potentials: A review of research on hedonic and eudaimonic well-being. *Annual Review of Psychology, 52*, 529–565.

Ryan, R. M., Sheldon, K. M., Kasser, T., & Deci, E. L. (1996). All goals are not created equal: An organismic perspective on the nature of goals and their regulation. In P. M. Gollwitzer & J. A. Bargh (Eds.), *The psychology of action: Linking cognition and motivation to behavior* (pp. 7–26). New York: Guilford.

Schultheiss, O. C. (2001). An information processing account of implicit motive arousal. In M. L. Maehr & P. Pintrich (Eds.), *Advances in motivation and achievement: New directions in measures and methods* (Vol.12, pp. 1–41). Greenwich, CT: JAI Press.

Schultheiss, O. C. (2007). A biobehavioral model of implicit power motivation: Arousal, reward and frustration. In E. Harmon-Jones & P. Winkielman (Eds.), *Fundamentals of social neuroscience* (pp. 176–196). New York: Guilford.

Schultheiss, O. C., & Brunstein, J. C. (1999). Goal imagery: Bridging the gap between implicit motives and explicit goals. *Journal of Personality, 67*, 1–38.

Schultheiss, O. C., & Brunstein, J. C. (2001). Assessment of implicit motives with a research version of the TAT: Picture profiles, gender differences, and relations to other personality measures. *Journal of Personality Assessment, 77*, 71–86.

Schultheiss, O. C., Jones, N. M., Davis, A. Q., & Kley, C. (2008). The role of implicit motivation in hot and cold goal pursuit: Effects on goal progress, goal rumination, and emotional well-being. *Journal of Research in Personality, 42*, 971–987.

Schultheiss, O. C., Yankova, D., Dirlikov, B., & Schad, D. J. (2009). Are implicit and explicit motive measures statistically independent? A fair and balanced test using the Picture Story Exercise and a cue- and response-matched questionnaire measure. *Journal of Personality Assessment, 91*, 72–81.

Sheldon, K. M. (2002). The self-concordance model of healthy goal striving: When personal goals correctly represent the person. In E. L. Deci & R. M. Ryan (Eds.), *Handbook of self-determination research* (pp. 65–86). Rochester, NY: University of Rochester Press.

Weinberger, J., & McClelland, D. C. (1990). Cognitive versus traditional motivational models: Irreconcilable or complementary? In E. T. Higgins & R. M. Sorrentino (Eds.), *Handbook of motivation and cognition: Foundations of social behavior* (Vol. 2, pp. 562–597). New York: Guilford.

Wessman, A. E., & Ricks, D. F. (1966). *Mood and personality.* New York: Holt, Rinehart, and Winston.

Winter, D. G. (1991). *Manual for scoring motive imagery in running text* (3rd. ed.). Unpublished scoring manual. University of Michigan, Ann Arbor.

Winter, D. G., John, O. P., Stewart, A. J., Klohnen, E. C., & Duncan, L. E. (1998). Traits and motives: Toward an integration of two traditions in personality research. *Psychological Review, 105*, 230–250.

Wurf, E., & Markus, H. (1991). Possible selves and the psychology of personal growth. In R. Hogan (Series Ed.) & D. Ozer, J. M. Healy, & A. J. Stewart (Vol. Eds.), *Perspectives in personality: Vol. 3A. Self and emotion* (pp. 39–62). London: Jessica Kingsley.

Wrosch, C., Scheier, M. F., Miller, G. E., Schulz, R., & Carver, C. S. (2003). Adaptive self-regulation of unattainable goals: Goal disengagement, goal reengagement, and subjective well-being. *Personality and Social Psychology Bulletin, 29*, 1494–1508.

Chapter 13

Implicit Motives: A Look from Personality Systems Interaction Theory

NICOLA BAUMANN
University of Trier

MIGUEL KAZÉN
University of Osnabrück

JULIUS KUHL
University of Osnabrück

During the "long past and the short history" of scientific psychology (Boring, 1929), motivation has been seen in contrast to cognition: Whereas cognition refers to the cognitive machinery that generates knowledge about the world, motivation is about what drives this machinery, its velocity, direction, and persistence (Atkinson, 1958; Heckhausen, 1991; McClelland, Atkinson, Clark, & Lowell, 1953; McDougall, 1932; Murray, 1938). Cognition relates to *how* questions (function) whereas motivation concerns *why* questions. The distinction between mechanisms causing behavior and purpose giving it direction and energy can be traced back to the distinction between causa efficiens and causa finalis in medieval thinking, a distinction underlying the dualistic world view of ancient philosophers (especially Aristotle). Today, the sharp distinction between mechanism and purpose ceases to be a useful position. Purposive behavior depends on mechanisms. An example for the close relationship between motivation and mechanism can be found in the work by the pioneers of motivational science cited above: The functional basis of motives can, at least in part, be explained on the basis of simple learning mechanisms such as classical conditioning and instrumental learning. For example, the achievement motive, which directs perception and action toward opportunities for meeting standards of excellence, can be related to acquired habits to associate an affective change with clues that were associated with such a change in the ontogenetic past (McClelland et al., 1953).

In addition to being supported by associationistic learning mechanisms, motives also include a cognitive component that adds a higher level of intelligence to them. Specifically, some researchers conceived of motives as extended networks of experiential knowledge acquired during early childhood years (e.g., Trudewind, 1989; Winterbottom, 1958). From a theoretical point of view, associative networks that bind innumerable personal episodes cannot reasonably be conceptualized in terms of verbally explicable analytical knowledge: Their extendedness would overtax any limited capacity system. The notion that motive-related knowledge is rooted in preconceptual (partly even preverbal) states of development suggests conceptualizing this knowledge component of motives in terms of implicit experiential networks (McClelland, 1985). Later in this chapter, we will expand this view applying the concept of motive across preconceptual, conceptual, and self-regulatory levels of analysis. As elaborated in other chapters of this volume (e.g., chapters 11 and 12), this theoretical conception of implicit motives was confirmed by research that demonstrated that explicit (i.e., self-reported) motive strength fails to predict the frequency of motive-related spontaneous thought and action (McClelland, Koestner, & Weinberger, 1989). In this chapter we will expand on an elaboration of those early attempts to connect motivation with function. Specifically, we will provide an outline of personality systems interactions (PSI) theory and lay out how this theory relates to implicit motives. In a subsequent section, we will describe how the Operant Motive Test (OMT) attempts to extend Murray's (1938) classical Thematic Apperception Test (TAT) and its empirically developed elaborations (Atkinson, 1958; Winter, 1994) to encompass cognition–motivation interactions up to the highest levels of cognitive-volitional mechanisms (Kuhl & Scheffer, 1999). In a final section, we will provide some recent results on the interaction between motives and cognitive mechanisms.

A Brief Summary of PSI Theory

In a nutshell, PSI theory proposes the following cognitive-emotional architecture in order to accommodate previous and more recent research on motives, goals, and self-regulation (Kuhl, 2000, 2001): Two motivational orientations (i.e., approach and avoidance) can be distinguished within each of seven levels of personality functioning (Kuhl & Koole, 2008). Positive and negative affects modulate the interactions among low-level and high-level systems. The seven levels are (1) intuitive/automatic behavior control and object perception, (2) motor activation and sensory arousal ("temperament"), (3) positive and negative affect, (4) stress- and coping-dependent progression (top-down) versus regression (bottom-up) between higher levels (5–7) and lower levels (1–3),

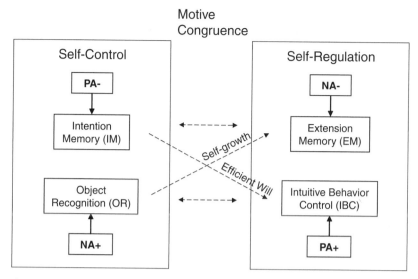

Figure 13.1 Cognitive systems of PSI theory and their modulation by high (+) versus low (−) positive (PA) or negative (NA) affect.

Note: Dashed arrows indicate antagonisms between cooperating systems that can only be overcome through an affective change.

(5) preconceptual motives, (6) conceptually represented specific and global goals, and (7) a disciplined versus an integrative form of volition (self-control involving intention memory vs. self-regulation).

According to PSI theory, affect-based modulation of the interaction between these levels of processing becomes especially evident at Level 4, the interface between low and high level processes: Presumably, Level 4 compares low-level inputs (behavioral tendencies aroused by habits, global activation, and/or positive or negative affect) with inputs from higher-level systems (motives, goals, and intentions) and "computes" whether top-down or bottom-up forces are stronger to be allowed to determine ongoing behavior. The two affect modulation assumptions of PSI theory are depicted in Figure 13.1. The *first modulation assumption* explains how high versus low positive affect (PA) modulates the interaction between intention memory (Level 7) and intuitive behavior control (Level 1). Specifically, intention memory is activated when a difficulty of enactment is encountered (e.g., when an individual has committed himself to an unpleasant activity): One does not form an intention unless there is some difficulty associated with performing an activity (without any difficulty one would simply go ahead and do it). The confrontation with difficulty (which is characteristic of achievement-related contexts) is typically associated with an initial dampening of positive affect (low PA). When an intention is to be performed, facilitating positive affect has to be generated, either from external sources (encouragement) or on the basis of a self-regulatory effort (self-motivation).

Experimental evidence confirms that positive primes (especially achievement-related ones) facilitate the enactment of difficult intentions, even to the extent that they remove the well-known Stroop interference effect (Kazén & Kuhl, 2005; Kuhl & Kazén, 1999). This principle of positive affect (PA assumption) facilitating the interaction (i.e., information transfer) between intention memory and an enactment-oriented system also works outside the laboratory: When people are asked to alternate between positive fantasies about goal attainment and a focus on difficult or unpleasant steps to be taken, the rate of enactment of difficult intentions (e.g., and success criteria such as losing weight, taking medicine, etc.) is significantly increased (Oettingen, Pak, & Schnetter, 2001).

The *second modulation assumption* of PSI theory concerns the interaction between perception of isolated objects and their integration into an extended ("holistic") experiential network. This network is called *extension memory*, and the part of it that integrates information about the person's autobiographical memory, preferences, values, and so forth, is called the *integrated self* (see Fig. 13.3). This integration process is regarded as the functional basis of self-growth. PSI theory holds that negative affect (NA) facilitates *object perception*. An object is defined as an isolated (i.e., "decontextualized") cognitive representation of a new, unexpected, or even threatening experience as a separate entity apart from its context. Abstraction from context helps recognize objects across different contexts, which can be especially useful for avoiding threatening objects. Active down-regulation of negative affect then facilitates integration of isolated experience into extension memory and the self. This process is called self-growth because the integrated representation of personally relevant knowledge (i.e., the self) grows through the integration of novel and sometimes even painful experience.

An empirical test of this NA assumption has been attempted on the basis of the self-infiltration technique. This method is based on the assumption that access to the integrated self, and thus to extension memory, can be measured by the extent to which a person can tell apart self-chosen goals from externally assigned goals. Confusions about the source of a goal or intention, called false self-ascription, can be a sign of impaired self-access. Empirical findings from self-infiltration experiments are in accordance with the NA assumption: When participants scoring low on a scale that assesses the ability to down-regulate negative affect (i.e., so-called state-oriented participants) are put into a negative mood, the rate of false self-ascriptions increases (Baumann & Kuhl, 2003; Kuhl & Kazén, 1994). In contrast, participants who are able to down-regulate negative affect (i.e., action-oriented participants) do not confuse assignments as self-selected when being put into a negative mood. A scale assessing individual differences in self-access confirms our interpretation of the relationship between excessive negative affect and self-integration as an indication of impaired self-access (Quirin, Koole, & Kuhl, 2009): Self-access (but not self-consciousness) correlates negatively with scales related to negative affect such as neuroticism, threat-related state orientation, life stress, and physical complaints.

Motives Across the Three Levels of
Higher-Order Processing

In this section we will apply the distinction between the three highest levels of personality functioning to the motive concept. In a nutshell, motives can be discussed in terms of preconceptual, conceptual, or self-regulatory levels of personality functioning, which helps distinguish different conceptualizations of implicit motives and may explain why different methods can be used to assess them. More specifically, PSI theory provides a functional interpretation of the commonalities and differences between three levels of motive measurement. The commonalities between the three levels of motive organization relate to three criteria defining a motive: (1) extended network representation, (2) implicit level of awareness, and (3) *apperception* in terms of need-related interpretation of perceptual input, a meaning-providing process that presumably results from close interaction between perception and higher-level representations (which modulate the interpretation of perceptual input). The three methods of motive assessment (i.e., the classical TAT/PSE, the OMT, and the grid technique) discussed in this section clearly satisfy those three criteria (albeit to various degrees). After briefly discussing the preconceptual and conceptual levels and the two instruments related to them (i.e., the TAT/PSE, and the grid technique, respectively), we introduce a third level of motive measurement, which will be elaborated in the next section.

The original concept of a motive refers to preconceptual or even preverbal stages of development. Presumably, motives are acquired at a developmental stage when children use words that do not refer to clear-cut concepts. The Russian psychologist Vygotski (1978) has described this stage in terms of pre-conceptual language, in which words denote associative conglomerations of images, emotional episodes, actions, and cognitions. For example, a child might say "I want cap" and mean "I want to go out to the playground." In this example, a word does not signify a concept as defined by a logical hierarchy of more general and more specific terms (e. g., a cap is a piece of clothing comprising a variety of exemplars) but refers to an idiosyncratic conglomeration of images and memories from personal experience (as when mother asked the child to put on a cap before she took her to the playground and met many friends, etc.). In PSI theory, the term *extension memory* denotes such an extended experiential network (including preconceptual and conceptual networks). McClelland (1985) defined a motive in terms of a similar network with affective and imagery components as well as "cognitive overtones." Through its close association between need-related affect and "perceptual imagery," a motive should be "observable" in *apperception*, which can be defined as a process of understanding something perceived in terms of high-level representation of previous experience.

Extension memory is not confined to the preconceptual level. In fact, in his theory of personal constructs, George Kelly (1955) used the term "extension" to describe the widening of a construct or *concept* (e.g., when a therapist helps a compulsive patient to widen his narrow definition of "order" from "putting all pencils on his desk in an exactly parallel arrangement" to "being able to find everything on his desk without having to search for it"). It goes without saying that need-related cognition is not confined to the preconceptual level. Goals can be considered the most important example of motivationally relevant conceptual representations (Brunstein, 2001; Brunstein, Schultheiss, & Grässmann, 1998; Elliot & McGregor, 2001). With his distinction between definition and extension of constructs, Kelly (1955) reminded us of two different types of concepts or constructs that we might also want to take into account when we talk about goals. Specifically, narrowly defined conceptual representations of goals (i.e., concrete goals such as "staying away from fattening food") can be distinguished from global goals that refer to an extended network of acceptable actions (e.g., "losing weight" or "being thin"). Sometimes specific goals can outperform global goals (Gollwitzer, 1999). Under other conditions (to be specified yet), positively charged global goals (e.g., "staying thin") can have a more powerful effect on behavior than concrete goals (Ferguson, 2007).

The conception of extension memory as a parallel (connectionistic) network can accommodate global goals and the network of conceptually represented actions and outcomes associated with it. When the "cognitive overtones" of a motive (McClelland, 1985) are to include extended networks of conceptually represented outcomes (i.e., global goals), assessment procedures should be adapted to that purpose. Since Kelly (1955) developed a valid method for assessing constructs on a conceptual level, one might think of using this "role repertory grid" for the assessment of global goals and all conceptual and emotional components associated with them. The grid technique developed by Schmalt (1999) and his associates is based on this rationale. From a terminological point of view, one could argue whether network representations of conceptually represented constructs can be called motives. We do not see any problem in extending the narrow definition of motives from the preconceptual to the conceptual level as long as the crucial characteristics of a motive are preserved. Schmalt's grid technique clearly satisfies the three criteria of a motive defined above (i.e., based on an extended network of need-related episodes, having an implicit component, an affecting apperception). As long as one knows which subtype of motive one refers to in a given context, it becomes a futile discussion whether one should insist on a strict and narrow or permit an extended definition of the motive concept. Note that our theoretical approach to a multilevel conceptualization of motives does not require substantial correlations among motives across levels of representation: Whether or not a preconceptual motive is also supported by conceptual or self-regulatory networks remains an empirical question.

In the remainder of this chapter, we will focus on the third, self-regulatory, level of motive operation. On this level (i.e., Level 7 in PSI theory), motives are associated with self-regulatory functions (plus Levels 3, 4, and 5, i.e., affect, regression, and preconceptual elements). Since neither the TAT nor the PSE assesses the degree to which preconceptual motives are connected with self-regulatory functions, we developed the Operant Motive Test (OMT).

The Operant Motive Test (OMT)

The Operant Motive Test (OMT) uses a modified TAT technique that extends the assessment of basic social needs (*n* Affiliation, *n* Achievement, *n* Power) from the preconceptual and conceptual levels to the level of self-regulatory support of motive enactment. It is not the aim to assess self-regulatory strategies per se, but to assess the extent to which motives are integrated in self-referential representations. For example, when the need for achievement is integrated with the self, self-regulatory competencies can be employed even at the level of apperception. On this level, a strong achievement motive not only facilitates detecting challenging tasks in the environment, but also down-regulates perceived difficulty (self-motivation) or negative cues associated with fear of failure (self-relaxation). This type of integration should implicitly affect the way people interpret motivationally relevant scenes and respond to them, albeit in a somewhat different manner compared to preconceptual or conceptual motive representations.

Participants are presented with 15 ambiguous pictures depicting social and nonsocial episodes (see Fig. 13.2). They are to choose one character from those depicted in the picture as the protagonist. Identification of the participant with a single character serves to facilitate elaboration of *personal* needs in fantasy behavior. The OMT pictures have a clear-cut, albeit implicit relation to motive themes in order to activate implicit representations of motives (Kuhl, Scheffer, & Eichstaedt, 2003; Scheffer, Kuhl, & Eichstaedt, 2003). Participants are asked to invent a story. In contrast to classical measures (i.e., TAT; PSE, "Picture Story Exercise"), participants do not have to write down the full story. Instead, they are instructed to write down their spontaneous associations (e.g., very short sentences or even single words rather than full narrative accounts) to four questions: (1) "What is important for the person in this situation and what is the person doing?" (2) "How does the person feel?" (3) "Why does the person feel this way?" (4) "How does the story end?" The reduction of the *explicit* response format to verbal associations rather than full stories was chosen to reduce distortions caused by logical reasoning (similar to distortions that occur when dreams are verbalized in a story format). The response format has the additional advantage that it cuts both administration and scoring time considerably while allowing for presentation of more pictures (e.g., 15 or more in OMT vs. 3–8 in PSE).

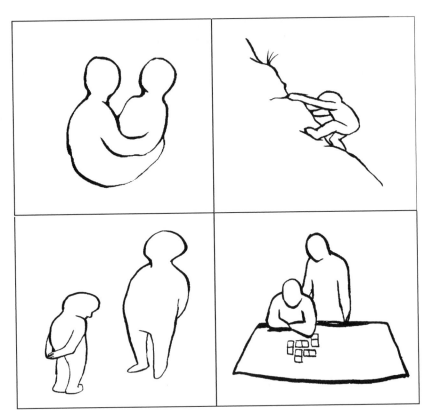

Figure 13.2 Four sample pictures of the Operant Motive Test (OMT).

In addition to motive contents (i.e., "what" a person is striving for), the OMT assesses the interaction between motives and volitional functions, that is, "how" a person is striving to meet his or her needs. Thus, the OMT coding system takes theoretical advances into account that are derived from the integration of self-regulatory processes into motivation psychology (Elliot & Church, 1997; Elliot & McGregor, 2001; Heckhausen, 1991; Kuhl, 1981, 1983, 2000): Extending the classical distinction between approach and avoidance motivation (e.g., hope for success vs. fear of failure), the OMT further differentiates four approach components for each motive (i.e., OMT Levels) on the basis of crossing two affective sources of motivation (positive vs. negative) with self-determined versus incentive-focused forms of motivation (see Table 13.1).

A full introduction into OMT scoring would be beyond the scope of this chapter. We will confine this description to a brief summary of the coding procedure (see Kuhl & Scheffer, 1999, for an elaborated coding manual). For each picture story, the OMT coding procedure starts by checking whether one of the three basic motives (affiliation, achievement, power) is present or not (cf. Winter, 1994) and whether approach or avoidance behavior is present (OMT

Table 13.1   Five-Level Model and Content Categories of the Operant Motive Test (OMT)

| Dominant Macrosystems | Motive | | |
	Affiliation	Achievement	Power
PA (self-regulated) → Task-involvement: context-sensitive switching among macrosystems	**1.1 Intimacy,** *affective sharing* – Interaction (mutual, joyful-intuitive exchange) – Process-like relation: love – Empathy	**2.1 Flow** – Curiosity and interest; feedback – Learning something – Being absorbed, concentrated – Fun with a task, variety	**3.1 Guidance** – Helping and protecting others – Pass on knowledge; educate – Convey values – Convince; calmness
PA (incentive-based) → Incentive-orientation: **intuitive behavior control**	**1.2 Sociability** – Extroverted contact (superficial) – Interest; entertainment – Good mood – Erotic; flirt	**2.2 Inner standards** – Pride; focused on results – Doing something well – Solving tasks – Persistence in thinking	**3.2 Status** – Being the focus of attention – Receiving recognition – Having prestige and authority – Observing others
NA (self-regulated) → Self-regulated coping: **extension memory** (acknowledging problems or NA and constructive coping)	**1.3 Coping with rejection** – Positive reevaluation of a rejection – Attempts to restore an attachment (positive outcome) – Delimitation, dislike, disgust	**2.3 Coping with failure** – Positive reevaluation of failure – Perception of threat associated with active coping – Identification of problems – Task rejection ("disengagement")	**3.3 Coping with power-related threats** – Asserting wishes – Having influence – Expressing feelings – Relaxing – Making decisions

(continued)

Table 13.1 (Continued)

Dominant Macrosystems	Motive		
	Affiliation	Achievement	Power
NA (incentive-based) → Goal-oriented behavior: **intention memory & intuitive behavior control** (denial of anxiety by acting)	**1.4 Avoiding insecurity**, *familiarity* *Acting with hope for:* – Safety – Security – Closeness – Being loved	**2.4 Pressure to achieve** – Social standards: trying to be best – Effort (with success); hope – Relief (after success) – Avoiding failure: passing exams – Persistence: solving difficult tasks	**3.4 Inhibited power, dominance** – Fear of using power – Denial: sense of duty ("must") – Many actions; having "survived" – Dominance
Low PA & high NA → Passive fear (rumination): **object recognition & intention memory** (conscious focus on fear)	**1.5 Dependence** – Being lonely – Feeling left alone, abandoned – Desperate, hopeless, sad – Rejected – Not being understood	**2.5 Failure** – Stressed – Helpless – Disappointed – Anxiety – Getting help	**3.5 Powerlessness** – Obedient, guilty, sick – Being a petitioner

PA = positive affect; NA = negative affect.

384

Levels 1–4 vs. OMT Level 5, respectively). If an approach tendency is apparent, the next step is to code whether more internal, self-regulatory processes (i.e., participation of the integrated self) or more external triggers (e.g., incentives present in the situation) are involved in the motive-specific approach tendencies (OMT Levels 1 and 3 vs. OMT Levels 2 and 4, respectively). For example, when a person in the story is confronted with a threat to need satisfaction, participation of the self is coded if he or she generates a creative solution. Whether or not the self is involved is derived from the functional profile of the integrated self (i.e., the self-related part of extension memory) spelled out in PSI theory (Kuhl, 2001; Kuhl & Koole, 2004): For example, feeling satisfied with own actions (i.e., self-positivity), having access to multiple and creative action alternatives (i.e., extended network structure), and perceiving and down-regulating negative affect (i.e., integrative capacity).

The final step in the assessment of self-determined and incentive-focused forms of motivation is to code whether they are based on positive (OMT Levels 1 or 2) or negative affect (OMT Levels 3 or 4). The affective sources of motivation do not have to be consciously experienced or explicitly reported in participants' associations to OMT pictures. For example, the effects of latent negative affect that is not associated with self-integration (i.e., OMT Level 4) can be inferred from rather "tight" or rigid forms of behavior even if negative affect is not directly mentioned (e.g., "she wants to be close to the other person"; "he just wants to beat his competitor"). The narrowness criterion is derived from the second modulation assumption, which states that excessive negative affect impairs access to extension memory and the integrated self. As a result, need satisfaction is associated with implicit avoidance and/or narrow scope of goal maintenance if no creative and socially integrated forms of need satisfaction are apparent (which would be OMT Level 3). Examples for Level 4 codings are: (1) reduction of affiliation motivation to receiving security and closeness from a person (Cell 1.4) rather than engaging in an extensive personal exchange; (2) competitive achievement motivation that is reduced to "trying to be better than others" (Cell 2.4) rather than developing one's own skills independent of social norms; (3) dominant implementation of power needs according to an "all-or-nothing-principle" (Cell 3.4) rather than responsible and socially integrative forms of power.

In contrast, if participants explicitly mention negative affect in conjunction with a creative search for solutions, OMT Level 3 is coded: Active and creative coping with rejection (cell 1.3), failure (cell 2.3), or power-related threats (cell 3.3). Thus, negative affect is not always associated with avoidance (OMT Level 5) but may motivate approach behavior and creative coping attempts, even if it is not mentioned (as on OMT Level 4).

Similarly, positive affective sources of motivation are differentiated into a form involving participation of the self and its volitional mechanisms (OMT Level 1) and a form without participation of the self (OMT Level 2). The self-determined form of positively oriented motivation is coded if needs are implemented in a creative, integrative, and flexible manner. In this case both creativity and flexibility are associated with positive incentives that seem to "flow" out of the activity itself: affective sharing and intimacy in the affiliation domain (Cell 1.1), flow in mastering difficult tasks in the achievement domain (Cell 2.1), and prosocial and socially integrative influences on others in the power domain (Cell 3.1). Thus, according to PSI theory, the intrinsic motivation associated with OMT Level 1 results from mainly unconscious workings of self-regulatory functions that maintain the fun and interest in the task (Kuhl & Koole, 2004). In contrast, if positive affect is not self-generated but primarily elicited by incentives, OMT Level 2 is coded: social contact motivated by social incentives such as having fun together (Cell 1.2), achievement incentives based on doing well according to inner standards rather than within a flow context (Cell 2.2), and explicit reference to power-related incentives such as being the focus of attention and having status (Cell 3.2).

In addition to four approach components, the OMT also includes a "classical" avoidance component for each motive (OMT Level 5): fear of rejection (Cell 1.5), failure (Cell 2.5), and powerlessness (Cell 3.5). The protagonist in participants' OMT associations consciously experiences negative affect and is passively fixated on it. Whereas negative affect may motivate active approach behavior on OMT Level 4 (without being mentioned) or creative coping attempts after being acknowledged (OMT Level 3), avoidance is coded when participants explicitly mention negative affect in their associations to OMT pictures without any active or creative coping attempt. Note that the fourth question of the OMT ("How does the story end?") sometimes elicits an unexpected "happy ending" of a story that is not derived in a plausible way from previous answers but seems to come "out of the blue." Such instances of good luck are not coded as active approach (but OMT Level 5).

In the OMT, no correction for length of protocol is necessary because only one of the 15 cells (3 motive contents × 5 levels) can be coded per picture. If no motive theme is apparent, a "zero" is coded. To assess implicit motives, the OMT can be used in multiple ways. First, computing a sum of OMT Levels 1–4 for each motive allows assessing rather "traditional" measures of approach motives in affiliation, achievement, and power. Second, the combination of OMT Levels 1 and 2 and OMT Levels 3 and 4 for each motive assesses the effects of positive versus negative affective sources of motivation, respectively. Third, the combination of OMT Levels 1 and 3 and OMT Levels 2 and 4 assesses the effects of primarily self-determined versus more incentive-focused forms of motivation, respectively. Finally, each cell resembles a unique interaction between motives and volition that is expected to have its own predictive power. Whereas the individual cells are often not normally distributed, the compound measures typically are. In sum, the five-level model of the OMT allows to test theoretically interesting differences in the type of self-regulation involved in need satisfaction.

Scorers are able to learn the 3×5 coding scheme of the OMT within several weeks of training. We usually have two independent scorers and calculate interrater agreement following the same procedure as outlined by Winter (1994) for the PSE. In previous OMT studies, interrater agreement was above .85. Furthermore, the OMT has been used successfully not only for research but also for applied purposes (cf. Kaschel & Kuhl, 2004).

Reliability and Validity of the OMT

Operant tests were criticized because they do not satisfy classical psychometric criteria, especially internal consistency and test–retest reliability, which fluctuate around .30 (e.g., Entwisle, 1972; Fineman, 1977; Tuerlinckx, De Boeck, & Lens, 2002). Recent work with the OMT suggests that reliability and validity of operant tests can be improved by its separating the assessment of need and implementation components (Baumann, Kaschel, & Kuhl, 2005; Chasiotis, Hofer, & Campos, 2006; Hofer, Busch, Chasiotis, Kärtner, & Campos, 2008; Kazén & Kuhl, 2005; Kuhl & Kazén, 2008; Scheffer, 2005; Scheffer, Eichstaedt, Chasiotis, & Kuhl, 2007; Scheffer et al., 2003). The OMT shows sufficient reliability even according to indices based on classical test theory (Scheffer et al., 2003): (a) internal consistencies (Cronbach's Alpha) of .74, .70 and .78 across the four levels of affiliation, achievement, and power, respectively, when looking at the lower and higher quartile of the distribution, and (b) sufficient retest stability across the four approach components (around $r = .72$) as well as for individuals cells of the OMT (around $r = .60$). Furthermore, recent studies by Chasiotis, Bender, Kiessling, and Hofer (in press), Chasiotis et al. (2006), and Hofer et al. (2008) show that the OMT is cross-culturally applicable and free of cultural biases.

Chasiotis and Hofer (2003) did not find a convergent validity between PSE and OMT in their cross-cultural sample of German, Costa Rican, and Cameroonian participants ($N = 370$). Only in the Cameroonian subsample ($N = 126$) were there significant relationships between PSE nPow and OMT nPow ($r = .21$) as well as OMT Category 3.4 (inhibited power/dominance, $r = .27$) and between PSE nAch and OMT Category 2.3 (coping with failure, $r = .23$). Both PSE and OMT demonstrated predictive validity. When entering both instruments at the same time, the OMT showed incremental validity in more outcome criteria than the PSE (Chasiotis & Hofer, 2003), which may be due to the higher initial correlation with the selected criteria. More importantly, there is a pattern of consistent relationships between compound measures as well as individual cells of the OMT and external criteria. For example, the OMT category of *guidance* (Cell 3.1: prosocial power motivation) significantly predicted parenthood across different cultures and gender (Chasiotis et al., 2006). The OMT category of achievement flow (Cell 2.1) accounted for unique variance in daily flow experience whereas the established PSE construct of *n*Ach did not correlate with flow experience (Baumann & Scheffer, 2008, in press). It goes without saying that these incremental aspects of OMT validity do not discount the merits of PSE measurement: Our theoretical analysis of the three levels of motive measurement provided in the first part of this chapter helps explain when which level of motive measurement should be appropriate. Furthermore, the evaluation of the discriminant, convergent, and unique validity of each of the 15 OMT components (plus sum scores) represents a monumental task that at this point is far from finished.

Congruence Between Explicit and Implicit Motives

Congruence between explicit and implicit motives has been identified as an important factor for emotional well-being and health (e.g., Baumann et al., 2005; Brunstein et al., 1998; Hofer & Chasiotis, 2003). Whereas goal imagery (Schultheiss & Brunstein, 1999) and self-determination (Thrash & Elliot, 2002) seem to foster congruence between the implicit and explicit motive systems, state orientation and stress have detrimental effects on motive congruence (Baumann et al., 2005; Brunstein, 2001). These findings can be functionally explained within the framework of PSI theory (Kuhl, 2000, 2001).

According to PSI theory, explicit goal orientations and implicit motives are associated with two different cognitive systems. Goal orientations are associated with the explicit and verbal format of intention memory whereas implicit motives are associated with implicit representations in extension memory, an extended semantic network operating according to connectionist principles and supported by intuitive-holistic processes (Beeman et al., 1994). According to PSI theory, extension memory provides access to preconceptual or conceptual implicit representations of one's own needs, values and wishes. Within the PSI framework, motive dispositions can be defined as "intelligent needs," that is, as implicit cognitive-emotional networks of need-related affective experiences and possible actions that can be performed to satisfy basic social needs in a context-sensitive way across a variety of situations. This explication of the motive construct can be regarded as an elaboration of earlier conceptualizations of the motive construct (Heckhausen, 1991; Kuhl, 2001; McClelland, 1980; Winter, 1996). According to this definition, motives can be considered the need-related part of the implicit self-system (Greenwald & Banaji, 1995), which in turn can be regarded as the self-related part of extension memory (see Fig. 13.3).

Within the framework of PSI theory, congruence between explicit and implicit motive measures is expected to occur when information can be

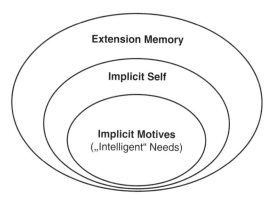

Figure 13.3 Theoretical relationship between extension memory, the implicit (integrated) self, and implicit motives.

exchanged between the two processing systems. More specifically, intention memory needs to "communicate" with extension memory in order to form valid representations of implicit needs in terms of self-congruent goals (cf. Fig. 13.1). An asymmetric activation of intention memory or—even worse— an inhibition of extension memory (e.g., through self-incongruent external demands) is expected to disturb the communication process and reduce congruence between explicit orientations and implicit needs.

The two affect modulation assumptions of PSI theory described earlier in this chapter specify conditions that disturb the communication process between intention and extension memory: (1) Reduced positive affect (frustration) is associated with an asymmetric activation of intention memory and consequently reduces the influence of extension memory in action control, for example, on explicit orientations (Kuhl & Beckmann, 1994). (2) Unattenuated negative affect is even worse for information exchange because it directly inhibits extension memory (Baumann & Kuhl, 2002; Bolte, Goschke & Kuhl, 2002), thereby impeding access to implicit needs. The empirically identified moderators of motive congruence (see Chapter 11) support this functional explanation of motive incongruence: The finding by Thrash and Elliot (2002) that implicit and self-attributed motives are only positively correlated for individuals high in self-determination underlines the crucial role of access to extension memory and the implicit self because, on a phenomenological level, self-inhibition should be experienced as low self-determination. Furthermore, individuals with deficits in self-regulation of affect (i.e., state-oriented individuals) tend to build commitment to unrealistic and motive-incongruent goals (Brunstein, 2001) especially when stressful conditions are naturally present or experimentally induced (Baumann et al., 2005): The finding of increased motive incongruence for individuals with self-motivation deficits under demanding (low positive affect) conditions supports the assumption of detrimental effects of an asymmetrical (over-) activation of intention memory whereas the relationship between self-relaxation deficits under threatening (high negative affect) conditions is a further example of the detrimental effects of self-inhibition (Baumann et al., 2005).

Whereas unattenuated stress seems to reduce cognitive balance and motive congruence, Schultheiss and Brunstein (1999) found goal imagery to bridge the gap between implicit motives and explicit goals. According to PSI theory, imagery can be conceived of as activating extension memory whereas the goal content of the imagery can be conceived of as activating intention memory. Findings are consistent with the assumption that the interaction between intention and extension memory is a central aspect of motive congruence: Equal activation of both memory systems enables a balanced communication process. In contrast, imagery about something neutral (i.e., goal-irrelevant) does not seem to foster motive congruence (Schultheiss & Brunstein, 1999).

Motive incongruence has been identified as a "hidden stressor" that mediates the relationship between unattenuated stress and psychosomatic symptoms (e.g., Baumann et al., 2005). According to PSI theory, the chronic need frustration associated with striving for unwanted (motive-incongruent) goals can be conceived of as an unspecific stress factor that may increase the "stress hormone" cortisol. Consistent with this assumption, Quirin, Koole, Bauman, Kazén, and Kuhl (in press) found a significant (albeit correlational) relationship between self-infiltration (i.e., a tendency to misperceive external assignments as self-selected activities) and cortisol level. Excessive levels of cortisol have been associated with a variety of psychosomatic symptoms (Sapolsky, 1992). Therefore, in addition to any symptom-specific causes, motive incongruence can be conceived of as a general mechanism that contributes to the chronification of stress and psychosomatic symptoms as confirmed by our empirical findings (Baumann et al., 2005): The relationship between unfavorable conditions (a combination of state orientation and stressful life events) and chronification of psychosomatic symptoms over a period of 3 months was partially mediated by motive-incongruent achievement orientations (see Fig. 13.4). Because of the stress-contingent inhibition of extension memory, state-oriented participants tend to over- or underestimate their implicit achievement motive when experiencing high levels of stress. Both types of mismatch between implicit and explicit modalities were associated with a chronification of psychosomatic symptoms. Furthermore, motive incongruence partially mediated between unattenuated stress and psychosomatic sysmptoms.

The functional explanation of motive congruence within the framework of PSI theory underlines the importance of a dynamic view on motivation: "Healthy" goal striving, self-integration, and intrinsic motive components are based on flexible and balanced interactions between basic cognitive and affective systems (cf. Table 13.1). In contrast, fixations on affective or cognitive

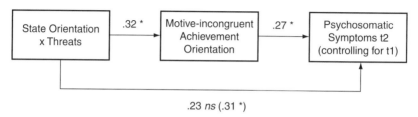

.23 *ns* (.31 *)

Figure 13.4 Motive-incongruent achievement orientation as a partial mediator between the direct effect of perceived life stress (i.e., threats) and failure-related state orientation (i.e., low self-relaxation) on chronification of psychosomatic symptoms over a period of 3 months reported by Baumann, Kaschel, & Kuhl (2005, *JPSP, 89,* 781–799).

systems are associated with alienation from own preferences (e.g., motive incongruence) and rigidity in goal striving (e.g., OMT Level 4).

Self-Determined Versus Incentive Focused OMT Levels

Implicit motives have been described as rooted within the implicit self (cf. Fig. 13.3). Nevertheless, the implicit self does not have to be equally involved in different strategies or levels of motive enactment (cf. Table 13.1). According to PSI theory, incentive-focused forms of motivation, for example, are more strongly supported by intuitive behavior control and/or intention memory than by extension memory and the implicit self. However, the distinction between primarily self-determined versus more incentive-focused forms of motivation as measured by the OMT requires validation: Are scorers able to distinguish between self-determined and incentive-focused forms of motivational orientations on the basis of content analysis? A positive answer to this question would require measures of self-access to be positively related to levels 1 and 3 of the OMT, that is, to the three approach components associated with self-regulation of positive affect (OMT Level 1: intimacy, flow, guidance) and to the three self-regulated forms of coping with negative affect (OMT Level 3: self-confrontational coping with rejection, with failure, and with power-related threats). In contrast, approach components associated with positive *incentives* (OMT Level 2: sociability, inner standards, status) and negative incentives (OMT Level 4: security, competitive achievement, dominant/inhibited power) are expected to show no significant relationships with measures of self-access.

How can we measure self-access? In previous research, two nonreactive measures of self-access have been used. Koole and colleagues (Koole, Dijksterhuis, & van Knippenberg, 2001; Koole & Jostmann, 2004) used short latencies during a self-evaluation task as an indicator of intuitive access to the self. In their studies, participants were to decide as quickly as possible whether they themselves possessed a trait or not by pushing either a *"me"* or *"not me"* button. Target traits were 15 positive (e.g., creative, reliable) and 15 moderately negative traits (e.g., silent, impulsive). Participants who can easily evaluate whether various adjectives describe themselves or not are assumed to have intuitive self-knowledge and to easily access it, that is, they are clear and certain about features related to themselves (McGregor & Marigold, 2003). This measure focuses on the *intuitive* characteristic of the self and will be labeled "intuitive self-access" in the remainder of this chapter.

In contrast to intuitive self-access, Kazén and colleagues (Kazén & Baumann, 2005; Kazén, Baumann, & Kuhl, 2003) focused more strongly on the *integrative* ability of the implicit self that is especially visible in counterpreferential decisions, that is, when participants have rejected something attractive (e.g., reject having a positive trait) or have accepted something unattractive (e.g., accept having a negative trait). Individuals with high self-regulatory abilities and valid self-representations (i.e., action orientation) take significantly more time to make such counterpreferential decisions than individuals low in self-regulation (i.e., state orientation), presumably because they perform a more thorough self-compatibility checking, which should in turn increase the likelihood of detecting the implicit conflict associated with counterpreferential decisions (Kazén et al., 2003). Therefore, we used increased self-evaluation latencies in counterpreferential compared to preferential decisions in a self-classification task as an indicator of "integrative self-access" (as a measure of the conflict-sensitive and self-confrontational Level 3 of the OMT).

Why is the integrative (deeper) measure of self-access expected to be more relevant for the active coping component of the OMT (Level 3)? Self-integration of negative traits and coping with negative affect may require deeper integrative competence. This hypothesis is confirmed by findings that demonstrate a close relationship between the ability to cope with negative affect (i.e., action orientation) and integrative competence as assessed by remote-associates tasks that require comprehending semantic overlap between remotely associated words (Baumann & Kuhl, 2002). Furthermore, Showers and Kling (1996) found that participants who have a superior ability to integrate positive and negative self-aspects into a coherent self (i.e., participants who describe themselves with positive as well as negative traits in their various life domains) are better able to down-regulate experimentally induced negative affect when confronted with the self (i.e., writing a story about who they are) compared to a condition when distracted from the self (i.e., working on easy numerical tasks) and compared to participants with a low ability to integrate positive and negative self-aspects. The finding supports the theoretical link between integrative competence of the self and coping with negative affect as assessed on OMT Level 3. In contrast, the intuitive (easy) measure of self-access is expected to be more relevant on OMT Level 1, which is driven by positive rather than negative affect.

In a study with $N = 58$ psychology undergraduates, we applied the OMT and a self-evaluation task with 18 positive (e.g., creative, tolerant) and 18 moderately negative traits (e.g., lazy, moody). Participants had to decide whether the traits described themselves or not. Both intuitive and integrative measures of self-access were calculated from self-evaluation latencies as described above. The nonparametric correlations (Spearman-Rho) between OMT scores and intuitive as well as integrative self-access are listed in Table 13.2. Consistent with expectations, participants with high scores in self-determined motive components (OMT Levels 1 and 3) showed significantly better self-access in a subsequent self-evaluation task. More specifically, the positively charged intrinsic components (OMT Level 1) of n Affiliation (i.e., intimacy) and n Power (i.e., guidance) were associated with intuitive ("easy") self-access as defined by Koole et al. (2001). These findings are consistent with the assumption that intuitive self-regulatory functions are involved in intrinsic motivation associated with this motive level, which is associated with positive affect. Furthermore, the active and self-confrontational coping components (OMT Level 3) of n Affiliation (i.e., coping with rejection) and n Power (i.e., coping with power-related threat) were associated with integrative self-access as defined by Kazén et al. (2003). The pattern is consistent with our theoretical expectations: Coping with negative affect (OMT Level 3) requires more integrative competencies than self-generation of positive affect (OMT Level 1).

Consistent with our assumptions, neither measure of self-access showed significantly positive correlations with incentive-oriented or avoidant motive levels. However, Table 13.2 shows an additional finding concerning the

Table 13.2 Spearman-Rho Correlations Between Intuitive and Integrative Measures of Self-Access and Content Categories of the Operant Motive Test (OMT).

OMT	Intuitive Self-Access[a]				Integrative Self-Access[b]			
	All	nAff	nAch	nPow	All	nAff	nAch	nPow
Level								
1	**.50****	**.48****	.12	**.41****	−.21	.11	−.16	−.21
2	.04	.25	.11	−.24	.09	−.06	−.18	.25
3	−.13	−.11	.03	−.13	**.39***	**.45****	−.01	**.32***
4	−.12	−.36*	.02	.10	−.14	−.05	−.05	−.15
5	−.06	.01	.00	−.09	−.05	−.02	−.25	.11

Note: The OMT levels indicate five different strategies to implement basic social needs (cf. Table 13.1). Levels 1 and 3 are theoretically associated with self-access. Correlations in boldface signify theoretically expected relationships. $N = 58$

[a] Shorter self-evaluation latencies indicate better intuitive self-access (cf. Koole et al., 2001). Mean self-evaluation latencies were reversed so that higher scores indicate better intuitive self-access.

[b] Longer self-evaluation latencies for counterpreferential (i.e., accepting negative and rejecting positive items) compared to preferential decisions (i.e., accepting positive and rejecting negative items) indicate better integrative self-access (cf. Kazén et al., 2003).

* $p < .05$ ** $p < .01$.

affiliation motive: A negative relationship between need for security (Cell 1.4) and the measure of simple (nonconfrontational) self-access. Apparently, seeking contact based on a need for security, closeness, and being loved is an affiliative concern that does not require extensive self-access because a deeply *personal* interaction is not central or even avoided by security-seeking individuals. Taken together, findings are consistent with our assumption that implicit motives encompass enactment strategies that vary in their degree of participation of the self.

In contrast to *n*Aff and *n*Pow, self-determined levels of *n*Ach did not correlate with intuitive and integrative self-access (see Table 13.2). Is there any theoretical reason that the self plays a different role in self-determined achievement compared to its role in the other two motivational domains? The latency measures of self-access based on positive and negative trait self-ascription may tackle a rather broad tendency to activate the self. Is it possible that individuals who are self-determined in affiliation and power domains activate intuitive and integrative functions of the self rather broadly whereas individuals who are self-determined in the achievement domain do not activate their intuitive and integrative abilities on a general basis, but only when they encounter task-related difficulty? It can be hypothesized, indeed, that self-access is useful during specific moments of achievement-related episodes only: When confrontation with some difficulty reduces positive affect, self-access may be needed to recruit counterregulation through reviving confidence based on past experiences of success (i.e., self-motivation).

Within the achievement domain, participation of the self may thus be a necessary but not a sufficient condition for self-determination. According to this view, self-access per se is not central to the satisfaction of achievement needs. Self-access is important only to the extent that the self provides emotional support for self-motivation when tackling difficult tasks (Level 1) or for self-relaxation when confronted with failure (Level 3). The central functional basis of achievement motivation is the maintenance of difficult goals in intention memory and their attainment through appropriate action. *Volitional facilitation* is our term for the enactment of difficult intentions through mobilizing positive affect (i.e., through self-motivation). If achievement flow (Cell 2.1) is about the ability to self-generate positive affect when the going gets tough, the effects of self-determined levels of *n*Ach on cognitive processing may only be revealed on difficult tasks. Coping with failure (Cell 2.3) is expected to be less relevant for volitional facilitation because it is about down-regulation of negative affect as opposed to up-regulation of positive affect.

In order to test the hypothesis about the relationship between volitional facilitation and self-access as assessed by the OMT (Level 1), an experimental paradigm was used to operationalize enactment of difficult intentions. Specifically, removal of the Stroop interference effect has been found to be a good measure of volitional facilitation (Kazén & Kuhl, 2005; Kuhl & Kazén,

1999), as discussed in the next section of the chapter. Thus, achievement flow (Cell 2.1) may not predict self-activation (and the ability to regulate affect) per se but rather a tendency to activate the self in conjunction with intention memory. Consistent with this assumption, Baumann and Scheffer (in press) found significant relationships between OMT achievement flow (Cell 2.1) and volitional facilitation (i.e., removal of Stroop interference): Participants with higher scores on achievement flow had significantly reduced reaction times, $\beta = -.33$, $p < .01$, and errors rates, $\beta = -.28$, $p < .05$, in response to incongruent compared to control stimuli. Consistent with expectations, the correlation between coping with failure (Cell 2.3) and volitional facilitation was not significant. This motive component may be more important when a task is not only difficult (i.e., reduces positive affect) but entails a threat (i.e., increases negative affect).

External observations of participants' overt behavior in an outdoor assessment center further support the assumption that achievement flow (Cell 2.1) predicts self-activation only when intention memory is active (Baumann & Scheffer, 2008): During several team tasks, participants high in the achievement flow motive (Cell 2.1) showed a unique pattern of overt behaviors indicative of joint activation of intention memory (i.e., "seeing difficulty": generating hypothesis, planning, analytical problem solving) and self-related functions (i.e., "mastering difficulty": high commitment to the task, spreading optimism and generating positive affect, motivating the team). The achievement flow motive predicted the product (seeing × mastering difficulty) after controlling for main effects of seeing and mastering difficulty. Findings contribute to the validity of the achievement flow motive. On a more general level, the presented findings support the assumption of PSI theory that individual OMT cells can be conceived of as entailing very specific interactions of cognitive and affective systems.

Need Specificity Hypothesis

According to our theoretical account of motives, each need is associated with a specific bodily and mental configuration that includes specific goal objects. In this section we elaborate on the role played by need content on the specific modulation of cognitive behavioral systems. The *need specificity hypothesis* (Kazén & Kuhl, 2005; Kuhl, 2001) asserts that when a need is activated (e.g., through need-related imagery or external cues), a particular configuration of the mental apparatus is aroused that supports need-specific cognition and behavior. For example, when one gets hungry, there is a configuration of one's mental resources that supports efficient processing of need-related cues (such as noticing the word "cake" or its picture on an advertisement or smelling it out of a hot oven), as well as instrumental behavior to obtain food (the specific goal object) and consume it. In the following paragraphs, this hypothesis is explained for achievement, affiliation, and power needs. Actually, it should be applicable to other social needs, such as those included in the original list by Murray (1938): "recognition," "autonomy," "defendance," "nurturance," and so forth, assuming that they represent valid constructs.

From the perspective of PSI theory, activation of a need or motive generates a specific system configuration, that is, activation of the macrosystem(s) specialized in the satisfaction of that need or motive. For example, if the achievement need is aroused through an external stimulus (e.g., a cue signaling a difficult task to be mastered), it is assumed that intention memory rather than intuitive behavior control will be engaged first because the former system is specialized in sequential-analytic thinking and maintaining difficult intentions active in memory whereas the latter is specialized in generating intuitive behavior patterns that can be executed instantaneously. Confrontation with a difficult task means that ready-to-go intuitive behaviors are not available (otherwise the task would not be called *difficult*). In contrast, when the need of affiliation is aroused, the opposite system-activation pattern is expected: Spontaneous behavior such as smiling and small talk (that does not involve explicit planning or difficult goals) is typical of affiliative interactions. In a similar vein, the need for power does not necessarily require difficulties to be mastered: Having an impact on others can satisfy the power motives even if no difficulties are encountered.

Empirical studies support the need specificity hypothesis across achievement, power, and affiliation domains. This research involved short presentation of need-related cues (words or pictures), and we measured their impact on subsequent cognitive performance. We assume that the need content of the cues exerts its influence on cognitive processes very quickly, even to the extent that it overrides the effect of stimulus valence (positivity or negativity). In that sense, the need specificity hypothesis entails a *primacy of motivation over affect* in motives' effects on attention, cognition, and behavior. This motivational primacy hypothesis is implied by the conceptual relationship between affect and need: To the extent that positive and negative affect indicates need satisfaction or frustration, respectively, there is a prototypical sequence starting with a need state, which is followed by an affective state whose valence depends on the degree of satisfaction or frustration encountered.

In a series of experiments on the Stroop effect (Kazén & Kuhl, 2005; Kuhl & Kazén, 1999), we examined the assumption that achievement but not affiliation-related primes activate a specific system configuration related to dealing with a difficult task. The first series of studies (Kuhl & Kazén, 1999) was designed to test the positive affect modulation assumption of PSI theory. If intention memory is activated by confrontation with a difficult task, the link between intention memory and intuitive behavior control is inhibited as long as problem solving is needed to overcome the difficulty. When an external cue eliciting positive affect is presented, it should signal "ready-to-go" (e.g., solution found) and re-establish the interrupted link between intention memory and the behavior control system (i.e., volitional facilitation). Two successive Stroop tasks, each requiring a response, were presented within a single trial (e.g., the word "GREEN" in blue, and then the word "RED" in yellow). We looked at the effects of different types of primes shown at the beginning of each trial on response latencies at the first Stroop task. In accordance with our expectations, we found that positive primes (e.g., "good luck" or "success") eliminated Stroop interference (6 ms in Study 1), measured as the latency difference between the incongruent (e.g., responding to the color blue of the word "GREEN") and the control condition (e.g., responding to the color blue of a meaningless series of characters: "XXXX"). Stroop interference was found with neutral and negative primes.

To examine the need specificity hypothesis, in the next series of studies (Kazén & Kuhl, 2005) we varied not only the valence of the primes (positive, negative) but also their need content (achievement, affiliation, and power). We presented on each trial a Stroop and a sentence evaluation task. Our main prediction was that positive achievement primes (e.g., "success") would reduce or eliminate Stroop interference (because they should predominantly activate intention memory), whereas positive affiliation primes (e.g., "love") would even increase Stroop interference (because they should first activate the intuitive behavior system, which could inhibit intention memory). We confirmed these expectations. Figure 13.5 shows the results of three studies (with

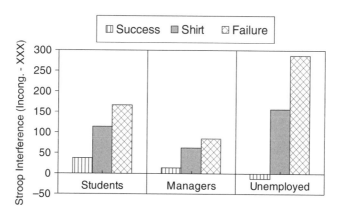

Figure 13.5 Latency differences (ms) between incongruent (e.g., word "GREEN" in blue) and control (e.g., "XXXX" in blue) Stroop conditions in three of the studies reported by Kazén & Kuhl (2005, *JPSP*, *89*, 426–448) as a function of prime valence (positive, neutral, or negative). Positive achievement primes (e.g, "erfolg") significantly *reduced or eliminated* Stroop interference in each study not only as indicated by these difference scores but also comparing their mean latencies with those obtained with neutral (e.g., "shirt") or negative achievement primes (e.g., "failure"). Only in the study with unemployed participants was the latency difference after negative primes significantly higher than after neutral primes.

students, managers, and unemployed graduates) for achievement: After positive achievement primes, there was a significant reduction or elimination of Stroop interference, as measured by latency differences between incongruent and control (XXXX) Stroop conditions. This volitional facilitation was also confirmed comparing positive versus neutral or negative achievement primes. Notably, the unemployed participants showed increased Stroop interference after negative achievement primes compared to the neutral condition, indicating failure-dependent volitional inhibition, which can be a cause or an effect of their previous negative experiences in achieving their professional goals.

To test the need specificity hypothesis thoroughly, we need to compare performance after positive achievement and positive affiliation primes with performance in the neutral prime condition. As already seen, Stroop latencies after positive *achievement* primes were significantly *faster* than those in the neutral prime condition (Fig. 13.5). Stroop performance after positive affiliation primes was different: In two studies (with students and unemployed graduates, but not managers), Stroop performance (incongruent Stroop minus XXXX) after positive *affiliation* primes was significantly *slower* (277 and 240 ms, for students and unemployed, respectively) compared to that in the neutral prime condition (114 and 157 ms). Finally, neither the negative *affiliation* nor the positive or negative *power* prime conditions influenced Stroop interference in any study. The previous results show (a) that the removal of the Stroop interference (volitional facilitation) effect is specific to the achievement domain, and (b) that needs have a processing priority compared to valence, because the effect of the positivity of the primes on cognitive performance was subordinated to the effect of need content within the same groups of participants (i.e., positive achievement primes reduced and positive affiliation primes increased interference).

The third study (with managers), provided a second way of testing the need specificity hypothesis. The effect of external need-related cues should be stronger in persons in which the corresponding need is more strongly aroused. This can be expected in individuals scoring high on an implicit motive test, such as the OMT. Therefore, we asked participants to fill out the OMT, as well as an explicit test measuring self-attributed motives (the motive enactment test; Kuhl & Henseler, 2003). We carried out a median split of the 63 managers according to their OMT scores (averaging Levels 1 to 4) and classified them into high ($n = 31$) versus low ($n = 32$) in need for achievement. After repeating the analyses including this factor, we found elimination of Stroop interference after positive achievement primes only for participants with high nAch (-8 ms, which was also significantly faster than to the neutral condition: 74 ms). In contrast, there was only a small reduction of the expected Stroop interference for participants with low nAch ($+37$ ms, which did not significantly differ from the neutral condition: 52 ms). Notably, a median split using the self-attributed achievement motive measure did not produce significant results. The overall pattern of findings thus confirms again the need specificity hypothesis.

Conclusion

The theoretical, methodological, and empirical work described in this chapter suggests that motives may be distinguished on at least three levels of higher cognitive-emotional functioning. Existing methods of motive assessment can be related to these three levels: Classical methods (TAT and PSE) focus on the preconceptual level with its impact on imagery and apperception (i.e., need-related interpretation of perceived scenes). The grid technique developed by Schmalt, Sokolowski, Langens and associates may help assess more differentiated cognitive elaborations of motives (although systematic research delineating commonalities and differences among the grid technique and classical methods is still missing).

Finally, the operant motive test (OMT) focuses on the self-integration level of motive measurement. The empirical findings reported suggest that the degree to which the self participates in motive-guided fantasy and action can be reliably and validly assessed from content analysis. Future research would greatly benefit from comparisons between the three methods to further explore their commonalities and differences. Our theoretical comparison of the three levels involved suggests that, despite of their commonalities, each of the three methods should have distinct behavioral correlates. Because of the close interaction expected among the preconceptual, conceptual, and self-regulatory levels, the three methods of motive measurement may show converging relationships with many behavioral measures and converging lack of relationships with self-report measures and some of their correlates. Note that the three levels mentioned do not coincide with different levels of explicit awareness ("consciousness"): Each of them relates to an implicit source of motivation. Even more interestingly, the three methods may sometimes show unique relationships when behavioral measures are taken that are dependent upon preconceptual imagery, conceptually elaborated extensions, or self-regulatory functions, respectively. Because interactions among mental systems are expected to be facilitated by participation of the self, self-regulatory dependence of motive effects are expected when one observes behavior that critically depends on systems interactions (e.g., interaction among intention memory and intuitive behavior control).

References

Atkinson, J. W. (1958). *Motives in fantasy, action, and society*. Princeton, NJ: Van Nostrand.

Baumann, N., Kaschel, R., & Kuhl, J. (2005). Striving for unwanted goals: Stress-dependent discrepancies between explicit and implicit achievement motives reduce subjective well-being and increase psychosomatic symptoms. *Journal of Personality and Social Psychology, 89*, 781–799.

Baumann, N., & Kuhl, J. (2002). Intuition, affect and personality: Unconscious coherence judgments and self-regulation of negative affect. *Journal of Personality and Social Psychology, 83,* 1213–1223.

Baumann, N., & Kuhl, J. (2003). Self-infiltration: Confusing assigned tasks as self-selected in memory. *Personality and Social Psychology Bulletin, 29,* 487–497.

Baumann, N., & Scheffer, D. (2008). Operanter Motivtest und Leistungs-Flow [Operant motive test and achievement flow]. In W. Sarges & D. Scheffer (Eds.), *Innovative Ansätze für die Eignungsdiagnostik [Innovative approaches to aptitude measurement]* (pp. 65-76). Göttingen, Germany: Hogrefe.

Baumann, N., & Scheffer, D. (in press). Seeing and Mastering Difficulty: The Role of Affective Change in Achievement Flow. *Cognition and Emotion.*

Beeman, M., Friedman, R. B., Grafman, J., Perez, E., Diamond, S., & Lindsay, M. B. (1994). Summation priming and coarse semantic coding in the right hemisphere. *Journal of Cognitive Neuroscience, 6,* 26–45.

Bolte, A., Goschke, T., & Kuhl, J. (2002). Emotion and intuition: Effects of positive and negative mood on implicit judgments of semantic coherence. *Psychological Science, 14,* 416–421.

Boring, E. G. (1929). *A history of experimental psychology.* New York: Appleton-Century-Crofts.

Brunstein, J. C. (2001). Persönliche Ziele und Handlungs- versus Lageorientierung: Wer bindet sich an realistische und bedürfniskongruente Ziele? [Personal goals and action versus state orientation: Who builds a commitment to realistic and need-congruent goals?] *Zeitschrift für Differentielle und Diagnostische Psychologie, 22,* 1–12.

Brunstein, J. C., Schultheiss, O. C., & Grässmann, R. (1998). Personal goals and emotional well-being: The moderating role of motive dispositions. *Journal of Personality and Social Psychology, 75,* 494–508.

Chasiotis, A., Bender, M., Kiessling, F., & Hofer J. (in press). The emergence of the independent self: Autobiographical memory as a mediator of false belief understanding and motive orientation in Cameroonian and German preschoolers. *Journal of Cross-Cultural Psychology.*

Chasiotis, A., & Hofer, J. (2003). *Die Messung impliziter Motive in Deutschland, Costa Rica und Kamerun* [Measurement of implicit motives in Germany, Costa Rica, and Cameroon]. Research report to the German Research Foundation (DFG).

Chasiotis, A., Hofer, J., & Campos, D. (2006). When does liking children lead to parenthood? Younger siblings, implicit prosocial power motivation, and explicit love for children predict parenthood across cultures. *Journal of Cultural and Evolutionary Psychology, 4,* 95–123.

Elliot, A. J., & Church, M. A. (1997). A hierarchical model of approach and avoidance achievement motivation. *Journal of Personality and Social Psychology, 72,* 218–232.

Elliot, A. J. & McGregor, H. A. (2001). A 2 × 2 achievement goal framework. *Journal of Personality and Social Psychology, 80,* 501–519.

Entwisle, D. R. (1972). To dispel fantasies about fantasy-based measures of achievement motivation. *Psychological Bulletin, 77,* 377–391.

Ferguson, M.J. (2007). On the automatic evaluation of end-states. *Journal of Personality and Social Psychology, 92*, 596–611.

Fineman, S. (1977). The achievement motive construct and its measurement: Where are we now? *British Journal of Psychology, 68*, 1–22.

Gollwitzer, P. M. (1999). Implementation intentions: Strong effects of simple plans. *Journal of Personality and Social Psychology, 73*, 186–197.

Greenwald, A. G., & Banaji, M. R. (1995). Implicit social cognition: Attitudes, self-esteem, and stereotypes. *Psychological Review, 102*, 4–27.

Heckhausen, H. (1991). *Motivation and action.* New York: Springer.

Hofer, J., Busch, H., Chasiotis, A., Kärtner, J., & Campos, D. (2008). Concern for generativity and its relation to implicit power motivation, generative goals, and satisfaction with life: A cross-cultural investigation. *Journal of Personality, 76*, 1–30.

Hofer, J., & Chasiotis, A. (2003). Congruence of life goals and implicit motives as predictors of life satisfaction: Cross-cultural implications of a study of Zambian male adolescents. *Motivation and Emotion, 27*, 251–272.

Kaschel, R., & Kuhl, J. (2004). Motivational counseling in an extended functional context: Personality systems interaction theory and assessment. In W. M. Cox & E. Klinger (Eds.), *Handbook of motivational counseling: Concepts, approaches, and assessment* (pp. 99–119). New York: Wiley & Sons.

Kazén, M., & Baumann, N. (2005, July). *Distinguishing associative from integrative implicit measures of self-access.* Proceedings of the "Third International Biennial SELF Research Conference," Max-Planck Institut of Human Development, Berlin. (CD; ISBN 1 74108 073 8).

Kazén, M., Baumann, N., & Kuhl, J. (2003). Self-infiltration and self-compatibility checking in dealing with unattractive tasks: The moderating influence of state vs. action-orientation. *Motivation and Emotion, 27*, 157–197.

Kazén, M., & Kuhl, J. (2005). Intention memory and achievement motivation: Volitional facilitation and inhibition as a function of affective contents of need-related stimuli. *Journal of Personality and Social Psychology, 89*, 426–448.

Kelly, G. A. (1955). *The psychology of personal constructs.* New York: Norton.

Koole, S., & Jostmann, N. (2004). Getting a grip on your feelings: Effects of action orientation and external demands on intuitive affect regulation. *Journal of Personality and Social Psychology, 87*, 974–990.

Koole, S. L., Dijksterhuis, a., & van Knippenberg, A. (2001). What's in a name: Implicit self-esteem and the automatic self. *Journal of Personality and Social Psychology, 80*, 669–685.

Kuhl, J. (1981). Motivational and functional helplessness: The moderating effect of state vs. action orientation. *Journal of Personality and Social Psychology, 40*, 155–170.

Kuhl, J. (1983). Motivation, Konflikt und Handlungskontrolle [Motivation, conflict, and action control]. Berlin: Springer.

Kuhl, J. (2000). A functional-design approach to motivation and volition: The dynamics of personality systems interactions. In M. Boekaerts, P. R. Pintrich, & M. Zeidner (Eds.), *Self-regulation: Directions and challenges for future research* (pp. 111–169). New York: Academic Press.

Kuhl, J. (2001). Motivation und Persönlichkeit: Interaktionen psychischer Systeme [Motivation and personality: Interactions of mental systems]. Göttingen, Germany: Hogrefe.

Kuhl, J., & Beckmann, J. (1994). *Volition and personality: Action versus state orientation.* Göttingen, Germany: Hogrefe.

Kuhl, J., & Henseler, W. (2003). Entwicklungsorientiertes Scanning (EOS). [Development-oriented scanning (EOS)] In L. Rosenstiel & J. Erpenbeck (Eds.), *Handbuch der Kompetenzmessung* [Handbook of competence measurement] (pp. 428–453). Heidelberg: Schäffer-Poeschel.

Kuhl, J., & Kazén, M. (1994). Self-discrimination and memory: State orientation and false self-ascription of assigned activities. *Journal of Personality and Social Psychology, 66,* 1103–1115.

Kuhl, J., & Kazén, M. (1999). Volitional facilitation of difficult intentions: Joint activation of intention memory and positive affect removes stroop interference. *Journal of Experimental Psychology: General, 128,* 382–399.

Kuhl, J., & Kazén, M. (2008). Motivation, affect, and hemispheric asymmetry: Power versus affiliation. *Journal of Personality and Social Psychology, 95,* 456–469.

Kuhl, J., & Koole, S. L. (2004). Workings of the will: A functional approach. In J. Greenberg, S. L. Koole, & T. Pyszczynski (Eds.), *Handbook of experimental existential psychology* (pp. 411–430). New York: Guilford.

Kuhl, J., & Koole, S. L. (2008). The functional architecture of approach and avoidance motivation. In A. Elliot (Ed.), *Handbook of approach and avoidance motivation* (pp. 535–553) New York: Psychology Press.

Kuhl, J., & Scheffer, D. (1999). *Der operante Multi-Motiv-Test (OMT): Manual* [Scoring manual for the Operant Multi-Motive Test (OMT)]. University of Osnabrück, Osnabrück, Germany.

Kuhl, J., Scheffer, D., & Eichstaedt, J. (2003). Der Operante Motiv-Test (OMT): Ein neuer Ansatz zur Messung impliziter Motive [The operant motive-test (OMT): A new approach to the assessment of implicit motives]. In F. Rheinberg & J. Stiensmeier-Pelster (Eds.), *Diagnostik von Motivation und Selbstkonzept* [*Diagnostic of motivation and self-concept*] (pp. 129–149). Göttingen, Germany: Hogrefe.

McDougall, W. (1932). *The energies of man: A study of the fundamentals of dynamic psychology.* New York: Methuen.

McClelland, D. (1980). Motive dispositions: The merits of operant and respondent measures. In L. Wheeler (Ed.), *Review of personality and social psychology, Vol. 1* (pp. 10–41). Beverly Hills, CA: Sage.

McClelland, D. C. (1985). *Human motivation.* Glenview, IL: Scott, Foresman, & Co.

McClelland, D. C., Atkinson, J. W., Clark, R. A., & Lowell, E. L. (1953). *The achievement motive.* New York: Appleton-Century-Crofts.

McClelland, D. C., Koestner, R., & Weinberger, J. (1989). How do self-attributed and implicit motives differ? *Psychological Review, 96,* 690–702.

McGregor, I., & Marigold, D. C. (2003). Defensive zeal and the uncertain self: What makes you so sure? *Journal of Personality and Social Psychology, 85,* 838–852.

Murray, H. A. (1938). *Explorations in personality.* New York: Oxford University Press.

Oettingen, G., Pak, H. J., & Schnetter, K. (2001). Self-regulation of goal-setting: Turning free fantasies about the future into binding goals. *Journal of Personality and Social Psychology, 80*, 736–753.

Quirin, M., Koole, S. L., Bauman, N., Kazén, M., & Kuhl, J. (in press). You can't always remember what you want: The role of cortisol in self-ascription of assigned goals. *Journal of Research in Personality.*

Quirin, M., Koole, S. L., & Kuhl, J. (2009). *Intuiting the self: Development and validation of the experiential self-access questionnaire.* Manuscript in preparation. University of Osnabrueck, Osnabrueck, Germany.

Sapolsky, R. M. (1992). *Stress, the aging brain, and the mechanism of neuron death.* Cambridge, MA: MIT Press.

Scheffer, D. (2005). *Implizite Motive* [Implicit motives]. Göttingen, Germany: Hogrefe.

Scheffer, D., Eichstaedt, J., Chasiotis, A., & Kuhl, J. (2007). Towards an integrated measure of need affiliation and agreeableness derived from the Operant Motive Test. *Psychology Science, 49*, 308-324.

Scheffer, D., Kuhl, J., & Eichstaedt, J. (2003). Der Operante Motiv-Test (OMT): Inhaltsklassen, Auswertung, psychometrische Kennwerte und Validierung. [The operant motive-test (OMT): Contents, scoring, psychometric values, and validation] In J. Stiensmeier-Pelster & F. Rheinberg (Eds.), *Diagnostik von Motivation und Selbstkonzept* [*Diagnostic of motivation and self-concept*] (pp. 151–167). Göttingen, Germany: Hogrefe.

Schmalt, H.-D. (1999). Assessing the achievement motive using the grid technique. *Journal of Research in Personality, 33*, 109–130.

Schultheiss, O. C., & Brunstein, J. C. (1999). Goal imagery: Bridging the gap between implicit motives and explicit goals. *Journal of Personality, 67*, 1–38.

Showers, C. J., & Kling, K. C. (1996). Organization of self-knowledge: Implications for recovery from sad mood. *Journal of Personality and Social Psychology, 70*, 578–590.

Thrash, T. M., & Elliot, A. J. (2002). Implicit and self-attributed achievement motives: Concordance and predictive validity. *Journal of Personality, 70*, 729–755.

Trudewind, C. (1989). Die Entwicklung der Leistungsmotivation [The development of achievement motivation]. In H. Keller (Ed.), *Handbuch der Kleinkindforschung* [*Handbook of infancy research*] (pp. 491–524). Berlin: Springer.

Tuerlinckx, F., De Boeck, P., & Lens, W. (2002). Measuring needs with the Thematic Apperception Test: A psychometric study. *Journal of Personality and Social Psychology, 82*, 448–461.

Vygotsky, L. S. (1978). *Mind in society: The development of higher psychological processes.* Cambridge, MA: Harvard University Press.

Winter, D. G. (1994). *Manual for scoring motive imagery in running text* (version 4.2). Department of Psychology: University of Michigan, Ann Arbor.

Winter, D. G. (1996). *Personality: Analysis and interpretation of lives.* New York: McGraw-Hill.

Winterbottom, M. R. (1958). The relation of need for achievement to learning experiences in independence and mastery. In J. W. Atkinson (Ed.), *Motives in fantasy, action and society* (pp. 453–478). Princeton, NJ: Van Nostrand.

SECTION 4

Interdisciplinary and Applied Aspects

Chapter 14

Political and Historical Consequences of Implicit Motives

DAVID G. WINTER
Department of Psychology, University of Michigan

Some of the most interesting and elusive questions of history involve the personalities of political leaders and nations. Why did Woodrow Wilson, from the presidency of Princeton University to the presidency of the United States, repeatedly spurn compromise, thereby failing to reach his most cherished political goals (George & George, 1956)? How did Richard Nixon, during the course of his long political career, change from a college student who was "very liberal, almost populist" (Nixon, 1978, p. 17) to a first-term member of Congress who zealously hunted suspected Communists, to a president who capped his political career by toasting Chinese Communist Party Chairman Mao Zedong in Beijing's Great Hall of the People? Why are some crises peacefully resolved or contained (e.g., the U.S.-Canada border dispute in 1846, the Bosnian annexation crisis of 1909, or the independent line of the Polish Communist Party in 1956), whereas other, similar crises escalate to aggression and war (e.g., the U.S.-Mexican War of 1846, the Sarajevo assassination crisis of 1914, or the Hungarian revolution of 1956)? Why do some nations experience rapid economic development at the same time that other, similar nations stagnate? What are the collective psychological antecedents of dictatorship and democracy?

Traditionally, these questions have been answered by speculative or "armchair" methods, because most political and historical actors, as well as national populations, are usually not available for traditional direct personality measurement. Current political leaders are inaccessible to psychologists (which is what makes the 1967 movie, "The President's Analyst," so funny); dead historical figures have taken their Oedipus complexes, their n Power and authoritarianism, with them.[1] As a result, the psychological study of history has proceeded by applying personality concepts (often drawn from psychoanalysis) to known biographical or historical facts, in order to produce psychobiographical (Greenstein, 1969/1987, Chapter 3) or psychohistorical (Cocks and Crosby, 1987) interpretations.

In recent decades, political psychologists have developed a variety of rigorous and objective methods of measuring personality at a distance (Winter, 2003b; see also Post, 2003; Slatcher, Chung, & Pennebaker, 2007; Winter, Hermann, Weintraub, & Walker, 1991b). Typically, these methods involve content analysis of spoken or written texts. Implicit motives are measured with the experimentally-derived content analysis systems pioneered by McClelland and his colleagues (see Winter, 1998b), and so they can be measured at a distance.

Measuring the motives of past or present groups, institutions, or whole societies presents additional problems. Using implicit motive measures in surveys of representative national populations is possible (Veroff, Atkinson, Feld, & Gurin, 1960; Veroff, Depner, Kulka, & Douvan, 1980) but expensive. To overcome these difficulties, psychologists have turned to the analysis of cultural products and archival materials. The first adaptation of implicit motive measures to historical materials was an undergraduate honors thesis by Berlew (1956; see also McClelland, 1958), who scored classical Greek texts for n Achievement and related the results to the growth and decline of Greek trade and economic activity. Bradburn and Berlew (1961) made a similar study of British economic development during the period 1550–1850, relating n Achievement scores of popular drama, accounts of sea voyages, and street ballads to subsequent economic growth. Cortes (1961) used a similar technique to study economic changes in Spain before and during its "golden age." McClelland scored children's primary school readers for n Achievement, n Affiliation, and n Power in his landmark study, *The Achieving Society* (1961), in order to study economic development in twentieth century nations.

In his undergraduate honors thesis, Donley (1968; Donley & Winter, 1970) scored the first inaugural addresses of twentieth-century U.S. presidents for n Achievement and n Power. This was the first systematic application of implicit motive measures to the study of historical individuals. Winter and Stewart (1977a) added scores for n Affiliation.

The Integrated Running Text Scoring System

The original motive implicit scoring systems were developed for use with modified Thematic Apperception Test or Picture Story Exercise responses— typically a series of brief (50–200 words) imaginative stories. Each story is typically scored for presence/absence of basic motive imagery; if imagery is scored, then several additional subcategories can also be scored for presence/absence. Imagery and each subcategory can only be scored once per story; the total score is the sum of categories scored as present in the story. Text materials, however, may range from brief interview responses to lengthy speeches, letters, or works of fiction. Usually there are no natural divisions analogous to separate TAT stories. In many of the early studies mentioned above, therefore, researchers modified the original full scoring systems. Typically they dropped the subcategories and scored only motive imagery. In lengthy texts, they used the sentence as the unit of scoring; thus imagery for a given motive could be scored only once per sentence (in some studies, only once in any two consecutive sentences).

Winter (1991a; see also Winter, 1994) codified these ad hoc modifications into an integrated system for scoring all three motives (achievement, affiliation, and power) at once, in all kinds of "running text," such as speeches, letters, interviews, diplomatic messages, fiction, drama, and television programs. Scores from this system were highly correlated with scores based on the original scoring systems. They successfully differentiated aroused and neutral stories from the original motive arousal experiments. They possessed high retest reliabilities (rs = .46 to .60, using pooled "same" and "no instructions" conditions from Winter & Stewart, 1977b). Finally, they predicted motive-relevant behaviors. This *Manual for Scoring Motive Imagery in Running Text* (Winter, 1994) has subsequently been used in many of the historical and political studies reviewed below. Using this system, Winter (1987b, 2002) subsequently rescored the U.S. presidential inaugural addresses and extended them backward to George Washington and forward to Barack Obama (Winter, 2001, 2005a, 2009b).

Implicit Motives and Economic Development

The Achieving Society and Its Critics

As research on *n* Achievement took root in the early 1950s, McClelland began to explore the social consequences of that motive. Laboratory studies showed that *n* Achievement was correlated with high standards, choosing tasks of intermediate difficulty, and using feedback to modify performance. McClelland linked these behaviors to Weber's (1920/1958) concept of a Protestant Ethic, and went on to hypothesize a causal sequence involving religious beliefs, child-rearing practices, *n* Achievement, and entrepreneurial activity (McClelland, 1955). *The Achieving Society* (McClelland, 1961) was an extensive elaboration of this chain of hypotheses. Among preindustrial cultures, *n* Achievement scored from folktales was associated with religious beliefs emphasizing individual contact with the divine (pp. 370–372), competitive games (pp. 323–324), and the presence of full-time entrepreneurs (pp. 65–70). Among modern nations, *n* Achievement scored from two waves (1929 and 1946–1950) of primary school readers predicted subsequent (but not prior) economic development (Chapter 3). In a smaller sample of industrial nations, *n* Achievement was associated with lower capital-output ratios—that is, with more efficient use of financial capital in the production process (pp. 422–423). McClelland supplemented his analysis of collective cultural documents with laboratory research theoretically related to entrepreneurial behavior (Chapter 6), as well as studies of individual managers and professionals in several different countries (Chapter 7).

McClelland's ambitious study was not without its critics. Some economists (Schatz, 1965) quarreled with his use of growth in electricity production (kWh per capita) as a measure of economic development. A sociologist reviewer (Eisenstadt, 1963) lamented what he saw as McClelland's neglect of situational and structural factors in the operation of *n* Achievement and economic development.

To bolster *The Achieving Society* thesis, and drawing on a demonstration that *n* Achievement could be increased through deliberate teaching based on operant reinforcement (Burris, 1958), McClelland (1965) developed programs to raise people's *n* Achievement and thereby to increase their individual economic performance and thus collective levels of economic development. McClelland and Winter (1969) demonstrated that this training led to significant economic improvements (time and effort, capital invested, labor employed, output, and sales) among owners and managers of various-sized enterprises in Mumbai and South India. However, their efforts to achieve greater collective (i.e., community or regional) economic development were largely frustrated by administrative and political problems that led to the discontinuation of the training project. Internal analysis showed that *n* Achievement training only led to improved economic performance among those who were in charge of their firm—that is, people with sufficient scope and control to carry out the improvement they had imagined (pp. 250–255). By incorporating the interactive effects of structural position on motivation, such a conclusion responded to the sociological criticism of McClelland thesis mentioned above. Winter (2008) has developed this point further in connection with his discussion of *n* Achievement in politics, cited below.

Other Studies of Motivation in Economics

Studies of individual firms and groups of firms have confirmed the relationship between *n* Achievement and entrepreneurial performance. In a 7-year longitudinal study of several small Finnish knitwear firms, Kock (1965) measured the motives of owner-managers and, where relevant, other executives involved in decision making. He found significant correlations between managerial *n* Achievement and several measures of economic performance: investment, growth in employment, value of output, and sales. In a study of small, high-technology research and development firms, Wainer and Rubin (1969) found that firms headed by presidents or owner-managers high in *n* Achievement showed significantly higher growth rates than other firms. Varga (1975) studied state-owned chemical and pharmaceutical companies in Hungary, during the years of socialist economic organization, and found that projects tended to be more successful in both technical and economic terms when staff members were high in *n* Achievement. Similar studies have been carried out in Australia (Morris & Fargher, 1974) and India (Hundal, 1971; Nandy, 1973). In a study of small business owners in Washington DC, Durand and Shea (1974) found that *n* Achievement predicted engagement in specific entrepreneurial activities over the next 18 months, but only for those owners or managers who were above the median in a measure of internal control of reinforcement.

For managers in progressive companies, *n* Achievement is associated with more rapid promotion and salary increases (Company *X* in Andrews, 1967; Cummin, 1967). Wormley (1976; quoted in McClelland, 1985, p. 255) found that portfolios managed by mutual fund managers with high *n* Achievement showed better than average performance over a 5-year period. In a U.S. national sample survey, Crockett (1962) found that *n* Achievement was associated with greater intergenerational occupational mobility. Even among farmers—if they have sufficient control over land and other necessary resources—*n* Achievement predicts being innovative and achieving higher crop yields per unit of land in Australia (Chamala & Crouch, 1977), Colombia (Rogers & Svenning, 1969), and India (Singh, 1969; Singh, 1979; Singh & Gupta, 1977). A meta-analysis of 18 studies by Collins, Hanges, and Locke (2004) showed a mean correlation of .20 between implicit *n* Achievement and entrepreneurship.

Using an adaptation of the integrated running text manual, Chusmir and Azevedo (1992) scored CEO annual reports to stockholders of the 50 largest U.S. corporations in 1988. They found that the level of *n* Achievement in a corporation's report was correlated significantly with its financial return on sales, return on equity, and future growth in sales volume. Diaz (1982) found a similar relationship in a large Japanese automobile manufacturing company. (Chusmir and Azevedo also found that the level of *n* Power in a corporation's annual report was correlated with subsequent profit.)

Implicit Motives and Leadership

Implicit motives play an important role in leadership, both in the world of politics and also in corporate and informal settings. First of all, motives affect how leaders construe their leadership position. Consider the differences in how the office of President of the United States was viewed by three occupants who had very different motive profiles (quotations from Tourtellot, 1964): Herbert Hoover (1929–1933), whose highest motive score was achievement (1.5 standard deviations above the mean of all U.S. presidents); Dwight Eisenhower (1953–1961), whose highest score was affiliation (.5 *SD* above the mean); and Harry Truman (1945–1953), whose highest score was power (2.3 *SD* above the mean).

Leadership: Not Just an Arena for Power

Consistent with his motive profile, Hoover had a conception of the president's role that emphasized excellence, in an explicit analogy to business. The president is "the Chief Executive of the greatest business in the world" who "must, within his capacities, give leadership . . . for betterment of our country" (p. 61). In accomplishing this task, he should consult "the fine minds of our citizens" (p. 122) but should avoid direct displays of anger: "Presidents cannot always kick evil-minded persons out of the front door [because they] are often selected by the electors" (p. 251).

For Truman, the power of the presidency was just that—to exercise power. "I believe the power of the President should be used in the interest of the people, and in order to do that the President must use whatever power the Constitution does not expressly deny him" (p. 68). Often presidents must "prevent career men from circumventing presidential policy" (p. 129). In battles with Congress, "the veto power of the President is one of the most important instruments of his authority, even though the legislation he rejects may be passed over his veto by the Congress" (p. 257).

In contrast, Eisenhower saw himself as a conciliator, avoiding partisan disagreement in order to bring the groups together. Early on, he told the press that "I have no intention of going out and getting into partisan struggles in any district or in any State" (p. 69). He later added that "when the Executive and Legislative Branches are politically in conflict, politics in Washington runs riot. . . . In the eyes of the world, we appear divided in council and uncertain in purpose" (p. 258).

Leaders' motive profiles are related to their leadership skills and styles. Motives determine the satisfactions, frustrations, and stresses arising from the leadership experience; they can therefore be sources of opportunity and vulnerability to leaders. For example, power-motivated leaders are vulnerable to flattery and ingratiation by subordinates (Fodor and Farrow, 1979); they tend to neglect moral considerations in making policy decisions (Fodor and Smith, 1982) and suffer diminished creativity after negative feedback (Fodor, 1990). As discussed below, they are also prone to aggression and violence. Achievement-motivated leaders are especially sensitive to issues of personal control, and affiliation-motivated leaders are vulnerable to scandal.

Motives of Successful Business Leaders

Studies of the implicit motives of business leaders illustrate important differences between *n* Achievement and *n* Power. Whereas implicit *n* Achievement predicts *entrepreneurial* success (combining labor, materials, and capital to produce innovative products), particularly in small "high technology" companies, several studies suggest that in larger corporate bureaucracies, implicit *n* Power is related to successful leadership. Thus Andrews (1967) also found that *n* Power predicted rank and past promotions and current rank in "Company Y," a very power-oriented company run "like a feudalistic hacienda" (p. 165). McClelland and Boyatzis (1982) found that controlled *n* Power was correlated with promotion history among executives in the vast AT&T corporation of the 1950s and 1960s, a finding that Winter (1991b) later confirmed with a combination of *n* Power and implicit responsibility.

A study of top managers in a large American corporation (McClelland, 1975, pp. 300–302; see also McClelland & Burnham, 1976) suggests the mechanism underlying these results. Subordinates of those managers high in *n* Power, low in affiliation, and high in activity inhibition (see McClelland, Davis, Kalin, & Wanner, 1972) had higher morale (combined organizational climate ratings of "team spirit" and "organizational clarity"). They experienced greater pressure for responsibility and less pressure for conformity. Taken together, these climate effects make up the "emotional form of communal relationship" that, according to Weber (1922/1968), grows out of charismatic leadership. To their followers, such leaders may appear to have almost supernatural, superhuman, or magical powers (pp. 241–243 passim). Although McClelland's study suggests that such leaders can be found in business, they are usually identified with the leadership in politics, to which we now turn.

At-a-Distance Studies of Political Leaders

United States presidents

House, Spangler, and Woycke (1991) studied charismatic leadership among U.S. presidents, using an archival analogue to McClelland's climate ratings by subordinates. They developed a composite measure of charisma, based on coding of biographies of cabinet members for presidential *charismatic behaviors* and *charismatic effects* on associates, as well as other measures developed by Simonton (1988). In a regression including all three implicit motives, as well as number of crises and year of inauguration, presidential *n* Power scores were positively associated with the composite charisma cluster.

Winter (2002) explored the relation of implicit motives to a wide variety of presidential outcome measures, as shown in Table 14.1. For Presidents Washington through Lyndon Johnson, *n* Power is positively associated with

Table 14.1. Motives and Leadership Performance among U.S. Presidents

	Correlation with Motive:		
Variable	Achievement	Affiliation	Power
Overall performance			
Rated greatness[a]	.07	.09	.40*
Made great presidential decisions[a]	.09	.29	.51**
Overall assessment by Greenstein (2000)	−.66*	.08	−.13
Specific dimensions of performance			
Greenstein (2000) ratings ($n = 10$):			
Effectiveness as a public communicator	.19	−.34	.45
Organizational capacity	−.52	.35	−.01
Political skill	−.72*	.01	−.21
Emotional maturity	−.70*	.03	.10
Consistent overarching vision	−.05	−.04	−.23
Strategic cognitive style	−.11	.20	−.62†
Historians' ratings ($n = 29$)[a]			
Idealism	.51**	.19	.19
Flexibility	−.22	.27	.26
Barber (1992) typology ($n = 11$):			
Active positive	−.07	.37	.87***
Active negative	.84***	.03	−.32
White House reporters' ratings (Shearer, 1982; $n = 6$):			
Combative skill	.25	.59	.76†
Sense of humor	.23	.19	.91*
Specific presidential outcomes[a]			
Electoral success: % vote in first election	.02	−.15	−.12
War entry	−.03	.16	.52**
Arms limitation treaty	.13	.40	−.05
Scandal	.15	.40*	.01

[a] From Winter (1987b).
†$p < .10$
*$p < .05$
**$p < .01$
***$p < .001$

overall ratings of presidential greatness by historians (based on Maranell, 1970), whereas *n* Achievement is unrelated to performance ratings. The *n* Power relationship to overall performance does not hold up in Greenstein's (2000) intensive scrutiny of presidents from the last half of the twentieth century (F. Roosevelt through Clinton). Nevertheless, in this small group *n* Power does predict communication effectiveness, which is one important dimension of political success. Moreover, the relationship of *n* Achievement to presidential performance is more strongly negative than in the total presidential sample.[2] According to Greenstein, these presidents *lacked* organizational capacity, political skill, and emotional maturity; other historians rate them as idealistic but inflexible. Barber (1992) categorized them as active-negative, meaning that although they are quite active, they seem to draw frustration instead of pleasure from being president.

How can the great contrast between the role of n Achievement in politics and business be explained? One likely possibility involves the issue of control: in the contexts in which n Achievement predicts success (small entrepreneurial firms), the entrepreneur has considerable control over structures and procedures. Thus, McClelland and Winter (1969, Chapter 9) found that n Achievement training only increased economic activity among people in control of their business. Political leaders, however, often do not have this level of control: because other leaders have their own power base and their own ideas of "the best," it is usually necessary to compromise the "one best plan." In addition, the best often costs too much and must be implemented by a civil service that the leader did not appoint, does not trust, and cannot remove (see Winter, 2008). Faced with these frustrations, achievement-motivated presidents may try to go over the heads of Congress (as did Wilson, who ruined his health in the process), micromanage (as did Carter), or turn to illegal means (as did Nixon). In a study of world leaders, Winter (2002) found that n Achievement (and not n Power) was associated with coming to power through a coup d'état—a tactic that can be seen as the ultimate extralegal assertion of personal control.

Power-motivated presidents, in contrast, use their communication and combative skills, as well as their sense of humor, to deal with these problems. They have the capacity to draw pleasure from the scrimmages of politics. As a result, they end up in Barber's active-positive category. Winter (2002) has developed motivational case studies of individual presidents. He used Richard Nixon's high n Achievement to explain some of the paradoxes of his political career (see also Winter & Carlson, 1988). John F. Kennedy responded to threatening situations such as the 1961 Berlin crisis and the 1962 Cuban Missile Crisis with speeches significantly higher than usual in n Power. Bill Clinton's dramatic turnaround after the defeat of his party in the 1994 midterm Congressional elections was related to increased n Power in his speeches. Finally, several predictions based on George W. Bush's 2001 inaugural address have been confirmed by subsequent events (Winter, 2005a): that he would enjoy being president and would be more politically effective than expected, that he would involve the U.S. in wars (high n Power), and further, that his administration would be vulnerable to scandal (high n Affiliation).

Motives are also related to certain specific presidential actions and outcomes. N Power is significantly related to the likelihood of the U.S. entering a war, whereas n Affiliation predicts U.S. adherence to treaties for the limitation or elimination of major weapons systems. On the other hand, the president's level of n Affiliation is also related to whether major administration officials will be involved in political scandals.

Electoral Success

No single motive is related to political success in the sense of getting elected—that is, the percent of the vote received in the first election. Rather, this kind of "sociometric" success is related to the congruence of the president's motive profile with that of United States society (as measured through content analysis of popular fiction and other literary texts; see Winter, 1987b, and McClelland, 1975, Chapter 9). Ethington (2001) demonstrated the same effect in a microstudy of the 2000 presidential campaign. The candidate (George W. Bush or Albert Gore) whose motive profile was closer to that of nighttime television host Jay Leno's opening monologue (on the "Tonight" show) on one day showed a significant relative increase in the polls five days later. Schmitt and Winter (1998) found traces of the reverse relationship in the Soviet Union: after a new General Secretary of the Communist Party assumed office, the motive profile of Soviet society (measured through content analysis of popular literature) tended to change toward his profile. In a study of the heads of winning and losing parties in 10 Canadian Parliamentary elections between 1945 and 1974, Suedfeld, Bluck, Ballard, and Baker-Brown (1990) found a significant winner–society congruence only with respect to n Power scores ($r = .71$, $p < .01$).

Members of the United States Congress

Hyman (2006) expanded the study of political motivation to the legislative branch of the American government, using motive scores of the "maiden speeches" of Senators or Representatives newly elected to the 80th or 81st Congresses in 1946 or 1948, respectively—two postwar elections that produced a large turnover in the membership of the Congress after World War II.

Among Democrats, n Power significantly predicted voting support for key aspects of Democratic President Truman's domestic program, whereas among Republicans, support for Truman's domestic program was significantly related to n Achievement. These contrasting results are actually consistent with previous research: n Power as involving networks of loyalty and support (Winter, 1973, pp. 114–115), and n Achievement reflecting independence of personal judgment and a lack of concern for political orthodoxy (see McClelland, 1961, pp. 228–230 and Chapter 8 *passim*). Voting on international and foreign policy issues, however, showed no relationship to implicit motives—perhaps reflecting the growth of a genuinely bipartisan foreign policy in the years after World War II.

Although implicit motives were unrelated to the career length or success with the House of Representatives, among Democrats they did predict "external" political career mobility (moving from the House to the Senate, or to the executive branch by appointment or election): n Power positively ($r = .25$, $n = 100$, $p < .001$; in a regression that included age, a crude measure of social class, and the other two motives, $\beta = .27$, $p < .01$), and n Affiliation showing a near-significant negative trend ($r = -.16$, $\beta = -.18$). These results suggest that the two major components of the "leadership motive pattern" (McClelland, 1975, Chapter 8)—high n Power and low n Affiliation—actually do predict the trajectory of political careers over time, at least for Democrats. Among Republicans, political career mobility is apparently related to other variables (e.g., social class, as measured by prestige of college attended).

United States Governors

Ferguson and Barth (2002) scored motive imagery in the first inaugural addresses of 44 U.S. governors who were in office during 1993–1994. The combination of high n Power and high n Achievement predicted success, measured by the proportion of gubernatorial legislative priorities passed by their state legislature. The difference from presidents in the role of n Achievement suggests that U.S. governors may be operating in a slightly different political structure and situation—one that entails greater personal control. Such a consideration would explain some of the problems that successful governors such as Jimmy Carter and Bill Clinton encountered when they became president. (The governors' scores on n Affiliation were negatively related to success.)

United States Supreme Court Justices

Aliotta (1988) scored implicit motives of the 15 U.S. Supreme Court justices appointed between 1925 and 1984 for whom there was a verbatim transcript of their testimony at Senate confirmation hearings and then related these scores to variables reflecting subsequent performance. She found that n Power predicted writing majority opinions, which is perhaps the most direct way for a justice to have impact and acquire prestige. Justices high in n Affiliation tended to avoid writing majority opinions, perhaps because they are reluctant to jeopardize amicable relationships with their dissenting colleagues. N Achievement is also negatively related to writing majority opinions, but positively related to writing *separate* opinions when casting either concurring *or* dissenting votes. As Aliotta concluded, achievement-motivated justices express an independent judicial philosophy by writing a separate opinion—appealing to history over the heads of the majority opinion that they could not successfully influence (pp. 279–280). The number of justices in this study was small, suggesting that the results should be interpreted with caution. Still, Aliotta did study virtually the entire population of U.S. Supreme Court nominees over a 59-year period—an important group of people whose actions had major social and political consequences.

The difference between judicial and presidential n Achievement can perhaps be explained by the extraordinary independence and therefore personal control enjoyed by Supreme Court justices: once confirmed, they serve for life; as the ultimate arbiters of the law, they are immune from any formal veto or influence on the part of the president, Congress, or public opinion. Like governors and in contrast to presidents, their structural position appears to entail more of the sense of personal control that people high in *n* Achievement require for effective performance.

Case Studies of Individual Leaders

At-a-distance implicit motive scores can contribute to psychological portraits of individual leaders and historical figures. Examples include John F. Kennedy (Winter, 2002); Richard Nixon (Winter & Carlson, 1988); Ronald Reagan (Hermann, 1983); Bill Clinton (Winter, 1998a); George H. W. Bush and Mikhail Gorbachev (Winter, Hermann, Weintraub, and Walker, 1991b, 1991a); the major candidates for U.S. president in 1976 (Winter, 1976, 1982), 1988 (Winter, 1988), and 1992 (Winter, 1995); Saddam Hussein (Winter, 2003c); former Syrian president Hafez-al-Assad (Hermann, 1988); 10 sub-Saharan African leaders (Hermann, 1987); the five major 1996 candidates for President of Russia (Valenty & Shiraev, 2001); and former Iranian president Sayyed Khatami (Taysi & Preston, 2001).

For example, Winter (2003c) found that Saddam Hussein, compared to other world leaders, scored quite high in *n* Power (almost one standard deviation above the mean), somewhat above average in *n* Affiliation (one-half *SD* above the mean), and very low in *n* Achievement (more than 1 *SD* below the mean). The profile of high power and low achievement seems consistent with many of his actions as leader of Iraq: taking extreme (rather than moderate) risks, in the pursuit of prestige (rather than economic progress); confusing *feelings* of omnipotence with genuine social power; being vulnerable to ingratiation by sycophants (Fodor & Farrow, 1979); and ignoring moral considerations (Fodor & Smith, 1982). For Saddam, just like the power-motivated experimental leaders studied by Fodor (1990), success encouraged his aspirations, but (in contrast to achievement-motivated leaders) he failed to learn from failures. Taken together, these behaviors add up to the ancient Greek concept of *hubris*, or overreaching ambition.

What about Saddam Hussein's above-average score on *n* Affiliation? Surely he displayed little "concern for warm, friendly relationships." Actually, people high in *n* Affiliation *are* drawn into warm, friendly, and cooperative relationships, but *only* with people they perceive as similar to themselves, and *only* when they feel safe. Under threat, they are often quite "prickly" and defensive. In the turbulent and dangerous world of Iraqi politics, Saddam Hussein did act in many respects like an affiliation-motivated person under threat, surrounding himself with "his own" like-minded people (literally people from his own village and family).

Implicit Motives and War and Peace

Expressed Implicit Power

World Leaders

Several lines of evidence suggest a connection between implicit motives, violence, and war. As noted above, presidential n Power is significantly correlated with U.S. entry into war. Hermann (1980b) scored press conference transcripts of 45 world leaders and found that n Power predicted maintaining an independent (versus interdependent) foreign policy, whereas n Affiliation predicted the opposite. Hermann (1980a) found similar results in a study of mid-1970s members of the Politburo of the Communist Party of the Soviet Union. In a study of 19 heads of state, opposition leaders, and Black nationalist leaders of southern Africa during the mid-1970s, Winter (1980) found a very strong relationship between n Power and experts' ratings of "likely to support the initiation, continuation, or escalation of armed conflict" ($r = .71$, $p < .001$). At the time, it seemed surprising that White leaders in South Africa did not score particularly high compared both to Black leaders and also to a world sample of leaders. In retrospect, of course, this was consistent with the ultimately peaceful dismantling of the South African apartheid system and the advent of Black majority rule in the early 1990s (see also Winter, 2005b).

Comparing Crises

Using content analysis of diplomatic documents and media broadcasts, as well as speeches and press conferences, Winter explored the role of implicit motives in several studies of crises that escalated to war, compared to crises that were peacefully resolved. An initial study (Winter, 1993) showed that over a 385-year period, n Power levels in the annual British "Sovereign's Speech" to Parliament increased significantly in the years just before Great Britain entered a war, compared to other years. As shown in Figure 14.1, communications between the German and British governments showed increased power-minus-affiliation significantly during the crisis that began with the assassination of Archduke Franz Ferdinand at Sarajevo (June 28, 1914) and ended with the outbreak of World War I 6 weeks later. During the peacefully resolved Cuban Missile Crisis of 1962, on the other hand, Soviet and U.S. communications showed the opposite pattern: power-minus affiliation significantly decreased. Consistent with these results, archival and laboratory studies by Langner and Winter (2001) showed that low n Power and high n Affiliation were related to making concessions and thereby avoiding escalation and war.

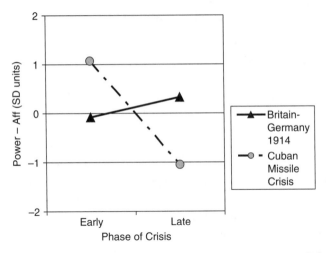

Figure 14.1. Motive imagery in British–German communications in July 1914 and US–Soviet communications during the Cuban Missile Crisis.

Winter (2004) added several further case studies. Comparison of the outbreak of the U.S.-Mexican war and the peaceful resolution of the Oregon boundary dispute (both during 1845–1846), using content analysis of relevant passages from President James K. Polk's diary and two major speeches to Congress, showed similar differences in motive patterns over time. Major documents from the South Carolina convention of 1860, which began the secession of Southern U.S. states to form the Confederacy, were significantly higher in n Power than major documents from the "Nashville Convention" 10 years earlier, at which the Southern states discussed but did not vote for secession. And despite his reputation for toughness and threats, President Andrew Jackson's 1833 speech against South Carolina's attempted "nullification" of the Tariff Acts of 1828 and 1832 was actually significantly lower in n Power than President James Buchanan's January 1861 message (considered by historians to be passive and weak) in response to the secession crisis that led to the outbreak of the Civil War.

Finally, Winter (2007b) published a systematic comparison of eight crises that escalated to war and eight matched crises that did not (for example, World War I versus the 1909 Bosnia crisis, Soviet violent suppression of "national communism" in Hungary in 1956 versus peaceful acceptance of it in Poland that same year, and the 1964–1965 U.S. military escalation in Vietnam versus its 1954 avoidance of intervention in Indochina). As shown in Figure 14.2, documents (e.g., speeches, press conferences, diplomatic communications) from the "war" crises were significantly higher in n Power, nonsignificantly lower in n Affiliation, and marginally lower in n Achievement than were documents from the "peace" crises.

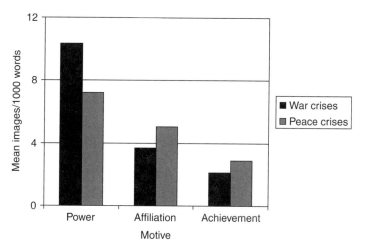

Figure 14.2. Motive scores of documents from crises that escalate to war and matched crises that are peacefully resolved.

Motives of Groups Resorting to Terrorism

The terrorist attacks that marked the first few years of the twenty-first century have reinvigorated political psychologists' studies of terrorism. Smith (2008) scored the writings of 13 groups that engaged in terrorism and 13 matched groups, of the same political orientation, that did not. The groups ranged from the Sicarii versus Pharisees in Roman Palestine (66–73 C.E.) to al-Qaeda versus the Movement for Islamic Reform in Arabia (1996–2002). As might be expected from the results above about war, the terrorist groups scored significantly higher in *n* Power than the nonterrorist control groups. Perhaps surprisingly, they also scored higher in *n* Affiliation. However, when the n Affiliation scores were divided into affiliation directed within the ingroup and affiliation directed toward an outgroup, the terrorist groups were significantly higher on the former, and the nonterrorist groups were higher on the latter. Based on these results, the motivational formula for terrorism could be described as high n Power and n Affiliation directed only toward the close circle of one's colleagues. Smith, Suedfeld, Conway, and Winter (2008) extended these findings in a comparative case study of two terrorist and two nonterrorist groups.

Blocked *n* Achievement and Internal Unrest

Southwood (1969) analyzed the relationship of national motive scores (from McClelland, 1961) to internal political instability (demonstrations, political assassinations, mass arrests, coups d'état, and civil war). Using educational opportunity (proportion of school-age children registered for secondary education) as a moderator, he found that *n* Achievement predicted political instability among countries low in opportunity but not among the high-opportunity countries. This finding is consistent with the "blocked control" interpretation of the results for *n* Achievement in individual leaders presented above.

Perceived n Power

The research cited above involves implicit motives as expressed in a variety of texts. However, the diplomacy of war and peace is a two-handed (or multi-handed) game. Anything that is *expressed* by one side also has to be *perceived* and then acted upon by the other side; the resulting gap between expression and perception is a site for the operation of many different kinds of distortion and misperception, including both "cold" mechanisms arising from limitations of cognitive capacity and also "hot" mechanisms resulting from perceivers' motives and emotions.

Winter (1987a) observed that during the months leading up to the U.S. Civil War in 1861, newspapers of the North and the South accentuated the level of threat (defined as "power density" or power images per 1,000 words) in their accounts of speeches of leaders from the other side, relative to those of their own side. Winter (2003a) found the same pattern of threat accentuation during the July 1914 crisis leading up to World War I, both in German and British newspapers and in the accounts of German–British diplomatic conversations by each side. In contrast, there was no threat accentuation in Soviet and U.S. newspapers during the 1962 Cuban Missile Crisis. Winter and Sweet (2009) studied how *The Times* (London) reported speeches of Adolf Hitler between the conclusion of the Munich agreement on September 30, 1938 and the German invasion of Poland in September 1, 1939. Comparing power densities of *Times* accounts with those of original texts, they found a significant increase in threat accentuation after the German occupation of Prague and the rest of Czechoslovakia on March 15, 1939—a surprise action that violated the Munich agreement and caused a complete turnaround of British policy. A similar change was observed in British diplomats' reports of meetings with Hitler and other top Nazi leaders. Whether accentuation of power density (hence of threat) is actually a distortion or "misperception" can be debated. In the case of Hitler's speeches and negotiation with the Nazis, it would likely be seen nowadays as a prescient and prudent amplification of threat signals (consistent with Winston Churchill's argument at the time). At the time, however, all sides in most conflicts probably believe they are seeing (and doing) the right thing.

In order to study factors that increase or decrease threat accentuation via perceived *n* Power, Peterson, Winter, and Doty (1994) designed a laboratory simulation of summarizing communications during crises. Winter (2007a) summarized research using this procedure, finding that *n* Power arousal and role involvement in the crisis increased threat accentuation, whereas psychological and temporal distance decreased it.

Problems and Issues in the Study of Motives in Politics and History

The availability of Winter's "running text" scoring manual makes it possible to carry out implicit motive research with historical and archival materials. At the same time, such research involves conceptual problems that should be recognized and addressed, in future work.

What Is Being Measured?

Although any written or spoken text *can* be scored for implicit motive imagery, the conceptual status of the resulting "motive scores" is not clear. Consider the first inaugural address of a U.S. president. Should the motive scores be attributed to the president's own personality? Since the actual speech was almost certainly written by one or more speechwriters, perhaps the motive scores should be attributed to them. Yet these speechwriters worked with material suggested by an indefinitely large circle of presidential advisors. Perhaps, then, the scores really represent the collective motives of the loosely defined "administration," for which the president's name is only eponymous label.[3] Thus Winter's (1998a) finding that U.S. President Bill Clinton's *n* Power increased after 1994 may reflect the personnel changes in the Clinton administration (replacing his press secretary, polling consultant, and media advisor, as well as bringing in a new political advisor), rather than any change in Bill Clinton's personality. Finally, McClelland (1976, pp. E–F) even suggested that implicit motive imagery scores derived from public sources and archival documents may represent collective *ideological climate variables* rather than motives in the sense of aspects of individuals' personality.

Reflecting on the speechwriter issue, Winter (1995) noted that speechwriters are selected by the leader for their ability to represent ideas in nuanced words and phrases—the stuff of motive imagery—that the leader feels comfortable and "natural" speaking. For important speeches, the leader generally reviews final drafts, often suggesting changes of phrasing and imagery. (For example, John F. Kennedy made several changes, involving motive imagery, on Theodore Sorensen's late draft of his 1961 inaugural address.) In the end, for many researchers the conceptual issue comes down to an empirical question: do the scores derived from collective and public sources predict the actions and outcomes one would expect on the basis of the established construct validity of the various implicit motives? From the empiricist perspective, if they do, then their conceptual status may not matter; if they don't, who cares?

Individual Motive Scores and Interactive History

Traditionally, motive scores are based on the PSE stories or other verbal behavior of individuals and are then related to other behavior of those individuals. But history and politics is bilateral or multilateral—that is, an interactive game. Each move by one player changes the environment of all other players, thereby affecting their subsequent moves. Over time, this unfolding process continually feeds back upon itself. Thus, on every day of the July 1914 crisis, the political leaders of each country had to take account of the previous day's actions by the six major powers (Germany, Austria-Hungary, Russia, France, Italy, and Great Britain) and several minor powers (Serbia, Belgium, Rumania, Turkey).

Two studies of implicit motives in international relations have attempted to deal with this inherent interactive complexity. Peterson, Doty, and Winter (1994) sketched a model of conflict escalation that integrated the expressed motives and perceived motives of each side, and Langner and Winter (2001) showed how the motives and explicit concessions of one side affect the motives and concessions of the other. Using time-series analysis, Ethington (2000) traced the web of relationships between U.S. and Iraqi motive imagery (scored from daily statements) and aggressive actions (coded by the Global Event-Data System; see Davies & McDaniel, 1993) during the autumn 1990 Gulf Crisis that led to the outbreak of the First Gulf War in January, 1991. Further progress along these lines will probably depend on adapting methodsand models from chaos theory and complexity theory (see Vallacher & Nowak, 1997).

Emerging Themes

The curious role of *n* Achievement discussed above—it predicts success in entrepreneurial roles but lack of success or even failure in politics—suggests that in motivational terms, there may be several different "kinds" or arenas of leadership; further, that mismatches between leaders' motive profiles and the affordances and pressures of the leadership arena may lead to unfortunate consequences. Winter has alluded to this possibility (2002) and is developing a comprehensive analysis of *n* Achievement in politics (Winter, 2008). As suggested above, achievement motivation can lead to success in business, but mostly under conditions of personal control of outcomes. Since politicians usually do not have such comprehensive control, achievement motivation may lead them to illegal behavior, micromanagement, or frustration and rigidity.

N Power also presents interesting challenges to academic analysis and political practice. Power clearly has "two faces" (McClelland, 1970): one that inspires and empowers followers; the other leading to dehumanization, exploitation, and oppression (Kipnis, Castell, Gergen, & Mauch, 1976). Sometimes these two faces are fused together; thus, for a time Adolf Hitler was an inspiring charismatic leader to many Germans, while presiding over the deliberate extermination of millions of innocent people. Perhaps the survival of the human race will depend on finding ways—whether intrapsychic or social-structural—to tame power. Winter (2006, 2009a) has reviewed some problems of taming power and suggested new approaches.

Understanding the Motivational Roots of Globalization and Climate Change

While it is risky to predict future social trends, the related themes of *globalization* and *climate change* have certainly been prominent in the scientific, political, economic, and social discourses of the twenty-first century. Research on implicit motives can play an important role in the psychological understanding of these trends. For example, will the same *n* Achievement that helped drive the dramatic industrial development of the nineteenth and twentieth centuries, thus creating both the opportunities and problems, continue to push globalized market capitalism toward further depletion of resources and global warming? Or can the *n* Achievement incentive of "excellence" be redefined or reconceived in terms of innovations and improvements that will enhance the sustainability of human life on earth? Will *n* Affiliation continue to be associated with high birth rates and population growth, as McClelland (1961, pp. 160–167) found during the mid-twentieth century? Or, in the interest of avoiding an over-populated earth, can it be directed toward quality rather than quantity of relationships? Will the intranational and international inequalities of globalization increase *n* Power levels and thereby set off renewed wars of resource control? Perhaps this was Shakespeare's dark vision, in *Titus Andronicus*, of a "wilderness of tigers" (III, 1, 53) or the lament that he put into the mouth of Ulysses, in *Troilus and Cressida*:

> Then everything includes itself in power,
> Power into will, will into appetite;
> And appetite, an universal wolf . . .
> Must make perforce an universal prey,
> And last eat up himself. (I, 3, 109–111, 119–124)

Or can *n* Power somehow be "tamed," so that we can enjoy the blessings of this motive while somehow guarding its shadow (Winter, 2006, 2009a)?

This chapter has reviewed many of the political and historical consequences of implicit motives. Recognizing their importance, it is nevertheless appropriate to conclude with a warning about the dangers of "overpsychologizing"—that is, exaggerating the importance of individual psychological factors in human society and history. It may be true, as Joll (1968) argued, that "it is only by studying the minds of men that we shall understand anything" (p. 24). Still, once individual intentions become embodied in institutions and structures, they take on a life of their own, no longer based or dependent on the minds of their makers. This reality calls for a certain amount of humility on the part of psychologist academics—as well as political leaders.

Notes

1. This phrase is adapted from Glad (1973, p. 313).
2. Spangler and House (1991) combined the presidential dependent variables in different ways and regressed these combination variables on all three motive scores, activity inhibition, n Power $\times$ activity inhibition interaction, and the leadership motive pattern. Such an analysis preserves the positive relationship between n Power and presidential effectiveness, and increases the negative relationship of n Achievement to effectiveness.
3. Along these lines, in his study of Finnish cloth mills Kock (1965) aggregated PSE scores of individual managers of each mill into a single set of scores that he attributed to the collective "management" of the mill.

References

Aliotta, J. M. (1988). Social backgrounds, social motives, and participation on the U. S. Supreme Court. *Political Behavior, 10,* 267–284.

Andrews, J. D. W. (1967). The achievement motive and advancement in two types of organizations. *Journal of Personality and Social Psychology, 6,* 163–168.

Barber, J. D. (1992). *The presidential character: Predicting performance in the White House, 4th ed.* Englewood Cliffs, NJ: Prentice-Hall.

Berlew, D. E. (1956). *The achievement motive and the growth of Greek civilization.* Unpublished honors thesis, Wesleyan University, Middletown, CT.

Bradburn, N. M., & Berlew, D. E. (1961). Need for achievement and English economic growth. *Economic Development and Cultural Change, 10,* 8–20.

Burris, R. W. (1958). *The effect of counseling on achievement motivation.* Unpublished doctoral dissertation, University of Indiana, Bloomington, IN.

Chamala, S., & Crouch, B. (1977). *Patterns of adaptation and factors associated with economic success in the wool industry, northwest Queensland, 1967/68–1971/72.* Brisbane, Australia: University of Queensland Department of Agriculture.

Chusmir, L. H., & Azevedo, A. (1992). Motivation needs of sampled Fortune-500 CEOs: Relations to organization outcomes. *Perceptual and Motor Skills, 75,* 595–612.

Cocks, G., & Crosby, T. (Eds.). (1987). *Psycho/history: Readings in the method of psychology, psychoanalysis, and history.* New Haven, CT: Yale University Press.

Collins, C. J., Hanges, P. J., & Locke, E. A. (2004). The relationship of achievement motivation to entrepreneurial behavior: A meta-analysis. *Human Performance, 17,* 95–117.

Cortes, J. B. (1961). The achievement motive in the Spanish economy between the 13th and 18th centuries. *Economic Development and Cultural Change, 9,* 144–163.

Crockett, H. J., Jr. (1962). The achievement motive and differential occupational mobility in the United States. *American Sociological Review, 27,* 191–204.

Cummin, P. C. (1967). TAT correlates of executive performance. *Journal of Applied Psychology, 51,* 78–81.

Davies, J. L., & McDaniel, C. K. (1993). The Global Event-Data System. In R. L. Merritt, R. G. Muncaster, & D. A. Zinnes (Eds.), *International event data developments* (pp. 19–44). Ann Arbor, MI: University of Michigan Press.

Diaz, A. J. (1982). *An empirical study of the effect of CEO motives on intra-industry performance with examples drawn from US and Japanese auto manufacturers.* Unpublished honors thesis, Harvard University, Cambridge, MA.

Donley, R. E. (1968). *Psychological motives and the American Presidency.* Unpublished honors thesis, Wesleyan University, Middletown, CT.

Donley, R. E., & Winter, D. G. (1970). Measuring the motives of public officials at a distance: An exploratory study of American presidents. *Behavioral Science, 10,* 227–236.

Durand, D., & Shea, D. (1974). Entrepreneurial activity as a function of achievement motivation and reinforcement control. *Journal of Psychology, 88,* 57–63.

Eisenstadt, S. N. (1963). *The achieving society* [review]. *Economic development and cultural change, 11,* 420–431.

Ethington, L. (2000, July). *Motive imagery and conflict escalation: A time-series study of the Gulf Conflict and the Gulf War.* Paper presented at the annual meeting of the International Society of Political Psychology, Seattle, WA.

Ethington, L. (2001, July). *Campaign 2000: A Time-Series Study of Motive Profiles in the U.S. Presidential Elections.* Paper presented at the annual meeting of the International Society of Political Psychology, Cuernavaca, Mexico.

Ferguson, M. R., & Barth, J. (2002). Governors in the legislative arena: The importance of personality in shaping success. *Political Psychology, 23,* 787–808.

Fodor, E. (1990). The power motive and creativity of solutions to an engineering problem. *Journal of Research in Personality, 24,* 338–354.

Fodor, E. M., & Farrow, D. L. (1979). The power motive as an influence on the use of power. *Journal of Personality and Social Psychology, 37,* 2091–2097.

Fodor, E. M., & Smith, T. (1982). The power motive as an influence on group decision making. *Journal of Personality and Social Psychology, 42,* 178–185.

George, A. L., & George, J. (1956). *Woodrow Wilson and Colonel House.* New York: John Day.

Glad, B. (1973). Contributions of psychobiography. In J. Knutson (Ed.), *Handbook of political psychology* (pp. 296–321). San Francisco: Jossey-Bass.

Greenstein, F. I. (1987). *Personality and politics.* Princeton, NJ: Princeton University Press. (Original work published 1969).

Greenstein, F. I. (2000). *The presidential difference: Leadership style from FDR to Clinton*. New York: Free Press.

Hermann, M. G. (1980a). Assessing the personalities of Soviet Politburo members. *Personality and Social Psychology Bulletin, 6,* 332–352.

Hermann, M. G. (1980b). Explaining foreign policy behavior using the personal characteristics of world leaders. *International Studies Quarterly, 24,* 7–46.

Hermann, M. G. (1983). Assessing personality at a distance: A profile of Ronald Reagan. *Mershon Center Quarterly Report, 7*(6), 1–8.

Hermann, M. G. (1987). Assessing the foreign policy role orientations of sub-Saharan African leaders. In S. G. Walker (Ed.), *Role theory and foreign policy analysis* (pp. 161–198). Durham, NC: Duke University Press.

Hermann, M. G. (1988). Syria's Hafez al-Assad. In B. Kellerman & J. Z. Rubin (Eds.), *Leadership and negotiation in the Middle East.* (pp. 70–95). New York: Praeger.

House, R. J., Spangler, W. D., & Woycke, J. (1991). Personality and charisma in the U.S. presidency: A psychological theory of leader effectiveness. *Administrative Science Quarterly, 36,* 364–396.

Hundal, P. S. (1971). A study of entrepreneurial motivation: Comparison of fast- and slow-progressing small-scale industrial entrepreneurs in Punjab, India. *Journal of Applied Psychology, 55,* 317–323.

Hyman, M. A. (2006). *Achievement, affiliation, and power in the United States Congress.* Unpublished honors thesis, Organizational Studies Program, University of Michigan, Ann Arbor, MI.

Joll, J. (1968). *1914: The unspoken assumptions*. London: Weidenfeld & Nicolson.

Kipnis, D., Castell, J., Gergen, M., & Mauch, D. (1976). Metamorphic effects of power. *Journal of Applied Psychology, 61,* 127–135.

Kock, S. E. (1965). *Företagsledning och motivation [Management and motivation].* Helsinki, Finland: Affärsekonomisk Förlagsförening.

Langner, C., & Winter, D. G. (2001). The motivational basis of compromise and concessions: Archival and experimental studies. *Journal of Personality and Social Psychology, 81,* 711–727.

Maranell, G. (1970). The evaluation of presidents: An extension of the Schlesinger poll. *Journal of American History, 57,* 104–113.

McClelland, D. C. (1955). Some social consequences of achievement motivation. In M. R. Jones (Ed.), *Nebraska symposium on motivation 1955* (pp. 41–65). Lincoln, NB: University of Nebraska Press.

McClelland, D. C. (1958). The use of measures of human motivation in the study of society. In J. W. Atkinson (Ed.), *Motives in fantasy, action, and society* (pp. 518–552). Princeton, NJ: Van Nostrand.

McClelland, D. C. (1961). *The achieving society.* Princeton, NJ: Van Nostrand.

McClelland, D. C. (1965). Toward a theory of motive acquisition. *American Psychologist, 20,* 321–333.

McClelland, D. C. (1970). The two faces of power. *Journal of International Affairs, 24,* 29–47.

McClelland, D. C. (1975). *Power: The inner experience.* New York: Irvington.

McClelland, D. C. (1976). *The achieving society—With a new introduction.* New York: Irvington.

McClelland, D. C. (1985). *Human motivation*. Glenview, IL: Scott, Foresman.

McClelland, D. C., & Boyatzis, R. E. (1982). The leadership motive pattern and long-term success in management. *Journal of Applied Psychology, 67,* 737–743.

McClelland, D. C., & Burnham, D. H. (1976, March–April). Power is the great motivator. *Harvard Business Review,* pp. 100–110, 159–166.

McClelland, D. C., Davis, W. N., Kalin, R., & Wanner, E. (1972). *The drinking man.* New York: Free Press.

McClelland, D. C., & Winter, D. G. (1969). *Motivating economic achievement.* New York: Free Press.

Morris, J. L., & Fargher, K. (1974). Achievement drive and creativity as correlates of success in small business. *Australian Journal of Psychology, 26,* 217–222.

Nandy, A. (1973). Motives, modernity and entrepreneurial competence. *Journal of Social Psychology, 91,* 127–136.

Nixon, R. M. (1978). *RN: The memoirs of Richard Nixon.* New York: Grosset & Dunlap.

Peterson, B. E., Doty, R. M., & Winter, D. G. (1994). Laboratory tests of a motivational-perceptual model of conflict escalation. *Journal of Conflict Resolution, 38,* 719–748.

Post, J. M. (Ed.). (2003). *The psychological assessment of political leaders: With profiles of Saddam Hussein and Bill Clinton.* Ann Arbor, MI: University of Michigan Press.

Rogers, E. M., & Svenning, L. (1969). *Modernization among peasants: The impact of communication.* New York: Holt, Rinehart & Winston.

Schatz, S. P. (1965). Achievement and economic growth: A critique. *The Quarterly Journal of Economics, 79,* 234–245.

Schmitt, D. P., & Winter, D. G. (1998). Measuring the motives of Soviet leadership and Soviet society: Congruence reflected or congruence created? *Leadership Quarterly, 9,* 293–307.

Shearer. L. (1982, January 17). Intelligence report: Pierpoint's presidential report card. *Parade: The Sunday Newspaper Magazine,* p. 8.

Simonton, D. (1988). Presidential style: Personality, biography, and performance. *Journal of Personality and Social Psychology, 55,* 928–936.

Singh, N. P. (1969). N Achievement among successful-unsuccessful and traditional-progressive agricultural entrepreneurs of Delhi. *Journal of Social Psychology, 79,* 271–272.

Singh, S. (1979). Relation among projective and direct verbal measures of achievement motivation. *Journal of Personality Assessment, 43,* 45–49.

Singh, S., & Gupta, B. S. (1977). Motives and agricultural growth. *British Journal of Social and Clinical Psychology, 16,* 189–190.

Slatcher, R. B., Chung, C. K., & Pennebaker, J. W. (2007). Winning words: Individual differences in linguistic style among U.S. presidential and vice presidential candidates. *Journal of Research in Personality, 41,* 63–75.

Smith, A. G. (2008). The implicit motives of terrorist groups: How the needs for affiliation and power translate into death and destruction. *Political Psychology, 29,* 55–75.

Smith, A. G., Suedfeld, P., Conway, L. G., & Winter, D. G. (2008). The language of violence: distinguishing terrorist from nonterrorist groups by thematic content analysis. *Dynamics of Asymmetric Conflict, 1,* 142–163.

Southwood, K. E. (1969). *Some sources of political disorder: A cross-national analysis.* Unpublished doctoral dissertation, University of Michigan, Ann Arbor, MI.

Spangler, W. D., & House, R. J. (1991). Presidential effectiveness and the Leadership Motive Profile. *Journal of Personality and Social Psychology, 60,* 439–455.

Suedfeld, P., Bluck, S., Ballard, E. J., & Baker-Brown, G. (1990). Canadian federal elections: Motive profiles and integrative complexity in political speeches and popular media. *Canadian Journal of Behavioural Science, 22,* 26–36.

Taysi, T., & Preston, T. (2001). The personality and leadership style of President Khatami: Implications for the future of Iranian political reform. In O. Feldman & L. O. Valenty (Eds.), *Profiling political leaders: Cross-cultural studies of personality and behavior* (pp. 57–77). Westport, CT: Praeger.

Tourtellot, A. B. (1964). *The presidents on the presidency.* Garden City, NY: Doubleday.

Valenty, L. O., & Shiraev, E. (2001). The 1996 Russian presidential candidates: A content analysis of motivational configuration and conceptual/integrative complexity. In O. Feldman & L. O. Valenty (Eds.), *Profiling political leaders: Cross-cultural studies of personality and behavior* (pp. 37–56). Westport, CT: Praeger.

Vallacher, R. R., & Nowak, A. (1997). The emergence of dynamical social psychology. *Psychological Inquiry, 8*(2), 73–99.

Varga, K. (1975). N Achievement, *n* Power and effectiveness of research and development. *Human Relations, 28,* 571–590.

Veroff, J., Atkinson, J. W., Feld, S. C., & Gurin, G. (1960). The use of thematic apperception to assess motivation in a nationwide interview study. *Psychological Monographs, 74*(12), Whole number 499.

Veroff, J., Depner, C., Kulka, R., & Douvan, E. (1980). Comparison of American motives: 1957 versus 1976. *Journal of Personality and Social Psychology, 39,* 1249–1262.

Wainer, H. A., & Rubin, I. M. (1969). Motivation of research and development entrepreneurs. *Journal of Applied Psychology, 53,* 178–184.

Weber, M. (1958). *The Protestant ethic and the spirit of capitalism.* New York: Scribner's. (Original work published 1920).

Weber, M. (1968). The types of legitimate domination. In *Economy and society* (pp. 212–264). New York: Bedminster Press. (Original work published 1922).

Winter, D. G. (1973). *The power motive.* New York: Free Press.

Winter, D. G. (1976, July). What makes the candidates run. *Psychology Today, 10,* 45–49, 92.

Winter, D. G. (1980). Measuring the motive patterns of southern Africa political leaders at a distance. *Political Psychology, 2*(2), 75–85.

Winter, D. G. (1982). Motivation and performance in presidential candidates. In A. J. Stewart (Ed.), *Motivation and society* (pp. 244–273). San Francisco: Jossey-Bass.

Winter, D. G. (1987a). Enhancement of enemy's power motivation as a dynamic of escalation in conflict situations. *Journal of Personality and Social Psychology, 52,* 41–46.

Winter, D. G. (1987b). Leader appeal, leader performance, and the motive profiles of leaders and followers: A study of American presidents and elections. *Journal of Personality and Social Psychology, 52,* 196–202.

Winter, D. G. (1988, July). What makes Jesse run? [Motives of the 1988 candidates]. *Psychology Today*, pp. 20ff.

Winter, D. G. (1991a). Measuring personality at a distance: Development of an integrated system for scoring motives in running text. In A. J. Stewart, J. M. Healy, Jr., & D. J. Ozer (Eds.), *Perspectives in personality, Vol. 3, Part B: Approaches to understanding lives* (pp. 59–89). London: Jessica Kingsley, Publishers.

Winter, D. G. (1991b). A motivational model of leadership: Predicting long-term management success from TAT measures of power motivation and responsibility. *Leadership Quarterly, 2,* 67–80.

Winter, D. G. (1993). Power, affiliation and war: Three tests of a motivational model. *Journal of Personality and Social Psychology, 65,* 532–545.

Winter, D. G. (1994). *Manual for scoring motive imagery in running text* (version 4.2). Department of Psychology, University of Michigan, Ann Arbor.

Winter, D. G. (1995). Presidential psychology and governing styles: A comparative psychological analysis of the 1992 presidential candidates. In S. A. Renshon (Ed.), *The Clinton presidency: Campaigning, governing and the psychology of leadership* (pp. 113–134). Boulder, CO: Westview.

Winter, D. G. (1998a). A motivational analysis of the Clinton first term and the 1996 presidential campaign. *Leadership Quarterly, 9,* 367–376.

Winter, D. G. (1998b). "Toward a science of personality psychology:" David McClelland's development of empirically derived TAT measures. *History of Psychology, 1,* 130–153.

Winter, D. G. (2001). Measuring Bush's motives. *ISPP News: International Society of Political Psychology, 12*(1), 9.

Winter, D. G. (2002). Motivation and political leadership. In L. Valenty & O. Feldman (Eds.), *Political Leadership for the New Century: Personality and Behavior among American Leaders* (pp. 25–47). Westport, CT: Praeger.

Winter, D. G. (2003a). Asymmetrical perceptions of power in crises: A comparison of 1914 and the Cuban Missile Crisis. *Journal of Peace Research, 40,* 251–270.

Winter, D. G. (2003b). Personality and political behavior. In D. O. Sears, L. Huddy, & R. Jervis (Eds.), *Handbook of Political Psychology* (pp. 110–145). New York: Oxford University Press.

Winter, D. G. (2003c). [Saddam Hussein:] Motivations and mediation of self-other relationships. In J. M. Post (Ed.), *The psychological assessment of political leaders: With profiles of Saddam Hussein and Bill Clinton* (pp. 370–374). Ann Arbor, MI: University of Michigan Press.

Winter, D. G. (2004). Motivation and the escalation of conflict: Case studies of individual leaders. *Peace and Conflict: Journal of Peace Psychology, 10,* 381–398.

Winter, D. G. (2005a). Continuity and change in George Bush's motive profile. *ISPP News: International Society of Political Psychology, 16*(1), 10–11.

Winter, D. G. (2005b). Things I've learned about personality from studying political leaders at a distance. *Journal of Personality, 73,* 557–584.

Winter, D. G. (2006). Taming power. In D. Rohde (Ed.), *Moral leadership: The theory and practice of power, judgment, and policy* (pp. 159–175). San Francisco: Jossey-Bass.

Winter, D. G. (2007a, July). *Psychological factors affecting threat accentuation in perceiving the intentions of leaders.* Paper presented at the annual meeting of the International Society of Political Psychology, Portland, OR.

Winter, D. G. (2007b). The role of motivation, responsibility, and integrative complexity in crisis escalation: Comparative studies of war and peace crises. *Journal of Personality and Social Psychology, 92*, 920–937.

Winter, D. G. (2008). *Why does achievement motivation lead to success in business but failure in politics?* Unpublished paper, University of Michigan, Ann Arbor, MI.

Winter, D. G. (2009a). How can power be tamed? In D. Tijosvold & B. Wisse (Eds.), *Power and interdependence in organizations.* (pp. 33–51). New York: Cambridge University Press.

Winter, D. G. (2009b, Spring). Predicting the Obama presidency. *ISPP News: International Society of Political Psychology, 20*(1), 6–8.

Winter, D. G., & Carlson, L. (1988). Using motive scores in the psychobiographical study of an individual: The case of Richard Nixon. *Journal of Personality, 56*, 75–103.

Winter, D. G., Hermann, M. G., Weintraub, W., & Walker, S. G. (1991a). The personalities of Bush and Gorbachev measured at a distance: Follow-up on predictions. *Political Psychology, 12*, 457–464.

Winter, D. G., Hermann, M. G., Weintraub, W., & Walker, S. G. (1991b). The personalities of Bush and Gorbachev measured at a distance: Procedures, portraits, and policy. *Political Psychology, 12*, 215–245.

Winter, D. G., & Stewart, A. J. (1977a). Content analysis as a technique for assessing political leaders. In M. G. Hermann (Ed.), *A psychological examination of political leaders* (pp. 28–61). New York: Free Press.

Winter, D. G., & Stewart, A. J. (1977b). Power motive reliability as a function of retest instructions. *Journal of Consulting and Clinical Psychology, 45*, 436–440.

Winter, D. G., & Sweet, B. E. (2009). Implicit British perceptions of German leaders in 1938–1939. *Political Psychology, 30*, 839–862.

Wormley, W. (1976). *Portfolio manager preference in an investment decision-making situation: A psychophysical study.* Unpublished doctoral dissertation, Harvard University, Cambridge, MA.

Chapter 15

Research on Implicit Motives Across Cultures

JAN HOFER
University of Osnabrück, Germany

Current personality psychology distinguishes three major elements of personality that affect and shape an individual's mental processes, social behavior, and life adaptations, namely, (a) relatively stable personality traits and temperament; (b) cognitions such as attitudes, beliefs, goals, and values; and (c) implicit motivation (Winter, 1996). Unfortunately, these different components of personality have led basically separate lives with little opportunity for stimulating exchange. Particularly, the conception of motivation as implicit has more and more frequently been ignored in favor of an almost entirely self-report-based approach in theorizing and empirical research on motivation. Yet, rejection of this implicit component of personality is premature because implicit motives predict important mental processes and are a decisive determinant of developmental pathways and long-term behavioral trends (e.g., Brunstein & Maier, 2005; Schultheiss et al., 2005; Woike, McLeod, & Goggin, 2003).

Happily, recent years have witnessed a renewed interest in nonconscious aspects of cognition, emotion, and behavior that help to explain the complex pattern of human functioning. It has become increasingly evident that experiences, thoughts, and actions can be influenced by mental contents (e.g., percepts, memories, thoughts, feelings, and desires) or some event in the current stimulus environment of which we are unaware (Bargh & Chartrand, 1999; Kihlstrom, 2002; Kuhl, 2001). Empirical research is rediscovering the fact that unconscious psychological forces can have profound effects on our behavior.

This renewed interest has been sparked off in part by McClelland, Koestner, and Weinberger (1989), whose model proposes that behavior is energized and directed by two distinct types of motive systems, namely implicit motives and explicit or self-attributed motives. The development of the latter motivational system requires advanced mastery of language, as it is shaped by explicit teaching of what is socially desirable and results in values and goals of which the actor is consciously aware. Given their conscious representation, explicit motives can be easily assessed via self-reports.

On the other hand, representing a disposition to have an affectively toned, goal-centered, associative network aroused and activated (Winter & Stewart, 1978), implicit motives develop based on experience and learning by processes of classical and instrumental conditioning. They are primarily shaped during early stages of cognitive development when language mastery has not yet been established. Consequently, implicit motives operate outside of conscious awareness and control. But they express themselves in individuals' fantasy and, thus, are measurable by indirect means. In particular, Picture Story Exercises (PSE; McClelland et al., 1989), which represent modifications of the classical TAT (Murray, 1943), have been established as a reliably scored and valid instrument for the measurement of implicit motives.

Implicit motives reflect humans' biological heritage as shaped by evolutionary forces—human motives direct and energize life-sustaining behavior (Winter, 1996). This is obvious not only for so-called primary or viscerogenic needs (e.g., hunger, thirst, and avoidance of pain; Murray, 1938), but also for secondary or psychogenic needs, that is, social motives, representing facets of the evolved human, enhancing personal survival and reproductive success (MacDonald, 1991). So, for instance, the need for affiliation and intimacy, as reflected by seeking contact and closeness to others, increases the likelihood for survival (by contributing toward enhanced mental and physical health) and successful reproduction by facilitating bonding with potential mates. Similarly, a desire for efficacy and competence (n Achievement) and having an impact on others (n Power) are considered to involve fitness-maximizing strategies (e.g., privileged access to mates and material resources by high-status males). Thus, evolution seems to have resulted in affective motive dispositions that are activated by specific types of stimulation or incentives. As such, motive dispositions might be conceptualized as open genetic programs (MacDonald, 1991).

Evolved motive dispositions show high plasticity by being sensitive toward the presence or absence of environmental events. Hence, differences in (evolved) personality dispositions may be considered to have both genetic and environmental sources of variance (Plomin & Daniles, 1987). In line with this argument, theorizing and empirical research related to individual differences in psychological and behavioral outcomes have provided evidence for the significance of the sociocultural context in which individuals think, feel, and act (e.g., Markus & Kitayama, 1991).

While research has indicated that certain behavioral and cognitive dispositions are common to human beings everywhere (e.g., Brown, 1991), the existence of pronounced variation in human personality and developmental pathways within a given cultural group but also across cultural samples is a widely acknowledged fact (e.g., Cheung, 2006; Keller, 2007). Consistent with this argument, differences in child-rearing practices (e.g., parenting style) and socialization patterns (e.g., social control) across cultures (e.g., Keller & Greenfield, 2000; McClelland, 1985) may result in distinct types of programming of development to meet specific environmental and sociocultural demands (MacDonald, 1991). Thus, it seems essential to include the sociocultural context in any model of human functioning in order to achieve a richer foundation from which mental processes and observed behavior may be described, interpreted, and predicted by interplay of internal (needs) and external forces, or presses, as Murray (1938) called them.

Acknowledging not only the postulated universality of human needs but also their potentially culture-bound programming, David McClelland was one of the pioneers who studied implicit motives and their antecedents and correlates in various cultures over historical periods, and his contribution to the literature on culture and personality is highly significant (see particularly McClelland, 1961, and McClelland, Atkinson, Clark, & Lowell, 1953), even if findings are not unchallenged (e.g., Mazur & Rosa, 1977).

In what follows, I wish to take the opportunity to illustrate the methodological and substantial progress that has been made in the field of cross-cultural studies on implicit motives. In the first part, after having discussed the concept of culture, I will present a theoretical framework for cross-cultural research that stresses the significance of a multicultural and multivariate approach in conducting research. Secondly, I will describe the concepts of equivalence and bias of measurements, and will illustrate methodological means to remedy systematic error in measurements. In the third part, I will give an overview of early cross-cultural research on implicit motives. In doing so, I will describe different approaches, that is, measuring implicit motives at the collective or at the individual level, highlighting recent findings in the field.

Conclusions will be drawn in the final part; I will argue that cross-cultural research is indispensable to understand universal and culture-specific variations in individuals' mental processes and behavioral acts. As such, studies should be designed to integrate conceptual models and advanced methodological and statistical tools, moving beyond the dichotomy of qualitative and quantitative approaches. Finally, I will outline future directions for cross-cultural research on motives.

Personality Develops and Is Set in a Sociocultural Context

Today, most psychologists would agree that personality develops by a complex interaction of genetic and environmental factors, with cultural influences being among the most important of the contextual influences (Benet-Martínez & Oishi, 2008). Developmental processes and outcomes are interpreted by an integration of biological opportunities and constraints with cultural norms, beliefs, and values (Keller & Greenfield, 2000). Moreover, culture affects an individual in a given situation by shaping the representation of immediate environmental pressures and demands (Hofer & Bond, 2008) and also the incentives for goal-oriented activities (Weinberger & McClelland, 1990). Nonetheless, recurrent calls to make culture vital to theory and research in psychology (e.g., Cole, 1996) seem to be largely unnoticed: Most research is still conducted in Euro-American cultures. Research involving individuals from diverse cultures requires scrutinizing well-known assumptions about psychological phenomena and their valid assessment. First of all, however, it requires elaborating on the concept of culture and its relationship with psychological phenomena.

The Concept of Culture

Culture is an intimidating concept: It is hard to grasp in definitional terms, and it comprises a vast array of facets that affect the shaping of personality components and interpersonal interactions (Bond, 2004, 2005). Accordingly, there has been a long argument on whether culture and personality are best viewed as interdependent or mutually constitutive, or as relatively distinct entities. The former view (the cultural approach) is often connected with a critique of the Western concept of personality with its focus on internal attributes such as preferences, desires, and traits (e.g., Kitayama & Park, 2007) and an advocacy of more qualitative and indigenous assessment methods; the latter view (the cross-cultural approach) seeks to identify culture-bound phenomena along with universals and advocates the use of standardized psychometric assessment methods, which requires the equivalence of measurements across cultures (Benet-Martínez & Oishi, 2008).

However, the two approaches should be seen as complementary because both have their merits and shortcomings (Van de Vijver, Hofer, & Chasiotis, 2009). As has already been done for empirical studies (e.g., Cheung, 2006; Keller, 2007), models of culture and personality should be utilized that integrate both perspectives by examining individual differences while advocating that personality and culture are mutually constitutive. In my view, such approaches are particularly appropriate to investigate human functioning at the interface between biology and culture. Particularly, if universal features of human functioning such as traits (e.g., McCrae & Costa, 1997), cognitions such as values (e.g., Schwartz, 1992) and beliefs (e.g., Leung & Bond, 2004), or innate motives (e.g., McClelland, 1985) are theoretically assumed, one needs to adopt frameworks allowing the investigation of both human universals and cultural-specific characteristics.

A Theoretical Frame for Research across Cultures

Bond (2005) has noted that the "honeymoon phase" in which culture was simply treated as a categorical variable is long finished. It is important that despite the many conceptualizations of culture that have been imported to the conceptual repertoire of psychological research from other scientific disciplines, psychologists must begin to analyze culture in psychologically relevant terms that reflect individuals' psychological experience and real life behavior.

Bond (2004) argues that ecological characteristics (e.g., type and depth of natural resources) predispose a group to develop a certain socioculturally constructed environment characterized by certain political, economic, legal, social, educational, and familial patterns, which in turn are likely to result in a certain *programming of the mind*, that is, the socialization for certain personality dispositions, norms, role expectations, values, and beliefs (see also Hofstede, 2000). Therefore, he psychologically defines culture as "a shared system of beliefs (what is true), values (what is important), expectations, especially about scripted behavioral sequences, and behavior meanings (what is implied by engaging in a given action) developed by a group over time" (Bond, 2004, p. 62). Certainly, idiosyncratic reasons, for example, biological, familial, and educational variations, are likely to produce variability within a given cultural group; that is, not all individuals will follow cultural pathways and acquire culture-specific personal propensities to the same extent (Kitayama & Park, 2007). Yet, sufficiently mutual socialization processes enhance communication of meaning and coordination of actions among a culture's members by reducing uncertainty and anxiety through making its members' behavior predictable, understandable, and valued (Bond, 2004; see also Tindale & Kameda, 2000).

Although Bond's (2004) definition of culture includes significant aspects highly relevant for research on personality and behavior across cultures, it does not explicitly refer to implicit processes and particularly implicit motivational systems, which, however, are decisive parts of our theoretical and empirical armamentarium for explaining and predicting psychological and behavioral differences across cultural groups: Many of the scripts, motivations, and expectations that guide our behavior are largely not amenable to rational analyses (Cohen, 1997; Nisbett & Wilson, 1977) either because they have become largely automatized or because they were only implicitly taught (Kitayama & Park, 2007). Thus, there is reason to believe that cultural patterns exercise their impact on human functioning in part by operating implicitly, that is, outside of awareness.

Following this line of argument, culture is more than a set of consciously represented social rules or norms for social behavior (e.g., Schwartz, 1992). It is very likely that culture is also reflected in implicit motivational propensities to strive for certain goals (e.g., closeness to other people). In other words, early socialization patterns created by parents foster the development of culture-conforming and adaptive implicit motives. Cultural fit (or deviance) may, for instance, be represented by particular motive strengths (e.g., high *n* Affiliation-Intimacy), patterns of incentives (e.g., anticipation of cooperative group activities), and behavioral correlates (e.g., engagement in activities with close others).

Thus, a multivariate and multicultural approach (see Bornstein, 2002), that is, cross-cultural research taking into account conscious and implicit variables simultaneously, may best be suited to examine the interplay of different, relatively stable facets of personality with social situations, defined in terms of their normative constitution, in research on the individual's inner experience and manifest behavior. Such a theoretical frame allows for examining not only universal relationships, but also culture-mediated linkages between psychological constructs and (psychological and behavioral) outcomes. Being the first motivational system to be shaped in human ontogeny (McClelland et al., 1989), implicit motives have far-reaching consequences for individuals' development, feelings, and behavior in everyday life and should therefore be a decisive factor in our endeavors to shed further light on human behavior and psychological features. Appropriately designed research can shed light on this claim.

Key Issues in the Methodology of Measuring Implicit Motives Across Cultural Groups

To consider motives and to study their impact on human functioning, we must measure them. However, when we apply test methods across ethnic and cultural groups, particularly when we intend to compare test scores for different groups, issues of equivalence (level at which scores can be compared across groups) and bias (all factors challenging the validity of group comparisons) become particularly relevant (Van de Vijver et al., 2009). Bias and equivalence are essential concepts in research across cultures, as without a careful examination of possible bias, it cannot be presumed that observed score differences (or similarities) across cultural groups reflect genuine findings. As Van de Vijver and Tanzer (2004) stated, "score differences observed in cross-cultural comparisons may have a partly or entirely different meaning than those in intracultural comparisons" (p. 131). Despite its importance, a review of (cross-) cultural studies regrettably shows that equivalence of measurements is insufficiently examined with Euro-American instruments, although culture-specific, often being applied as if they were universally valid (Van de Vijver &

Leung, 1997). Almost 50 years ago, Lindzey (1961) noted that it remains a task for future research to show that (projective) thematic apperception methods, even if valid techniques within our own society, possess cross-cultural validity. I hope the following section will show that this aim can be achieved despite all the challenges involved.

Bias and Equivalence

The pivotal concept in evaluating the adequacy of cross-cultural assessment procedures is bias, which generally refers to the occurrence of systematic error in a measure, that is, validity-threatening factors. Equivalence represents a second key concept that results in bias for comparing test scores; the level of equivalence is determined by the presence or absence of certain types of bias. Thus, bias and equivalence are two closely related concepts that are, in principle, the opposite of each other: Test scores are equivalent when they are unbiased (Van de Vijver & Leung, 1997). It should be noted that concepts of equivalence and bias do not refer to inherent characteristics of an instrument but rather to qualities of a particular comparison of test scores between (cultural) groups. For example, an instrument may show bias when comparing German and Cameroonian individuals but may be appropriate for comparing German and Chinese individuals (see Van de Vijver & Tanzer, 2004).

Dependent on its source of origin, three major types of bias can be distinguished that cause an incomparability of measures assessed in culturally different samples: construct bias, method bias, and item bias (Van de Vijver & Leung, 1997). In the following subsections, I will refer to these different sources of bias and the level of equivalence they challenge. In doing so, each type of bias will be described with particular attention being paid to issues relevant for the cross-cultural study of implicit motives. Furthermore, strategies to address and remedy types of bias will be given in each of the following sections.

I will illustrate these strategies by reference to an exemplary study on developing a bias-free picture set for measuring n Power and n Affiliation-Intimacy in three cultural groups from sub-Saharan Africa (Cameroon), Latin America (Costa Rica), and Europe (Germany) (Hofer, Chasiotis, Friedlmeier, Busch, & Campos, 2005). These cultural groups were selected because of well-documented differences in cultural dimensions (Hofstede, 2000), value orientations (Schwartz, 1992), and self-construal (Kağıtçıbaşı, 2005; Markus & Kitayama, 1991). As this study represents an integrated examination of construct, method, and item bias, it will be referred to for each type of bias.

Table 15.1 briefly summarizes the major issues related to bias (definition, consequences, examples, measures of caution) as elaborated upon in the following section.

Table 15.1 Major Sources of Bias: Construct, Method, and Item Bias.

Type of Bias	Origin	Consequence	Example	Remedies
Construct bias	Source of bias related to culture-bound meaning and/or behavioral indicators of psychological construct	Incomparability of measurements due to construct inequivalence	Indigenous facets of the need for achievement (e.g., possible social-oriented nature of n Achievement in non-Western cultures)	Development of indigenous measures (pessimistic approach), conduction of pretests, collaboration with local experts
Method bias:[a] sample bias, instrument bias, administration bias	Sources of bias related to methodological-procedural aspects of a cross-cultural research	No comparisons of means between groups due to an increase or decrease in test scores of at least one cultural group	Sample differences in knowledge of test language (sample bias), familiarity with test methods (instrument bias), or received test instructions (administration bias)	Careful planning and implementation of research (e.g., balancing of samples, use of standardized test administration and scoring procedures)
Item bias[a]	Source of bias related to characteristics of single test items	No comparisons of means between cultural groups due to differential item functioning	Picture cue elicits motive imagery to a different degree among participants characterized by similar motive strengths depending on their culture of origin	Identification of biased items by local experts (judgmental approach) and psychometric methods (statistical approach)

[a] Given construct equivalence, relationships between constructs may be examined within each of the cultural samples at hand when sources of method and item bias are presented.

Construct Bias

Definition

Construct bias is present when the phenomenon (construct) to be measured is conceptually not identical across cultural groups. Construct bias is caused by insufficient overlap of definitions of the construct across cultural groups, differential appropriateness of test content, or poor and incomplete sampling of relevant behavior and domains associated with the construct (Van de Vijver & Leung, 1997). In other words, individuals from different cultural groups do not ascribe the same meaning to the construct. Consequently, construct (structural and functional) equivalence is lacking.

A good example of possible construct bias from the domain of motivation is the debate about the nature of the need for achievement. *n* Achievement is defined as a disposition to strive for success in competition with a standard of excellence. Individuals characterized by a strong need for achievement typically seek challenging tasks, compete to do things better, and derive satisfaction from personal mastery (McClelland, 1987).

It has, however, been argued that this definition due to its focus on personal individual achievements neglects contextual and cultural determinants of achievement motivation that may lead to diverse cultural meaning and modes of achievement (Kornadt, Eckensberger, & Emminghaus, 1980; Maehr & Nicholls, 1980). For example, when socialization processes emphasize the group over the individual, achievement motivation is characterized by a pronounced, social-oriented element (De Vos, 1973; Yu, 1996): Rather than pushing oneself ahead of others and actively striving toward self-enhancement, which entails the personal risk of social isolation, the concept of a social-oriented achievement motive reflects an individual's need to conform to the values of an in-group by striving to meet the expectations of significant persons and groups, that is, family and peers. Thus, cultural specificities in child-rearing practices, socialization patterns, religious belief and value systems, and social rules to sanction individuals' behavior (Keller & Greenfield, 2000) result in distinct experiences of rewards and punishments. These differences in cultural practices may eventually lead to the development of differences in terms of concerns for achievement, achievement incentives, domains of action, and standards of evaluation. In other words, a monocultural approach may not be regarded a priori as qualified for a universal explanation of human motivation (Van de Vijver, 2000).

Dealing with construct bias

A careful study design helps to prevent the occurrence of construct bias. Of course, one could circumvent construct bias in cross-cultural research by developing culture-specific, indigenous measurements, which for the measurement of implicit motives has already been done, for example, by developing scoring categories that reflect culturally important variables and include contextual grounding of interpretations that allow for acknowledging culture-bound meanings of possibly universal needs (Dana, 1999; see also De Vos, 1973).

Additionally, culture-specific adaptations of the original TAT cards (e.g., Chowdhury, 1960; Leblanc, 1958; Wang, 1969) and of stimulus sets for PSEs are available (e.g., Kornadt & Voigt, 1970; Ostheimer, 1969; Singh, 1978). They are based on the reasoning that, provided with culturally adequate stimulus materials, respondents will be able to identify more easily with same-culture characters and settings and thus provide richer projective material. Although empirical evidence does not suggest a requirement for culturally adapted picture cards (e.g., Lefkowitz & Fraser, 1980; Murstein, 1965), such an approach may be particularly preferred by researchers who hold a skeptical view about the universal nature of personality constructs (Church, 2001). However, culture-specific measures cannot be used for comparisons across cultures and thus obstruct research on universal features of a phenomenon. Thus, if researchers aim to examine universal aspects by applying measurement methods that are cross-culturally applicable and if they are eager to achieve conceptual equivalence, different strategies are recommended.

For instance, cultural decentering, that is, simultaneous development of the same instrument in different cultures, is proposed to deal with construct bias. Similarly, an independent within-culture development of instruments and subsequent administration of all instruments across the constituent cultures, that is, the convergence approach, may also help to prevent problems of construct bias (Van de Vijver & Tanzer, 2004). Several statistical techniques, which are, however, not easily applicable for thematic apperception methods, are available to identify construct bias. Those techniques usually apply a comparison of data structures across cultural groups by the use of confirmatory factor analysis, structural equation models, and cluster analysis (see Van de Vijver & Leung, 1997). Cross-cultural comparisons of behavioral correlates represent another, rarely applied strategy for examining the equivalence of a construct. Regarding assessment of implicit motives across cultures, one could also scrutinize equivalence of conditions of motive arousal that played an important role in the development of content coding systems (e.g., McClelland et al., 1953; Winter, 1973; for arousal studies in different cultural contexts, see also Hofer, Busch, Bender, Li, & Hagemeyer, in press; Ng, 2006; Tedeschi & Kian, 1962).

Construct Bias Addressed by the Hofer et al. Study

Prior to conducting their main data collection, Hofer and colleagues (2005) examined issues concerning the cross-cultural equivalence of *n* Power and *n* Affiliation-Intimacy in pilot studies that explored the cross-cultural meaningfulness of established content-coding procedures in interviews with cultural experts and informants to gain essential information on the constructs under investigation (e.g., culture-specific characteristics, behavioral correlates). As Costa Rican collaborators were familiar with thematic apperception measures and the discussion with cultural experts showed high congruence with respect to the coding categories, questions related to construct bias were scrutinized in the Cameroonian subsample. By conducting a survey with local informants, coding categories that were critically reviewed, for example, giving unsolicited help and/or support as indicator of *n* Power, were further examined. Qualitative analyses of responses indicated the validity of established motive indicators also within the Cameroonian sample.

Method Bias

Definition

Even if a construct is well defined and all relevant aspects are represented by a test method, bias-free test scores are far from guaranteed. Presence of method bias may threaten measurement unit equivalence, the second level of equivalence. Method bias is a term that subsumes all sources of systematic error that occurs due to flaws in the procedural part of a study (e.g., sampling, instrument characteristics). For example, an assistant in culture A incidentally used the word "test" (an achievement-related cue) in the instruction for the Picture Story Exercise (PSE), while an assistant in culture B administered the test under neutral conditions. Thus, even if assessed scores have the same unit of measurement (e.g., number of achievement imageries corrected for number of words across cultural groups), a source of method bias, namely, arousal of achievement motivation in culture A caused by the wording of the instructions, caused differences in origin of measurement unit, that is, a shift in the mean scores in one of the cultures.

Depending on its source, it is useful to differentiate three types of method bias: sample bias, instrument bias, and administration bias.

Sample Bias

This type of method bias is most often caused by the dissimilarity of individuals from different ethnic and cultural groups on test-relevant background variables. For instance, differences in education and knowledge of the test language may negatively affect the equivalence of measurements across different groups. Hofer and Chasiotis (2004) addressed test language as a possible "nuisance" factor in a sample of Zambian male adolescents. The authors report that Zambian adolescents characterized by same educational background but differing in language use, that is, responding to picture cards either in English (the official language of Zambia) or Chitonga (the native language of the Gwembe Tonga), significantly differed in levels of n Achievement and n Affiliation-Intimacy after adjusting for protocol length. Thus, it seems doubtful whether the findings reflect genuine differences (or similarities) in motive strengths between Chitonga and English users because neither Zambian subgroup differed in age, gender distribution, or their familiarity with the stimulus material, and because they were surveyed under similar test conditions. Already Ervin (1964) has found that the language in which the response to thematic apperception measurement is given may affect the way personality is expressed in bilinguals; an individual's personality may appear different from language to language, since linguistic characteristics (e.g., linguistic register) may influence the coding of the written material.

Instrument Bias

The second type of method bias, namely instrument bias, includes characteristics of the instrument that generate distorted score differences between the groups under investigation, for example, differential response styles in self-report measures, such as social desirability and acquiescence. For thematic apperception measurements, the inappropriate scoring of responses is a further relevant source of instrument bias. Coding of implicit motives is usually straightforward by implementing well-established scoring conventions (e.g., Winter, 1994), but research on the validity of scoring rules for a given cultural and ethnic group is rather scarce.

Finally, instrument bias relates to differential familiarity with stimulus material, for example, pictorial material, and response procedures (e.g., talking about an ambiguous stimulus), that represents recurrent and general problems in cross-cultural research. Previous researchers describe tremendous problems when attempting to assess facets of personality by administering projective measures, either cultural adaptations of the classical Thematic Apperception Test (TAT) or the PSE in non-Western samples. For example, Fanon and Geronimi (1956; cited in Bullard, 2005) used the standard TAT in their study with Muslim women from North Africa. They concluded that the standard TAT was unsuited for use with North Africans (see also Planques, Blanc-Garin, & Collomb, 1956, cited in Bullard, 2005, for use of the Congo-TAT) based on their experience that participants consistently refused to invent or fictionalize. Likewise, Schneider & Schneider (1970) summarized their experiences with the use of a culturally adapted picture story test among the Aghem in West Cameroon as being most discouraging: "Under the most favorable circumstances, the subjects gave short descriptions of the pictures" (p. 542; see Chowdhury, 1960, for similar problems among a heterogeneous Indian sample).

Hofer and Chasiotis (2004) also reported that pretests in Zambia indicated that various subjects had difficulties in following the instruction to write fantasy stories and rather produced mere descriptions of picture cards. To reduce group differences in familiarity with stimulus material and testing, instructions for picture story tests were adapted in subsequent assessments of motives (see also Hofer et al., 2005). Participants were given a detailed and vivid introduction to a picture story test designed to elicit greater fantasy production; for instance, the difference between a mere description of a depicted social situation and a fantasy story about it was illustrated by an example.

Administration Bias

The third type of method bias, namely administration bias, is caused by sources associated with the particular form of test administration. It either stems from differences in physical (e.g., noisy versus quiet environment) and/or social environmental test conditions (e.g., presence of other people), amount of space between participants, gender of the test administrator, or is provoked by personal characteristics of the test administrator and his or her interaction with respondents (see the example given at the beginning of the "Method Bias" section), particularly if they come from a different culture. Characteristics of the administrators may involve differential skills in interviewing and test assessment, for example, ambiguous instructions for respondents, or variations in the guidelines for administrators. The administrators' implicit attitudes toward the cultural groups under investigation could also exercise considerable impact on the outcome of testing, for example, creation of a hostile atmosphere for the assessment of implicit motives. Communication problems may arise either because of language problems when, for example, the testing language is not the first language of the interviewer and/or respondent or because of violation of cultural norms by the use locally inappropriate address (e.g., Goodwin & Lee, 1994; see also Van de Vijver & Leung, 1997).

Dealing with Method Bias

To remedy method bias, various steps can be taken in the design and implementation of a cross-cultural study, such as an intensive training of test administrators; detailed instructions and manuals for administration, scoring, and interpretation (e.g., Smith, Feld, & Franz, 1992); and balancing samples with respect to important participant and context variables (Van de Vijver, 2000). These general guidelines to prevent method bias in data collection will be illustrated next.

Method Bias Addressed by the Hofer et al. Study

Hofer and colleagues (2005) took various precautions in their study design. For example, to prevent sample bias, cultural samples were balanced with regard to important background characteristics, for example, gender, age, and level of education. This control also led to the exclusion of all Cameroonian participants who did not respond in English (the official language in the Anglophone part of Cameroon) from analyses, so that this possible source of bias could be controlled. To avoid administration bias, all local test administrators were well trained, for example, in cultural sensitivity, by the use of detailed manuals for administration.

For the scoring and interpretation of PSE stories, too, manuals were employed to guarantee that the same scoring rules were put into practice, thus preventing instrument bias. Moreover, both during the training phase and the actual scoring, interrater agreements were repeatedly examined. Participants from all cultural groups were given a detailed and vivid introduction to picture story tests, including a sufficient number of examples to minimize group differences in familiarity with the stimulus material and the testing situation. However, despite this careful implementation of recommendations given for research on implicit motives (e.g., Smith et al., 1992), a strict standardization of test administration could not be realized in the main data collection, as some illiterate Cameroonian participants had to respond verbally to picture stimuli. If such exceptions are included in analyses, it is vital to test whether such differences in data collection actually bias the results. In this case, analyses within the Cameroonian subsample did not point to bias associated with those differences in test administration.

Item Bias

The highest level of equivalence, that is, scalar or full score equivalence, that is indispensable for comparisons of means across cultural samples, is only guaranteed when, in addition to construct and method bias that globally affects the assessment and interpretation of data from cross-cultural studies, item bias is absent. Item bias or differential item functioning (DIF; Holland & Wainer, 1993) exerts a more local influence on test scores and derives from characteristics of single items.

An item is considered biased when respondents with the same underlying psychological construct (e.g., n Power) from different (cultural) groups react differently to a given item (e.g., a particular picture or verbal cue). Item bias can be produced by various sources such as a poor translation and adaptation of items (nonequivalent content or wording; e.g., use of verbal cues) or, when considering the assessment of implicit motives by PSE, divergent appropriateness of the picture content across cultures.

The problem of item bias has regularly been examined for self-report measurements, for example, personality scales, and educational and cognitive tests. However, to my knowledge the only studies examining item (picture) bias of thematic apperception measurements have been conducted by Hofer and colleagues (e.g., Hofer et al., 2005; Hofer & Chasiotis, 2004). Hofer and Chasiotis

(2004) found that picture cues noticeably differed in their capacity to elicit motive imagery across cultural samples from Germany and Zambia.

For example, one of the picture cards depicted a white-collar employee in an office with a family picture at his desk (architect at a desk; see Smith, 1992, for a reprint). While the picture card elicited motive imagery scored for greater affiliation-intimacy among German participants, stories written by Zambian respondents scored higher for the achievement motive. It seems that among Zambian participants, the family picture at the desk (pull for affiliation-intimacy) was less prominent than the depicted office situation, a highly achievement-related context.

Similarly, motive imagery scored for n Power was much more present in stories written by Cameroonian and German adults to a picture cue that shows a ship captain wearing a uniform (see Smith, 1992, for a reprint) than in stories written by Costa Rican participants (Hofer et al., 2005). Obviously, participants with different cultural backgrounds differ from each other in how far they perceive a person in uniform as representing a power-related cue. In this context, it is noteworthy that Costa Rica abolished its military by constitution in 1948. Both examples indicate that different elements of the depicted situation became salient in given cultural samples.

Dealing with Item Bias

To detect item bias, two main approaches have been suggested: the judgmental approach, that is, identifying inappropriate items by cultural experts (see, e.g., Rosen, 1962) and the statistical approach (see, e.g., Melikian, 1964). To date, the majority of studies have made use of the latter approach and examined item bias by employing different statistical methods such as Analysis of Variance, Mantel-Haenszel Procedure, or Item Response Theory, depending on the measurement level of items, number of (cultural) groups, or sample size (for an overview on statistical techniques and different forms of item bias, see Van de Vijver & Leung, 1997; Van de Vijver & Tanzer, 2004).

Despite the existence of numerous statistical tools to detect item bias, our knowledge about factors that cause item bias is still limited, as no particular item features have been found to increase or decrease item bias. Moreover, evidence indicates that findings from judgmental and statistical approaches do not sufficiently converge (e.g., Plake, 1980). Thus, it is advisable to combine both strategies for detection of item bias: Local cultural experts may initially scrutinize wording and content of items, and statistical procedures used later for examining bias.

Item Bias Addressed by the Hofer et al. Study

Such a combined procedure was chosen by Hofer and colleagues (2005) to identify picture stimuli that elicit motive imagery to an equal extent among participants, regardless of their culture of origin. Thus, the applicability of picture material was scrutinized by local experts as a first step, and statistical techniques to detect item bias were applied next. By statistical means, bias-free picture sets were identified as being suitable for cross-cultural comparisons of n Affiliation-Intimacy and n Power. The quality of the resulting picture sets was further scrutinized, revealing that age, gender, educational level, and value orientations (*openness to change* and *conservation*; Schwartz, 1992) caused no systematic error (item bias) in the data.

Some Final Words on Bias

To address bias, an integrated examination of construct, method, and item bias represents the gold standard for enhancing our understanding of cultural differences and universals of implicit motives (Van de Vijver, 2000). The study described above (Hofer et al., 2005) demonstrates that an extended methodological approach can lead to unbiased culture-independent sets of picture stimuli that allow for comparisons of data on n Affiliation-Intimacy and n Power across cultural samples, thus showing that Lindzey's (1961) concerns can indeed be met. Given the unique contribution that implicit motive measures may add to the cross-cultural study of personality, this achievement is of great value for motivational research.

However, the study also demonstrated that marked cross-cultural differences exist concerning stimulus cards with respect to triggering n Affiliation-Intimacy and n Power. In pretests, half of the picture cards had to be removed because of item bias. Thus, even if individuals have a general need for close interpersonal relationships and for having impact on other peoples' behavior and emotions, contexts for motive realization, as depicted in the picture cards, differ to some extent across cultures. Even if the biased items may not be suited for use in cross-cultural research, a close examination of their content may help to identify cultural peculiarities of a phenomenon under investigation, for example, a culture-relevant situation for the realization of implicit motives (Van de Vijver & Tanzer, 2004).

Research on Implicit Motives Across Cultural Contexts

Until the mid-1960s, the use of thematic apperception methods was popular in cultural and cross-cultural research investigating national character or various facets of personality, like attitudes, values, and role behavior (e.g., Henry, 1947; Leblanc, 1958; Sherwood, 1957); they obviate problems of self-report such as participants' unwillingness or inability to give relevant information and true attitudes, or fear of social disapproval (e.g., Joshi, 1965). However, these studies often were seriously biased (Lindzey, 1961).

Cross-cultural studies on implicit motives in this narrower sense were probably set off by the groundbreaking work of McClelland and colleagues on *n* Achievement (McClelland, 1961; McClelland, Clark, Roby, & Atkinson, 1949; McClelland et al., 1953). So, it seems barely surprising that most work on motivation in different cultural contexts focused on *n* Achievement. In principle, two lines of research are distinguishable, that is, the assessment of implicit motives at the collective level and at the individual level, respectively.

Motives at the Collective Level

Metaphorically speaking, this approach demonstrates between-subject and within-subject differences, that is, cultures, like individuals, not only differ greatly from each other, but from themselves at different moments in time. McClelland and his associates used the innovative method of content-coding folk tales, literature, children's readers, and artistic expression (see Aronson, 1958) to measure the level of implicit motives of a certain cultural group at a certain period of time in their history. Stories read by children in public schools were chosen as material indicative of collective achievement concern because of their comparability across countries in story length, imaginativeness, and in the extent to which stories were relatively uninfluenced by historical events. Furthermore, it was assumed that material that educational authorities think is right for children to read in school may well represent the basic (motivational) ideas or spirit of the times in a country (McClelland, 1985). The measured national level of, for example, *n* Achievement, was then related to various societal/cultural outcomes indicative of economic growth or decline.

According to McClelland (1961), *n* Achievement precedes and presumably determines economic development rather than arising from it. He suggested that the development of a strong need for achievement in children results in the growth of a group of energetic entrepreneurs who can bring about economic and technological progress (Bradburn & Berlew, 1961). In other words, a pronounced level of *n* Achievement within a society will lead to a higher level of economic and other forms of cultural achievement within a certain period of time (approximately 20 to 25 years).

McClelland (1961) reports substantial evidence supporting his basic assumptions on the relationship between *n* Achievement and economic development. For example, a positive relationship between achievement imagery in folk tales and the level of entrepreneurial activity was reported for a sample of over 40 preliterate small-scale societies located in Africa, Asia, South Pacific, and South and North America. Moreover, McClelland showed that amount of achievement imagery scored in children's readers in 1925 predicted economic growth in 1950 among modern societies (e.g., Argentina, Hungary, Japan, Spain, Turkey, U.K.; see also Engeser, Rheinberg, & Möller, 2009, for findings on differences between federal states in contemporary Germany). Further evidence on the significant link between n Achievement and economic growth and decline is added by a number of historical analyses of different cultures (e.g., England before the Industrial Revolution—Bradburn & Berlew, 1961; USA from 1800 to 1950—de Charms & Moeller, 1962), which reveal that motives change over time within the same society and that such changes are related to subsequent systematic changes in economic activities.

McClelland (1961) also considered the possibility that an increase in the general level of n Achievement may lead to social disruption within a society. In drawing on data on cross-national n Achievement levels 1925 and 1950, Feierabend, Feierabend, and Sleet (1973) could show that countries increasing in implicit achievement motivation were predominantly characterized by instability (e.g., political unrest, coerciveness of regime) in the period from 1948 to 1954, whereas those decreasing in n Achievement were primarily stable. The authors suggest that n Achievement may represent a general "energizer" for societal change and growth and thus may produce desired (economic growth) and undesired (social unrest) effects. In particular, if a high level of n Achievement is paired with limited opportunities to achieve, that is, when there is a considerable gap between rising n Achievement within a society and the actual attainment of achievement strivings (e.g., preindustrial societies) or when the urge to go ahead is blocked, for example, by discrimination against minority groups, a society is apt to experience political unrest and strife; deprived or oppressed groups that seek to satisfy their achievement aspirations then clash with dominant groups in society (McClelland, 1961; Southwood, 1969; see also LeVine, 1966, for the case of the Ibo in Nigeria).

Aside from n Achievement, n Power was also found to be related to certain societal and political characteristics of countries. Even if a high need for power does not reflect "a loss of human value and a willingness to engage in violence," as proposed by Rudin (1968, p. 903), high collective scores on n Power seem to entail some unwanted effects for the population if not "tamed" (see, e.g., Winter, 1991). For example, higher country scores on n Power when paired with low scores for activity inhibition, that is, the degree of restraint over emotional and motivational impulses as reflected by the frequency of using the word *not*, were cross-nationally related to heavy drinking of the population (McClelland, Davis, Kalin, & Wanner, 1972). Indicating that inhibiting a dispositional need to be assertive might entail harmful consequences, for example, elevated blood pressure, McClelland (1975, 1985) also reported that the highest death rates from heart disease and hypertension were found in countries characterized by high collective scores on both n Power and activity inhibition. Moreover, countries characterized by high levels of n Power and low levels of n Affiliation scored high on political violence.

Societal characteristics related to collective levels of n Affiliation have been rarely studied. Yet, available evidence seems to fit with predictions. For example, cultural groups characterized by a high need for affiliation seem to place greater emphasis on care and respect for other people, as reflected in an absence of marital violence and infanticide, closeness of familial relationships, interest in having children, and prosocial adult behavior (McClelland, 1961, 1985). There is also suggestive evidence that countries high in n Affiliation tend to have lower psychogenic death rates from homicide, suicide, ulcers, cirrhosis of the liver, and hypertension (see Barrett & Franke, 1970; Lester, 1971). Moreover, a high collective concern for affiliation potentially moderates the expression of n Power, thus protecting individual rights against suppression by the government (McClelland, 1961, 1985). Totalitarian regimes, for example, Russia during the Stalin reign and China in 1955 after the Communist takeover, seem to be characterized by high collective levels of n Power and low levels of n Affiliation.

Another focus of research on collective-level scores of motives highlighted developmental issues of implicit needs, in particular socialization practices associated with the formation of n Achievement. According to Winterbottom (1958; Rosen & D'Andrade, 1959), n Achievement is most likely to become high when a child is urged to obtain independence and mastery, accompanied by rewards and few restrictions after mastery has been acquired. For example, McClelland and Friedman (1952) reported that amount of achievement imagery in folk tales told in various American Indian tribes was significantly associated with stress on early independence training. Child, Storm, and Veroff (1958) also found a positive relationship between amount of n Achievement in folk tales and socialization practices directly related to achievement, for example, reward for achievement behavior, across 52 cultural groups. However, a focus on general self-reliance in child-rearing practices showed no association with amount of achievement imagery (see "Motives at the Individual Level," below).

Finally, Parker (1962) examined the relationship between child-rearing practices, social behavior, and collective levels of implicit motives as reflected in Eskimo and Ojibwa myths. According to ethnographic evidence, Ojibwa society is characterized by a pronounced striving for individual achievement and power. Competitiveness and mutual suspicion were described as main features of interpersonal relations. In order to foster those strivings, children were exposed to an early and severe socialization process yielding a high level of independence and assertiveness. In contrast, cooperative and communicative values were stressed in socialization of Eskimo children, with little emphasis on striving for individual achievement or acquisition of power as means of enhancing self-esteem. Thus, Parker predicted that these cultural groups would significantly differ in collective levels of implicit motives, such that Ojibwe myths should reflect lower levels of affiliation imagery and higher levels of achievement and power imagery than Eskimo myths. Findings were in remarkable agreement with predictions, indicating a significant association between collective motive patterns, child-rearing practices, and the social behaviors of adults. The findings reported by Parker (1962) also provide support for a direct relationship between culture-level socialization patterns and motive development, a relationship that might hold true not only for the shaping of *n* Achievement but also for *n* Power and *n* Affiliation (see McClelland & Pilon, 1983).

Though studies focusing on psychological aspects shared by all or most members of a culture (e.g., modal personality or national character) were often criticized for underemphasizing individual difference within a given cultural sample, McClelland's and others' work indicates that dominant motives or motive patterns within a cultural group are meaningfully related to societal outcomes, including modal behaviors of its members. Child-rearing practices may, thus, result in the development of culture-adequate motive patterns, which in turn represent a source for divergent developmental pathways across cultures (Keller, 2007). Nonetheless, respective findings also demonstrate that implicit motives are far from representing a stable or uniform national character, but are open to changing patterns of socialization within a given society, as described below.

Motives at the Individual Level

Early research on implicit motives across cultures at the individual level is more difficult to evaluate, as concerted research efforts were rarely present. As with research on the collective level of motives, most research at the individual level focused on antecedents and correlates of *n* Achievement. A significant research issue already mentioned before (see discussion of construct bias) concerns the nature of achievement motivation as understood by different cultural groups. Whereas some studies point to culture-bound facets of achievement (e.g., Kagan & Knight, 1981; Yu, 1996), other studies indicate that the definition of *n* Achievement (e.g., McClelland, 1987) is sufficiently general to grasp achievement motivation of individuals in non-Western societies. A number of studies could show that achievement motivation can be successfully aroused among non-Western participants by the use of experimental manipulations typically used in Western contexts (e.g., Angelini, 1966; Hayashi, Yamauchi, & Sudo, 1972; however, for a failure of arousal of *n* Achievement among Arab students, see Botha, 1971).

Considerable work on *n* Achievement also produced findings that are generally in agreement with the theory of achievement motivation. For example, high levels of *n* Achievement were longitudinally related to increases in agricultural productivity by Indian farmers (Singh, 1978). The relationship between economic development and *n* Achievement is also affirmed by a study conducted in four different regions in Brazil: Angelini, Bitencourt, and Rosamilha (1970) could show that adolescents' level of *n* Achievement was related to the degree of industrialization of their area of living.

Studies on developmental antecedents of n Achievement across cultural and ethnic groups, assessing motive scores at the individual level, generally confirm the significance of emphasis on mastery and autonomy in childhood. Self-reliance training seems to exercise an important influence in the range from 6 to 10 years with an optimum at 8 (Moss & Kagan, 1961). Demands made earlier or later than age 8 may result in lower levels of n Achievement and, in the case of premature demands, in increased levels of fear of failure (see McClelland, 1961). Support for the link between child-rearing practices and n Achievement has been found in several studies with various cultural and ethnic samples: Heckhausen and Kemmler (1957) were able to confirm the hypothesized link between self-reliance training and strength of n Achievement in a study with German preschoolers; according to Rosen (1962), Brazilian mothers were less likely to train their sons in self-reliance, autonomy, and achievement, which was regarded as explanation of their markedly low n Achievement when compared to U.S. American boys.

Rosen's study (1962) further illustrates the effect of two additional factors on the development of n Achievement, namely the roles of the father and of social class. Referring to the former, lack of concern for independence and achievement was associated with a common type of family structure in Brazil, the authoritarian, father-dominated family. Rather than encouraging independence, authoritarian fathers seem to thwart their sons' striving for self-reliance and autonomy. A similar negative relationship between father dominance and level of n Achievement is reported by Bradburn (1963) for Turkey (see also Kornadt & Voigt, 1970, for Kenyan boys' increases in n Achievement after being separated from their families while at boarding school). Thus, an optimal pattern for the development of high levels of n Achievement seems to be a somewhat dominating and demanding mother and a father who allows his son autonomy (LeVine, 1966). Unfortunately, research on developmental antecedents of n Achievement in girls is lacking.

With respect to social class, findings reported by Rosen (1959, 1962) also indicate that socioeconomic status and ethnicity interact in influencing implicit motivation. Rosen (1959), who examined different ethnic subgroups in the United States and Canada, found a link between n Achievement and independence training in early childhood (see also McClelland & Pilon, 1983). However, the link could not be established for participants characterized by a low socioeconomic background. Generally, members of the middle class tended to have considerably higher n Achievement than individuals in the lower social strata. Thus, prerequisites for the development of a pronounced n Achievement may be particularly characteristic of middle-class families (for effect of family size and birth order on n Achievement, see Angelini, 1967).

Several studies have shown statistically significant differences in n Achievement between groups of individuals drawn from culturally divergent groups and societies. It is likely that genuine differences in n Achievement were reported by those studies (e.g., Bradburn, 1963; Rosen, 1959, 1962) that linked its findings on motive strength meaningfully to, for example, antecedents of motive formation, such as dominant child-rearing practices, thus considering the motive's nomological network.

Other findings on cross-cultural differences or similarities in motive strength with culturally divergent samples (e.g., Botha, 1971; Morsbach, 1969; Salili, 1996) seem to be more problematic as methodological flaws cannot be ruled out (e.g., nonequivalence of stimulus materials; language differences, etc.). Similarly, sporadic early research across cultures focusing on needs for power and affiliation (e.g., Sanders, Scholz, & Kagan, 1976; Singh, 1986) must await methodologically sophisticated replications before a comprehensive evaluation of these research efforts may be attempted.

Recent Cross-Cultural Research on Implicit Motives

With the recent resurgence of interest in implicit processes, research on implicit motives in divergent cultural contexts has increased, too (e.g., McAuley, Bond, & Ng, 2004). This has led to methodological (e.g., Hofer et al., 2005) progress as well as to the emergence of various new theoretical and empirical approaches. For example, Langens (2001) reanalyzed available data (McClelland & Winter, 1969) and was able to show that change in business activity of Indian entrepreneurs is best explained by the interplay of implicit motives and self-discrepancies. Also, Pang and Schultheiss (2005) reflected on differences in strength of implicit motives by comparing student samples from two so-called individualistic cultures, namely Germany and the USA. Summarizing their findings, the authors conclude that despite different methods used for data collection, samples, and historic contexts, data are in agreement with those presented by McClelland (1961, 1975), suggesting that Americans continue to have a stronger concern with achievement and a weaker concern with power than Germans, and that they are less inhibited in the expression of their motivational needs than Germans.

Cross-cultural studies conducted by scholars at the University of Osnabrück in Germany provide evidence for a number of replicable relationships between implicit motives and both psychological and behavioral correlates. For example, findings that commitment to and successful pursuance of goals that are aligned to one's implicit needs predict enhanced emotional well-being among Euro-American individuals (e.g., Brunstein, Schultheiss, & Grässmann, 1998) have been replicated within a non-Western sample (Hofer & Chasiotis, 2003). For the motivational domains of achievement and affiliation-intimacy, congruence between implicit motives and life goals was associated with enhanced life satisfaction in a study sample of Zambian male adolescents.

Further evidence of a possibly universal relationship between the alignment of different types of motives and subjective well-being was provided by a cross-cultural investigation that collected data from Cameroonian, German, and Costa Rican participants (Hofer, Chasiotis, & Campos, 2006; see Fig. 15.1). Higher levels of life satisfaction were related to congruence between implicit need for affiliation-intimacy and values that reflect a concern for close, positive interactions with others, namely, benevolence (Schwartz, 1992), across three cultural samples that were fairly heterogeneous with respect to their composition (e.g., age, educational level, and vocational status).

Again drawing on samples from Cameroon, Costa Rica, and Germany, further relationships among psychological constructs that might reflect basic processes of human functioning common to cultural samples under investigation could be identified. Hofer, Busch, Chasiotis, Kärtner, and Campos (2008) examined the cross-cultural applicability of core assumptions constituting an integrative model of generativity proposed by McAdams and de St. Aubin (1992). According to this theoretical framework, the desire to foster the succeeding generations' well-being originates from two motivational sources, culture-specific normative expectations and an inner (implicit) need to act in a generative manner. These constructs feed a disposition for contributing to the next generation, which initiates the setting of conscious generative goals. Referring to findings that highlight the role of n Power for generative behavior, Peterson and Stewart (1993) hypothesized that a prosocial type of n Power

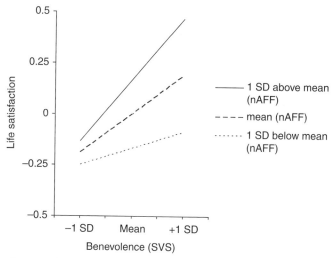

Figure 15.1 Level of life satisfaction and its relationship to the association of benevolence and n Affiliation. From "Congruence between social values and implicit motives: Effects on life satisfaction across three cultures," by J. Hofer, A. Chasiotis, & D. Campos, 2006, *European Journal of Personality*, *20*, 305–324. Copyright 2006 by John Wiley & Sons Limited. Reproduced with permission.

serves as a motivational source for generative concern (disposition). Using bias-free data assessed by use of implicit and self-report measures, it could be verified that the psychological mechanisms of generativity are the same in the cultures under examination: A pronounced desire to have a positive impact on other people's emotions or behavior is turned into a generative disposition, which in turn determines to what extent the individual develops generative goals.

The high cross-cultural reliability of the instruments also allowed testing for differences on the relevant measures between the cultural groups (see also Hofer et al., 2006, for cultural differences in n Power and n Affiliation-Intimacy). In short, a much stronger emphasis on consciously represented facets of generativity, that is, concern and goals, was present in cultures emphasizing social relatedness. Moreover, German participants scored significantly lower than Cameroonian and Costa Rican subjects in implicit, prosocial power motivation. Differences in socialization practices between cultures with a collectivist versus individualist orientation (e.g., teaching of cultural norms and values) may be a significant factor in this pattern of results. Increasing individualization in Western cultures (e.g., lower relatedness to relatives and non-relatives) may entail the risk of lessened investment in coming generations, thus threatening intergenerational links and important sources of well-being in old age.

Regarding prosocial n Power, it has been argued that having younger siblings influences the development of a prosocial power motive, as this family context provides important responsibility training (e.g., Winter & Barenbaum, 1985). By assuming that the childhood context is important for the emergence of a caregiving motivation, that is, prosocial power motivation, Chasiotis, Hofer, and Campos (2006) tested a model across cultural groups (Cameroon, Costa Rica, Germany) in which being exposed to interactive experiences with younger siblings in childhood elicits implicit nurturant motivations, which, in turn, lead to more conscious feelings of affection toward children in adulthood, with these feelings being linked to the probability of having own children in adulthood. The proposed model describing this developmental pathway was valid in all cultures under investigation and hence supported the view that childhood context variables such as birth order might exert similar influences on programming of psychological, somatic, and reproductive developments across different cultures.

Finally, another set of recent studies examined possible differences of motive arousal among participants from different cultures of origin. Ng (2006) reported that students from China (from both Beijing and Hong Kong) and from the United States differ in the antecedents of n Power arousal. Whereas n Power was primarily aroused by the status aspect of power among Chinese students (sitting in a professor's seat while responding to PSE), U.S. American students were mainly motivated by the decision-making aspect of power (taking the PSE after allocating bonuses to other employees).

Similarly, Hofer et al. (in press) assumed that the type of situational context in which the PSE is embedded will affect the arousal of *n* Achievement in students from Cameroon, China, and Germany depending on proposed differences in self-construal between cultural groups. Two arousal conditions were applied in the study: Whereas one group was informed that the best performance/stories written by single individual would be identified (me-oriented instruction), the other group was told that only the performance of the whole group (we-oriented instruction) would be evaluated. As expected, Cameroonian students who received the we-oriented instructions scored higher for *n* Achievement than did participants in the me-oriented condition. Thus, the appeal to contribute to the accomplishment of the group represents a noticeable incentive for Cameroonian participants because showing achievement-related behavior demonstrates solidarity and affirms social connectedness. In contrast, Chinese and German students scored higher for *n* Achievement in contexts that emphasize competition and personal success. Considering the German sample, the finding fits the notion that, in Western cultural contexts, individuals strive for personal agency and autonomy.

For the Chinese sample, *n* Achievement was expected to be aroused in contexts of competition as well as collaboration. However, personal agency may be particularly esteemed by the highly educated everywhere. So, the sample of university students may have been biased toward stressing me-oriented achievement as, typically, child-rearing practices in China do emphasize not only social and moral virtues like obedience, respect, and responsibility but also academic and professional success as important socialization goals. However, the findings may also reflect changes in culturally defined achievement-related values and norms that occurred in the course of recent social and economical changes in the People's Republic of China (Egri & Ralston, 2004).

Conclusions and Future Perspectives

Research in diverse cultural contexts, focusing either on motive scores at the collective or at the individual level, has provided valuable insight into universal features and culture-specific aspects of implicit motives and their developmental antecedents and behavioral and psychological correlates. However, cross-cultural research on implicit motives based on methodologically sound designs and test methods is a fledgling development within cross-cultural psychology.

Recent studies conducted in Euro-American cultural contexts continuously enhance our knowledge on various aspects of implicit motives and their significance for human functioning (see this volume). However, a critical review clearly shows the large backlog of work that has to be done on implicit motives in cross-cultural context. For example, fundamental work must be conducted with respect to the arousability of motives, and their developmental antecedents and behavioral correlates, particularly focusing on *n* Affiliation-Intimacy and *n* Power, which have received much less scientific attention compared to *n* Achievement. Also, the generalizability of linkages of implicit motives to other psychological constructs, for example, autobiographical memories, psychobiological correlates, as well as the genuineness of reported cross-cultural differences in motive strengths, still awaits future research efforts in non-Western cultures.

In general, multivariate research, that is, the combined consideration of various significant components of personality (e.g., Winter, John, Stewart, Klohnen, & Duncan, 1998) should be extended multiculturally, preferably assessing more than two cultural groups (see Bornstein, 2002). Such a step would broaden scientific knowledge of the human psyche.

Even though latitude for variation in personality components among members of a given cultural group exists, human motives and other such personality components are not distributed randomly among various cultural groups. Individuals in a given geographical or societal niche tend to have similar learning and life experiences (e.g., socialization patterns fostering or sanctioning specific motive-related behavior) and thus are likely, within genetically preset constraints, to develop similarities in basic personality structure (e.g., in patterns of motives).

Moreover, cultural context molds beliefs and values regarding the consequences of actions in the day-to-day environment. Of course, the process of behaviorally implementing implicit motives is conditioned by those beliefs and values that determine what is desirable or should be avoided in a given culture, and by contextual conditions that may accentuate certain role obligations, communication styles, or norms for displaying behavior in a given situation. Consequently, associations between an implicit motive and specific goals as well as behavioral acts may, for example, differ in strength across cultures, as main value orientations and beliefs constrain the thoughts and behavior of those who interact within these collective entities (Hofer & Bond, 2008).

Thus, a motive in its original form is probably an evolved and innate aspect of humans' biological heritage. As a fully matured social motive, however, it represents a complex learned pattern of eliciting stimuli, emotional responses, and behaviors, with these elements culturally defined or at least influenced. Hence, social constraints and environmental demands in a given culture may determine particular instrumental means by which a motive is realized in a given situation. For example, onset of sexual activity and number of sexual partners may function as a possible outlet of an untamed need for power (Winter, 1973) in Western sociocultural contexts that exercise relatively little social control over individuals' sexual behavior, but may be dissociated from *n* Power in many other cultures that hold authoritarian ideologies emphasizing sexual restraint.

In some cases, dominant cultural ideologies may even act as a source of motivation, potentially in conflict with evolved motive dispositions, but in conformity with externally imposed social control (MacDonald, 1991; see also Kuhl, 2001). Hence, in cross-cultural research, attention should be given to universal as well as culture-specific aspects of human motivation to understand the ways in which motives are nurtured and elaborated across cultural groups. Particularly, cross-cultural work needs to intensify research on behavioral correlates of implicit motives by integrating our understanding of the "pull-power" exercised by different types of situations into the prediction of behavior within and across cultural groups (Bond, 2005).

Finally, revitalizing research on collective motive patterns would add further insight into the value of implicit motives for predicting human functioning across cultures. Recently, studies have verified that country-level indicators can be successfully linked to individuals' behavior across cultures (e.g., Van de Vliert, Huang, & Levine, 2004). The assessment of collective motive scores, scored from past or current material representative for a given cultural group (e.g., readers, popular books), may help to explain current societal characteristics and behavioral trends within and across cultures, and also to predict how the motives of future generations are shaped. Conceiving of collective motive patterns as a significant facet of the person's daily environment, then comparing collective-level and individual-level motive scores may also allow conclusions about an individual's level of enculturation, that is, adjustment to common environmental and sociocultural demands. Whereas satisfaction of individual motives, which are in conflict with societal needs, may involve rather short-term effects on well-being, a good motivational fit between the individual and the culture's normative expectations, given sufficient opportunities for need satisfaction, might represent an important prerequisite for a happy and successful life over the life course (Kitayama & Park, 2007). Thus, the inclusion of country-level motive scores would facilitate a reliable and valid integration of culture and motives into a single theoretical and empirical frame.

Taken together, I hope the present chapter has raised awareness of the manifold challenges that cross-cultural research on implicit motives faces, such as the careful creation of an unbiased stimulus set for motive assessment or the identification of appropriate behavioral instantiations of a motive in specific cultural groups. These challenges, however, can successfully be mastered given sound methodological and conceptual preparation. Moreover, facing these challenges is worthwhile, given the many valuable insights and predictive purchase that cross-cultural research on implicit motives promises.

Author Note

I am grateful to Holger Busch and Michael Harris Bond for their helpful comments on an earlier version of this manuscript.

References

Angelini, A. L. (1966). Measuring the achievement motive in Brazil. *Journal of Social Psychology, 68,* 35–40.

Angelini, A. L., Bitencourt, L. J. F., & Rosamilha, N. (1970). Motivation for achievement and economic development. *Revista Interamericana de Psicologia, 4,* 33–41.

Angelini, H. R. (1967). Family structure and motivation to achieve. *Revista Interamericana de Psicologia, 1,* 115–125.

Aronson, E. (1958). The need for achievement as measured by graphic expression. In J. W. Atkinson (Ed.), *Motives in fantasy, action and society* (pp. 249–265). Princeton, NJ: Van Nostrand.

Bargh, J. A., & Chartrand, T. L. (1999). The unbearable automaticity of being. *American Psychologist, 54,* 462–479.

Barrett, G. V., & Franke, R. H. (1970). "Psychogenic" death: A reappraisal. *Science, 167,* 304–306.

Benet-Martínez, V., & Oishi, S. (2008). Culture and personality. In O. P. John, R.W. Robins, & L. A. Pervin (Eds.), *Handbook of personality: Theory and research* (pp. 542–567). New York: Guilford Press.

Bond, M. H. (2004). Culture and aggression - from context to coercion. *Personality and Social Psychology Review, 8,* 62–78.

Bond, M. H. (2005). A cultural-psychological model for explaining differences in social behavior: Positioning the belief construct. In R. M. Sorrentino, D. Cohen, J. M. Olson, & M. P. Zanna (Eds.), *Culture and social behavior* (Vol. 10, pp. 31–48). Mahwah, NJ: Lawrence Erlbaum.

Bornstein, M. H. (2002). Toward a multiculture, multiage, multimethod science. *Human Development, 45,* 257–263.

Botha, E. (1971). The achievement motive in three cultures. *Journal of Social Psychology, 85,* 163–170.

Bradburn, N. M. (1963). n Achievement and father dominance in Turkey. *Journal of Abnormal and Social Psychology, 67,* 464–468.

Bradburn, N. M., & Berlew, D. E. (1961). Need for achievement and English industrial growth. *Economic Development and Cultural Change, 10,* 8–20.

Brown, D. E. (1991). *Human universals.* New York: McGraw-Hill.

Brunstein, J. C., & Maier, G. W. (2005). Implicit and self-attributed motives to achieve: Two separate but interacting needs. *Journal of Personality and Social Psychology, 89,* 205–222.

Brunstein, J. C., Schultheiss, O. C., & Grässmann, R. (1998). Personal goals and emotional well-being: The moderating role of motive dispositions. *Journal of Personality and Social Psychology, 75,* 494–508.

Bullard, A. (2005). The critical impact of Frantz Fanon and Henri Collomb: Race, gender, and personality testing of North and West Africans. *Journal of the History of the Behavioral Sciences, 41*, 225–248.

Chasiotis, A., Hofer, J., & Campos, D. (2006). When does liking children lead to parenthood? Younger siblings, implicit prosocial power motivation, and explicit love for children predict parenthood across cultures. *Journal of Cultural and Evolutionary Psychology, 4*, 95–123.

Cheung, F. (2006). A combined emic–etic approach to cross-cultural personality test development: The case of the CPAI. In Q. Jing, H. Zhang, & K. Zhang (Eds.), *Psychological science around the world* (Vol. 2, pp. 91–103). London: Psychology Press.

Child, I. L., Storm, T., & Veroff, J. (1958). Achievement themes in folk tales related to socialization practice. In J. W. Atkinson (Ed.), *Motives in fantasy, action, and society* (pp. 479–492). Princeton, NJ: Van Nostrand.

Chowdhury, U. (1960). An Indian modification of the Thematic Apperception Test. *Journal of Social Psychology, 51*, 245–263.

Church, T. A. (2001). Personality measurement in cross-cultural perspective. *Journal of Personality, 69*, 979–1005.

Cohen, D. (1997). Ifs and thens in cross-cultural psychology. In R. S. Wyer, Jr. (Ed.), *The automaticity of everyday life* (pp. 121–131). Mahwah, NJ: Lawrence Erlbaum.

Cole, M. (1996). *Cultural psychology*. Cambridge, MA: Harvard University Press.

Dana, R. H. (1999). Cross-cultural, multicultural use of the thematic apperception test. In L. Gieser & M. I. Stein (Eds.), *The thematic apperception test and the art of projection* (pp. 177–190). Washington, DC: American Psychological Association.

de Charms, R., & Moeller, G. H. (1962). Values expressed in American children's readers: 1800–1950. *Journal of Abnormal and Social Psychology, 64*, 136–142.

De Vos, G. (1973). *Socialization for achievement: Essays on the cultural psychology of the Japanese*. Berkeley, CA: University of California Press.

Egri, C. P., & Ralston, D. A. (2004). Generation cohorts and personal values: A comparison of China and the United States. *Organization Science, 15*, 210–220.

Engeser, S., Rheinberg, F., & Möller, M. (2009). Achievement motive imagery in German schoolbooks: A pilot study testing McClelland's hypothesis. *Journal of Research in Personality, 43*, 110–113.

Ervin, S. M. (1964). Language and TAT content in French-English bilinguals. *Journal of Abnormal and Social Psychology, 68*, 500–507.

Fanon, F., & Geronimi, C. (1956). Le T.A.T. chez les femmes musulmanes: Sociologie de la perception et de l'imagination. Congrès des Médecins Aliénistes et Neurologistes de France, LIV session, pp. 364–368.

Feierabend, R. L., Feierabend, I. K., & Sleet, D. A. (1973). Need for achievement, coerciveness of government, and political unrest: A cross-national analysis. *Journal of Cross-Cultural Psychology, 4*, 314–325.

Goodwin, R., & Lee, I. (1994). Taboo topics among Chinese and English friends: A cross-cultural comparison. *Journal of Cross-Cultural Psychology, 25*, 325–338.

Hayashi, T., Yamauchi, H., & Sudo, W. (1972). The effect of experimental arousal of achievement motivation on imaginative stories. *Japanese Journal of Educational Psychology, 20,* 179–183.

Heckhausen, H., & Kemmler, L. (1957). Entstehungsbedingungen der kindlichen Selbständigkeit. *Zeitschrift für Experimentelle und Angewandte Psychologie, 4,* 603–622.

Henry, W. E. (1947). The thematic apperception technique in the study of culture-personality relations. *Genetic Psychology Monographs, 35,* 3–135.

Hofer, J., & Bond, M. H. (2008). Do implicit motives add to our understanding of psychological and behavioral outcomes within and across cultures? In R. M. Sorrentino & S. Yamaguchi (Eds.), *The handbook of motivation and cognition within and across cultures* (pp. 95–118). Amsterdam: Elsevier/Academic Press.

Hofer, J., Busch, H., Bender, M., Li, M., & Hagemeyer, B. (in press). Arousal of achievement motivation among student samples in three different cultural contexts: Self and social standards of evaluation. *Journal of Cross-Cultural Psychology.*

Hofer, J., Busch, H., Chasiotis, A., Kärtner, J., & Campos, D. (2008). Concern for generativity and its relation to implicit pro-social power motivation, generative goals, and satisfaction with life: A cross-cultural investigation. *Journal of Personality, 76,* 1–30.

Hofer, J., & Chasiotis, A. (2003). Congruence of life goals and implicit motives as predictors of life satisfaction: Cross-cultural implications of a study of Zambian male adolescents. *Motivation and Emotion, 27,* 251–272.

Hofer, J., & Chasiotis, A. (2004). Methodological considerations of applying a TAT-type picture-story-test in cross-cultural research: A comparison of German and Zambian adolescents. *Journal of Cross-Cultural Psychology, 35,* 224–241.

Hofer, J., Chasiotis, A., & Campos, D. (2006). Congruence between social values and implicit motives: Effects on life satisfaction across three cultures. *European Journal of Personality, 20,* 305–324.

Hofer, J., Chasiotis, A., Friedlmeier, W., Busch, H., & Campos, D. (2005). The measurement of implicit motives in three cultures: Power and affiliation in Cameroon, Costa Rica, and Germany. *Journal of Cross-Cultural Psychology, 36,* 689–716.

Hofstede, G. (2000). *Culture's consequences. International differences in work-related values.* Newbury Park, CA: Sage.

Holland, P. W., & Wainer, H. (1993). *Differential item functioning.* Hillsdale, NJ: Lawrence Erlbaum.

Joshi, V. (1965). Personality profiles in industrial and preindustrial cultures: A TAT study. *Journal of Social Psychology, 66,* 101–111.

Kagan, S., & Knight, G. P. (1981). Social motives among Anglo American and Mexican American children: Experimental and projective measures. *Journal of Research in Personality, 15,* 93–106.

Kağitçibaşi, C. (2005). Autonomy and relatedness in cultural context: Implications for self and family. *Journal of Cross-Cultural Psychology, 36,* 403–422.

Keller, H. (2007). *Cultures of infancy*. Mahwah, NJ: Lawrence Erlbaum.

Keller, H., & Greenfield, P. M. (2000). History and future development in cross-cultural psychology. *Journal of Cross-Cultural Psychology, 31*, 52–62.

Kihlstrom, J. F. (2002). The unconscious. In V. S. Ramachandran (Ed.), *Encyclopedia of the human brain* (Vol. 4, pp. 635–646). San Diego, CA: Academic.

Kitayama, S., & Park, H. (2007). Cultural shaping of self, emotion, and well-being: How does it work? *Social and Personality Psychology Compass, 1*, 202–222.

Kornadt, H.-J., Eckensberger, L. H., & Emminghaus, W. B. (1980). Cross-cultural research on motivation and its contribution to a general theory of motivation. In H. C. Triandis & R. W. Brislin (Eds.), *Handbook of cross-cultural psychology* (Vol. 3, pp. 223–321). Boston: Allyn & Bacon.

Kornadt, H.-J., & Voigt, E. (1970). *Situation und Entwicklungsprobleme des Schulsystems in Kenia*. Stuttgart, Germany: Ernst Klett Verlag.

Kuhl, J. (2001). *Motivation und Persönlichkeit. Interaktionen psychischer Systeme*. Göttingen, Germany: Hogrefe.

Langens, T. A. (2001). Predicting behavior change in Indian businessmen from a combination of need for achievement and self-discrepancy. *Journal of Research in Personality, 35*, 339–352.

Leblanc, M. (1958). Acculturation of attitude and personality among Katangese women. *Journal of Social Psychology, 47*, 257–264.

Lefkowitz, J., & Fraser, A. W. (1980). Assessment of achievement and power motivation of Blacks and Whites, using a Black and White TAT, with Black and White administrators. *Journal of Applied Psychology, 65*, 685–696.

Lester, D. (1971). Suicide and homicide rates and society's need for affiliation. *Journal of Cross-Cultural Psychology, 2*, 405–406.

LeVine, R. A. (1966). *Dreams and deeds: Achievement motivation in Nigeria*. Chicago: University of Chicago Press.

Leung, K., & Bond, M. H. (2004). Social axioms: A model for social beliefs in multi-cultural perspective. *Advances in Experimental Social Psychology, 36*, 119–197.

Lindzey, G. (1961). *Projective techniques and cross-cultural research*. New York: Appleton-Century-Crofts.

MacDonald, K. B. (1991). A perspective on Darwinian psychology: The importance of domain-general mechanisms, plasticity, and individual differences. *Ethology and Sociobiology, 12*, 449–480.

Maehr, M. L., & Nicholls, J. G. (1980). Culture and achievement motivation: A second look. In N. Warren (Ed.), *Studies in cross-cultural psychology* (Vol. 2, pp. 221–267). New York: Academic Press.

Markus, H. R., & Kitayama, S. (1991). Culture and the self: Implications for cognition, emotion, and motivation. *Psychological Review, 98*, 224–253.

Mazur, A., & Rosa, E. (1977). An empirical test of McClelland's "achieving society" theory. *Social Forces, 55*, 769–774.

McAdams, D. P., & de St. Aubin, E. (1992). A theory of generativity and its assessment through self-report, behavioral acts, and narrative themes in autobiography. *Journal of Personality and Social Psychology, 62*, 1003–1015.

McAuley, P. C., Bond, M. H., & Ng, I. W.-C. (2004). Antecedents of subjective well-being in working Hong Kong adults. *Journal of Psychology in Chinese Societies, 1*, 25–49.

McClelland, D. C. (1961). *The achieving society*. Princeton, NJ: Van Nostrand.

McClelland, D. C. (1975). *Power: The inner experience*. New York: Irvington.

McClelland, D. C. (1985). *Human motivation*. New York: Cambridge University Press.

McClelland, D. C. (1987). Characteristics of successful entrepreneurs. *Journal of Creative Behavior, 3*, 219–233.

McClelland, D. C., Atkinson, J. W., Clark, R. A., & Lowell, E. L. (1953). *The achievement motive*. New York: Appleton-Century-Crofts.

McClelland, D. C., Clark, R. A., Roby, T. B., & Atkinson, J. W. (1949). The effect of need for achievement on thematic apperception. *Journal of Experimental Psychology, 37*, 242–255.

McClelland, D. C., Davis, W. N., Kalin, R., & Wanner, E. (1972). *The drinking man*. New York: The Free Press.

McClelland, D. C., & Friedman, G. A. (1952). Child-rearing practices and the achievement motivation appearing in folk tales. In T. M. Newcomb, E. L. Hartley, & G. E. Swanson (Eds.), *Readings in social psychology* (pp. 243–249). New York: Holt, Rinehart, and Winston.

McClelland, D. C., Koestner, R., & Weinberger, J. (1989). How do self-attributed and implicit motives differ? *Psychological Review, 96*, 690–702.

McClelland, D. C., & Pilon, D. A. (1983). Sources of adult motives in patterns of parent behavior in early childhood. *Journal of Personality and Social Psychology, 44*, 564–574.

McClelland, D. C., & Winter, D. G. (1969). *Motivating economic achievement*. New York: Free Press.

McCrae, R. R., & Costa, P. T. Jr. (1997). Personality trait structure as a human universal. *American Psychologist, 52*, 509–516.

Melikian, L. H. (1964). The use of T.A.T. cards among Arab university students: A cross-cultural study. *Journal of Social Psychology, 62*, 3–19.

Morsbach, H. (1969). A cross-cultural study of achievement motivation and achievement values in two South African groups. *Journal of Social Psychology, 79*, 267–268.

Moss, H. A., & Kagan, J. (1961). Stability of achievement and recognition-seeking behaviors from early childhood through adulthood. *Journal of Abnormal and Social Psychology, 62*, 504–513.

Murray, H. A. (1938). *Explorations in personality*. New York: Oxford University Press.

Murray, H. A. (1943). *Thematic Apperception Test manual*. Cambridge, MA: Harvard University Press.

Murstein, B. I. (1965). The stimulus. In B. I. Murstein (Ed.), *Handbook of projective techniques* (pp. 509–546). New York: Basic Books.

Ng, I. (2006). *A cross-cultural study of power and power motivation in China and the United States*. Unpublished doctoral dissertation, University of Michigan, Ann Arbor.

Nisbett, R. E., & Wilson, T. D. (1977). Telling more than we can know: Verbal reports on mental processes. *Psychological Review, 84*, 231–259.

Ostheimer, J. M. (1969). Measuring achievement motivation among the Chagga of Tanzania. *Journal of Social Psychology, 78*, 17–30.

Pang, J. S., & Schultheiss, O. C. (2005). Assessing implicit motives in U. S. college students: Effects of picture type and position, gender and ethnicity, and cross-cultural comparisons. *Journal of Personality Assessment, 85*, 280–294.

Parker, S. (1962). Motives in Eskimo and Ojibwa mythology. *Ethnology, 1*, 516–523.

Peterson, B. E., & Stewart, A. J. (1993). Generativity and social motives in young adults. *Journal of Personality and Social Psychology, 65*, 186–198.

Plake, B. S. (1980). A comparison of a statistical and subjective procedure to ascertain item validity: One step in the test validation process. *Educational and Psychological Measurement, 40*, 397–404.

Planques, L., Blanc-Garin, J., & Collomb, H. (1956). Le Congo-T.A.T. chez les noires d'Afrique. *Congrès des Médecins Aliénistes et Neurologistes de France, LIV* session, pp. 191–198.

Plomin, R., & Daniles, D. (1987). Why are children in the same family different from each other? *Behavioral and Brain Sciences, 10*, 1–16.

Rosen, B. C. (1959). Race, ethnicity, and the achievement syndrome. *American Sociological Review, 24*, 47–60.

Rosen, B. C. (1962). Socialization and achievement motivation in Brazil. *American Sociological Review, 27*, 612–624.

Rosen, B. C., & D'Andrade, R. (1959). The psychological origins of the achievement motive. *Sociometry, 22*, 185–218.

Rudin, S. A. (1968). National motives predict psychogenic death rates 25 years later. *Science, 160*, 901–903.

Salili, F. (1996). Achievement motivation: A cross-cultural comparison of British and Chinese students. *Educational Psychology, 16*, 171–179.

Sanders, M., Scholz, J. P., & Kagan, S. (1976). Three social motives and field independence-dependence in Anglo American and Mexican American children. *Journal of Cross-Cultural Psychology, 7*, 451–462.

Schneider, M. R., & Schneider, J. F. (1970). The use of projective pictures in a preliterate African community. *Rural Sociology, 35*, 542–543.

Schultheiss, O. C., Wirth, M. M., Torges, C. M., Pang, J. S., Villacorta, M. A., & Welsh, K. M. (2005). Effects of implicit power motivation on men's and women's implicit learning and testosterone changes after social victory or defeat. *Journal of Personality and Social Psychology, 88*, 174–188.

Schwartz, S. H. (1992). Universals in the content and structure of values: Theoretical advances and empirical tests in 20 countries. In M. Zanna (Ed.), *Advances in experimental social psychology* (Vol. 25, pp. 1–65). Orlando, FL: Academic Press.

Sherwood, E. (1957). On the designing of TAT pictures, with special reference to a set for an African people assimilating Western culture. *Journal of Social Psychology, 45*, 161–190.

Singh, S. (1978). Achievement motivation and entrepreneurial success: A follow-up study. *Journal of Research in Personality, 12*, 500–503.

Singh, S. (1986). Values and personality correlates of projective measure of power motivation. *British Journal of Projective Psychology and Personality Study, 31*, 32–38.

Smith, C. P. (Ed.) (1992). *Motivation and personality: Handbook of thematic content analysis.* New York: Cambridge University Press.

Smith, C. P, Feld, S. C., & Franz, C. E. (1992). Methodological considerations: Steps in research employing content analysis systems. In C. P. Smith (Ed.), *Motivation and personality: Handbook of thematic content analysis* (pp. 515–536). New York: Cambridge University Press.

Southwood, K. E. (1969). *Some sources of political disorder: A cross-national analysis.* Ph.D. dissertation, University of Michigan, Ann Arbor, MI.

Tedeschi, J. T., & Kian, M. (1962). Cross-cultural study of the TAT assessment for achievement motivation: Americans and Persians. *Journal of Social Psychology, 58*, 227–234.

Tindale, R. S., & Kameda, T. (2000). "Social sharedness" as a unifying theme for information processing in groups. *Group Processes & Intergroup Relations, 3*, 123–140.

Van de Vijver, F. J. R. (2000). The nature of bias. In R. H. Dana (Ed.), *Handbook of cross-cultural and multi-cultural personality assessment* (pp. 87–106). Mahwah, NJ: Lawrence Erlbaum.

Van de Vijver, F. J. R., Hofer, J., & Chasiotis, A. (2009). Methodological aspects of cross-cultural developmental studies. In M. H. Bornstein (Ed.), *Handbook of cross-cultural developmental science* (pp. 21–37). Mahwah, NJ: Lawrence Erlbaum.

Van de Vijver, F. J. R., & Leung, K. (1997). *Methods and data analysis for cross-cultural research.* Newbury Park, CA: Sage.

Van de Vijver, F. J. R., & Tanzer, N. K. (2004). Bias and equivalence in cross-cultural assessment: An overview. *European Review of Applied Psychology, 54*, 119–135.

Van de Vliert, E., Huang, X., & Levine, R. V. (2004). National wealth and thermal climate as predictors of motives for volunteer work. *Journal of Cross-Cultural Psychology, 35*, 62–73.

Wang, M.-J. (1969). Report on the revision of the Thematic Apperception Test. *Acta Psychologica Taiwanica, 11*, 24–41.

Weinberger, J., & McClelland, D. C. (1990). Cognitive versus traditional motivational models. Irreconcilable or complementary? In E. T. Higgins & R. M. Sorrentino (Eds.), *Handbook of motivation and cognition: Vol. 2: Foundations of social behavior* (pp. 562–597). New York: Guilford Press.

Winter, D. G. (1973). *The power motive.* New York: Free Press.

Winter, D. G. (1991). Power, affiliation, and war: Three tests of a motivational model. *Journal of Personality and Social Psychology, 65*, 532–545.

Winter, D. G. (1994). *Manual for scoring motive imagery in running text.* Ann Arbor, MI: University of Michigan.

Winter, D. G. (1996). *Personality: Analysis and interpretation of lives.* New York: McGraw-Hill.

Winter, D. G., & Barenbaum, N. B. (1985). Responsibility and the power motive in women and men. *Journal of Personality, 53*, 335–355.

Winter, D. G., John, O. P., Stewart, A. J., Klohnen, E. C., & Duncan, L. E. (1998). Traits and motives: Toward an integration of two traditions in personality research. *Psychological Review, 105,* 230–250.

Winter, D. G., & Stewart, A. J. (1978). The power motive. In H. London & J. E. Exner (Eds.), *Dimensions of personality* (pp. 391–447). New York: Wiley.

Winterbottom, M. R. (1958). The relation of need for achievement to learning experiences in independence and mastery. In J. W. Atkinson (Ed.), *Motives in fantasy, action, and society* (pp. 453–478). Princeton, NJ: Van Nostrand.

Woike, B., McLeod, S., & Goggin, M. (2003). Implicit and explicit motives influence accessibility to different autobiographical knowledge. *Personality and Social Psychology Bulletin, 29,* 1046–1055.

Yu, A.-B. (1996). Ultimate life concerns, self, and Chinese achievement motivation. In M. H. Bond (Ed.), *The handbook of Chinese psychology* (pp. 227–246). Hong Kong: Oxford University Press.

Chapter 16
Clinical Implications of Implicit Motives

JOEL WEINBERGER, TANYA COTLER, AND DANIEL FISHMAN
Adelphi University

In this chapter, we attempt to apply what is known about implicit motives to clinical psychology. We must admit at the outset that the answer is "very little." This is partly because the two fields have developed independently of one another. Clinicians and clinical researchers tend to be ignorant of the implicit motives literature. Similarly, those who study implicit motives come from a background of personality and/or social psychology and are largely unfamiliar with the clinical literature. This is unfortunate, as we believe that each has much to contribute to the other. We hope that this chapter represents a modest beginning to putting the two fields in touch with one another to the betterment of both.

We address this issue in two ways. First, we discuss what implicit motives may be able to tell us about emotional well-being and psychopathology. The focus here will be on the expression of implicit motives. We assume that people function most adaptively if they focus on expressing those implicit motives that are most characteristic of them rather than those that occupy a relatively low position in their hierarchy of motives. Additionally, once they have identified the relevant motives, inhibition or blocking of them can lead to psychopathology. Traits, goals, and explicit motives are the variables that have been most investigated as encouraging or inhibiting relevant motive expression.

We also review how integrating findings in clinical psychology with those of implicit motives can contribute to an understanding of psychotherapy.

No matter what kind of psychotherapy is investigated, the therapeutic relationship carries a great deal of the variance in treatment outcome (Weinberger, 1995; Weinberger & Rasco, 2007). Researchers are not quite sure why. We discuss an implicit motive we term "oneness motivation" that may underlie some of the effectiveness of the therapeutic relationship.

How Implicit Motives Affect Well-Being and Psychopathology

Defining Implicit Motives as They May Relate to Psychopathology

McClelland, Koestner, and Weinberger (1989) and Weinberger and McClelland (1990) have offered a theoretical account of the place of implicit motives in human functioning. First, they argue, there are a limited number of implicit motives. These are usually identified as achievement, power, and various forms of affiliative motives (Smith, 1992; Weinberger, Cotler, & Fishman, this volume). Next, implicit motives are biologically based. That is, they exist in all of us to varying degrees and are part of what it means to be a human being. Third, we have an inherent need to express them. Doing so feels pleasurable; frustration of these needs is experienced as unpleasurable. Fourth, although all of us have all of these motives and need to express them, there are individual differences in their strength and therefore their pull to be expressed. That means that we spend more time and energy attending to and trying to express motives that are stronger in us than we do trying to express those having relatively less strength. Satisfying our stronger motives results in more pleasure than satisfying relatively weak motives. Similarly, frustration of strong motives results in more unpleasure than frustrating relatively weak motives. Next, implicit motives are unconscious. That is, we are generally not able to report what our implicit motives are or how strong they are. As a result, they cannot be measured through self-report. Instead, they must be measured indirectly. This is usually accomplished through stories people tell to standardized cards (McClelland, 1985) or through publicly available writings or verbalizations (Winter, 1992). A consequence of implicit motives not being conscious is that we may not be aware of one of the main internal factors that affects our behavior (i.e., drives us). This can lead to all sorts of problems and frustrations. Finally, implicit (unconscious) motives are qualitatively different from reportable (conscious or self-attributed) motives. In support of this qualitative difference, the correlation between implicit motives and self-reported motives, bearing the same names and described similarly, is essentially zero. Further, their behavioral correlates are different. Implicit motives predict spontaneous and long-term behaviors whereas explicit motives predict short-term behaviors related to a person's consciously held self-image (McClelland et al, 1989; Weinberger & McClelland, 1990).

Expressing Implicit Motives Is Satisfying

Brunstein, Schultheiss, and Grassman (1998) tested the hypothesis that feelings denoting positive well-being (e.g., happiness) should follow activities that satisfy a person's implicit motives. Specifically, they predicted that pleasurable feelings would follow successful advancement of a goal that resulted in gratification of an implicit motive. Conversely, unpleasurable feelings were predicted to follow failure to advance such goals. Further, these feelings would only result if the goal advanced or frustrated an implicit motive that was highly characteristic of the person. Thus, they tested three aspects of the model described above: that satisfaction of implicit motives is satisfying; that frustration of implicit motives is unpleasurable; and that these outcomes are especially likely if the motive is strong in the person.

In order to test their hypotheses, Brunstein et al. conducted two experiments. In the first, they divided their participants into those whose motivations were primarily agentic (power and achievement) and those whose motivations were primarily communal (affiliative/intimacy). They then had the participants rate their moods twice a day for 6 days as their measure of well-being. Agentically motivated individuals reported more positive mood when they made progress toward agentic goals but showed no mood effects when progressing toward the attainment of communal goals. The reverse was true for those characterized by primarily communal motives. That is, they showed more positive mood when progressing toward communal goals but no effects when agentic goals were being met.

Study 2 measured implicit motives in students beginning a semester of college who were asked to list two agentic and two communal goals. Well-being at the end of the semester was predicted by the interaction of implicit motives and the attainment of the listed goals. Motive congruent goals (agentic motive/agentic goal; communal motive/communal goal) predicted reported well-being when those goals proved attainable. When they did not, well-being decreased. When participants pursued goals that were not congruent with their dominant motive (agentic motive/communal goal; communal motive/agentic goal), feelings of well-being were not increased. In fact, when participants were strongly committed to motive-incongruent goals, their sense of well-being diminished.

This study therefore supported all three parts of the model it tested. It also indicated that pursuit of goals not related to predominant motives can result in unpleasure. Presumably, this is because it prevents satisfaction of relevant implicit motives. It may also just be that such pursuits are inherently unsatisfying and result in disappointment. We return to this when we discuss discrepancies between implicit and explicit motives. This adds another aspect to the model. Nondominant implicit motives also have an effect on well-being. Specifically, pursuing goals related to them reduces the subjective sense of well-being.

Schultheiss, Jones, Davis, and Kley (2008) obtained findings similar to those of Brunstein et al. (1998). Their measures of well-being were scores on a depression measure (depressive symptomatology). They therefore came a bit closer than Brunstein et al. (1998) to studying psychopathology. In parallel to Brunstein et al., Schultheiss et al. reported that progress in attaining motive-congruent goals resulted in low depression scores whereas lack of progress toward congruent goals resulted in relatively high depression scores. Goal progress had no meaningful effects when implicit motives were weak. Thus, the model's predictions, that progress in expressing motive-congruent goals or the lack thereof would be related to well-being, were replicated. The Brunstein et al. finding that pursuit of motive-incongruent goals results in lower well-being was not replicated. This discrepancy therefore needs further study.

Traits Mediate Motive Effects

Winter, John, Stewart, Klohnen, and Duncan (1998) also tested whether easy expression of implicit motives results in well-being whereas difficulty in such expression reduces well-being. They found a theoretically important interaction between traits and implicit motives. In their model, motives are rather flexible drives with no fixed object of expression. They are general wishes or desires seeking expression however they can. Other psychological variables then channel or fail to channel these motives into satisfying arenas for expression. This is similar to Freud (1915a) and Hull's (1943) classic models of drives. Brunstein et al. and Schultheiss et al. as well as Weinberger and McClelland (1990) have made similar theoretical points. But Winter et al. went further and posited that traits, more specifically introversion and extroversion, would channel implicit motives. Their data supported this hypothesis. They hypothesized that extroversion would facilitate motive expression and therefore well-being whereas introversion would inhibit motive expression and therefore negatively affect well-being. They examined life outcomes for implicit affiliation and power motivation in interaction with introversion and extroversion to test this hypothesis.

Winter et al. (1998) examined a sample of women studied at age 21 and then followed up at age 48 (the Mills sample of 1958 and 1960—Helson & Wink, 1992). They found, as predicted, that women high in affiliation and extroversion had more successful interpersonal relationships; women high in affiliation and introversion, on the other hand, had more unsuccessful interpersonal relationships. Moreover, these latter women experienced a great deal of interpersonal stress. Winter et al. obtained parallel results for power. Extroverted individuals high in implicit power motivation had more successful, high-impact careers than those who were high in implicit power but were introverted.

Winter et al. (1998) concluded that extroversion facilitated relatively free and easy implicit motive expression. Introversion, on the other hand, led to difficulties in expressing motives and therefore resulted in problematic goal attainment. This supports the idea that implicit motive expression is satisfying and leads to well-being whereas difficulty in satisfying implicit motives negatively affects well-being. In our view, the picture is not necessarily this simple, however. We are not sure that extroversion is invariably a positive force in implicit motive satisfaction. That extroversion had this effect makes sense for the motives Winter et al. studied. Power requires that a person impact on another. This would be difficult for an introvert to do. Extroverts would have a leg up because they naturally seek to interact and communicate with others. It would be easier for them to enjoy the steps one must take to express implicit power motivation. A similar argument can be made for affiliation. Extroversion would be an advantage to someone looking to make interpersonal contact. An introvert would have to overcome a natural hesitancy to do so. His or her motive would therefore be harder to satisfy and would be accompanied by discomfort even when satisfied (approaching another and starting a conversation; going to a social event, etc.). But does this hold for all motives? Achievement motivation is characterized by competition with oneself. Unlike power and affiliation, another person is not necessary to satisfy this motive. It might even be problematic to involve another in what is essentially an intrapersonal event. We would therefore predict that for achievement, introversion might supply an advantage over extroversion. The person would experience no pull to find others and interact with them. This would make the often solitary activity of achievement easier to do. An extrovert would be distracted by his or her need to be around others and to assert him or herself. This detracts from achievement-type activities like reading maps, doing crossword puzzles, writing computer programs, and so forth. Alternatively, a high-achievement extrovert could seek out an activity that involved social approval so that the above prediction would not necessarily be borne out. This is an empirical question that can be answered by attempting to replicate the Winter et al. findings with people characterized by high achievement motivation. The results would have important clinical implications, which we will address below. But whether our speculations are accurate or not, the idea that satisfaction of an implicit motive is related to well-being, whereas frustration of it is not, has been supported by this study, too.

The Interaction of Implicit and Explicit Motives

We said earlier in this paper that implicit and explicit motives are roughly orthogonal. That is, knowing one provides little to no ability to predict the other. Further, they seem to be two completely independent psychological entities. This suggests that they would evidence few interactive effects. This turns out not to be the case, however. Weinberger and McClelland (1990) hypothesized that people are better off when their explicit and implicit motives are of similar strength. They would have problems when they were dissimilar. Weinberger and McClelland were basically offering a conflict model. That is, there would be problems when conscious and unconscious motives were in conflict with one another. That would be because a person would consciously want something while unconsciously not being motivated to work at it.

Alternatively, the person might unconsciously desire something and find him/herself spontaneously working toward something that he or she consciously does not value or even devalues. An example may make this clearer. A person may consciously want to rise within the corporation for which he works. He would have high explicit power motivation. If he also had high implicit power motivation, there would be no problem. He would find himself naturally and spontaneously working to create the kinds of impacts that lead to increased status and rank. But if he had low implicit power motivation, he would not spontaneously work at increasing his rank. He would only do so when the relationship of a task to his conscious desire was clear. There would, therefore, be a lot of missed opportunities. He would also not enjoy the kinds of things that increase power. We would have a frustrated and unhappy corporate executive. Let us take the opposite kind of conflict. Now the person has no conscious wish to rise in the ranks. But unconsciously she enjoys doing things that result in exactly that. Now we have a person who does things that lead to consciously unwanted outcomes. Again, an unhappy person.

These hypotheses are no longer simply speculation. There are data that bear on them. Kehr (2004; Kehr & von Rosenstiel, 2006) has reported findings that indirectly support this hypothesis. He found that implicit/explicit discrepancies can negatively impact performance in an Industrial/Organizational setting. He did not employ the PSE, however, so his work would have to be replicated with the PSE to directly support our hypothesis. More direct support has been provided by Hofer and Chasiotis (2003), who reported that affiliative/initimacy motive congruence and incongruence were related in the expected ways to subjective well-being and life satisfaction. Brunstein et al. (1998) found the same for communion and agency. And Thrash and Elliot (2002) found a relation between concordance in achievement motivation and self-determination. Thus, the relation hypothesized by Weinberger and McClelland (1990) seems to hold for the major implicit motives.

Kuhl (2000) offered a model to explain how the explicit and implicit systems come to be concordant or discrepant. This model is contained in his personality systems interaction (PSI) theory. According to PSI, the implicit and explicit motivational systems are congruent when they have free and easy access to one another, that is, when they can exchange information. This kind of exchange takes place without much difficulty unless the person is having problems regulating affect, especially negative affect (like stress). Stress interferes with affect regulation. When this happens, the exchange of information does not take place, and the two motive systems become incongruent. This is a dynamic model closely akin to Freud's (1915b, 1923) conflict model of unconscious and conscious processing. In Freud's model, what is desired by the unconscious system or id causes anxiety because is it at odds with reality or with society. It must therefore be rejected. This is accomplished through defenses that prevent that content from reaching consciousness. The result is a discrepancy between what is consciously known and unconsciously desired. This discrepancy even-tuates in psychological suffering. The solution is to make the unconscious conscious. That is, open the lines of communication or bring the unconscious content under the province of the conscious system. Kuhl's model does not see stress as an inherent conflict between a rapacious unconscious system and reality-based (ego) and socially valued (superego) systems. According to Kuhl, the stress can be environmental or internal. The result is the same, however. The lack of communication between the two systems results in a discrepancy between them, which, in turn, negatively impacts emotional well-being. The "cure" is similar as well. Open the lines of communication through lessening of stress and improving affect-regulatory coping mechanisms. Both the PSI and Freud models add to the Weinberger and McClelland model by specifying how and why discrepancies come to be and how and why they lead to negative psychological consequences. They also offer ways of addressing the problem.

The Freud model has generally not been experimentally tested. The Kuhl model has. In three experiments, Baumann, Kaschel, and Kuhl (2005) showed that the inability to generate positive affect and to reduce negative affect resulted in decreases in subjective well-being. This relationship increased as stress levels increased. In one of these experiments, symptomatology increased as well. Furthermore, the effect was carried by increases in motive discrepancy. That is, the personality characteristic of difficulty with affect regulation inter-acted with stress to increase motive incongruence. This incongruence, in turn, directly affected subjective well-being and symptomatology. Motive congru-ence was related to the ability to generate positive affect as well as the ability to reduce negative affect (strong affect-regulation coping mechanisms). Level of stress had no direct effect on this relationship. Thus, the model received empirical support. More work is required to understand this phenomenon more completely, but this is a promising beginning.

To summarize the findings relating to subjective well-being and psycho-pathology: Expressing implicit motives is healthy but only if the motive is central to the person. Frustrating implicit motives results in negative effects; again, this is especially so if the motive is central to the person. Motive expression is not something that takes place easily. Certain personality traits can aid in such expression. Extroversion seems to help in the healthy expression of power and affiliative motivation. Finally, the person is better off if the implicit and explicit motive systems are coordinate. Discrepancies between the systems result in reduced well-being. Stress in combination with poor affect regulation can increase such discrepancies. All of this work has just begun and much more is needed, but the work thus far is promising.

We turn now to the second part of this paper, the relationship of implicit motivation to the effectiveness of the therapeutic relationship.

The Oneness Motive (OM), the Therapeutic Relationship, and Therapeutic Success

There is now general agreement that psychotherapy is effective (Weinberger & Rasco, 2007). This agreement breaks down when the question of how and why psychotherapy works is raised. There are many brand name therapies, all claiming that they provide the answers to these questions. Often, these answers and the techniques they lead to contradict one another. Despite the apparent and real differences between the different major schools of psy-chotherapy, all seem to work and to be about equally effective. Meta-analyses beginning with the classic work of Smith, Glass, and Miller (1980) almost routinely find no differences between apparently diverse treatments. Thus, Lipsey & Wilson (1993), Wampold et al. (1997) and Luborsky et al. (2002) all have replicated the findings of Smith et al. When meta-analyses and indivi-dual studies do not seem to support this equivalency effect, Luborsky et al. (1999) have shown that allegiance effects may be responsible. That is, the treatment identified with the researchers invariably "won." Not everyone has accepted the above understanding of the literature (e.g., Chambless, 2002; DeRubeis, Brotman, & Gibbons, 2005), but no one has been able to refute it (cf. Weinberger & Rasco, 2007).

One way of understanding these findings has been termed "the common factors approach." (See Arkowitz, 1992; Goldfried, 1982; Kleinke, 1994; and Weinberger, 1993, for a history of this approach. See Weinberger, 1995, and Weinberger & Rasco, 2007, for efforts to apply it.) This approach basically states that all therapies work because of what they all have in common, rather than because of what differentiates them from one another. That is, different kinds of psychotherapy do not necessarily achieve their effects through the principles they espouse. Instead, their effectiveness is due to, often unacknowledged, factors that they share, (i.e., common factors).

The Therapeutic Relationship

The therapeutic relationship is, by far, the most written about common factor. Wolfe and Goldfried (1988) termed it "the quintessential integrative psychotherapeutic factor." Empirical data strongly support the efficacy of the therapeutic relationship. Beutler (1989) and Lambert (1992) reported that the therapeutic alliance accounted for more of the variance in psychotherapeutic outcome than did technical interventions. Gaston, Marmar, Gallagher, and Thompson (1991) found that the alliance accounted for more than 35% of the variance in outcome after controlling for initial symptom levels and symptom change. Blatt and Zuroff (2005) obtained highly significant effects for the therapeutic relationship when they controlled for contemporaneous clinical improvement. Hovarth and Symonds (1991) conducted a meta-analysis and found a small but reliable effect of the working alliance on therapeutic outcome. Additionally, the effect was similar in size across the various schools of therapy examined (psychodynamic, cognitive, eclectic/mixed) and across a wide variety of diagnoses. A more recent meta-analysis (Martin, Garske, & Davis, 2000) reported the same results. Finally, a task force commissioned by Division 29 (Psychotherapy) of the American Psychological Association concluded that the therapeutic relationship was a critical factor in psychotherapy. They enumerated many studies and a host of data to support this conclusion (Norcross, 2002). These data and more are reviewed in Norcross and Lambert (2006).

Oneness Motivation

We would like to propose am implicit motive as, at least partly, underlying the efficacy of the therapeutic relationship. (See Safran & Muran, 2000, and Hilsenroth, Peters & Ackerman, 2004, for research programs on other aspects of the therapeutic relationship.) The origin of this motive lies in psychoanalytic theory. Some psychoanalytic theorists (e.g., Bergmann, 1971; Limentani, 1956; Mahler, Pine, & Bergman, 1975; Searles, 1979; L. Silverman, Lachmann, & Milich, 1982) argued that people harbor a wish for oneness or merger with what they termed "the good mother of early childhood" (i.e., mother when she was experienced early in life as comforting, protective, and nurturing). They went on to argue that gratifying this wish in psychotherapy (symbolically and unconsciously) is causally relevant to positive outcome.

The relationship of such wishes to infant experience is unsupported at best and doubtful at worst (D. Silverman, 2003, 2005; Lachman & Beebe, 1989; Stern,1985; Siefert & Weinberger, 2006). The existence of such wishes or at least the effects of activating or priming such content in adults is strongly supported, however. Data collected by L. Silverman and his colleagues (L. Silverman et al., 1982; L. Silverman & Weinberger, 1985) have shown that subliminally presenting the message MOMMY AND I ARE ONE led to all sorts of positive effects, including improvements in outcome in educational and psychotherapeutic settings. Meta-analyses by Hardaway (1990) and by Weinberger and Hardaway (1990) demonstrated that these effects were reliable and had respectable effect sizes.

Weinberger (1992; Siegel & Weinberger, 1998) reconceptualized this wish as an implicit motive, termed the "oneness motive" (OM), operative to a greater or lesser degree in all individuals. OM is conceptualized as a need to become part of, at one with, or belong to, a larger whole. People are not normally aware of their OM and its operation. It is therefore an implicit motive like achievement, power, affiliation, and intimacy. It is most clearly (but not exclusively) manifest in interpersonal relationships, including that of psychotherapy. The scoring system was developed, in line with the general logic of other implicit motive systems, by arousing the motive and then looking at stories people told to standardized pictures (the PSE). The manner of arousal was a bit different from that used with the other motives, however. The OM was aroused by subliminally presenting subliminal messages to three groups. One got MOMMY AND I ARE ONE; the other two viewed the control messages PEOPLE ARE WALKING and MOMMY IS GONE. Stories written subsequent to this stimulation yielded systematic and theoretically meaningful differences between the groups. A scoring system, structurally patterned after those capturing other implicit motives (see Smith, 1992), was then constructed (Weinberger, Stefanou, Scroppo, & Siegel, 1996). In order to validate this system, a second study was run. In this second study, individuals were subliminally presented with either MOMMY AND I ARE ONE or PEOPLE ARE WALKING. They then wrote stories to a set of standardized pictures. People trained in the new OM scoring system scored these stories blindly. The MOMMY AND I ARE ONE group had significantly higher OM scores than did the PEOPLE ARE WALKING group. Thus, the system developed in the first study was able to differentiate the two groups in the second study and was therefore validated. Weinberger therefore concluded that OM was a viable motive that now needed to be tested for reliability and validity.

The Oneness Motive Scoring System (Weinberger et al. 1996) defines oneness (as stated above) as a need to become part of, at one with, or belong to, a larger whole. In order to score for oneness, a story must have one or more of the following themes:

1. Emotionally close interpersonal relationship: an ongoing positive and emotionally close interpersonal relationship (e.g., this couple feel really close to one another).

2. Oneness attainment: A character or force that, while retaining its own bounded identity, is explicitly described as joining with another person or entity to form a unity or larger whole (e.g., they are a team and work as one).
3. Merger or Flow Experience: a nonaversive softening of boundaries between a character and the outside world (e.g., the music flowed through his fingers).

If any of the above three themes is present in a story, it has basic oneness imagery. A point is awarded for each theme present in a story. If a story has none of these themes, it gets no points and no further scoring is done. If a story does have one or more of these themes, further subcategories are scored. These are: (a) wish—a stated hope, need, desire, or wish related to oneness imagery; (b) focus—strong concentration on oneness imagery; (c) block—explicit concern about obstacles to the fulfillment of oneness; (d) fulfillment – an experience of a pleasurable, homeostatic end state of inner peace or satisfaction, or of being recharged or refueled; (e) thema—the story qualifies for more than a single oneness theme, or the entire story concerns a oneness experience or is saturated with oneness imagery (oneness is the leitmotif of the story). (See Weinberger et al., 1996, for more detail.) Each category and each subcategory can be awarded a single point or no points. That means that scores of stories can range from 0 to 8.

Data Supportive of OM

Data attesting to the reliability of the OM system are reported in Siegel and Weinberger (1998). There is more than adequate interrater and test–retest reliability. The former ranges from .81 to .95 whereas the latter has been measured at .80 for people tested one week apart. We will focus the rest of this chapter on the validity of the system as it related to psychotherapeutic interventions in an effort to support our argument that OM may underlie some of the effectiveness of the therapeutic relationship. To this end, we therefore describe two studies relating to the relationship of OM to psychotherapeutic effectiveness. The first relates to a meditation treatment designed to help people adjust to and cope with physically based disorders. The second relates to intensive inpatient treatment of chronic mental illness.

Siegel and Weinberger (1998) described a study wherein participants were part of a stress reduction and relaxation program housed in a major hospital in Massachusetts. Participants were referred by their physicians to learn to better cope with their medical conditions. All participants suffered from diseases and conditions that were either life threatening (e.g., cancer, heart disease, AIDS) or difficult to treat and chronically painful (e.g., chronic headaches, digestive problems, arthritis). Thus, they had to learn to "live with it." Treatment lasted 8 weeks and involved learning and practicing mindfulness meditation techniques (Kabat-Zinn, 2005). Meetings were held weekly for 2 hours, with a group leader. There were homework assignments and audiotapes to reinforce the practice. There was also a single full day session.

Effects of the treatment were assessed immediately at its completion and at a 2-year follow-up. Measures included the Symptom Check List Revised (SCL 90-R—Derogatis & Melisaratos, 1983), and the Profile of Mood States (POMS). Stories scored for OM were collected before and after the treatment.

First, results indicated that the treatment was effective in its own right. Additionally and more to the point of this chapter, OM scores were related to the outcome measures as predicted. Table 16.1 shows the correlations of OM with outcome measures immediately at the end of treatment. Table 16.2 shows the correlations at the 2-year follow-up.

Table 16.1 shows that OM correlated negatively with most of the subscales of the SCL-90-R. That is, the higher the OM score, the fewer reported symptoms at the end of treatment. Similarly, The higher the OM score, the lower participants' anger and hostility on the POMS. OM was also positively correlated with feelings of being resourceful and loved-friendly on the POMS. Thus, participants' symptoms and moods were related to OM scores in a theoretically sensible fashion. Table 16.2 shows that these relationships remained relatively stable for 2 years. Again, OM was negatively correlated with the subscales of the SCL-90-R. The magnitude of the correlations was similar, although the statistical significance was less, probably due to lesser power at time 2 (a smaller sample size). The POMS results did not replicate completely. Anger-Hostility was still negatively related to OM, but the positive correlations

Table 16.1 Correlations of Oneness Motive (OM) with Outcome in Stress Reduction Program

Variable	Correlation (r)
SCL-90-R (n = 43)	
Somatization	−.31**
Obsessive-Compulsive	−.37**
Interpersonal Sensitivity	−.34**
Depression	−.32**
Anxiety	−.33**
Hostility	−.46***
Phobic Anxiety	*ns*
Paranoid Anxiety	−.46***
Psychoticism	−.33**
General Severity Index	−.38**
POMS (n = 50)	
Anger-Hostility	−.32**
Loved-Friendly	.48***
Resourceful	.29**

Source: From Weinberger & Siegel (1998).
*p < .10; ** p < .05; *** p < .01

Table 16.2   Correlations of Oneness Motive (OM) with Outcome in Stress Reduction Program at 2-Year Follow-Up

Variable	Correlation (r)
SCL-90-R (n = 27)	
Somatization	−.34*
Interpersonal Sensitivity	−.35*
Anxiety	ns
Obsesssive-Compulsive	−.45**
Depression	ns
Hostility	ns
Phobia	−.37*
Paranoia	−.43**
Psychoticism	ns
POMS (n = 26)	
Loved-Friendly	ns
Tense	−.40**
Depressed	ns
Resourceful	ns
Anger-Hostility	−.47**
Fatigue	ns
Confused	ns
Positivity	ns
Negativity	−.39**

Source: Weinberger & Siegel (1998).
*p < .10; ** p < .05; *** p < .01

dropped out. Statistical power may have been an issue here as well, but further research will be necessary to sort this out. Finally, as predicted, OM scores increased over the course of the treatment (t (30) = 2.81, p < .01; d = 1.00). Thus, the sense of being part of something larger than the self increased as a result of the treatment, presumably reflecting a positive change in the therapeutic relationship. A second study (Weinberger, Bonner, & Barra, 1999) examined more traditional psychotherapeutic treatment. These data were collected at an inpatient treatment center. The patients suffered from severe mental illness, largely character disorders. They were treated with intensive psychodynamic psychotherapy for one year and were evaluated with a battery of measures before and after that year of treatment. Among these measures were storytelling tasks (TATs in this case). These stories were scored for OM. The data were not collected with our study in mind, so that the TAT stories and the outcome evaluations were collected completely blind to our hypotheses. We, in turn, were blind as to outcome when we scored the stories for OM. Among the outcome measures collected (described in a bit more detail below) were assessments of behavior and of interpersonal functioning on the ward.

The sample consisted of 64 inpatients (31 males and 33 females), ages 18–29 (mean age 21). As stated above, most were diagnosed with character disorders. Forty (63%) had severe character disorders, including Borderline Personality Disorder. Eighteen (28%) were diagnosed as psychotic, and six (9%) suffered from major depression or were severely neurotic (grab bag of diagnoses on Axis I of the DSM-IV). As stated above, all were assessed at intake and again at the end of one year. Treatment consisted of four times a week psychodynamic psychotherapy.

The ward behavior measures we report on here were the Strauss-Harder Case Record Rating Scale (Strauss & Harder, 1981) and the Fairweather Ward Behavior Rating Scale (Fairweather et al. 1960). The Strauss-Harder scale measures what is termed neurotic and psychotic behavior on the ward. Neurotic behavior is defined as anxiety, depressed mood, and so forth. That is, it essentially assesses unhappy affect exhibited on the ward. Psychotic behavior is defined as hallucinations, hypomanic, or manic behavior, and pathological hygiene or severely unkempt appearance. That is, it assesses bizarre behavior and features. The Fairweather Ward Behavior Rating Scale is a measure of interpersonal communication on the ward. The higher the score, the poorer the communication. Items assess things such as whether or not the patient engages in conversation on the ward, if so, how coherent he or she is, and how often such conversations involve conflict with others. All of these scales are filled out by workers on the ward who had daily contact with the patients.

The data were analyzed via mixed model (both independent and repeated measure) Analyses of Covariance, with initial scores of OM as the covariate. The independent measures were OM (high or low) and time (before and after the year of treatment). The dependent measures were the ward behavior measures described above. Table 16.3 shows the results of the ANCOVA for the neurotic subscale of the Strauss-Harder Case Record Scale.

Table 16.4 shows the results of the ANCOVA for the psychotic subscale of the Strauss-Harder Case Record Scale.

Table 16.3   ANCOVA of Neurotic Subscale of the Strauss-Harder

	Means & SDs	
	Low OM at Posttest	High OM at Posttest
Time 1	−0.14 (0.82)	0.34 (0.88)
Time 2	0.04 (.99)	−0.14 (0.85)
	ANCOVA Table	
Source		F
Time		0.87 (*ns*)
OM post		1.17 (*ns*)
Time × OM post		4.09**

*p < .10; **p < .05

Table 16.4   ANCOVA of Psychotic Subscale of Strauss-Harder

	Means & SDs	
	Low OM at Posttest	High OM at Posttest
Time 1	2.53 (1.67)	2.79 (2.22)
Time 2	3.03 (1.75)	1.94 (1.34)
	ANCOVA Table	
Source		F
Time		0.34 (*ns*)
OM Post		1.29 (*ns*)
Time × OM post		6.16**

*p <.10; **p < .05

Table 16.3 shows the expected interaction between time and OM at the end of treatment. Deconstructing the interaction (Rosenthal & Rosnow, 1998) reveals that high OM was related to low neurotic behavior at the end of the year but not at the beginning whereas low OM was unrelated to neurotic behavior at either time. This supports the idea that when OM increases, psychopathology decreases. One caveat is in order, however. Examination of the means suggests that this effect might have been due to pre-existing differences. The group with high OM at the end of the year started out with higher pathology than did the group with low OM. That is, regression toward the mean may have been operative. Further study is therefore required.

The results depicted by Table 16.4 are more clear-cut. Again, there is a significant interaction between time and OM. As with neurotic behavior, deconstructing the interaction (Rosenthal & Rosnow, 1998) reveals that high OM was related to low psychotic behavior at the end of the year but not at the beginning whereas low OM was unrelated to psychotic behavior at either time. This supports the idea that when OM increases, severe psychopathology decreases. This time, the means clearly support this interpretation of the interaction. Psychotic behavior at time one is virtually identical for both low and high OM participants. At the end of the year, however, psychotic behavior has clearly dropped significantly for those with high OM whereas, if anything, it has increased for those with low OM.

Table 16.5 shows the results of the ANCOVA for the Fairweather Ward Behavior Rating Scale.

The results depicted in Table 16.5 parallel those reported above. There is a significant interaction between time and OM that indicates that problematic interpersonal interactions decrease over the course of the year for those with high OM and do not change for those with low OM. The means clearly support this interpretation of the results. Thus, OM is related to quality of interpersonal interactions of severely disturbed inpatients as they are treated for their problems.

Table 16.5   ANCOVA of Fairweather Rating Scale

	Means & SDs	
	Low OM at Posttest	High OM at Posttest
Time 1	1.33 (0.23)	1.29 (0.30)
Time 2	1.37 (0.27)	1.17 (0.28)
	ANCOVA Table	
Source		F
Time		0.11 (NS)
OM post		0.16 (NS)
Time × OM post		8.19***

*p < .10; **p < .05; ***p < .01

Conclusions

To quickly summarize the results of the two studies reviewed here: OM was related to positive change in two vastly different kinds of interventions. In one case, it was related to coping with chronic medical conditions treated with short-term meditation training. In the second case, it was related to improved functioning in severely disturbed psychiatric inpatients treated with long-term intensive psychodynamic psychotherapy. Thus, it can be argued that OM is relevant to diverse forms of psychotherapeutic treatments.

As we discussed above, the therapeutic relationship is powerfully related to positive change in psychotherapy. The studies just reviewed indicated that an implicit motive (OM) related to the therapeutic relationship by some psycho-analytic theorists was related to improved functioning in two vastly different therapeutic settings and treatments. This supports the idea that the desire to be part of something larger or beyond the self may underlie some of the ameliora-tive power of the therapeutic relationship.

Obviously, this conclusion requires much more support before we can confidently assert that it had been conclusively demonstrated. Future studies will have to provide this support or prove the model wrong. For example, patient and therapist assessments of the therapeutic relationship, as well as outside observer assessments of it should be compared to OM scores. The pattern of relationships among these variables would go a long way toward clarifying the role of oneness in the psychotherapeutic relationship. But, we hope you will agree that there has been a beginning.

References

Arkowitz, H. (1992). Integrative theories of therapy. In D. K. Freedheim (Ed.), *History of psychotherapy: A century of change* (pp. 261–303). Washington, DC: American Psychological Association.

Baumann, N., Kaschel, R., & Kuhl, J. (2005). Striving for unwanted goals: Stress-dependent discrepancies between explicit and implicit achievement motives reduce subjective well-beiung and increase psychosomatic symptoms. *Journal of Personality and Social Psychology, 89,* 781–799.

Bergmann, M. S. (1971). On the capacity to love. In J. B. McDevitt & C. S. Settlage (Eds.), *Separation-individuation: Essays in honor of Margaret S Mahler* (pp. 15–40). New York: International Universities Press.

Beutler, L. E. (1989). Differential treatment selection: The role of diagnosis in psychotherapy. *Psychotherapy, 26,* 271–281.

Blatt, S. J., & Zuroff, D. C. (2005). Empirical evaluation of the assumptions in identifying evidence based treatments in mental health. *Clinical Psychology Review, 25,* 459–486.

Brunstein, J. C., Schultheiss, O. C., & Grassmann, R. (1998). Personal goals and emotional well-being: The moderating role of motive dispositions. *Journal of Personality and Social Psychology, 75,* 494–508.

Chambless, D. L. (2002). Beware the dodo bird: The dangers of overgeneralization. *Clinical Psychology: Science and Practice, 9,* 13–16.

Derogatis, L. R., & Melisaratos, N. (1983). The brief symptom inventory: An introductory report. *Psychological Medicine, 13,* 595–605.

DeRuubeis, R. J., Brotman, M. A., & Gibbons, C. J. (2005). A conceptual and methodological analysis of the nonspecifics argument. *Clinical Psychology: Science and Practice, 12,* 174–183.

Fairweather, T., Fairweather, G. W., Simon, R., Gebhard, M. E., Weingarten, E., Holland, J. L., et al. (1960). Relative effectiveness of psychotherapeutic programs: A multicriteria comparison of four programs for three different patient groups. *Psychological Monographs, 74* (5, Whole No. 492).

Freud, S. (1915a/1958). Instincts and their vicissitudes. In J. Strachey (Ed.), *The standard edition* (Vol. 14, pp. 111–140). London: Hogarth Press. (Original work published 1915).

Freud, S. (1915b/1958). The unconscious. In J. Strachey (Ed.), *The standard edition* (Vol. 14, pp. 166–215). London: Hogarth Press. (Original work published 1915).

Freud, S. (1923, 1961). The ego and the id. In J. Strachey (Ed.), *The standard edition* (Vol. 19, pp. 3–69). London: Hogarth Press. (Original work published 1923).

Gaston, L., Marmar, C. R., Gallagher, D., & Thompson, L. W. (1991). Alliance prediction of outcome beyond in-treatment symptomatic change as psychotherapy processes. *Psychotherapy Research, 1,* 104–113.

Goldfried, M. R. (Ed.). (1982). *Converging themes in psychotherapy.* New York: Springer.

Hardaway, R. (1990). Subliminal symbiotic fantasies: Facts and artifacts. *Psychological Bulletin, 107,* 177–195.

Hilsenroth, M., Peters, E., & Ackerman, S., (2004). The development of therapeutic alliance during psychological assessment: Patient and therapist perspectives across treatment. *Journal of Personality Assessment, 83,* 332–344.

Helson, R., & Wink, P. (1992). Personality change in women from the early 40s to the early 50s. *Psychology and Aging, 7,* 46–55.

Hofer, J., & Chasiotis, A. (2003). Congruence of life goals and implicit motives as predictors of life satisfaction: Cross cultural implications of a study of Zambian male adolescents. *Motivation and Emotion, 27,* 251–272.

Hovarth, A. O., & Symonds, B. D. (1991). Relation between working alliance and outcome in psychotherapy: A meta-analysis. *Journal of Counseling Psychology, 38,* 139–149.

Hull, C. L. (1943). *Principles of behavior.* New York: Appleton-Century-Crofts.

Kabat-Zinn, J. (2005). *Full catastrophe living: Wisdom of your body and mind to face stress, pain, and illness: Fifteenth Anniversary Edition.* New York: Bantam.

Kehr, H. M. (2004). Implicit/explicit motive discrepancies and volitional depletion among managers. *Personality and Social Psychology Bulletin, 30,* 315–327.

Kehr, H. M., & von Rosenstiel, L. (2006). Self-management training (SMT): Theoretical and empirical foundations for the development of a metamotivational and metavolitional intervention program. In F. Dieter, M. Heinz, & L. Rosenstiel (Eds.), *Knowledge and action* (pp. 103–141). Ashland, OH: Hogrefe & Huber.

Kleinke, C. L. (1994). *Common principles of psychotherapy.* Pacific Grove, CA: Brooks/Cole.

Kuhl, J. (2000). A functional design approach to motivation and volition: The dynamics of personality systems interactions. In M. Boekaerts, P. R. Pintrich, & M. Zeidner (Eds.), *Self-regulation: Directions and challenges for future research* (pp. 111–169). New York: Academic Press.

Lachmann, F. M., & Beebe, B. (1989). Oneness fantasies revisited. *Psychoanalytic Psychology, 6,* 137–149.

Lambert, M. J. (1992). Implications of outcome research for psychotherapy integration. In J. C. Norcross & M. R. Goldstein (Eds.), *Handbook of psychotherapy integration.* New York: Basic Books.

Limentani, D. (1956). Symbiotic identification in schizophrenia. *Psychiatry, 19,* 231–236.

Lipsey, M., & Wilson, D. (1993). The efficacy of psychological, educational, and behavioral treatment: Confirmation from meta-analysis. *American Psychologist, 48,* 1181–1209.

Luborsky, L., Diguer, L., Seligman, D. A., Rosenthal, R., Johnson, S., Halperin, G., Bishop, M., & Schweizer, R. (1999). The researcher's own therapeutic allegiances: A "wild card" in the comparisons of treatment efficacy. *Clinical Psychology: Science and Practice, 6,* 95–132.

Luborsky, L., Rosenthal, R., Diguer, L., Andrusyna, T. P., Berman, J. S., Levitt, J. T., Seligman, D. A., & Krause, E. D. (2002). The dodo verdict is alive and well—mostly. *Clinical Psychology: Science and Practice, 9,* 2–12.

Mahler, M. S., Pine, F., & Bergman, A. (1975). *The psychological birth of the human infant. Symbiosis and individuation.* London: Hutchinson.

Martin, D. J., Garske, J. P., & Davis, M. K. (2000). Relation of the therapeutic alliance with outcome and other variables: A meta-analytic review. *Journal of Consulting and Clinical Psychology, 68,* 438–450.

McClelland, D. C. (1985). *Human motivation.* Glenview, IL: Scott Foresman.

McClelland, D. C., Koestner, R., & Weinberger, J. (1989). How do self-attributed motives differ? *Psychological Review, 96*(4), 690–702.

Norcross, J. C. (Ed.). (2002). *Psychotherapy relationships that work.* New York: Oxford University Press.

Norcross, J. C., & Lambert, M. J. (2006). The therapy relationship. In J. C. Norcross, L. E. Beutler, & R. F. Levant (Eds.), *Evidence-based practices in mental health* (pp. 208–218). Washington, DC: American Psychological Association.

Rosenthal, R., & Rosnow, R. L. (1998). *Essentials of behavioral research: Methods and data analysis* (3rd ed.). New York: McGraw-Hill.

Safran, J. D., & Muran, J. C. (2000). *Negotiating the therapeutic alliance: A relational treatment guide.* New York: Guilford Press.

Schultheiss, O. C., Jones, N. M., Davis, A. Q., & Kley, C. (2008). The role of implicit motivation in hot and cold goal pursuit: Effects on goal progress, goal rumination, and emotional well-being. *Journal of Research in Personality, 42,* 971–987.

Searles, H. F. (1979). Concerning the development of an identity. In H. F. Searles (Ed.), *Countertransference and related subjects* (pp. 45–70). Madison, CT: International Universities Press.

Siegel, P., & Weinberger, J. (1998). Capturing the "mommy and I are one" merger fantasy: The oneness motive. In J. M. Masling, & R. F. Bornstein (Eds.) *Empirical perspectives on the psychoanalytic unconscious.* (pp. 71–97). Washington, DC: American Psychological Association.

Siefert, C. J., & Weinberger, J. (2006). Psychoanalytic research: Progress and process (unconscious wishes for oneness: Observations from the couch becomes research in a lab). *Psychologist-Psychoanalyst, 26,* 28–31.

Silverman, D. (2003). Mommy nearest: Revisiting the idea of infantile symbiosis and its implications for females. *Psychoanalytic Psychology, 20,* 261–270.

Silverman, D. (2005). Early developmental issues reconsidered: Commentary on Pine's ideals on symbiosis. *Journal of the American Psychoanalytic Association, 53,* 239–251.

Silverman, L. H., Lachman, F. M., & Milich, R. H. (1982). *The search for oneness.* New York: International University Press.

Silverman, L. H., & Weinberger, J. (1985). Mommy and I are one: Implications for psychotherapy. *American Psychologist, 40,* 1296–1308.

Smith, C. E. (1992). *Motivation and personality: Handbook of thematic content analysis.* New York: Cambridge University Press.

Smith, M. L., Glass, G. V., & Miller, F. I. (1980). *The benefits of psychotherapy.* Baltimore, MD: Johns Hopkins University Press.

Stern, D. N. (1985). *The interpersonal world of the infant.* New York: Basic Books.

Strauss, J. S., & Harder, D. W. (1981). The Case Record Rating Scale: A method for rating symptoms and social function data from case records. *Psychiatric Research, 4,* 333–345.

Thrash, T. M., & Elliot, A. J. (2002). Implicit and self-attributed achievement motives: Concordance and predictive validity. *Journal of Personality, 70,* 729–755.

Wampold, B. E., Mondin, G. W., Moody, M., Stich, F., Benson, K., & Ahn, H. (1997). A meta-analysis of outcome studies comparing bona fide psychotherapies: Empirically, "all must have prizes." *Psychological Bulletin, 122,* 203–215.

Weinberger, J. (1992). Demystifying subliminal psychodynamic activation. In R. Bornstein & T. Pittman (Eds.), *Perception without awareness* (pp. 186–203). New York: Guilford.

Weinberger, J. (1993). Common factors in psychotherapy. In J. Gold & G. Stricker (Eds.), *Handbook of psychotherapy integration* (pp. 43–56). New York: Plenum.

Weinberger, J. (1995). Common factors aren't so common: The common factors dilemma. *Clinical Psychology: Science and Practice, 2,* 45–69.

Weinberger, J., Bonner, E., & Barra, M. (1999, August). Reliability and validity of the oneness motive. Paper delivered at American Psychological Association, Boston, MA.

Weinberger, J., & Hardaway, R. (1990). Separating science from myth in subliminal psychodynamic activation. *Clinical Psychology Review, 10,* 727–756.

Weinberger, J., & McClelland, D. C. (1990). Cognitive versus traditional motivational models: Irreconcilable or complementary? In R. M. Sorrentino & E. T. Higgins. (Eds.), *Handbook of motivation and cognition: Foundations of social behavior* (Vol. 2, pp. 562–597). New York: Guilford Press.

Weinberger, J., & Rasco, C. (2007). Empirically supported common factors. In S. G. Hoffman & J. Weinberger (Eds.), *The art and science of psychotherapy* (pp. 103–129). New York: Routledge.

Weinberger, J., Stefanou, S., Scroppo, J., & Siegel, P. (1996). *The oneness motive scoring system.* Unpublished manuscript, Adelphi University, Garden City, NY.

Winter, D. G. (1992). Content analysis of archival data, personal documents, and everyday verbal productions. In C. P. Smith (Ed.), *Motivation and personality: Handbook of thematic content analysis* (pp. 110–125). New York: Cambridge University Press.

Winter, D. G., John, O. P., Stewart, A. J., Klohnen, E. C., & Duncan, L. E. (1998). Traits and motives: Toward an integration of two traditions in personality research. *Psychological Review, 105,* 230–250.

Wolfe, B. E., & Goldfried, M. R. (1988). Research on psychotherapy integration: Recommendations and conclusions from NIMH workshop. *Journal of Consulting and Clinical Psychology, 56,* 448–451.

Chapter 17

Competencies as a Behavioral Manifestation of Implicit Motives

RICHARD E. BOYATZIS
Case Western Reserve University, Cleveland, OH, USA

STEPHEN P. KELNER, JR.
Egon Zehnder International Inc., Boston, MA, USA

The drive for effectiveness in organizations fuels the quest for understanding the talent and capability of the people that create or determine effectiveness. Of the many ways to address this need, competency research and applications arrived in 1973 with David McClelland's landmark article (1973). It built upon earlier work on skills, abilities, and cognitive intelligence (Campbell, Dunnette, Lawler, & Weick, 1970; McClelland, Baldwin, Bronfenbrenner, & Strodbeck, 1958) and preceded the work on emotional and social intelligence (Boyatzis, 2008, in press; Goleman, 1998, 2006; Salovey & Mayer, 1990). Emotional, social, and cognitive intelligence competencies account for a substantial and important amount of the variance in predicting or understanding performance in competency studies (Boyatzis, 2008).

Competencies and Performance

The concept of competency-based human resources has gone from a new technique to a common practice in the 36 years since David McClelland (1973) first proposed them as a critical differentiator of performance in publication. Today, almost every organization with more than 300 people uses some form of competency-based human resource management. Major consulting companies, such as The Hay Group, Development Dimensions International, and Personnel Decisions Incorporated, and thousands of small consulting firms and independent consultants have become worldwide practitioners of competency assessment and development. Competency research has emanated from universities, in particular Harvard and later Boston University (with David McClelland), Columbia (with Warner Burke), University of Minnesota (with Marv Dunnette), Henley Management College (with Victor Dulewicz), and Case Western Reserve (with Richard Boyatzis, David Kolb, Don Wolfe, Diana Bilimoria, and Melvin Smith). Even with these university sources of research, for the most part, the academic and applied research literature has trailed application. This has resulted in continued skepticism on the part of many academics and some professionals, and less guidance to practitioners from ongoing research than is helpful. Some of this is due to the observation that many of the competency validation studies have been done by consultants who have little patience for the laborious process of documenting and getting the results published even though the validation studies were done with great rigor.

What Is a Competency?

A competency is defined as a capability or ability that differentiates performance in a specific role, job, organization, or culture (Boyatzis, 1982, 2008; McClelland, 1973, 1985). Competencies are identified through a number of related but different sets of behavior organized around an underlying construct or implicit motive, which we call the "intent." The behaviors are alternate manifestations of the intent (i.e., implicit drive), as appropriate in various situations or times.

For example, listening to someone and asking him or her questions are several behaviors. A person can demonstrate these behaviors for multiple reasons or to various intended ends. A person can ask questions and listen to someone to ingratiate him or herself or to appear interested, thereby gaining standing in the other person's view. Or a person can ask questions and listen to someone because he or she is interested in understanding this other person, his or her priorities, or thoughts in a situation. The latter we would call a demonstration of *empathy*. The underlying intent is to understand the person. By contrast, the former underlying reason of gaining status demonstrates elements of what we may call *influence*. Similarly, the underlying intent of a more subtle competency like emotional self-awareness is self-insight and self-understanding.

This construction of competencies as requiring both action (i.e., a set of alternate behaviors) and intent called for measurement methods that allowed for assessment of both the presence of the behavior and inference of the intent.

They were documented from behavioral work samples, videotapes of simulations, or direct observation.

By the most literal use of the definition above, of course an implicit motive is itself a competency, in that it can be a characteristic that is "causally related to effective and/or superior performance in a job" (Boyatzis, 1982), which in practice can also be related to performance in a specific role, job, organization, or culture. For example, power motive has been shown consistently to correlate with success in management roles (McClelland & Burnham, 1972; Jacobs & McClelland, 1994). In practice, however, implicit motivation is normally the intent, and a competency requires a more limited and closely related set of behaviors than is possible to the broad-based motive.

To identify, define, and clarify each competency, an inductive method was used. Work performance or effectiveness criteria were developed for any job studies. A sample of outstanding or superior performers was identified. Another sample of "average" or "poor" performers was also identified from the remaining population depending on the objectives of the study. The criterion sampling was crucial for this inductive method to work. While work output data was best, like sales, profits, waste reduction, or new products launched, often jobs need something else.

For many management and staff jobs, nominations were developed to add to any output measures available. Nominations were collected from multiple perspectives: from bosses (i.e., people in jobs one or two levels above the target job being studied); from peers, which included the people who might be in the eventual sample; and subordinates. Nominations have been shown to be better predictors of performance than ratings (Lewin & Zwany, 1976) or performance appraisal results (Luthans et al., 1988). Typically, three or more sources of effectiveness are collected to obtain a consensual determination of distinctly effective people. The nomination forms are quite simple. At the top of a page is a statement like, "List the names of any Marketing Manager whom you see as outstanding in their performance. If you believe no one is outstanding, then leave the sheet blank, but please return it in the self-addressed stamped envelope." During the era of paper (pre-email and Internet data collection), the forms were color coded to indicate the category of judge while retaining confidentiality and anonymity.

In most competency studies, the sample of "outstanding" or "superior" performers is selected as those who are identified by multiple people from each of multiple sources of nominations and output data and/or morale climate scores (Boyatzis, 1982, 2008; Spencer & Spencer, 1993). They are typically the top 5%–7% of the population. For an extreme case design, the contrasting sample of "average" performers is a random sample selected from all of those job incumbents who have received no nominations from any source and are on the bottom 20% of any output measure or climate morale scores. This means that they did not even nominate themselves on the peer forms. This sample was often about 50% of the population. The remaining incumbents often had some nominations from some sources but not others and were not included in the extreme case studies. In other competency validation studies, the output and/or nomination criteria were collected and analyzed against competency data for everyone by using continuous statistics. This became easier once 360° informant-based surveys were used rather than the Behavioral Event Interview, but to develop the proper items for a rating survey, a direct assessment of real-life behavior is important, especially when identifying highly job-specific behavior.

To collect the behavioral data, a modification of the critical incident interview (Flanagan, 1954) was adapted using the inquiry sequence from the Picture Story Exercise (PSE) (Smith, McClelland, Atkinson, & Veroff, 1992) and the focus on specific events in one's life from the biodata method (Dailey, 1971). The method, called the Behavioral Event Interview (BEI), is a semistructured interview in which the respondent is asked to recall recent, specific events in which he or she felt effective (Boyatzis, 1982; Spencer & Spencer, 1993) and describe it using primarily the PSE probes. Once the person recalls an event, he or she is guided through telling the story of the event with a basic set of five questions: (1) What led up to the situation? (2) Who said or did what to whom? (3) What did you say or do next? What were you thinking and feeling? (4) How did you do that? and (5) What was the outcome or result of the event? An additional probe asked for illustrative examples of asserted capabilities (e.g., "You say you are a good coach—give me an example").

The contention that these interviews were getting an accurate recording of the person's behavior (and implicit motives while doing it) came from multiple sources. First, the critical incident methodology is well established to record behavioral details of events. Second, autobiographical memory research (Rubin, 1986) has shown the accuracy of recall of events is increased dramatically when the events are: (1) recent, (2) have a high valence or saliency to the person, and (3) the recall involves specific actions. Third, requiring the reporting of recent, salient events coupled with solicitation of specific, detailed actions explicitly in the interview protocol itself was believed to maximize accuracy. The interviewers were trained with repeated practice, supervision, and review of audiotapes and/or transcripts. They were trained to ask for behavioral details and occasionally ask what the person was thinking or feeling. All of these conditions were incorporated into the BEI.

The responses are audiotaped and transcribed and interpreted using a thematic analysis process (Boyatzis, 1998). Thematic analysis is a process for "coding" raw qualitative information, whether in written, video, or audio form (Atkinson, 1958; Smith, McClelland, Atkinson, & Veroff, 1992; Winter, 1973). Through the use of a "codebook" articulating specific themes and how to identify them, the researcher is able to convert open-ended responses or unstructured responses and behavior into a set of quantified variables for analysis. The method has been used in numerous studies showing predictive validity of the competencies demonstrated by the person during the events as coded from the interviews (Boyatzis, 1982; McClelland, 1998; Spencer & Spencer, 1993).

The process of developing behaviorally based codes to be used for assessment, known conventionally as "behavioral indicators," itself requires some skill (or competencies). This is particularly important when the codebook is used as the basis for a broadly administered questionnaire or interview protocol used not by highly trained experts but by a more general population, that is, managers rating their employees in an annual performance appraisal.

Many 360° tools and similar assessments do not reliably and validly assess competencies because the questionnaire items reflect *only* the observed behavior and not the implicit motive, or underlying intent. A major revision of the Emotional and Social Competency Inventory (Boyatzis & Goleman, 1996, 1999; Boyatzis, Goleman, & Hay Acquisition, 2001, 2007) was made to add intent into the framing of each question. For example, in repeated inductive competency studies from BEIs, one of the behavioral manifestations of Empathy was discovered to be listening to others carefully and intently. So one of the earlier items was, "Listens attentively to others." In the 2007 version, the item was changed to "Understands others by listening attentively." This is an attempt to build the implicit motive or intent into the item. So the 360° informant who is not a trained coder can account for someone's differential uses of listening.

Because later informant assessment, through 360° tools or assessment centers and simulations coded by reliable "experts," is so essential, care must be taken in the development of behavioral indicators so that they truly reflect the competency. Because the competencies are derived from performance inductively, they reflected effective job performance. Since they were identified and articulated in terms of the actions and intent (i.e., implicit motives), they are a behavioral approach to a person's talent.

The anchor for understanding which behaviors and which intent are relevant in a situation emerges from predicting effectiveness. The construction of the specific competency is a matter of relating different behaviors that are considered alternate manifestations of the same underlying construct. But simple similarity is not sufficient; it also requires similarity of the context of use and of the intended consequence in social or work settings. In other words, the behaviors must not only be similar, but accomplishing a similar objective.

The Basis for the Competency Concept, Beyond Motivation

To differentiate it from a theory of motivation, a theory of performance is the basis for the concept of competency. The theory used in this approach is a basic

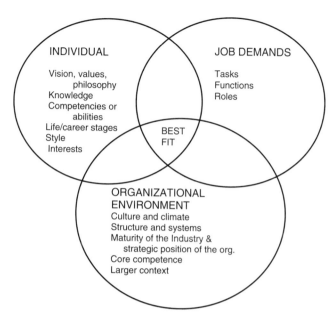

Figure 17.1 Theory of action and job performance: Best Fit (maximum performance, stimulation, and commitment) = Area of Maximum Overlap or Integration (Boyatzis, 1982, 2008).

contingency theory, as shown in Figure 17.1. Maximum performance is believed to occur when the person's capability or talent is consistent with the needs of the job demands and the organizational environment (Boyatzis, 1982). You can describe a person's talent by his or her values, vision, and personal philosophy; knowledge; competencies; life and career stage; interests; and style. Job demands can be described by the role responsibilities and tasks needed to be performed. Aspects of the organizational environment that are predicted to have important impact on the demonstration of competencies and/ or the design of the jobs and roles include: culture and climate; structure and systems; maturity of the industry and strategic positioning within it; and aspects of the economic, political, social, environmental, and even religious milieu surrounding the organization.

Research published over the last 30 years or so shows us that outstanding leaders, managers, advanced professionals, and people in key jobs, from sales-people to bank tellers, appear to require three clusters of behavioral habits as *threshold* abilities and three clusters of competencies as *distinguishing outstanding performance*. The threshold clusters of competencies include:

1) Expertise and experience;
2) Knowledge (i.e., declarative, procedural, functional, and metacognitive); and
3) Basic cognitive competencies, such as memory and deductive reasoning.

Table 17.1 The Scales and Clusters of the Emotional and Social Competency Inventory (ESCI)

Emotional Intelligence Competencies

Self-Awareness Custer   Concerns knowing one's internal states, preferences, resources, and intuitions. The self-awareness cluster contains one competency:
Emotional Self-Awareness: Recognizing one's emotions and their effects

Self-Management Cluster   Refers to managing one's internal states, impulses, and resources. The self-management cluster contains four competencies:
Emotional self-control: Keeping disruptive emotions and impulses in check
Adaptability: Flexibility in handling change
Achievement orientation: Striving to improve or meeting a standard of excellence
Positive outlook: Seeing the positive aspects of things and the future

Social Intelligence Competencies

Social Awareness Cluster   Refers to how people handle relationships and awareness of others' feelings, needs, and concerns. The Social Awareness cluster contains two competencies:
Empathy: Sensing others' feelings and perspectives, and taking an active interest in their concerns
Organizational awareness: Reading a group's emotional currents and power relationships

Relationship Management Cluster   Concerns the skill or adeptness at inducing desirable responses in others. The cluster contains five competencies:
Coach and Mentor: Sensing others' development needs and bolstering their abilities
Inspirational Leadership: Inspiring and guiding individuals and groups
Influence: Wielding effective tactics for persuasion
Conflict Management: Negotiating and resolving disagreements
Teamwork: Working with others toward shared goals. Creating group synergy in pursuing collective goals.

Source: From Boyatzis and Goleman (1996, 1999) and Boyatzis, Goleman, and Hay Acquisition (2001, 2007).

There are three clusters of competencies that differentiate outstanding from average performers in many countries of the world, as defined in Table 17.1 (Boyatzis, 1982; Bray, Campbell, & Grant, 1974; Campbell, Dunnette, Lawler, & Weick, 1970; Goleman, 1998; Goleman, Boyatzis, & McKee, 2002; Howard & Bray, 1988; *JMD* special issue, 2008; Kotter, 1982; Luthans et al., 1988; Rosier, 1994–1997; Spencer & Spencer, 1993; Sternberg, 1996; Thorton & Byham, 1982). They are:

1) Advanced cognitive competencies, such as systems thinking and pattern recognition;
2) Emotional intelligence competencies, including self-awareness and self-management competencies, such as emotional self-awareness and emotional self-control;
3) Social intelligence competencies, including social awareness and relationship management competencies, such as empathy and teamwork.

Competencies can be considered to be a behavioral approach to emotional, social, and cognitive intelligence. To understand this, their empirical manifestations must be understood in greater detail.

Competencies as Behavioral Manifestations of Emotional Intelligence

Emotional intelligence and social intelligence (i.e., EI and SI) are convenient phrases with which to focus attention on the underlying emotional and social components of human talent. While the earliest psychologist to explore the related concept of "social intelligence" (SI; Thorndike in the 20s and 30s, cf. Goleman, 1995, 2006) offered the idea as a single concept, more recent psychologists have appreciated its complexity and described it in terms of multiple capabilities (Bar-On, 1992, 1997; Goleman, 1998; Saarni, 1988). Gardner (1983) conceptualized this arena as constituting intrapersonal and interpersonal intelligence—two of his seven "intelligences." Salovey and Mayer (1990) first used the expression "emotional intelligence" (EI) and described it in terms of two major areas: knowing and handling one's own and others' emotions. Other conceptualizations have used labels such as "practical intelligence" and "successful intelligence" (Sternberg, 1996), which often blend the capabilities described by other psychologists with cognitive abilities and anchor the concepts around the consequence of the person's behavior, notably success or effectiveness.

While other interpretations of "intelligence" are offered in the literature, Boyatzis and Sala (2004) claimed that to be classified as an "intelligence," the concept should be:

1) Behaviorally observable;
2) Related to biological and in particular neurobiological functioning. That is, each cluster should be differentiated as to the type of neural circuitry and systems involved, including but not limited to neuroendocrine pathways;
3) Related to life and job outcomes;
4) Sufficiently different from other personality constructs that the concept adds value to understanding the human personality and behavior; and
5) One with measures that, as a psychological construct, should satisfy the basic criteria for a sound measure, that is, show convergent and discriminant validity (Campbell & Fiske, 1959).

This set of criteria is different than the Mayer, Caruso, and Salovey (1999) three standards for "an intelligence." In their view, relevant criteria regarding components of a capacity that is indeed a specific kind of intelligence are that: (1) it should reflect a "mental performance rather than preferred ways of behaving" (pp. 269–270); (2) tests of it should show positive correlation with other forms of intelligence; and (3) the measures should increase with experience and age.

As a theory of emotional intelligence, we believe that there should be a link to neural (or possibly neuroendocrine) functioning. If the theory claims that there are multiple components of this emotional intelligence, then these different components should have different neurological pathways. This first proposed criterion is more specific than the Mayer et al. (1999) first and second criteria. The construct should actually be able to predict neural and endocrine (i.e., hormonal) patterns within the individual. Regarding the rationale for including criterion 2 (i.e., job and life outcomes), the American Psychological Association's Task Force on Intelligence (APA Public Affairs Office, 1997) reported that predicting real-life outcomes is an important part of the standard against which we should judge an intelligence. The task force added that there should be a consensus within a field as to the definition. Although the consensus is lacking in the field regarding emotional intelligence at this time, the link between EI and SI competencies and real-life outcomes is in fact testable.

While Mayer, Caruso, and Salovey (1999) seem to discard patterns of behavior as irrelevant to their concept of EI, this approach contends that EI and SI should predict behavioral patterns in life and work, as well as the consequences of these patterns in the form of life and work outcomes. This seems a more relevant test of the concept than merely showing a link to experience and age (i.e., as Mayer, Caruso, & Salovey's [1999] third criterion).

The competency and talent stream of research has focused on explaining and predicting effectiveness in various occupations, often with a primary emphasis on managers and leaders (Bray, Campbell, & Grant, 1974; Boyatzis, 1982; Kotter, 1982; Luthans et al., 1988; McClelland, 1973; McClelland et al., 1958; Spencer & Spencer, 1993; Thornton & Byham, 1982). As has been explained earlier in this chapter, in this competency approach, specific capabilities were identified and validated against effectiveness measures, or, often, inductively discovered and then articulated as competencies.

An integrated concept of emotional, social, and cognitive intelligence competencies offers more than a convenient framework for describing human dispositions (Boyatzis & Sala, 2004). It offers a theoretical structure for the organization of personality and links it to a theory of action and job performance. Goleman (1998) defined an "emotional competence" as a "learned capability based on emotional intelligence which results in outstanding performance at work." In other words, if a competency is an "underlying characteristic of the person that leads to or causes effective or superior performance" (Boyatzis,

1982), then: (a) an *emotional intelligence competency* is an ability to recognize, understand, and use emotional information about *oneself* that leads to or causes effective or superior performance; *(b)* a *social intelligence* competency is the ability to recognize, understand and use emotional information about *others* that leads to or causes effective or superior performance; and (c) a *cognitive intelligence competency* is an ability to think or analyze *information* and situations that leads to or causes effective or superior performance. In brief, the emotionally intelligent understand themselves, the socially intelligent understand others, and the cognitively intelligent understand information, all in ways that have an impact on performance.

If instead of making these distinctions, competence is defined as a single construct, the tendency to believe that more effective people have the vital ingredients for success invites the attribution of a halo effect. For example, person A is effective, therefore she has all of the right stuff, such as brains, savvy, and style. Like the issue of finding the best "focal point" with which to look at something, the dilemma of finding the best level of detail in defining constructs with which to build a personality theory may ultimately be an issue of which focal point is chosen. The separate competencies, like the clusters, are, we believe, the most helpful focal point for description and study of performance.

Even the articulation of one overall emotional or social intelligence might be deceptive and suggest a close association with cognitive capability (i.e., traditionally defined "intelligence" or what psychologists often call "g" referring to general cognitive ability) (Ackerman & Heggestad, 1997; Davies, Stankov, & Roberts, 1998). The latter would not only be confusing, but would additionally raise the question as to what one is calling emotional and social intelligence and whether it is nothing more than an element of previously defined intelligence or cognitive ability. We therefore feel it necessary to make more refined distinctions within each of these intelligence constructs, if only to ultimately determine the strength of the three larger categories more cleanly.

The Emotional Competency Inventory, version 2 (ECI-2) (i.e., the forerunner to the current Emotional and Social Competency Inventory, ESCI) and the closely related university version (ECI-U) showed desired levels of convergent validity in confirmatory factor analyses for both the theoretical clusters (Boyatzis & Goleman, 1996, 1999; Boyatzis, Goleman, & Hay, 2001, 2007; Goleman, Boyatzis, & McKee, 2005; Wolff, 2005) and empirical clusters (Boyatzis & Sala, 2004) in studies by Battista (2005) as well as Battista, Boyatzis, Guillen, and Serlavos (in press). In addition, a wide variety of validation studies showed strong and consistent validity in predicting or explaining life and job outcomes (Boyatzis & Sala, 2004; Wolff, 2005). This helps to establish this behavioral, competency approach to EI and SI as satisfying the second and fourth criteria of an emotional or social intelligence cited earlier in this chapter. The ESCI extends the measure of social as well as emotional competencies; while both are found in the ECI, they are better explained with the newer tool.

The latest version of the ESCI attempts to address the difference between coded behavior from Behavioral Event Interviews and informant-based 360° surveys. Construction of the ESCI (i.e., the 360° survey of behavior) focused away from including all of the behavioral manifestations ever found for the interview-based studies and, instead, focused on those that repeatedly arose in validation studies and were most central to the definition of the competency. In this way, some of the items are reflective of the competency, and some are formative, or as they were earlier called, alternate manifestations. To address the lack of context from the 360° informant (that the coder of interviews would have), a statement of the intent was incorporated into each item in the ESCI.

Meanwhile, Guillen, Saris, and Boyatzis (2009) revealed no statistically significant relationship between personality dimensions as measured by the NEO-PR and EI or SI competencies. Burkle (2000b) and Murensky (2000) showed small but significant correlations between selected personality dimensions as measured by the Myers Briggs Type Indicator and selected clusters of EI and SI competencies. These findings suggest that this behavioral competency approach to EI and SI satisfies the third criterion of an emotional or social intelligence mentioned earlier in this article, rather than a convergent validity criterion based on correlations with other personality tools.

In contrast, the model of EI offered through the MSCEIT (Mayer et al., 2003) has a total score of a person's EI, two area scores of Experiential and Strategic, and branches within each area of: (a) Perceiving (with subtests of Faces and Pictures) and Facilitating (with subtests of Facilitation and Sensations); and (b) Understanding (with subtests of Changes and Blends) and Managing (with subtests of Emotional Management and Emotional Relationships). Although data from studies comparing these tests are underway, conceptually we would expect small correlations between these two different measures. The MSCEIT assesses a person's direct handling of emotions, while the ESCI, which is intended to assess the EI and SI competencies described earlier, assesses how the person expresses his or her handling of emotions in life and work settings. Nonetheless, there may be correlation between: (1) Self-awareness competencies from the ESCI and the Experiential area, in particular the Facilitating branch from the MSCEIT; (2) Social Awareness competencies from the ESCI and the Understanding branch of the Strategic area; and (3) Relationship Management competencies from the ESCI and the Managing branch from the Strategic area of the MSCEIT. Similarly, although the data bearing on this issue are presently being collected, currently there is no documented relationship among the ESCI competencies and the subscales of Bar-On's EQ-i (Bar-On, 1992, 1997). Although we believe there will be little correlation between the self-report version of the EQ-i and the others' views of a person's competencies through the ESCI, if only because there is rarely a strong correlation between self-image and other-view on competence, there may be substantial correlation among the EQ-i subscales and ESCI when 360° measures of both are compared, meaning that data from comparable raters can be related directly.

Competencies and a Holistic Theory of Personality

The specification of a competency comes from the personality theory on which this approach is based. McClelland (1951) originally described a theory of personality as comprised of the relationships among a person's unconscious motives, self-schema, and observed behavioral patterns. Boyatzis (1982) offered this scheme as an integrated system diagram that showed concentric circles, with the person's *unconscious motives* and *trait dispositions* at the center. These affected, and were affected by, the next expanding circle of the person's *values* and *self-image*. The surrounding circle was labeled the *skill* level. The circle surrounding it included *observed, specific behaviors*.

The synthesis of Goleman (1995) in developing the concept of emotional intelligence and later in his (Goleman, 2006) conception of social intelligence provided yet another layer to this integrated system view of personality. In particular, Goleman's synthesis introduced the *physiological* level to this model by relating findings from neuroscience, biology, and medical studies to psychological states and resulting behavior. The result is a personality theory, as shown in Figure 17.2, that incorporates and predicts the relationship among a person's: (a) neural circuits and endocrine (i.e., hormonal) processes; (b) unconscious dispositions called motives and traits; (c) values and operating philosophy; (d) observed separate competencies; and (e) competency clusters.

This conceptualization of personality requires a more holistic perspective than is often taken. When integrating the physiological level with the psychological and behavioral levels, a more comprehensive view of the human emerges. The evidence of the causal sequence predicted in this personality theory is emerging but is slow due to the disparate nature of the different fields studying parts of the model. For example, arousal of a person's power motive both causes *and is affected by* arousal of his or her sympathetic nervous system (i.e., SNS) (Boyatzis, Smith, & Blaize, 2006). When a person's power motive is aroused, he or she is more likely to show behavior associated with a group of competencies called Influence, Inspirational Leadership, or Change Catalyst (McClelland, 1985; Winter, 1973). Boyatzis and Sala (2004) showed that these competencies form an empirical cluster of emotional and social intelligence competencies as assessed through the Emotional Competency Inventory and now Emotional and Social Competency Inventory (ECI, ESCI; Boyatzis & Goleman, 1996, 2006). These competencies are shown more

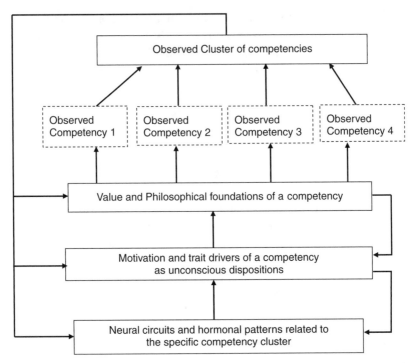

Figure 17.2 Levels within the personality structure structure (Boyatzis, 2008; Boyatzis, Goleman, & Rhee, 2000).

frequently when a person is operating from a humanistic versus a pragmatic operating philosophy (Boyatzis, Murphy, & Wheeler, 2000). When the power motive is aroused along with a person's self-control at the trait level (McClelland, 1985; McClelland & Boyatzis, 1982), the stressful effects of inhibiting one's urges add to the arousal of the SNS. The result is elevated blood pressure and decreased levels of both immunoglobulin A and natural killer cells (i.e., basic indicators of the immune system). Relatively recent research has shown that arousal of the SNS is associated with neural circuits passing predominantly through the right prefrontal cortex (Boyatzis & McKee, 2005).

Further, it is now the contention of leading researchers in affective neuroscience and genetic expression that experience overtakes genetic dispositions in determining the biological basis of behavior once in adulthood (Williams, personal communication, 2003). This would suggest that a person's experience and his or her arousal effect rewire or at least rechannel neural circuits and tendencies to invoke certain neuroendocrine pathways. Offering support for the observation, or prediction, is the proposed personality theory, that use of one's competencies (i.e., behavior in specific settings in life) becomes an arousal that over time creates different dispositions, even at the biological level.

Emerging Challenges in Competency Research

Although the field of competency research and applications is now over 40 years old, research uncovers as many questions as it answers. Of the many questions raised by current studies, three stand out as having major relevance for future research and applications: cross-cultural validation, tipping points, and development of competencies.

Competencies Across Cultures

The competency or behavioral approach to EI and SI is derived inductively from performance. As a result, when competency validation studies were first conducted in various countries in the 1970s and early 1980s, it was observed that the same or quite similar competencies appeared as valid predictors of performance regardless of the country or culture (Spencer & Spencer, 1993; see also the special issue of *Journal of Management Development, 2009*). In some studies, some of the competencies show more weight and predictive power than others. Further research will help reveal as to whether these are cultural differences emerging or they are merely the function of specific organizational samples. People conducting competency validation studies in many countries claim that the important, distinguishing competencies tend to be generic.

Cultural relativism would suggest that although specific items or certain behaviors may be reflective of the competency in a particular culture, other actions may reflect the competency in a different culture. Although the growing body of research on EI would support the notion of the relationship to performance as universal (see collection of articles on EI in the special issue of *Psicotema*, 2006), more research is needed to test the universality of competencies, the possibility of specific behavioral manifestations being different in different cultures, and the universality of EI/SI.

Tipping Points for Outstanding Performance

A major advancement in understanding the effect of competencies on performance came from catastrophe theory, which is now considered a subset of complexity theory. Instead of only asking the typical question, "Which competencies are needed or necessary for outstanding performance?" David McClelland, in a paper published posthumously in 1998, posed the question, "How often do you need to show a competency to 'tip' you into outstanding performance?" In other words, how frequently should a competency be shown to be sufficient for maximum performance? He reported that presidents of divisions of a large food company using competencies above the tipping points received significantly higher bonuses, which were proportional to the profitability of their divisions, as compared to their less profitable peers (McClelland, 1998).

Using this method, Boyatzis (2006) replicated significant findings regarding tipping points in an international consulting firm. The profits from accounts of senior partners were analyzed for seven quarters following assessment of their competencies. Senior partners using competencies above the tipping point more than doubled the operating profits from their accounts as compared to the senior partners below the tipping point. The measure of competencies was the average perceived frequency of use of each competency by others around the senior partner, using a 360° competency questionnaire. He showed that this method was superior to a simple median split or continuous analysis of the relationship between the frequency of competencies shown and financial performance of the senior partners, leaders, of this firm.

Knowing the point at which a person's use of a competency tips her or him into outstanding performance provides vital guidance to managers and leaders. It helps those coaching others to know which competencies are the closest to added value in stimulating outstanding performance. (The tipping point is sometimes referred to as a trigger point.)

The tipping point for each competency would be a function of the organizational environment. For example, the manager of an office of a strategy consulting company would have a tipping point of Adaptability—the ability to respond to changes in the working environment quickly—at the maximum level. To show sufficient Adaptability to be outstanding, he/she would have to be using it "frequently and consistently." Their business, projects, and clients change each year. They typically have high turnover in consulting staff as well. Meanwhile, the manager of a basic chemical processing plant may have a tipping point of only "occasional or often" of Adaptability. The certainty of their product line and predictability of their production processes do not create as much uncertainty as the consulting business. They probably have less turnover in the chemical plant as well, requiring even less adaptation to new staff. Analysis of tipping points should become a standard feature of competency assessment studies in the future.

Boyatzis (2006) also confirmed the earlier argument about the importance of clusters. It was shown that a dramatic increase in profit contributed to the company occurred when senior partners were using an assortment of the competencies from each cluster above the tipping point. It did not seem to matter which of the competencies were being using above the tipping point from each cluster. This allows for the differences in style observed from outstanding leaders while confirming the importance of competencies as predictors of performance.

Can Competencies Be Developed?

One of the benefits of the behavioral approach to EI and SI is that we enter a domain of human talent that can be developed in adulthood. Though the understanding of competencies has been steadily extended over the last 35 years, perhaps the most important contributions have come about in the last 15 years. The "honeymoon effect" of typical training programs might start with improvement immediately following the program, but within months it drops precipitously (Campbell et al., 1970). Only 15 programs were found in a global search of the literature by the Consortium on Research on Emotional Intelligence in Organizations to improve emotional intelligence. Most of them showed impact on job outcomes, such as number of new businesses started, or life outcomes, such as finding a job or satisfaction (Cherniss & Adler, 2000), which are the ultimate purpose of development efforts. But showing an impact on outcomes, while desired, may also blur *how* the change actually occurs. Furthermore, when a change has been noted, a question about the sustainability of the changes is raised because of the relatively short time periods studied.

Decades of research on the effects of psychotherapy (Hubble et al., 1999), self-help programs (Kanfer & Goldstein, 1991), cognitive behavior therapy (Barlow, 1988), training programs (Morrow, Jarrett, & Rupinski, 1997), and education (Pascarella & Terenzini, 1991; Winter, McClelland, & Stewart, 1981) have shown that people can change their behavior, moods, and self-image. But most of the studies focused on a single characteristic, like maintenance of sobriety, reduction in a specific anxiety, or a set of characteristics often determined by the assessment instrument, such as the scales of the MMPI (i.e., Minnesota Multiphasic Personality Inventory).

Even in the arena of development of motives, McClelland and Winter (1968), McClelland, Davis, Kalin, and Wanner (1970), Miron and McClelland (1979), Cutter, Boyatzis, and Clancy (1977), and McClelland (1977) showed significant improvement in life and job outcomes, but little data supporting that a person's motive scores on PSEs actually changed. As was said earlier, there are few models or theories of how individuals change and develop in sustainable ways (McClelland, 1965; Prochaska, DiClemente, & Norcross, 1992).

The few published studies examining improvement of more than one of these competencies show an overall improvement of about 10% in emotional intelligence abilities 3 to 18 months following training (Goleman, Boyatzis, & McKee, 2002). More recent meta-analytic studies and utility analyses confirm that significant changes can and do occur. But they do not show the impact that the level of investment would lead us to expect, nor do they show it with many types of training. There are, undoubtedly, other studies that were not found and reviewed, or not available through journals and books and, therefore, overlooked. We do not claim that this is an exhaustive review, but one suggestive of the percentage improvement as a rough approximation of the real impact. This approximation is offered to help in the comparison of relative impact of management training, management education, and self-directed learning.

The results appear no better from standard MBA programs, where there is no attempt to enhance emotional intelligence abilities. The best data here comes from a research project by the American Assembly of Collegiate Schools of Business. They found that levels of behavior of graduating students from two highly ranked business schools, compared to their levels when they began their MBA training, showed only improvements of 2% in the skills of emotional intelligence (Boyatzis, 2008). In fact, when students from four other high-ranking MBA programs were assessed on a range of tests and direct behavioral measures, they showed a gain of 4% in self-awareness and self-management abilities, but a *decrease* of 3% in social awareness and relationship management (Boyatzis & Saatchioglu, 2008; Boyatzis, Stubbs, & Taylor, 2002).

A series of longitudinal studies underway at the Weatherhead School of Management of Case Western Reserve University has shown that people can change on this complex set of competencies that we call emotional and social intelligence, competencies that distinguish outstanding performers in management and professions (Boyatzis, Stubbs, & Taylor, 2002). And the improvement lasted for years. A visual comparison of the percentage improvement in behavioral measures of emotional intelligence and social intelligence competencies from different samples is shown in Figure 17.3. This was achieved by MBAs taking a course designed on the basis of intentional change theory (Boyatzis, 2001, 2006).

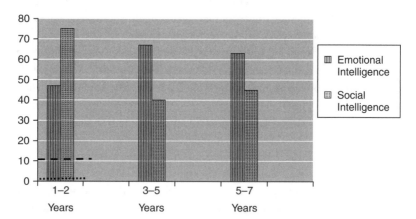

- - Indicates impact of company and government training programs 3–18 months after training on multiple emotional intelligence competencies.

.... Indicates impact of a variety of above-average MBA programs.

Figure 17.3 Percentage improvement of emotional and social intelligence competencies of different groups of MBA graduates taking the intentional change course (This figure is adapted from Goleman, Boyatzis, & McKee, 2002.)

The positive effects of this program were not limited to MBAs. In a longitudinal study of four classes completing the Professional Fellows Program (i.e., an executive education program at the Weatherhead School of Management), Ballou, Bowers, Boyatzis, and Kolb (1999) showed that these 45–55 year old professionals and executives improved on Self-confidence, Leadership, Helping, Goal Setting, and Action skills. These were 67% of the emotional intelligence competencies assessed in this study.

Concluding Thought

The study of competencies opens the door to insights about humans and human talent and potential applications for their development. Without implicit motives, the competencies would be nothing more than a list of skills or behaviors. Extending the study of implicit motives into the arena of competencies allows precision in observation, measurement, and development of human talent and the realm of emotions. Adults appear to be able to develop competencies so vital to outstanding performance in management, leadership, and many other occupations and professions. But many more challenges remain for future research on competencies to explore, like cross-cultural relevance, tipping points, and competency development.

Author Note

This chapter is adapted from Boyatzis, R. E. (2009). A behavioral approach to emotional Intelligence. *Journal of Management Development, 28*(9), 749–770.

References

Ackerman, P. L., & Heggestad, E. D. (1997). Intelligence, personality, and interests: Evidence for overlapping traits. *Psychological Bulletin, 121,* 219–245.

American Psychological Association Public Affairs Office. (1997). *Intelligence: Knowns and unknowns.* Washington DC: APA.

Atkinson, J. W. (Ed.) (1958). *Motives in fantasy, action, and society: A method of assessment and study.* New York: D. Van Nostrand.

Ballou, R., Bowers, D., Boyatzis, R. E., & Kolb, D. A. (1999). Fellowship in lifelong learning: An executive development program for advanced professionals. *Journal of Management Education. 23*(4), 338–354.

Barlow, D. H. (1988). *Anxiety and disorders: The nature and treatment of anxiety and panic.* New York: The Guilford Press.

Bar-On, R. (1992). *The development of a concept and test of psychological well-being.* Unpublished manuscript, Haifa University, Tel Aviv, Israel.

Bar-On, R. (1997). *Bar-On Emotional Quotient Inventory: Technical manual*. Toronto, Canada: Multi-Health Systems.

Battista, J. M. (2005). *Confirmatory factor analysis of ECI-2 (n=6,542) others' averaged observations of EI competencies demonstrated*. Unpublished research note, ESADE, Barcelona, Spain, June 1 2005.

Batista-Foguet, J. M., Boyatzis, R. E., Guillen, L., & Serlavos, R. (in press). Assessing Emotional Intelligence Competencies in Two Global Contexts. In P. Salovey, M. Mandal, V. Shanwal and R. Emmerling (Eds.) *Emotional intelligence: Theoretical and cultural perspectives*. San Francisco: Nova Science Publishers.

Boyatzis, R. E. (1982). *The competent manager: A model for effective performance*. New York: John Wiley & Sons.

Boyatzis, R. E. (1998). *Transforming qualitative information: Thematic analysis and code development*. Thousand Oaks, CA: Sage.

Boyatzis, R. E., (2001). How and why individuals are able to develop emotional intelligence. In C. Cherniss & D. Goleman (Eds.), *The emotionally intelligent workplace: How to select for, measure, and improve emotional intelligence in individuals, groups, and organizations* (pp. 234–253). San Francisco: Jossey-Bass.

Boyatzis, R. E. (2006). Intentional change theory from a complexity perspective. *Journal of Management Development, 25*(7), 607–623.

Boyatzis, R. E. (2008). Competencies in the 21st century. *Journal of Management Development, 27*(3), 5–12.

Boyatzis, R. E. (2009). A behavioral approach to emotional intelligence. *Journal of Management Development. 28*(9), 749–770.

Boyatzis, R. E., & Goleman, D. (1996, 1999). *Emotional Competency Inventory*. Boston: Hay Group.

Boyatzis, R. E., Goleman, D., & Hay Acquisition. (2001, 2007), *Emotional and Social Competency Inventory*. Boston: Hay Group.

Boyatzis, R., & McKee, A. (2005), *Resonant leadership: Sustaining yourself and connecting with others through mindfulness, hope, and compassion*. Boston: Harvard Business School Press.

Boyatzis, R. E., Murphy, A., and Wheeler, J. (2000). Philosophy as the missing link between values and behavior. *Psychological Reports, 86*, 47–64.

Boyatzis, R. E., & Sala, F. (2004), Assessing emotional intelligence competencies. In Glenn Geher (Ed.), *The measurement of emotional intelligence* (pp. 147–180). Hauppauge, NY: Novas Science Publishers.

Boyatzis, R. E., Smith, M., & Blaize, N. (2006). Sustaining leadership effectiveness through coaching and compassion: It's not what you think. *Academy of Management Learning and Education, 5*(1), 8–24.

Boyatzis, R. E., Stubbs, L., & Taylor, S. (2002). Learning cognitive and emotional intelligence competencies through graduate management education. *Academy of Management Journal on Learning and Education, 1*(2), 150–162.

Bray, D. W., Campbell, R. J., & Grant, D. L. (1974). *Formative years in business: A long term AT&T study of managerial lives*. New York: John Wiley & Sons.

Burckle, M. (2000a). Can you assess your own emotional intelligence? Evidence supporting multi-rater assessment. Hay/McBer Research Report. Boston, MA.

Burckle, M. (2000b). ECI and MBTI. Hay/McBer Research Report. Boston, MA.

Campbell, J. P., Dunnette, M. D., Lawler, E. E., III, and Weick, K. E., Jr. (1970). *Managerial behavior, performance, and effectiveness*, New York: McGraw-Hill.

Campbell, D. T., & Fiske, D. W. (1959). Convergent and discriminant validation by the multitrait-muiltimethod matrix. *Psychological Bulletin, 56*, 81–105.

Cherniss, C., & Adler, M. (2000). *Promoting emotional intelligence in organizations: Make training in emotional intelligence effective.* Washington, DC: American Society of Training and Development.

Cutter, H., Boyatzis, R. E., & Clancy, D. (1977). The effectiveness of power motivation training for rehabilitating alcoholics. *Journal of Studies on Alcohol, 38*(1), 131–141.

Dailey, C. A. (1971). *Assessment of Lives: Personality Evaluation in a Bureaucratic Society.* San Francisco: Jossey-Bass.

Davies, M., Stankov, L., & Roberts, R. D. (1998). Emotional intelligence: In search of an elusive construct. *Journal of Personality and Social Psychology. 75*, 989–1015.

Reserve University, Cleveland, OH.Flanagan, J. C. (1954). The critical incident technique. *Psychological Bulletin, 51*, 327–335.

Gardner, H. (1983). *Frames of mind: The theory of multiple intelligences.* New York: Basic Books.

Goleman, D. (1995). *Emotional Intelligence.* New York: Bantam Books.

Goleman, D. (1998). *Working with emotional intelligence.* New York: Bantam.

Goleman, D. (2006). *Social intelligence.* New York: Bantam Books.

Goleman, D., Boyatzis, R. E., & McKee, A. (2002). *Primal leadership: Realizing the power of emotional ntelligence.* Boston: Harvard Business School Press.

Guillen, L., Saris, W. E., & Boyatzis, R. E. (2009). The impact of emotional and social competencies on effectiveness of Spanish executives. *Journal of Management Development, 28*, 9, 771–793.

Howard, A., & Bray, D. (1988). *Managerial lives in transition: Advancing age and changing times.* New York: Guilford Press.

Hubble, M. A., Duncan, B. L., & Miller, S. D. (Eds.) (1999). *The heart and soul of change: What works in therapy.* Washington, DC: American Psychological Association.

Jacobs, R. L., & McClelland, D. C. (1994). Moving up the corporate ladder: A longitudinal study of the leadership motive pattern and managerial success in women and men. *Consulting Psychology Journal Practice and Research, 46*(1), 32–41.

Journal of Management Development, Special issue, February, 2008, Competencies in the 21st Century.

Journal of Management Development, Special issue, October, 2009 (in press), Competencies in the European Union.

Kanfer, F. H., & Goldstein, A. P. (Eds.) (1991). *Helping people change: A textbook of methods* (4th ed.). Boston: Allyn and Bacon.

Kolb, D. A., & Boyatzis, R. E. (1970). Goal-setting and self-directed behavior change. *Human Relations, 23*(5), 439–457.

Kotter, J. P. (1982). *The general managers.* New York: Free Press.

Lewin, A. Y. & Zwany, A. (1976). *Peer nominations: A model, literature critique and a paradigm for research.* Springfield, VA: National Technical Information Service.

Luthans, F., Hodgetts, R. M., & Rosenkrantz, S. A. (1988). *Real managers.* Cambridge, MA: Ballinger Press.

Mayer, J. D., Salovey, P., & Caruso, D. R. (1999). Emotional intelligence meets traditional standards for an intelligence. *Intelligence, 2*, 267–298.

Mayer, J. D., Salovey, P., Caruso, D. R., & Sitarenios, G. (2003). Measuring emotional intelligence with eh MSCEIT V2.0. *Emotion, 3*, 97–105.

McClelland, D. C. (1951). *Personality.* New York: William Sloane Associates.

McClelland, D. C. (1965). Toward a theory of motive acquisition. *American Psychologist, 20*(5), 321–333.

McClelland, D. C. (1973). Testing for competence rather than intelligence. *American Psychologist, 28*(1), 1–40.

McClelland, D. C. (1977). Another look at the impact of power motivation training. *Journal of Studies on Alcohol, 38*(1), 142–152.

McClelland, D. C. (1985). *Human motivation.* Glenview, IL: Scott, Foresman.

McClelland, D. C. (1998). Identifying competencies with behavioral event interviews. *Psychological Science, 9*, 331–339.

McClelland, D. C., Baldwin, A. L., Bronfenbrenner, U., & Strodbeck, F. L. (1958). *Talent and society.* New York: Van Nostrand.

McClelland, D. C., & Boyatzis, R. E. (1982). The leadership motive pattern and long term success in management. *Journal of Applied Psychology, 67*(6), 737–743.

McClelland, D. C., & Burnham, D. H. (1972). "Power is the great motivator." *Harvard Business Review* (reprint), January 2003.

McClelland, D. C., Davis, W. N., Kalin, R., & Wanner, E. (1972). *The drinking man: Alcohol and human motivation.* New York: Free Press.

Miron, D., & McClelland, D. C. (1979). The impact of achievement motivation training on small business. *California Management Review, 21*(4), 13–28.

Morrow, C. C., Jarrett, M. Q., and Rupinski, M. T. (1997). An investigation of the effect and economic utility of corporate-wide training. *Personnel Psychology, 50*, 91–119.

Murensky, C. L. (2000). *The relationship between emotional intelligence, personality, critical thinking ability, and organizational leadership performance at upper levels of management.* Dissertation, George Mason University, Fairfax, VA.

Pascarella, E. T., & Terenzini, P. T. (1991). *How college affects students: Findings and insights from twenty years of research.* San Francisco, CA: Jossey-Bass.

Psicotema, Special issue on emotional intelligence, 2006.

Prochaska, J. O., DiClemente, C. C., & Norcross, J. C. (1992). In search of how people change: Applications to addictive behaviors. *American Psychologist, 47*(9), 1102–1114.

Rosier, R. H. (Ed.) (1994–1997). *The competency model handbook: Volumes 1–4.* Lexington, MA: Linkage.

Rubin, D. C. (1986). *Autobiographical memory.* New York: Cambridge University Press.

Saarni, C. (1988). Emotional competence: How emotions and relationships become integrated. In R. A. Thompson (Ed.), *Nebraska symposium on motivation, 36* (pp. 115–182).

Salovey, P., & Mayer, J. D. (1990). Emotional intelligence. *Imagination, Cognition and Personality, 9,* 185–211.

Smith, C. P. in association with Atkinson, J. W., McClelland, D. C., & Veroff, J. (Eds.) (1992). *Motivation and personality: Handbook of thematic content analysis.* New York: Cambridge University Press.

Spencer, L. M., Jr., & Spencer, S. M. (1993). *Competence at work: Models for superior performance.* New York: John Wiley & Sons.

Sternberg, R. J. (1996). *Successful intelligence: How practical and creative intelligence determine success in life.* New York: Simon and Shuster.

Thornton, G. C., III, & Byham, W. C. (1982). *Assessment centers and managerial performance.* New York: Academic Press.

Winter, D. G., (1973). *The power motive,* New York: Free Press.

Winter, D. G., McClelland, D. C., & Stewart, A. J. (1981). *A new case for the liberal arts: Assessing institutional goals and student development.* San Francisco, CA: Jossey-Bass.

Wolff, S. B. (2005). *Emotional competence inventory: Technical manual.* Boston: The Hay Group.

Chapter 18
Motive Training and Motivational Competence

FALKO RHEINBERG
University of Potsdam, Germany

STEFAN ENGESER
Technishe Univesität München

McClelland and the Beginnings of Scientifically Informed Motive Training

Theoretical Background

The first targeted attempts to modify people's implicit motives were made by McClelland and colleagues in the 1960s (McClelland & Winter, 1969). Their work was inspired by the idea that economically underdeveloped countries could be more effectively supported by targeting the motivational basis of entrepreneurial behavior than by providing financial and technological aid.

There were empirical reasons to assume that the achievement motive plays a decisive role in the business world: (1) Individuals high in the achievement motive show characteristics that are essential for successful entrepreneurial behavior: constantly seeking to improve processes and procedures, a willingness to take calculated risks, actively seeking out information on the results of their actions, a tendency to feel responsible for those outcomes, and so forth. (see Chapter 2). (2) Businessmen—especially active and successful ones—scored higher on the achievement motive than other occupational groups (McClelland, 1961). These early findings have been substantiated by a recent meta-analysis (Collins, Hages, & Locke, 2004). (3) The more achievement oriented a society is overall (measured in terms of the frequency of achievement-related themes in popular literature or school textbooks), the more it stimulates and facilitates entrepreneurial activity in the upcoming generations. Indicators of societal achievement orientation thus predict subsequent economic growth and productivity (McClelland, 1961). Research attention has recently been drawn back to this relationship between societal achievement orientation and economic growth (Harrison & Huntington, 2000), sparking heated discussions. After all, this explanatory approach assigns societies partial responsibility for their developmental status, a conclusion that not everyone considers "politically correct" or accurate. (4) Because there seemed no point in trying to change the achievement orientation of whole societies given the limited resources available, programs were developed to foster the achievement-motivated experience, thinking, and behavior of those active in the business world at least.

Design of the Training Program

To this end, a training program was designed and first implemented in a group of Indian businessmen from the province of Andhra Pradesh in Kakinada. The core element of the intervention was a 2-week training program involving self-awareness exercises, theoretical modules, and the development of a personal action plan. The program targeted the affective network of the achievement motive, which it aimed to (1) extend and strengthen, (2) render more clearly perceptible and identifiable, (3) relate to participants' everyday behavior and experience, and finally (4) align with participants' superordinate values of self-definition and cultural norms (McClelland, 1965; McClelland & Winter, 1969). The participants thus learned to think, feel, talk, and act like someone with a strong achievement motive.

Measured in terms of its economic effects, the program was a huge success. Participants who had completed the training program worked harder, invested more, and created more new jobs than businessmen in an untrained control group. Moreover, measured against the economic development of a parallel control group from another city in the region, the program proved to have far-reaching effects: 2 years later, there were almost one-third more jobs in Kakinada than in the control city. Yet the psychological intervention was extremely cost effective: state job creation schemes had to invest 12 times more to create one new job.

Was There Motive Change?

In view of this compelling evidence for the economic effects of McClelland's motive training program, the United Nations Industrial Development Organization (UNIDO) initiated successful follow-up studies (Varga, 1977). From the theoretical perspective, however, it is not the programs' economic success that was astonishing, but the fact that the participants' achievement motive could apparently be modified at all. In fact, the training approach was entirely at odds with McClelland's own theorizing: McClelland conceived of motives as stable personality traits (McClelland, 1958) and later even assumed them to be partly genetically determined (Weinberger & McClelland, 1990).

Any attempt to change a personality trait of this kind within a 2-week training program must surely be doomed to failure.

But was the participants' achievement motive, in fact, changed? The answer to this question depends on how "motive change" is defined. There is, in fact no, way of evaluating motive change in McClelland's pioneering study. Granted, the mean Thematic Apperception Test (TAT) scores for the achievement motive were higher after training than before training. Because participants in the program had learned to write stories that would score high in achievement motivation on the TAT coding system, however, the validity of the procedure was trivially reduced. Against this background, it is hardly surprising that the motive scores measured after the training program were unrelated to participants' subsequent entrepreneurial activity. Given that variants of his training program developed for use in schools proved to have inconsistent effects, McClelland (1972) concluded that it was not the achievement motive itself that was fostered by his program, but life management skills.

If a motive is understood to describe, on a very basal level, a typical pattern of affective arousal elicited by certain natural incentives that are integrated within an extensive network of relevant stimulus cues during preverbal development, McClelland's interpretation seems reasonable. However, researchers soon noted that the direction of the action tendency elicited can differ, and that an approach motive could thus be distinguished from an avoidance motive. Atkinson (1957) distinguished hope of success (HS) versus fear of failure (FF) as the approach-versus-avoidance tendencies of the achievement motive.

In English-language research, an anxiety questionnaire (TAQ, Mandler & Sarason, 1952) was used to assess the tendency to avoid failure. Heckhausen (1963) took a different approach, developing a German coding system for the TAT procedure that assessed the hope and fear components of the achievement motive separately (see Chapter 2). McClelland's participants were not familiar with this coding system and had not been trained to write stories with a certain profile of HS and FF scores. A reanalysis of their TAT protocols showed that the training program (a) had particularly favorable effects on participants who were initially high in fear of failure (FF > HS) and that (b) the direction of the motive (net hope = HS − FF) was indeed related to participants' subsequent entrepreneurial activity. Participants whose HS came to outweigh their FF over the course of the program were subsequently more active (Heckhausen & Krug, 1982). Varga (1977) reported similar findings from replication studies in Indonesia, Pakistan, Persia, and Poland.

Thus, if motive change is defined as change in the *direction* of the achievement motive (HS > FF), it can be concluded that McClelland's early motive training programs indeed stimulated motive change. As mentioned above, McClelland (1985) saw things differently. His interpretation was that the changes elicited by his program amounted to increased self-confidence and perhaps improved life management skills.

Programs Designed to Reduce Fear of Failure

Heckhausen's Self-Evaluation Model

McClelland's motive training program was relatively complex. Moreover, not all of the 12 elements of his program were derived directly from motivation theory. Rather, the program included any and all techniques used by therapists or religious groups such as the Mormons or Jesuits to effect personality change (McClelland, 1985, p. 554). The question thus arose of whether—if the objective was "just" to change the direction of the achievement motive (HS > FF), rather than its strength relative to other motives (power or affiliation)—it might be possible to develop more streamlined approaches that were more compatible with motivation theory. This question became increasingly urgent as it emerged that, despite the time and energy invested in McClelland's training program, its effects in other contexts, especially schools, were inconsistent (for a summary, see Heckhausen & Krug, 1982; McClelland, 1985).

A more direct and parsimonious concept for motive training programs could indeed be derived from Heckhausen's self-evaluation model of achievement motivation (Heckhausen, 1975). This model integrated three important process variables known to distinguish individuals higher in hope for success (HS > FF) from individuals higher in fear of failure (HS < FF): (1) *goal setting*, (2) *causal attribution*, and (3) *self-evaluative emotions* (pride and shame): (1) Research on the risk-taking model (Atkinson, 1957) had shown that success-motivated individuals prefer tasks of moderate difficulty and set themselves realistic standards ($P_s \approx .50$) (Heckhausen, Schmalt, & Schneider, 1985; Schneider, 1973). The fit between task demands and personal abilities makes the relationship between effort and outcomes (success vs. failure) very clear. Moreover, individuals who choose tasks of moderate difficulty are able to see their abilities developing over time. (2) This leads them to develop a pattern of causal attributions that is conducive to motivation: failure is attributed to variable and controllable causes, especially lack of effort, and success to internal causes, especially ability and effort (Heckhausen, 1972; Heckhausen, 1975; Weiner & Kukla, 1970). Attribution of failure to variable causes stops them from giving up too soon, and attribution of success to internal factors maximizes positive affect in cases of success. (3) Highly positive affective responses after success and chances for improvement after failure make achievement-related situations attractive and exciting. This, in turn, supports the strategy of setting realistic standards and preferring tasks of moderate difficulty ($p = .50$). Thus, three key characteristics of success-oriented achievement motivation can be seen as a self-reinforcing system of three processes (goal setting, causal attribution, and self-evaluation). Table 18.1 gives a schematic representation of these processes.

Table 18.1   Hope of Success Versus Fear of Failure as Self-Reinforcing Processes in Heckhausen's Self-Evaluation Model (1972, 1975)

Components of Self-Evaluation

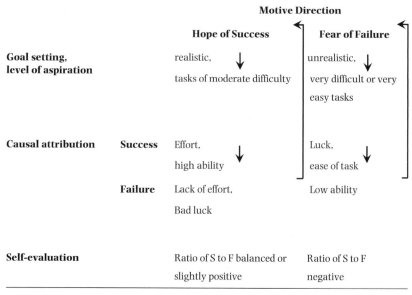

		Motive Direction	
		Hope of Success	**Fear of Failure**
Goal setting, level of aspiration		realistic, ↓ tasks of moderate difficulty	unrealistic, ↓ very difficult or very easy tasks
Causal attribution	**Success**	Effort, high ability ↓	Luck, ease of task ↓
	Failure	Lack of effort, Bad luck	Low ability
Self-evaluation		Ratio of S to F balanced or slightly positive	Ratio of S to F negative

Note: S = experiences of success; F = experiences of failure.

Heckhausen (Heckhausen, 1975; Heckhausen & Weiner, 1972) proposed an analogous pattern of self-reinforcement for failure-oriented achievement motivation. Individuals high in failure motivation tend to set themselves unrealistic standards, meaning that they are more likely to choose tasks that are far too easy or too difficult for them. As a result, the relationship between their effort and the outcome is far from clear, and it is hard for them to see their abilities developing over time. They are thus more likely than individuals high in success motivation to attribute their successes to external causes (luck in the case of difficult tasks, ease of task otherwise). Because they are less aware of their abilities developing over time, they are less protected against the threatening attribution "lack of ability" that soon presents itself after failure on easy tasks. Moreover, because failure on overly difficult tasks is a relatively regular occurrence, it invites attribution to stable causes (lack of ability, excessive demands). Attribution of success to external causes is unlikely to elicit positive self-evaluative emotions (pride). When failures are attributed to stable causes, making them seem inevitable, and attributions to "lack of ability" additionally threaten self-esteem, achievement-related situations seem threatening rather than challenging.

Against this background, it is only rational that failure-motivated individuals avoid challenges and instead choose tasks that are either too easy or too difficult for them (Heckhausen, 1972, 1975; Heckhausen et al., 1985).

Implications for Training Programs

Within the framework of the self-evaluation model of achievement motivation, various findings on motive-specific differences in goal-setting behavior, causal attribution, and self-evaluative emotions fell into place like pieces of a jigsaw puzzle. The great advantage of using this model as a framework for the development of training programs was that it identified three processes that have to be targeted in order to reduce FF and boost HS. The focus on just these three processes meant a considerable reduction on the 12 elements of McClelland's original motive training program (see below).

At the same time, Rheinberg and Krug (1978) emphasized that enduring change in motive direction could not be achieved by targeting a single component in isolation. If failure-motivated individuals are encouraged to set themselves realistic standards, but their causal attributions of failure are not addressed at the same time, achievement-related situations become even more threatening for them, as the failure to be expected on the serious challenges now facing them is attributed to their own failings. Such aversive experiences are incompatible with stable, self-reinforcing change. If, on the other hand, only causal attributions are addressed, the new explanatory strategy will soon come into conflict with reality unless realistic goal setting ensures that the "new" causal attributions are in keeping with real-life events. Only if the goal-setting strategy is modified will the new pattern of causal attributions be realistic. Thus, training programs exclusively targeting patterns of causal attribution cannot be expected to bring about permanent motive change either. Finally, the invitation to experience more pleasure in one's successes than displeasure in one's failures, and indeed, to reward oneself for success, seems rather out of place if the causal interpretation of events suggests that there is, in reality, little reason to be proud of one's performance.

Thus, it follows from Heckhausen's self-evaluative model that training programs focusing exclusively on the behavioral aspect of realistic standard setting, the cognitive aspect of causal attribution, or on self-reward measures cannot possibly succeed, but that all three processes must be targeted at once to effect lasting change in the direction of the achievement motive (Rheinberg & Krug, 1978). Better goal-setting skills can enable people to structure everyday situations in ways that arouse their (achievement) motive more frequently. New patterns of causal attribution can make it easier for people to interpret the outcomes of their achievement-related behavior in a way that is conducive to motivation. It is only when both of these requirements are in place that achievement-related situations elicit the positive (self-evaluative) emotions that essentially mobilize behavior in everyday life, and that make these situations attractive rather than threatening.

Model-Based Training Programs

Krug and Hanel (1976) first implemented a training program based on these principles in a group of failure-motivated underachievers. In 16 training sessions, the fourth graders learned to set realistic goals, to identify causal attributions conducive to motivation, and to experience more pleasure in their successes than displeasure at their failures. The exercises were first conducted in the context of games (e.g., ring toss game), then with paper-and-pencil material (e.g., labyrinth tasks), and finally with school tasks. At each stage of the program, the trainer served as a model, demonstrating realistic goal-setting behavior and beneficial causal attributions, and verbalizing his or her thoughts aloud in both instances. In addition to demonstrating these behavioral and cognitive characteristics of success-motivated achievement behavior, the model expressed strong positive affect after success and only mild displeasure after failure.

The children then repeated the exercises in small groups. They also verbalized their cognitions aloud to begin with, later continuing them in "internal speech" (Meichenbaum & Goodman, 1971). Their expressions of positive affect were loud and joyful. Thus, although McClelland (1985, p. 553) suggested otherwise, this training approach did *not* target only cognitive variables, but also impacted behavioral and affective elements.

The intervention led to a decrease in fear of failure and an increase in hope of success. In other words, there was a change in the dominant direction of the achievement motive as directly expressed by the "net hope score" (NH): the difference between HS and FF. Figure 18.1 shows the pre- and posttest scores for the training group and two control groups in the Krug and Hanel (1976) study. HS and FF were measured using Schmalt's (1976a) AM grid (see below).

The failure-motivated students who participated in the training program (high-FF students with motive training) showed significantly higher NH scores at posttest. In contrast, a control group of failure-motivated students (high-FF students without motive training) who had worked on some of the same task material, but without the typical elements of the motive training program (training in goal setting, attribution, self-evaluation), showed no motive change. An unselected control group of students (total sample) showed the same mid-level NH scores as at pretest. The training program thus proved highly effective.

Motive Measurement in Training Studies

With the exception of one pilot study (see below), Schmalt's (1976a, 1976b) Achievement-Motive grid (AM grid) was used to measure the effects of this and all subsequent training programs based on Heckhausen's self-evaluation model

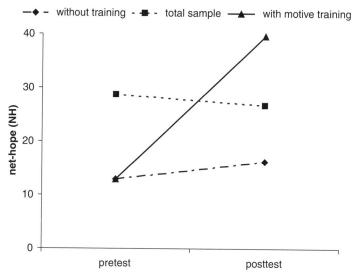

Figure 18.1. NH scores for a training group (high-FF students with motive training, $N = 9$) and a control group high in failure motivation (high-FF students without motive training, $N = 21$) and for an unselected control group (total sample, $N = 91$) (based on Krug & Hanel, 1976).

on participants' motives. This measurement technique uses achievement-related pictures to activate the achievement motive. Respondents do not generate stories of their own about these pictures, however, but are presented with a list of statements borrowed from the content categories of the TAT and asked to check those that apply to the person shown in the picture. The AM grid thus shares the component of motive arousal by means of picture cues with the TAT/PSE (see Chapters 2–6) but does not include the component of active imagery and language production.

Correlations between AM and TAT/PSE scores have been shown to be weak or nonexistent. According to Langens & Schmalt (2008), however, the AM grid predicts similar criteria as the TAT/PSE and can thus also be considered a measure of implicit motives. It would go beyond the scope of this chapter to discuss this point in detail (see Chapters 5–7 and Schmalt, 2005). However, findings from numerous studies with samples of students unmistakably show that, in this population at least, the AM grid is sensitive to the *direction* of the achievement motive (HS vs. FF). Because the motive training programs based on Heckhausen's self-evaluation model indeed targeted motive *direction*, the AM grid—with its greater parsimony and objectivity—was used in preference to the TAT/PSE.

In one early pilot study, however, the TAT/PSE was used instead of the AM grid (Hecker, Kleine, Wessling-Lünnemannn, & Beier,1979). The findings (decrease in FF scores) were in line with those emerging from subsequent studies with the AM grid.

Combined Training Programs

Numerous training programs based on the Krug and Hanel (1976) approach were conducted, replicating the findings reported above in various samples, including students with learning disabilities (Krug, Peters, & Quinkert, 1977; for summaries, see Heckhausen & Krug, 1982, and Rand, 1987). Later versions of the program, in which the principles of realistic goal setting, beneficial causal attributions, and positive self-evaluative emotions were applied to learning- and achievement-related material proved particularly effective. Rheinberg and Schliep (1985) first tested this approach with fifth graders who had not yet learned to write. Remedial literacy materials were first broken down into numerous elements that were clearly graded by their level of difficulty. Having completed the game-based task devised by Krug and Hanel (1976), the students learned to set themselves realistic goals for the spelling exercises, to provide positive causal explanations for their performance, and to apply constructive self-evaluative strategies in this context as well. Relative to a control group that did not receive training, the participating students showed significant increases in both their NH scores as measured by Schmalt's (1976a) AM grid and their spelling skills (Rheinberg & Schliep, 1985).

Fries, Lund, and Rheinberg (1999) combined the principles of the motive training program with training tasks developed by Klauer (1991) to foster *inductive reasoning*. The fifth and sixth graders in the training group showed significant increases in both their NH scores as measured by Schmalt's AM grid (1976a) and their inductive reasoning as measured by Weiß's (1987) CFT 20 intelligence test. These findings have since been replicated in numerous studies (Fries, 2002).

Combined training programs of this kind probably have particularly sustained effects because students not only learn to act like success-motivated individuals in achievement-related situations, but also—through the specific content of the training program—acquire competencies that make school learning objectively easier for them. These programs thus preclude the counterproductive effects that may occur when participants in training programs return to their school work with great enthusiasm, but still lacking in the necessary academic skills, meaning that their increased effort does not lead to recognizably improved learning outcomes. The feeling that there is no change in one's achievement, irrespective of the effort invested, can lead to experiences of helplessness, as described by Dweck (1975). Indeed, training programs have occasionally been found to have such negative effects (Kraeft & Krug, 1979). To foster the achievement motive on the long term, it is thus vital that participants are able to see the effects of their increased efforts in the form of improved learning outcomes.

Programs Integrated in Classroom Instruction

Such perceptions are likely to be facilitated if the specific training situations are not entirely different from the everyday learning situations of regular classroom instruction. Some training programs have thus been integrated into regular lessons and implemented in cooperation with the participating students' teachers. This strategy had previously been attempted by scholars such as DeCharms (1976) and Mehta (1968), who trained teachers to integrate aspects of the motive training program for Indian businessmen (McClelland & Winter, 1969; see above) into their lessons. These effects on student motives proved to be inconsistent, however. As in McClelland's original training program, many of the components implemented were not derived directly from motivation theory; moreover, they could not always be meaningfully integrated within regular instruction.

Based on Heckhausen's self-evaluation model, it was now possible to take a much more targeted approach to motive training. Instead of floundering through the various quasitherapeutic and indoctrinatory elements of McClelland's original training program, the training procedure could focus on the three core elements of goal setting, causal attribution, and self-evaluation. In a 17-week training program reported by Rheinberg and Günther (2005), these three elements were consistently applied to regular classroom material. Figure 18.2 shows change in NH scores as measured by Schmalt's (1976a) AM grid for trained and untrained fifth graders.

Relative to the untrained control students, the trained students showed a significant increase in NH scores. They also set more realistic goals, as assessed by a standardized measurement procedure. The same effect was observed when aspired school grades, rather than the standardized psychodiagnostic procedures, were used as the criterion for goal setting. Moreover, the students in

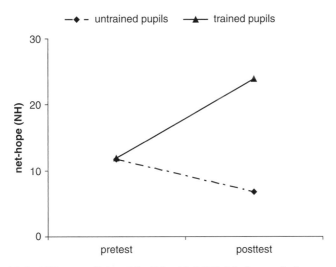

Figure 18.2. NH scores (Schmalt's AM grid, 1976a) before and after a motive training program integrated in classroom instruction (trained students, $N = 35$; untrained students, $N = 24$) (data from Rheinberg & Günther, 2005, p. 64).

the training group were significantly more likely to attain the grades to which they aspired than their peers in the control group (see Rheinberg & Günther, 2005, p. 66).

The contents of physical education lessons proved a particularly favorable combination for the motive training elements of the self-evaluative model. The criteria for success and failure are especially visible in this context, and students can feel the effects of their increased effort and persistence directly and physically. Motive training programs were successfully integrated in physical education lessons from an early date (Hecker, Kleine, Wessling-Lünnemann, & Beier, 1979), and numerous studies have replicated the findings of an increase in NH scores as measured by the AM grid (Kleine, 1980; Krug, Mrazek, & Schmidt, 1980; Winterstein, 1991).

The Concept of Reference Norm Orientation

Social and Individual Reference Norms

Observations of classroom instruction revealed that some teachers implemented certain principles of the motive training programs described above, although they were not familiar with either the programs themselves or the concept of motivation underlying the self-evaluation model. A research program conducted in the 1970s and 1980s established that the decisive variable was the type of reference norm that these teachers applied when evaluating their students' achievement.

Since McClelland, Atkinson, Clark, and Lowell (1953), the theme of achievement motivation has been defined as "concern with a standard of excellence." Yet standards of excellence differ not only in their levels, but also in their origins, that is, the reference system within which they are anchored. Much of the experimental research on achievement motivation has used socially defined standards to manipulate success versus failure or task difficulty: Standards achieved by few are deemed to be difficult, those achieved by many to be easy; outcomes that are above average are deemed to be good, those that are below average to be poor. This approach is in line with the concept of *social comparison*, as formulated by Festinger (1954).

Application of social comparison standards is by no means mandatory in the achievement context, however. When the achievement motive is assessed by means of the TAT/PSE, the first decision to be made in the coding process is whether a story contains any achievement imagery. One important criterion for this decision is whether the story generated by the participant describes something as being done particularly well or better (Atkinson, 1958), where "better" may mean either *better than others* or *better than before*. Whereas in the first case, a social comparison is made as described above (i.e., a social reference norm is applied), in the second case, an entirely different comparison is made, namely with a person's own previous achievements (i.e., an individual reference norm is applied).

Veroff (1969) was probably the first to investigate the application of these two standards of reference empirically. Although the coexistence of these different standards for evaluating students' learning outcomes had long been noted in the field of education (e.g., Herbart, 1831; Pestalozzi, 1807), they had not been theoretically derived or empirically investigated, but understood in purely normative or prescriptive terms. It was Heckhausen (1974) who systematically linked these two distinct approaches to the "standard of excellence" to achievement motivation, and who coined the terms social versus individual reference norms (Veroff, 1969, referred to "autonomous" rather than "individual" standards).

Teachers' Reference Norm Orientations

Drawing on Heckhausen's (1974) theoretical considerations, the distinction between social and individual reference norms was then applied to teachers' evaluations of their students' learning outcomes, leading to the establishment of an independent research program (Rheinberg, 1977, 1980, 2001). The great appeal of this research was that, based on the teachers' approach to performance evaluation, it was possible to derive, by relatively stringent means, further differences in their teaching practice that could in turn be expected to impact aspects of their students' achievement motivation—most specifically, the direction of the achievement motive.

Research first showed that teachers differ in the reference norm (RN) they consider fair and appropriate: a social reference norm or an individual reference norm. This difference in personal preferences was termed *reference norm orientation* (RNO; Rheinberg, 1980). Teachers who prefer to apply a social RN want to be able to compare the students in a class. They thus assign all students the same tasks and provide the same instruction for all. Comparing the students then makes it very clear which students perform consistently better or worse than others. Perceptions of stable achievement invite stable causal attributions (Heider, 1958). Teachers with a social RNO thus prefer to attribute their students' learning outcomes to *stable causal factors* (ability), which in turn generate *long-term expectations*. As a result, teachers with a social RNO are relatively quick to decide which students are likely to show positive or less positive development over time. Their *sanctions* (praise and criticism) are highly dependent on whether a learning outcome is above or below the class average. They thus communicate to their students what is important in life, namely to be better than others. Numerous studies have provided empirical evidence in support of these theoretically derived predictions (Rheinberg, 1980, 2001). Being taught by teacher with a social RNO is likely to prove extremely

Table 18.2 Prototypical Characteristics of the Social Versus Individual RNO

Variable	Social	Individual
Comparisons of student achievement	Cross-sectional comparisons *between* students	Longitudinal comparisons *within* a student
Causal attribution	More—and phenomenally more valid—attributions, especially of interindividual differences in achievement to stable factors	Attributions tend to be kept pending; relative preference for instructional factors
Expectations	Longer term, based on general levels of achievement	Short term, based on the current level of knowledge
Sanctions	Based on differences in students' achievement	Based on individual development
Individualization	Same instruction for all	Principle of fit

discouraging for students whose performance is below average. Table 18.2 provides an overview of the prototypical characteristics of the two RNOs.

Teachers with an *individual RNO* compare a student's current learning outcomes with his or her previous performance. Because achievement tends to fluctuate intraindividually, they have a much more *variable conception of achievement* than teachers with a social RNO. When a student's current performance is measured against his or her previous learning outcomes, even slight improvements are highlighted, as if seen through a magnifying glass. Of course, the same holds in principle when performance deteriorates. But because students tend to learn cumulatively over time, *intra*individual comparison generally casts students' overall achievement in a positive light, showing more gains than declines. In contrast to the *inter*individual comparisons of teachers with a social RNO, class learning gains are irrelevant. Because teachers with an individual RNO are more attuned to the variability in student achievement, they are more likely to attribute their students' learning outcomes to *variable causes* (effort, learning strategies, etc.). Their *sanctions* (praise and criticism) depend on whether or not a student's performance has improved over time. They thus establish realistic standards for each individual student. Because the emphasis is on individual students improving their own knowledge and skills, rather than on outperforming others, below-average students also see chances for positive evaluation. Because teachers with an individual RNO are more sensitive to whether or not a student is making progress, they soon ascertain that assigning all students the same tasks and providing the same instruction for all overstretches some students and fails to stretch others enough. Instead, they seek to *individualize* instructional demands as far as practically possible. They do not necessarily award better grades, but students in their classes can be proud of having raised their grade from a D to a C, for example, and can nurture the hope that, with continued effort, they can do even better.

The parallels between the characteristics of the instruction delivered by teachers with an individual RNO, on the one hand, and the content of the motive training programs inspired by Heckhausen's self-evaluation model, on the other, are clear. The individualized demands of these teachers show students how to set realistic goals; the tasks they assign are achievable only if effort is applied. At the same time, the teachers' attributions correctly communicate the belief that learning outcomes depend on the effort invested, and students' perceptions of consistent learning gains reflect their increasing competence. These perceptions make it more likely that they will experience positive rather than negative affect in achievement-related contexts and that experiences of failure will not undermine their hope of future success. Finally, positive affect in achievement-related situations is further supported by the students themselves adopting an individual RNO, which they use as a basis for their own self-evaluation. Taken together, exposure to teachers with an individual RNO can be expected to function as a "natural" motive training program (Rheinberg, 1980).

Effects of Teachers' Individual Reference Norm Orientations

Because the instruction of teachers with an individual RNO shares certain characteristics with motive training programs, it seemed reasonable to expect these teachers to foster a success-oriented achievement motivation in their students over time. A series of studies confirmed these predictions (Rheinberg, 1982). Figure 18.3 shows a typical pattern of results. Trudewind and Kohne (1982) constructed parallel comparison groups from a large sample of elementary students. One-half of the students were taught by teachers with a pronounced social RNO over their first 4 years at school, the other half by teachers with a pronounced individual RNO.

The NH scores—as measured by Schmalt's (1976a) AM grid—of students who had been allocated teachers with a strong social RNO decreased in the first year of schooling; those of students taught by teachers with an individual RNO increased. The difference in the two groups' NH scores remained significant across the 4 years of the study.

These effects of teacher RNO on student motives have also been replicated in various samples of older students. Detailed analyses revealed that the effects of exposure to an individual RNO are most favorable in weaker students, who showed a marked decrease in fear of failure as measured by Schmalt's (1976a) AM grid. Figure 18.4 illustrates this pattern of results for fifth graders who were split into tertiles based on their scores on an intelligence test, and whose motive development was tracked from the start (T1) to the end (T2) of the school year. (In the German education system, students transfer to secondary school after fourth grade, with students from different elementary school classes being allocated to new classes at secondary level.)

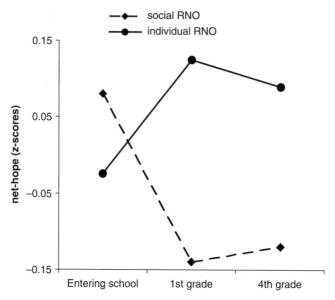

Figure 18.3. Development of the direction of the achievement motive over 4 years of elementary schooling in students taught by teachers with a social RNO ($N = 143$) versus an individual RNO ($N = 168$) (based on Trudewind & Kohne, 1982, p. 129).

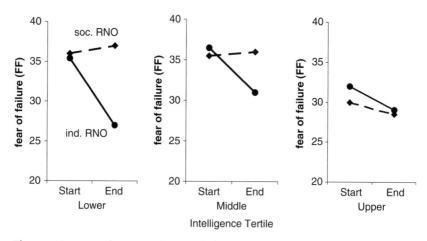

Figure 18.4. Development of fear of failure in fifth grade students of different intelligence levels taught by teachers with a social RNO ($N = 106$) versus an individual RNO ($N = 91$) (Rheinberg, 1979).

Students taught by teachers with a social RNO showed little change in fear of failure over the study period. After all, the instruction they were given was in keeping with what most of them had become accustomed to in elementary school. Students taught by teachers with an individual RNO showed decreasing fear of failure, with the most pronounced decrease being observed in the lower intelligence tertile. It is this group of students that experiences the greatest change when their performance is no longer compared with that of their better-performing classmates, but with their own previous performance. Irrespective of their intelligence level, students allocated to teachers with an individual RNO showed a greater awareness of their increased proficiency at the end of the school year. And after 2 years, their self-concept of ability had also improved (Rheinberg & Peter, 1982). This finding has since been replicated for mathematics in samples representative of the German secondary school system (Köller, 2005).

Interventions Designed to Change Teachers' Reference Norm Orientations

Once the favorable effects of an individual RNO on students' motives had been established, interventions were developed to foster a stronger individual RNO in teachers (for a summary, see Rheinberg & Krug, 2005). The underlying strategy was borrowed from Mehta (1968) and DeCharms (1976). However, the interventions were no longer based on the complex programs developed by McClelland and Winter (1969) for the business context, some aspects of which could not be integrated in classroom instruction. Rather, there was a specific focus on individualized task setting, patterns of causal attribution, and applying an individual RN to evaluate student learning outcomes.

As reported above for programs targeting students directly, effects on the achievement motive were most salient in physical education lessons. Weßling-Lünnemann (1982) trained 21 physical education teachers to apply an individual RN in their lessons. However, Rheinberg's questionnaire for determining reference norm orientation (FEBO; Rheinberg, 1980) showed that not all teachers benefited from the program as intended. Seven of the participating teachers picked up some motivation techniques for their lessons but continued to evaluate their students applying social norms. Figure 18.5 shows how the NH scores of students in the two training groups developed in the following school year relative to the scores of a control group whose teachers did not receive training.

The NH scores of the control students decreased significantly over the school year. This pattern is typical of fourth graders in Germany: at the end of fourth grade, students are selected to the different tracks of the three-tiered secondary system, and many students worry that they will fail to meet their parents' high educational expectations. This typically leads to an increase in mean FF scores in fourth grade.

It emerged that only the successfully trained physical education teachers were able to reverse this unfavorable trend (training group 1). The students of the seven teachers who still applied a social RNO, even after the training

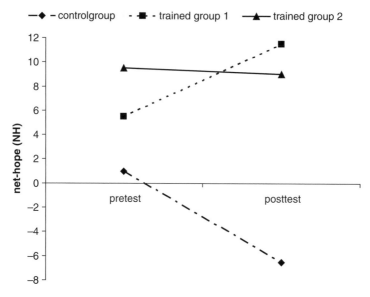

Figure 18.5. NH scores (Schmalt's AM grid) of two training groups and a control group over a school year (based on data from Weßling-Lünnemann, 1982; training group 1, teachers applied an individual RN, $N = 249$; training group 2, teachers still applied a social RN, $N = 132$; control group, $N = 123$).

program (training group 2), showed a somewhat more favorable development in NH than the control group, but the difference between the two groups was not significant.

Some studies conducted detailed investigations of training effects on student motivation over a short-term period. Of course, short-term interventions of this kind cannot be expected to affect students' motives, but interesting patterns of change in certain motivation-relevant student characteristics can be observed. In an instructional experiment reported by Rheinberg and Krug (2005), a teacher was trained to apply either an individual RN or a social RN in his classes. After a pretest (*zero* in Fig. 18.6) he then delivered history lessons to two parallel classes for 5 weeks, applying an individual RN in one class and a social RN in the other. The students in each class were split into tertiles based on their learning outcomes. Figure 18.6 illustrates the students' responses to the question of how encouraged they felt to participate actively in class by performance tertile.

As shown by the three curves in the right panel, relatively little change was observed overall when the teacher applied a social RNO, though the weaker students felt even less encouraged to participate toward the end of the intervention. In contrast, some intriguing effects were seen in the class where the teacher applied an individual RNO (the three curves in the left panel). Both the above-average and the below-average students first showed sharp decreases in

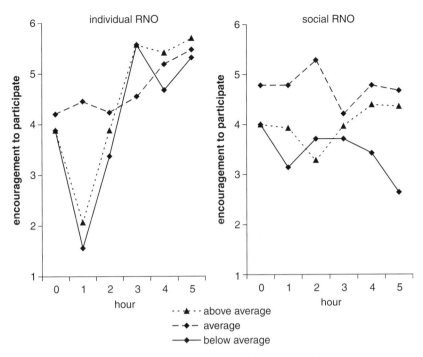

Figure 18.6. Perceived encouragement to participate actively in class when exposed to an individual RNO (N = 17) versus a social RNO (19): findings from a 6-week instructional experiment (based on Rheinberg & Krug, 2005, p. 104).

perceived encouragement to participate. In contrast to standard practice in the German education system, these students were no longer compared with the class average, but with their own prior performance. This makes a considerable difference, both to students who were previously always above average or "good," and to below-average students, who tend not to be called on very often in class. After just 2 weeks, however, the students no longer seemed to be irritated by the new RNO. By the end of the intervention, all three groups of students—even the below-average group—felt more encouraged to participate than did the above-average group in the social RNO class. Similar patterns of results emerged when oral participation in class discussions or objective performance data were taken as criteria (Rheinberg & Krug, 2005, pp. 100–111).

Training Programs for Parents

Because children's motivational development is influenced not only by their teachers, but of course also by their parents, the principles of the teacher training program have since also been applied to training programs for parents (Lund, Rheinberg, & Gladasch, 2001). In these programs, parents learn how to

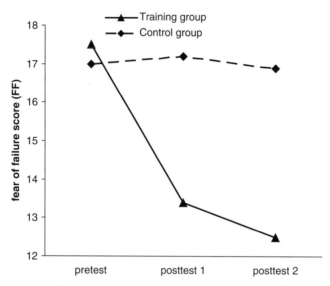

Figure 18.7. Development in fear-of-failure scores (FF, Schmalt, 1976a) at three points of measurement (posttest 1 after 8 weeks, posttest 2 after 8 months) for the training group ($N = 28$) and the control group ($N = 53$) in a parent-training program (Lund et al., 2001).

help their children set realistic goals, how to help them identify positive causal attributions for successes and failures, and how to encourage them to base their self-evaluation on an individual RN, without losing sight of whether their performance is better or worse than that of their peers (social RN).

Parents attended evening training sessions for 6 to 9 weeks. Relative to control groups, students whose parents participated in the training program showed a significant improvement in NH scores as measured by Schmalt's (1976a) AM grid. This development was the result of a reduction in fear of failure (FF; Schmalt, 1976b), which had declined even further at a follow-up test 8 months later. Figure 18.7 shows change in fear of failure (FF) in the control and training groups. The effects of parental training were thus particularly sustained. The core elements of the training program have now been standardized and are available on CD (Lund, 2002).

Reference Norm Orientation and Related Concepts

The concept of RNO was proposed by Heckhausen (1974) and investigated and developed in the school context by Rheinberg (1975, 1977, 1980, 2001). Independently of this German research program, similar concepts were later developed in the English-language literature, namely Nicholls' (1984) concept of *task versus ego orientation* and Dweck's concept of *learning versus performance goal orientation* (Dweck & Leggett, 1988). *Ego and performance goal orientation* involve a social RNO; *task or learning goal orientation*, an individual RNO.

Although there is broad overlap between these concepts and RNO, the approaches are not identical (Dickhäuser & Rheinberg, 2003). In particular, we are not aware of any studies taking a goal orientation approach that have attempted to modify the implicit achievement motive. As such, we do not address these concepts in any further detail in this chapter.

What Do the Training Programs Achieve?

Our brief accounts of the training studies outlined above have focused on findings relating to the implicit achievement motive. (Some favorable training effects on measures of the explicit achievement motive have also been reported; for full accounts, see Heckhausen & Krug, 1982, and Rand, 1987). But precisely what effects did the programs have on students' achievement motives? Importantly, the programs did not aim to extend, strengthen, or reinforce the associative network of the achievement motive acquired in preverbal development, thus moving it to the top of the motive hierarchy. In other words, the objective was *not* to make strongly affiliation- or power-motivated people into strongly achievement-motivated people. Quite apart from the difficult ethical questions that such endeavors would raise, it is extremely doubtful that motive change of this kind would be at all feasible within such a short space of time.

Instead, the training programs based on the self-evaluation model and individual RNOs aimed to change not the *strength* of the implicit achievement motive, but its *direction*. The key objective was to enable participants to experience less fear of failure and more hope of success in everyday achievement-related situations, and to act accordingly.

There is no doubt that the training programs also impacted cognitive elements of motivation, especially causal attribution. Furthermore, they contained a habit formation component, with students being taught (a) to start by setting goals in achievement-related situations and (b) to make those goals realistic. The combination of these goal-setting habits with the belief that success and failure are largely dependent on one's own actions leads to a change in the quality of experience of everyday school situations, which now tend to be interpreted as challenges rather than threats. There is no question that this changed perception of the situation amounts to more than just enhanced life management skills. Indeed, precisely these perceptions play a key role in the assessment of implicit motives in projective measures such as the TAT, PSE, or AM grid.

Of course, the implicit motive as a construct comprises more than the procedure used to measure it. But the motive-specific perception of situations that are open to different interpretations is also an important defining component of implicit motives on the construct level. From this perspective, the motive training programs described above certainly effected change in the implicit achievement motive: change in favor of success-oriented experience and behavior in open or ambiguous situations.

Training Programs Designed to Promote Motive Congruence

Motive Congruence and Motivational Competence

Given that it is probably not possible to change the hierarchy of implicit motives, the question arises of whether and to what extent people are aware of their relative motive strengths. If I have no way of influencing which motive-specific activity characteristics I find attractive and satisfying, it would at least be useful to know which forms of activity and types of situations are in line with my activity preferences. Indeed, this is one (of many) requirements for a self-determined way of life.

Surprisingly, it cannot be taken for granted that people are aware of their implicit motives and the associated activity preferences. In fact, the correlations between people's self-reports on what is important and attractive to them, as measured by motivation questionnaires, and their implicit motives, as assessed by the TAT/PSE, are very weak (Spangler, 1992; for a summary, see Brunstein, 2003). This remarkable finding was first reported by DeCharms, Morrison, Reitman, and McClelland (1955) and has since been discussed from various angles.

The perspective that guides current research draws on the work of McClelland, Koestner, and Weinberger (1989) and McClelland (1985). According to this approach, implicit motives are preferences for motive-typical classes of incentives that are partly genetically predetermined and that develop early in life via preverbal experiences. They are manifested in the individual's affective responsiveness to motive-congruent situations and activities. In contrast, self-reports on one's preferred incentives and value beliefs derive from the self-concept ("motivational self-concept," Rheinberg, 2002a, 2002b). The motivational self-concept is represented in the medium of language, is thus acquired later, and contains not only accurate self-perceptions, but also rosy illusions, others' impressions, and adopted value beliefs of what is considered good and desirable in life.

The interrelations between affect-based, implicit motives and the cognitively represented value beliefs and perceived preferences of motivational self-concepts can be theoretically conceptualized in various ways (Brunstein, 2003; McClelland, 1985, see also Chapters 11 and 12). Heckhausen's (1977)

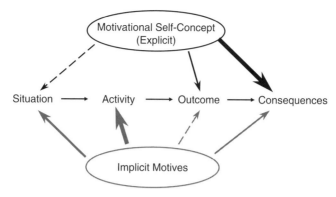

Figure 18.8. The hypothesized effects of implicit motives and motivational self-concepts in Heckhausen's (1977) extended cognitive model of motivation (based on Rheinberg, 2002b).

"extended cognitive model of motivation" illustrates the influences of the two motive systems during a given action episode. The model breaks an action episode down into four stages: the *situation*, which is likely to unfold in a certain way, affording various action alternatives and temptations, the actual *activity*, which can take various forms and bring about specific *outcomes*, which may, in turn, have desired or undesired *consequences*. In contrast to the affect immediately associated with the outcome (e.g., pride or shame), the elaboration of an activity's consequences, their probabilities, and desirability is a cognitive act. Augmented by some additional assumptions, this episode-specific model has proved a powerful predictor of school learning motivation, even at the individual level (Heckhausen & Rheinberg, 1980; Rheinberg, 1989).

Figure 18.8 illustrates the hypothesized effects of implicit motives and motivational self-concepts in an action episode. At the first station of the model, the *situation*, implicit motives influence the perception of the situation, determining which incentives are most salient to the individual. At the next station, the *activity*, implicit motives have a strong impact on the perceived attractiveness of different types of activity and serve to mobilize behavior. If the activity is congruent with the individual's motives (e.g., efficient task completion in someone with a strong achievement motive), implicit motives energize the necessary behavior and facilitate a positive quality of experience, keeping goal-directed behavior on course almost effortlessly. Implicit motives are thus sources of *activity-specific incentives* that are independent of the foreseeable consequences of the desired end states (Rheinberg, 1989). The thicker arrows to *situation* and *activity* in Figure 18.8 highlight the particular influence of implicit motives on these two stations of the action model. In keeping with the predictions of the model, empirical findings show that respondents with a strong achievement motive are significantly more likely to select achievement-related goals when they are instructed to make sure that striving for that goal will be "enjoyable and exciting." When, on the other hand, they are instructed to select goals that are "suitable" for them, the implicit achievement motive does not have the same effect (Job, 2007).

How the outcome of an activity is evaluated depends on the desirability of its potential *consequences* and on the perceived probability of their occurrence. These evaluations are thus the results of cognitive processes. If an activity is motivated solely by the attractiveness of its probable consequences, it will have to rely on value and efficacy beliefs, which are more or less consciously accessible. It is here that motivational self-concepts take effect; as cognitive schemata, motivational self-concepts contain information on what seems important and valuable to me, what seems to suit me, and what seems to be within the realm of my potential. Whenever people deliberate long and hard on whether or not to pursue a certain goal, their decision is based on their motivational self-concept. But how easy they then find it to engage in the necessary activities, and their quality of experience in doing so, depends on their implicit motives.

The ideal configuration is thus one in which individuals, based on their value orientations and self-knowledge, decide on goals and life projects that entail activities and situations that are in keeping with their implicit motives. The precondition for their making such choices is that their motivational self-concept is not radically at odds with their implicit motives. Someone with a strong implicit achievement motive and a weak implicit affiliation motive, but whose self-concept says quite the reverse, will frequently find him- or herself in situations and activities that require conscious effort and bring little or no enjoyment. Supposing herself to be someone who flourishes in social contexts, a student may opt to prepare for a test with a group of classmates, only to be constantly reminded how annoying it is when people keep chatting and having fun, rather than studying efficiently. Or she will talk herself into going to student parties and trying to maneuver herself into friendly conversations, although she soon finds the whole thing boring and loud, and would much rather be at home working out a complex problem on her computer. If her motivational self-concept and her implicit motives were congruent, she would have been able to spare herself such experiences.

The capacity to make motive-congruent decisions can also be termed *motivational competence*: a person's ability to reconcile current and future situations with his or her activity preferences such that he or she can function effectively, without the need for permanent volitional control (Rheinberg, 2002a). The components of motivational competence are (1) an accurate motivational self-concept (congruence between one's implicit motives and self-attributed motives), (2) the ability to evaluate the potential incentives of future situations and, if necessary, (3) to endow situations with motive-congruent incentives. (4) Moreover, when committing to longer-term projects, a person high in motivational competence does not consider only the benefits to be expected upon its completion, but also the pleasure to be derived from the activities themselves. (5) Metamotivational knowledge, that is, knowledge of the internal and external conditions that influence one's motivational processes, is also important (e.g., "I'd better not think about phoning my new girlfriend while I'm in the middle of preparing a difficult presentation"). An additional component in achievement-oriented societies may be knowledge of how to elicit a success-oriented motivational state (Rheinberg, 2002b). (This last component is less relevant in conflict-driven societies or societies based on inherited privileges.)

The Flow Hypothesis of Motivational Competence

Only the first of the five theoretically postulated components of motivational competence—congruence between implicit motives and motivational self-concept—has as yet been subject to close empirical investigation. The concept of congruence is by no means new; motivational competence is essentially a specification within motivation theory of the general idea of congruence presented by Rogers (1961). Brunstein's research group has been foremost in investigating what happens when people pursue goals that are congruent or incongruent with their implicit motives. As expected, the affective well-being of students who set themselves motive-congruent goals at the start of the semester was observed to increase as the semester progressed (Brunstein, Schultheiss, & Grässmann, 1998). Moreover, respondents whose implicit motives were congruent with their motivational self-concepts were shown to be particularly adept at dealing with critical feedback under ego-involving conditions (Brunstein, 2001). See Chapters 11 and 12 of this volume for further evidence of the favorable effects of high motive congruence on well-being.

We now address a specific hypothesis that provides further theoretical justification for interventions designed to increase the congruence between implicit motives and motivational self-concept. As shown in Figure 18.8, implicit motives have a particularly strong impact on the performance of the activity. Motive-congruent activities are supported and energized by implicit motives. People can become completely absorbed in these activities; because they enjoy what they are doing, they do not have to keep pushing themselves to complete a prespecified plan of action. Csikszentmihalyi (1975) labeled this joyful absorption in a seemingly effortless activity *flow*. People are far more likely to enter flow states when involved in motive-congruent activities than when pursuing motive-incongruent activities, where the realization of goal-directed activities requires constant monitoring and volitional control.

Of course, even people with high motivational competence are not always able to pursue motive-congruent activities that have intense experiences of flow; the objective conditions of our lives state otherwise. However, it is reasonable to assume that people high in motivational competence do not engage *unnecessarily* in motive-incongruent activities. This should be especially apparent in leisure time, but also observable whenever people have a certain freedom of choice in how to go about their everyday activities.

People with low motivational competence, in contrast, can be expected to engage in motive-incongruent activities even when it is not necessary. Especially when they put a great deal of thought into whether the expected consequences of their involvement are in keeping with their person and their values, their decisions are made on the basis of the motivational self-concept. Because their motivational self-concept deviates from their implicit motives, however, it is under precisely these conditions that they are drawn into activities that do not correspond with their implicit motives. Given the desired consequences of these actions, they then have to force themselves to do what is necessary to attain their goal by means of permanent volitional control. Of course, it is quite possible to live this way, but it means doing without the recurrent experiences of flow that can make even the most difficult activities succeed as if of their own accord. Rather, people with low motivational competence are more likely to feel that their activities are not really self-determined, and that performance of these activities requires high levels of self-control. Given this background, the flow hypothesis of motivational competence predicts a positive relationship between motive congruence and flow experience, provided that the individual's way of life is not fully subject to the control of others.

The flow hypothesis of motivational competence was first investigated by Clavadetscher (2003) in a sample of $N = 60$ adult members of a Swiss cultural organization. The members supported the organization by volunteering for certain activities involved in the staging of cultural events (e.g., concerts). These activities ranged from inviting well-known artists to doing the organization's accounts or running the bar in concert intermissions. Members volunteered for activities that appealed to them. The respondents' implicit motives were measured using the Multi-Motive Grid by Schmalt, Sokolowski, and Langens (2000); their motivational self-concepts were assessed using the PRF by Stumpf, Angleitner Wieck, Jackson, and Belloch-Till (1985). Clavadetscher used the sum of the z-score differences between the explicit and implicit measure of each motive as a negatively valenced measure of motivational competence (the lower the differences between the respective measures of implicit and explicit motives, the higher a respondent's motivational competence). In addition, the Flow Short Scale (FSS; Rheinberg, Vollmeyer, & Engeser, 2003) was used to assess how often the respondents reported flow experience while performing their voluntary activities. The mean flow scores for the voluntary activities were above average (mean T-value of 55 on the FSS). Moreover, as predicted by the flow hypothesis of motivational competence, the better the volunteers' motivational self-concepts corresponded with their implicit motives, the more flow they experienced in their chosen projects ($r = .34; p < .01$).

Most of the following studies on the flow hypothesis of motivational competence were conducted in achievement-related situations (e.g., in sporting,
academic, and occupational contexts) and thus examined motive congruence
with respect to the achievement motive. Rheinberg, Vollmeyer, and Manig
(2005) used the experience sampling method (ESM, Csikszentmihalyi &
Larson, 1987) to examine 28 scientists/managerial staff members and 53
secretaries/administrative assistants over a 1-week period. The participants
were given a "pager" that emitted signals seven times per day, prompting
them to rate their momentary flow state (FSS, Rheinberg et al., 2003) and to
note down where they were and what they were doing. The TAT/PSE had
previously been administered to assess the participants' implicit achievement
motive, and the Achievement Motives Scale (AMS, Gjesme & Nygard, 1970) to
assess their self-attributions of success-oriented achievement motivation. Based
on the difference between the two z-standardized motive measures, the sample
was divided by median split into groups, high verus low in motive congruence.

Across the total sample, participants with high motivational competence
reported significantly higher flow scores than participants with low motivational competence. As shown in Figure 18.9, this effect was observed in both
groups: the scientists/managerial staff and the secretaries/administrative assistants. There was one notable difference between the two groups, however. The
flow scores of the scientists/managers were particularly high in achievement-
related situations (writing papers, planning studies, running analyses, etc.),
differing significantly from their flow scores in non-achievement-related situations ($p < .01$).

This situational effect was not observed in the group of secretaries/admin-
istrative assistants, whose flow scores were independent of whether they were

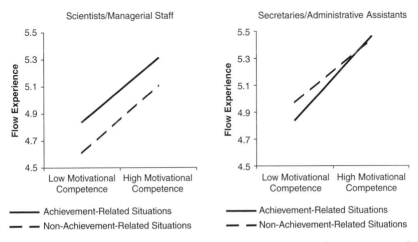

Figure 18.9. Flow experience of the two groups by motivational competence and
type of situation.

engaging in achievement-related activities or talking to colleagues, taking a break, and so forth. At the same time, their overall flow scores were as high as those of the scientists/managerial staff. In other words, flow experience at work is not confined to the higher levels of the hierarchy, as had already been reported by Csikszentmihalyi and LeFevre (1989). This finding was now extended to the flow effect of motivational competence, which was shown to occur irrespective of the respondents' level in the occupational hierarchy. It should be noted, however, that the sample of secretaries/administrative assistants in the institutions examined (universities, research institutes) probably enjoyed a relatively high level of self-determination in their work.

Other researchers have not worked with difference measures, but with interactions between implicit motives and motivational self-concepts. One example is Steiner's (2006) study of badminton players. The players first imagined that they were playing a game of badminton and explored what exactly it was about the game that gave them particular pleasure. They then completed the FSS for badminton (Rheinberg et al., 2003). Figure 18.10 shows the findings for N = 83 male players.

The players' implicit achievement motive had previously been assessed using the MMG (Schmalt et al., 2000); their self-concept of achievement motivation using the PRF (Stumpf et al., 1985). A significant interaction ($p < .01$) emerged between the two motive measures. Players with high scores on both motive measures reported the highest levels of flow, followed by players with low scores on both motive measures. The lowest levels of flow were reported by players

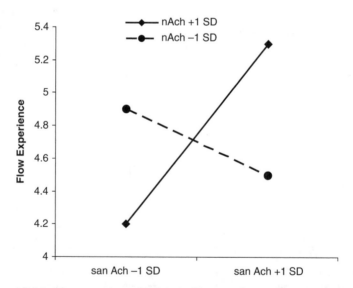

Figure 18.10. Flow experience (FSS) in badminton players (N = 83) by implicit achievement motive (*nAch*) and self-attributed achievement motive (*sanAch*) (data from Steiner, 2006, p. 65).

whose scores on the two motive measures were incongruent. This pattern of findings is exactly what is predicted by the flow hypothesis of motivational competence.

It also emerged that motive congruence is particularly relevant to flow experience when the implicit motive is strong. The contrast between high verus low motive congruence was only significant for respondents with a strong implicit achievement motive, and not for those whose implicit achievement motive was weak (for details, see Steiner, 2006, p. 65).

Findings from a study by Engeser (2005) made this pattern of results even clearer. Engeser assessed the implicit achievement motives (TAT/PSE after Winter, 1991) and self-attributed achievement motivation (PRF, Stumpf et al.) of $N = 273$ psychology students enrolled in a statistics course. In addition, the Volitional Components Inventory (VCI) by Kuhl and Fuhrmann (1998) was administered to assess the students' self-regulation competence and feelings of self-determination in everyday situations (sample item: "I feel that most of the time I really want to do the things I do.")

Of course, harmonious self-regulation cannot be equated with flow experience; rather, it is the state that makes it easy to become effortlessly absorbed in an activity and to enter flow. It is this reasoning that informed the flow hypothesis of motivational competence. Figure 18.11 shows the interaction between implicit achievement motive (*nAch*) and self-attributed achievement motivation (*sanAch*) for harmonious self-regulation.

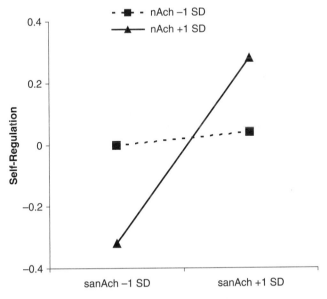

Figure 18.11. Harmonious self-regulation in $N = 273$ students: interaction between the implicit and self-attributed achievement motive (z-scores; based on Engeser, 2005, p. 198).

The interaction between implicit and self-attributed achievement motivation is significant. As is clearly shown by the data presented in Figure 18.11, motive congruence is irrelevant to harmonious self-regulation if the implicit achievement motive is weak. In the case of a strong implicit achievement motive, however, whether or not the self-attributed achievement motive is accurate makes a considerable difference to harmonious self-regulation.

How Can Motivational Competence Be Increased?

The findings outlined above show that the congruence between implicit and self-attributed motives not only has positive effects on emotional well-being (see Brunstein, 2003; Brunstein et al., 1998) but is also conducive to effective functioning in everyday life (flow experience and harmonious self-regulation). There is no doubt that motive congruence is a highly desirable personal characteristic, especially when the implicit motive in question is strong. So what can be done to increase motive congruence in oneself and in others?

Of course, it is possible to start by assessing people's motives using methods such as the PSE technique. However, it is important to note that, for various reasons, the PSE's accuracy on the individual level is low; it is less reliable than intelligence tests, for example. Nevertheless, PSE data, as far as they are available, can be expected to facilitate the development of a realistic self-concept (Rheinberg, 2004).

Alternatively, individuals facing an imminent decision on whether or not to engage in a certain activity can benefit from an experimental manipulation developed by Schultheiss and Brunstein (1999). In this experiment, participants were assigned the goal of counseling another person in a directive manner. This scenario activated both the affiliation motive and the power motive. One group of respondents participated in a goal imagery exercise before the counseling session, imagining how precisely they would go about counseling the client, how the client would respond, and how they themselves would feel during the exchange. Immediately before the session, participants' goal commitment was measured, that is, how committed they felt to attaining the goal of providing directive counseling. Findings showed scores on the implicit affiliation and power motives to be much more powerful predictors of goal commitment in the imagery group than in a control group. Participants high in affiliation and power motivation reported stronger goal commitment to engage in the—for them—motive-congruent activity than did participants low in these motives. The mental elaboration of the imminent situation evidently rendered it better "readable" for the participants' implicit motives. In the control group that did not participate in the goal imagery exercise, no such relationship was found between implicit motives and goal commitment.

Table 18.3 Practical Recommendations for Enhancing Motivational Competence

I. Retrospective Diagnosis

- Which activities do I prioritize and return to again and again even without the promise of reward?
- When has my work been particularly unproblematic and enjoyable; when could I have carried on endlessly? What was so special about that situation, task, or activity?
- When have I been particularly pleased with an outcome; when have I found myself unable to enjoy an outcome, despite its objective success?
- Which incentives/conditions must be in place for my involvement in an activity to be joyful, effective, and flowlike? (Discomfiting answers are also important here.)

II. Prospective Incentives

- Before adopting a goal, do not focus exclusively on its desirable consequences.
- Instead, imagine exactly what you will have to do to achieve that goal and how performing these activities will make you feel ("translation" into a form "readable" by your motives).
- Only then decide for or against the goal (provided you have the freedom to do so).

Note: From Rheinberg (2002a).

In more general terms, imagery techniques of this kind can be applied to increase motivational competence in a given situation. In terms of the extended cognitive model of motivation (see Fig. 18.8), the imagery exercise forces people faced with a decision to elaborate the *situation* and *activity* stations, rather than basing their decision solely on the *outcome* and *consequences* stations. In so doing, the influence of the motivational self-concept is temporarily weakened and that of the implicit motives strengthened. This intervention can also be expected to help people low in motivational competence to make motive-congruent decisions.

More specific recommendations for increasing one's motivational competence can be derived from the findings of Schultheiss and Brunstein (1999). Table 18.3 presents a list of practical recommendations proposed by Rheinberg (2002a).

The Clarificatory Training Approach of Krug and Kuhl

The evident stability of implicit motives has implications for current motive training programs. Krug and Kuhl (2005) have continued to develop and refine the training program originally proposed by McClelland and Winter (1969) and Varga (1977), adapting it to European conditions. Like McClelland and Burnham (1976), they found that it is less the achievement motive than the power motive that predicts European (German) managers' success in large organizations. The managers' implicit power motive (PSE, Winter, 2001) was found to correlate significantly with employee satisfaction with their management ($r = .65$), satisfaction with working in the team ($r = .58$), and satisfaction with the team's performance ($r = .49$) ($N = 122$; Krug & Kuhl, 2005, p. 177). No such relationships were found for the managers' implicit achievement motive.

Had the stability of implicit motives not been established, researchers might have attempted—like McClelland—to strengthen the implicit power motive in training programs. Krug and Kuhl have now moved from such a modificatory approach to a clarificatory one: Although it is clear that training cannot modify the strength of implicit motives in the short to medium term (Krug, 1983), measures should at least be taken to ensure that individuals are properly aware of their implicit motives. This would increase the congruence between implicit motives and motivational self-concept, thus bolstering the main component of motivational competence. Interventions of this kind would help managers to understand (a) why they feel uncomfortable with certain managerial tasks and tend to avoid them more often than is advisable. They would also gain a better awareness of (b) how they can modify the scope of their duties through restructuring and delegating tasks, thus tailoring themselves a new sphere of activity that is a better fit to their implicit motives and motive-specific activity preferences. Finally, it would (c) give them a sound basis for predicting whether the new tasks that will face them if they accept a promotion or move to a higher paid position in another company are in keeping with their motive structure.

The question is whether a 4- to 5-day training program using methods of self-exploration can succeed in modifying participants' motivational self-concept. All participants in the training studies reported by Krug and Kuhl were administered the PSE prior to the training program, meaning that scores on the achievement, power, and affiliation motive were available for each participant. Like the program devised by McClelland and Winter (1969), the Krug and Kuhl program includes theoretical modules on the motive constructs as well as "games" and self-awareness exercises. The participants reassess their own motive profile every day of the program.

In a sample of $N = 63$ managers, Krug and Kuhl examined how well the participants' motivational self-concepts corresponded with their PSE scores in terms of the dominant motive identified. At the beginning of the first day, only 32% of participants were able to identify their dominant motive—very nearly the percentage to be expected if answers were given at random. Most managers made the mistake of ascribing themselves a dominant achievement motive, when in fact they had a dominant power motive. By the end of the training period, before they were told their actual PSE scores, 80% of participants were able to identify their dominant motive (Krug & Kuhl, 2005). What is important is that this considerable increase in motivational competence was facilitated by guided self-exploration. It seems reasonable to assume that the effects of the participants' new knowledge about themselves are sustained.

Whether and how the increase in the participants' motivational competence impacted their success as managers will be a subject of future research (Krug & Kuhl, 2006). The findings presented in the section "The Flow Hypothesis of Motivational Competence" suggest that positive effects are to be expected on the managers' emotional well-being and effective functioning. Kehr (2005) has since developed a similar training approach.

A Potential Problem of Modified Self-Evaluations

Given the stability of implicit motives and their considerable effects on behavior and experience, this chapter has recommended that motivational competence be enhanced by bringing self-concepts into line with implicit motives. We do not now intend to withdraw this recommendation. However, it is important to draw attention to a problem potentially entailed in this approach. Because motivational self-concepts are embedded within an overarching self-concept that also contains many other self-evaluations and value beliefs, the possibility cannot be excluded that a change in motivational self-concept may cause conflict with a person's core value beliefs.

A participant in a training program who gradually comes to realize that, contrary to what he had always believed, his behavior is not in fact achievement motivated, but driven by a dominant power motive, may—against the background of his value orientations—experience this new knowledge of himself as shameful. In this case, our recommendations would be to make him aware (a) that there is no way of changing the dominance of his implicit power motive anyway, (b) that a strong power motive can take a very positive form that he can choose to cultivate ("socialized power motive"), and (c) that he can enhance his emotional well-being and effective functioning by ensuring that his (working) life is endowed with motive-congruent contexts and situations.

Of course, recommendations of this kind only make sense if implicit motives are considered to be of greater consequence than cognitive self-definitions and value orientations. An alternative view might be that it is important not to "capitulate" to one's basal biopsychological incentive systems, or motives. Instead, one might ascribe to a view of humanity in which we humans, as rational beings, are challenged to define ourselves on the basis of our reasoned values. The value-oriented formation of our self would then be a guiding goal in our lives and we would actualize ourselves on a daily basis by acting in accordance with our self-created self-definition.

Of course, people may choose to live according to this noble principle of cognitive self-creation. But they should be warned that, if their self-definition is in stark contradiction to their dominant implicit motive, life will be relatively joyless and devoid of flow experiences. Rather, the realization of their values and aspirations will necessitate constant volitional self-control (as Martin Luther pointed out, the Old Adam has to be drowned anew each day). There is no doubt that life is easier, more joyful, and more successful if one's self-definition corresponds with one's implicit motives.

References

Atkinson, J. W. (1957). Motivational determinants of risk-taking behavior. *Psychological Review, 64*, 359–372.

Atkinson, J. W. (Ed.). (1958). *Motives in fantasy, action, and society*. Princeton, NJ: Van Nostrand.

Brunstein, J. C. (2001). *Implizite und explizite Formen des Leistungsstrebens. Validierung eines Zwei-Komponenten-Modells der Leistungsmotivation* [Implicit and explicit forms of achievement striving. Validation of a two-component model of achievement motivation] (DFG Report). University of Potsdam, Institute for Psychology, Potsdam, Germany.

Brunstein, J. C. (2003). Implizite Motive und motivationale Selbstbilder: Zwei Prädiktoren mit unterschiedlicher Gültigkeit [Implicit motives and motivational self-concepts: Two predictors with differing validity]. In J. Stiensmeier-Pelster & F. Rheinberg (Eds.), *Diagnostik von Motivation und Selbstkonzept (Tests and Trends*, Vol. 2, pp. 59–88). Göttingen, Germany: Hogrefe.

Brunstein, J. C., Schultheiss, O. C., & Grässmann, R. (1998). Personal goals and emotional well-being: The moderating role of motive dispositions. *Journal of Personality and Social Psychology, 75*, 494–508.

Clavadetscher, C. (2003). *Motivation ehrenamtlicher Arbeit im Verein Mahogany Hall, Bern* [Motivation for voluntary work in the Mahogany Hall Society, Berne, Switzerland]. Unpublished final thesis, Berne University of Applied Sciences, Berne, Switzerland.

Collins, C. J., Hages, P. J., & Locke, E. A. (2004). The relationship of achievement motivation to entrepreneurial behavior: A meta-analysis. *Human Performance, 17*, 95–117.

Csikszentmihalyi, M. (1975). *Beyond boredom and anxiety*. San Francisco: Jossey-Bass.

Csikszentmihalyi, M., & Larson, R. (1987). Validity and reliability of the Experience Sampling Method. *Journal of Nervous and Mental Disease, 175*, 529–536.

Csikszentmihalyi, M., & LeFevre, J. (1989). Optimal experience in work and leisure. *Journal of Personality and Social Psychology, 56*, 815–822.

DeCharms, R. (1976). *Enhancing motivation: Change in the classroom*. New York: Irvington.

DeCharms, R., Morrison, H. W., Reitman, W., & McClelland, D. C. (1955). Behavioral correlates of directly and indirectly measured achievement motivation. In D. C. McClelland (Ed.), *Studies in Motivation* (pp. 414–423). New York: Appleton-Century-Crofts.

Dickhäuser, O., & Rheinberg, F. (2003). Bezugsnormorientierung: Erfassung, Probleme, Perspektiven [Reference norm orientations: Measurement, problems, perspectives]. In J. Stiensmeier-Pelster & F. Rheinberg (Eds.), *Diagnostik von Motivation und Selbstkonzept* (*Tests and Trends*, Vol. 2, pp. 41–56). Göttingen, Germany: Hogrefe.

Dweck, C. S. (1975). The role of expectations and attributions in the alleviation of learned helplessness. *Journal of Personality and Social Psychology, 31,* 674–685.

Dweck, C. S., & Leggett, F. L. (1988). A social-cognitive approach to motivation and personality. *Psychological Review, 95,* 256–273.

Engeser, S. (2005). *Lernmotivation und volitionale Handlungssteuerung: Eine Längsschnittuntersuchung beim Statistik Lernen im Psychologiestudium.* [Learning motivation and volitional action regulation: A longitudinal study on learning elementary statistics]. Unpublished doctoral dissertation, University of Potsdam, Germany.

Festinger, L. (1954). A theory of social comparison processes. *Human Relations, 7,* 117–140.

Fries, S. (2002). *Wollen und Können: Ein Training zur gleichzeitigen Förderung des Leistungsmotivs und des induktiven Denkens* [Volition and ability: A training program simultaneously fostering the achievement motive and inductive reasoning]. Münster, Germany: Waxmann.

Fries, S., Lund, B., & Rheinberg, F. (1999). Läßt sich durch gleichzeitige Motivförderung das Training des induktiven Denkens optimieren? [Does simultaneous motive modification optimise the teaching of inductive reasoning?] *Zeitschrift für Pädagogische Psychologie, 13,* 37–49.

Gjesme, T., & Nygard, R. (1970). *Achievement-related motives: Theoretical considerations and construction of a measuring instrument.* Unpublished manuscript, University of Oslo, Norway.

Harrison, L. E., & Huntington, S. P. (2000). *Culture matters.* New York: Basic Books.

Hecker, G., Kleine, W., Wessling-Lünnemann, G., & Beier, A. (1979). Interventionsstudien zur Entwicklungsförderung der Leistungsmotivation im Sportunterricht [Intervention studies to foster development of achievement motivation in physical education lessons]. *Zeitschrift für Entwicklungspsychologie und Pädagogische Psychologie, 11,* 153–169.

Heckhausen, H. (1963). *Hoffnung und Furcht in der Leistungsmotivation* [Hope and fear in achievement motivation]. Meisenheim, Germany: Hain.

Heckhausen, H. (1972). Die Interaktion der Sozialisationsvariablen in der Genese des Leistungsmotivs [The interaction of socialization variables in the genesis of the achievement motive]. In C. F. Graumann (Ed.), *Handbuch der Psychologie* (Vol. 7/2, pp. 955–1019). Göttingen, Germany: Hogrefe.

Heckhausen, H. (1974). *Leistung und Chancengleichheit* [Achievement and equality of opportunity]. Göttingen, Germany: Hogrefe.

Heckhausen, H. (1975). Fear of failure as a self-reinforcing motive system. In I. G. Sarason & C. Spielberger (Eds.), *Stress and anxiety* (pp. 117–128). Washington, DC: Hemisphere.

Heckhausen, H. (1977). Achievement motivation and its constructs: A cognitive model. *Motivation and Emotion, 1,* 283–329.

Heckhausen, H., & Krug, S. (1982). Motive modification. In A. J. Stewart (Ed.), *Motivation and society* (pp. 274–318). San Francisco: Jossey-Bass.

Heckhausen, H., & Rheinberg, F. (1980). Lernmotivation im Unterricht, erneut betrachtet [A new look at motivation to learn in the classroom]. *Unterrichtswissenschaft, 8,* 7–47.

Heckhausen, H., Schmalt, H.-D., & Schneider, K. (1985). *Achievement motivation in perspective.* New York: Academic Press.

Heckhausen, H., & Weiner, B. (1972). The emergence of a cognitive psychology of motivation. In P. C. Dodwell (Ed.), *New horizons in psychology* (pp. 126–147). London: Penguin Books.

Heider, F. (1958). *The psychology of interpersonal relations.* New York: Wiley.

Herbart, J. F. (1831). Pädagogische Briefe oder Briefe über die Anwendung der Psychologie auf die Pädagogik [Pedagogical letters or letters on the application of psychology to pedagogy]. Leipzig, Germany: Osterwick.

Job, V. (2007). *Antecedents and consequences of motive-goal congruence.* Unpublished doctoral thesis, University of Zurich, Switzerland.

Kehr, H. (2005). Das Kompensationsmodell der Motivation und Volition als Basis für die Führung von Mitarbeitern [The compensation model of motivation and volition as a basis for managing employees]. In R. Vollmeyer & J. C. Brunstein (Eds.), *Motivationspsychologie und ihre Anwendung* (pp. 131–150). Stuttgart, Germany: Kohlhammer.

Klauer, K. J. (1991). *Denktraining für Kinder II* [Reasoning training for children II]. Göttingen, Germany: Hogrefe.

Kleine, W. (1980). *Leistungsmotivschulung im Grundschulsport* [Training the achievement motive in elementary school physical education lessons]. Schorndorf, Germany: Hofman.

Köller, O. (2005). Bezugsnormorientierung von Lehrkräften: Konzeptuelle Grundlagen, empirische Befunde und Ratschläge für praktisches Handeln [Teachers' reference norm orientations: Conceptual framework, empirical findings, and recommendations for classroom practice]. In R. Vollmeyer & J. C. Brunstein (Eds.), *Motivationspsychologie und ihre Anwendung* (pp. 189–202). Stuttgart, Germany: Kohlhammer.

Kraeft, U., & Krug, S. (1979). Ursachenzuschreibung in schulischen Lernsituationen [Causal attributions in school learning situations]. In L. H. Eckensberger (Ed.), *Bericht über den 31. Kongress der DGfPs* (pp. 59–60). Göttingen, Germany: Hogrefe.

Krug, S. (1983). Motivförderprogramme: Möglichkeiten und Grenzen [Motive enhancement programs: Potential and limitations]. *Zeitschrift für Entwicklungspsychologie und Pädagogische Psychologie, 15,* 317–346.

Krug, S., & Hanel, J. (1976). Motivänderung: Erprobung eines theoriegeleiteten Trainingsprogrammes [Motive modification: Testing a theory-based training program]. *Zeitschrift für Entwicklungspsychologie und Pädagogische Psychologie, 8,* 274–287.

Krug, S., & Kuhl, U. (2005). Die Entwicklung von Motivförderprogrammen [The development of motive enhancement programs]. In R. Vollmeyer & J. C. Brunstein (Eds.), *Motivationspsychologie und ihre Anwendung* (pp. 167–188). Stuttgart, Germany: Kohlhammer.

Krug, S., & Kuhl, U. (2006). *Macht, Leistung, Freundschaft* [Power, achievement, friendship]. Stuttgart, Germany: Kohlhammer.

Krug, S., Mrazek, J., & Schmidt, C. (1980). Motivationsförderung im Sportunterricht durch Leistungsbewertung unter individueller Bezugsnorm [Enhancing motivation in physical education lessons by applying individual reference norms in performance evaluation]. *Psychologie in Erziehung und Unterricht, 27,* 278–284.

Krug, S., Peters, J., & Quinkert, H. (1977). Motivförderungsprogramm für lernbehinderte Sonderschüler [A motive enhancement program for students with learning disabilities]. *Zeitschrift für Heilpädagogik, 28,* 667–674.

Kuhl, J., & Fuhrmann, A. (1998). Decomposing self-regulation and self-control: The volitional component inventory. In J. Heckhausen & C. S. Dweck (Eds.), *Motivation and self-regulation across the life span* (pp. 15–45). Cambridge, UK: Cambridge University Press.

Langens, T. & Schmalt, H.-D. (2008). Motivational traits: New directions and measuring motives with the Multi-Motive-Grid (MMG). In G. Boyle, G. Matthews, & D. Saklovske (Eds.) *The Sage handbook of personality theory and assessment* (pp. 517–540). London: Sage Publications.

Lund, B. (2002). Aspekte der Leistungsmotivation: Lehr- und Lernmaterial für Lehrer, Lehramts- und Psychologiestudenten und interessierte Eltern [Aspects of achievement motivation: Teaching and learning material for teachers, candidate teachers, psychology students, and interested parents] [CD]. University of Potsdam, Potsdam, Germany.

Lund, B., Rheinberg, F., & Gladasch, U. (2001). Ein Elterntraining zum motivationsförderlichen Erziehungsverhalten in Leistungskontexten [Teaching parents how to reduce children's fear of failure]. *Zeitschrift für Pädagogische Psychologie, 15,* 130–142.

Mandler, G., & Sarason, S. B. (1952). A study in anxiety and learning. *Journal of Abnormal and Social Psychology, 47,* 166–173.

McClelland, D. C. (1958). Methods of measuring human motivation. In J. W. Atkinson (Ed.), *Motives in fantasy, action and society* (pp. 7–42). Princeton, NJ: Van Nostrand.

McClelland, D. C. (1961). *The achieving society.* Princeton, NJ: Van Nostrand.

McClelland, D. C. (1965). Toward a theory of motive acquisition. *American Psychologist, 20,* 321–333.

McClelland, D. C. (1972). What is the effect of achievement motivation training in the schools? *Teachers College Record, 74,* 129–145.

McClelland, D. C. (1985). *Human motivation.* Glenview, IL: Scott, Foresman, & Co.

McClelland, D. C. (1995). Achievement motivation in relation to achievement-related recall, performance, and urine-flow, a marker associated with release of vasopression. *Motivation and Emotion, 19,* 59–76.

McClelland, D. C., Atkinson, J. W., Clark, R. A., & Lowell, E. L. (1953). *The achievement motive.* New York: Appleton-Century-Crofts.

McClelland, D. C., & Burnham, D. (1976). Power is the great motivator. *Harvard Business Review, 25,* 159–166.

McClelland, D. C., Koestner, R., & Weinberger, J. (1989). How do self-attributed and implicit motives differ? *Psychological Review, 96,* 690–702.

McClelland, D. C., & Winter, D. G. (1969). *Motivating economic achievement*. New York: Free Press.

Mehta, P. (1968). Achievement motivation training for educational development. *Indian Educational Review, 3*, 1–29.

Meichenbaum, D. H., & Goodman, J. (1971). Training impulsive children to talk to themselves: A means of development self-control. *Journal of Abnormal Psychology, 77*, 115–126.

Nicholls, J. G. (1984). Achievement motivation: Conceptions of ability, subjective experience, task choice, and performance. *Psychological Review, 91*, 328–346.

Pestalozzi, H. (1807). *Über den Aufenthalt in Stanz* [On the time in Stanz]. Liegnitz, Germany: Seyffart.

Rand, P. (1987). Research on achievement motivation in school and college. In F. Halisch & J. Kuhl (Eds.), *Motivation intention and volition* (pp. 215–232). Berlin, Germany: Springer.

Rheinberg, F. (1975). Zeitstabilität und Steuerbarkeit von Ursachen schulischer Leistung aus der Sicht des Lehrers [Temporal stability and controllability of the causes of school outcomes from the teacher's perspective]. *Zeitschrift für Entwicklungspsychologie und Pädagogische Psychologie, 7*, 180–194.

Rheinberg, F. (1977). Bezugsnorm-Orientierung: Versuch einer Integration motivierungsbedeutsamer Lehrervariable [Reference norm orientations: An attempt to integrate teacher variables relevant to motivation]. In W. H. Tack (Ed.), *Bericht über den 30. Kongress der DGfPs* (pp. 318–319). Göttingen, Germany: Hogrefe.

Rheinberg, F. (1979). Bezugsnorm und Wahrnehmung der eigenen Tüchtigkeit (Reference norm and perception of own ability). In S. H. Filipp (Ed.), *Selbstkonzeptforschung: Probleme. Befunde, Perspektiven* (pp. 237–259). Stuttgart, Germany: Klett.

Rheinberg, F. (1980). *Leistungsbewertung und Lernmotivation* [Achievement evaluation and motivation to learn]. Göttingen, Germany: Hogrefe.

Rheinberg, F. (1982). Bezugsnormen zur Schulleistungsbewertung: Analyse und Intervention [Reference norms for the evaluation of student learning outcomes]. *Jahrbuch für Empirische Erziehungswissenschaft 1982*. Düsseldorf: Schwann.

Rheinberg, F. (1989). *Zweck und Tätigkeit* [Purpose and activity]. Göttingen, Germany: Hogrefe.

Rheinberg, F. (2001). Bezugsnormen und schulische Leistungsbeurteilung [Reference norms and evaluation of student learning outcomes]. In F. E. Weinert (Ed.), *Leistungsmessung in Schulen* (pp. 59–71). Weinheim, Germany: Beltz.

Rheinberg, F. (2002a). Freude am Kompetenzerwerb, Flow-Erleben und motivpassende Ziele [Enjoyment of learning, flow experience, and motive-congruent goals]. In M. v. Salisch (Ed.), *Emotionale Kompetenz entwickeln* (pp. 179–206). Stuttgart, Germany: Kohlhammer.

Rheinberg, F. (2002b, September). *Motivationale Kompetenz* [Motivational competence]. Paper presented at the 22nd MPK, Siegen, Germany.

Rheinberg, F. (2004). *Motivationsdiagnostik* [Measurement of motivation]. Göttingen, Germany: Hogrefe.

Rheinberg, F., & Günther, A. (2005). Ein Unterrichtsbeispiel zum lehrplanabgestimmten Einsatz individueller Bezugsnormen [Application of individual reference norms within the curriculum: An example from classroom instruction]. In F. Rheinberg & S. Krug (Eds.), *Motivationsförderung im Schulalltag* (3rd ed., pp. 55–68). Göttingen, Germany: Hogrefe.

Rheinberg, F., & Krug, S. (1978). Innere und äußere Differenzierung, Motivation und Bezugsnorm-Orientierung [Internal and external differentiation, motivation and reference norm orientation]. In K. J. Klauer & H. J. Kornadt (Eds.), *Jahrbuch für empirische Erziehungswissenschaft 1978* (pp. 165–195). Düsseldorf, Germany: Schwann.

Rheinberg, F., & Krug, S. (2005). *Motivationsförderung im Schulalltag* [Fostering motivation in school] (3rd ed.). Göttingen, Germany: Hogrefe.

Rheinberg, F., Manig, Y., & Vollmeyer, R. (2005). *Flow-Erleben: Untersuchungen zu einem populären, aber unterspezifizierten Konstrukt* [Flow experience: Studies on a popular, but unspecific construct] (Final DFG Report). University of Potsdam, Institute for Psychology, Potsdam, Germany.

Rheinberg, F., & Peter, R. (1982). Selbstkonzept, Ängstlichkeit und Schulunlust von Schülern: Eine Längsschnittstudie zum Einfluß des Klassenlehrers [Self-concept, anxiety, and school aversion: A longitudinal study on the influence of the form tutor]. In F. Rheinberg (Ed.), *Jahrbuch für Empirische Erziehungswissenschaft 1982* (pp. 143–160). Düsseldorf, Germany: Schwann.

Rheinberg, F., & Schliep, M. (1985). Ein kombiniertes Trainingsprogramm zur Förderung der Rechtschreibkompetenz älterer Schüler [A combined training program to enhance the spelling skills of older students]. *Heilpädagogische Forschung, 12,* 277–294.

Rheinberg, F., Vollmeyer, R., & Engeser, S. (2003). Die Erfassung des Flow-Erlebens [Measuring flow experience]. In J. Stiensmeier-Pelster & F. Rheinberg (Eds.), *Diagnostik von Motivation und Selbstkonzept* (Tests and Trends, Vol. 2, pp. 261–279). Göttingen, Germany: Hogrefe.

Rogers, C. R. (1961). *On becoming a person.* Boston: Houghton Mifflin.

Schmalt, H.-D. (1976a). *Das LM-Gitter* [The AM Grid]. Göttingen, Germany: Hogrefe.

Schmalt, H.-D. (1976b). *Die Messung des Leistungsmotivs* [Measurement of the achievement motive]. Göttingen, Germany: Hogrefe.

Schmalt, H.-D. (2005). Validity of a short form of the achievement-motive grid (AMG-S): Evidence the three-factor structure emphasizing active and passive forms of fear of failure. *Journal of Personality Assessment, 84,* 172–184.

Schmalt, H.-D., Sokolowski, K., & Langens, T. (2000). *Das Multi-Motiv-Gitter (MMG)* [The Multi-Motive Grid (MMG)]. Lisse, The Netherlands: Swets.

Schneider, K. (1973). *Motivation unter Erfolgsrisiko* [Motivation under the risk of success]. Göttingen, Germany: Hogrefe.

Schultheiss, O. C., & Brunstein, J. D. (1999). Goal imagery: Bridging the gap between implicit motives and explicit goals. *Journal of Personality, 67,* 1–38.

Spangler, W. D. (1992). Validity of questionnaire and TAT measures of need for achievement: Two meta-analyses. *Psychological Research, 112,* 140–154.

Steiner, M. (2006). *Motivationale Kompetenz und Anreize im Badminton* [Motivational competence and intentives in badminton]. Unpublished Lizensiat thesis. University of Zürich, Switzerland.

Stumpf, H., Angleitner, A., Wieck, T., Jackson, D. N., & Beloch-Till, H. (1985). *Deutsche Personality Research Form (PRF)* [German Personality Research Form (PRF). Göttingen, Germany: Hogrefe.

Trudewind, C., & Kohne, W. (1982). Bezugsnorm-Orientierung des Lehrers und Motiventwicklung: Zusammenhänge mit Schulleistung, Intelligenz und Merkmalen der häuslichen Umwelt in der Grundschulzeit [Teachers' reference norm orientation and motive development: Relationships with school achievement, intelligence, and characteristics of the home environment in the elementary years]. In F. Rheinberg (Ed.), *Jahrbuch für Empirische Erziehungswissenschaft 1982* (pp. 115–142). Düsseldorf, Germany: Schwann.

Varga, K. (1977). Who gains from achievement motivation training? Indian Institute of Management, Ahmedabad. *Vikalpa (The Journal for Decision Makers), 2*, 187–200.

Veroff, J. (1969). Social comparison and the development of achievement motivation. In C. P. Smith (Ed.), *Achievement-related motives in children* (pp. 46–101). New York: Russel Sage Foundation.

Weinberger, J., & McClelland, D. C. (1990). Cognitive versus traditional motivational models. In E. Higgins & R. M. Sorrentino (Eds.), *Handbook of motivation and cognition: Foundations of social behavior* (pp. 562–597). New York: Guilford Press.

Weiner, B., & Kukla, A. (1970). An attributional analysis of achievement motivation. *Journal of Personality and Social Psychology, 15*, 1–20.

Weiß, R. H. (1987). *Grundintelligenztest Skala 2, CFT-20* [Culture Fair Intelligence Test Scale 2, CFT-20] (3rd ed.). Göttingen, Germany: Hogrefe.

Weßling-Lünnemann, G. (1982). Individuelle Bezugsnorm-Orientierung: Ein didaktischer Grundsatz für den Sportunterricht [Individual reference norm orientations: A didactic principle for physical education]. In F. Rheinberg (Ed.), *Jahrbuch für Empirische Erziehungswissenschaft* (pp. 221–234). Düsseldorf, Germany: Schwann.

Winter, D. G. (1991). *Manual for scoring motive imagery in running text* (3rd ed.). Michigan: Unpublished manuscript, University of Michigan, Department of Psychology.

Winter, D. G. (2001). *Manual for scoring motive imagery in running text* (4 ed.). Unpublished manuscript, University of Michigan, Ann Arbor, Department of Psychology.

Winterstein, P. J. (1991). *Leistungsmotivationsförderung im Sportunterricht* [Enhancing achievement motivation in physical education lessons]. Hamburg, Germany: Kovac.

INDEX

Note: Page Numbers followed by *f* denotes Figures, *t* denotes Tables and n denotes Notes.

Motive congruence (*Continued*)
goals, explicit (personal), 351–54, 354, 365, 367
motivational-congruence hypothesis, 357, 359
satisfaction of motives, 350–51
empirical research, 310–15, 311*f*, 312*t*–313*t*, 339n3
explicit influences upon implicit, processes, 327–29, 340n6, 368–69, 473–75
extensity in, 328–29
feedback in, 323, 330
imagery in, 315, 323
implicit influences upon explicit, processes, 323–27, 339n5, 368–69, 473–75
information integration in, 332
integration *vs.*, 335–36
memory system organization in, 331–32
neuroplasticity in, 333
normative, temporal, and configural, individual differences in, 336–38
organizational framework, 315–19, 316*f*, 318*t*
design issues, 333–35
explicit influences upon implicit, processes, 327–29, 340n6, 368–69, 473–75
implicit influences upon explicit, processes, 323–27, 339n5, 368–69, 473–75
methodological influences, 319–23
related literature integration, 331–33
PSI theory, 388–91, 389*f*, 391*f*
social desirability in, 320–21
translation in, 332
Motive Dictionary, 200
Motive enactment test, 398
Motive incongruence, 366, 390, 391*f*
Motive training
achievements of, 529–30
congruence development, 530–33, 531*f*
(*see also* motive congruence)
fear of failure reduction program design, 513–20, 514*t*, 517*f*, 519*f*
classroom instruction integration, 518–20, 519*f*
combined programs, 518
Heckhausen's self-evaluation model, 513–16, 514*t*, 519
measurement methods, 516–17, 519*f*
model-based programs, 516, 517*f*
feedback in, 521–22, 522*t*
history, 510–11
motivational competence, 532–33
(*see also* motive congruence)
clarificatory approach, 539–41
enhancement methods, 538–39, 539*t*
flow hypothesis of, 533–38, 535*f*–537*f*
self-evaluation issues, 541–42

program design, 511
reference norm orientation
changing, interventions, 525–27, 526*f*, 527*f*
individual RNO effects, 523–25, 524*f*
learning *versus* performance goal orientation, 529
parents, 527–28, 527*f*, 528*f*
social, individual norms, 520–21, 522*t*
task *versus* ego orientation, 529
teachers, 521–23, 522*t*
UNIDO follow-up studies, 511–12
Moulton, R. W., 192
MSCEIT, 498
Mücher, H. P., 289
Mueller, E. F., 289
Mullen, M. K., 232
Multi-Motive Grid (MMG), 77–78, 314–15
Murensky, C. L., 498
Murray, H., 7, 32, 75, 152, 154, 354

Nacos, B. L., 199–200
Naglieri, J. A., 199
Natural killer cell activity studies, 285
Need specificity hypothesis, 395–98, 397*f*
Negaction tendency, 188*t*
Negation. *see* activity inhibition
"Neo-instinctive" model, 157
Neural systems, 279, 290–91, 291*f*
activation in response to stress, 105, 109–10
amygdala, 280, 290–93, 291*f*, 299n, 333
association cortex structures, 295
emotional intelligence, 495, 499
hypothalamus, 290, 291*f*, 292, 295
insula, 291*f*, 295
neuroimaging studies, 295–98, 297*f*
orbitofrontal cortex, 280, 290, 291*f*, 294–95, 333
striatum, 280, 287, 290, 291*f*, 293–94, 333
Neuroimaging studies, neural systems, 295–98, 297*f*
Neutral expressions, FEE studies, 262–63
Ng, I., 456
Nicholls, J. G., 528–29
Nissen, M. J., 255
Nixon, Richard, 415, 418
Nonverbal incentives as behavior influence, 15. *see also* incentive cues
Noradrenaline, 78
Norcross, J. C., 476
Norepinephrine, 15–16, 228, 280–81
Nosek, B. A., 332
Nucleus accumbens, striatum, 293, 299n, 333
Nuttin, J., 354